UNLOCKING TORTS

Tort law is a foundation subject in every law degree in England and Wales. *Unlocking Torts* will ensure you grasp the main concepts of this subject with ease.

Containing accessible explanations in a clear and logical structure, it provides an excellent foundation for learning and revising, and incorporates the following features to support learning:

- Clear learning outcomes at the beginning of each chapter set out the skills and knowledge you will need to get to grips with the subject.
- Key Facts summaries throughout each chapter allow you to progressively build and consolidate your understanding.
- End-of-chapter summaries provide a useful checklist for each topic.
- Cases and judgments are highlighted to help you find them and add them to your notes quickly.
- Frequent activities, self-test questions and sample essay questions are included so you can put your knowledge into practice and prepare yourself for assessment.
- A 'Critiquing the Law' feature is designed to foster essential critical thinking skills.

The sixth edition has been comprehensively updated throughout to reflect numerous recent developments and changes in the law, including significant updates to chapters on duty of care, psychiatric harm, defences, vicarious liability and nuisance. This edition includes commentary on cases such as *Chief Constable of Northamptonshire Police v Woodstock* [2025] EWCA Civ 13, *Paul v Wolverhampton* [2024] UKSC 1, *Lewis-Ranwell v G4S Health Services (UK) Ltd and Devon Partnership NHS Trust and Devon County Council* [2026] UKSC 2, *Fearn v Tate Gallery* [2023] UKSC 4, and *CCC v Sheffield Teaching Hospitals NHS Foundation Trust* [2026] UKSC 5.

This book forms part of the *Unlocking the Law* series; it is essential reading for all core modules on tort law.

Sanmeet Kaur Dua is Professor of Legal Education at Queen Mary. She is the Deputy Head and Director of Education for the Department of Law.

UNLOCKING THE LAW

UNLOCKING TORTS

6th edition

Sanmeet Kaur Dua

Routledge
Taylor & Francis Group
LONDON AND NEW YORK

Designed cover image: Shutterstock

Sixth edition published 2027
by Routledge
4 Park Square, Milton Park, Abingdon, Oxon, OX14 4RN

and by Routledge
605 Third Avenue, New York, NY 10158

Routledge is an imprint of the Taylor & Francis Group, an informa business

First edition published by Hodder Education 2004

Fifth edition published by Routledge 2019

British Library Cataloguing-in-Publication Data
A catalogue record for this book is available from the British Library

Library of Congress Cataloging-in-Publication Data
Names: Kaur Dua, Sanmeet author
Title: Unlocking torts / Sanmeet Kaur Dua.
Description: Sixth Edition. | Abingdon, Oxon [UK] ; New York, NY : Routledge, 2026. | Series: Unlocking the law | Includes index.
Identifiers: LCCN 2026020032 | ISBN 9781032064581 hardback | ISBN 9781032061290 paperback | ISBN 9781003202417 ebook
Subjects: LCSH: Torts—England | Torts—Wales
Classification: LCC KD1949 .T875 2026
LC record available at https://lccn.loc.gov/2026020032

ISBN: 978-1-032-06458-1 (hbk)
ISBN: 978-1-032-06129-0 (pbk)
ISBN: 978-1-003-20241-7 (ebk)

DOI: 10.4324/9781003202417

Typeset in Palatino
by Apex CoVantage, LLC

Contents

Guide to the book

In the Unlocking the Law books, all the essential elements that make up the law are clearly defined to bring the law alive and make it memorable. In addition, the books are enhanced with learning features to reinforce learning and test your knowledge as you study. Follow this guide to make sure you get the most from reading this book.

AIMS AND OBJECTIVES

Defines what you will learn in each chapter.

SECTION

Highlights sections from Acts.

Definition

Find key legal terminology at a glance

ARTICLE

Defines Articles of the EC Treaty or of the European Convention on Human Rights or other Treaty.

CASE EXAMPLE

Illustrates the law in action.

JUDGMENT

Provides extracts from judgments on cases.

ACTIVITY

Enables you to test yourself as you progress through the chapter.

CRITIQUING THE LAW

Highlights academic debate within controversial areas of the law.

SAMPLE ESSAY QUESTIONS

Provide you with real-life sample essays and show you the best way to plan your answer.

SAMPLE PROBLEM QUESTIONS

Sample problem questions include some of the more complicated issues within a topic and consider ways of resolving them.

SUMMARY

Concludes each chapter to reinforce learning.

Acknowledgements

I would like to thank Routledge, particularly Emily Kindleysides and Sanika Shah for their support and time, as well as a number of colleagues who have helped develop ideas and offered invaluable advice.

My thanks and gratitude to those around me from the youngest to the eldest, who have offered their time, support and good humour in allowing me the space to write this edition. A very special thanks to Ashwin and Sienna for patiently listening to me explain, often in detail, some of the fundamental principles in Tort Law. Thank you to my husband, Amar, who is my greatest supporter. The three of you inspire me everyday.

Sanmeet Kaur Dua

Preface

The study of torts can prove fascinating because it is really all about people, the problems that they have and the ways that these might be overcome in law. Tort law covers civil wrongs and in this way the topic areas vary widely in their content and context, from basic negligence actions for motoring accidents to assaults encountered in sporting activities or interference of problem neighbours. Since tort is also essentially a common law area, much of this book is devoted to cases. Case notes and judgments are separated out in the text for easy reference.

The sixth edition has been updated throughout to include developments in the law since the last edition. In particular, this edition includes cases that develop the law on the liability of public authorities including *HXA v Surrey County Council* [2023] UKSC 52, *Tindall v Chief Constable of Thames Valley Police* [2024] UKSC 33, *Chief Constable of Northamptonshire Police v Woodstock* [2025] EWCA Civ 13, as well as the law on the application of the defence of illegality following the decision in *Lewis-Ranwell v G4S Health Services (UK) Ltd, Devon Partnership NHS Trust, Devon County Council* [2026] UKSC 2. This edition also includes updates to the law in psychiatric harm in relation to claims made by secondary victims who witness a medical crisis, now clarified in *Paul v Wolverhampton* [2024] UKSC, updates in the law of nuisance following the decision in *Fearn v Tate Gallery* [2023] UKSC 4 as well as updates on how damages should be calculated when considering 'lost years' following the decision in *CCC v Sheffield Teaching Hospitals NHS Foundation Trust* [2026] UKSC 5.

I hope that you will gain as much enjoyment in reading about torts and testing your understanding with the various activities and features in the book, as I have had in writing it.

The law is stated as I believe it to be on 1 March 2026.

Tables

Figures

Table of cases

Table of statutes and other instruments

Statutes

Statutory Instruments

EU Legislation

1

The origins and character of tortious liability

AIMS AND OBJECTIVES

After reading this chapter you should be able to:

- Explain the basic character of torts
- Identify the basic principles of tortious liability
- Explain the aims of tortious liability
- Distinguish the interests protected by the Law of Torts
- Recognise the relevance of specific mental states in pursuing tort actions
- Discriminate between fault liability and no fault liability
- Discriminate between joint liability and several liability and recognise when and why contributions can be made between different tortfeasors
- Identify when human rights legislation impacts on the Law of Torts

tort
Tort is a French word meaning 'wrong' – so it is a general word used to describe civil wrongs

trespass
Torts based on trespass tend to involve interference, e.g. with rights over land, or property or indeed with their 'bodily integrity'

1.1 The origins of tort

The law of **tort**, or torts, is part of the English common law which has developed incrementally since Norman times. Academic writers are not agreed whether there is a law of tort or a law of torts. A law of tort implies some general common rules relevant to all parts of the law. A law of torts recognises that there are various separate and distinct aspects but also implies that the separate parts have something in common. The writer of this book inclines to the idea that there is a law of torts, each tort being governed by similar underlying principles.

Although some modern torts have been created by statute, the law is still generally to be found in common law principles. The origins of torts can be traced back to the fourteenth century when the word '**trespass**' was given a much wider legal meaning than it has today. It originally referred to 'any direct and forcible injury to the person, land or property (chattels)'.

DOI: 10.4324/9781003202417-1

Trespass was one of two medieval forms of action, the second being 'trespass on the case' or simply 'case'. Case covered 'injury which was consequential to a wrong but the wrong was neither forcible nor direct'.

actionable *per se*
An action for a tort where the claimant does not have to prove that damage occurred only that the tort occurred

The distinction can still be seen in the law of torts today – torts which are **actionable *per se***, i.e. without proof of damage, such as trespass to land and trespass to the person, generally originate from the old form of trespass, while those torts which require proof of damage, for example negligence and nuisance, generally come from case. This distinction is based on the notion that torts which are actionable *per se* aim to vindicate the claimant's rights so can be established without proof of damage, whereas torts that require proof of damage such as a claim in negligence aim to provide compensation hence why proof of some harm is required.

claimant
The person who brings an action in tort

In the past, the distinction was of crucial importance as using the wrong form of action could result in the **claimant** being left without any remedy. Today, although there may be cost penalties, the Rules of Court allow for the amendment of pleadings (subject to the provisions of the Limitation Act 1980 which are discussed in Chapter 19). The legal historian will be able to find traces of the old rules in modern law but for practical purposes the distinction is of little relevance. In his judgment in *United Australia Ltd v Barclays Bank* [1941] AC 1, Lord Atkin said at 28:

JUDGMENT

'When these ghosts of the past stand in the path of justice clanking their medieval chains the proper course for the judge is to pass through them undeterred.'

In *Letang v Cooper* [1965] 1 QB 232, Lord Denning MR remarked at 239:

JUDGMENT

'These forms of action have served their day. They did at one time form a guide to substantive rights; but they do so no longer. Lord Atkin told us what to do about them.'

CASE EXAMPLE

Letang v Cooper [1965] 1 QB 232

The claimant decided to sunbathe on a grass area which was also used as a car park. The defendant drove in. He did not see the claimant lying on the grass and ran over her legs. The problem for the claimant was caused by the date on which she tried to commence her action. She was out of time to bring an action for negligence (a descendant of case) where the usual time limit is three years. If she was able to use trespass, then the action could stand as the time limit was six years. It was argued that the old rules should apply, her injury was direct and forcible.

The Court of Appeal held that the old rules no longer apply. Intentional injury will give a claim based in trespass, but unintentional injury gives a claim based in negligence. The claimant was unsuccessful.

Before leaving this introduction, mention should be made of the tort of defamation. Slander has its roots in the old ecclesiastical law. Libel stems from the old prerogative law which regarded certain written statements as prejudicial to the state. Both libel and slander eventually found a home in the common law courts. As will be seen in Chapter 14, the tort of defamation continues to have its own unique characteristics.

1.2 General principles of liability

1.2.1 The character of torts

Anyone who teaches law is certain to be asked 'What does tort mean?' If only there was an easy answer! It seems to be generally accepted that the word itself is a surviving relic of Norman French and means simply 'wrong'. This does not tell us very much. Winfield defines the meaning as follows: 'Tortious liability arises from the breach of a duty primarily fixed by law; this duty is towards persons generally and its breach is redressible by an action for unliquidated damages' (*Winfield and Jolowicz on Tort*, Goudkamp and Nolan, 21st edn, Sweet & Maxwell 2025, p 2).

The definition is helpful in that it shows that there are three elements:

1 a duty fixed by law – as we shall see this does not necessarily, or indeed usually, mean fixed by statute but a duty which the courts have recognised;

2 the duty must be owed generally – as we shall see individual torts have been developed so that a general duty is owed to any person in a position to bring an action based on that tort;

3 the breach of duty must entitle the claimant to general **damages**.

damages
Refers to the compensation awarded by the court in a successful claim

The nature of the duty varies from tort to tort. For example, where negligence is alleged, the duty is to take reasonable care; in the case of trespass to the person the duty is to refrain from infringing a person's bodily integrity.

The class of persons to whom a duty is owed may be limited. For example in negligence, a duty is owed only to those who ought reasonably have been foreseen as likely to be affected by failure to take reasonable care; in trespass to the person the duty is owed only to those directly affected by the action.

The injury sustained must be of a type recognised by the law. In negligence for example it took many years for the courts to recognise that psychiatric harm was as much an injury as physical damage. In trespass to the person and other torts which are actionable per se it is unnecessary to prove damage, the infringement of the right being regarded as injury enough.

1.2.2 The functions and purposes of torts

The aim of the law of torts is twofold:

1 to compensate someone who has suffered a wrong at the hands of the **defendant**; and

2 to deter persons from acting in such a way that another person's rights are infringed.

defendant
The person against whom a claim in tort is made

Compensation

Clearly a person who has suffered injury is entitled to financial compensation which is intended, so far as possible, to put them in the position they would have been in but for the wrongdoing of the defendant. Where the damage is purely to property this may be possible, but real difficulty arises in cases of personal injury. The rules which guide the courts in such matters are discussed in detail in Chapter 19. The award of damages can also be regarded as ensuring that an injured party receives justice in that loss caused by the tort is compensated. In some cases the 'victim' would not agree that justice has been done. How often does the media report a case where a 'victim' makes it clear that the money is in reality no compensation for the loss which has occurred? While the finding of liability may go some way to satisfy the injured party's desire for vengeance, having 'had their day in court', it is only rarely that a punitive element of damages is payable.

From the defendant's point of view, the concept of justice is also debatable. The amount of damages is assessed purely by the effect on the claimant. A defendant who has caused serious personal injury to the particular victim because of some personal characteristic of that victim will find that the award far exceeds the amount which would have been payable to another, less vulnerable, victim.

Sometimes, establishing liability will be avoided doing away with any notion of compensation so as to prevent opening the 'floodgates' of litigation. In some circumstances, there is a fear that if liability is established a precedent will be set and so a multitude of claims will follow, imposing crushing liability on the defendant. Now a lot of this depends on the current state of affairs of the UK and the type of defendant. Consider for instance a claim against a large oil and gas company; should we be concerned about opening the floodgates or do we think that they are financial able to absorb the impact of such a claim? What if a similar claim was levelled against the NHS or a small high street chain? A balance must be struck between ensuring deserving claimants receive compensation as well as ensuring that a claim will not prove to be economically crushing on the tortfeasor.

The law does not compensate a person for all types of damage. We shall see, for example in Chapter 14, that generally there is no duty to respect another's privacy. A person who publishes something which is true is not liable for defamation no matter how detrimental the publication may be to the 'victim'.

The law does not always regard a person as having a legal claim. In negligence, for example, a person who suffers psychiatric damage as a result of the defendant having negligently caused harm to someone else, will only be able to bring an action when certain very strict conditions have been complied with (see Chapter 6).

Deterrence

Tort law can operate to impose a higher standard of care and to change behaviour for the better. This may be done for example by imposing punitive damages on a tortfeasor. Others will see this and this will deter them from engaging in similar conduct and ideally, strive for higher standards. However, the deterrent effect of torts is debatable. This is illustrated by the decision of certain publishers to go ahead and publish defamatory material in the belief that, if the 'victim' brings an action, the profit will outweigh any possible compensation. In such cases if an action is brought damages can include a punitive element, but such a publisher may also calculate that the 'victim' is unlikely to bring an action. An action for defamation frequently has the effect of ensuring that the material becomes known to many more people, no legal aid is available and the outcome is unpredictable. None of these are matters that a 'victim' is likely to ignore.

Where insurance is required, for example in relation to motor vehicles (Road Traffic Act 1988), the deterrent effect is perhaps more effective. A person who is liable may well find that once the insurance company has paid the compensation, the premium goes up. Defendants may or may not care that their actions have caused injury to someone else, but all are likely to be very concerned about the effect to their pockets. Equally, if the payee is not the tortfeasor in that it is an insurance company, the deterrent effect may be muted.

The deterrent effect is also reinforced in the case of professionals who are subject to strict codes of practice, for example healthcare professionals, lawyers and accountants. Professional governing bodies usually have powers to prevent future practice where the code is not obeyed thus preventing a wrongdoer from earning a living.

1.2.3 The interests protected by the law of torts

Common law develops incrementally by virtue of the doctrine of precedent but it is possible to classify, in broad terms, the general nature of interests which the law of torts protects:

- personal security;
- property;
- reputation;
- economic interests.

Reference should be made to the various chapters for more detail. The following paragraphs simply draw the reader's attention to the specific torts which may be relevant to the particular interests.

Personal security is most obviously protected by the torts of trespass to the person and trespass to land. The tort of negligence now also has a large part to play in ensuring that an individual does not suffer harm by the unreasonable acts or omissions of others. Nuisance helps to protect an **occupier** of land from activities on neighbouring land which are detrimental to health or comfort. Statutory torts created by the Protection from Harassment Act 1997 and the Consumer Protection Act 1987 also contribute in protecting personal security.

occupier
In liability for damage caused by the state of premises the occupier is the person in actual control of the premises when the damage occurs – so there can be dual occupation

Property is protected by the torts of trespass to land and interference with goods. The torts of nuisance and the rule in *Rylands v Fletcher* [1868] LR 1 Exch 265 also help by providing a remedy for wrongful interference with the use of land or damage caused to land, in both cases caused by some activity or omission on the wrongdoer's land. Negligence also has a role to play where property is damaged as a result of failure to take reasonable care.

A person's reputation is protected by the tort of defamation. The equitable remedies available for breach of confidentiality, although not strictly part of tort law, and the influence of the European Convention on Human Rights cannot be ignored in this context. These may help to protect privacy by preventing publication of true but detrimental information.

economic loss

Refers to a loss that is purely financial, e.g. loss of profit – in contrast to personal injury or damage to property

Economic loss is an oddity. Damages are calculated to take account of financial loss sustained by the victim of a tort (see generally Chapter 19) but, as will be seen in Chapter 6, there are restrictions on the availability of a claim in negligence for what is described as 'pure economic loss'. The 'economic' torts of deceit, malicious falsehood, passing off and interference with trade (see Chapter 15), may ensure that a business is protected from unfair competition. Economic loss may also be compensated where the law of contract can be used.

1.2.4 The parties to an action in tort

Capacity generally

The usual principle applies to torts as to any other part of the civil law. In order to bring or defend an action, the party concerned must have legal capacity. A minor (a person under 18 years of age) can neither bring nor defend an action in their own name but must rely on representation by a suitable adult. Similar rules apply to those of unsound mind. Special rules apply to certain other groups, for example corporations and trade unions. Until the twentieth century, married women were also included as a slightly different case, but now they are generally treated as any other person!

The state

As the Crown is traditionally regarded as the fount of all justice, it is not surprising that special rules have evolved as to the liability of the state and its officials. In relation to the monarch, the old idea that the 'King can do no wrong' is maintained and no action can be brought against the sovereign personally, nor in respect of certain prerogative and statutory powers.

Until 1947 the only remedy against the Crown was by way of petition of right asking the monarch for redress of a wrong. This anomaly was dealt with by the Crown Proceedings Act 1947. The present position is that the Crown is usually in the same position as any other legal person and can therefore sue or be sued in relation to torts in much the same way as anyone else.

vicarious liability

Not a tort in itself but a means of imposing liability on somebody who is responsible for the tortfeasor usually an employer

There are nevertheless, some peculiarities. For example, the doctrine of **vicarious liability** cannot apply to heads of government departments as all servants of the Crown are fellow employees. The head of department cannot therefore be regarded as employing subordinate officials. In practice this was of little importance as the wrongdoer remained personally liable and the Treasury Solicitor would satisfy any judgment. Theoretically, however, it was possible for the Crown to plead immunity when an allegation of tortious behaviour was made. This has been dealt with by the Crown Proceedings Act 1947 which brought Crown immunity in tort to an end in most circumstances.

Foreign sovereigns and their servants have long enjoyed what is popularly known as 'diplomatic immunity' for tortious actions. Such immunity can always be waived but its existence can and does cause problems. By way of example, a person whose vehicle has been damaged by the negligent driving of a chauffeur employed by a foreign embassy will be unable to obtain compensation if the chauffeur can show that the accident occurred in the course of employment by the embassy unless immunity is waived.

Minors

A person does not become legally adult until their eighteenth birthday is reached (Family Law Reform Act 1969 s1). Until that time a minor may only sue or defend an action by a responsible adult known as a 'litigation friend'. Apart from this procedural requirement a minor has exactly the same rights and duties in torts as an adult. We shall see, however, that certain allowances may be made, particularly in relation to the defences of voluntary assumption of risk and contributory negligence, for a less mature understanding.

The general rule is that minors may be liable for their own tortious activities. The fact of immaturity is relevant in some cases. For example in a case of negligence, the actions of the child will not be judged by the usual standard of the reasonable man but by the standard of a reasonable and prudent child of the same age. This can be seen in the case of *Mullin v Richards* [1997] EWCA Civ 2662 where two 15-year girls were play fighting with plastic rulers when one snapped and a piece of plastic from that ruler went into the claimant's eye causing her permanent vision loss in one that eye. It was held that the conduct of the defendant must be measured by that which is reasonably expected of a reasonable 15-year-old child.

Victims of child tortfeasors might well hope that the minor's parents would be liable for the child's wrongdoing. This is not the case unless:

- the parent can be shown to have vicarious liability; or
- the parent has personally been negligent, for example in *Bebee v Sales* [1916] 32 TLR 413 by failing to exercise reasonable control over a 15-year old who injured another child's eye with an airgun given to him by his father. The father had failed to exercise proper control when he did not remove the gun from the boy's possession after he had smashed a neighbour's window.

Unborn child

There is no general rule that a child may not sue its parent.

A child born with disabilities due to injuries suffered whilst in the womb, or because of injury suffered by either parent which impacts on their ability to have a normal baby, may bring a claim if certain conditions are satisfied. These conditions are found in the Congenital Disabilities (Civil Liability) Act 1976 which provides:

1. the child must be born alive and disabled;
2. the defendant must have potential tort liability to the child even if the mother was not harmed and has no cause of action;
3. the mother herself cannot be liable for any injury to her unborn child.

In relation to the second point, this means that the cause of action is derivative. So, even if the mother does not suffer harm but the unborn child does say because of a drug that is negligently manufactured and subsequently taken by the mother, the child may bring a claim against the manufacturer for any disability caused.

The third point makes clear that a mother is effectively immune from liability due to policy reasons. A child cannot bring a claim against their mother for any acts or omissions which may cause the child harm, whether that be through consuming excessive alcohol through the pregnancy, engaging in risky sporting activities, by excessive smoking or otherwise. This immunity is however lost if the unborn child suffers harm caused by the negligent driving of the mother as per s2 of the 1976 Act as the mother is required by law to be insured.

Note that the law does not extend the same immunity to a father for any acts or omissions committed against his unborn child. A child born alive and disabled, would therefore be able to bring a claim against their father due to the father's acts or omissions. This difference in treatment is due to policy. Imagine if the father strikes the mother whilst pregnant, harming the unborn child resulting in it being born disabled, would it be acceptable for the father to have a shield of immunity against a claim brought by the child?

Married persons

As far as claims by or against third parties are concerned, married people are in the same position as anyone else. Where a claim is made by one spouse against the other, proceedings are not subject to any special rules except that the court has power to stay any proceedings if no substantial benefit is likely to be obtained by either party if the matter continues. This provision, found in the Law Reform (Husband and Wife) Act 1962 s1(2)(a), is designed to ensure that the courts do not become yet another forum in which husband and wife can fight purely personal battles for the sake of it.

Corporations

A corporation is an artificial person having legal personality by virtue of incorporation. A corporation can sue for any tort which is committed against it save for those where commission of the tort is clearly impossible, for example false imprisonment. Similarly, the corporation is an appropriate defendant, usually by virtue of vicarious liability as the employer of someone who has in fact committed the tort.

Partnerships

Partnerships do not have legal personality and cannot therefore sue or be sued. A right of action vests in the partners who sue as individuals. Where a tort has been committed by the firm, the individual partners have joint and **several liability** to the claimant. The Rules of Court make special provision to ensure that legal actions are not duplicated or unduly prolonged.

several liability

Where there are joint tortfeasors, each one can be separately liable for the whole damage – so if one lacks funds to pay compensation the claimant can bring the action against the one that can pay

It should be noted that a new type of partnership was brought into being by the Limited Liability Partnerships Act 2000. Where a partnership is formed by virtue of the Act, it has its own legal personality and can sue or be sued in the same way as any other corporation.

Persons of unsound mind

A person who is of unsound mind may sue, through the services of a litigation friend, for any tort committed against them. Where such a person has allegedly committed a tort the position is not straightforward.

If a tort requires a particular state of mind, then evidence will be needed that the person had that state of mind.

CASE EXAMPLE

***Henderson v Dorset Healthcare University NHS Foundation Trust* [2020] UKSC 43**

The claimant, Mrs Henderson had suffered from paranoid schizophrenia and at the relevant time, suffered a deterioration in her condition. The defendants were responsible for her care and should have been more alert to the claimant's mental collapse. When the claimant's mother came to see her, the claimant stabbed her to death. Experts confirmed that the claimant knew what she was doing. She was charged with murder which was ultimately considered as manslaughter on the grounds of diminished responsibility. The claimant then brought a claim against the defendants for damages on the grounds that but for their breach of duty, she would not have killed her mother. This argument was defeated by the defence of illegality and on public policy grounds. This is to say, that there is something abhorrent in awarding damages to someone who has committed an illegal act.

Where the actions are involuntary, the person is unlikely to be liable.

Death

There are two issues that can arise after the death of one of the parties.

The first is to do with the survival of an existing right of action or indeed liability. In 1934, the Law Reform (Miscellaneous Provisions) Act was introduced to address the common law position of extinguishing a claim upon the death of one of the parties. It used to be the case that the right of action dies with the person. The unfairness of this position was corrected by the 1934 Act which provides that claims can survive the death of one of the parties to the action.

SECTION

Effect of death on certain causes of action.

s1(1) Subject to the provisions of this section, on the death of any person after the commencement of this Act all causes of action subsisting against or vested in him shall survive against, or, as the case may be, for the benefit of, his estate. Provided that this subsection shall not apply to causes of action for defamation.

This provision does not provide for a cause of action but rather states that an action will survive the death of one of the parties. For example, if the claimant dies as a result of the negligence of the defendant, the claimant's estate may bring an action on behalf of the deceased for the loss the deceased suffered. In other words, for the deceased's estate to bring a claim, they must establish that the deceased had a cause of action and all of the elements of that cause of action can be made out including proof of damage.

This provision does not allow for claims for defamation to survive the death of the party defamed. This difference in approach is attributable to the different types of loss suffered e.g. harm to reputation versus death caused by negligent driving.

The second is to do with potential claims that may be brought by dependents of the deceased for the loss of their dependency or in other words, for the deprivation of their financial support. So here this can create a cause of action but only for the dependents of the deceased pursuant to the Fatal Accidents Act 1976.

SECTION

S.1 Right of action for wrongful act causing death.

(1) If death is caused by any wrongful act, neglect or default which is such as would (if death had not ensued) have entitled the person injured to maintain an action and recover damages in respect thereof, the person who would have been liable if death had not ensued shall be liable to an action for damages, notwithstanding the death of the person injured.

(2) . . . every such action shall be for the benefit of the dependants of the person ("the deceased") whose death has been so caused.

There are two points to make here. The first is that dependants of the deceased can recover damages provided that the deceased would have been able to do the same had they not died. The deceased would be able to prove that the defendant's act or omissions caused their death. The second is that dependants who may bring a claim are defined in s1(3) as the following:

(a) the wife, husband or civil partner or former wife, husband or civil partner of the deceased;

(b) a cohabitant of the deceased provided that they were living with the deceased in the same household for at least two years and were living during the whole of that period as the husband, wife or civil partner of the deceased;

(c) any parent or other ascendant (i.e. grandparents) of the deceased;

(d) any person who was treated by the deceased as his parent;

(e) any child or other descendant of the deceased;

(f) any child (not being a child of the deceased) by marriage or civil partnership who was treated by the deceased as a child of the family in relation to that marriage or civil partnership;

(g) any person who is, or is the issue of, a brother, sister, uncle or aunt of the deceased.

In determining such a claim put forward by the dependant, the court will have to make an assessment as to what would have happened if the deceased had lived. This inevitably means that an assessment of the dependency itself needs to be undertaken or put in another way, dependants need to demonstrate their loss. In the case of *Franklin v South Eastern Railway* (1858) 3 H&N 211, at 214 Pollock CB set the relevant test that continues to be applied today, that damages should be calculated in reference to a reasonable expectation of pecuniary benefit, as of right or otherwise, from the continuance of the life. Each dependent claimant will need to demonstrate that they had a reasonable expectation of pecuniary benefit from the deceased had they not died.

1.2.5 Tort and mental state

In torts, two mental states are relevant:

- intention;
- **malice**.

malice

Motive is generally unimportant in most torts but in some circumstances acting maliciously is an element of the tort, e.g. malicious falsehood and nuisance

Intention

In the criminal law, the general principle is that a person must intend to commit the crime if they are to be found guilty (the element of *mens rea*). It is very rarely the case that a person must be shown to have intended to commit a tort, although where this can be shown, the claimant may find it easier to establish a case.

Having said this, many torts require the defendant to have intended to do the act which amounts to the tort. In trespass to the person, for example, the defendant must have intended to touch the claimant in order to be liable although they need not have intended to commit battery. A trespass to land cannot be committed by a parachutist who is blown onto land by the wind.

In the tort of negligence, the defendant is liable for unintended consequences of an act. Liability rests on the fact that the defendant failed to foresee the potential consequences and thus failed to guard against them. If the consequences are intended, then some other tort may have been committed. By way of example, if a motorist deliberately rams another vehicle, there may be liability for trespass to the person or trespass to goods, but there will be no liability for negligence.

Malice

In some rare circumstances, the defendant's motive may be relevant. An improper motive is usually referred to as malice and its presence can have the effect of rendering what might otherwise be a reasonable action unreasonable and therefore unlawful. Examples of this are found in the tort of malicious falsehood (see Chapter 15) and in nuisance (see Chapter 9). Malice may also defeat the defence of qualified privilege available in defamation (see Chapter 14).

1.2.6 Alternative methods of obtaining compensation

Alternative dispute resolution (ADR)

While a person may be able to bring legal action to seek a remedy for some injury or damage which has been suffered, this can be fraught with difficulty. Despite the recent reforms, the court system is slow and expensive. The availability of legal aid has been substantially curtailed. Perhaps most importantly, there can never be any true certainty as to the outcome. While the victim of wrongdoing may well wish to see the defendant publicly found liable by a judge in a court of law, most will think long and hard before venturing into such uncharted waters.

Over recent years other methods to resolve issues have been developed so that there are now various methods of ADR available. These include

- arbitration;
- adjudication;

- conciliation;
- mediation.

Each may be relevant in the context of torts; for example, conciliation and mediation schemes have been created by a number of local authorities to deal with complaints of statutory nuisance (see Chapter 9).

For full discussion of ADR the reader should consult a text on the English legal system.

Insurance

The purpose of insurance from a defendant's point of view is to protect them from personally having to foot the bill. From the claimant's point of view, the fact that a defendant is insured will mean that there are resources from which any damages will be met.

As the level of damages for personal injury can be very high, insurance is compulsory in certain circumstances. The Road Traffic Act 1988 makes third party insurance compulsory for all motor vehicles while the Employers' Liability (Compulsory Insurance) Act 1969 requires employers to have insurance against liability for injury to employees. Professionals, for example solicitors and doctors, are required to have third party insurance as a condition of practice although they will be covered by their employers' insurance if employed. Insurance against public liability may be required as a term in a standard form contract, for example the 'Standard Form of Building Contract' (commonly known as the JCT contract) which is widely used by the construction industry.

Individuals may choose to obtain no-fault insurance to protect themselves and/or their property in the event of accidental damage. Common examples are household insurance policies which protect the buildings and contents. Other policies protect against redundancy, ill health and death.

The judges are of course aware that many awards of damages will in fact be paid by insurance companies and that individuals may have chosen to protect themselves against misfortune. This may in some cases influence the way in which a case is approached. In the context of road traffic accidents, the courts can impose a very high standard of care.

The availability of insurance may also be relevant. One of the policy reasons influencing the decision on **nervous shock** arising from the Hillsborough cases (see Chapter 6) was the need to ensure that the number of potential claims was limited. This means that insurance companies are in a position to make a realistic assessment of potential liability, an essential first step to setting the amount of a premium!

nervous shock
A recognised psychiatric injury such as clinical depression and post-traumatic stress disorder caused by a single shocking event

1.2.7 Relationships with other areas of law

Crime

In one sense, torts are the civil equivalent of crimes. Each requires a certain standard to be observed and breach of the 'code' leads to consequences. Tortious behaviour may entitle a 'victim' to compensation or some other remedy while criminal behaviour will lead to punishment of the person convicted and may also lead to compensation of the victim by means of a criminal compensation order, or by payment of compensation by the Criminal Injuries Compensation Authority. The distinction between crime and torts is essentially one of degree. A crime is generally regarded by society as wrongdoing of a sufficiently extreme nature that it requires punishment, while tortious behaviour leaves the 'victim' to decide whether or not to pursue a private remedy.

In some circumstances, the two areas of law overlap. This is particularly evident in cases involving trespass to the person which overlaps with criminal assaults and torts such as conversion and trespass to goods. In such cases it may be possible for civil action to be brought using tort even though the wrongdoer has been punished by the criminal law. It was partly to avoid such duplication of actions that the criminal courts have been given power to award compensation to the victim in straightforward cases.

Contract

Both the law of contract and the law of torts are concerned to ensure that a person fulfils a duty whether this is imposed freely by agreement (contract) where the parties negotiate risks and responsibilities or by law (torts) where parties have no say. There are a number of areas where there is some overlap between the two areas such as misrepresentation and consumer protection. However, where there is a choice between bringing a claim in contract law or tort, it should be noted that there are differences in proving the claim including differences in the limitation periods which can be more generous under tort law, and in the measure of damages that may be awarded.

Academic writers are divided over the issues raised. Some believe that the separate law is evolving into a new category, a general law of obligations which gives rise to a remedy whenever an obligation is breached. This is so whether the obligation arises from agreement between the parties or from a duty imposed by law.

Land law

While torts are rarely concerned with rights relating to the title to land, many torts, for example trespass to land and *Rylands v Fletcher*, depend on the legal status of the parties in relation to the occupation of the land affected or from which the problem emanates. The torts lawyer needs to be fully aware of the basic principles of land law. This text generally assumes such knowledge although the reader's attention will be drawn to specific problems where necessary.

1.3 Fault and no-fault liability

1.3.1 Fault liability

'There can be no liability without fault.' This old legal adage was reworded by Lord Atkin in *Donoghue v Stevenson* [1932] AC 562 when he said that the law of tort is (at 580):

JUDGMENT

> 'based upon a general public sentiment of moral wrongdoing for which the offender must pay'.

Case law, as readers will see as they progress through this book, upholds Lord Atkin's view. Although not all torts require intention to do wrong, each in reality imposes an expected standard of behaviour and a defendant who fails to meet that standard, whether by being insufficiently careful (negligence) or by doing something which is regarded as an infringement of another's rights (trespass to the person or to land), may find that an aggrieved person has a legal remedy.

The tort of negligence provides perhaps the best example of the problems of torts which require a claimant to prove fault. Among the problems which such a claimant faces are:

- evidential difficulties – it is not always possible to prove that the defendant was at fault even though damage has been suffered;
- the need in some cases, for example where the damage suffered is nervous shock, to bring the claimant within a recognised class of 'victim' – failure may mean that although the actual damage is the same, some claimants may succeed while others fail.

Arguments in favour of a fault-based system include:

- the potential deterrent value of a finding of fault (see section 1.2.2);
- the possibility that the defendant will in fact be punished for the wrongdoing although punitive damages are rarely awarded.

1.3.2 Strict liability

While most torts contain an element of fault in the sense of failure to meet a required standard or intention to do a particular act, some are described as bearing **strict liability**. In such cases there is no requirement to show that the defendant was at fault or exercised reasonable care to avoid causing the claimant harm. Torts of strict liability include liability under the Consumer Protection Act 1987 and the Animals Act 1971. Where the requirements of the tort have been fulfilled, the defendant will be liable even though in reality there is no fault in the sense of intention or negligence. It would, however, be wrong to say that a defendant who is in breach of a particular requirement is always liable. While the torts may impose 'strict liability' defences are usually available even if they are limited. Liability is 'strict', not 'absolute'.

strict liability

Refers to torts where the claimant does not have to show fault on the part of the defendant – the most obvious ones are under the Animals Act 1971 and the Consumer Protection Act 1987

For a detailed discussion of the merits and demerits of a fault-based system in the context of negligence where it causes most difficulty, see Chapter 3. The reader is also referred to Chapter 10 on *Rylands v Fletcher* for an interesting tort which started life as a tort of strict liability but now appears to have changed its character to become fault based!

1.3.3 No-fault schemes

The problems faced by claimants who need to prove fault have already been highlighted. The question arises: 'Is the law always an appropriate tool to deal with wrongful behaviour which causes damage?'

This question was considered by the Royal Commission on Civil Liability and Compensation for Personal Injury (Cmnd 7054, 1978), which is from now on referred to as the Pearson Committee. The report showed that at that time the number of people suffering serious injury or death was around 3 million each year, of whom something under 250,000 made a claim in torts. Taking into account all sources of compensation, this small proportion of the total number of victims actually received about 25 per cent of all monies paid for accidental injury. The Pearson Committee also found that the costs of the torts system were disproportionate to the amount paid to claimants and that administrative costs swallowed up a larger percentage of the budget than the costs of other sources for compensation, for example the social security system. There was no doubt then, nor is there now, that where compensation for a tort is paid, the claimant will in fact receive a greater sum than from other sources. In summary the Pearson Committee found that

- the torts system gives disproportionate benefits to a minority of people suffering accidental injury;
- the system is expensive in terms of cost;
- court action is slow and complex.

It was recommended that a no-fault system of compensation should be introduced to deal with accident compensation. This has not been done in England, but a scheme was set up in New Zealand in 1974 and corresponding rights of action in tort were abolished. Under the scheme the claimant originally received a lump sum for bodily impairment in addition to a weekly payment of a sum equivalent to 80 per cent of earnings subject to a statutory maximum amount. The scheme proved too expensive to continue, and in 1992 the payment of a lump sum ceased and was replaced by an additional weekly payment in cases of permanent disability. The New Zealand scheme has proved more costly than had been anticipated and is criticised as the focus is still on the cause of the injury, disability resulting from degeneration being excluded. Blindness is blindness whether it is caused by an accidental injury or by a disease, but only the victim of the accident will benefit under the scheme.

The Pearson Committee made many recommendations but most have not been implemented. Some have been partially implemented – the court system has been reformed in recent years and some provisions have been made to recoup at least part of the cost of compensation borne by the social security system. Little else has happened or is likely to happen.

In spite of the failures of torts, people who suffer personal injury may be entitled to compensation from other sources provided they are able to fulfil the relevant criteria applicable to each.

1 More people are now taking out insurance policies which will pay out in the event of ill health, accidental injury or unemployment. Such policies are not inexpensive and tend to be subject to strict conditions making them sometimes less effective than the insured might expect.
2 There is some limited provision for compulsory liability insurance, for example in relation to road traffic accidents and accidents at work.
3 A person injured as a result of a criminal act may be entitled to payment under the Criminal Injuries Compensation Scheme although this is sometimes criticised as inadequate, as awards are made on a 'tariff' basis rather than on the basis of the extent of the victim's actual loss.

4 Social security benefits are payable to all those who qualify and not only to all who suffer injury. The level of such benefits is not generous, the criteria for qualification are rigorously enforced and many benefits are means-tested.

The system is not perfect and many people will continue to receive no compensation at all. The consequences of medical accidents cause particular concern and the British Medical Association advocates a no-fault scheme for the victims of such accidents (No Fault Compensation Working Party Report 1991). The government has contributed to the debate by consultations over the way in which compensation for clinical negligence should be awarded. In 2001 the Department of Health published a paper – 'Clinical negligence: what are the issues and options for reform?' – outlining the perceived problems and suggesting that the solution might be found in:

- no-fault compensation which would save time and costs;
- structured settlements which would mean weekly or monthly payments;
- fixed tariffs for specific injuries;
- more use of mediation or other methods of ADR.

The debate will no doubt continue as it has since the Pearson Committee published its report in 1978.

joint tortfeasors
Where the wrongful act is carried out by more than one person they are joint tortfeasors and any or all of them can be sued

1.4 Joint and several tortfeasors

1.4.1 Joint and several liability

Injury can be caused by more than one person. Where it results from one act caused by more than one person, the persons responsible are called 'joint' tortfeasors. This will be the case where a person carries out a tortious act on the instructions of another person. In cases where the injury results from the cumulative effect of more than one person acting independently, the wrongdoers are known as 'several concurrent' tortfeasors. Provided the injury results from the combined actions, in other words the claimant has a single, indivisible injury, any or all of the wrongdoers are liable to the claimant for the full extent of the injury.

From the claimant's point of view, this may have advantages as the choice of defendant can be dictated by the extent to which each defendant is likely to be able to meet any award of damages. Defendants on the other hand may take a different view as the one defendant in a position to pay may find that the entire sum has to be found if co-tortfeasors are insolvent.

Not surprisingly defendants may well consider this to be unjust and the rules, while ensuring that the claimant is fully compensated, make provision for allocation of financial liability between defendants.

1.4.2 Contributions between tortfeasors

We have seen that the distinction between joint tortfeasors and several concurrent tortfeasors is in practice of little importance to a claimant. Full compensation is recoverable. This means that if the defendant against whom judgment is given is unable to satisfy the claim, the claimant is free to sue another defendant. Clearly this runs counter to the desire to minimise any potential waste of court time and costs. This problem is dealt with by the provision that costs cannot be obtained by a claimant for a second or subsequent action unless the court is satisfied that the action is reasonable in all the circumstances (Civil Liability (Contribution) Act 1978 s4).

None of this helps the defendant who may find that a substantial amount is owed in circumstances where others share responsibility. Help is, however, available by virtue of the Civil Liability (Contribution) Act 1978. This provides in s1(1) that a person liable for damage can recover a contribution from any other person who is also liable for that damage, whether that other person has joint or several liability. Rules exist to make sure that the claimant can only recover the actual loss – there is no chance of suing more than one defendant and getting damages twice over!

The amount of any contribution should reflect the extent to which each defendant bears responsibility for the damage. The way this works is similar to the basis on which contributory negligence apportions blame between the claimant and the defendants by virtue of the Law Reform (Contributory Negligence) Act 1945, which is discussed in Chapters 5 and 19.

1.5 Tort and human rights

1.5.1 An innovation in English law?

Legal and political influences

The development of English tort law has been impacted by the Human Rights Act 1998 which gives effect to the European Convention on Human Rights. There was some resistance to the idea of legislative protection of human rights primarily because it was felt that the common law, for example through principles enshrined in the Magna Carta 1215 and the Bill of Rights 1688, was able to give adequate protection by means such as the prerogative orders (*habeas corpus, mandamus, certiorari*) and the process of judicial review. Each of these could restrain the abuse of a citizen's rights by the state. In addition, the doctrine of precedent allows for the incremental development of the law in this area.

The twentieth century saw the growth of powers vested in the state, for example in the areas of social welfare, health and control of the environment, so that the potential for abuse of the individual by the state increased or was perceived to do so. State control of many aspects of individual life was also perceived to have increased when the United Kingdom joined the European Union in 1973; this may be what narrowly tipped the nation into voting for the UK to leave the EU.

The issue of human rights is therefore a political one as it is for Parliament to decide whether, and if so to what extent, individual rights and freedoms and protection from abuse need to be enshrined in statute rather than relying on the common law.

The Convention and its basis in the law of the United Kingdom

The Convention for the Protection of Human Rights and Fundamental Freedoms (hereinafter 'the Convention') is an international treaty which the United Kingdom was the first country to sign as long ago as 1951, but, until Parliament acted, the Convention had little effect in the United Kingdom.

From 1966 British citizens were able to petition the European Court of Human Rights (referred to hereinafter as ECtHR) to obtain rulings as to whether or not fundamental rights had been abrogated by the activities of the state. The problem with this was that the British Government was not bound to have any regard for the decisions of the ECtHR. This meant that whether or not the decisions led to change in the United Kingdom depended largely on political decisions.

From the 1970s onwards debate raged as to the need for a modern Bill of Rights for the United Kingdom, and in 1997 the Labour Party won a general election on the basis that the Convention would be incorporated as part of United Kingdom law. The manifesto promise was fulfilled when the Human Rights Act 1998 was passed, bringing most of the Convention into effect as part of the law of the United Kingdom in October 2000.

1.5.2 The Human Rights Act 1998

The Act is said to have incorporated the Convention into national law. While this is true to a substantial extent, some important provisions of the Convention have not been incorporated, for example Article 13 which gives a right to an effective remedy in a national court, and for the time being the incorporation of certain other articles has been delayed.

The main provisions of the Act are as follows:

- Section 2 – requires any court or tribunal hearing any case which involves a question of Convention rights to take into account the jurisprudence (case law) of the ECtHR whenever it is relevant to the issue.
- Section 3 – requires the courts to interpret all legislation in a way which is compatible with the rights enshrined in the Convention, giving the courts the right to make a 'declaration of incompatibility' where a statute is found to be inadequate to uphold a Convention right (a 'fast track' procedure for the amendment of offending legislation is found in s10 and Sched. 2).
- Section 6 – makes it unlawful for a public authority to act in a way which is incompatible with Convention rights unless constrained to do so by primary legislation. The term public authority is widely construed and can include bodies carrying out functions on behalf of a public authority and exercising the powers conferred upon such an authority. It is not clear when these 'quasi' public bodies will be treated as public bodies. The following contrasting cases demonstrate the difficulty which at present remains unresolved.
- Section 7 – gives a right to challenge decisions or actions by a public authority, the courts having power to declare that decision or action unlawful and, by s8, to grant appropriate remedies, for example, damages.

CASE EXAMPLE

R(A) v Partnerships in Care Ltd [2002] 1 WLR 2610

Managers of a private psychiatric hospital altered the care and treatment of a patient. This was held to be an act of a public nature as the managers were acting in accordance with statutory regimes imposed by the Registered Homes Act 1984 and the Mental Health Act 1983.

CASE EXAMPLE

R (Heather) v Leonard Cheshire Foundation [2002] EWCA Civ 366

The Leonard Cheshire Foundation decided to close one of its homes. Despite the fact that it was in part publicly funded and was regulated by the state, it was held that it was not a public body.

The Human Rights Act 1998 has introduced what can be regarded as an umbrella over the rights of individuals, enabling them to resist oppression by the state by challenging the legitimacy of acts and omissions by the state and/or failures of the law to give effective protection of those rights which the Convention sets out as fundamental.

While protection from abuse by the state or a public body is perhaps the primary aim of the Convention, indirectly it may be of benefit in disputes between private individuals, as the court has a positive obligation to enforce Convention rights. This can involve:

- exercising judicial discretion in a way which gives effect to such rights;
- interpreting legislation in accordance with the Convention;
- developing the common law so that it is compatible with Convention rights;
- creating a remedy in private disputes where it is necessary in order to protect an individual's rights.

CASE EXAMPLE

Venables and Thompson v Newsgroup Newspapers and Associated Newspapers Ltd [2001] 2 WLR 1038

Injunctions were continued to prevent the two boys convicted of the killing of James Bulger from being identified, the court being satisfied that this was necessary to safeguard their rights under Article 2 (the right to life) and Article 8 (the right to respect for private life).

1.5.3 Incorporation of human rights into the law of tort

The general requirement, set out in s2 of the Act, takes account of the ECtHR case law. It must be remembered that this has been developed since the early 1950s. This means that modern cases may well be decided in a rather different way than if reliance had been placed only on common law. It is not possible at this time to anticipate the long-term effect of this requirement but in the context of the law of tort, as will be seen, some old ideas have had to be reconsidered and in some cases, abandoned. Specific reference to relevant cases will be made as appropriate as individual torts are discussed later in this book. In this chapter, the intention is merely to give a flavour of how the Convention is influencing the development of this particular area of law.

Figure 1.1 Human rights are like an umbrella that provides basic rights that overarch the law.

1.5.4 Human rights and trespass to the person

The tort is one of the oldest in the common law and has served to protect individuals from unlawful threats of violence (assault), unlawful violence (battery) and unlawful detention (false imprisonment) (see Chapter 13 of this book). This gives no remedy in English common law to those who are lawfully subjected to what they perceive as unwarranted and unpleasant behaviour. The Convention, in Article 3, imposes an additional requirement by which the lawfulness of behaviour can be judged.

ARTICLE

'No one shall be subjected to torture or to inhuman or degrading treatment or punishment' (Art. 3).

This Article has been important in cases involving medical treatment which show that it does not extend as far as some people would like.

CASE EXAMPLE

Pretty v United Kingdom [2002] 35 EHRR 1, EHtCR

Diane Pretty suffered from a degenerative disease and wanted her husband to be allowed to help her to take her own life. The Director of Public Prosecutions ('DPP') refused to give an undertaking that Mr Pretty would not be prosecuted under the Suicide Act 1961 s2(1), so Mrs Pretty sought judicial review alleging that the decision of the DPP was unlawful and seeking a declaration that the Suicide Act was incompatible with Article 3 and other parts of the Convention. When her case was heard by the House of Lords her appeal was dismissed and she appealed to the ECtHR. It was held at 12:

JUDGMENT

'the absolute and unqualified prohibition on a Member State inflicting the proscribed treatment requires that "treatment" should not be given an unrestricted or extravagant meaning. It cannot . . . be plausibly suggested that the [DPP] or any other agent of the United Kingdom is inflicting the proscribed treatment on Mrs Pretty, whose suffering derives from her cruel disease' (para. 13).

Diane Pretty's suffering was clearly the result of her disease rather than the result of any treatment. She was left with no legal redress using either the common law or the Convention. Presently, the Terminally Ill Adults (End of Life) Bill (commonly known as the assisted dying Bill) is heading towards the final stages of becoming a law and which would now assist those in Diane Pretty's position. There is some concern that this will introduce a licence to kill whereas others feel that this will give those who are terminally ill, a choice.

There are however other cases in which the treatment itself, while lawful under English law, has been found to be 'inhuman or degrading'. Two cases, which were heard by the ECtHR before the Human Rights Act 1998 became law, give an idea of the way in which such claims will be considered in the future. In both cases, the English courts would now be able to hear the complaints pursuant to s6 and would have regard to these and other cases in which the compass of Article 3 has been considered.

CASE EXAMPLE

Keenan v United Kingdom [2002] 33 EHRR 38, ECtHR

Mark Keenan committed suicide while in prison. Throughout his detention it was clear that he suffered from a chronic psychiatric problem. Nine days before his expected release date, he received an additional 28 days in prison for an assault on prison officers. He hanged himself the day after he received the sentence that meant that his release would be delayed. His mother complained to the court that among other matters of concern, the way in which his medical care had been delivered and the delay in his discharge amounted to inhuman and degrading treatment.

The court held that there had been a violation of Article 3 stating at 915:

JUDGMENT

'The lack of effective monitoring of Mark Keenan's condition and lack of informed psychiatric input into his assessment and treatment disclose significant defects in the medical care provided to a mentally ill person known to be a suicide risk. The belated imposition on him in those circumstances of a serious disciplinary punishment . . . is not compatible with the standard of treatment required in respect of a mentally ill person. It must be regarded as constituting inhuman and degrading treatment and punishment within the meaning of Article 3 of the Convention'.

CASE EXAMPLE

Price v United Kingdom [2002] 34 EHRR 53, ECtHR

Ms Price, a thalidomide victim who also had kidney problems, was imprisoned for failure to pay a civil debt. She had to spend the first night at a police station in a cell which was not designed to accommodate those with disability. She was forced to sleep in her wheelchair, was unable to reach the emergency button and unable to use the toilet. Despite her deteriorating condition a doctor was not called for over four hours. Once moved to a prison she stayed in a Health Care Centre where the facilities were better adapted to her needs. However, she complained that she was forced to allow male officers to assist her to clean herself after using the toilet and that a female officer later exposed her to male officers when helping her to the toilet. She complained that her treatment was humiliating and degrading.

The court held that while

JUDGMENT

'there is no evidence in this case of any positive intention to humiliate or debase the applicant . . . the court considers that to detain a severely disabled person in [such] conditions constitutes degrading treatment contrary to Article 3' (para. 30).

In both Keenan and Price, the detention was lawful and there could be no remedy for false imprisonment, nor had either been assaulted or battered to enable the tort of trespass to the person to be used. It is clear that the way each was treated, while lawful, was wholly inappropriate having regard to their respective needs. The Human Rights Act 1998 can therefore provide a remedy where the common law fails to do so.

1.5.5 Human rights and negligence

To date this area of tort law has been most affected by the requirements of Article 13. Article 13 is not incorporated by the Human Rights Act 1998, the view being taken that a sufficient remedy exists by virtue of ss7 and 8. Decisions of the ECtHR are, however, relevant in the United Kingdom by virtue of s2 which expressly requires ECtHR case law to be taken into account in deciding cases before the English courts and tribunals.

ARTICLE

'Every one whose rights and freedoms as set forth in this Convention are violated shall have an effective remedy before a national authority notwithstanding that the violation has been committed by persons acting in an official capacity' (Art. 13).

In the case of *Keenan v United Kingdom* [2002] 33 EHRR 38, ECtHR described above, it can be suggested that an allegation of negligence could have been made on the basis that, in the light of his psychiatric condition, the way in which he was treated was inappropriate and caused him injury. As can be seen in Chapter 4, he would have had to prove that his treatment caused psychiatric injury and this is not clear. He undoubtedly suffered anguish, fear and even terror but the ECtHR held that 'There is no evidence that this would be regarded as "injury" in the sense recognised by domestic law' (para. 128). On this basis the ECtHR held that there had been a violation of Article 13 as there was no effective remedy for violation of his rights under Article 3.

In the context of child care, issues under Article 13 have arisen from the idea that a local authority could not be sued in negligence for decisions made as to the care of children which, with hindsight, proved to be inappropriate and to have caused the children injury (*X and Others v Bedfordshire County Council* [1995] 3 All ER 353). The reason behind this view was that local authorities act for the benefit of society as a whole and would be unduly inhibited by the possibility of being held to account in negligence, unless the circumstances were wholly exceptional. The case came before the ECtHR as *Z and Others v United Kingdom* [2001] 2 FLR 612.

CASE EXAMPLE

Z and Others v United Kingdom [2001] 2 FLR 612; [2001] 34 EHRR 3, ECtHR

Z and her siblings first came to the attention of social services in October 1987. Thereafter there was a string of concerns as to the children's welfare raised by neighbours, the police, teachers, the children's GP and health visitor. In December 1992 the local authority at last applied for and obtained an interim care order. The consultant child psychiatrist who examined the children in January 1993 stated that the case was the worst case of neglect and emotional abuse that she had seen in her professional career. A full care order was made in April 1993. In June of that year, the Official Solicitor started an action on behalf of the children against the local authority for damages for negligence and/or breach of statutory duty. At all stages, right through to the House of Lords, the English courts held that the children's claim must fail. The Children Act 1989 cannot be construed to confer a private law cause of action and the claim in negligence was struck out on the public policy ground that it was not just and reasonable to impose a duty of care on a local authority when dealing with child care cases. The merits of the children's case could not therefore be investigated by the English court.

Having found violation of Articles 3 and 6 (the right to a fair trial), the ECtHR found that

JUDGMENT

'the applicants did not have available to them an appropriate means of obtaining a determination of their allegations that the local authority failed to protect them from inhuman and degrading treatment and the possibility of obtaining an enforceable award of compensation for the damage suffered thereby . . . [T]here has accordingly been a violation of Article 13 of the Convention' (para. 111).

The result of *Z and Others v United Kingdom* has been to change the previously held view that cases of negligence against public authorities should only exceptionally give rise to a right to claim. In effect this meant that such authorities were usually regarded as having *immunity* from legal action but actually this is better understood as a duty not being owed by the authorities so there is an *absence of duty*. Immunity invites notions of policy whereas an assessment of the presence of a duty, invites a sense of neutrality of treatment. (For a detailed discussion of this issue, see Chapter 3.)

1.5.6 Human rights and nuisance

Common law nuisance does not always provide a remedy for un-neighbourly behaviour, particularly where the defence of statutory authority can be used or the public interest demands that an activity should continue. By Article 8 the right to privacy and family life is guaranteed subject to legal and necessary interference. The courts have interpreted this very broadly to include problems with night flights into airports, sewage and low flying military aircraft as interference, but even so a remedy is not always available.

ARTICLE

'1. Everyone has the right to respect for his private and family life, his home and his correspondence.
2. There shall be no interference by a public authority with this right except such as is in accordance with the law and is necessary in a democratic society in the interests of national security, public safety or the economic well-being of the country, for the prevention of disorder or crime, for the protection of health or morals, or for the protection of the rights and freedoms of others' (Art. 8).

It seemed in 2001 that, as a result of the application of Article 8, night flights into and out of Heathrow Airport might be ended or at the least rigorously curtailed.

CASE EXAMPLE

Hatton v United Kingdom [2001] 11 BHRC 634 (Chambers judgment)

Mrs Hatton and others complained that night flights into and out of Heathrow meant that they all suffered sleep deprivation and consequential health problems. They were unable to bring a case before the English courts against the Civil Aviation Authority as the airport was operated by statutory authority found in the Civil Aviation Act 1982 which, by s76, specifically excluded civil liability arising from the operation of the airport. Having found that the noise was capable of being an infringement of Article 8, the ECtHR had to consider whether the state had fulfilled its positive duty 'to take reasonable and appropriate measures to secure the applicants' rights under Article 8(1)' (para. 95).

The court held:

JUDGMENT

'regard must be had to the fair balance that has to be struck between the competing interests of the individual and the community as a whole' . . . 'the State failed to strike a fair balance between the United Kingdom's economic well-being and the applicants' effective enjoyment of their right to respect for their homes and their private and family lives' (paras 96 and 107).

The hope that night flights might be curtailed was short-lived. In *Hatton and Others v United Kingdom* ECtHR 8 July 2003 (Application No. 36022/97) the government appealed to the Grand Chamber, arguing that the economic well-being of the country meant that night flights into the airport were necessary and that the interference with the right under Article 8(1) went no further than was necessary for this purpose. The Grand Chamber agreed with the British Government that the interference was justified under the provisions of Article 8(2).

JUDGMENT

'The question is whether . . . a fair balance was struck between the competing interests of the individuals affected by the night noise and the community as a whole.'

The court held that a fair balance had in fact been achieved. The court also found that domestic remedies had been inadequate to review the position and therefore amounted to a breach of Article 13. This meant that the claimants were entitled to costs.

It is interesting to note that five of the judges, in a court of 17, held that the 'concern for environmental protection shares a common ground with the general concern for human rights' and that 'one of the important functions of human rights protection is to protect "small minorities" whose "subjective element" makes them different from the majority'. The five judges held that compensation should be payable to the claimant.

Night flights continue and, indeed, currently there are plans to expand Heathrow airport, and there is talk to expand Gatwick airport.

Two cases were later decided in which the English courts considered the impact of Article 8.

CASE EXAMPLE

Marcic v Thames Water Utilities [2003] UKHL 66

This was an important test case concerning the potential liability of water service providers for failure to resolve problems experienced by those receiving their services.

Mr Marcic's property was regularly flooded with sewage as the drains provided by Thames Water were inadequate to cope when there was heavy rainfall. The fabric of the house and his gardens were damaged by regular flooding from 1992 onwards. There was no prospect that Thames Water would undertake remedial work in the foreseeable future using the criteria by which priorities were decided.

In the High Court it was held that Thames Water had no liability in nuisance but that Mr Marcic was entitled to a remedy for breach of his Article 8 rights. The Court of Appeal held that Mr Marcic had a valid claim in nuisance at common law but went on to discuss the human rights issue. Although Mr Marcic's rights under Article 8(1) had been violated, the issue turned on Article 8(2) – did the interference go beyond what was necessary in a democratic society? The Court of Appeal held that it did and that Thames Water was liable for infringement of Mr Marcic's Article 8 rights. The matter then went to the House of Lords which held that Mr Marcic could not succeed in his claim using nuisance nor had there been an infringement of his Article 8 rights. Lord Hoffmann explained:

JUDGMENT

'[*Hatton v The United Kingdom*] makes it clear that the Convention does not accord absolute protection to property or even to residential properties. It requires a fair balance to be struck between the interests of persons whose homes and property are affected and the interests of other people, such as customers and the general public' (para. 71).

Mr Marcic's action was dismissed. (For further discussion of the nuisance aspect of this case see Chapter 9.)

In the second case, the English court considered the impact of Article 1 First Protocol as well as Article 8.

ARTICLE

'Every . . . person is entitled to the peaceful enjoyment of his possessions. No one shall be deprived of his possessions except in the public interest and subject to the conditions provided for by law and by the general principles of international law' (Art. 1 First Protocol).

CASE EXAMPLE

Dennis and Dennis v Ministry of Defence [2003] EWHC 793 (QB)

The case concerned the effect of noise from RAF Harrier jet fighters which regularly overflew the neighbouring estate. Having found that a nuisance was established, Mr Justice Buckley further held (at para. 48) 'that the public interest clearly demands that RAF Wittering should continue to train its pilots'. No remedy of injunction was thus available using the common law.

It was argued that the noise interference was a breach of Article 8 and that the impact on the market value of the estate was a breach of Article 1 First Protocol. Having found that there was interference with Article 8 rights, the judge referred to *S v France* [1990] 65 D & R 250 in which it was stated:

JUDGMENT

'Noise nuisance which is particularly severe . . . may seriously affect the value of real property . . . and thus amount to a partial appropriation . . . a fair balance would not be struck in the absence of compensation. I would thus award damages under section 8 in respect of Articles 8 and 1' (paras 61 and 63).

1.5.7 Human rights and other torts

The fact that only three aspects of the impact of human rights into tort law have been highlighted does not mean that there will be no impact in other torts. As has been seen, the fact that the Convention does not have obvious effect is not relevant (e.g. who would have thought, prior to 1998, that flooding by sewage would be regarded as a breach of the right to respect for privacy and a family home?).

The rights protected by the Convention are expressed as principles enforced by a duty on the state to ensure that they are protected. This means that where the law of tort fails to provide a remedy but a person's Convention right has been violated, it may be the case that the state is under a duty to rethink the issue in order to provide the required protection. Developments have been rapid and this is likely to continue.

KEY FACTS

Definition **The Convention**	**Case**
Effective from 1951 but only incorporated into UK law from October 2000.	
Incorporates most of the Convention but not Article 13.	
Allows reliance on Convention rights in the UK courts.	
Human rights and trespass to the person	
Article 3 prohibition of inhuman and degrading treatment.	*Keenan v UK* [2002]; *Price v UK* [2001]
Human rights and negligence	
Although Article 13 right to a remedy not incorporated, public authorities no longer have blanket immunity from actions for negligence.	*Z v UK* [2001]
Human rights and nuisance	
Article 8 capable of wide interpretation: • night flights; • flooding by sewage. Article 1 First Protocol – peaceful enjoyment of property noise interference from aircraft a breach of Article 8 and loss of value of home a breach of First Protocol – compensation payable.	*Hatton v UK* [2003] *Marcic v Thames Water* [2003] *Dennis v Ministry of Defence* [2003]

SUMMARY

- Tort law concerns civil wrongs and developed out of the old writ system.
- Torts involve duties fixed by law.
- The main aims of tort are to compensate the victim and to deter wrongdoing.
- Tort protects personal security, reputation, property and some economic interests.
- Tort interrelates with both Contract Law and Criminal Law but also differs from both.
- Tort generally involves fault liability but there are also some strict liability torts.
- Human rights can affect torts through the European Convention of Human Rights and the Human Rights Act 1988 which incorporates much of the Convention into English law.

2

Negligence: Duty of care

AIMS AND OBJECTIVES

After reading this chapter you should be able to:

- Describe the basic origins and character of negligence
- Identify the essential elements of a negligence claim
- Explain the reasons for retreating from the *Anns* two-part test
- Recognise the role of policy in establishing the existence of a duty of care
- Critically analyse the concept of duty of care
- Apply the relevant tests to factual situations to determine the existence of a duty of care

2.1 Negligence

2.1.1 The origins of negligence and the neighbour principle

The historical background

The origins of negligence lie in other torts in a process known as an action on the case, a method of proving tort through showing negligence or carelessness. Traditionally most torts depended on proof of an intentional and direct interference with the claimant or with his property. Where this was impossible a claimant could make out a special case for liability based on careless deeds.

Long before the twentieth century judges had begun to recognise that many more people suffered loss or injury through careless acts than through intentional ones. Judges towards the end of the eighteenth century established the principle that defendants in certain specific situations might be considered liable for their careless act where they caused foreseeable loss or injury to a claimant. However, there was no general duty of care and there was no means of establishing one. One attempt to establish

DOI: 10.4324/9781003202417-2

a formula through which duty situations could be identified came in *Heaven v Pender* [1883] 11 QBD 503.

In the case Brett MR suggested at 509:

JUDGMENT

'wherever one person is . . . placed in such a position with regard to another that everyone of ordinary sense . . . would at once recognise that if he did not use ordinary care and skill . . . he would cause danger or injury to the person or property of the other, a duty arises to use ordinary care and skill to avoid such danger.'

The development of a general test for establishing the existence of a duty of care

The modern tort of negligence begins with Lord Atkin's groundbreaking judgment in *Donoghue v Stevenson* [1932] AC 562. A new approach was necessary in the case because no other action was available.

The judgment is important not just for the decision itself, or only for identifying negligence as a separate tort in its own right, but also for devising the appropriate tests for determining whether negligence has actually occurred.

CASE EXAMPLE

Donoghue v Stevenson [1932] AC 562

The claimant argued that she had suffered shock and gastroenteritis after drinking ginger beer from an opaque bottle out of which a decomposing snail had fallen when the dregs were poured. A friend had bought her the drink and so the claimant was unable to sue in her own right in contract. She nevertheless claimed £500 from the manufacturer for his negligence and was successful. The House of Lords was prepared to accept that there could be liability on the manufacturer. Two major objections were discussed in the case. The first of these is referred to as the 'contract fallacy'. A previous case, *Winterbottom v Wright* [1842] 10 M & W 109, appeared to contain a clear rule preventing a duty of care from being established in the absence of a contractual relationship. The parties to the action were the manufacturer of the ginger beer and the eventual consumer of his product, the ginger beer actually having been bought by the claimant's friend from the owner of a roadside café. The judges rejected the application of this principle in the case. The second potential problem was one raised by Lord Buckminster, who objected to the possibility of a general test for establishing duty of care, and indeed to the specific duty established in the case. He did so on the basis that it would be destructive to commerce and would only harm consumers by the cost of paying damages in successful actions being added to the price of the manufacturer's goods. Again the majority rejected this argument.

Lord Atkin's judgment contained five critical elements:

(i) Lack of privity of contract did not prevent the claimant from claiming.

(ii) Negligence was accepted as a separate tort in its own right.

(iii) Negligence would be proved by satisfying a three-part test:
- the existence of a duty of care owed to the claimant by the defendant;
- a breach of that duty by falling below the appropriate standard of care;
- damage caused by the defendant's breach of duty that was not too remote a consequence of the breach.

(iv) The method of determining the existence of a duty of care is the so-called **neighbour principle**. This is not the *ratio* of the case but is rather *obiter dicta*. Nevertheless it is a vital guiding principle on which the actual *ratio* was ultimately dependent.

neighbour principle
A test used in negligence to establish whether a duty of care is owed

As Lord Atkin put it at 580:

JUDGMENT

'You must take reasonable care to avoid acts or omissions which you can reasonably foresee would be likely to injure your neighbour. Who then in law is my neighbour? . . . persons who are so closely and directly affected by my act that I ought reasonably to have them in my contemplation as being affected so when I am directing my mind to the acts or omissions in question.'

(v) A manufacturer would owe a duty of care towards consumers or users of his or her products not to cause them harm. This is commonly referred to as the 'narrow *ratio*' of the case.

So from the 'neighbour principle' of Lord Atkin the tort of negligence is identified as being based on foreseeability of harm. The case gives us one clear example of a relationship where possible harm is foreseeable and a duty of care then exists – the duty of a manufacturer to the consumers or users of his or her products.

In one sense, then, the case of *Donoghue v Stevenson* gives us a very simple way of looking at negligence (see Figure 2.1).

In establishing duty the court must be certain that the case involves not just a risk of a type recognised by the law as leading to a duty but that the resulting risk is a type envisaged by the law. In *Bourhill v Young* [1943] AC 92 the court would not accept the existence of a duty in nervous shock because the claimant was not within the area of foreseeable harm. In doing so it approved the judgment of Cardozo J in the American case *Palsgraf v Long Island Railway Co* [1928] 284 NY 339. In imposing a duty, then, a judge must be certain not just that the circumstances are those where a duty is commonly accepted but that the particular defendant owes a duty in the circumstances to the particular claimant.

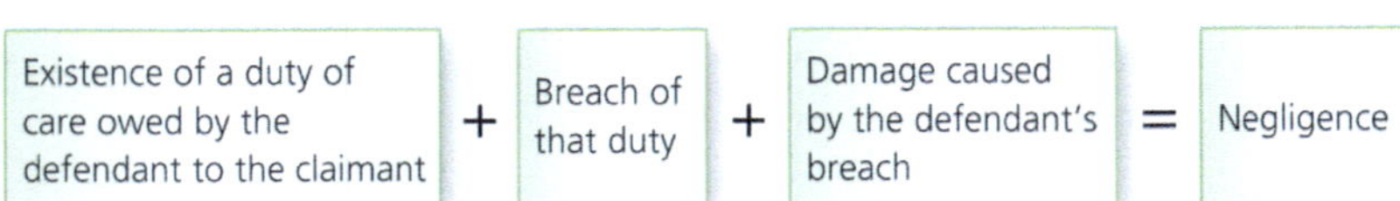

Figure 2.1 The basic elements of an action for negligence.

ACTIVITY

Quick quiz

In the following situation, state which types of loss are recoverable from the manufacturer under the principle in *Donoghue v Stevenson*.

Sacha bought a new toaster last week and on the second time of using the toaster it burst into flames. When she bought it the toaster was in a sealed package, and on both occasions that she has used it she has followed the manufacturer's instructions precisely. Sacha is not in any way to blame for the damage that has resulted:

- The toaster was completely destroyed and Sacha wants a replacement.
- The decorating in the kitchen has suffered smoke damage and needs redecorating.
- A cupboard behind the toaster was burnt so badly that it needs replacing.
- Sacha's arm was badly burnt as she tried to put out the fire and she would like compensation for the injury.

2.1.2 Development in defining duty and the two-part test in *Anns*

Over many years the tort of negligence developed incrementally, case by case, with a duty of care being established in numerous relationships. Lawyers were able to use the neighbour principle to argue for the extension of negligence into areas previously not covered by the tort where damage was a foreseeable consequence of the defendant's acts or omissions.

proximity
Refers to the fact that the defendant should contemplate that his actions may have an effect on potential claimants – rather than physical closeness

At a much later stage in time the test was simplified. The new test did not depend on a duty of care being determined in a given case according to how the case fitted in with past law. Under the new test a duty would be imposed because of the **proximity** of the relationship between the two parties unless there were policy reasons for not doing so. This of course means legal proximity (the extent to which the deeds of one can affect the other), not proximity based on physical closeness.

CASE EXAMPLE

Anns v Merton London Borough Council [1978] AC 728

The local authority had failed to ensure that building work complied with the plans, and as a result the building had inadequate foundations. The claimant, a tenant who had leased the property after it had changed hands many times, claimed that the damage to the property threatened health and safety and sued successfully. The decision was clearly arrived at on policy grounds.

Lord Wilberforce, in framing the 'two-part' test, suggested that the appropriate method of determining whether or not the defendant owed a duty of care in a given case was as follows.

- First it should be established that there is sufficient proximity between defendant and claimant for damage to be a foreseeable possibility of any careless act or omission.

- If this was established, then it was only for the court to decide whether or not there were any policy considerations that might either limit the scope of the duty or remove it altogether.

Lord Wilberforce explained the position in the following terms at 751:

JUDGMENT

> 'the position has now been reached that in order to establish that a duty of care arises in a particular situation, it is not necessary to bring the facts of that situation within those of previous situations in which a duty of care has been held to exist. Rather the question has to be approached in two stages. First one has to ask whether, as between the alleged wrongdoer and the person who has suffered damage there is a sufficient relationship of proximity or neighbourhood such that, in the reasonable contemplation of the former, carelessness on his part may be likely to cause damage to the latter – in which case a prima facie duty of care arises. Secondly, if the first question is answered affirmatively, it is necessary to consider whether there are any considerations which ought to negative, or to reduce or limit the scope of the duty or the class of person to whom it is owed or the damages to which a breach of it may give rise.'

Lord Wilberforce's two-part test led to some significant developments in the law of negligence in the 1980s, particularly in relation to economic loss and nervous shock (see later for instance *Junior Books v Veitchi* [1983] 1 AC 520 in section 6.2). However, these developments were not always considered appropriate and the 'two-part' test caused distress among many judges. Academics such as *J Murray* in Street on Torts (11th edn, Butterworths, 2003) have commented: 'The two part test looked deceptively simple. In effect the plaintiff, having established foreseeability, raised a presumption of the existence of a duty which the defendant then had to rebut on policy grounds.'

The clear problem with the two-part test is the amount of discretion given to judges to determine whether or not a duty should exist in a given situation. As a result of a general unease with the test, the judgments in a series of cases in the 1980s display criticism by senior judges of the two-part test.

Lord Keith in *Governors of the Peabody Donation Fund v Sir Lindsay Parkinson & Co Ltd* [1985] AC 210 suggested that whether or not it was just and fair to impose a duty was a more appropriate test than mere policy considerations.

Lord Oliver in *Leigh and Sillavan Ltd v Aliakmon Shipping Co Ltd (The Aliakmon)* [1986] 1 AC 785 considered that the test should not be considered as giving the court a free hand to determine what limits to set in each case.

misfeasance
This is where the defendant has acted wrongly

In *Curran v Northern Ireland Co-ownership Housing Association Ltd* [1987] AC 718 Lord Bridge indicated that the courts should be wary of extending those cases where a statutory body could be under a duty to control the activities of third parties. He also commented that the *Anns* test 'obscured the important distinction between **misfeasance** and **non-feasance**'.

non-feasance
This is where the defendant has a duty to act and is liable for a failure to act

In this last case Lord Bridge approved the judgment of Brennan J in the High Court of Australia in *Sutherland Shire Council v Heyman* [1985] 60 ALR 1. In this case the judge argued that it was 'preferable that the law should develop novel categories of negligence incrementally and by analogy with established categories'.

In *Yuen Kun Yeu v Attorney General of Hong Kong* [1987] 2 All ER 705 Lord Keith also argued that the *Anns* test had been 'elevated to a degree of importance greater than its merits', and this he felt was probably not Lord Wilberforce's original intention.

These judgments all show a much more cautious approach in determining the existence of a duty of care than need be the case under the two-part test. As a result of this the two-part test was in fact later discarded and the case of *Anns* also overruled.

CASE EXAMPLE

Murphy v Brentwood District Council [1990] 2 All ER 908

A house had been built on a concrete raft laid on a landfill site. The council had been asked to inspect and had approved the design of the raft. The raft was actually inadequate and cracks later appeared when the house subsided. The claimant sold the house for £35,000 less than its value in good condition would have been and sued the council for negligence in approving the raft. The House of Lords held that the council was not liable on the basis that the council could not owe a greater duty of care to the claimant than the builder. In doing so the court also overruled *Anns* and the two-part test, preferring instead a new three-part test suggested by Lords Keith, Oliver and Bridge in *Caparo v Dickman* [1990] 1 All ER 568.

2.1.3 The retreat from *Anns* and the three-part test from *Caparo*

In *Caparo v Dickman* the House of Lords had in fact shown some dissatisfaction with the two-part test and preferred a return to the more traditional incremental approach by reference to past cases. The test was able to change in *Murphy* because they had identified an incremental approach with three stages.

CASE EXAMPLE

Caparo v Dickman [1990] 1 AC 605

Shareholders in a company bought more shares and then made a successful takeover bid for the company after studying the audited accounts prepared by the defendants. They later regretted the move and sued the auditors claiming that they had relied on accounts which had shown a sizeable surplus rather than the deficit that was in fact the case.

The House of Lords decided that the auditors owed no duty of care since company accounts are not prepared for the purposes of people taking over a company and cannot then be relied on by them for such purposes. The court also considered a three-stage test in imposing liability appropriate.

First, it should be considered whether the consequences of the defendant's behaviour were reasonably foreseeable.

Second, the court should consider whether there is a sufficient relationship of proximity between the parties for a duty to be imposed.

Last, the court should ask the question whether or not it is fair, just and reasonable in all the circumstances to impose a duty of care.

In *Caparo* Lord Bridge at 617–618 explained the flaws in the *Anns* two-part test, the need for the modern three-part test and also for a return to an incremental development in the law of negligence.

JUDGMENT

'since the *Anns* case a series of decisions of the Privy Council and of your Lordship's House have emphasised the inability of any single general principle to provide a practical test which can be applied to every situation to determine whether a duty of care is owed and, if so what is its scope. What emerges is that, in addition to the foreseeability of damage, necessary ingredients in any situation giving rise to a duty of care are that there should exist between the party owing the duty and the party to whom it is owed a relationship characterised by the law as one of "proximity" or "neighbourhood" and that the situation should be one in which the court considers it fair, just and reasonable that the law should impose a duty of a given scope upon the one party for the benefit of the other. We must now, I think, recognise the wisdom of the words of Brennan J in the High Court of Australia in *Sutherland Shire Council v Heyman* [1985] 60 ALR 1 where he said:

"It is preferable, in my view, that the law should develop novel categories of negligence incrementally and by analogy with established categories, rather than by a massive extension of a prima facie duty of care restrained only by indefinable "considerations which ought to negative or to reduce or limit the scope of the duty or the class of the person to whom it is owed".'

remoteness of damage

Also known as causation in law – refers to damage which is foreseeable and therefore which the courts are prepared to compensate – they would not compensate for damage that was too remote a consequence of the defendant's breach

Reasonable foresight

The basic requirement of foresight is simply that the defendant must have foreseen the risk of harm to the claimant at the time he or she is alleged to have been negligent. This is to say, what would a reasonable person in the position of the defendant, ought to have foreseen?

This is slightly confusing given the fact that a claimant must then go on and satisfy the **remoteness of damage** test. It is also confusing because foreseeability of harm is also a necessary ingredient of proximity. However, although the two are quite closely linked they are still distinct concepts.

Foresight is always critical of course in determining whether or not there is a duty of care owed. It should also be remembered that there is no general, all-embracing duty of care. The existence of the duty depends on the individual circumstances.

CASE EXAMPLE

Haley v London Electricity Board [1965] AC 778

Workers dug a hole in the ground to access cables but only left it guarded by a long-handled hammer. The claimant, who was blind, did not see that there was a hole and fell into it sustaining injuries. It was foreseeable that such precautions were inadequate to prevent those who were blind, from being injured by the hole. This is to say that, it was foreseeable that there could be blind people or those with partial sight in the vicinity that could be injured.

CASE EXAMPLE

Bourhill v Young [1943] AC 92

The claimant, who was pregnant, was alighting from a tram, some 50 feet away from the scene of an accident negligently caused by the defendant. The claimant did not see the accident but heard it. Shortly after, the claimant went past the scene of the accident and claimed she suffered nervous shock with the result that her baby was stillborn. It was held that there was no duty owed because the claimant was not within the area of foreseeable harm such that the defendant could have envisaged causing the claimant harm.

CASE EXAMPLE

Topp v London Country Bus (South West) Ltd [1993] 1 WLR 976

A bus company did not owe a duty of care when leaving a bus unattended and joyriders stole the bus and injured the claimant.

CASE EXAMPLE

Bhamra v Dubb [2010] EWCA Civ 13

It was held that there was a breach of duty when a caterer supplied eggs at a Sikh wedding and a guest died as a result of an allergy to eggs. Harm from consuming eggs was not in itself foreseeable but the duty existed because Sikhs are not allowed to consume eggs because of their religion so should not have been in the food provided.

Proximity

Proximity was a major part of both the neighbour principle and Lord Wilberforce's two-part test and is still a factor in identifying the existence of a duty of care. Proximity of course means legal rather than factual proximity, exactly what Lord Atkin's neighbour principle explained. There are nevertheless, different ways in which proximity may manifest including, through the relationship between the claimant and defendant, whether the defendant assumed responsibility for the claimant and whether the claimant is part of a class of people that could be potentially impacted.

CASE EXAMPLE

Geary v JD Wetherspoon plc [2011] EWHC 1506 (QB)

The claimant was at the defendant's pub in which there was a grand open staircase in the centre of the building. When the claimant was leaving, she hoisted herself onto the left banister and attempted to slide down it like Mary Poppins. Unfortunately she fell backwards and landed on the marble floor just less than 4 metres below. She sustained a fracture to her spine, resulting in tetraplegia. Proximity of relationship could not be established in this case not least because there was no assumption of responsibility on the part of the defendant. The claimant was injured as a result of her own actions and the mere existence of a occupier-entrant cannot in itself give rise to sufficient proximity.

Where there is an assumption of responsibility by the defendant in relation to the claimant, this can go to establishing that there is sufficient proximity.

CASE EXAMPLE

Kent v Griffiths [2001] QB 36

The claimant suffered from an asthma attack whilst at home. The claimant's GP attended her home and determined that she needed urgent hospital treatment. The doctor called 999 at 16.25 to request for an ambulance, the call was accepted and acknowledged by the call operator. However, by 16.38 no ambulance had arrived, so the claimant's husband made a second call. The operator's response was that one was on its way. There again no ambulance had arrived, and a third call was made at 16.54 and the operator said that the ambulance was only a few minutes away now. The ambulance did not arrive until 17.05 and the claimant arrived at the hospital at 17.17. The ambulance took 34 minutes to arrive. In the absence of any reasonable excuse for the delay, it was found that the ambulance did not reach the claimant's home within a reasonable time. It could and should have arrived at the claimant's home at least 14 minutes sooner than it did. If it had arrived in a reasonable time, as it should have done, there was a high probability that the miscarriage and respiratory arrest from which the claimant suffered would have been averted.

Here, once the emergency call was placed and accepted the emergency service assumed responsibility for the well-being of the patient not least because the class of people to which such a patient belongs is so narrow that proximity can be clearly asserted.

Determining whether there is proximity also inevitably seems to be influenced by policy considerations as illustrated by the following case which has been very influential in determining whether proximity is present:

CASE EXAMPLE

Hill v Chief Constable of West Yorkshire [1988] 2 All ER 238

A serial killer known as the 'Yorkshire Ripper' murdered young women in the Leeds area. He had been questioned by the police several times before being caught and identified as the Yorkshire Ripper. The mother of his last victim brought a claim against the police authority arguing that the police should have apprehended him sooner and if they had, her daughter would still be alive. It was held that there was insufficient proximity between the police and the public for a duty to be imposed to protect individual members of the public from specific crimes. So relatives of victims of the Yorkshire Ripper had no claim against the police for any careless or ineffective handling of the case. The argument that the claimant's daughter would not have died but for the negligence of the police investigation was therefore rejected.

The size of the class to which the victim belonged was appreciably too large for it to be practical to establish proximity in any meaningful way.

The distinction between foreseeability and proximity can be shown when examining the area of liability for nervous shock particularly in the rules relating to secondary victims (see section 6.1.4). Where physical damage is caused by the defendant's negligence it is not difficult to establish proximity. There is quite clearly physical as well as legal proximity. However, where the damage is nervous shock and the claimant is a secondary victim physical proximity may be much more tenuous. The foreseeability of harm may not be problematic. Nevertheless, the claimant in this situation then needs to go on to establish the relationship with the primary victim, the closeness in time and space and the witnessing of the event or its immediate aftermath with his own unaided senses in order to establish liability.

Fair, just and reasonable

This requirement is in reality identifying that there must be a limit to liability and no duty will be imposed unless it is just in all the circumstances. In other words, what are the policy reasons for avoiding the imposition of liability? The thinking since *Caparo* until recent times has been that this limb of the test has stood for the proposition that usually it will not be fair, just or reasonable to impose a duty of care on a public authority when it is engaged in one of its core functions. This has effectively created what is referred to as a 'blanket immunity' for public authorities particularly the police. See further below for examples of the policy reasons advanced to avoid the imposition of liability on public authorities. Before we move on to policy reasons for precluding liability, we need to review the position on liability imposed for positive acts and omissions.

2.2 *Robinson v Chief Constable of West Yorkshire Police* – the evolution of the imposition of a duty of care, policy-based reasoning in negligence and the incremental test

2.2.1 Policy and the three-part test

A major concern expressed about Lord Wilberforce's test from *Anns* was that it put too much power in the hands of judges to decide cases on policy issues alone. While the test may have been flawed, policy considerations have still played a part in determining liability. The major difference is that under *Anns* this was openly done, whereas under *Caparo* it was done covertly through the third part of the *Caparo* test, that it must be fair, just and reasonable in the circumstances to impose a duty. In this manner policy was clearly a consideration in the decision in *Hill* even though that very aspect of the test in *Anns* was subject to wider criticism. Even when *Robinson* reached the Court of Appeal, Lord Hallett LJ expressly made clear at paragraph 46 that 'most claims against the police in negligence for their acts and omissions in the course of investigating and suppressing crime and apprehending offenders will fail the third stage of the *Caparo* test . . . [That is to say,] it will not be fair, just and reasonable to impose a duty'.

The so-called modern three-part test as developed in *Caparo* was such a welcome move away from the two-part test in *Anns* that emphasis was placed heavily on the notion that the courts will only impose a duty of care where it is considered fair, just and reasonable to do so on the facts. This, however, is an interpretation of the decision which is very much mistaken. In *Robinson v Chief Constable of West Yorkshire Police*, the Supreme Court went to great length to set out the correct interpretation of the decision in *Caparo* and how the *Caparo* test should be applied. The decision in *Robinson* effectively tells us to stop anchoring an established duty on policy-based reasoning i.e. the third limb of *Caparo* and to approach establishing duty in the same way regardless of whether the defendant is a private or public authority. Per Lord Reed at 21:

CASE EXAMPLE

***Robinson v Chief Constable of West Yorkshire Police* [2018] UKSC 4**

The proposition that the *Caparo* test applies to all claims in the modern law of negligence, and that consequently a duty of care will only be imposed where it is considered fair, just and reasonable to do so in relation to particular facts, is mistaken. As Lord Toulson pointed out in his landmark judgment in *Michael v Chief Constable of South Wales Police (Refuge and others intervening)* [2015] UKSC 2; [2015] AC 1732, para. 106, that understanding of the case mistakes the whole point of *Caparo*, which was to repudiate the idea that there is a single test which can be applied in all cases in order to determine whether a duty of care exists, and instead to adopt an approach based, in the manner characteristic of the common law, on precedent, and on the development of the law incrementally and by analogy with established authorities.

Indeed, Lord Bridge in *Caparo* highlighted the following at 617:

JUDGMENT

'. . . [there is an] inability of any single general principle to provide a practical test which can be applied to every situation to determine whether a duty of care is owed.'

Lord Bridge went on to explain that foreseeability and proximity are necessary ingredients in establishing a duty of care as well as exploring whether it is also fair, just and reasonable to impose a duty of care. He further explains that since such concepts are difficult to actually define, these should not be used as practical tests but rather as labels to attach to features of the situation in determining whether this is a type of situation which should give rise to a duty of care. This is in addition to recognised categories in which a duty should be recognised as a matter of course. The crucial point that was made by Lord Bridge at 633–634 is:

JUDGMENT

'the law should develop novel categories of negligence incrementally and by analogy with established categories, rather than by a massive extension of a prima facie duty of care restrained only by indefinable "considerations which ought to negative, or to reduce or limit the scope of the duty or the class of person to whom it is owed".'

Lord Toulson in *Michael v Chief Constable of South Wales* [2015] UKSC 2 explained that the incremental approach which was adopted by Lord Bridge in *Caparo* has almost entirely been overshadowed by the so-called three-part test which has been given an elevated level of importance and yet lacks utility as a practical test. With increasing frustration, the Supreme Court at 106 in *Michael* explained that:

JUDGMENT

'[There is an] inability of any single general principle to provide a practical test which could be applied to every situation to determine whether a duty of care is owed and, if so, what is its scope . . ., the concepts both of "proximity" and "fairness" were not susceptible of any definition which would make them useful as practical tests, but were little more than labels to attach to features of situations which the law recognised as giving rise to a duty of care. Paradoxically, this passage in Lord Bridge's speech has sometimes come to be treated as a blueprint for deciding cases, despite the pains which the author took to make clear that it was not intended to be any such thing.'

The ultimate clarification of the test in how to establish a duty of care has been given in the decision in *Robinson*. The Supreme Court has unambiguously set out the current test for establishing a duty of care including how to understand judgments that have been determined using the *Caparo* test at paragraph 100:

JUDGMENT

'. . . it is neither necessary nor appropriate to treat *Caparo Industries v Dickman* [1990] 2 AC 605 as requiring the application of its familiar three-stage examination afresh to every action brought. Where the law is clear that a particular relationship, or recurrent factual situation, gives rise to a duty of care, there is no occasion to resort to *Caparo*, at least unless the court is being invited to depart from previous authority.'

In summary, this decision tells us to look for a precedent and established principles and if a direct precedent exists then to apply that without any need to engage in further reasoning in the merits of whether a duty exists. The precedent will either say that a duty exists in a given scenario or it does not. If a precedent does not exist and we are dealing with a novel type of case, then whether a duty exists can be determined by going beyond existing principles to determine whether a duty of care should be established. Lord Reed summarised this position at paragraph 27 of *Robinson*:

JUDGMENT

'It is normally only in a novel type of case, where established principles do not provide an answer, that the courts need to go beyond those principles in order to decide whether a duty of care should be recognised. Following *Caparo*, the characteristic approach of the common law in such situations is to develop incrementally and by analogy with established authority. The drawing of an analogy depends on identifying the legally significant features of the situations with which the earlier authorities were concerned. The courts also have to exercise judgement when deciding whether a duty of care should be recognised in a novel type of case. It is the exercise of judgement in those circumstances that involves consideration of what is "fair, just and reasonable".

What is an established principle? The case of *Robinson* itself did not turn on a direct precedent but rather established principles. These serve as examples of established principles:

- At common law, public authorities are generally subject to the same liabilities in tort as private individuals and bodies so if conduct would be tortious if committed by a private person or body, it is generally equally tortious if committed by a public authority.
- Public authorities, like private individuals and bodies, are generally under no duty of care to prevent the occurrence of harm unless (i) A has assumed a

responsibility to protect B from that danger, (ii) A has done something which prevents another from protecting B from that danger, (iii) A has a special level of control over that source of danger, or (iv) A's status creates an obligation to protect B from that danger.

- Public authorities, like private individuals and bodies, generally owe no duty of care towards individuals to prevent them from being harmed by the conduct of a third party much like in *Smith v Littlewoods*.'

Where an established principle does not exist or does not assist in determining whether a duty of care should be recognised in the circumstances, then the court will have to consider whether it would be fair, just and reasonable to recognise a duty.

The application of *Robinson* can be further demonstrated in Figure 2.2:

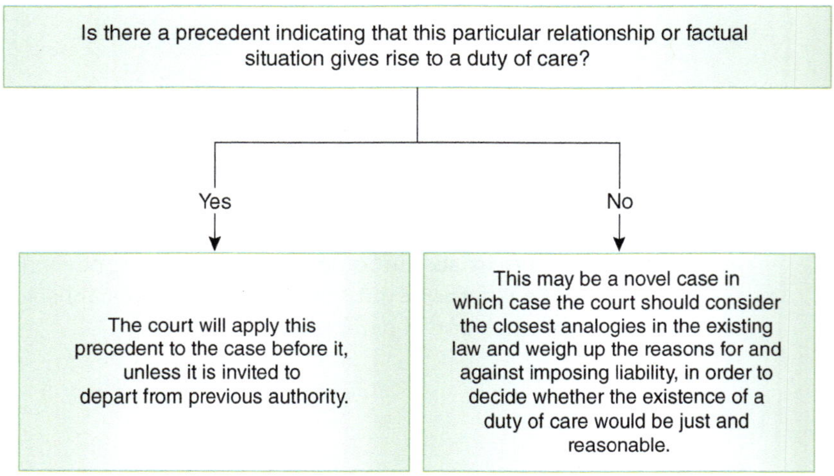

Figure 2.2 Establishing the duty of care incrementally and by analogy with established authorities.

Having had this reset on the law establishing a duty of care following the decision in *Robinson*, we can consider how the courts have moved forward.

The case of *Sumner v Colborne and Others* [2018] EWCA Civ 1006 concerned a road traffic accident in which the defendant argued, *inter alia*, that visibility at the junction was impaired due to the presence of vegetation that the defendant claimed Denbighshire County Council had negligently maintained. One question to be determined in this case was whether the Council did indeed owe a duty of care to the defendant in this respect. This is addressed at paragraph 29:

JUDGMENT

'It seems to me in the light of those various authorities that the existence or otherwise of a duty of care in circumstances of the kind that arise in the present case has not been established by previous decision and that it falls to us to apply the incremental approach summarised in *Robinson v Chief Constable of West Yorkshire Police* to decide whether a duty of care should be recognised in this novel situation . . . As regards analogies, *Yetkin* comes closest on its facts and gives some support to the defendant's case.'

The Court of Appeal found that there were no direct precedents that could be applied although there were some useful precedents which can be considered for guidance, they were too far removed from the facts of this case. There were no established principles that could assist, therefore this case is classified as a novel case and so the Court had to consider whether there was a close analogy. In weighing up the factors for and against the imposition of a duty of care, it was determined that there were powerful reasons for not imposing liability upon the council. These included setting a precedent that owners of land would in the future have to ensure that vegetation in their fields and gardens did not affect sightlines on neighbouring highways and that is just too onerous. It would also extend to the erection of buildings and such things should be managed through planning controls rather than through the imposition of a duty of care. Further, this case concerned an omission rather than a positive duty. There was concern that the finding of a duty would open the floodgates to defendants seeking contributions from owners of land adjacent to the highway in cases where visibility is an issue. In light of such considerations, the Court of Appeal determined that it would not be fair, just and reasonable to find a duty of care in circumstances of the kind that existed here.

It is arguable that the Court of Appeal may have reached the same conclusion using the three-part *Caparo* test in any case, i.e. that perhaps there would have been a lack of proximity between the parties and/or it would not have been fair, just or reasonable to establish a duty.

So the outcome would have been the same but perhaps the reasoning would have stopped one stage prior to getting to the third limb or even if proximity could be established, immunity would have been argued in favour of the public authority. The reasoning under *Robinson* gives more legitimacy to the reasoning than the 'blanket immunity argument'.

In the decision of *James-Bowen and others v Commissioner of Police of the Metropolis* [2018] UKSC 40 there is a further example of the incremental approach being applied to a novel situation where policy reasoning precluded a duty of care being established. Here the Supreme Court determined that the common law does not usually recognise a duty of care in the tort of negligence to protect reputational interests. In this case, police officers' identities were released in connection to allegations that were made against them by a suspected terrorist when he was arrested by them. The police officers contended that their reputation had been damaged and that the Police Commissioner owed them a duty of care to safeguard their interests. There was no direct precedent on this matter or an established principle, so the closest analogies were examined and thought was given to how such a duty would withstand considerations of legal policy in this domain. It was determined by the Supreme Court that it would not be fair, just and reasonable to recognise a duty in these circumstances as there would be a conflict of interest in the Commission trying to faithfully investigate allegations against police officers made by a third party while at the same time trying to protect the reputational interests of those police officers.

In *Darnley v Croydon Health Services NHS Trust* [2018] UKSC 50, the appellant took a blow to the head and attended the A&E department within the responsibility of the defendant. Upon arrival, the appellant explained that he was suffering from a significant head injury but he was told by the receptionist that there would be a 4–5 hour wait. Due to feeling very unsettled, after waiting only 19 minutes the appellant went home. Later, however, he suffered from permanent brain damage. The appellant brought proceedings on the basis that he should have been assessed as a high priority case upon arrival to the hospital and should not therefore have been told that he would have to wait 4–5 hours. The Supreme Court decided that this case is not concerned with the imposition of a duty of care in a novel situation. The common law in this jurisdiction has abandoned the search for a general principle capable of providing a practical test applicable in every situation in order to determine whether a duty of care is owed and, if so, what its scope is.

JUDGMENT

'It has long been established that such a duty is owed by those who provide and run a casualty department to persons presenting themselves complaining of illness or injury and before they are treated or received into care in the hospital's wards. The duty is one to take reasonable care not to cause physical injury to the patient. The duty is to take reasonable care not to cause physical injury to the patient' (para. 16).

The Supreme Court reminds us at paragraph 15 that in *Robinson* it was made clear that where the existence of a duty of care has previously been established, a consideration of justice and reasonableness has already been taken into account in arriving at the relevant principles and it is, normally, only in cases where the court is asked to go beyond the established categories of duty of care that it will be necessary to consider whether it would be fair, just and reasonable to impose such a duty. This was not one of those situations as we are not concerned with a novel duty but rather an established one namely, a duty to take reasonable care not to act in such a way as foreseeably to cause such a patient to sustain physical injury or in other words a duty to take reasonable care not to provide misleading information which may foreseeably cause physical injury.

Prior to the decision in *Robinson*, which of course involved a claim against a public authority, public authorities were effectively protected from claims in negligence as recourse was often had to the third limb of the three-part test in *Caparo*, namely that it would not be fair, just or reasonable to impose liability. We now know that this is an approach that is mistaken. Public authorities do not necessarily have a protected status and if the same duty would be owed by a private party, it could equally be owed by a public authority. It is to claims against public authorities to which we turn below after considering the role of omissions in establishing liability.

2.3 Liability for omissions

As explained above, a duty of care may be imposed for acts done to another which usually involved a positive act. Another way a duty may be imposed is as a result of a failure to act or a failure to prevent harm. This is typically known as an omission, and liability will not be imposed in negligence for pure omissions. Omissions are instances where there is a failure to act because there is no requirement or proximity between any of the parties prompting any action. Omissions should now be considered in a more modern context as espoused by Lord Reed in *Poole BC v GN* [2019] UKSC 25 at para 28. He explains that there is

> '. . . a distinction between causing harm (making things worse) and failing to confer a benefit (not making things better), rather than the more traditional distinction between acts and omissions, partly because the former language better conveys the rationale of the distinction drawn in the authorities, and partly because the distinction between acts and omissions seems to be found difficult to apply. As in the case of private individuals, however, a duty to protect from harm, or to confer some other benefit, might arise in particular circumstances, as for example where the public body had created the source of danger or had assumed responsibility to protect the claimant from harm'.

This tells us that there are two stages to consider when thinking about omissions. The first is that there is generally there is no liability for omissions and second, liability may be established in certain circumstances.

Referring to the first stage, a duty cannot be imposed upon a bystander to help a complete stranger who may be in danger or, put in the modern context, a duty cannot be imposed upon a bystander for failing to confer a benefit on a stranger. To cite some common examples, someone who watches and does nothing as a blind man approaches the edge of a cliff, or watches a child drown in a shallow pool, is not required to save either of them. The parties are strangers to one another and lack proximity of relationship and the situation has not been created by the party watching. There is no reason in law why someone watching such events unfold should be held liable in such situations. There are a number of reasons for this rule which include the following: impacting on one's freedom of choice; why should one bystander over and above another be expected to help; and why should a random bystander be expected to engage in potentially risky activity over another, amongst others. Taking this further as was explained in *Robinson*, using the example in *Hill*, if the police fail to arrest a suspected murderer before a potential future victim is killed or fail to respond to an emergency call in time to save the caller from an attack, as was the case in *Michael* (discussed further below), there can be no liability imposed on the police since they did not create the situation but merely failed to save the victim just like watching someone approach the edge of a cliff or watching a child drown in a shallow pool.

CRITIQUING THE LAW

Do you think that it is right that the law distinguishes between instances where things are made worse and instances where there is a failure to act? Is it right that the law does not impose a legal obligation to help someone in peril?

This is not to say of course, that one does not have a moral obligation or desire to help someone who is in distress. Note, however, that should a person decide to engage in assisting someone that is in peril and makes their position worse in that they assume responsibility for their welfare, then a duty may be owed (see further below on the police and making it worse). The second stage in considering omissions is to consider whether any of the limited exceptions to the proposition that a duty of care is not imposed for an omission apply. These exceptions are helpfully set out by Tofaris and Steel in "Negligence Liability for Omissions and the Police" (2016) 75 CLJ 128:

'In the tort of negligence, a person A is not under a duty to take care to prevent harm occurring to person B through a source of danger not created by A unless (i) A has assumed a responsibility to protect B from that danger, (ii) A has done something which prevents another from protecting B from that danger, (iii) A has a special level of control over that source of danger, or (iv) A's status creates an obligation to protect B from that danger.'

- **Assumption of responsibility** – a promise or assurance on which the claimant relies;

CASE EXAMPLE

Michael v Chief Constable of South Wales Police (Refuge and others intervening) [2015] UKSC 2; [2015] AC 1732

It was argued that the police owed a common law duty of care for the failure (omission) to prevent the perpetrator of the crime from carrying out his acts. The perpetrator killed his ex-girlfriend after she had placed an emergency 999 call which was downgraded in priority. By the time the police arrived, the perpetrator had already killed his ex-girlfriend. It was held that this was a pure omission, namely the failure to protect the victim from the acts of a third party. There was no assurance or promise given as to when the police would arrive.

- **Something which prevents another from protecting someone from a source of danger** – interference principle

  '[I]f A knows or ought to know that B is in need of help to avoid some harm, and A knows or ought to know that he has done something to put off or prevent someone else helping B, then A will owe B a duty to take reasonable steps to give B the help she needs.'

  The decisions in *Kent v Griffiths* can be explained using this exception. Lord Woolf MR at paragraph 49 accepted that, if wrong information had not been given about the arrival of the ambulance, the claimant would have been driven to the hospital and arrived before her respiratory arrest. In other words, the claimant would have been driven to the hospital and arrived prior to her respiratory arrest. This is also an argument that is advanced in *Tindall* which is discussed below.

- **Control** – where the defendant exercises a high degree of control or responsibility

  Control may be established because for instance because of the nature of the relationship between the parties such as parent and child whereby the parent is under a duty to help their child should they find themselves in danger. There are other less obvious scenarios where control is more difficult to establish. Compare and contrast the following cases.

CASE EXAMPLE

Dorset Yacht v Home Office [1970] AC 1004

Negligence against the Home Office was claimed when boys under the control of three guards escaped and caused significant damage to the claimant's yacht. Given the boys' criminal propensities and history of previous escapes, it was argued that the guards had failed to maintain effective control over them. The Home Office argued that the guards did not owe a duty of care to the claimants as this was an omission. A failure to act to prevent harm does not in itself lead to the imposition of a duty of care. However, the House of Lords held that there was a 'special relationship' present in that it was reasonably foreseeable to the officers who were in control over the boys, that they might well do some damage to property nearby.

In *Stansbie v Troman* [1948] 2 KB 48 a decorator who was engaged by the homeowner left the house to obtain materials closing but not locking the front door despite several reminders from the homeowner. A thief broke in and stole property including valuable jewellery. The homeowner sued the decorator in negligence. It was held that the decorator was in a position to exercise such control over the property that he ought to have had the safety of the homeowner's property in mind even though the theft was carried out by a third party.

This case can be compared with the following one in which the requisite level of control was not established.

CASE EXAMPLE

Smith v Littlewoods Organisation Ltd [1987] AC 241

The defendants bought a disused cinema which they intended to develop. Some vandals broke into the cinema and caused a fire which destroyed the property itself and some neighbouring properties. The owners of the neighbouring properties brought an action against the defendants on the basis that they were under a duty of care to prevent intruders entering the cinema and destroying other adjoining properties. It was held that it is implausible to impose such a duty of care on an occupier.

Cases in which such a duty would exist were likely to be rare; and that, since the defenders had not known of the previous acts of vandalism in their cinema involving fire and since the cinema had not otherwise presented an obvious fire risk, the defenders had not been under any duty to the pursuers to anticipate the possibility of the cinema being set on fire by vandals by keeping the premises lockfast or otherwise taking steps to prevent their entry. The defendant had not been under any duty to the pursuers to anticipate the possibility of the cinema being set on fire by vandals by taking the steps which the pursuers contended should have been taken. These were third parties over whom the defender has no control in considering the consequences of acts or omissions on the defender's part.

The requisite level of control and supervision was not found in the following two difficult cases.

CASE EXAMPLE

Palmer v Tees Health Authority [1999] EWCA Civ 135

The claimant's daughter Rosie Palmer, aged 4, was abducted, sexually assaulted, murdered and her body mutilated by a man called Armstrong who is the third party in this scenario. Armstrong had a history of mental illness and was under the psychiatric care of the defendants. He had stated during his admission to hospital that he had sexual feelings towards children and that a child would be murdered after his discharge. After he was discharged, he failed to attend all of his out-patient appointments following his discharge. The claimant and Rosie lived nearby to where Armstrong lived, they did not know each other and there was no history of previous attacks. The claimant argued that the defendant health authority failed to provide the treatment that Armstrong needed and failed to diagnose that there was a real, substantial and foreseeable risk of Armstrong committing serious sexual offences against children. The claim was struck out as disclosing no cause of action. Merely living nearby is insufficient to establish the requisite proximity required to generate a duty of care especially given that Rosie and Armstrong were unknown to each other or in other words, there was no reason why Rosie stood out as being in a category of special risk of harm.

In the next case, an innocent driver was killed by a child straying onto the middle of a busy main road. It was held that the nursery looking after the child failed to exercise sufficient control over its premises which permitted the child to escape and cause an accident in which a driver was killed. The nursery did, therefore, owe a duty of care to the driver.

CASE EXAMPLE

Carmarthenshire v Lewis [1955] AC 549

A 4-year boy (who is the third party in this scenario) attended a nursery which was managed by the local authority, left the nursery premises and wandered onto a main road. The nursery gates were not locked, and the nursery teacher was attending to another child at the relevant time. The claimant's husband was driving a lorry and saw the child in the middle of the road and took evasive action to avoid hitting him but in so doing, crashed into a lamppost and was killed in the crash. The claimant argued that her husband's death was caused by the negligence of the teacher and sued the nursery for being vicariously liable to the negligent actions of the teacher. It was held that the nursery was liable to the claimant in damages given the lack of explanation as to how it was so easily possible for a child to leave the nursery premises and end up in the middle of the road.

- **The defendant's status creates an obligation to protect another from danger**

  This exception is not one that has been particularly effective or successful. The argument advanced by Tofaris and Steel is that the police have special status as they are the body who are tasked with intervening and using force to protect citizens in a way that the members of the public cannot be reasonably expected to do for themselves. This is not an argument that proved consistent with the decision in *Michael* and is one that is unlikely to be successful moving forward. It is far better to consider the following argument which has a greater chance of being successfully argued.

- **Creation of the risk or making the situation worse**
  Additionally, a duty of care may be found in cases of omissions involving a third party where the defendant should have been aware of the risk they have created.

CASE EXAMPLE

Haynes v Harwood [1935] 1 KB 146

A person had left their two-horse van unattended in a busy street. Children (third party) nearby threw stones at the horses which caused them to bolt down the street. The claimant police officer saw that there was a woman and child directly in the path of the horse and ran to stop the horses which he did but suffered injury in doing so. He brought a claim against the defendant horse owners. It was held that the defendant did owe a duty of care since they created a source of danger by leaving the horses unattended and it was foreseeable that leaving the horses in this way could result in injury to another.

CASE EXAMPLE

Topp v London Country Bus (South West) Limited [1993] 1 WLR 976

The defendant bus company would ordinarily leave some of its buses with the keys in the ignition near its depot to assist with the change-over of drivers which usually does not take very long. However, one bus had been left unattended for a significant period of time and was stolen by an unknown party (third party) who unfortunately crashed it into Mrs Topp, killing her. The bus was found abandoned around the corner from the sight of the crash. Mrs Topp's husband brought a claim against the defendant bus company for negligence given that there would be a threat that a bus left unattended with the keys in the ignition might be stolen and cause harm. The question for the Court of Appeal was whether there was a duty of care to protect against the wrongful acts of third parties. On the facts, leaving the keys in the ignition of a bus was not an inherently dangerous thing so it did not create a source of danger in the same way that leaving horses unattended in a busy street did. This did not fall within a special category of risk, so no duty of care was established.

CASE EXAMPLE

Goldman v Hargrave [1967] 1 AC 645 (PC)

In this case lightning struck a tree which caught fire on the defendant's land. The defendant cut down the tree but left it to burn out and took no further steps to douse the tree with water. Later the wind picked up and the fire revived and spread across to the claimant's land. It was held that the defendant was liable for increasing the risk of fire (not for starting it).

On this last exception see the discussion on *Tindall* below, where the police were not held to make matters worse when they attended the scene of a road traffic accident by taking with them the 'police slow' sign when leaving which alerted other drivers to the incident.

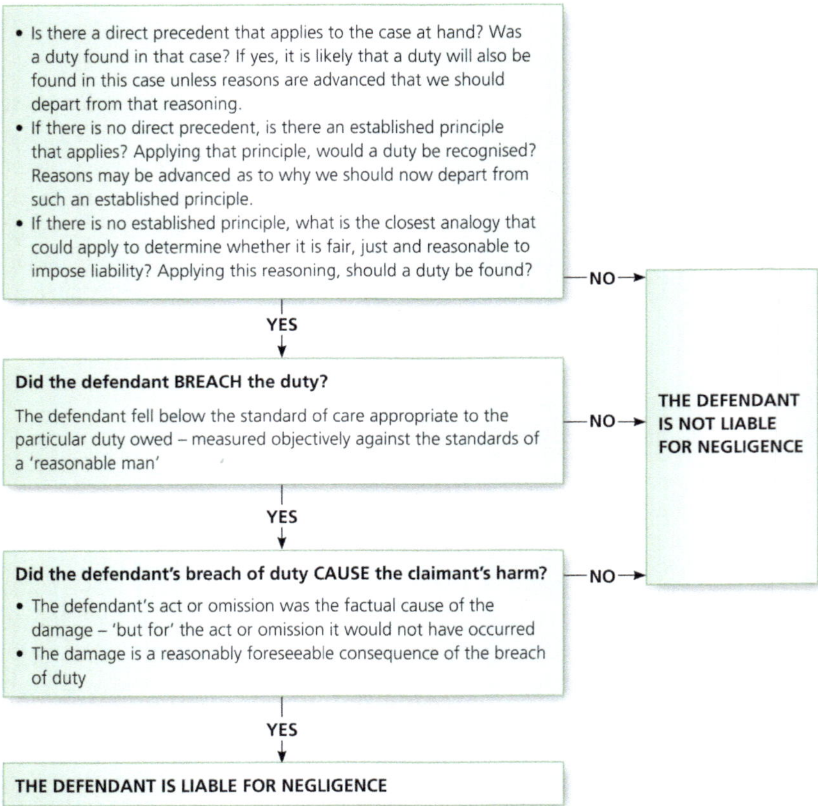

Figure 2.3 The essential elements for proof of negligence with particular emphasis on the establishment of a duty of care.

SAMPLE ESSAY QUESTION

Discuss the extent to which the concept of the duty of care in negligence has developed so that both claimant and defendant are treated fairly.

Outline the essential elements of a negligence claim arising from *Donoghue v Stevenson*

- Duty of care
- Breach of duty
- Foreseeable damage caused by the breach

Discuss the means of establishing duty

- Is there a direct precedent that applies to the case at hand?
- If there is no direct precedent, is there an established principle that applies?
- If there is no established principle, what is the closest analogy that could apply to determine whether it is fair, just and reasonable to impose liability?

Discuss the fairness of the incremental approach

- Based on real situations and relationships
- No general duty of care – so fair

Discuss the fairness of the two-part test from *Anns*

- First part same as neighbour principle
- Second part based on policy – so could work unfairly
- But main criticism was that it gave too much discretion to judges – so overruled

Discuss the fairness of the *Caparo* three-part test

- Based on foreseeable harm, legal proximity and fair, just and reasonable to impose a duty
- So first two very close to neighbour principle
- Question whether the third is just a secret way of reaching policy decisions which can be unfair
- The *Caparo* test did not intend for rigid adherence to the tripartite test but rather intended for there to be an incremental approach to the development of the duty of care

Discuss how *Robinson* has clarified the role of public policy

- Emphasis is now on reviewing established authorities before engaging in an analysis of policy-based reasoning
- If the case is truly novel and an established authority does not provide an answer, then it is right to consider of whether it will be fair, just and reasonable to impose a duty of care (*Darnley v Croydon Health Services NHS Trust*)

ACTIVITY

Self-assessment questions

- Why is *Donoghue v Stevenson* such an important case?
- Exactly who or what in the law of negligence is a 'neighbour'?
- What are the three main ingredients that must be proved for a successful claim of negligence?
- In what ways was the test in *Anns* such a radical change from before?
- Why did the House of Lords discard this test in *Murphy*?
- What is the current test for identifying that there is a duty of care?
- Is the new test actually any better than what went before?
- What is the role of policy in establishing a duty of care?
- To what extent does the duty of care concept act as a control device in negligence claims?

Essay writing

Using the guide in Appendix 1, try the following essay title.

In *McLoughlin v O'Brian* [1982] 2 All ER 298 Lord Wilberforce suggested that 'at the margins, the boundaries of a man's responsibilities for acts of negligence have to be fixed as a matter of policy'.

In the light of subsequent developments, consider the extent to which policy is a major factor in determining the existence of a duty of care.

2.4 Types of defendants: public authorities

2.4.1 Public authorities and policy

Negligence claims by individuals against public authorities such as local authorities, education authorities, and emergency and rescue services must be considered carefully as public authorities are funded by the state and have limited resources. Actions may be brought against a public authority directly or based on vicarious liability for the actions of its employees such as social service workers, police officers or educational psychologists amongst others. Further, claims are brought against public authorities for the actions of third parties e.g. a criminal who they have failed to arrest and has gone on to cause harm or kill another. Since the third party is rarely worth suing if they can be found, a claim is brought against the relevant public authority who will inevitably have deeper pockets and is argued to have had some level of control over the third party. The question that needs to be addressed in such scenarios is, what is it that the public authority has done or failed to do that will attract liability in negligence. Further, if the bar is not set high enough and too many claims of this nature progress, then already stretched public services will be placed under further strain in meeting their core obligations.

There are some preliminary points to consider before reviewing the liability of public authorities which contextualise and inform the direction of judicial thinking in this area.

2.4.2 The *East Suffolk* principle

Public authorities are subject to the same liabilities in tort as private individuals so that if conduct would be tortious if committed by a private person, it would also be tortious if committed by a public authority. Public authorities are under a duty of care to avoid causing harm but like private individuals are under no duty of care to prevent the occurrence of harm as the law does not generally impose liability for pure omissions. Public authorities may have statutory powers or duties enabling or requiring it to prevent the harm in question. This is explained in and is thus often referred to as the *East Suffolk* principle.

CASE EXAMPLE

East Suffolk Rivers Catchment Board v Kent [1941] AC 74

Owing to a very high tide there were several breaches in the sea wall which led to the respondents' land being flooded. Even though this damage was caused by an act of nature, East Suffolk in exercising their statutory *powers* to enter the land undertook to repair of the wall. The repair was carried out poorly, so flooding continued for 178 days causing serious damage to the respondents' land. Had the wall been repaired with reasonable skill, the wall could have been repaired in 14 days. The question was whether they owed a common law duty in negligence for their actions. It was held that the appellants were under no obligation to repair the wall or to complete the work after having begun and so owed no liability to the respondents, the damage suffered by them being due to natural causes. They were not liable in negligence just because they used a method to repair the wall that was unreliable.

JUDGMENT

Lord Romer at 102 explained that 'Where a statutory authority is entrusted with a mere power it cannot be made liable for any damage sustained by a member of the public by reason of a failure to exercise that power. If in the exercise of their discretion they embark upon an execution of the power, the only duty they owe to any member of the public is not thereby to add to the damages that he would have suffered had they done nothing. So long as they exercise their discretion honestly, it is for them to determine the method by which and the time within which and the time during which the power shall be exercised; and they cannot be made liable, except to the extent that I have just mentioned, for any damage that would have been avoided had they exercised their discretion in a more reasonable way.'

This case tells us that just because a public authority negligently exercises its powers, this does not attract a common law duty in negligence unless in so doing, that action makes the claimant worse off than they were before the damage occurred. Something more or extra is required to trigger the imposition of a common law duty of care when exercising their discretion.

2.4.3 Omissions

General rule

This section should be read in conjunction with the general discussion on omissions. This section concentrates on omissions in the context of public authorities in particular.

The law distinguishes two ways of establishing tortious liability:

- making things worse (misfeasance)– the infliction of damage or injury by a positive act; and
- failing to confer a benefit (non-feasance) – causing harm by failing to prevent it or allowing it to happen.

The law does not include any general liability for failing to act or non-feasance. There are of course those that believe that the law should include a 'good neighbour' principle, but this idea has generally not been accepted and in any case would be very difficult and unfair to enforce in most circumstances.

There are two fairly obvious historical reasons for the courts taking this position:

- the problem of showing causation – showing that somebody failed to prevent harm is much more difficult than showing that they caused it;
- the problem of imposing onerous burdens – it is hard to define the situations in which it could be said that a defendant should act and there is a distinct possibility of unfairness in doing so. For instance, should a person who sees someone drowning be obliged to jump in to attempt a rescue even if they cannot swim themself?

In the context of a public authority, a duty of care does not arise just because a public authority fails to exercise a statutory power or duty or fails to prevent an individual being harmed by a third party.

CASE EXAMPLE

Stovin v Wise [1996] AC 923

The claimant had an accident at a junction which was known to the defendant council as being dangerous as road users' view was restricted by a bank on adjoining land (raised part of the road). Accidents had occurred at this junction a few times before. The council resolved to removing part of the bank to improve the junction for road users. The council had not done this at the time of the claimant's accident. The claimant argued that the council had therefore failed to make this improvement and should be held liable for this omission. The House of Lords held that despite there being a statutory power, it is within the council's discretion whether to do this and this did not equate to a duty to act. Lord Hoffmann at 943 highlights that

'There are sound reasons why omissions require different treatment from positive conduct. It is one thing for the law to say that a person who undertakes some activity shall take reasonable care not to cause damage to others. It is another thing for the law to require that a person who is doing nothing in particular shall take steps to prevent another from suffering harm from the acts of third parties . . . or natural causes.'

Where it is argued that a public authority failed to confer a benefit, in other words it is argued that duty of care should be found because of an omission, this will only be the case if the public authority's act falls within one of the exceptions. An explanation of these exceptions has been provided in the previous chapter and is only recounted here in brief. These exceptions will be referenced as appropriate in the context of different public authorities below.

(i) assumption of responsibility – a promise or assurance on which the claimant relies;
(ii) something which prevents another from protecting someone from a source of danger – interference principle;
(iii) control – where the defendant exercises a high degree of control or responsibility;
(iv) the defendant's status creates an obligation to protect another from danger;
(v) creation of the risk or making the situation worse

For further discussion of the intersection of liability between public authorities and these exceptions see Morgan, J, 'Maintaining the elegant façade of the acts-omissions distinction' [2022] *Cambridge Law Journal* 245–248.

2.4.4 Policy and public authorities

Since public money is involved in meeting claims against public authorities, policy becomes a major consideration in determining whether such claims in negligence are possible. Establishing a duty of care and liability in favour of the individual will set a precedent that this type of defendant will owe a duty of care. As these bodies are funded by the state, any resources diverted towards meeting claims will inevitably mean that these services have less resources available to provide services necessary. Decisions in the past have usually rested on whether it is fair, just and reasonable in the circumstances to impose a duty and/or, it has been argued that there is a lack of proximity between the public body and claimant.

Prior to the guidance provided in *Robinson*, the approach generally was to deny the finding of a duty of care on public policy grounds. It is for this reason that public authorities have in the past been said to have a 'blanket immunity' against a finding of liability. The decision in *Robinson* has now made clear that no such immunity exists and that whilst policy will continue to be important, public authorities do not retain a special status by which policy could be used to shield them from a finding of a duty and that, policy will really only ever be considered in a truly novel case.

Policy factors considered by judges

Policy has always been a major consideration in determining liability in negligence. The court has to decide not just whether there is or is not a duty, but whether there should or should not be one. Navigating policy considerations in relation to claims against public authorities continues to be difficult given their status and funding.

Policy factors that can influence the determination of whether a duty should exist or not include:

- Loss allocation – inevitably judges have been more likely to impose a duty on a party who is able to stand the loss, the role of insurance clearly is a major determining factor also.

- Practical considerations – the courts for instance have been willing to impose vicarious liability on companies that can then plan effective policies for the future avoidance of liability.
- Moral considerations – for instance the public might be more prepared to accept a 'good Samaritan' law than would the judges.
- Protection of professionals – Lord Denning in particular expressed concern here that professionals should not be prevented from working by restrictive rulings.
- Constitutional considerations – the judges are not keen to be seen as law makers, which they acknowledge is Parliament's role.
- The 'floodgates' argument – judges are reluctant to impose liability where to do so might encourage large numbers of claims on the same issue – this does not appear to be a morally justifiable position and it has particularly hampered the development of liability for nervous shock.
- The beneficial effects of imposing a duty for future conduct – in *Smolden v Whitworth and Nolan* [1997] PIQR P133 the court imposed a duty on a rugby referee who failed to properly control a scrum.

In summary, when considering the liability of public authorities, it is important to remember the following points.

(i) Public authorities may owe a duty of care in the same way that a private individual might.

(ii) Just because a public authority is under a statutory duty or power to prevent the harm occurring, does not automatically mean that a parallel duty of care arises. Something extra is required for a duty in negligence to arise.

(iii) Public authorities, like private individuals, are generally under no duty of care to prevent the occurrence of harm. This was confirmed in *Michael* at paragraph 97 by Lord Toulson who stated 'the common law does not generally impose liability for pure omissions'.

(iv) A claim might be brought against a public authority for the actions of a third party against the claimant but there is no general duty to prevent others from causing harm.

The rest of this chapter will explore the circumstances in which different public authorities have come under a duty of care to prevent harm, relevant policy considerations and the application of exceptions to the omissions rule.

2.4.5 Liability of local authorities

This section explores the liability of local authorities when discharging their statutory functions which has triggered a claim in negligence. Local authorities have many responsibilities that stretch across many areas including the provision of social services especially in the context of child welfare, housing, healthcare provisions and beyond which is reflected in the cases below.

Child welfare

Over a long period of time, it was the case that judges used policy as a means of ensuring that there is not an unrestricted expansion of liability in tort.

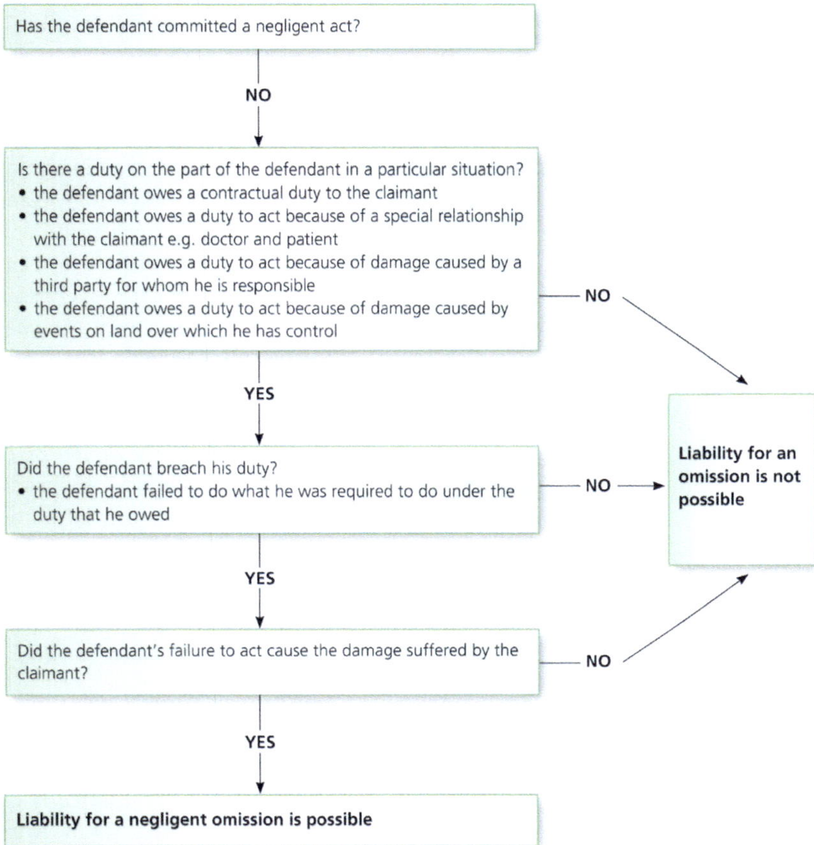

Figure 2.4 The essential elements for a claim for an omission to act.

This policy-based position and reasoning has firmly been rejected in the decision of *Poole v GN* which provides the most recent position of the law in this area. *Poole* strongly shifts away from using public policy–based reasoning in favour of the assumption of responsibility test.

CASE EXAMPLE

Poole BC v GN and another [2019] UKSC 25

This case concerned the liability of a local authority for an alleged negligent failure to exercise its social services functions so as to protect children from harm caused by third parties. In this case the claimant children, one of whom is severely disabled both mentally and physically, were placed in an area in which it was known to the council that there was a family that engaged in anti-social behaviour. The children were subjected to appalling treatment by this family and one of the children attempted suicide as a result of the treatment. The claimants including the mother argued that the council, in the exercise of its housing functions, owed them a duty of care to protect them from abuse and anti-social behaviour by rehousing them. Second, the children argued that the council owed them a duty of care to protect them from harm by allowing them to continue to live on the estate. The Court of

Appeal determined that no duty should be owed to prevent such harm by taking such children into care to protect them.

The Supreme Court unanimously agreed that the local authority could not be held liable. At paragraph 74, Lord Reed states that: '. . . the decision in *X (Minors) v Bedfordshire* can no longer be regarded as good law in so far as it ruled out on grounds of public policy the possibility that a duty of care might be owed by local authorities or their staff towards children with whom they came into contact in the performance of their functions . . . or in so far as liability for inflicting harm on a child was considered, to depend upon an assumption of responsibility. Whether a local authority or its employees owe a duty of care to a child in particular circumstances depends on the application in that setting of the general principles most recently clarified in the case of *Robinson*. Following that approach, it is helpful to consider in the first place whether the case is one in which the defendant is alleged to have harmed the claimant, or one in which the *defendant is alleged to have failed to provide a benefit to the claimant, for example by protecting him from harm*. The present case falls into the latter category (emphasis added).'

The principal question of law was: whether a local authority or its employees may owe a common law duty of care to children affected by the manner in which it exercises or fails to exercise its social services functions, and if so, in what circumstances.

Since the claim concerned a failure to confer a benefit, a duty would only arise here if the council had assumed a responsibility to protect the claimants which it did not. Just because the council had a statutory obligation to investigate and monitor the claimant, that did not automatically convert into or give rise to an assumption of responsibility to protect them from their neighbours. For a claim to be successful against the local authority, the claimant will need to show that an assumption of responsibility has been established but this is difficult especially in cases where there has been a failure or omission to remove children.

Moreover, the decision in *Poole* is not to be taken to mean that assumption of responsibility is a developing or uncertain area of law. The decision in *Poole* has clarified that where appropriate, it remains prudent to strike out applications that do not disclose circumstances giving rise to a duty of care.

CASE EXAMPLE

HXA v Surrey County Council [2023] UKSC 52

In this case there were two claims brought by children in negligence against local authorities for a failure to protect them from the sexual or physical harm that they suffered by their parent or parent's partner. They argued that the local authorities owed them a duty of care to protect them from harm as they were under their care. Following *Poole*, given that the claims concerned a failure to benefit the claimants by protecting them from harm by a third party they needed to establish that there was an assumption of responsibility undertaken by the local authority to protect them from harm. Moreover, they needed to specify the precise nature of the assumption of responsibility. What did the defendant assume responsibility to use reasonable care, to do? The local authority had failed to do what it had resolved to do as next steps in investigating the position in relation to the claimants but, this does not in and of itself evolve into an assumption of responsibility. At paragraph 101 it is confirmed that: 'The denial of an assumption of responsibility in these two cases is, in any event, dictated by the decision that there was no assumption of responsibility in *N v Poole*. Given that in *N v Poole* there was no assumption of responsibility to protect children from their abusive neighbours, it is hard to see how there was an assumption of responsibility in our cases to protect the children from the abuse by a parent or parent's partner.'

However, the Supreme Court at paragraph 105 did say that the denial of a duty of care in this case does not mean that there can never be an assumption of responsibility, and hence a duty of care owed, by the social services department of a local authority to protect a child from harm. See for example the case of *Barrett v Enfield* discussed further below. Two examples were given by the Supreme Court. The first is that is where the local authority has taken a child into care (e.g. foster or respite care) and has thereby taken on parental responsibility for a child. In that situation, the local authority has assumed responsibility to use reasonable care to protect the child from harm including harm from third parties. The second is where an assumption of responsibility flows from the fact that the child's safety has been entrusted to the local authority by the parents, the local authority has accepted that responsibility, and indeed the parents may be said to have delegated parental responsibility to the local authority such as in the case of *Barrett*.

In terms of whether the older cases survive the decisions in *HXA* and *Poole*, the older cases still have relevance and should not be side-lined. Lord Reed explains at paragraph 73 of *Poole* that the reasoning in the older cases that came before *Poole* can be reframed or understood in the context of the assumption of responsibility test. The imposition of a common law duty of care towards the parents in cases such as *JD v East Berkshire* would still be inconsistent with the statutory framework, since it would interfere with the performance by the authority of its statutory powers and duties in the manner intended by Parliament. So, the reasoning in many of the cases before *Poole* is still relevant but crucially, the well-known decision *X v Bedfordshire* is no longer good law because it was decided on the basis of public policy.

CASE EXAMPLE

X v Bedfordshire County Council [1995] 3 All ER 353

This was a series of appeals for striking out actions against public authorities. One involved child abuse where the local authority failed to act after the children were referred to them by social workers who worked for the local authority. The argument was that the children suffered long-term damage that could have been avoided had the council acted promptly. The other group involved a failure to provide special needs facilities. In the case concerning child abuse, it was held that it would not be just or reasonable to impose a duty, since it would cut across the council's other statutory obligations and remove resources that could otherwise be used for child protection. The justification given by the judges in the House of Lords was that the statute that the council were allegedly in breach of was for the benefit of the public generally, not only individuals.

The case of *X v Bedfordshire* was later taken to the European Court of Human Rights (under a different name) *Z and others v United Kingdom* [2001] 34 EHRR 3 and a different decision was provided. The European Court of Human Rights accepted that the children had been subjected to inhuman and degrading treatment contrary to Article 3, and that they had been refused an effective remedy contrary to Article 13. The English courts had to rethink the blanket immunity from liability that they have in the past been prepared to offer public bodies. Clearly now, especially following *Robinson* and *Poole*, we have come a long way away from policy-based reasoning and offering blanket immunity to public authorities. In *Poole* it was held at paragraph 74 that:

> 'In the light of the cases [Lord Reed has] discussed, the decision in *X (Minors) v Bedfordshire* can no longer be regarded as good law in so far as it ruled out on grounds of public policy the possibility that a duty of care might be owed by local authorities or their staff towards children with whom they came into contact in the performance of their [statutory] functions'.

CASE EXAMPLE

The Supreme Court in *Poole* has reaffirmed the status of the decision in *D v East Berkshire* as one that remains good law.

D v East Berkshire [2003] EWCA Civ 1151

This case involves three separate cases heard jointly. Here the parties are parents who brought proceedings against their respective local authorities for incorrectly determining that they had been abusing their children where in fact, there were medical reasons underlying their children's ill-health. In the first case, the mother suffered psychiatric harm after being wrongly accused of suffering from a mental illness; in the second case a father was wrongly accused of sexual abuse against his daughter preventing him from seeing her; and in the third case, parents were wrongly accused on inflicting injuries on their daughter which led to them being separated from her.

The Court of Appeal had to consider how the local authority must manage the potential conflict between the interests of the parents and the interests of the children. It is important that healthcare professionals are not inhibited from acting in the best interests of the children by a concern that they may be in breach of duty owed to the parents. For this reason, it was concluded that for public policy reasons, where child care decisions are being taken, no common duty of care should be found in favour of the parents at the same time but that where it is fair, just and reasonable to find a duty of care with respect to such children, this may be possible depending on the facts. This formulation of the test using policy has now been reframed by the Supreme Court in *Poole* as the following (paragraph 54): '. . . the imposition of a common law duty of care towards the parents would be inconsistent with the statutory framework, since it would interfere with the performance by the authority of its statutory powers and duties in the manner intended by Parliament'.

Cases prior to *Poole* such as *D v East Berkshire* where policy was used to deny a duty of care should be compared with cases where a duty was established but now, following *Poole*, can be understood in terms of finding an assumption of responsibilities, and this is illustrated by the following two cases.

CASE EXAMPLE

Phelps v London Borough of Hillingdon [2000] 4 All ER 504

As a result of breaches of statutory duties under the 1944 and 1981 Education Acts by educational psychiatrists, children were not diagnosed as special educational needs with the result that they did not receive the educational facilities which would otherwise have been provided. This inevitably has an impact on their employment prospects. This was a failure to confer a benefit. The House of Lords held that there was a duty of care owed by the educational psychologist.

In *Poole* at paragraph 69, the Supreme Court held that the reasoning in *Phelps* can be understood as the educational psychologist having assumed responsibility for the professional advice which he provided about a child in circumstances where it was reasonably foreseeable that the child's parents would rely on that advice.

CASE EXAMPLE

Barrett v Enfield London Borough Council [2001] 2 AC 550

The claimant had been taken into care of the local authority since he was 10 months old until he reached 18 years old. The claimant argued that the defendant authority via its various support services had failed to safeguard his welfare resulting in multiple placements, failed to consider adoption as well as failed to make proper arrangements to reunite him with his mother. He claimed that this left him with a deep psychological illness. He argued that the local authority was under a duty to show him the standard of care which would be expected of a responsible parent. The local authority sought to strike out the claim on the basis that the exercise of the authority's statutory functions fell within their discretion and so it was non-justiciable and that it would be contrary to policy (or not fair just or reasonable) to impose a duty of care on the authority. The House of Lords held the case that the case should not be struck out without proper investigation into the facts and that the authority did owe a duty of care.

In *Poole* at paragraph 73, it was explained that in *Barrett v Enfield,* the local authority assumed responsibility for the welfare of a child when it took him into its care.

This area of law in relation to local authorities and their duties to children is now clearer following the decision in *Poole*. Nevertheless, it is concerning that this decision makes it difficult for already vulnerable people to hold local authorities and other relevant decision-making bodies liable. The preferred outcome from the Supreme Court's decision would have been the recognition of a duty in some limited circumstances perhaps restricted to situations involving third parties such as children.

2.4.6 Police

Liability of the police to the public

Prior to the decision in *Robinson*, absent special circumstances such as an assumption of responsibility, the police usually did not owe a duty of care to individuals when performing their duty of investigating and preventing crime. As discussed in the previous chapter in *Hill v Chief Constable of West Yorkshire*, one argument for this proposition of course is that there is an alternative means of compensating through a claim to the Criminal Injuries Compensation Authority as opposed to finding a private duty of care.

Claims against the police can be considered from three different standpoints. The first is when the police discharge its operation or core function. The second is when the police assume responsibility for a person's welfare. The third is under a human rights perspective.

Operational negligence

CASE EXAMPLE

Robinson v Chief Constable of West Yorkshire Police [2018] UKSC 4

An elderly lady, Mrs Robinson was walking along a street but was knocked over in a struggle between two police officers and a man whom they were trying to arrest. During the struggle, they knocked into Mrs Robinson and fell on top of her causing her personal injuries. The question that arose in this case was whether the police owed Mrs Robinson a duty of care, and if they did, were they in breach of that duty. This injury was caused when the police were performing their core operational activities. The Supreme Court decided that the police were nevertheless liable for the injuries caused as there is no general rule that the police are not under any duty of care when discharging their function of preventing and investigating crime. They generally owe a duty of care when such a duty arises under ordinary principles of the law of negligence, unless statute or the common law provides otherwise. Applying those principles, they may be under a duty of care to protect an individual from a danger of injury which they have themselves created, including a danger of injury resulting from their own actions.

When establishing a claim in negligence, if there is an analogous precedent or a particular relationship which gives rise to a duty of care, then there should be no recourse to the three-part test in *Caparo* and there is certainly no need for consideration of whether it is fair, just and reasonable to impose such a duty *unless* the argument is being made that the court should depart from previous authority. The police like anyone else, may be liable in tort to a person who is injured as a direct result of their acts or omissions. Courts are prepared to impose a specific duty on bodies such as the police where for instance there is clear and outrageous negligence.

CASE EXAMPLE

Rigby v Chief Constable of Northamptonshire
[1985] 1 WLR 1242

The claimant's shop was burnt out when police fired a canister of CS gas into the building to force out a dangerous psychopath who had broken into it and was firing from inside it. The canister set the shop on fire and there was no firefighting equipment in attendance.

It was held that a duty of care was owed in such a circumstance as the police created the danger.

The cases of *Robinson* and *Rigby* dispense with any suggestion of there being a rule that the police owe no duty of care when engaged in their core operational activities, or that 'outrageous negligence' or an assumption of responsibility must be established. On the contrary, these cases are examples of the application to the police of the ordinary common law duty of care to avoid causing reasonably foreseeable injury to persons and reasonably foreseeable damage to property.

In the case of *Brooks v Commissioner of Police for the Metropolis*, the House of Lords explains that in non-operational matters, to impose a duty of care on the police, would cut across the freedom of action the police ought to have when investigating serious crime.

CASE EXAMPLE

Brooks v Commissioner of Police for the Metropolis
[2005] UKHL 24; [2005] 1 WLR 1459

This involved the friend of the murdered teenager Stephen Lawrence. He claimed that he had suffered post-traumatic stress disorder both as a result of the handling of the crime investigation and as the result of his own treatment as a witness and as a victim. The House of Lords would not accept that the police owed any duty in these respects. The reasoning is not unlike that in *Hill*, that to allow potential liability to witnesses and victims of crime would prevent the police from concentrating on their primary functions and would lead to a very defensive approach to tackling crime.

Assumption of responsibility by the police

Generally, the police do not appear to owe a duty of care towards 'informers', on whose support they rely extensively in the investigation of crime. However, the police may owe a duty of care if it can be demonstrated that they have assumed responsibility for the welfare of particular individuals.

CASE EXAMPLE

Marsh v Chief Constable of Lancashire Constabulary [2003] EWCA Civ 284

Here a car dealer who was an informer for the police sought damages when his former business associate assaulted him. The former partner had been arrested but subsequently released by the police. The court held that it would not be 'fair, just and reasonable' to impose a duty on the police to take into account the claimant when considering releasing the business partner on bail. There was a duty to take the safety of the public into account in ordering release but there was no special relationship between the police and informers that would entitle the claimant to be owed a personal duty.

Compare this decision with that of the decision in *Swinney*.

CASE EXAMPLE

Swinney v Chief Constable of Northumbria Police [1997] QB 464

In this case, the claimant had supplied the police with the name of the person who had hit and killed a police officer. The details of the name of the claimant were recorded in a document which was left in a police vehicle from which it was stolen and somehow came into the hands of the person who had killed the police officer. The claimant subsequently received threats of violence and arson and suffered from significant psychological harm. The claimant argued that the defendant owed her a duty of care to ensure that the recorded information was securely stored as opposed to being secured in an unattended car.

Initially it was determined that the police were immune from such an action and did not owe a duty of care to the claimant as there was not a sufficient relationship of proximity and it would not be fair, just and reasonable to impose the duty upon one party for the benefit of the other. The claimant's position was deemed to be no different from the many thousands of citizens who supply information to the police. The Court of Appeal, however, took a different view and held that the policy arguments that applied in *Hill* for instance, do not apply in this case as retention of a confidence does not involve any diversion of resources, matters of policy and discretion or reopening investigations. In this case an individual was clearly identifiable and, in the circumstances, there are strong public policy considerations favouring the imposition of a duty namely to encourage the public to inform about crime with confidence in the system. It was held that a special relationship could be established between the claimant and the police through the assumption by the police of responsibility to preserve the confidentiality of information supplied by the claimant which was likely to expose them a risk greater than the ordinary risk to the general public. This position was confirmed Lord Brown of Eaton-under-Heywood in the House of Lords delivering the judgment in *Van Colle v Chief Constable of Hertfordshire Police* [2008] UKHL 50 at para 135:

Judgment

JUDGMENT

'True it is that in *Brooks* both Lord Nicholls of Birkenhead and Lord Steyn contemplated the possibility of exceptional cases on the margin of the *Hill* principle which might compel a different result. If, say, the police were clearly to have assumed specific responsibility for a threatened person's safety – if, for example, they had assured him that he should leave the matter entirely to them and so could cease employing bodyguards or taking other protective measures himself – then one might readily find a duty of care to arise. That, however, is plainly not this case. There is nothing exceptional here unless it be said that this case appears exceptionally meritorious on its own particular facts – plainly not in itself a sufficient basis upon which to exclude a whole class of cases from the *Hill* principle.'

In *Sherratt v Chief Constable of Greater Manchester Police* [2018] EWHC 1746 (QB), it was established that the police had assumed a responsibility for the welfare of the deceased and a duty of care was established. In this case the mother of the deceased called the police concerned for the welfare of her daughter who was suicidal. The call handler gave a specific assurance to the mother that they would have the police attend her daughter's house and if necessary, arrange for her daughter to be transferred to hospital and that she, the mother, need not do anything else. This assurance induced reliance and met the requisite level of proximity required to establish a duty of care as the focus was on the welfare of one specific individual. This case illustrates the significance of what the call handler says or what assurances they offer to the caller. This case is similar to the decision in *Kent v Griffiths* but distinct from cases where a person takes their own life because here the police were specifically contacted about the deceased's welfare and then assumed responsibility for her welfare including transferring her to hospital if necessary. This case appears to fall within the example provided in *Van Colle*. In cases that involve suicide and where that is the very risk that the police have been made aware, if that risk should materialise, the police are unlikely to succeed by arguing that either there was a break in the chain of causation or that the deceased had willingly taken that risk. This is illustrated by the cases that follow.

CASE EXAMPLE

Reeves v Commissioner of the Metropolitan Police [1999] 3 WLR 363

Police were holding a prisoner who was a known suicide risk. When the prisoner did commit suicide the court rejected the police defence of *novus actus interveniens*. The suicide was the very risk that the police should have been guarding against.

A similar approach was taken in *Kirkham*.

CASE EXAMPLE

Kirkham v Chief Constable of the Greater Manchester Police [1989] 3 All ER 882

The defendant police authority was made aware at the time of taking the prisoner into their custody that he had suicidal tendencies. The prisoner managed to hang himself whilst in custody, the very risk which the police were informed about. The victim's wife brought an action against the police authorities claiming that by taking a man into custody the police assume a duty to pass on to the prison authorities all information regarding his well-being. The police knew that the prisoner was a suicide risk but failed to pass this information on to the prison authorities. The prisoner, who was suffering from clinical depression, committed suicide. Had the prison authorities known of the risk they would have taken steps to prevent his suicide. Held, that by taking the husband into custody the police had assumed a duty of passing information that might affect his well-being on to the prison authorities. As the husband was clinically depressed he could be said to have waived any claim by reason of his suicide and his act was the very occurrence that the duty imposed upon the police should have prevented. Therefore, a plea of *volenti non fit injuria* could not succeed.

Claims against the police and the Human Rights Act

The sort of blanket immunity from negligence actions enjoyed by the police has led to the issue being challenged in a human rights context. This is to say that where it has been held that the police do not owe a duty of care, a parallel claim has been explored under the Human Rights Act 1998. In *Hill*, the House of Lords confirmed that there is no general duty of care owed by the police to individual members of the public in the investigation and suppression of crime and public policy provided immunity from such a claim.

CASE EXAMPLE

Osman v United Kingdom [2000] ECtHR, 29 EHRR 245; [1999] Crim LR 82

Osman's teacher, Mr Paul Paget-Lewis, formed an unnatural attachment to him. His teacher started a campaign of harassment against Osman and his family which included taking pictures of Osman, following him home and acts of vandalism to the Osman family home and property. Through this period, the Osmans had contacted the police regularly and the police had cause to interview Paget-Lewis but did not arrest him. These events culminated in Paget-Lewis stealing a gun and shooting and killing Osman's father and injuring Osman. Paget-Lewis was convicted and later detained in a mental hospital. In a civil action for negligence against the police for failure to prevent the attack on the family, the court rejected and struck out the claim on the basis of the immunity in *Hill*. Subsequently, the Osmans took their case to the European Court of Human Rights on the grounds of the State's failure to protect the lives of Osman and his father under Article 2 (right to life) and that they had no access to a court in respect of that failure. The ECtHR held that with respect to the Article 2 claim, whilst the State's obligation is to secure the right to life by putting in place effective criminal provisions to deter the commission of offences against the person and enforcement mechanisms to support these provisions, Article 2 goes further an in some defined circumstances, there may be a positive duty to take further preventative measures to protect an individual whose life is at risk. This duty however must not impose a disproportionate burden upon the authorities taking into account resources, priorities and the unpredictability of human conduct. This duty will only be deemed to have been violated if the authorities knew or ought to have known of a *real and immediate right to life* of an identified individual from the criminal acts of a third party and they failed to take measures to avoid that risk. On the facts, Osman was unable to identify a particular point in the sequence of events where it could be said that the police knew or ought to have known that his life or the lives of his family were at real or immediate risk from Paget-Lewis. In other words, is there anything to demonstrate that the police have assumed responsibility for the welfare of the individual concerned, created the danger or are in some way responsible for the third party?

Moving on to the Article 6 (right to a fair trial) claim, the ECtHR held that this approach to striking out the claim contravened Article 6. While the court appreciated that the rule was in place to ensure the effectiveness of the police, it had not been balanced with the rights of the public. This is considered further in the context of claims against local authorities and the decision in *Z and others v UK* (2001) 34 ECRR 3.

The reasoning in *Hill v Chief Constable of West Yorkshire* was followed in the joined appeals *Chief Constable of Hertfordshire v Van Colle; Smith v Chief Constable of Sussex* [2008] UKHL 50. Both cases involved prospective witnesses in criminal proceedings who had been attacked and murdered by the accused.

In the first case, the House of Lords rejected a claim that the police had breached the deceased's right to life under Article 2 of the European Convention of Human Rights because the test in *Osman v UK* was not satisfied. There was no *real and immediate right to life* of an identified individual from the criminal acts of a third party, and they failed to take measures to avoid that risk. The murderer was a seriously disturbed and unpredictable person and the court concluded that the police could not have anticipated his behaviour. In the second case, there were no 'special circumstances' as required by *Hill* to impose a duty on the police.

CASE EXAMPLE

Michael v Chief Constable of South Wales [2015] UKSC 2

The victim made a 999 call detailing that her former partner was threatening her with violence and would be returning to her house soon to kill her. The call handler asked her to keep her line free. The call was classified as a high priority call because of the threat. When the call was passed on, the threat was not mentioned and the call was downgraded. About 15 minutes after her first call, the victim called 999 again and the call handler heard a scream. When the police attended her house, they found the victim had been stabbed to death. The victim's dependants brought a claim under Article 2 of the ECHR, namely the victim's right to life. The police applied to strike out the claim on the basis of their immunity i.e. they did not owe a duty of care to prevent the actions of a third party and because a duty is not owed for a pure omission which this was. Further there was no assumption of responsibility as the call handler had done nothing to give rise to an assurance but merely an expectation.

At paragraph 114, the Supreme Court explained that:

JUDGMENT

'It does not follow from the setting up of a protective system from public resources that if it fails to achieve its purpose, through organisational defects or fault on the part of an individual, the public at large should bear the additional burden of compensating a victim for harm caused by the actions of a third party for whose behaviour the state is not responsible. To impose such a burden would be contrary to the ordinary principles of the common law.'

As to the Article 2 claim the direction that was given was that it is not necessary to develop the law of negligence to comply with the ECHR, Articles 2 and 3, particularly as ECHR claims have different objectives from civil actions such as negligence.

The police and making it worse

***Tindall v Chief Constable of Thames Valley Police* [2024] UKSC 33**

This case was brought by the widow of Mr Tindall who was killed in a road traffic accident. The claim was brought against the police for making matters worse after having earlier attended an accident on the same stretch of road where another driver, Mr Kendall lost control of his vehicle due to the presence of a patch of black ice on the road. Whilst Mr Kendall was waiting for the police, he flagged down other drivers alerting them to the presence of black ice. When the police arrived, they placed a 'police slow' sign on the road. Once Mr Kendall was taken away by ambulance and the police having cleared the debris from the accident, they removed the police slow sign, called for a gritter to come out without explaining the urgency of the situation and left the scene. Some minutes later another vehicle lost control on the same patch of black ice and careered across the road and crashed head on with Mr Tindall resulting in both drivers being killed. Crucially, Mr Kendall confirmed that had the police not arrived at the scene at all, he would have carried on trying his best to alert other drivers to the danger.

The claimant argued that the police intervention made matters worse and/or the police had assumed responsibility in a manner that gave rise to a duty of care to protect Mr Tindall from harm.

Lord Justice Stuart-Smith when delivering the judgment in *Tindall* in the Court of Appeal at paragraph 54, helpfully set out the principes derived from previous decisions in addressing the question whether the police are to be taken as having assumed responsibility to an individual member of the public so as to give rise to a duty to exercise reasonable care to protect them from harm. They are as follows:

(i) Where a statutory authority (including the police) is entrusted with a mere power it cannot generally be made liable for any damage sustained by a member of the public by reason of a failure to exercise that power. In general the duty of a public authority is to avoid causing damage, not to prevent future damage due to causes for which they were not responsible: see *East Suffolk, Stovin;*

(ii) If follows that a public authority will not generally be held liable where it has intervened but has done so ineffectually so that it has failed to confer a benefit that would have resulted if it had acted competently: see *Capital & Counties, Gorringe, Robinson;*

(iii) Principle (ii) applies even where it may be said that the public authority's intervention involves it taking control of operations: see *East Suffolk, Capital & Counties;*

(iv) Knowledge of a danger which the public authority has power to address is not sufficient to give rise to a duty of care to address it effectually or to prevent harm arising from that danger: see *Stovin;*

(v) Mere arrival of a public authority upon, or presence at, a scene of potential danger is not sufficient to found a duty of care even if members of the public have an expectation that the public authority will intervene to tackle the potential danger: see *Capital & Counties, Sandhar;*

(vi) The fact that a public authority has intervened in the past in a manner that would confer a benefit on members of the public is not of itself sufficient to give rise to a duty to act again in the same way (or at all): see *Gorringe;*

(vii) In cases involving the police the courts have consistently drawn the distinction between merely acting ineffectually (e.g. *Ancell, Alexandrou*) and making matters worse (e.g. *Rigby, Knightly, Robinson*);

(viii) The circumstances in which the police will be held to have assumed responsibility to an individual member of the public to protect them from harm are limited. It is not sufficient that the police are specifically alerted and respond to the risk of damage to identified property (*Alexandrou*) or injury to members of the public at large (*Ancell*) or to an individual (*Michael*);

(ix) In determining whether a public authority owes a private law duty to an individual, it is material to ask whether the relationship between the authority and the individual is any different from the relationship between the authority and other members of the same class as the individual: see *Gorringe*, per Lord Scott.

Lord Justice Stuart-Smith highlights at paragraphs 66 and 67 that there is a distinction to be drawn between the police merely acting ineffectually and making matters worse. In terms of making things worse, all that could be said is that the arrival of the police led Mr Kendall to assume that they would act in a certain way namely, to somehow alert other drivers to the danger which influenced him to get into the ambulance. The arrival of the police could not be said to have been negligent, and it cannot be said that they made matters worse by putting out the 'police slow' sign clearing the debris and then removing it when they left. At most these actions can be described as a public authority acting ineffectually and failing to confer a benefit that may have resulted if they had acted more competently. An argument was advanced that the police did make matters worse under the interference principle at paragraph 50:

> "[I]f A knows or ought to know that B is in need of help to avoid some harm, and A knows or ought to know that he has done something to put off or prevent someone else helping B, then A will owe B a duty to take reasonable steps to give B the help she needs.

This is another way of saying that there exists a duty of care not to make matters worse by acting in a way that creates an unreasonable and reasonably foreseeable risk of physical injury to the claimant. There is no reason in principle why the conduct which creates this risk should not consist in acts which are foreseeably likely to have the effect of putting off or preventing someone else from taking steps to protect the claimant from harm. On the facts of the case, the claimant would need to show that the police knew or ought reasonably to have known that their conduct had or might have had the effect of putting off or preventing Mr Kendall from warning other motorists of the ice hazard. The claimant could not show that the police knew what role Mr Kendall was playing in altering other drivers to the risk or that he would have continued to do so had they not arrived.

This scenario did not fit into either of the two exceptions (control or assumption of responsibility) to the general rule that there is no duty of care to prevent harm caused by a third party or a hazard that they had not created. It cannot be said that the police exercised any control over the accident scene. It was held that police did not do anything which could on any view be characterised as taking control of the patch of ice which represented the source of danger. In fact, they did nothing at all about that source of danger. They did not cordon off or close the road. This is an example of the police behaving ineffectually, but that cannot be turned around to say that there was a duty of care consequent on their having taken control of the patch of ice. There was nothing to suggest that the police assumed responsibility to Mr Tindall or any other road users by the occurrence of black ice on that stretch of road. An ineffectual response by the police officers does not give rise to a duty of care in negligence to protect road users from hazards or dangers on the road which they had not created. The appeal was dismissed by the Supreme Court.

The decision in *Tindall* has subsequently applied by the Court of Appeal in *Chief Constable of Northamptonshire Police v Woodcock* [2025] EWCA Civ 13.

This appeal combined two unrelated cases that raised issues as to whether the police may be liable in damages for failing to protect a person from harm caused by the criminal actions of a third party.

CASE EXAMPLE

Chief Constable of Northamptonshire Police v Woodcock [2025] EWCA Civ 13

In the first case of *Woodcock* the claimant argued that the police failed to protect her from her on/off boyfriend, Guzelyurt. Woodcock had made complaints to the police about his behaviour towards her and her children as well as reporting that he had threatened to kill her. There was significant police involvement following a series of incidents involving Guzelyurt harassing Woodcock and her family with neighbours becoming aware of the situation. One morning the neighbours alerted the police to the presence of Guzelyurt loitering outside the house even suggesting that he would attack Woodcock. The police treated this as an emergency and attended Woodcock's house but did not alert her that Guzelyurt was seen outside. When Woodcock left her house that morning, Guzelyurt near-fatally stabbed Woodcock. Woodcock claimed damages for negligence on the basis that the police had failed to protect her from the attack, to arrest Guzelyurt earlier than they did or to warn her that he was outside her house.

The second case, *HD, PD, CJ, PJ, OB v Chief Constable of Wiltshire Police* ("*CJ*"), concerned MP, who possessed indecent images of children and had committed sexual offences against minors. A laptop containing indecent images was passed on to the police by MP's mother in December 2012. The police suspected that the images were downloaded by MP's father BP who had already been convicted of sexual offences. The task was given middle to low priority and the examination of the laptop was completed and reported on in May 2014 confirming that the person who downloaded the indecent images was in fact MP. The police did not take any action against MP. In February 2015, OB's mother complained to the police that MP forced her son to watch rude pictures. In April 2015 HD's mother reported MP for sexual abuse of HD. In June 2015, the police connected the review of the laptop with the reports of the abuse. There were three other victims. A claim was brought for the breach of their Article 3 rights (prohibition of torture) together with a claim that police negligence had led to MP being able to avoid detection for so long so he could go on to commit the offences against the claimants.

Consideration was given to the nine points set out in the Court of Appeal judgment in *Tindall*. In *Woodcock*, the central question was whether the Chief Constable had a duty to warn Ms Woodcock about her neighbour's information that Guzelyurt was loitering nearby. As per the rules, Woodcock would have to demonstrate that her claim fell within one of the exceptions to the rule that there cannot be liability for an omission or failure to act. On the facts the police did nothing which can be regarded as an assumption of responsibility to warn Woodcock or to prevent any attack upon her by Guzelyurt. They had not promised Woodcock that they would warn her of any sighting of Guzelyurt near her home and had not promised to pass on to her any information they received alerting them to a danger. They had not promised to respond within any particular time to any information alerting them to a risk of attack. Compare this with the decision in *Kent* where there was an assumption of an ambulance arriving. Following on from the reasoning in *Tindall* where the interference principle was confirmed by the Supreme Court, Woodcock argued that the call handler caused her neighbour to refrain from taking action that she would have taken thereby making matters worse. However, there was no evidence as to what the neighbour would have done. In fact, the neighbour said that she did not want to get involved. Contrast this with what Mr Kendall said he would have done in *Tindall*, which was to continue to draw the hazard on the road to the attention of other drivers. Finally, it could not be said the police had any more control over Guzelyurt than the police have over persons they suspect of a crime but have not yet been able to arrest. Therefore, no liability against the police could be established. Woodcock's case is a case of an omission by the police to act, which did not make matters worse.

In *CJ* there were two central arguments raised. The first was that the police had been negligent and that the failings and delay of the police to act upon reviewing the contents of the laptop meant that MP could avoid detection and go on to commit the offences against the claimants. The failings of the police were omissions and failures to act rather than positive acts making things worse. As such, the actions do not fall within any of the exceptions to the rule that a person is not under a duty to take care to prevent harm occurring to another person through a source of danger not created by them. The next claim advanced was that there was a breach of Article 3 of the ECHR (prohibition of torture). It was held that as the images on the laptop were not numerous nor of the most serious kind to meet the threshold to engage Article 3, and if it did, it would be to those in the images rather than the claimants in this case. The facts did not present a real and immediate risk to the individuals concerned but rather a generalised risk, which is insufficient to engage Article 3. The claim was therefore dismissed.

2.4.7 Emergency services

NHS

The NHS may be held liable for the negligent acts of its employees by being vicariously liable for their conduct. This includes the actions of A&E receptionists, nurses and doctors.

The case of *Darnley* has already been discussed above but it is worth mentioning it again here in the context of a patient attending an accident and emergency unit at a hospital. The Supreme Court highlights that a duty of care is owed by those who run a casualty department to persons presenting themselves complaining of illness or injury and before they are treated. So even though work at the reception desk of an A&E can be delegated to non-medically trained staff, liability for damage may be established if such staff through their negligence including the negligent provision of information cause damage to a patient even if they are yet to be treated.

Judgment

JUDGMENT

***Darnley v Croydon Health Services NHS Trust* [2018] UKSC 50**

Lord Lloyd-Jones explained at paragraph 21 that: '. . . what a reasonable person would have done and could reasonably be expected to have done in the context of a busy A & E department . . . [drawing] attention to the difficult conditions in which staff at such departments often have to work . . . A & E department waiting areas are not always havens of tranquillity . . . if there is a duty to provide "precise and accurate information" about the length of time before a patient might be seen by a triage nurse, it is difficult to see why it does not extend to an obligation to correct such information as changing pressures on resources arise . . . . The question under consideration is whether the respondent owes a duty to take reasonable care when providing, by its receptionists, information as to the period of time within which medical attention is likely to be available.'

Fire brigade

The liability of the fire brigade was considered in the following case in which four appeals were heard together as they all raised the question whether the fire brigade owe a duty of care for its negligent acts or omissions.

CASE EXAMPLE

Capital Counties Plc v Hampshire [1997] QB 1004

This case concerned a conjoined appeal. In two of the cases, the fire brigade attended to tackle a fire and turned off the sprinkler system which was in operation. Whilst the mere attendance of the fire brigade at the scene of the fire alone could not create sufficient proximity between the claimants and the defendants, there must be some more, something that makes it worse or creates the danger. By switching off the sprinkler system, the fire brigade created the risk of the fire spreading beyond that what it would have done had the sprinklers not been turned off. The fire did indeed spread and destroy the buildings. The fire brigade did therefore make the situation worse and did therefore owe a duty of care.

In the third claim, the fire brigade attended to deal with a fire on premises adjacent to the claimant's building. It was alleged that the fire brigade did not adequately inspect that the fire had been properly extinguished with the result that it reignited damaging the claimant's property. In the fourth claim, the claimant's property had been destroyed by a fire which the fire brigade had failed to extinguish owning to a lack of proper water supply.

The third and fourth claims are instance of omissions; there was not an assumption of responsibility and therefore a lack of proximity between the fire brigade and the owner of the adjacent property. There was no positive act on the part of the fire brigade. There was an ineffectual response. Nothing that the fire brigade did made the situation worse than it would have been had they not attended the scene. The fire brigade did not therefore owe a duty of care in the third or fourth claim.

In summary (at 1030): '. . . the fire brigade are not under a common law duty to answer the call for help, and are not under a duty to take care to do so. If, therefore, they fail to turn up, or fail to turn up in time, because they have carelessly misunderstood the message, got lost on the way or run into a tree, they are not liable.'

Ambulance service

CASE EXAMPLE

Kent v Griffiths (No 3) [2001] QB 36

The facts of this case are discussed above.

JUDGMENT

'The mere existence of public duties does not of itself create a special relationship imposing a duty in private law; there is no special relationship or assumption of responsibility merely because a statutory body has embarked upon the performance of its statutory functions, even in relation to an identified individual . . . There is a specific assumption of responsibility when an ambulance is said to be on its way, equivalent to that of a doctor to a patient in a casualty department. The fact that, following a 999 call, an ambulance may always be sent does not negative that assumption of responsibility. Once an ambulance is allocated there is no position of conflict' (paras 38 and 40).

What this case tells us is that unlike the police or fire brigade, the public policy grounds that have precluded the existence of a duty of care do not apply to the ambulance service when responding to a 999 telephone call; that the ambulance had been called for the claimant alone and it was foreseeable that she would suffer further injuries if its arrival was delayed and there was no reason why it should not have been provided within a reasonable time. The ambulance therefore assumed responsibility towards the claimant who was relying on the ambulance to attend.

ACTIVITY

Self-assessment questions

1 What exactly is 'failure to confer a benefit'?
2 Why did English law traditionally reject the idea of liability for a failure to act?
3 In which situations will courts impose liability where there has been an omission to act?
4 What is the common factor in those situations where the courts will impose such liability?
5 In what circumstances could the police owe a duty of care to another?
6 What is the difference between the decision in *Kent v Griffiths* and *Tindall v Chief Constable of Thames Valley Police*?

ACTIVITY

Quick quiz

Which of the following is an omission creating a duty of care?

1 A man sees another man bleeding to death in the street and walks past.
2 A doctor refuses to attend to a sick patient who then dies.
3 An electrician paid to fit new lights for a householder leaves some bare wires overnight and a child of the house is electrocuted.
4 A person who has borrowed a book from a friend leaves the book on the bus and it is lost.
5 I could help my nephew revise for his A Level Law but I do not and he fails.
6 Sparks from my barbecue are blown by a high wind and set fire to my next door neighbour's shed.

KEY FACTS

The development of the duty of care in negligence	Case
Negligence requires the existence of a duty of care, which is breached by the defendant and causes damage to the claimant that is not too remote a consequence of the breach – Lord Atkin. The existence of a duty is established by reference to Lord Atkin's 'neighbour principle' – neighbours are those people who are so closely affected by our deeds that we should take care to avoid harming them.	*Donoghue v Stevenson* [1932]

(*Continued*)

(Continued)

A development of the test was Lord Wilberforce's 'two-part' test – first, see if there is sufficient proximity between claimant and defendant to impose a duty; second, decide whether policy reasons will prevent a duty being imposed.	*Anns v Merton LBC* [1978]
This test was later overruled.	*Murphy v Brentwood District Council* [1990]
The 'three-part' test for establishing a duty – 'Is there proximity?', 'Is the damage foreseeable?', 'Is it just and reasonable to impose a duty?', are mere labels and should not be used with rigidity	*Caparo v Dickman* [1990]
The law should develop novel categories of negligence incrementally and by analogy with established categories	*Robinson v Chief Constable of West Yorkshire Police* [2018] UKSC 4
• Post-*Robinson* application of an existing precedent (established category of duty of care) or closest analogy • No analogy or established principle	*Darnley v Croydon Health Services NHS Trust* [2018] UKSC 50 *Sumner v Colborne and Others* [2018] EWCA Civ 1006 *James-Bowen and Others v Commissioner of Police of the Metropolis* [2018] UKSC 40
Liability will not be imposed for pure omissions which is distinct from arguments about policy. These decisions involve pure omissions not a determination of policy. Liability for public authorities no blanket immunity exists under the disguise of policy There is a shift away from using public policy–based reasoning when analysing the potential liability of public authorities using in favour of the assumption of responsibility test	*Mitchell v Glasgow City Council* [2009] 2 WLR 481; UKHL 11; *Michael v Chief Constable of South Wales* [2015] UKSC 2 *Poole BC v GN* [2019] UKSC 25 *HXA v Surrey County Council* [2023] UKSC *Poole BC v GN* [2019] UKSC 25 *D v East Berkshire* [2003] EWCA *Phelps v Hillingdon BC* [2000]

SUMMARY

- Prior to 1932 there was no specific action for negligence available – although there was a similar action called 'on the case'.
- *Donoghue v Stevenson* established the elements for a successful claim in negligence: duty of care owed by the defendant to the claimant, breach of that duty and foreseeable damage caused by the breach.
- It also established the neighbour principle (a means of identifying when a duty of care is owed).
- A later two-part test devised by Lord Wilberforce was based on (1) whether there was legal proximity between the parties and (2) whether there were any policy reasons to refuse to impose a duty.
- Judges were unhappy with the excess of power this test gave them so it was later overruled and replaced with a three-part test for establishing duty from *Caparo v Dickman*: foreseeable harm, legal proximity of the parties and that it is fair, just and reasonable to impose a duty.
- *Caparo v Dickman* was not intended to be adhered to as a rigid three-stage test and now the incremental approach as explained in *Robinson* is to be applied in determining whether a duty of care exists.
- There are certain situations where the courts are reluctant to impose a duty because of policy reasons.
- The law does not include any general liability for omissions or failing to act unless an exception applies. Public authorities may owe a duty of care in the same way that a private individual might.
- Public authorities may be under a statutory duty or power to prevent the harm occurring, but that does not automatically mean that a parallel duty of care arises. Something extra is required for a duty in negligence to arise.
- Public authorities may be responsible for the actions of a third party but there is no general duty to prevent others from causing harm.

Further reading

Cornford, T, 'The negligence liability of public authorities for omissions' (2019) *78(3) CLJ* 545–569.

Denning, L, *The Discipline of Law* (Butterworths, 1979), Part 6 Chapter 1.

Morgan, J, 'Maintaining the elegant façade of the acts-omissions distinction' [2022] *Cambridge Law Journal* 245–248.

Nolan, D, 'Negligence and human rights law: The case for separate development' (2013) *76 MLR* 286.

Tofaris, S, and Steel, S, 'Negligence liability for omissions and the police' (2016) *75(1) The Cambridge Law Journal* 128–157.

von Hagen, D, 'Oral references: Careless talk costs money' [2001] *DJ Freeman Litigation Review* 9.

3

Negligence: Breach of duty

AIMS AND OBJECTIVES

After reading this chapter you should be able to:

- Identify the relevant measure of care applicable to non-professionals and professionals
- Explain and apply the general standard of care
- Explain and apply the standard of care applicable to professionals, particularly doctors
- Identify the factors used in determining whether a defendant has fallen below the standard of care appropriate to the duty owed
- Critically analyse the concepts of standard of care and breach of duty of care
- Identify the appropriate standard of care in factual situations
- Apply the factors for determining breach to factual situations in order to establish if a breach has occurred
- Describe the requirements for a plea of *res ipsa loquitur*, and the effects of a successful plea

3.1 The standard of care and the 'reasonable person' test

3.1.1 The standard of care

To establish a claim in negligence, there needs to be a duty of care owed to another person, a breach of that duty which causes damage which is not too remote a consequence of the breach of duty.

Breach of duty, the second element of negligence, refers to the standard of care that is appropriate to the duty owed. A breach of duty simply

DOI: 10.4324/9781003202417-3

occurs when the party owing the particular duty falls below the standard of behaviour that is required by the particular duty in question.

There are two steps here. The first is to determine the standard of care, and the second is to determine whether or not the defendant's behaviour has fallen below that standard according to established tests. While the standard of care in any situation is a question of law, whether or not the defendant has fallen below the standard is a question of fact that will be determined by reference to all of the circumstances of the case.

The standard of care required is generally measured according to an objective method of testing. In this way, while what is the appropriate standard is obviously determined factually according to the circumstances of the case, it is nevertheless the standard that would have been adopted by a 'reasonable person' confronted by the same circumstances that will be taken as the measure by which the defendant's actions will be judged.

3.1.2 The 'reasonable person' test – the objective standard

The objective standard measured according to the standards of the 'reasonable person' was first identified in the following case:

CASE EXAMPLE

Blyth v Proprietors of the Birmingham Waterworks [1843–60] All ER Rep 478

A water main was laid in which there was a 'fire plug'. This was a wooden plug in the main that would allow water to flow through a cast iron tube up to the street when necessary. A severe frost loosened the plug and water flooded the claimant's house, the cast iron tube being blocked with ice. The frost was beyond normal expectation. There was nothing that the defendants could have reasonably done to prevent the damage and there was no liability.

In explaining how the standard of care is measured and identifying the significance of the 'reasonable person' in objectively measuring the standard Alderson B made the following observation (at 478):

JUDGMENT

'Negligence is the omission to do something which a reasonable [person], guided upon those considerations which ordinarily regulate human affairs, would do, or doing something which a prudent and reasonable [person] would not do.'

The test on the face of it seems simple enough. The question is, who is the reasonable person by whose standards we are supposed to judge our behaviour?

Judges have over time attempted to define the character of the reasonable person in order that the objective standard can be more closely understood.

In *Hall v Brooklands Auto-Racing Club* [1933] 1 KB 205 Greer LJ defined the reasonable person as follows (at 224):

JUDGMENT

'The person concerned is sometimes described as "the [person] on the street", or as the "[person] on the Clapham Omnibus", or, as I recently read in an American author, the "[person] who takes the magazines at home and in the evening pushes the lawnmower in his shirt sleeves".'

The use of the 'reasonable person' is an objective measure but it is also a means of placing that test in the context of human characteristics. The standard does not always reflect average behaviour. Precise characteristics that can be associated with the reasonable person have also been considered.

CASE EXAMPLE

Glasgow Corporation v Muir [1943] AC 448

Here small children were scalded when a tea urn was dropped. The urn was being carried through a narrow passage where the children were buying ice creams when the corporation allowed a church picnic to come inside on a rainy day. Liability was assessed according to the 'reasonable person' test.

In establishing on what to base an objective standard Lord Macmillan concluded that at 457:

JUDGMENT

'The standard of foresight of the reasonable [person] is an impersonal test. It eliminates the personal equation and is independent of the idiosyncrasies of the particular person whose conduct is in question. Some persons are by nature unduly timorous and imagine every path beset by lions; others, of more robust temperament, fail to foresee or nonchalantly disregard even the most obvious dangers. The reasonable [person] is presumed to be free from both over-apprehension and from over-confidence.'

In fact, breach of duty is another way of saying that the defendant is at fault and is therefore liable for the damage caused. The issue of whether liability should always be based on fault or whether there should be a no-fault liability system is a controversial question and one that we will return to.

Certainly, in practice who the reasonable person is and what constitutes an objective standard are concepts determined by the judges in a case. Judges in reaching a decision will also base their judgment on either policy or expediency as the need arises.

Policy considerations that can influence a judge include:

- Who can best stand the loss – clearly a claimant needs to claim from a party who can afford to pay. The key rule in deciding whether or not to bring a case is 'Never sue a person of straw' (a person of no means).
- Whether or not the defendant is insured – in most circumstances in the modern day it will be an insurance company rather than the actual defendant who will pay the compensation. This would be the case for instance of motorists, employers, professional bodies, manufacturers, etc.
- The extent to which the decision will prevent similar behaviour in the future – the tort system is mainly about compensating for loss and damage suffered but it should also have a deterrent element.
- Whether or not the decision would 'open the floodgates' to further cases.
- Whether or not particular types of actions should be discouraged – for instance against the police or administrators of the law.
- Whether or not there are alternative means of gaining a remedy.

CASE EXAMPLE

Nettleship v Weston [1971] 2 QB 691

The claimant offered to give the defendant driving lessons in her husband's car after confirming that she was insured on the car. During a lesson, the defendant turned a corner but failed to straighten out and mounted the pavement and struck a lamppost whereupon the defendant suffered personal injury.

The insurance position of the defendant was a consideration in reaching a conclusion but most importantly, the standard against which the defendant's driving should be measured was a crucial consideration. Ask yourself, are you able to tell how good a driver is and if so, should the standard of their driving be judged using a variable standard? Would that be fair for someone who is injured as a result of a driver's negligence to say that they only had a few month's experience? Lord Justice Megaw commented at 709:

JUDGMENT

'In my judgment, in cases such as the present it is preferable that there should be a reasonably certain and reasonably ascertainable standard of care, even if on occasion that may appear to work hardly against an inexperienced driver, or his insurers. The standard of care required by the law is the standard of the competent and experienced driver: and this is so, as defining the driver's duty towards a passenger who knows of his inexperience, as much as towards a member of the public outside the car; and as much in civil as in criminal proceedings.'

3.2 Determining the standard of care

Through the case law a number of rules have emerged concerning those things that should be taken into account in setting the standard by which the defendant's behaviour should be measured.

3.2.1 Foreseeability of harm

There is no obligation on the defendant to guard against risks other than those that are within their reasonable contemplation. It would be unfair to make a defendant responsible for the unforeseeable. If the harm suffered by the claimant is not foreseeable, the defendant will not be liable.

CASE EXAMPLE

Roe v Minister of Health [1954] 2 QB 66

A patient became paralysed after being injected with nupercaine, a spinal anaesthetic. This had been stored inside glass ampoules themselves stored in a sterilising fluid, phenol. Evidence at the trial showed that the phenol solution had entered the anaesthetic through hairline cracks in the ampoules, contaminating it and causing the paralysis. There was no liability because such an event had not previously occurred and was unforeseeable as a result. At the relevant time when this occurred in 1947, it was not known that contamination could occur in this way but by the time that the case came to trial in 1954 this was a known risk. Denning LJ at 84 highlighted that we must not look at the 1947 accident with 1954 spectacles.

Nevertheless, if the defendant is aware of the possibility of harm he must guard against it, and it will be a breach of the duty of care to fail to do so.

CASE EXAMPLE

Walker v Northumberland County Council [1995] 1 All ER 737

Here a senior social worker had suffered a nervous breakdown. His employers knew that he might suffer another breakdown when he returned to work if the pressures of his work were too severe and stressful. They took insufficient steps to reduce the pressures of his workload and, when he was again made ill, they were in breach of their duty to take reasonable steps to avoid psychiatric injury knowing of his state of health.

3.2.2 The magnitude of the risk

Likelihood of harm

Wherever we owe a duty to another person, we must all guard against the risk of doing harm. This is only reasonable. The degree of caution that we must exercise will obviously be dictated by the **likelihood** of the risk and seriousness of the consequences of the risk materialising. The magnitude of the risk then can be balanced against the extremes that must be taken in order to avoid it.

CASE EXAMPLE

Bolton v Stone [1951] AC 850 HL

Miss Stone was standing outside a cricket ground and was hit by a cricket ball that had been hit out of the ground. She was actually 100 yards from where the batsman had struck the ball. The batsman was 78 yards from a 17-foot-high fence over which the ball had travelled. This was quite incredible and it was shown that balls had only been struck out of the ground six times in 28 years. There was no negligence. The cricket ground had done everything reasonably possible to avoid risks of people being hit.

Lord Radcliffe identified the connection with the basic 'reasonable person' test:

JUDGMENT

'the fact remains that, unless there has been something which a reasonable [person] would blame as falling beneath the standard of conduct that he would set for himself and require of his neighbour, there has been no breach of legal duty' (at 868–869).

This case is further discussed below in the context of practicalities of taking precautions.

The defendant though must take into account any factors that might increase the risk of harm occurring.

CASE EXAMPLE

Haley v London Electricity Board [1965] AC 778

Here a hole was being dug along a pavement and a hammer was left propped up on the pavement to warn passers-by of the presence of the hole. A blind man was passing and his stick failed to touch the hammer and he tripped and fell which left him deaf. The precautions taken were sufficient for sighted people but not so for blind people. It was held that there was a sufficiently large proportion of blind people in the community for precautions to be taken that would protect blind people and the cost would be very low. The defendants were liable for negligence.

Statutory health and safety law means that formal risk assessment is now a common requirement in all industries and this creates an obligation in relation to specific incidents as well as in general terms.

CASE EXAMPLE

Davis v Stena Line [2005] EWHC 420 (QB)

A passenger on a ferry fell overboard. The likelihood of such accidents was high and well known to the company which had failed to provide adequate training for the crew in such events. The captain of the ferry attempted a risky rescue, involving throwing the man a rope and pulling him up the high-sided vessel and through a door. Weather conditions were very bad and the man died in the swell created by the ferry. A passing ship which had previously spotted the man alive in the water had been in a position to launch its fast rescue boat. The court held that (1) the rescue attempted by the ferry captain would have had very little chance of success and it was negligent of the captain not to consider the better alternative option and (2) negligence on the part of the company not to have provided the captain with the training that would have enabled him to make that decision.

Seriousness of harm

The risk of a very small harm must be considered in relation to the seriousness of the consequences of that risk materialising.

CASE EXAMPLE

Paris v Stepney Borough Council [1951] AC 367

The claimant here who was a mechanic was already blind in one eye. He was employed as a garage hand at the defendant's garage. When dismantling a chassis of a vehicle a fragment of metal broke off and lodged in his good eye with the result that he was then blinded in that eye. His employers had failed to supply him with safety goggles that they were actually legally required to do. They were then liable to the defendant to the extent of causing his total blindness rather than merely for the loss of the sight in the one eye. The claimant's partial sight meant that the duty towards him was necessarily greater than normal. Though the likelihood of becoming totally blind and suffering such an injury in this job was low, the seriousness of the consequences should this happen were clearly very high for the claimant given his already reduced vision.

The same principle can apply even though the foreseeable harm is psychiatric rather than physical.

CASE EXAMPLE

Walker v Northumberland County Council [1995] 1 All ER 737

An area social services officer had particularly onerous and stressful responsibilities and suffered a nervous breakdown. He returned to work after three months on the understanding that there would be a lighter workload and less pressure. He was nevertheless expected to clear up the backlog and suffered a further breakdown leading to eventual dismissal on ill health. The employers were held to have breached their duty to protect his psychiatric well-being and health.

3.2.3 The practicability of precautions

The reasonable person only needs to do what is reasonable to avoid risks of harm. This means that there is no obligation to go to extraordinary lengths, particularly if the risk is slight.

Lord Normand in *Bolton v Stone* stated at 860–861: 'It is not the law that precautions must be taken against every peril that can be foreseen by the timorous'.

CASE EXAMPLE

***Latimer v AEC Ltd* [1953] AC 643**

A factory became flooded after a torrential rainstorm. The water mixed with oil and grease on the floor making the surface very slippery and dangerous. When the water subsided sawdust was spread over the floors to make them secure. There was not enough to cover the whole floor and Latimer slipped on an uncovered patch and was injured. The House of Lords held that everything reasonable had been done in the circumstances and, balancing out the possible risks, it was unreasonable to expect the factory to be closed. It was held that there was no negligence.

In *Bolton v Stone,* it was argued that the defendants had failed to take sufficient precautions to prevent the escape of cricket balls from the ground.

JUDGMENT

Lord Oaksey at 863:

'Cricket has been played for about ninety years on the ground in question and no ball has been proved to have struck anyone on the highways near the ground until the [claimant] was struck, nor has there been any complaint to the [defendants]. In such circumstances was it the duty of the defendants, who are the committee of the club, to take some special precautions other than those they did take to prevent such an accident as happened? The standard of care in the law of negligence is the standard of an ordinarily careful [person], but in my opinion an ordinarily careful [person] does not take precautions against every foreseeable risk. He can, of course, foresee the possibility of many risks, but life would be almost impossible if he were to attempt to take precautions against every risk which he can foresee. He takes precautions against risks which are reasonably likely to happen. Many foreseeable risks are extremely unlikely to happen and cannot be guarded against except by almost complete isolation.'

The precaution suggested by the claimant in this case was to erect a very high fence to prevent the balls from being hit out of the ground. The only option here being to stop playing cricket altogether. A balance must be struck between the efficacy of the suggested precaution and the cost. The suggestions here were out of proportion and go beyond what is expected of a reasonable person in such circumstances.

The context in which the damage occurs may very often dictate that the defendant has little chance to protect against it. In this way there was no liability when an inmate in a young offenders' institution was injured in a knife attack by another inmate: *Thompson v Home Office* [2001] EWCA Civ 331.

Generally, though where the defendant has sufficient control of circumstances to be able to avoid the harm, he would be obliged to act. This is particularly so where the welfare of the claimant is entrusted to the defendant.

CASE EXAMPLE

***Bradford-Smart v West Sussex County Council, The Times*, 29 January 2002**

The Court of Appeal accepted that a school would be in breach of its duty of care to its pupils if it failed to take steps that were within its power to put a stop to bullying. The Court accepted that this could apply even to incidents that arose off the school premises, although in general it was accepted that only rare exceptions would give rise to a breach of duty, and that the present case was not such an occasion.

3.2.4 The social utility of the activity

A defendant can sometimes escape liability in a case because it is possible to show that there was a justification for taking the risk in question. This might be so for instances where the defendant acts to avoid a potentially worse event.

CASE EXAMPLE

***Watt v Hertfordshire County Council* [1954] 1 WLR 835**

A woman was trapped in a car crash. The fire station summoned to the incident had a special heavy jack for using in such circumstances. It would normally be taken to the scene properly secured in its own vehicle, but the vehicle was elsewhere. The jack was taken unsecured in another vehicle because of the emergency and when the driver was forced to brake sharply the jack moved injuring a fireman. There was no negligence because the situation was an emergency and justified the risk.

However, this will not mean that the taking of any risk at all can be justified. Only the precise circumstances can justify the taking of the risk.

CASE EXAMPLE

***Griffin v Mersey Regional Ambulance* [1998] PIQR P34**

There was liability when an ambulance crossing a red light crashed. However, the other motorist was held to be 60 per cent contributorily negligent.

The usefulness of a defendant's behaviour, social utility, has also been considered in an entirely different context. In *The Scout Association v Barnes* [2010] EWCA Civ 1476 it was raised when a 13-year-old scout was injured while playing a game in the scout hut called 'objects in the dark'. It was held that since playing the game was only to increase its excitement rather than for any educational or social value the added risk was not justified.

Further the government had cause to believe that people are deterred from helping others in an emergency situation for fear of being sued should something go wrong when offering such help. To that end, it introduced the Social Action, Responsibility and Heroism Act 2015. This seeks to reassure those who help in an emergency situation that their efforts to help will be considered against three things:

i. Social Action – was the defendant acting for the benefit of society?
ii. Responsibility – did the defendant demonstrate a responsible approach to protecting the safety of others?
iii. Heroism – was the defendant acting heroically in an emergency situation to help another without regard to their own safety?

In 2006 the Compensation Act was introduced. This Act is designed to balance the actions of the defendant in meeting the standard of care in a given scenario and the prevention of a desirable activity from being undertaken. Often people and organisations undertake socially worthwhile activities for the benefit of the community and they should not be deterred from engaging in such activities by an unrealistic fear of negligence liability.

3.2.5 Common practice

A negligent activity cannot be excused merely because it is common practice. Nevertheless, the fact that something is generally practised may be strong evidence that it is not negligent, otherwise it would not normally be carried out.

This of course is not an absolute principle and it will not necessarily be negligent merely to fail to follow common practice.

CASE EXAMPLE

Brown v Rolls-Royce Ltd [1960] 1 WLR 210

An employee contracted dermatitis. The employers provided adequate washing facilities but they did not provide a barrier cream that was commonly used in the industry. They were not negligent in not providing the barrier cream because it could not be shown in the case that using the cream was guaranteed to prevent the condition.

CRITIQUING THE LAW

The objective standard of care is designed to work in many scenarios in changing environments. Do you think that the objective standard of care is one that is attainable?

3.3 The standard of care and different classes of defendant and characteristics

The standard of care is measured objectively but the courts have often looked at whether the standard may differ according to the type of person who owes the duty.

3.3.1 Children

Traditionally there was little case law involving the standard of care owed by children. Case law from other jurisdictions indicated that a child was not expected to have the same skill or understanding as an adult and therefore the standard of care owed was that appropriate to the age of the child in question.

CASE EXAMPLE

McHale v Watson [1966] 115 CLR 199

A 12-year-old boy injured a girl in the eye when he threw a steel rod at a post. There was held to be no negligence.

This seems to be more of a subjective than an objective test but the English courts have tended to follow it.

CASE EXAMPLE

Mullin v Richards [1998] 1 All ER 920

Here two 15-year-old schoolgirls were 'fencing' with plastic rulers. A piece of the ruler broke off and hit one of the girls in the eye. The Court of Appeal held that since such games were commonplace and would normally not lead to injury then the injury was unforeseeable to girls of that age and there was no negligence. Would an ordinarily careful and reasonable 15-year-old be able to foresee that this game carried such a risk?

In *Orchard v Lee* [2009] EWCA Civ 295 it was held that the mere fact that a risk of harm was insufficient on its own to make a 13-year-old boy liable for injuries he caused to a lunch break supervisor when he was running backwards in a school playground. The reasoning was that the school did not prohibit running in the playground so that the defendant was merely doing what any boy of the same age would do in a designated play area.

However, the judges have been willing on occasions to make awards of contributory negligence against child claimants.

CASE EXAMPLE

Armstrong v Cottrell [1993] PIQR P109 CA

The judge in this case was prepared to reduce damages for a 12-year-old by a third because he felt that children of that age should know the Highway Code.

And this can even be to a high level of reduction with quite young children.

CASE EXAMPLE

Morales v Eccleston [1991] RTR 151

Damages were reduced by 75 per cent when an 11-year-old ran into the road to recover his football.

One further aspect of the standard expected of children is that the law expects that young children should be supervised. This can be seen as a precise aspect of the duty owed to young children in the case of occupiers' liability (see *Phipps v Rochester Corporation* [1995] 1 QB 450 (s8.2.3)).

CASE EXAMPLE

Jenny v North Lincolnshire CC [2000] LGR 269

The Court of Appeal held that the local authority was liable for the injuries to a young school pupil who was injured as the result of being on a major road during school hours.

3.3.2 The disabled

Where a person is sick or suffering from a disability it is likely that the standard of care owed is what would be appropriate in the case of the reasonable person suffering the same illness or disability. It is inevitable that the same degree of care will not be expected as would for a person in normal health.

A person suffering from a disability of the mind may be liable for the torts he commits if sufficiently aware of the quality of the act.

CASE EXAMPLE

Morriss v Marsden [1952] 1 All ER 925

Here the defendant was a schizophrenic who attacked a claimant and was thus accused of battery. It was held that persons suffering from a mental illness could be liable for intentional torts even if unaware that their actions were wrong if they knew the quality of the act they committed.

See below the decision in *Mansfield v Weetabix* where a driver was unaware of his disability.

3.3.3 Motorists

In general, the same standard of care is expected of all motorists regardless of their age or experience, and even of learner drivers.

CASE EXAMPLE

Nettleship v Weston [1971] 2 QB 691

A learner driver on her third lesson crashed into a lamp post injuring the person teaching her to drive. The Court of Appeal found that she was liable despite being a learner driver.

In identifying that the standard of care of all motorists is the same and that there is no reduction in the standard because of inexperience. Lord Denning commented as follows (at 699):

JUDGMENT

'[The law] requires of him the same standard of care as of any other driver. The learner driver may be doing his best, but his incompetent best is not good enough. He must drive in as good a manner as a driver of skill, experience and care, who is sound in mind and limb, who makes no errors of judgment, has good eyesight and hearing, and is free from any infirmity.'

Lord Denning identified in the case that this is probably to do with the fact that motorists are obliged to carry compulsory insurance and therefore the degree of risk associated with the particular class of driver can be reflected in the insurance premium they are expected to pay.

The principle might even extend to a motorist who becomes physically incapable of controlling the vehicle because of a physical impairment.

CASE EXAMPLE

Roberts v Ramsbottom [1980] 1 All ER 7

A driver crashed into a stationary vehicle after suffering a cerebral haemorrhage (a stroke). He continued to drive after the seizure and the court felt that he was negligent for doing so. The court accepted that a defendant would have a defence if his actions were entirely beyond his control, but that here the driver should have stopped driving immediately.

However, a motorist will not be liable if he is unaware of the disabling condition that causes the loss of control.

CASE EXAMPLE

Mansfield v Weetabix Ltd [1997] PIQR P526

Here it was held that the driver could not have reasonably known of the infirmity that led to his loss of control and the subsequent accident so there was no fault. The standard of care that the driver was obliged to show in these circumstances was that which is to be expected of a reasonably competent driver unaware that he is or may be suffering from a condition that impairs his ability to drive. The driver did not know and could not reasonably have known of his infirmity which was the cause of the accident. Therefore, he was not at fault. His actions did not fall below the standard of care required.

3.3.4 People engaged in sport

The standard of care appropriate to participants in sport is the ordinary standard of reasonable care. The level of care required will depend on the circumstances of the case including whether the player is a professional or an amateur.

CASE EXAMPLE

Condon v Basi [1985] 2 All ER 453

Here the ordinary standard of reasonable care was applied when a footballer was injured in a dangerous and unacceptable tackle during an amateur football match. Sir John Donaldson MR suggested in the case that a much higher degree of care would be expected of a professional footballer.

Professional players are assumed to be more knowledgeable of the potential risks and consequences of injury and are thus more likely to be found in breach of their duty of care to fellow professionals.

CASE EXAMPLE

McCord v Swansea City AFC Ltd and another, The Times, 11 February 1997

Here a tackle by a player of the defendant football club ended the claimant's career. While the judge was not prepared to consider the tackle as reckless, it was a serious mistake of judgment that amounted to a breach of his duty of care to fellow players.

However, the level of care required is always taken in the context of the individual circumstances because of the inherent risk of injury of which each player is aware.

CASE EXAMPLE

Pitcher v Huddersfield Town Football Club Ltd [2001] All ER (D) 223

The claimant, a professional football player, suffered a knee injury ending his career after a rash tackle. The judge did not accept that the defendant player had fallen below an appropriate standard. He had mistimed his tackle but such errors of judgment were commonplace in the sport.

While participants in sport are inevitably aware of the risks of engaging in sporting activities, particularly contact sports of any kind, they are nevertheless to be protected from unnecessary harm by the officials in the game. In this way a referee in a sporting contest owes a duty of care to the players.

CASE EXAMPLE

Smolden v Whitworth [1997] PIQR P133

In a colts rugby match, that is one involving young and inexperienced players, the referee had been approached by the coaches about repeated collapsing of the scrum by players on the other side. He failed to properly control the scrums and eventually one player was seriously injured, leading to paralysis, when the scrum collapsed. The Court of Appeal agreed that the referee had fallen below the standard of care that he owed to the players. They were, however, eager to emphasise that the judgment was appropriate to the colts but not to the senior game where the players would be more experienced. (The existence of this duty and the appropriate standard have been recently affirmed in *Vowles v Evans and Another* [2003] EWCA Civ 318.)

Sporting authorities may also fall below the appropriate standard of care when they fail to provide the proper facilities to deal with sporting injuries.

CASE EXAMPLE

Watson v British Boxing Board of Control [2001] QB 1134

The claimant suffered severe head injuries after a blow to the head during a boxing match as a result of which he also suffered brain damage. The organisers were held to be in breach of their duty of care by failing to provide adequate medical facilities at the ringside that could have reduced the extent of the damage.

A spectator at a sporting contest is generally said to consent to the risks associated with being present at the sport. A person engaged in the sport, then, will not be liable in negligence to a spectator for any injuries or damage caused in the normal course of the sport unless the sportsman has shown a blatant and reckless disregard for the safety of the spectator.

CASE EXAMPLE

Wooldridge v Sumner [1963] 2 QB 43

A photographer stood behind a line of shrubs marking the perimeter of the arena at the National Horse Show at White City Stadium. The defendant tried to take a corner too fast on his horse with the result that the horse plunged through the shrubs and injured the claimant. The Court of Appeal held that the defendant was not liable for negligence but had merely made an error of judgment in how fast he should be going at the time.

In *Mountford v Newlands School and Another* [2007] EWCA Civ 21 the Court of Appeal held that a school would be liable for injury sustained in a seven-a-side under-15 rugby game because the referee did not prevent a boy over 15 from playing in breach of the rules.

The duty of care owed to a disabled participant in sporting events will be greater than that owed to an able-bodied sportsman, simply because the disability will require a greater degree of care.

CASE EXAMPLE

Morrell v Owen, The Times, 14 December 1993

Here athletics coaches were held to be in breach of their duty of care to a paraplegic archer. The disabled athlete was hit on the head by a discus and suffered brain damage as a result.

3.3.5 Emergency situations: acting in the agony of the moment

There are occasions where the defendant may act in the agony of the moment as they are placed in an unexpected situation of danger giving them limited opportunity to respond with the standard care that they might otherwise exhibit under normal circumstances. An example is when a passenger has to choose between staying on a coach which appears to be about to overturn or choosing a perilous alternative namely to jump off and, in all likelihood, sustaining personal injury. These were the facts in *Jones v Boyce* (1816) 1 Starkie 493 where it was held that there was no negligence on the part of the passenger who chose the more perilous of two alternatives. Consider further the following two cases.

CASE EXAMPLE

Ng Chun Pui v Lee Chuen Tat [1988] R.T.R. 298 (PC)

The defendant was driving a coach on a dual carriageway when a car cut across in front of it. To avoid hitting the car, the coach driver had to brake and take evasive action which led the coach to skid across the dual carriageway colliding with a bus travelling in the opposite direction resulting in injury to the claimants. It was held that the coach driver's driving had to be judged in the light of the emergency in which he had been placed by the driver of the car. There was nothing to criticise in the driving of the coach driver before the emergency arose and when the emergency arose, he was attempting to extricate himself, his coach and his passengers from a situation which appeared to him as a situation of extreme danger. He did what any careful driver would instinctively have done in the circumstances, and he acted with the alertness, skill and judgment which could reasonably have been expected.

This decision should be compared with the following decision in which breach was established despite the defendant acting in an emergency situation.

CASE EXAMPLE

Das International v Manley [2002] EWCA Civ 1638

This case involved two successive road accidents. The defendant was driving along a dual carriageway when he saw a pedestrian in the road and had to swerve to avoid him which resulted in his car crashing into the central reservation and ending up down the embankment. The defendant was not seriously injured and was able to make his way back up the embankment to the road to flag down some help. The claimant was driving along the same stretch of road when he saw a pedestrian, which on this occasion was the defendant dressed in dark clothing and took action to avoid hitting him. The claimant also ended up crashing his car which was beyond economical repair but he was not seriously injured. The question for the court was whether the defendant was negligent in his manner of flagging down help. It was accepted that the same standard of care is not expected of persons faced with emergency situations. Such people should behave in a way which is not unreasonable, taking into account the exigencies of their situation. Even where the situation allows some time for reflection but still presents a person with a dilemma, the courts will be prepared to make allowances. However, having said all that, breach was established as it cannot be reasonable to move suddenly from the side of the road straight into the path of a fast-moving vehicle when it is pitch dark, wearing dark clothing which made it even more difficult to be seen.

Quite often, it will be those responding to an emergency such as a police or ambulance service where the standard of care may need to be supressed. For example, in *Mashall v Osmond* [1983] QB 1034, the police were chasing a suspected criminal travelling in a car. The car eventually pulled up in a lay-by and the officer driving the police car, intended to pull up alongside the car, but ended up skidding into the vehicle and catching the suspect who ended up lying between the two car with serious leg injuries. The claimant suspect claimed damages for injuries sustained as a result of the negligent driving of the police officer. The Court of Appeal held that the police officer's driving could not be judged according to the same standard of care as if he had time to consider his actions given that he was driving in no doubt stressful circumstances.

3.3.6 People lacking specialist skills

If a person carries out a task requiring a specialist skill he will be judged according to the standard of a person reasonably competent in the exercise of that skill. This does not mean that an amateur will be expected to show the same degree of skill as a professional.

CASE EXAMPLE

Wells v Cooper [1958] 2 QB 265

A tradesman delivering fish was injured when a door handle fitted by the householder came off in his hand. The Court of Appeal held that the appropriate standard of care was that of a reasonably competent carpenter. The claimant's complaint was that the handle was fixed to the door with three-quarter-inch screws that he claimed were inadequate. Since these were the screws that a carpenter would have used there could be no negligence.

Nevertheless, a person not possessing specialist skills will not be expected to exercise the same standard of care as a skilled person unless that standard is appropriate to the circumstances.

CASE EXAMPLE

Phillips v Whiteley [1938] 1 All ER 566

A jeweller pierced ears in a whitewashed room using sterilised equipment. When the claimant contracted a blood disorder the jeweller was not negligent. He had taken all reasonable steps in the circumstances to avoid the risk of harm and could not be fixed with the same standard of care as a surgeon performing an operation. The appropriate standard of care was the degree of care that should be taken by a jeweller carrying out the procedure, not that which would be appropriate to a surgeon.

3.3.7 People using equipment

In general, where people use equipment they are taken to know how to use it properly, unless it is very specialist equipment requiring specialist skills. So where a person suffers injury, loss or damage while using the equipment there is no requirement by the other party to check that they are able to use it properly, and so no breach.

CASE EXAMPLE

Makepeace v Evans, The Times, 13 June 2000, CA

The claimant was a decorator hired by the first defendant sub-contractors, who in turn were hired by the second defendant main contractors. The claimant used a scaffolding tower provided by the second defendants. Their site agent did not enquire whether the claimant was competent to use it. When the claimant was injured his action against the second defendants failed. It was a standard piece of equipment in the trade, and they were entitled to assume that he was able to use it or seek advice. The court held that to say otherwise would be to 'extend the nursemaid school of negligence too far'.

ACTIVITY

Quick quiz

Consider how it will be decided whether there has been a breach of a duty of care in the following situations.

1 Jamie is an 11-year-old boy who has caused a crash by running out in front of cars while playing 'chicken'.
2 Tom has been injured when stones from a quarry have hit him on his head after blasting. He was walking on a pavement a mile away from the quarry.

The quarry face is shielded by a high hill, and no previous explosions from the quarry have ever caused this to happen before.

3 Tan, an acupuncturist, has been treating Rachel for pain in her shoulders. Tan has followed normal methods precisely but Rachel has suffered a rare infection.

4 During a forest fire Tristram used explosives to blow up his neighbour Ali's trees in order to prevent the fire from spreading to his own farm and also to the nearby village of Trumpton.

ACTIVITY

Self-assessment questions

1 Who exactly is a 'reasonable person'?

2 In what ways does a 'reasonable person' differ from an average person?

3 How big a part does policy play in determining the standard of care in negligence?

4 When will a standard of care be lowered due to inexperience of the person owing the duty?

5 What standard of care does a child usually owe?

6 What effect does the fact that the acts leading to the damage were common practice have on deciding whether there is a breach of duty?

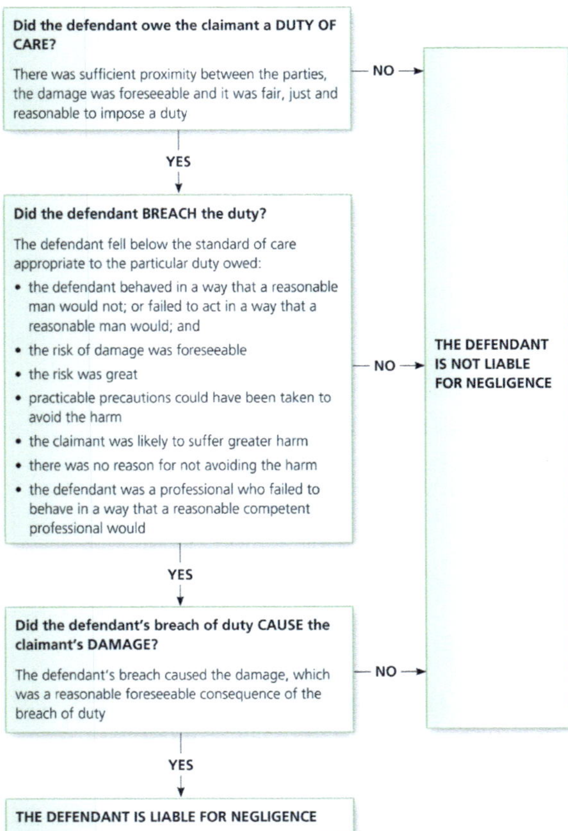

Figure 3.1 The essential elements for proof of negligence with particular emphasis on the breach of the duty of care.

KEY FACTS

The standard of care and testing breach of duty	Case
A breach of duty occurs where a person falls below the standard of care appropriate to the duty he owes.	
The standard of care is that appropriate to the 'reasonable person'.	*Blyth v Birmingham Waterworks* [1856] *Nettleship v Weston* [1971] 2 QB 691
The reasonable person is free from both over-apprehension and over-confidence.	*Glasgow Corporation v Muir* [1943]
Policy considerations often govern what the standard will be, e.g. the floodgates argument.	

Factors to be taken into consideration	Case
Many factors are taken into account in determining whether the duty is breached: • foreseeability of harm • the magnitude of the risk • the practicability of precautions • the social utility of the act	*Roe v Minister of Health* [1954] *Bolton v Stone* [1951] *Paris v Stepney BC* [1951] *Latimer v AEC* [1953] *Watt v Herts CC* [1954] Social Action, Responsibility and Heroism Act 2015

Different types of defendant	Case
Consideration will be made for different types of defendant, e.g. • children – are expected to be less cautious • the disabled • motorists – all owe the same duty even if inexperienced • sportsmen – will depend on rules of sport being observed • people lacking specialist skills • people using equipment	*Mullin v Richards* [1998] *Morriss v Marsden* [1952] *Nettleship v Weston* [1971] *Smolden v Whitworth* [1997] *Wells v Cooper* [1958] *Makepeace v Evans* [2000]

3.4 The standard of care appropriate to experts and professionals

3.4.1 Breach of the duty of care and medical negligence claims

Medical negligence is in many ways a specialist type of negligence action and is important because recent years have seen a dramatic increase in the numbers of claims against doctors and health authorities. This has also led to the worry that the UK will follow the USA, where medical malpractice claims and the so-called ambulance chasing by lawyers is commonplace.

However, it is still quite difficult in England and Wales to bring successful medical negligence claims. The major reasons for this are twofold:

- the difficulties that are experienced when trying to prove both breach of the duty of care (the subject of this chapter), and
- the problem of causation (an area subject to its own particular problems and considered in detail in Chapter 4).

Doctors are not exempt from the law and, just as with anybody, if they fall below the standard of care that is appropriate to them, they may be found liable in negligence for a breach of their well-established duty of care to their patients. This well-established duty of care has been applied to the situation where receptionists at an A&E department gave misleading information about waiting times to a patient who relied on this information to his detriment. The Supreme Court, in *Darnley v Croydon Health Services* (NHS Trust) [2018] UKSC 50 held that applying the established principle that a duty is owed by those who provide and run a casualty department, no further enquiry into whether a duty of care exists need to be undertaken as per the decision in *Robinson*. This serves as a further example post-*Robinson* that where a case does not raise a novel situation, the *Caparo* criteria need not be considered anew as such factors that the criteria would have raised have already been considered in this situation hence it is an established duty. What this case turned on was whether non-medically trained staff breached their duty and therefore, to what standard should non-medically trained staff be held? At paragraph 26:

JUDGMENT

'The standard required is that of an averagely competent and well-informed person performing the function of a receptionist at a department providing emergency medical care . . . the standard procedure was that anyone complaining of a head injury would be seen by a triage nurse . . . within 30 minutes of arrival.'

Unfortunately in this case, the claimant was misinformed that he would have to wait 4–5 hours. The claimant waited 19 minutes and then left thinking he would have to wait a long time. The claimant suffered permanent brain damage as a result of his injuries which he may not have done if he had waited to be seen upon arrival within 30 minutes and of course had his injuries treated. It was held in this case that it was foreseeable that being told incorrect waiting times may result in the claimant leaving the A&E department and the provision of such misleading information is negligent. The receptionists were not held to the professional standard of care but rather the ordinary standard of care of an averagely competent and well-informed person performing the function of a receptionist. Compare this with the standard of care owed by medically trained staff such as doctors.

Whilst the decision is welcomed in terms of serving as an example of an established principle post-*Robinson*, it does remind us that there is not a blanket immunity for those who work in public services and whilst resources may be a factor in the decision-making process, it does not tie the hands of the judiciary.

Having said that, professionals, and in particular doctors, who are a very specific 'body of professionals', do not conform to the usual rules on the breach of duty in negligence and therefore are more appropriately considered as a special category on their own.

As McNair J identified in *Bolam v Friern Hospital Management Committee* [1957] 1 WLR 582 at 582:

JUDGMENT

'In the ordinary case which does not involve any special skill . . . negligence . . . means a failure to do some act which a reasonable [person] in the circumstances would do, or the doing of some act which a reasonable [person] in the circumstances would not do . . . . But where you get a situation which involves the use of some special skill or competence, then the test as to whether there has been negligence or not is not the test of the [person] on the top of a Clapham omnibus, because he has not got this skill.'

The standard of care appropriate to professionals then is not judged according to the reasonable person test, so his actions are not compared with those of the 'person on the Clapham omnibus'. Rather they are compared against the accepted standards of members of their own profession. This in itself complicates the objective measure that is normally used to determine negligence and leads on also to many criticisms.

3.4.2 The *Bolam* test

The *Bolam* test has two aspects. The first is that the *standard of care appropriate to professionals* is not judged according to the reasonable person test, so their actions are not compared with those of the 'person on the Clapham omnibus'. A person exercising such specialist skills will be judged instead by comparison with his natural peer group, in other words other people who exercise the same skill and who have the same expertise. This test originates in a case alleging medical negligence but it is equally appropriate to all professionals.

CASE EXAMPLE

Bolam v Friern Hospital Management Committee [1957] 1 WLR 582

Mr Bolam suffered from depression and entered hospital to undergo electro-convulsive therapy. The practice, as the name suggests, causes possibly quite severe muscular spasms. The doctor giving the treatment failed to provide either relaxant drugs or any means of restraint during the treatment. The claimant suffered a fractured pelvis and the question for the court was whether there was negligence in the practice of providing neither restraint nor relaxants. The court received evidence that a number of different practitioners carrying out the type of treatment took different views on the use of restraints or relaxant drugs. McNair J established the standard of care appropriate to doctors as 'the standard of the ordinary skilled [person] exercising and professing to have that special skill'. Since there were doctors who would have carried out the therapy in the same manner the doctor here had acted in accordance with a competent body of medical opinion and there could be no negligence.

The second limb of the test is that a professional (in this case a doctor) will be considered negligent when he has failed to act in a way that would be accepted as being appropriate by a 'competent body of medical opinion'. Taking the situation in *Bolam* as an example, since there were a number of different practices that were adopted and accepted as appropriate by different doctors, then the role of the court was to listen to the expert evidence of other doctors and to determine on the basis of that evidence whether or not the practice conformed to that acceptable to a 'competent body of medical opinion'.

3.4.3 Criticism of the *Bolam* test

Although the test is the appropriate method of determining whether a professional has fallen below an appropriate standard of care and is therefore negligent in a given case, it has been subject to judicial criticism and it has also been a wider source of criticism for academic commentators.

As Sally Sheldon points out, the test is very different from cases involving non-professionals where, having heard evidence from experts, the court will reach its own conclusions on whether or not the duty of care has been breached by falling below the acceptable standard. The situation is somewhat different for doctors: 'Once the court is convinced that two (or more) different schools of thought exist within the profession, it seems that all the defendant must do is to show that he has acted in accordance with one of them, subject to the caveat that such a school must constitute a "responsible body of opinion".' (S Sheldon and M Thompson, *'"A responsible body of medical men skilled in that particular art . . .": Rethinking the Bolam test', Feminist Perspectives on Health Care Law,* S Sheldon and M Thompson (eds) (Cavendish Publishing, 1998), p. 16.)

M Brazier and J Miola comment that: 'Many academic commentators and organisations campaigning for victims of medical accidents perceive [that] the Bolam test . . . has been used by the courts to abdicate responsibility for defining and enforcing patient rights . . . Bolam out of control came close to acquiring demonic status in some quarters.' (*'Bye-bye Bolam: A medical litigation revolution?'* (2000) Medical Law Review 8, pp. 85–114 at p. 85.)

Some of the issues with the *Bolam* test are as follows:

- The test allows professionals to set their own standard in negligence actions – in the case of people other than professionals the standard is an objective one, measured against the 'reasonable person'. In this case the court will decide what the appropriate standard is. In the case of professionals, however, the standard is measured subjectively according to what other professionals, brought to court as expert witnesses, say it is. Professions become self-regulating.
- As such it protects professionals to a greater degree than is the case for anyone else – it is sufficient for a professional to bring to court a fellow professional to say that he would have done the same in the circumstances for the allegation of negligence to fail.

- Practices that are only marginal may be accepted as a result – the danger is that the test can legitimise practices that are highly experimental without real credibility, or at the least practices that few other responsible practitioners would carry out.
- There is a danger that professionals will close ranks – even if this is not the case the criticism will certainly be made and this can have the obvious effect of undermining confidence in the profession.
- It is impossible to say what a reasonable, competent body of professional opinion is – in some cases this can just amount to a question of numbers. The judges in any case are in effect leaving the definition to be made by those accused of the negligence.

The House of Lords attempted to meet these criticisms in *Bolitho v City and Hackney Health Authority* [1998] AC 232. The House of Lords explained that it is for the court in each individual case to determine what is the standard of care appropriate to the professional against whom the negligence is alleged, and not for professional opinion.

CASE EXAMPLE

Bolitho v City and Hackney Health Authority [1997] 4 All ER 771

A two-year-old boy was in hospital being treated for croup. His airways became blocked and, despite being summoned on more than one occasion by nursing staff, a doctor failed to attend. The boy suffered a cardiac arrest and brain damage as a result. This could have been avoided if a doctor had intubated and cleared the obstruction. The hospital admitted that the doctor was negligent in failing to attend. Nevertheless, it claimed that it was not liable because the doctor stated that even if she had attended she would not have intubated and so the cardiac arrest and brain damage would in any case have occurred. Evidence was introduced to show that there were at the time two schools of thought as to whether or not to intubate in such circumstances. The case is ultimately one of causation and whether the *Bolam* test applies at that point, but the House of Lords rejected the view that because certain medical opinion accepted the practice of the doctor in question that they were bound to accept it because of Bolam.

In *Bolitho v City and Hackney Health Authority* the House of Lords rejected the idea that a doctor should escape liability for negligence merely because of evidence put forward by a number of experts on medical practices who claimed to represent a 'reasonable' or 'responsible' or 'respectable' body of opinion. Lord Browne-Wilkinson explained their rejection in this way at 778:

JUDGMENT

'The use of these adjectives – responsible, reasonable and respectable – all show that the court has to be satisfied that the exponents of the body of medical opinion

> relied upon can demonstrate that such opinion has a logical basis . . . if, in a rare case, it can be demonstrated that the professional opinion is not capable of withstanding logical analysis, the judge is entitled to hold that the body of opinion is not reasonable or responsible'.

But he still accepted the significance of using *Bolam* in stating at 779:

JUDGMENT

> 'It is only where a judge can be satisfied that the body of expert opinion cannot be logically supported at all that such opinion will not provide the benchmark by reference to which the defendant's conduct falls to be assessed.'

As the above demonstrates, judges cannot substitute their preferred views of expert evidence and opinion over another responsible expert so long as the expert evidence can withstand a logical basis. If the evidence does not have a logical basis it may be rejected. This is sometimes referred to as the *Bolitho* gloss and qualifies the *Bolam* test.

Professional standard of care summary

(i) Where a person professes to have a special skill, their conduct will be judged according to the standard of a reasonable person having that same skill rather than the reasonable lay person.

(ii) A professional will not be considered as falling below the standard of care if they have acted in a way that would be accepted as being proper by one responsible body of professional opinion even if there are other competing views.

(iii) If it can be demonstrated that the professional opinion is not capable of withstanding logical analysis, the judge is entitled to hold that the body of opinion is not reasonable or responsible.

CRITIQUING THE LAW

> Does the professional standard give too much deference to professionals, or does it now strike the right balance using the *Bolitho* gloss?

3.4.4 Applying the test

The test not surprisingly has caused controversy. Judges have been prepared to disregard the expert evidence of doctors where they feel that there is no real basis for the medical opinion.

CASE EXAMPLE

Marriott v West Midlands AHA and Others [1999] Lloyd's Rep Med 23

A claimant became seriously ill after his GP failed to respond to the claimant's wife's call for help. The claimant had been injured in a fall downstairs and had been admitted to hospital but released the following day, despite his protests that he was feeling unwell. When his condition deteriorated his wife contacted the GP who said that there was no need to attend, after which the claimant became seriously unwell. The Court of Appeal rejected the claim that the doctor was not negligent based on the evidence of other doctors. The court felt that the *Bolam* test could only apply where there was a logical basis for the arguments of the expert witnesses.

On the significance of *Bolitho* to the application of the *Bolam* test is also worth noting that:

> 'A very important point has emerged from the House of Lords decision with regard to the position of defending doctors. Their Lordships focused on the words used in earlier medical negligence judgments and found the adjectives "responsible", "reasonable" and "respectable" being used to describe a body of opinion which would act as a successful defence. They held that this "showed that the court had to be satisfied that the exponents of the body of opinion relied upon could demonstrate that such opinion had a logical basis". This means that it will become increasingly difficult for doctors to justify their actions on the basis of producing colleagues who will say that they would have done the same. To escape liability they will have to present a convincing and logical argument to a judge who has little or no medical knowledge.' *W Scott, 'Bolam and Bolitho: A new standard of care for doctors?' (1998) 148 NLJ 64.*

The following case serves as a reminder that the judges will be prepared to reject expert evidence that does not withstand a logical basis.

JUDGMENT

Hodgson v Hammond [2025] EWHC 1261 (KB)

The claimant brought a claim for clinical negligence against two GPs whom she had seen but failed to act upon a potential diagnosis of pelvic inflammatory disease. Duty was not in dispute, but beach of duty was. The claimant argued that one doctor failed to undertake a pelvic examination whilst the other failed to refer her for urgent pelvic exam. Both doctors argued that their actions were reasonable in the circumstances and would be supported as proper by a responsible body of medical opinion per *Bolam.* The judge had to weigh up the expert witness evidence. The judge explained at paragraphs 85 and 88 that: '. . . given that there is a low threshold both for considering and excluding PID, and given that, as all the experts accepted, PID is a diagnosis that a GP cannot afford to miss, as the breach of duty experts accept, no responsible body of GPs could support not even considering carrying out an examination which could test that potential diagnosis, when measured against the risks of non-treatment . . . . in my judgment this is the rare case where the claimant has demonstrated that . . . the professional opinion [for the defendant] is not capable of withstanding logical analysis, per *Bolitho*.'

Consent and the Bolam test

Adults

One of the difficult areas for judges to determine is the degree of information that should be given to a patient in advance of any form of intrusive medical treatment. The courts are now prepared to take a more active view in determining what level of information is appropriate to give a patient in advance of treatment.

When seeking consent to medical treatment and the information given to a patient to make about their proposed treatment, used to be governed by the decision in *Sidaway* and the *Bolam* test. This test told us that a doctor's duty to warn patients of risks was based on whether they had acted in line with a responsible body of opinion in line with the *Bolam* test. This has now been superseded by the decision in *Montgomery v Lanarkshire Health Board* discussed below. This case tells us that doctors now have a duty to take reasonable care to ensure that patients are aware of 'material risks' as well as any risks to which the patient may attached significance.

CASE EXAMPLE

Sidaway v Governors of the Bethlem Royal & Maudsley Hospitals [1985] AC 871

Mrs Sidaway had suffered persistent pain in her right arm and shoulder and had on advice of her surgeon consented to a spinal operation to relieve the pain. On obtaining consent, the doctor had accurately informed her that there was a less than 1 per cent risk of something going wrong. What Mrs Sidaway claimed the doctor had not told her was the potentially catastrophic consequences if something did go wrong. In the event, while the operation was carried out without negligence, the damage did occur and she was left paralysed. She sued on the grounds that the surgeon had been negligent in failing to properly warn of the possible extent of the damage. The House of Lords held that the degree of information given by the doctor conformed to 'a practice accepted as proper by a responsible body of neuro-surgical opinion' so that there was no negligence. They also rejected the idea that there should be a doctrine of 'informed consent' as there is in other jurisdictions because this would make operation of the *Bolam* test impossible. Lord Diplock at 895:

JUDGMENT

'The only effect that mention of risks can have on the patient's mind, if it has any at all, can be in the direction of deterring the patient from undergoing the treatment which in the expert opinion of the doctor it is in the patient's best interests to undergo. To decide what risks the existence of which a patient should be voluntarily warned . . . is as much an exercise of professional skill and judgement as any other part of the doctor's comprehensive duty of care.'

In *Sidaway* it was further explained by Lord Bridge that when questioned specifically by a patient about risks involved in a particular treatment proposed, the doctor's duty must be to answer both truthfully and as fully as the questioner requires. This was the issue in *Chester v Afshar.*

CASE EXAMPLE

Chester v Afshar [2004] UKHL 41; [2004] 4 All ER 587

The claimant, who suffered from back pain, consulted a well-known neurosurgeon who recommended an operation. The claimant did not wish to undergo an operation and asked specifically about the risks of the operation. Instead of being given the risk levels involved he was persuaded by the surgeon to go ahead with the operation. In fact, there was a small risk, between 1 and 2 per cent, of nerve damage resulting from the operation that might range from minor effects to paralysis. The court accepted that the doctor had failed to warn of these risks and in fact the claimant did suffer fairly serious nerve damage, although there was no question of negligence in the operation. The Court of Appeal held that the surgeon had fallen below the appropriate standard in failing to give full information which, if it had been given, would have meant that the claimant would not have had the operation at that time. Thus, she would not have suffered the nerve damage at that time either. The Court felt that if it did not establish liability in the case then it would be to undermine the duty on doctors to warn of risks that no reasonable patient would refuse even after advice of risks was given.

This is taken much further by the Supreme Court in leading case in this area.

CASE EXAMPLE

Montgomery v Lanarkshire Health Board [2015] UKSC 11

The claimant sought damages on behalf of her son who was born severely disabled. The claimant was deemed to be a high-risk pregnancy patient and was dependent on insulin as she suffered from diabetes. Diabetes during pregnancy usually means that babies are larger than normal. The claimant is of a small stature of no more than 5 feet tall. The claimant maintained that she should have been given more information about having an ordinary delivery, the risk of the baby being unable to pass through the pelvis and developing shoulder dystocia, and information about the alternative possibility of delivery by elective caesarean section. Shoulder dystocia is the prime concern in diabetic pregnancies and can result in permanent disability. The doctor in charge of the claimant's care said that she would not discuss such risks as a matter of course with her patients. The claimant however contended that had she known about the risks, she probably would have elected to have a caesarean section. The question here was whether a failure to disclose the risks of the birth through a normal delivery breached the doctor's duty of care. There was a 9–10 per cent chance of shoulder dystocia occurring. Had the claimant been informed of this risk, she would have elected to have a caesarean section. Lords Kerr and Reed explained at paragraphs 87–88:

JUDGMENT

'An adult person of sound mind is entitled to decide which, if any, of the available forms of treatment to undergo, and her consent must be obtained before treatment interfering with her bodily integrity is undertaken. The doctor is therefore under a duty to take reasonable care to ensure that the patient is aware of any material risks involved in any recommended treatment, and of any reasonable alternative or variant treatments. The test of materiality is whether, in the circumstances of the particular case, a reasonable person in the patient's position would be likely to attach significance to the risk, or the doctor is or should reasonably be aware that the particular patient would be likely to attach significance to it.

The doctor is however entitled to withhold from the patient information as to a risk if he reasonably considers that its disclosure would be seriously detrimental to the patient's health. The doctor is also excused from conferring with the patient in circumstances of necessity, as for example where the patient requires treatment urgently but is unconscious or otherwise unable to make a decision.'

This case is important because it overturns the previous House of Lords decision in *Sidaway v Board of Governors of the Bethlem Royal Hospital and the Maudsley Hospital* [1985] AC 871. The General Medical Council commended the decision as consistent with current guidance on obtaining informed consent from patients. This is important due to the number of developments including the ease at which patients can access medical information on the internet and have a greater ability to take on board such information. Further patients are increasingly seen as holding rights and being capable of making decisions based on the information before them. To be able to make these decisions, they need all relevant information. As highlighted above, this is subject to the exception that is known as 'therapeutic privilege'. This is where a doctor may decide to withhold information from a patient because such disclosure would actually be more harmful than helpful to the patient.

This case makes clear that the *Bolam* test of professional practice, does **not** apply in determining whether a doctor should inform a patient of the risks of a procedure. On that matter, the courts impose their required standard of reasonable care on the medical profession, and a doctor cannot avoid liability by establishing that their view is supported by a responsible body of medical opinion, and so would not have disclosed the risk involved to the patient. The duty of care to inform a patient about the material risks of a procedure was to enable the patient to make an informed choice. This is a move away from medical paternalism to protecting a patient's autonomy and right to self-determination. There is therefore a difference between the role of a doctor in *diagnosis and treatment,* which rests entirely on professional skill and judgment, and the doctor's *advisory role* where the doctor must also take into account the patient's right to decide on the risks to their health which they are willing to run. There are therefore two stages to the analysis as confirmed by the Court of Appeal following *Montgomery* in *Duce v Worcestershire Acute Hospitals NHS Trust* [2018] EWCA Civ 1307 (paras 33 and 34):

(i) What risks associated with an operation were or should have been known to the medical professional in question. That is a matter falling within the expertise of medical professionals.

(ii) Whether the patient should have been told about such risks by reference to whether they were material. That is a matter for the Court to determine . . . . This issue is not therefore the subject of the *Bolam* test and not something that can be determined by reference to expert evidence alone . . . whether, in the circumstances of the particular case, a reasonable person in the patient's position would be likely to attach significance to the risk, or the doctor is or should reasonably be aware that the particular patient would be likely to attach significance to it.

This point is further explored and explained in *McCulloch and others (Appellants) v Forth Valley Health Board (Respondent)* [2023] UKSC 26 at paragraphs 57–58:

JUDGMENT

'A hypothetical example may help to explain, in more detail, how we regard the law as working. A doctor will first seek to provide a diagnosis (which may initially be a provisional diagnosis) having, for example, examined the patient, conducted tests, and having had discussions with the patient. Let us then say that, in respect of that diagnosis, there are ten possible treatment options and that there is a responsible body of medical opinion that would regard each of the ten as possible treatment options. Let us then say that the doctor, exercising his or her clinical judgment, and supported by a responsible body of medical opinion, decides that only four of them are reasonable. The doctor is not negligent by failing to inform the patient about the other six even though they are possible alternative treatments. The narrowing down from possible alternative treatments to reasonable alternative treatments is an exercise of clinical judgment to which the professional practice test [*Bolam*] should be applied. The duty of reasonable care would then require the doctor to inform the patient not only of the treatment option that the doctor is recommending but also of the other three reasonable alternative treatment options (plus no treatment if that is a reasonable alternative option) indicating their respective advantages and disadvantages and the material risks involved in such treatment options.

It is important to stress that it is not being suggested that the doctor can simply inform the patient about the treatment option or options that the doctor himself or herself prefers. Rather the doctor's duty of care, in line with *Montgomery*, is to inform the patient of all reasonable treatment options applying the professional practice [*Bolam*] test.'

Children

Where consent is required in respect of children who are incapable of giving a valid consent it is customary for doctors to seek the consent of the parents of the child. If this is withheld doctors commonly seek the consent of the courts either through care proceedings or through the inherent jurisdiction of the High Court. A failure to do so could result in a breach of Article 8 of the European Convention of Human Rights. This was the case in *Glass v UK* [2004] 39 EHRR 15.

Examination and diagnosis

The original test in *Bolam* had its context in situations where the medical professionals had a range of potential clinical practices to choose from. It was quite rightly used to determine whether or not the choice was legitimate according to the standards accepted by doctors. The rule, however, has been extended well beyond this simple context and has also been accepted and held to apply to the diagnosis of illness.

CASE EXAMPLE

Maynard v West Midlands Regional Health Authority [1985] 1 All ER 635

Here consultants operated before the results of certain tests they had ordered became available. They both considered that the patient had pulmonary tuberculosis but also felt that she might have Hodgkin's disease and decided to operate immediately without benefit of the information from the tests. She claimed that the operation damaged her vocal cords unnecessarily. The court determined that there was no negligence because the doctors had followed a practice approved by a responsible body of medical opinion, even if it was true that quite conflicting practices were possible at the time.

In the above case Lord Scarman stated at 638:

JUDGMENT

'There is seldom any one answer exclusive of all others to problems of professional judgement. A court may prefer one body of opinion to the other; but that is no basis for a conclusion of negligence.'

The application of the test to diagnosis may be critical. This is because one potential result of misdiagnosis is that the wrong treatment may be given or wrong operation carried out, leading to even further problems.

CASE EXAMPLE

Ryan v East London and City HA [2001] WL 1890334

Here a child suffered a permanent spinal disability following an operation that had been carried out after a misdiagnosis of a spinal tumour. The court accepted that if the diagnosis had not been negligent the child would have had the correct treatment and not suffered the disability.

In this way failing to take proper account of technical information which then leads on to mistreatment is also falling below the appropriate standard of care if a competent body of medical opinion would have reacted to the information differently.

CASE EXAMPLE

Hunt v NHS Litigation Authority [2002] WL 1480071

Here the doctor failed to fully realise the implications of a cardiotocograph and gave a woman in labour drugs to speed up her labour, then left her in the care of midwives, attending periodically. In fact the doctor should have noticed that the baby had an irregular heartbeat and that something was wrong. The baby suffered brain damage when it was born with the cord tight around its neck. The doctor should have carried out a forceps delivery at a much earlier stage if she had reacted correctly to the information from the tests.

The test will inevitably be appropriate in terms of the examination given by a doctor as well as the diagnosis resulting from it.

CASE EXAMPLE

Reynolds v North Tyneside HA [2002] Lloyd's Rep Med 459

A baby suffered injury and it was shown that a vaginal examination of the mother by the midwife at an appropriate time would have lessened the chance of injury. The judge accepted evidence that a reasonably prompt examination would have been expected of midwives at the time of the case and the health authority thus fell below the appropriate standard of care in failing to provide one.

Choice of treatment

It is also long since accepted that the test applies to medical treatment, so that all aspects of medicine fall within the scope of the rule.

CASE EXAMPLE

Whitehouse v Jordan [1981] 1 All ER 267

A senior registrar had carried out a forceps delivery of a baby. The baby had become wedged and suffered asphyxia and brain damage. The allegation was that the doctor had used the forceps with too much force and that was the cause of the damage. The mother gave evidence that she had been lifted off the bed when the forceps were applied to the baby's head. In the House of Lords, Lord Edmund-Davis rejected the view put forward by Lord Denning in the Court of Appeal that an error of clinical judgment should not necessarily be treated the same as negligence.

Lord Denning considered (at 267):

JUDGMENT

'while some errors may be completely consistent with the due exercise of professional skill, other acts or omissions . . . may be so glaringly below proper standards as to make a finding of negligence inevitable'.

Nevertheless, he confirmed that the *Bolam* test was the appropriate test by which to measure standards of professional activity.

Level of expertise

The standard of care will not necessarily reduce because of the lack of expertise of the doctor. The standard is that appropriate to the doctor or professional exercising and professing to possess the skill in question. It is not, therefore, possible to argue that the standard is reduced because the defendant lacks experience. A junior doctor must exercise the same degree of skill as the experienced doctor.

CASE EXAMPLE

Wilsher v Essex Area Health Authority [1988] 1 All ER 871

A baby was born prematurely and with an oxygen deficiency. A junior doctor then administered excess oxygen by mistake. The junior doctor inserted a catheter in an artery rather than a vein and a registrar failed to spot the mistake. The baby was later found to be nearly blind. A possible cause of the blindness was the excess oxygen. The House of Lords rejected the health authority's argument that the standard of care expected should be reduced because it was a junior doctor. Accepting such an argument would then mean that the care a patient was entitled to would depend on the experience of the doctor who treated them. This was unacceptable and negligence was held to have occurred in the case.

While the same standard of skill is expected of the doctor (professional) regardless of his level of experience, in circumstances where the defendant lacks the resources that might generally be available the court will recognise that the same standard of care cannot be expected. However, this is recognition of the resource implications.

CASE EXAMPLE

Knight v Home Office [1990] 3 All ER 237

A prisoner had committed suicide while in a prison hospital. In NHS hospitals there would be a general duty of care to protect suicide risks from harm. The court recognised that because of the greater difficulty of supervising prisoners who might attempt suicide and the lack of resources available to deal with the problem, the same standard of care could not be expected of the prison doctors.

However, this principle may depend on the type of care in question. For instance a prisoner might expect the same standard of obstetric care as would generally be available (see *Brooks v Home Office* [1999] 2 FLR 33).

3.4.5 The *Bolam* principle and professionals generally

The rule that the appropriate standard of care in relation to professionals is measured against the standard held by a reasonable, competent body of professional opinion is not a rule exclusive to doctors. It can be applied to professionals generally.

A person professing to exercise a particular professional skill will be expected to act in accordance with the standards accepted by a competent body of opinion, expert in the particular skill in question, and again it will be measured against the practices accepted as competent within that profession.

CASE EXAMPLE

Luxmoore-May v Messenger May and Baverstock [1990] 1 All ER 1067

Auctioneers sold paintings at auction for £840. Some months later the paintings were then resold for £88,000. It was alleged that the auctioneers were negligent in failing to recognise that the paintings were the work of a famous artist. The Court of Appeal held that the auctioneers should be judged according to the standards of a competent body of opinion skilled in the profession of the auctioneers. In the event they were not negligent because it was shown that there could be divergence of opinion on the origins of the paintings.

The *Bolam* test may in any case apply even though the defendant lacks the appropriate professional qualifications and is not applying the same reasoning that a professional would apply.

CASE EXAMPLE

Adams and another v Rhymney Valley District Council, The Times, 11 August 2000, CA

The defendant council fitted double-glazed windows in the claimant's council flat. The windows had removable keys and the council did not fit smoke alarms in the flat. The keys were not kept in the windows. During a fire one of the claimants was badly injured breaking the windows trying to get out and three of the claimant's children died in the fire. The trial judge rejected the claim on the basis that the council had exercised the skill of a competent window designer in fitting windows with removable keys. The Court of Appeal dismissed the appeal and rejected the argument that *Bolam* had been wrongly applied. Even though the council had not consulted the police or the fire brigade they had not produced a negligent design for the windows.

The standard expected of the professional is that of a competent body of professional opinion, not of professional opinion generally. So that it is possible for the practice of the professional in question to be accepted in fact by only a minority of professionals.

CASE EXAMPLE

***Defreitas v O'Brien and Connolly* [1995] 6 Med LR 108**

A doctor specialising in spinal surgery considered an intricate exploratory operation necessary. The argument that there was negligence because as it was shown only 11 out of over 1,000 surgeons who regularly performed the operation would have operated in this case was rejected. The Court of Appeal held that the number involved was capable of being seen as a competent body of medical opinion in the circumstances.

This might include even unorthodox or unusual practices.

CASE EXAMPLE

***Shakoor v Situ (t/a Eternal Health Co)* [2001] 1 WLR 410**

The claimant, who suffered from a skin condition, went to a Chinese herbalist who prescribed a remedy. The claimant later died of acute liver failure that was found to be a rare and unpredictable reaction to the remedy. Shakoor's widow brought proceedings alleging negligence in prescribing the remedy, or alternatively, in failing to provide warning of the risks. The court held that it was necessary to consider the standard of care of a practitioner of alternative medicine. It was implied that (1) he was presenting himself as competent to practice within the system of law and medicine under which his standard of care would be judged; (2) he knew, rather than believed, that the remedy was not harmful; and (3) if a patient reacted adversely to the remedy and as a result sought orthodox medical help then this would be discussed in an orthodox medical journal. In the instant case, the actions of the herbalist were consistent with the standard of care appropriate to traditional Chinese herbal medicine in accordance with established requirements. So there was no breach of duty.

Common practice among a profession is often cited as indicating that the practice is acceptable and not negligent. There are of course some practices that can be seen as negligent regardless of whether they are commonly carried out or not.

One final aspect of the standard of care expected of professionals is that they should keep reasonably abreast of changes and developments in their profession. They would not, however, be expected to be immediately aware of all new ideas.

However, it is important that where guidelines are issued by government or by the professional bodies governing the professions that indicate best practice, then professionals should act according to those guidelines.

CASE EXAMPLE

Thomson v James and Others [1996] 31 BMLR 1

A GP failed to follow government guidelines in advising parents on vaccinations for rubella, measles and mumps. A child was then not vaccinated following the advice of the GP and contracted first measles and later meningitis and was brain damaged as a result. The doctor was negligent in failing to issue proper advice.

ACTIVITY

Quick quiz

Using *Bolam* criteria in each of the following situations, consider whether or not the doctor defendant is likely to have breached his duty of care, giving reasons for your answers.

1 A patient has suffered paralysis when the doctor carried out a treatment which on statistical evidence available to the court is only generally carried out by 11 out of 1,000 doctors, although the 11 contain many very experienced and well-respected doctors.

2 A patient has suffered paralysis when a doctor carried out experimental treatment which has not previously been performed. The doctor is an eminent surgeon.

3 A patient has suffered paralysis when he received what he alleged to be negligent treatment and the defence was that the doctor carrying out the treatment was a junior and very inexperienced doctor.

4 A patient has suffered paralysis following an operation carried out by a doctor carrying out a standard procedure and where there were known risks of paralysis. However, the claimant is arguing that the doctor was negligent because an article in an American journal in the month the operation was carried out explained a new procedure which tests showed reduced the risk of paralysis to very low proportions.

Self-assessment questions

1 How does the test used for measuring the standard of care appropriate to a professional differ from the normal test?

2 What justifications does McNair J give for departing from the principles that are generally used to determine what the standard of care is and whether or not it has been breached?

3 How widely has the application of the *Bolam* test spread in the context of the original case?

4 What is the value of expert witness evidence in determining whether or not a professional has breached his duty of care?

5 What do you think that Lord Scarman meant in *Maynard* when he said, 'A court may prefer one body of opinion to the other; but that is no basis for a conclusion of negligence'?

6 Why do you think that the judges were not prepared to reduce the standard of care for inexperience in *Wilsher*?

7 In what ways do you think that Brazier and Miola are correct to say that the *Bolam* test 'has been used by the courts to abdicate responsibility for defining and enforcing patient rights'?

8 What is the value of expert witness evidence in determining whether or not a professional has breached his duty of care?

9 In what ways has *Bolitho* not really made any inroad on the *Bolam* test?

10 What criticisms can be made of the test used for establishing the standard of care owed by professionals?

ACTIVITY

Applying the law

Consider how the courts would determine whether there was a breach in the following situations:

1 Harold is a gynaecologist who when called by midwives because of a difficult birth nevertheless persuades the midwives to continue. The baby dies during delivery. Certain doctors suggest that only a caesarean section delivery was appropriate in the case but Harold states that, even if he had attended he would not have carried out a caesarean and other doctors say that they would have reacted similarly.

2 During a forceps delivery of Martha's baby, Harold, an inexperienced doctor who has never performed a forceps delivery before, damages the baby's head so badly that the baby suffers almost total brain damage and dies.

SAMPLE ESSAY QUESTION

'The rules governing breach of duty are inconsistently applied so that they have the potential to be unfair to either party.' Discuss the accuracy of the above statement.

Explain breach and describe how the standard of care is measured

- Breach is falling below the standard that is appropriate to the duty owed
- Based on the reasonable man test *Blyth v Birmingham Waterworks* – so is an objective test
- And the standard does not reduce merely because of, e.g. inexperience *Nettleship v Weston*

Explain the factors that the court will take into account in assessing breach

- Foreseeability of the risk of harm *Roe v Minister of Health*
- The magnitude of harm *Bolton v Stone, Haley v London Electricity Board*
- The effects of the 'thin skull' rule *Paris v Stepney BC, Page v Smith*
- The practicability of any possible precautions *Latimer v AEC, Bolton v Stone*
- Possible effect of common practice *Brown v Rolls Royce, Re Herald of Free Enterprise*

Discuss whether these cause inconsistency or injustice

- Objective measure should lead to consistency and justice
- Inexperience will not excuse – the same standard is expected so creates consistency and is fairer to claimant but could appear unfair to defendant
- Recovery only possible for foreseeable damage – so fair
- The 'thin skull' rule may cause inconsistency or appear unfair
- And common practice may apply inconsistently

Explain the different approach applied to professionals, particularly doctors

- Measured against 'a competent body of professional opinion' *Bolam v Friern Hospital Management Committee*
- So more subjective than objective

Discuss whether this leads to inconsistency or injustice

- Allows them in effect to set their own standards which may mean that claims are easier to defeat
- Definitely inconsistent with reasonable man standard
- Risky practices may still be accepted
- A danger of professionals 'closing ranks' to defeat claims
- Harder to determine what 'a competent body of professional opinion' actually is until it is tested

KEY FACTS

The standard of care of professionals	Case
A breach of duty occurs where a person falls below the standard of care appropriate to the duty he owes.	
The standard of care is usually that appropriate to the 'reasonable person'.	*Blyth v Birmingham Waterworks* [1856]
But the standard appropriate to professionals is judged according to the standards of a competent body of professional opinion.	*Bolam v Friern Hospital Management Committee* [1957]
This is because the 'reasonable person' does not share those skills.	
And all aspects of medicine are tested against this rule, including even complementary medicine. The disclosure of information which must be tested against is whether, in the circumstances of the particular case, a reasonable person in the patient's position would be likely to attach significance to the risk, or the doctor is or should reasonably be aware that the particular patient would be likely to attach significance to it.	*Whitehouse v Jordan* [1981]; *Shakoor v Situ* [2001] *Montgomery v Lanarkshire Health Board* [2015]
Though there is no lowering of standard to take account of inexperience.	*Wilsher v Essex AHA* [1988]
The rule is criticised for allowing doctors to set their own standards while standards generally are measured according to an objective standard.	
It is felt that the standard should not be applied to hypothetical situations.	*Bolitho v City & Hackney HA* [1997]

res ipsa loquitur
Literally, 'the thing speaks for itself' – where the claimant is unable to show details of the negligence but the damage was obviously caused negligently the defendant will be required to show that he was not negligent

3.5 Pleading *res ipsa loquitur*

One of the common threads throughout all law is the general maxim that 'he who accuses must prove'. In this way the party claiming the negligence has the burden of proof and must show the defendant's breach of the duty of care.

The burden of proof can work very harshly on a claimant who is bound to collect all of the necessary evidence in order to show that there is negligence. This can be particularly difficult for instance in a medical negligence claim where a mass of highly technical evidence may need to be produced in order to satisfy the burden.

There are certain rare circumstances in which this burden of proof can be made less demanding. The first of these is the rule that it is possible to introduce criminal convictions as evidence in a civil claim.

A second possibility, which may have an impact on the burden of proof, is an old common law maxim ***res ipsa loquitur***. Literally translated, *res ipsa loquitur* means 'the thing speaks for itself'. The maxim therefore acts as a mechanism whereby the claimant can be relieved of the burden of proving the negligence and the court can infer negligence in those situations where the factual circumstances of the case would make proving it almost impossible.

The rule is easily justified. M A Milner, *Negligence in Modern Law* (Butterworths, 1967), pp. 89–93e explains that 'Res ipsa loquitur is an immensely important vehicle for importing strict liability into negligence cases. In practice, there are many cases where res ipsa loquitur is properly invoked in which the defendant is unable to show affirmatively either that he took all reasonable precautions to avoid injury or that the particular cause of the injury was not associated with negligence on his part.'

3.5.1 The effects of the doctrine

There is some argument as to the exact means by which the principle works. The simplest explanation is that it straightforwardly reverses the burden of proof and instead of the claimant having to prove the negligence, the burden is on the defendant to prove that he was not negligent.

In *Wilsher v Essex Area Health Authority* [1986] 3 All ER 801, CA, on the other hand, it was suggested that the maxim does not in fact reverse the burden of proof. Instead it was suggested that invoking the maxim raises a *prima facie* presumption of negligence. The result of this presumption is that the defendant is then required to rebut the presumption by introducing evidence to show that in the circumstances he was not negligent. Nevertheless, the court held that the burden remains throughout with the claimant. This though does not appear to be the standard view.

In more general fashion Lord Justice Hobhouse in *Ratcliffe v Plymouth & Torbay HA, Exeter & North Devon HA* [1998] PIQR stated at 189 that the doctrine:

JUDGMENT

'is not a principle of law; it does not relate to or raise any presumption. It is merely a guide to help to identify when a *prima facie* case is being made out.'

Whatever the precise mechanism is, it does at least give a claimant who alleges negligence the opportunity to demand some contrary proof from the defendant in circumstances where the collection of evidence would prove difficult if not impossible.

CASE EXAMPLE

Henderson v H E Jenkins & Sons [1970] AC 282

The claimant's husband was killed when the brakes of a lorry failed while it was on a steep hill. The defendants argued that this was to do with a latent defect which caused corrosion in the brake pipes. This defect could only be detected once the pipes were removed, which was a practice not recommended by the manufacturers. The court would not accept this as sufficient to rebut the claimant's argument that there was negligence involved. The court held that the defendants should have gone on to show that there was nothing else in the vehicle's history that could account for the corrosion of the brakes. The defendants were required to prove that they were not negligent, had failed to do so and so were held liable.

Because the maxim can be equally harsh on the defendant the maxim is very narrowly construed by the courts and it will only be accepted as an appropriate plea if the facts of the case fit specific criteria that have been laid down by the courts.

CASE EXAMPLE

Scott v London and St Katherine's Dock Co [1865] 3 H & C 596

Here the claimant was standing outside the defendant's warehouse when several large bags of sugar fell on him. There was little or no explanation for the incident and no evidence that could be introduced that would show that any particular person had been negligent. The trial judge initially found for the defendant since there was no proof of negligence. However, on appeal this was reversed and the criteria for dealing with such claims were established.

Erle CJ explained the application of the maxim at 601:

JUDGMENT

'where the thing is shewn to be under the management of the defendant or his servants, and the accident is such that in the ordinary course of things could not happen if those who have the management use proper care, it affords reasonable evidence, in the absence of explanation by the defendants that the accident arose from want of care'.

3.5.2 The criteria for claiming *res ipsa loquitur*

The criteria arising from the judgment in the last case are quite clear and give a systematic means of applying the maxim and determining the circumstances in which it can be used.

There are then three specific criteria for successfully pleading *res ipsa loquitur*:

- At all material times the thing causing the harm must have been in the control of the defendant.
- The incident must be of a type that could only have been caused by negligence.
- The cause of the incident is not known and there is no other obvious explanation for the incident.

The incident was in the control of the defendant

The basis of the plea is that there is no explanation available for proof of negligence but that the defendant caused the damage. Inevitably the defendant must be in control of the situation that has led to the damage, or there can be no liability.

What does actually fall within the defendant's control is a question of fact in each case for the court to decide.

CASE EXAMPLE

Gee v Metropolitan Railway Co [1873] LR 8 QB 161

A passenger leaned on a train door shortly after it left the station. The door opened and the passenger fell out and was injured. The defendants were responsible for ensuring that all doors were properly closed before the train left the station. There was no reasonable explanation for why the door opened. However, the defendants were in control at the material time and the court thus held that they were liable.

Actual control is a question of fact. As a result it is possible to show from the circumstances that it would be unfair to suggest that the defendant had actual control. In the absence of control then the defendant cannot be said to be the cause without proof.

CASE EXAMPLE

Easson v London and North Eastern Railway [1944] KB 421

Here a boy passenger fell through the door of a train when it was a long way from its last stop. There may well have been other reasons why the door was open or not secure. For instance it was possible that another passenger had opened the door. The court certainly felt that it was impossible to say that the doors were under the control of the railway company throughout the entire journey and as a result *res ipsa* could not apply.

It seems only fair that if the defendant is in control of the circumstances in which the damage occurred he should be called on to give some explanation of the incident.

The incident is of a type usually associated with negligence

It is also obviously of critical importance to show also that the incident causing the damage is of a type that would not normally occur if proper care were taken. If this is so then the incident can be seen as one of a type that would commonly be caused only by negligence. The absence of a reasonable explanation by the defendant means that it is reasonable to assume that the event occurred because of lack of care.

CASE EXAMPLE

Scott v London and St Katherine's Dock Co [1865] 3 H & C 596

Here the facts really do speak for themselves. Large bags of sugar are inanimate objects and it is unlikely that they could fall from a hoist without a lack of care being taken. They may well have been stacked carelessly and too close to the opening. It could be that a careless employee brushed against them causing them to fall. What is certain is that, if they had been stacked safely, they would not have fallen and injured the claimant.

Res ipsa is often pleaded in medical negligence cases because the claimant is entitled to an explanation of how the damage occurred if not by negligence.

CASE EXAMPLE

Glass v Cambridge Health Authority [1995] 6 Med LR 91

A man who was shown to have a normal healthy heart nevertheless went into cardiac arrest while under a general anaesthetic. The maxim was held to have been appropriately pleaded in the case although the Health Authority was able to introduce evidence to show why it had not been negligent.

In medical negligence cases the plea is common because of the difficulties of showing the precise negligence and the plea may often be used because the precise party responsible for the damage is unknown.

CASE EXAMPLE

Mahon v Osborne [1939] 2 KB 14

Here after an operation a patient later died. It was discovered that a swab was inside him. It was clear that the swab must have been left in the patient during an operation and that it could not have been there but for negligence, although the precise member of the medical staff who was actually responsible could not be identified. Scott LJ, however, felt that some positive evidence of neglect of duty in the operation was needed in such cases.

The maxim in such cases may be used when the claim is that a particular body is vicariously liable for the acts of the tortfeasor.

CASE EXAMPLE

Ward v Tesco Stores Ltd [1976] 1 WLR 810

A customer slipped on yoghurt that had been spilt on to the supermarket's floor. Tesco claimed that they had a procedure in place whereby the floors were cleaned regularly throughout the day and staff were instructed to stay with such spillages when they were found until they were cleaned. Nevertheless the customer was also able to show evidence of other spillages that were not immediately cleaned up. The court accepted that such occurrences could only result from negligence.

There is no other explanation for the incident causing damage

The third and final criterion for the plea to have effect is that it is impossible for the claimant to introduce evidence to give any explanation of the incident. If the circumstances of the incident are capable of explanation by the claimant then the usual burden applies and the claimant should show how the facts prove negligence.

A plea of *res ipsa loquitur* can only apply because there are no other means available to explain the true cause of the incident. It is thus fairer in the circumstances to ask the defendant to introduce some evidence to rebut the presumption that negligence has occurred.

CASE EXAMPLE

Barkway v South Wales Transport Co Ltd [1950] 1 All ER 392

Without apparent reason a bus mounted a pavement and this resulted in injury to the claimant. In fact it was discovered that a tyre had burst because of a defect in the wall of the tyre that could not have been discovered earlier. *Res ipsa* was shown to be inappropriate, however, when it was discovered that the bus company gave no instructions to drivers to report heavy blows suffered by the tyres. As a result the court held that it was possible for negligence to be shown and the defendants were liable.

Comment

We have already seen that there is debate among the judiciary as to the proper role of the maxim in relation to medical negligence cases.

It has been argued at different points that the maxim should always apply because the three criteria will generally be satisfied and because the claimant may otherwise face a very difficult time collecting the appropriate evidence.

The courts, nevertheless, have been reluctant to accept such widespread application of the maxim. The Pearson Report in 1978 also rejected general application because of the fear of an escalating number of claims resulting and the consequent rise in insurance premiums for medical staff.

3.5.3 Strict liability in negligence

Res ipsa was formerly very often used in cases involving foreign bodies in foodstuffs. Clearly while it may be difficult to show how the material got there it is nevertheless something that should not happen if proper care is taken.

The Consumer Protection Act allows that any person within the chain of distribution of a product is strictly liable if a consumer suffers harm as the result of defects in the product. The customer has the option to sue without showing fault but merely proving the defect and the existence of the defendant in the chain of distribution.

While fault is in a sense abolished in the Act causation is still an issue.

ACTIVITY

Self-assessment questions

1 *Res ipsa loquitur* means the thing speaks for itself, but what does this mean precisely in relation to the incident in question?
2 What three elements must always be present for a judge to accept that the doctrine applies in the case?
3 To what extent is it accurate to speak of a reversal of the burden of proof?
4 What sorts of things indicate that the loss or damage suffered could only have been the result of negligence?
5 Why has the doctrine regularly been pleaded in medical negligence cases?
6 What is the effect of the doctrine in consumer protection law?

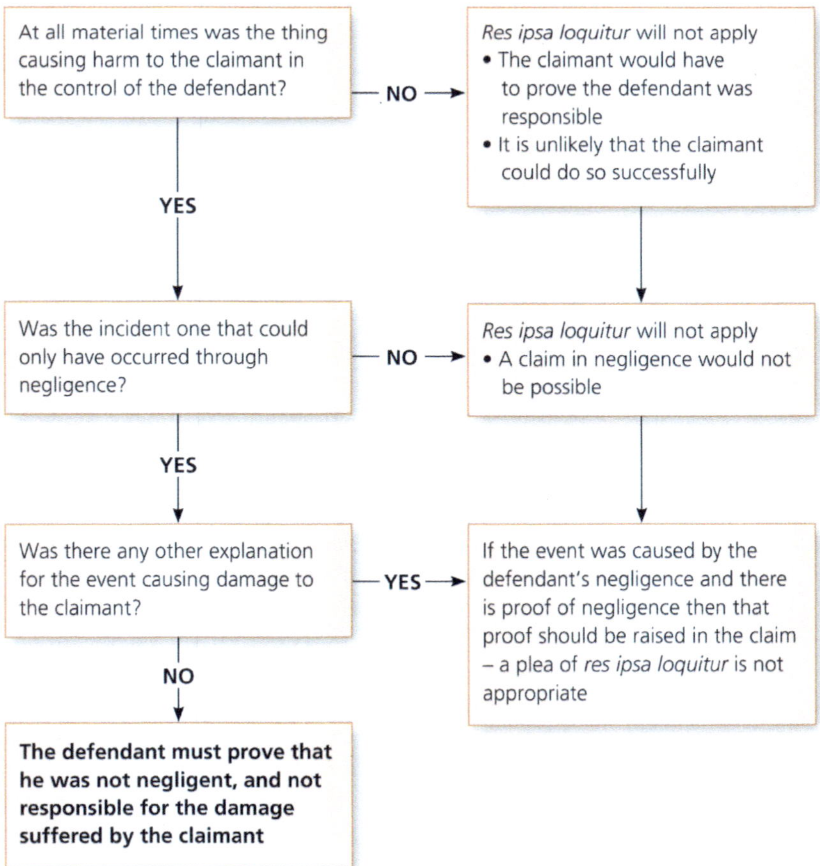

Figure 3.2 The requirements for making a plea of *res ipsa loquitur*.

KEY FACTS

Res ipsa loquitur	**Case**
Res ipsa loquitur means the thing speaks for itself – it is a means of establishing negligence where proof is hard to come by. The doctrine in effect means that the defendant has to prove that he was not negligent if the plea is raised successfully.	
There are three essential aspects to the plea: • at all material times events leading to the damage were under the control of the defendant • the incident is of a type usually associated with negligence • there is no other explanation. It can be particularly appropriate to medical negligence claims.	*Gee v Metropolitan Railway* [1873] *Scott v London and St Katherine's Dock* [1865] *Barkway v South Wales Transport* [1950]

3.6 Fault liability and the need for reform

Fault liability, particularly in the case of medical negligence as we have seen, seems unfair to claimants because of the problems associated both with amassing evidence and of actually proving fault.

It seems obviously wrong to impose liability on a body such as a health authority unless that body can be shown to have done wrong. The fact that the defendant satisfies legal tests on fault is nevertheless scant comfort to a person who places his safety in the hands of professional people and finds himself later to have suffered irreversible and disabling damage.

Fault liability can also be seen as unfair to victims who have suffered harm because the degree to which a person can easily gather evidence and therefore present a winnable case may depend on the degree of publicity that the case has produced. Inevitably people involved in an event gaining media attention or involving a number of claimants may be in a better position to find suitable evidence.

In this way fault liability can also be unfair to society generally in not providing an adequate means of remedying wrongs since the fault based system can create classes of victims who can be compensated and classes who cannot. This can be particularly true of the victims of pure accidents and those suffering from genetic disorders.

It can also be seen as unfair to defendants since there are no identified degrees of culpability. This in turn means that a defendant will not be penalised according to the degree of negligence shown.

The rules concerning the standard of care as well as the imposing of duties mean that very often a claimant's ability to recover for the wrong suffered is determined according to the whims of policy and therefore can be subject to arbitrary and often inconsistent reasoning.

In fairness to the fault based system its major justification is that it does punish the wrongdoer and so is said to have some deterrent value.

However, no-fault systems have been advocated on a number of occasions. The Pearson Committee in 1978 suggested such a system in the case of personal injury claims, though this has never been accepted or implemented. Two no-fault based medical negligence bills have also been introduced unsuccessfully. The principle is not without precedent since such a system has operated in New Zealand (see section 1.3.3).

In the case of healthcare professionals it is interesting to note that the Chief Medical Officer has proposed a new system for claims against NHS Trusts in a June 2003 report 'Making amends'. The system advocated is an attempt to avoid the delays and costs of pursuing claims through the courts, although of course it will not prevent a claimant from pursuing a claim in this way. The substance of the proposals is for a 'right of redress' where investigation of a patient's complaint reveals 'serious shortcomings' and which result in 'harm which could have been avoided'. The proposed result would include appropriate care and rehabilitation and compensation up to £30,000. There are more complex provisions in the case of severely neurologically damaged babies.

For additional discussion of fault based liability, see section 1.3.

ACTIVITY

Essay writing

Using the guide in Appendix 1, try the following essay title.

Consider the extent to which the rules by which the courts determine whether there is a breach of a duty of care actually discourage people from engaging in activities that may harm or damage others.

SUMMARY

- A breach occurs when the defendant falls below the standard of care appropriate to the duty owed.
- Measured against the standard of the 'reasonable person'.
- So is an objective standard, e.g. the reasonable motorist.
- There is no lowering of the standard for those who lack experience.
- Judges take many factors into account:
- the foreseeability of the risk of harm
  - the magnitude and likelihood of the risk
  - the practicability of any possible precautions
  - the possible effect of common practice.

- Measured differently in the case of professionals:
  - measured against 'a competent body of professional opinion'
  - the *Bolam* test
  - which causes controversy.

Further reading

Elvin, J, 'Liability for negligent refereeing of a rugby match' (2003) *119 LQR* 560.

Mulheron, R, '*Trumping Bolam*: A critical legal analysis of Bolitho's gloss' [2010] *CLJ* 609.

Mulheron, R, 'Legislating dangerously: Bad Samaritans, good society, and the Heroism act 2015' (2017) *80(1) MLR* 88.

Stein, R, and Swaine, F, 'Ms B v an NHS Trust: The patient's right to choose' (2002) *152 NLJ* 642.

Toczek, L, 'A case of foul play' (2002) *152 NLJ* 868.

4

Negligence: Causation

AIMS AND OBJECTIVES

After reading this chapter you should be able to:

- Describe the usual means of establishing causation in fact, the but for test
- Recognise the problems that arise in proving causation in fact where there are multiple causes of the damage
- Explain the possible effects on the liability of the original defendant of a plea of *novus actus interveniens*, where the chain of causation has been broken
- Identify and apply the test for establishing causation in law, reasonable foreseeability of harm, so that the damage is not too remote a consequence of the defendant's breach of duty
- Critically analyse the concepts of causation in law and causation in fact
- Apply the tests to factual situations to determine whether the defendant has caused the damage suffered by the claimant

4.1 Introduction

Once the claimant has shown the existence of a duty of care and proved that it has been breached by falling below the appropriate standard of care, he must still prove on the balance of probabilities that the defendant's negligent act or omission actually caused the damage.

As with the other two elements of negligence, the burden is on the claimant to prove the causal link on a balance of probabilities. This may actually be quite difficult to do, particularly where the incident leading to the damage has been the result of multiple causes or where the damage suffered is of an unusual type.

Causation is also clearly appropriate to other torts, not just negligence. Even in those torts that are strict liability and where the claimant as a result is relieved only of the burden of proving fault causation is still an

DOI: 10.4324/9781003202417-4

issue and the claimant must still show a direct link between the defendant's acts or omissions and the damage suffered.

Causation is necessarily measured against the facts of the individual cases. Nevertheless, as in the other areas, policy can still play a big part in decisions.

In establishing negligence the courts will measure causation in two different ways:

but for test
The main test for establishing factual causation in an action for negligence – but for the defendant's breach of duty the damage would not have occurred

- according to the **but for test**, that the defendant's negligent act or omission did in fact cause the claimant's damage (causation in fact);
- by establishing that the damage is still sufficiently proximate in law to hold the defendant liable to compensate the victim (causation in law – more commonly referred to as remoteness of damage).

The rest of this chapter will set the test used to establish causation in fact, namely the but for test, and then set out the four exceptional circumstances in which it is permitted to depart from the but for test.

4.2 Causation in fact and the but for test

The simplest proposition, and the effective starting point in establishing causation, is to say that the defendant will only be liable in negligence if the claimant would not have suffered the damage but for the defendant's negligent act or omission.

In many cases where the negligence of the defendant is obvious the facts allow the test to operate simply and straightforwardly. The negligence either was the cause of the damage or there was some alternative cause, and the defendant is not liable.

The test was explained simply and precisely by Lord Denning in *Cork v Kirby MacLean Ltd* [1952] 2 All ER 402 at 407:

JUDGMENT

'. . . if the damage would not have happened but for a particular fault, then that fault is the cause of the damage; if it would have happened just the same, fault or no fault, the fault is not the cause of the damage'.

CASE EXAMPLE

***Barnett v Chelsea & Kensington Hospital Management Committee* [1969] 1 QB 428**

Three night watchmen from a college went to the casualty ward of the hospital at around 5.00 a.m. on the morning of New Year's Day complaining of vomiting and stomach pains after drinking tea. The doctor on duty, in clear breach of his duty towards the men, then refused to attend to them or examine them and told them to call on their own doctors in the morning. A few hours later one of the men died, as it was discovered later, through arsenic poisoning. The court found that the hospital was not liable for the failure to treat, even though this was a clear breach of their duty, because it was shown that the man would not have recovered even if he had received treatment. The failure to treat was not the cause of death.

It is of course possible that the defendant's injury follows naturally from the negligent omission because the events leading to the damage would not have occurred but for the negligent omission.

The interplay between the application of standard of proof (balance of probabilities and the but for approach can be depicted using a scale:

Essentially, any probability of the injury occurring that falls within the first segment does not attract any liability but anything that is over 50 per cent may.

4.2.1 The problem of multiple causes

The problem of proving a causal link between the defendant's negligent act and the damage is always made more difficult where there is the possibility of more than one cause. In such instances the court is forced into the position of trying to determine which of the possibilities is the actual cause of the damage suffered. Very often the court will find that it is impossible to do this with accuracy and the claimant may be left without compensation at all.

CASE EXAMPLE

Wilsher v Essex Area Health Authority [1986] 3 All ER 801 CA

Here a baby after being delivered was given excess oxygen as a result of the admitted error of the doctor and the baby then suffered blindness through retrolental fibroplasia. The House of Lords identified that the excess oxygen was just one of five possible causes of the condition and therefore it could not be said to fall squarely within the risk created by the defendants. The court would not impose liability on the defendant in these circumstances although this seems very unfair.

The difficulty of identifying precise cause means that the case law is often inconsistent. The risk then is that the decision will appear on the surface to be unfair to the claimant. This again is all too common where the chance of recovery may have been lost through negligence in medical treatment or diagnosis.

CASE EXAMPLE

Hotson v East Berkshire Area Health Authority [1987] 2 All ER 909

A young boy suffered a fractured hip when he fell out of a tree. The hospital negligently failed to make a correct early diagnosis so that he later developed avascular necrosis, a deformity of the hip. Expert evidence confirmed that he would have had a 75 per cent chance of the deformity even without the failure to diagnose promptly. On this basis the trial judge, and later the Court of Appeal, awarded him 25 per cent of the damages they would have considered appropriate for the condition for the loss of a chance of recovery. The trial judge commented that the hospital had translated the probability of the disability developing into a certainty by negligence in their failure to diagnose. However, the House of Lords allowed the Health Authority's appeal and would not consider the slim chance of recovery an issue of causation. Causation is either established on the balance of probabilities or not, and it was not in the case.

Lord Ackner summed up the issue of causation in the case quite succinctly at 922:

JUDGMENT

'the deformed hip . . . was not caused by the admitted breach by the defendants . . . but was caused by the separation of the left femoral epiphysis when he fell . . . I have sought to stress that this case was a relatively simple case concerned with the proof of causation, upon which the plaintiff failed, because he was unable to prove on the balance of probabilities that his deformed hip was caused by the defendant's breach of duty in delaying over a period of five days a proper diagnosis and treatment.'

However unfair the position of the House of Lords may appear there is nevertheless no disputing its legal logic.

Hill commented that: 'The emotive speech and obvious feelings for a "lost chance" plaintiff must not let us colour or obscure the real issue – the existence of an "evidentiary gap". Proof of causation should not be accepted on anything less than the balance of probabilities, as is common with all civil actions.' *(T Hill 'A lost chance for compensation in the tort of negligence by the House of Lords'[1991] 54 MLR 511.)*

In *Hotson*, the claimant only proved his case to 25 per cent and therefore did not prove his case on the balance of probabilities and recovered nothing.

The House of Lords had an opportunity to review the law on 'loss of a chance' in the next case.

CASE EXAMPLE

Gregg v Scott [2005] UKHL 2

The claimant was concerned about a lump under his arm but his GP failed to refer him to a hospital for tests, dismissing the lump as harmless fatty tissue. When the claimant saw another GP nine months later, by which time he was in considerable pain, he was referred to hospital for tests and cancer of the lymph glands was diagnosed which it was established had spread considerably during the delay. The claimant argued negligence on the part of the original doctor and it was shown that if his condition had been diagnosed on the first visit and treatment had started at that point he would have had a 42 per cent chance of being alive and disease free in ten years, whereas as a result of the delay in treatment his chances of being alive and disease free after ten years had reduced to 25 per cent. The House of Lords, on a split decision 3:2, was unwilling to depart from the principle in ***Hotson*** by awarding the claimant a proportion of what he would have recovered if the doctor's negligence had in fact caused his premature death. Interestingly the House added that, had the claimant sought damages for the pain and suffering experienced during the delay in treatment these might have been awarded.

The majority judges and the dissenting judges were clearly unconvinced by each other's irreconcilable reasoning.

Lord Hoffmann, delivering the leading judgment held at 84:

JUDGMENT

'Academic writers have suggested that in cases of clinical negligence, the need to prove causation is too restrictive . . . In the present case it is urged that Mr Gregg has suffered a wrong and ought to have a remedy [and that] the exceptional rule in ***Fairchild*** should be generalised and damages awarded in all cases in which the defendant may have caused an injury and has increased the likelihood of the injury . . . It should be first noted that adopting such a rule would involve abandoning a good deal of authority.'

Lord Nicholls dissenting, on the other hand stated at 24:

JUDGMENT

'Given the uncertainty of outcome, the appropriate characterisation of a patient's loss in this type of case must surely be that it comprises the loss of a chance of a favourable outcome, rather than the loss of the outcome itself. Justice so requires . . . And this analysis of a patient's loss accords with the purpose of the legal duty . . . to promote the patient's prospects of recovery by exercising due skill and care in diagnosing and treating the patient's condition. This approach also achieves a basic object of the law of tort. The common law imposes duties and seeks to provide appropriate remedies in the event of a breach of duty. If negligent diagnosis . . . diminishes a patient's prospects of recovery, a law which does not recognise this as a wrong calling for a claim for loss of life expectancy may give rise to compensation.'

Ultimately the legal justification for failing to provide a remedy in the 'loss of a chance' cases lies in the fact that the claimant's arguments on causation rests on a possibility rather than a probability of harm occurring, and on a simple balance of probabilities test the claims fail. In practical terms, it would become very difficult to manage awarding compensation for anything below the required threshold. For example, it would be hard to reconcile the position of two claimants where one has lost 40 per cent chance of recovering and is entitled to a proportionate amount and the other, has lost 51 per cent chance of recovery but has thereby proved their claim on the balance of probabilities, and is therefore entitled to 100 per cent of the damages. This matter is further explored in the case of *CNZ v Royal Bath Hospitals NHS Foundation Trust* [2023] EWHC 19 (KB), at 337 (Richie J).

JUDGMENT

'So the but for test is inherently imperfect. A defendant found liable because there was a finding that on the balance of probability, at say 55%, the breach caused the damage, will pay for all of the damage. Yet if the standard of proof fails, at say only a 45% likelihood that the breach caused the damage, no damages are awarded. This is the rough and ready nature of causation in tort law.'

CRITIQUING THE LAW

The but for test appears to be a blunt tool and appears generates some unfair outcomes. Do you agree with the decision in ***Hotson and Gregg v Scott***? Do you think that the claimants should have received some damages to reflect the negligence of the defendant?

4.3 Problems in proving causation

Very often the problem is not purely one of fact and the process of establishing cause is not so much scientific enquiry as attributing blame. Inevitably interpretation of the factual evidence may still depend on the value judgments used by the court. For instance, a pedestrian runs onto the road into the path of an oncoming vehicle that is travelling over the speed limit for the area and the pedestrian is injured. In purest scientific terms the actual cause of the accident is that both parties were present on the road at the same time. It is possible in the circumstances to feel that the pedestrian has done as much as, if not more than, the motorist in causing his own injuries. Inevitably, however, even allowing for a successful claim of contributory negligence, the motorist would be held to have caused the victim's injuries, because he is blameworthy by exceeding the speed limit.

Even greater problems may occur where the level of knowledge available to the court makes it impossible to pinpoint the precise cause. This may be particularly appropriate where medicine and medical technology is concerned.

The rest of this section considers the exceptions to the but for test and when they may be applied.

4.3.1 Material contribution to risk

If the damage is caused by multiple causes that are acting concurrently, or at the same time, then the but for test appears to be incapable of providing an absolute test of causation. The case law demonstrates the difficulties faced by the courts in trying to identify the precise cause.

On the one hand the court may decide that the negligence has 'materially contributed to the risk' of damage and that the defendant should therefore be liable for damages. The traditional but for test may not produce a just result in such instances and different causal requirements need to be applied.

CASE EXAMPLE

McGhee v National Coal Board [1973] 3 All ER 1008

Here the claimant worked in a brick kiln where he was exposed to brick dust, a possible cause of the dermatitis that he in fact contracted. The Board was not liable for exposure during working hours. They were held liable for materially increasing the risk of the claimant contracting the disease because of their failure to provide washing facilities, even though it could not be shown that he would have avoided the disease if there had been facilities. The reasoning of the court was that, since the employer was clearly negligent in failing to provide basic health and safety the burden should shift on to them to disprove the causal link. This type of test is clearly more advantageous to a claimant than the basic but for test applied so rigidly in ***Hotson v East Berkshire AHA*** [1987] 1 All ER 210.

In *McGhee,* it could not be said that on the balance of probabilities the additional negligent exposure to brick dust had been the cause of the dermatitis contracted by the claimant as it may have occurred in any event. So when it is proved, on a balance of probabilities, that an employer has been negligent and that their negligence has materially increased the risk of their employee contracting an industrial disease, then they are liable in damages to that employee if they contract the disease notwithstanding that the employer is not responsible for other factors which have materially contributed to the disease. Lord Wilberforce summarises the position at 6:

JUDGMENT

'. . . from the evidential point of view, one may ask, why should a man who is able to show that his employer should have taken certain precautions, because without them there is a risk, or an added risk, of injury or disease, and who in fact sustains exactly that injury or disease, have to assume the burden of proving more: namely, that it was the addition to the risk, caused by the breach of duty, which caused or materially contributed to the injury?'

The House of Lords was prepared to make the employer liable for the dermatitis suffered by the worker in the brick kiln. The court did so because it considered that the risk of the particular damage occurring had been materially increased by the defendant's negligent failure to provide adequate washing facilities, even though it was impossible to pinpoint the lack of washing facilities as the precise cause of the condition.

The courts appear to take a pragmatic approach where proof of causation is difficult.

CASE EXAMPLE

Bonnington Castings Ltd v Wardlaw [1956] AC 613

The claimant contracted pneumoconiosis after years of working in dusty conditions and without adequate washing facilities. There were two principal causes of dust, the one requiring no extraction system and the other which did, but no extractor was provided. It was impossible to prove accurately which dust the claimant had inhaled most of. Since the dust which should have been extracted legally was at least a partial cause of his illness the court were prepared to award compensation.

Where the courts use this 'material contribution to risk test' it can be difficult in any case to determine the exact extent of the defendant's contribution. By contrast, where there are several possible concurrent causes (sometimes referred to as agents) of the damage and it is impossible to identify one specific cause responsible for the damage, then it is unlikely that the court will hold that a single cause is ultimately responsible. The consequence of this of course could be that the claimant is left without an action at all, even though the damage must have resulted from one of the causes. While perhaps technically accurate it also seems potentially unfair.

CASE EXAMPLE

Wilsher v Essex Area Health Authority [1986] 3 All ER 801, CA

Here the court identified that there were at least five distinct possible causes of the baby's blindness and the claimant thus could not establish the necessary causal link with the defendant's negligence and was without a remedy.

In ***McGhee*** there was only one possible agent which could have caused the dermatitis, the brick dust, and there was no doubt that the dermatitis from which he suffered was caused by that brick dust.

In this case there was a number of different agents which could have caused the blindness. Excess oxygen was ***one*** of them. The defendants failed to take reasonable precautions to prevent one of the possible causative agents (e.g. excess oxygen) from causing blindness. It is not possible to tell in this case whether excess oxygen did or did not cause or contribute to the blindness suffered by the claimant. The claimant's blindness may have been caused by some completely different agent or agents, e.g. hypercarbia, intraventricular haemorrhage, apnoea or patent ductus arteriosus. In addition to oxygen, each of those conditions has been implicated as a possible cause of blindness. The claimant suffered from each of those conditions at various times in the first two months of his life. There is no satisfactory evidence that excess oxygen is more likely than any of those other four candidates to have caused blindness.

Essentially *Wilsher* is distinct from *McGhee* because there was only one candidate (brick dust) which could have caused the dermatitis, and the failure to take the precaution caused or contributed to the dermatitis. Whereas in *Wilsher* a failure to take preventative measures against one out of five possible causes is no evidence as to which of those five caused the injury.

The approach in *McGhee* was followed in the following case in which there was one agent but several potential *defendants*.

CASE EXAMPLE

Fairchild v Glenhaven Funeral Services Ltd and others [2002] 1 WLR 1052, CA

This case involved a number of appeals. The claimants suffered mesothelioma after exposure to asbestos dust over many years working for a number of different employees. The medical evidence identified that the inhaling of asbestos fibres was the cause of the disease. Nevertheless, it was impossible to identify in which particular employment the disease was actually contracted. The Court of Appeal accepted that medical evidence could not identify a single cause of the disease, which might be caused by contact with even a single asbestos fibre, or may involve cumulative exposure to fibres. As a result, the Court held that the precise employer responsible could not be identified and so the claim should be rejected. It is impossible to say with certainty how the disease begins, but it is possible to identify that prolonged exposure worsens the risk. It seems then that the Court of Appeal applied *Wilsher v Essex AHA* [1986] 3 All ER 801 inappropriately where *McGhee v NCB* [1973] 3 All ER 1008 might have been more fairly applied in the circumstances. The House of Lords has in any case subsequently reversed the Court of Appeal decision.

> The decision in the Court of Appeal inevitably led to criticism. Miller comments that: 'The "single hit" theory that one asbestos fibre alone is capable of initiating mesothelioma has been the source of incalculable harm . . . The key point is that the "single hit" theory presupposes a deterministic view which is not supported by science. It encourages a mindset much closer to criminal law – equating the "guilty" fibre with the knife or bullet which severs the victim's aorta. Of course, lawyers, like most non-scientists, find it hard to resist reducing a complex process to an easily visualised analogy. But they must not forget that the notion of the "guilty" fibre has no basis in the epidemiological evidence . . . The counter-argument that it is unjust to impose liability upon those not responsible for the "guilty" fibre . . . overlooks the role of tort in deterring all negligent behaviour not simply that which can be shown to result in actual injury.'
> *C Miller, 'Why the House of Lords must overturn the Fairchild decision' (2002) 152 NLJ 319.*

The House of Lords took a different approach to the Court of Appeal and accepted that in certain circumstances where there are a number of defendants all contributing to the same basic injury, then a modified approach to causation has to be taken.

CASE EXAMPLE

Fairchild v Glenhaven Funeral Services Ltd and others [2003] 1 AC 32

These three joined appeals, all concerned employees who had contracted mesothelioma as a result of prolonged exposure to asbestos dust with a number of different employers. Because of the difficulty of identifying during which employment the disease was actually contracted the Court of Appeal in fact rejected the claims. The House of Lords accepted the expert evidence that it is scientifically uncertain whether inhaling a single fibre or inhalation of many fibres causes the disease, so it is impossible to say accurately which employer caused the disease. However, the House of Lords held that, because it is evident that the greater the exposure to the dust the greater are the chances of the disease occurring, then each employer has a duty to take reasonable care to prevent employees from inhaling the dust. Besides this the House felt that any other cause of developing the diseases could be ignored in the case. On the basis that the claimants suffered the very injuries that the defendants were supposed to guard against, the House of Lords was prepared to impose liability on all employers. The House chose to apply the 'material risk' test from *McGhee*. In doing so the House held that because all of the defendants had contributed to a risk of mesothelioma (none of them over the required 50 per cent to satisfy the but for test), then no distinction should be drawn between the making of a material risk of causing the disease and a course of action that would materially increase the risk of the disease. Because the employers in the case never argued that they should only be liable for a proportion of the damages then each employer should be liable to compensate its employee in full, even though the employee may have inhaled more asbestos fibres while working for another employee.

At first sight it is quite difficult to see the precise differences between the three very significant cases of *Wilsher, McGhee* and *Fairchild*, all of which still stand as leading authorities. The House of Lords in *Fairchild* accepted that the sufferers of diseases such as mesothelioma, while inevitably deserving of compensation, are unable to satisfy the normal tests for causation because they will invariably be unable to point to a single party who is responsible.

The House of Lords stressed that there needs to be considerable restraint in any relaxation of the threshold but for test of causal connection. It is not the intention of this decision to lead to such a relaxation whenever a claimant has difficulty in establishing the but for test and there must be good reason for departing from the normal threshold but for test. Such reason can be demonstrated if the following can be established:

- Only one agent could have caused the harm and the claimant may have been exposed to that agent tortiously and innocently (e.g. by another source such as an employer or because of the environment);
- The defendants have failed to take precautions to protect against the risk of the agent causing the claimant harm;
- The claimant is unable to satisfy the normal tests for causation because of the current limit of state of scientific knowledge of the disease and so the claimant is unable to attribute as between several employers, the precise responsibility for the harm, although there could be no doubt that exposure to the asbestos fibres in whatever volume was at the root of the disease;
- It follows that it is fairer to give the defendants the burden of proving that their negligence could not be the actual cause rather than make the claimants prove the precise cause.

The majority of the judges were therefore prepared to accept an exceptional principle that where there was proof that a defendant's negligence materially increased the risk of a claimant suffering from a particular disease then this would be sufficient basis for a claim against that defendant. This was said to be based on the principle in *McGhee*.

The Court was not prepared to extend the principle in *McGhee* to factual circumstances such as those in *Wilsher* where the problem for causation was in fact that there was a number of very different potential causes of the injury other than the defendant's negligence, and evidence would be needed to show that the negligence was the actual cause.

As Lord Bingham stated at 57:

JUDGMENT

'It is one thing to treat an increase in risk as equivalent to the making of a material contribution where a single noxious agent is involved, but quite another where any one of a number of noxious agents may equally probably have caused the damage.'

The House of Lords appears to have engaged in a policy decision in order to ensure that there is compensation for asbestos related diseases contracted in the course of employment. Lowther comments: '[J]urisdictions worldwide have grappled with concerns regarding an effective formulation for determining causation, and, as far as authorities selected by Lord Bingham illustrate, they have concluded that effectively throwing one's hands into the air and retreating behind the convenient barrier of scientific uncertainty to deny a single remedy when there are multiple possible causes cannot be an effective or just solution as far as the injured third party is concerned.' *(Lowther, 'Fairchild clarifying rules on causation'* (2002) 14 ELM 4.)

In *CNZ v Royal Bath Hospitals NHS Foundation Trust* [2023] EWHC 19 (KB) [350] Richie J summarises this exception to the but for test.

JUDGMENT

'I take from these cases the principle that where the but for test cannot be satisfied due to scientific gap impossibility then the law will apply the material contribution to the injury test. If the Claimant can prove the breach made a material contribution to the Claimant's injury which was more than de minimis then damages are to be awarded against the Defendant. In certain (limited) circumstances material contribution to the risk of causing the injury will be used but in the current case before me material contribution to risk is not relevant.'

Table 4.1 The relationship between key cases on multiple consecutive causes.

	Wilsher v Essex AHA [1986]	*McGhee v National Coal Board [1973]*	*Fairchild v Glenhaven Funeral Services and Others [2001]*	*Hotson v East Berkshire AHA [1987]*
The damage suffered by the claimant	The baby suffered blindness through retrolental fibroplasia.	The employee contracted dermatitis, a painful skin disease.	Various employees contracted mesothelioma, a cancer affecting the lungs caused by exposure to asbestos fibres.	The boy suffered avuncular necrosis, a permanent deformity of the hip.
The breach of duty by the defendant	A junior doctor employed by the defendant health authority administered excess oxygen after a difficult birth.	The employer failed to provide adequate washing facilities in the workplace so the employee could not wash till he got home.	All of the employers had exposed the claimants to asbestos fibres, although some were no longer in business.	The doctor employed by the health authority failed to diagnose the greenstick fracture at the appropriate time.

(Continued)

Table 4.1 (Continued)

	Wilsher v Essex AHA [1986]	***McGhee v National Coal Board [1973]***	***Fairchild v Glenhaven Funeral Services and Others [2001]***	***Hotson v East Berkshire AHA [1987]***
Liability for harm	No liability	Liability	Liability	No liability
The reason for the decision	Scientific evidence showed that there were six possible causes of the condition suffered by the baby – so on a balance of probabilities it could not be proved that the doctor's breach of duty was the factual cause of the harm.	Even though it could not be shown that the employee would not have contracted the disease but for the employer's breach of basic health and safety duties, the employer had materially increased the risk of the employee catching the disease, and it was for the employer to disprove causation.	Although it is currently scientifically impossible to identify which particular asbestos fibre caused the disease or even whether it was more than one fibre, exposing the employee to asbestos by any of the employers was material contribution to the risk of harm so any could be liable.	Scientific evidence showed that there was a 75 per cent chance that the boy would have suffered the deformity as a result of his injury even if the fracture had been immediately diagnosed – on a balance of probabilities it could not be proved that the doctor's breach of duty was the factual cause of the deformity.
but for test applied	Yes	No	No	Yes

- Establishing liability in a case may depend on how broadly or how narrowly the particular duty is expressed.

CASE EXAMPLE

Barker v Corus (UK) (formerly Saint Gobain Pipelines plc); Murray v British Shipbuilders (Hydromatics) Ltd; Patterson v Smiths Dock Ltd and Others [2006] UKHL 20

This involved three appeals concerning questions left unanswered in *Fairchild*. Barker had died as a result of mesothelioma. He had been exposed to asbestos fibres during three different periods, once in the employment of the defendant, once during different employment and once during a period of self-employment.

The defendant argued that causation could not be proved since the disease could have been contracted solely during the period of self-employment, and alternatively that, although mesothelioma was an indivisible injury that damages should be apportioned between the different possible causes so that the defendant should not be bound to pay full damages. The trial judge allowed a claim under *Fairchild* subject to a 20 per cent reduction for contributory negligence for a failure by Barker to protect himself during his self-employment. The Court of Appeal also applied *Fairchild*, accepted that the defendant was **jointly and severally liable** and rejected the possibility of apportionment. The House of Lords held that in such circumstances a defendant could only be liable for the share of damages equivalent to the share of the risk of contracting mesothelioma created by his breach of duty, and therefore apportioned damages accordingly. This effectively means that liability is several and damages should be apportioned relative to each defendant's degree of contribution regardless of the fact that a defendant may now be insolvent.

ntly and verally liable

e defendants are ble to the claimant parately for the hole amount or ntly with the her defendants. efendants can aim a contribution om each other.

Lady Hale commenting on the potential injustice caused by the relaxation of standard rules of causation in *Fairchild* stated at 126:

JUDGMENT

'for the first time in our legal history, persons are made liable for damage even though they may not have caused it at all, simply because they have materially contributed to the risk'.

Lord Hoffmann explaining the position taken by the court stated at 43:

JUDGMENT

'since this is a case in which science can only deal with probabilities the law should accept that position and attribute liability according to probability'.

The decision was praised in certain quarters: 'The pragmatic decision . . . reflects a desire not only to ensure that the traditional causation tests remain the cornerstones for Tort based compensation claims but to redress the inequities thrown up by . . . Fairchild.' *J McManus, 'Playing it fair' (2006) 156 NLJ 871.*

However, the decision was reconsidered by Parliament and in effect, in the case of *mesothelioma claims only*, was reversed by a hastily included provision in section 3 of the Compensation Act 2006.

SECTION

3 Mesothelioma: damages

. . .

(2) The responsible person shall be liable –

(a) in respect of the whole of the damage caused to the victim by the disease (irrespective of whether the victim was also exposed to asbestos –

(i) other than by the responsible person, whether or not in circumstances in which another person has liability in tort, or

(ii) by the responsible person in circumstances in which he has no liability in tort), and

(b) jointly and severally with any other responsible person.

The effect of section 3 on the *Fairchild* exception to the normal rules on causation has subsequently been considered by the Supreme Court where only one defendant has negligently exposed the claimant to asbestos.

CASE EXAMPLE

Sienkiewicz v Greif (UK) Ltd [2011] UKSC 10

The claimant was the administratrix of the deceased's estate. The deceased had died from mesothelioma from exposure to asbestos fibres. She had worked for 18 years in premises in which asbestos was used and which the trial judge held it had negligently exposed her to. She was also exposed to higher than normal levels of asbestos dust in the town in which she lived, Ellesmere Port. Since the risk of contracting the disease from exposure in the town was of 24 people per million and her combined risk with her exposure at work rose to 28.39 cases per million, the trial judge also held that the risk from exposure in the work place was small and had not materially contributed to her risk of harm since it would need to at least double it to succeed under the *Fairchild* exception. The Court of Appeal reversed this and held that the *Fairchild* exception could be applied wherever the defendant negligently exposing the claimant to asbestos was a material contribution to the risk of harm and that section 3 Compensation Act 2006 defined the scope of the exception in this manner. The Supreme Court held that the *Fairchild* exception did apply in the case but that the Court of Appeal was wrong in its interpretation of section 3 Compensation Act 2006.

To summarise the current position, if the claimant is negligently exposed to asbestos by more than one defendant and contracts mesothelioma, s3 of the Compensation Act applies in that each defendant is jointly and severally liable to the claimant for all of the damage. If the claimant is negligently exposed by more than one defendant to some other substance that causes illness such as asbestosis, then the decision in *Barker v Corus* applies and each defendant is liable in proportion to their level of responsibility.

4.3.2 Material contribution to injury

Following *Bonnington v Castings v Wardlaw* as discussed above, if the claimant can show that the that the defendant's breach materially contributed to the injury suffered in that it has added to the severity of the injury suffered, then the defendant may be liable. A distinction is drawn between divisible and indivisible injuries. A divisible injury is one where it is possible to attribute different parts of the injury to different causes so for example, the greater the exposure to a harmful substance the worse the injury suffered. By contrast, an indivisible injury is one which cannot be divided and attributed to different causes so in this instance, greater exposure to a substance will not have an impact on the severity of the injury suffered. Such injury should be assessed using the but for test.

This distinction is helpfully explained by Stuart-Smith LJ in *Holmes v Poeton Holdings Ltd* [2023] EWCA Civ 1377 at 31:

JUDGMENT

'It is a characteristic of divisible diseases that, once initiated, their severity will be influenced by the total amount of the agent that has caused the disease. By contrast, once an indivisible disease is contracted, its severity will not be influenced by the total amount of the agent that caused it. The classic distinction in asbestos-related diseases is between asbestosis and mesothelioma. Mesothelioma is an indivisible disease because, although the risk of developing a mesothelioma increases in proportion to the quantity of asbestos dust and fibres inhaled, the condition once caused is not aggravated by further exposure and the severity of the condition, if it occurs, is not thought to be affected by variations in the victim's overall exposure. Asbestosis is a divisible disease because all of the victim's exposure to asbestos will contribute to the severity of his eventual disease.'

The categorisation of an injury as indivisible or divisible is therefore significant because where the tortfeasor has made a material contribution to a claimant's injury, they may be liable for all the damage suffered even if but for the breach of duty the injury or illness might still have occurred.

A further application of this exception to the but for test can be found in the decision of *Bailey v Ministry of Defence* [2008] EWCA Civ 883, where the Court of Appeal considers cumulative causes as indivisible harm where the defendant's negligence materially contributed to the injury. The defendant effectively was held to have caused the brain damage that the claimant suffered.

CASE EXAMPLE

Bailey v Ministry of Defence [2008] EWCA Civ 833

The claimant underwent an operation for acute pancreatitis (non-negligent cause) following which she received sub-standard post-operative care (negligent cause) leaving her in a very weakened state. Whilst still in hospital, the claimant was unable to clear her throat and aspirated her vomit leading to a cardiac arrest that caused her to suffer brain damage. The question for the Court of Appeal was whether the negligence had 'caused or materially contributed to' the injury. There were effectively two cumulative causes for the claimant's weakened state which prevented her from being able to clear her throat: one was pancreatitis and the other was the failure by the defendant to provide proper care leaving her in a weakened state.

It was held that if the evidence demonstrates on a balance of probabilities that the injury would have occurred because of the non-negligent cause, the claimant will have failed to establish that the negligent cause contributed to causing brain damage. If the evidence demonstrates that 'but for' the contribution of the negligent cause the injury would probably not have occurred, the claimant will have discharged the burden. In a case where medical science cannot establish the probability that 'but for' an act of negligence the injury would not have happened but can establish that the contribution of the negligent cause was more than negligible, the 'but for' test is modified, and the claimant will succeed.

So, the material contribution principle applies to cases of indivisible injury and that, where the principle applies, the claimant does not have to show that the injury would not have happened but for the tortious exposure for which the defendant is responsible. This position was reiterated in *Holmes* discussed below.

In another similar case, *Williams v Bermuda Hospitals Board* [2016] UKPC 4, the claimant was suffering from acute appendicitis when he arrived at the defendant's hospital where there was a negligent delay in treating him during which time, his appendix ruptured leading to sepsis and harm to his heart and lungs. It was held that on the balance of probabilities the delay materially contributed to the development of sepsis and resulting harm.

There is some argument that this approach to establishing causation is generous to claimants and that *Bailey* in particular, could have been argued on the basis of the traditional but for test and considered as an instance of taking your victim as you find them also known as the eggshell skull rule which is discussed further below. See further Stapleton, *Unnecessary Causes,* LQR 2013, 39–65; and Stapleton and Steel, *Causes and Contributions* LQR 2016, 132, 363–369; Steel, *Material Contribution to Damage*, again LQR 2022 138, 540–545 at 543); and S.H. Bailey, *Material Contribution after* Williams v The Bermuda Hospitals Board (2018) 38 L.S. 411.

The Court of Appeal had a recent opportunity to consider the application of the material contribution to injury principle.

CASE EXAMPLE

Holmes v Poeton Holdings Ltd [2023] EWCA Civ 1377

The claimant was diagnosed with suffering from Parkinson's disease. In the course of his employment with the defendant, the claimant was exposed to a solvent used for metal degreasing which was capable of causing Parkinson's disease. Parkinson's disease is considered to be an indivisible injury i.e. it can result from a single cause or exposure or cumulative causes or exposure. The defendant argued that the traditional but for test should apply to indivisible injuries rather than the material contribution to injury test. The Court of Appeal held that the material contribution to injury test can apply to indivisible injuries but on these facts, the claimant had failed to demonstrate that the exposure to the solvent had materially contributed to him developing Parkinson's disease. On the facts, the claimant could only establish that such exposure to the solvent was *one* risk factor in developing the disease and was unable to demonstrate that such exposure materially contributed to him developing Parkinson's disease.

The Court of Appeal considered the principle further in the following tragic case:

CASE EXAMPLE

Zgonec-Rozej & Ors V Dr Pereira [2025] EWCA CIV 171

John Jones QC (Mr Jones) took his own life following a period of suffering from mental illness. A claim was brought by his dependents under the Fatal Accidents Act 1976 and the Law Reform (Miscellaneous Provisions) Act 1934. It was argued that there were a number of failings which translated into breaches of duty in the care provided by the Mr Jones' psychiatrist. Those breaches of duty did not cause or contribute to the death of Mr Jones but it was argued these failings collectively contributed to the death of Mr Jones as per *Bailey* and *Williams*, and so the correct test to be applied here was not the 'but for test' but rather the material contribution to injury test. The Court of Appeal confirmed that but for principle is the correct test to be applied and that the material contribution test is an exception which should be applied in very narrow confines.

This recent case is a reminder that where the but for test can be applied to determine causation, it is not possible to defer to this exceptional rule. This rule should only be applied as per the parameters set out in *Bailey*, namely that if the evidence demonstrates on a balance of probabilities that the injury would have occurred as a result of the non-tortious cause or causes in any event, the claimant will have failed to establish that the tortious cause contributed. It is only where medical science cannot establish the probability that but for an act of negligence the injury would not have happened but can establish that the contribution of the negligent cause was more than negligible, the but for test is modified, and the material contribution to injury test may be applied.

4.3.3 Failure to warn

A further instance where the courts have departed from the but for test is where there is a failure to warn a claimant about the risks involved in a planned procedure.

CASE EXAMPLE

Chester v Afshar [2004] UKHL 41

Here as we have already seen in the previous chapter on breach of duty, the Court of Appeal held that the surgeon had fallen below the appropriate standard by failing to give full information on the risks of neurological damage from an operation. The Court accepted that there was evidence to show that the claimant would not have undergone the operation but for the failure to advise of the risks, even though she admitted that she may have been prepared to have the operation at a later stage. It was a simple logic for the Court to accept that the injuries arose directly from the operation, which, even though not carried out negligently, would not have taken place but for the omission to warn of the risks. The House of Lords acknowledged that the problem facing the claimant was that she had admitted that she would have had the operation at some point in the future but not at that time so that it is hard to say that the negligent omission to reveal the full extent of the risks by the doctor could be said to be the direct cause of the injury suffered. The claimant could not prove that but for the failure to inform, her disability would not have arisen.

Their Lordships appear to be inconsistent in their reasoning. Lord Steyn stated at 19:

JUDGMENT

'it is a distinctive feature of the present case that but for the surgeon's negligent failure to warn the claimant of the small risk of serious injury the actual injury would not have occurred when it did and the chance of it occurring on a subsequent occasion was very small. It could therefore be said that the breach by the surgeon resulted in the very injury about which the claimant was entitled to be warned.'

Lord Hoffmann dissenting, on the other hand stated at 31:

JUDGMENT

'this argument is about as logical as saying that if one had been told, on entering a casino, that the odds on number 7 coming up at roulette were only 1 in 37, one would have gone away and come back next week or gone to a different casino. The question is whether one would have taken the opportunity to avoid or reduce the risk, not whether one would have changed the scenario in some irrelevant detail.'

The House Lords was split 3:2 and for the majority, there was a need to consider policy and corrective justice to vindicate the patient's right to know.

Given the failure to warn the claimant, she was unable to give informed consent to the surgery, and her autonomy and dignity need to be vindicated by a departure from the traditional but for test to achieve a just result in this case.

It is crucial that in *Chester*, the claimant said that she if she had been warned of the risk that she would have taken time to reflect and consider whether to have that operation, and to consider whether to defer having the operation even though the evidence was that the risk could have been precisely the same if she had it at another time or by another surgeon.

CASE EXAMPLE

Duce v Worcestershire Acute Hospitals NHS Trust [2018] EWCA Civ 1307

The claimant underwent major surgery (a total hysterectomy and bilateral salpingo-oophorectomy) which left her with nerve damage and serious and permanent pain. The claimant argued that she had not been warned of these risks and had she been warned of these risks she would have considered whether to have the surgery. However, based on her previous discussions with doctors and insistence on having the surgery, she was unable to establish that she would not have gone ahead with the surgery had she been warned.

The exception to the but for test as developed in *Chester* is therefore a very limited exception. In *Duce* it was confirmed that *Chester* should not be understood as setting out a free-standing test, but rather the circumstances which justify the normal approach to the but for test being modified given the unusual circumstances of the case. This means that claimants must establish that but for the defendant's failure to warn, they would not have gone ahead with the surgery.

ACTIVITY

Self-assessment questions

1. What is the difference between causation in fact and causation in law?
2. How does the but for test work?
3. In what ways is causation a problem to a claimant trying to prove medical negligence?
4. What exactly is the effect of the judgment in ***Hotson v East Berkshire Area Health Authority***?
5. What is the difference in the judgments in ***McGhee*** and in ***Wilsher***?
6. What effect has the case of ***Fairchild v Glenhaven Funeral Services*** had on proving causation in fact?
7. How do courts react when there are multiple causes for the damage suffered?
8. How do the courts react when the claimant has a pre-existing condition?
9. What is the justification for the decision in ***Performance Cars v Abraham***?
10. Why exactly are ***Baker v Willoughby*** and ***Jobling v Associated Dairies*** decided differently?
11. Do these two judgments represent fair results both to claimants and defendants?

KEY FACTS

Causation in fact	Case
A defendant may be liable in negligence if but for his act or omission the damage would not have occurred.	*Barnett v Chelsea & Kensington Hospital Management Committee* [1969]
Multiple causes	**Case**
It may be difficult at times to prove causation and courts will not impose liability where the cause is uncertain.	*Wilsher v Essex AHA* [1986]
Courts are very reluctant to base liability on loss of a chance.	*Hotson v East Berks AHA* [1987]
Where there are multiple causes the court may feel that the defendant's act has materially increased the risk.	*McGhee v National Coal Board* [1973]
But where a number of defendants all contribute to the risk of harm no distinction should be drawn between creating a material risk of causing the disease and materially increasing the risk of the disease in determining liability.	*Fairchild v Glenhaven Funeral Services and others* [2001]

4.3.4 Multiple consecutive causes

Where causes leading to the loss or damage suffered are consecutive, or come one after the other, then ordinarily the liability will remain with the first event unless subsequent events have added to the damage. The but for test will be applied to the original defendant.

CASE EXAMPLE

Performance Cars Ltd v Abraham [1962] 1 QB 33

The defendant negligently drove his vehicle so that it collided with a Rolls-Royce car. When the Rolls-Royce was also later negligently struck by another car the court held that this did not relieve the original defendant of liability for a respray that had in any case been made necessary by the first collision.

In this way where a pre-existing condition of the claimant has contributed to the eventual damage it has been held that this may affect the extent of the liability of the defendant.

CASE EXAMPLE

Cutler v Vauxhall Motors [1971] 1 QB 418

The claimant suffered a grazed ankle following his employer's negligence. The claimant already suffered a varicose condition and when an ulcer formed on the area of the graze he required an operation. While the defendant was held liable for the negligence the court identified that the liability applied only in respect of the graze, not the operation.

However, a court when it is trying to determine where liability lies in the case of consecutive causes has inevitably at times been influenced by the desire to avoid in any way under-compensating the victim.

CASE EXAMPLE

Baker v Willoughby [1970] AC 467

The claimant was knocked down by a car and suffered a permanent stiff leg as a result. He was then forced to take work on a reduced income. At a later time he was shot in the injured leg during an armed robbery and this resulted in the leg having to be amputated. The House of Lords rejected the driver's claim that he was then only liable for damages up to the point of the amputation. The court identified that the loss of earnings was a permanent state of affairs and had resulted from the original injury. The armed robbery and amputation of the leg had not altered this fact even though the eventual damage was different and worse.

Lord Reid explained why in his judgment at 492:

JUDGMENT

'A man is not compensated for the physical injury; he is compensated for the loss which he suffers as a result of that injury. His loss is not in having a stiff leg; it is in his inability to lead a full life, his inability to enjoy those amenities which depend on freedom of movement and his inability to earn as much as he used to earn or could have earned if there had been no accident. In this case the second injury did not diminish any of these. So why should it be regarded as having obliterated or superseded them?'

Nevertheless, the picture is even less straightforward because the courts have also at times been keen to ensure that the victim is not over-compensated at the expense of the defendant. Again the principle is that the defendant should only be liable for the extent of the damage actually caused by him.

CASE EXAMPLE

Jobling v Associated Dairies [1982] AC 794

In 1973, and as a result of his employer's negligence, the claimant slipped on the floor of a refrigerator in his employer's butcher's shop and injured his back losing 50 per cent of his earning capacity as a result. Then in 1976 he later developed spondylotic myelopathy, a crippling back disorder which was in fact unrelated to the fall. The court held that the defendant employer was liable for damages only up to the condition developing in 1976, since the condition, and therefore any further loss of earnings, would have occurred anyway despite the original negligence. The court, while not overruling *Baker v Willoughby*, was nevertheless very critical of the case.

The two cases taken together demonstrate the important relationship between causation where there are multiple causes and the principles on which damages should be awarded.

- Where a claimant suffers damage from two separate consecutive causes the second tortfeasor should only be liable for any additional damage caused over that suffered as a result of the first tort.
- Where a claimant suffers from a condition that is unconnected with a tort that has also caused him to suffer injury or damage of a similar type then the damages imposed on the tortfeasor must be reduced to take into account the effect of the condition.

Interestingly the points that can be taken from the two cases are not necessarily mutually exclusive.

CASE EXAMPLE

Murrell v Healey [2001] 4 All ER 345

The claimant had been injured in two car accidents six months apart, both caused by the negligence of separate defendants. He was paid a settlement in respect of the first claim during which he alleged that it was possible he would be unable to work again. In the second claim, and prior to the actual settlement for the first, he claimed that he did in fact expect to return to work in two months but that the second incident had damaged his knees and hips and that would prevent him from returning to work. This fact was disputed by other evidence in the case of either claim. The trial judge in the second claim held that damages should be reduced by the amount that the settlement from the first covered the same damage. He also held that no post-trial loss of earnings should be allowed since the injuries to the knees and hips were not the cause of the second accident. The Court of Appeal held that the judge should have considered any additional damage caused by the second accident. In this way, if the claimant could have done light work after the first accident but that this was prevented by the second then damages should have been based on that. As the claimant had in effect removed this possibility by his evidence in the first claim, no further damages were awarded.

The fact that the courts are prepared to consider the impact that future foreseeable tortious acts may have on termination of the claimant's employment is yet another source of complication to establishing cause.

CASE EXAMPLE

Heil v Rankin [2000] 2 WLR 1173

Here a police officer who suffered post-traumatic stress disorder following a car crash was discharged from the police force. The court held that it was a foreseeable consequence of such employment that he would at some point suffer another event that might cause his retirement from the force and that they were entitled to take this into account when assessing damages.

4.4 *Novus actus interveniens*

novus actus interveniens

Means 'a new act intervenes' – refers to situations where the defendant is excused liability because another intervening act has broken the chain of causation

4.4.1 Breaking the chain of causation

Even though the defendant can be identified as negligent and the but for test satisfied in some senses, the chain of causation may be broken by a subsequent, intervening act. If the court accepts that this intervening act is the true cause of the damage suffered then the defendant may not be liable despite his breach of duty.

Such a plea by the defendant is known as ***novus actus interveniens***. Translated, it means 'a new act intervenes', and it is an effective defence. If, however, the intervening act is not accepted by the court as being the true cause of the damage then the chain is unbroken and the defendant remains liable for his breach.

CASE EXAMPLE

Kirkham v Chief Constable of Greater Manchester [1990] 3 All ER 882

Police who had transferred a prisoner to Risley remand centre had failed to inform the authorities there that the prisoner was a known suicide risk. When the prisoner did in fact commit suicide the police were held liable for their failure to warn the prison authorities. Their plea of *novus actus interveniens* by the prisoner failed, since he was suffering from clinical depression, not in full control and therefore the suicide was not as such a voluntary act.

The effects of an intervening act can easily be illustrated in diagram form (see Figure 4.1).

The area is full of difficulties and the possibility of the plea succeeding is entirely dependent on the facts of the individual case. The case law seems, however, to fall into three easily definable categories:

- where the intervening act is caused by the claimant himself;
- where the intervening act is an act of nature;
- where the intervening act is the cause of a third party in which case a new defendant may in effect be introduced into the case.

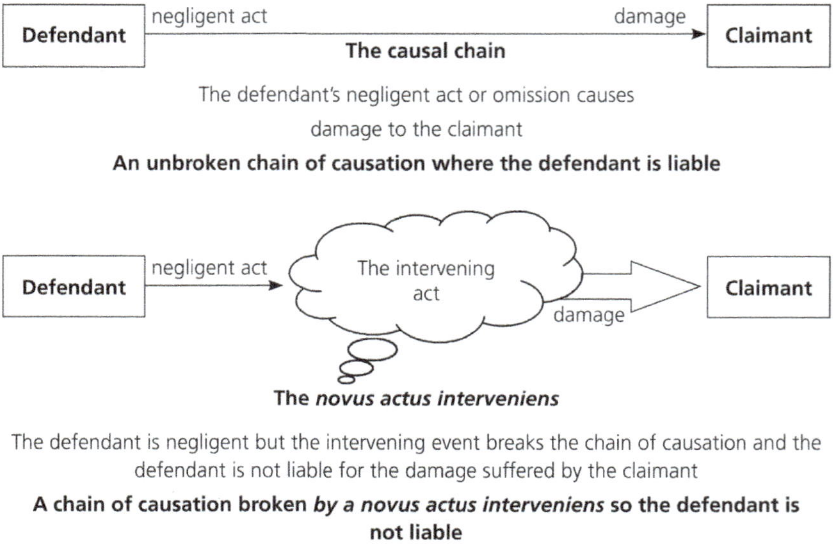

Figure 4.1 The effect of a break in the chain of causation.

4.4.2 An intervening act of the claimant

This is very closely connected with contributory negligence. Unlike contributory negligence, however, where the defendant is liable but damages are reduced by the extent to which the claimant is responsible for the harm he suffers, the plea here is that the claimant is actually responsible for his own damage. Therefore the chain of causation is broken and the defendant has no liability at all.

CASE EXAMPLE

McKew v Holland & Hannen & Cubitts (Scotland) Ltd [1969] 3 All ER 1621

The claimant suffered an injury to his leg leaving it seriously weakened as a resul of the defendants' negligence. When he later tried to climb a steep flight of step with no handrail without asking for help he fell and suffered further serious injuries. The court held that the defendants were not liable for this fall. The claimant act was a *novus actus interveniens*.

Lord Reid identified at 1623:

JUDGMENT

'A defender is not liable for a consequence of a kind which is not foreseeable. B it does not follow that he is liable for every consequence that a reasonable m could foresee.'

However, if the defendant's original breach is still the operating cause of the later damage and the claimant was not acting unreasonably, then the plea that the chain of causation is broken will fail.

CASE EXAMPLE

Wieland v Cyril Lord Carpets Ltd [1969] 3 All ER 1006

Mrs Wieland suffered an injury following the defendant's negligence causing her to have to wear a surgical collar. She wore bifocals and wearing the collar restricted her head movement and meant her use of her spectacles was also seriously impaired. When she then fell down a flight of stairs and sustained further injuries the defendants were liable for those injuries. The court held that there was no break in the chain of causation. The risk to Mrs Wieland in the circumstances was said to be foreseeable. The obvious difference with the last case was that the claimant did nothing unreasonable.

So providing the claimant's actions are reasonable there will not necessarily be a break in the chain of causation.

CASE EXAMPLE

Lord v Pacific Steam Navigation Co. Ltd (The Oropesa) [1943] 1 All ER 211

Here through the negligence of those sailing a ship, *The Oropesa*, another ship was damaged in a collision between the two. The captain of the other ship together with some crew members then put to sea in a lifeboat in order to consult with the captain of *The Oropesa* as to what to do to save their own ship. Some of the sailors drowned. The Court of Appeal held that the decision to take out the lifeboat was a perfectly reasonable one to make in the circumstances and so there was no break in the chain of causation.

It will not, however, be a *novus actus interveniens* by the claimant himself if the alleged intervening act is one that the defendant was under a duty to prevent.

CASE EXAMPLE

Reeves v Commissioner of the Metropolitan Police [1999] 3 WLR 363

Here police were holding a prisoner who was a known suicide risk. The prisoner did in fact commit suicide. While the police accepted that they owed the claimant a duty of care, they nevertheless denied liability, arguing a *novus actus interveniens* by the claimant himself. The court rejected the argument, as the suicide was the specific act that the police should have been seeking to prevent.

Article 2 of the European Convention on Human Rights (the right to life) might also be relevant in such circumstances since authorities responsible for the care of a known suicide risk owe a clear duty of care to do everything reasonable to avoid that suicide. Where they fail to take adequate steps to prevent the suicide then the authority in question is likely to be in breach of Article 2 as well as liable for negligence.

CASE EXAMPLE

Savage v South Essex Partnership NHS Foundation Trust [2008] UKHL 74

A patient who was detained under mental health legislation in a psychiatric ward and was a known suicide risk absconded and did commit suicide. It was accepted that there was a real and immediate risk of circumstances and that inadequate precautions had been taken to prevent the patient from absconding. As a result it was held not only that the Trust was in breach of its duty of care but also was in breach of Article 2.

4.4.3 An intervening act of nature

A plea that an act of nature has broken the chain of causation will rarely succeed. The reason for this is that the claimant in this instance is then left without any means of gaining a remedy for the wrong suffered.

However, the defendant may well be relieved of liability in those situations where he can show that the act of nature that he argues is breaking the chain of causation is unforeseeable and independent of his own negligence.

CASE EXAMPLE

Carslogie Steamship Co v Royal Norwegian Government [1952] AC 292

The claimant's ship was damaged following a collision with a vessel of the defendant's navy and through the defendant's fault. After a delay for repairs the ship then embarked on a voyage it would not otherwise have taken. On that voyage the ship suffered further damage during a heavy storm. The argument that the defendant should be liable for both the original damage and the damage caused by the storm failed. The House of Lords accepted that the storm was a genuine break in the chain of causation and the defendant could not be held liable for the full extent of the damage. The storm damage was not a consequence of the collision but was a quite separate occurrence that might have happened on any voyage.

4.4.4 An intervening act of a third party

In order to succeed with a plea of *novus actus interveniens* in these circumstances the defendant must show that the act of the third party was also negligent and was of such magnitude that it did in fact break the chain of causation. Furthermore, the defendant must not be under any duty to guard against the act of the third party.

CASE EXAMPLE

Knightley v Johns **[1982] 1 All ER 851**

The defendant, through his negligent driving, crashed and blocked a tunnel. The police officer in charge at the scene then negligently sent a police officer against the flow of traffic to block off the tunnel at the other end. There was a second accident and the police officer was injured as a result. The court held that the defendant was not liable for the injuries sustained by this policeman. They were the fault of the other police officer and his action amounted to a *novus actus interveniens*.

Stephenson LJ identified at 860:

JUDGMENT

'the original tortfeasor, whose negligence created the danger which invites rescuers, will be responsible for injury and damage which are the natural and probable results of the wrongful act'.

But in accepting that the chain of causation had been broken Stephenson LJ also commented at 865:

JUDGMENT

'Negligent conduct is more likely to break the chain of causation than conduct which is not.'

Furthermore, for the act of the third party to break the chain of causation, the consequences of the third party's act must be foreseeable.

CASE EXAMPLE

Lamb v Camden London Borough Council **[1981] QB 625**

Here the defendant council negligently broke a water main as a result of which the claimants' house suffered water damage and the claimants had to move out. While the claimants were out of the house squatters moved in and caused much more damage. The council was held not liable for the further damage. The actions of the squatters were a *novus actus interveniens*. It was not foreseeable.

As already mentioned above, for the chain of causation to be broken, the defendant must not have any duty to guard against the third party's act.

CASE EXAMPLE

Ward v Cannock Chase District Council [1986] 3 All ER 537

Here the defendant council negligently allowed a house to fall into general disrepair. The house adjoined the claimants' house. When the claimants were forced to move out of their house while the repairs to the adjoining house were carried out vandals and thieves who broke in damaged it. The council had failed to make proper repairs and act quickly enough in repairing the house next door. The court held that this meant that acts of vandalism were almost inevitable. There was no *novus actus interveniens* and the council was held liable.

Nevertheless, it is also possible that in such circumstances both the defendant and the third party have in fact contributed to the damage caused. In such circumstances both parties will be held individually liable accordingly.

CASE EXAMPLE

Rouse v Squires [1973] QB 889

The defendant drove negligently, causing his lorry to jackknife on a motorway, as a result of which an accident occurred in which many vehicles were involved, including the claimant. Another driver because he was driving much too fast then negligently collided with some of the stationary vehicles from the first incident, killing the claimant. Despite the obvious responsibility of the later driver, the chain of causation was held not to be broken. The damage in the second incident was held to be a foreseeable consequence of the first and the first driver was held to be 25 per cent responsible for the death of the claimant. The remaining liability was with the driver of the vehicle involved in the second collision. The court identified that the negligence of the lorry driver was an operative cause of the claimant's death and that the chain of causation could not be broken by the effect of a later driver driving too fast or not keeping a proper lookout for hazards ahead. It did accept that someone deliberately or recklessly driving into the crashed vehicles could break the causal chain.

So the effects of a successful plea of *novus actus interveniens* in simple terms would appear to be as follows:

- Where it is the claimant's own act that intervenes – the defendant is relieved of liability and the claimant has no possible remedy for the damage suffered.
- Where there is an intervening act of nature – it is likely that the claimant will have no defendant to sue and no remedy.
- Where a third party is responsible for the intervening act – the claimant will have no action against the original defendant – whether or not the claimant still has a possible action and a remedy will depend on whether the third party is also negligent.

ACTIVITY

Self-assessment questions

1 How do the courts react when the claimant has a pre-existing condition?
2 What is the justification for the decision in ***Performance Cars v Abraham***?
3 Why exactly are ***Baker v Willoughby*** and ***Jobling v Associated Dairies*** decided differently?
4 Do these two judgments represent fair results both to claimants and defendants?
5 In what ways does the case of ***Heil v Rankin*** cause complications?
6 What exactly does the phrase ***novus actus interveniens*** mean?
7 What are the necessary requirements for a successful claim of ***novus actus interveniens*** by a defendant?
8 What is the difference between a plea of ***novus actus interveniens*** and one of contributory negligence?
9 What are the three types of ***novus actus***?
10 Which is the least likely to be successful?
11 Which is the most likely to still give the claimant a remedy?
12 What happens to the claimant's claim when the defence proves successful?

KEY FACTS

	Novus actus interveniens	**Case**
Where there are multiple consecutive causes the liability remains with the first defendant unless the later cause increased the damage.	*Performance Cars v Abraham* [1962]	
Though they are careful not to undercompensate or to overcompensate.	*Baker v Willoughby* [1970]; *Jobling v Associated Dairies* [1982]	
	A defendant will not be liable where there is a *novus actus interveniens* (a new act intervening).	
	This is because the 'chain of causation' is broken by the intervening act.	
	An intervening act could be of three types: • an intervening act of the claimant • an intervening act of nature • an intervening act of a third party.	*McKew v Holland & Hannen & Cubitts* [1969] *Carslogie Steamship Co v Royal Norwegian Government* [1952] *Knightley v Johns* [1982]

(Continued)

(Continued)

	But there will be no break in the chain of causation where the intervening event is reasonable and foreseeable.	*Lord v Pacific Steam Navigation Co Ltd (The Oropesa)* [1943]
	Or where the defendant was under a duty to prevent the act that is alleged to break the chain of causation.	*Reeves v Commissioner of the Metropolitan Police* [1999]

ACTIVITY

Quick quiz

In the following situations consider which type of ***novus actus interveniens*** is involved and whether or not the defendant in the case is likely to be held liable.

1 During a very severe storm Atmar is driving well over the speed limit, loses control of his car and crashes into Jacquie's car causing some damage to the bumper and left side wing. The storm causes a large tree to uproot. This then falls on to Jacquie's car destroying it completely.
2 During a very severe storm Jacquie is driving well over the speed limit, loses control of her car and crashes into Sukhy's car causing the radiator to burst and leak water. Sukhy then drives home, a distance of 30 miles. The radiator leaks on the way and boils dry causing the engine to seize. The engine is completely destroyed as a result.
3 During a very severe storm Sukhy is driving well over the speed limit, loses control of his car and crashes into Chris's car which stalls and will not start. In fact only minimal damage was done to the front bumper of Chris's car. Chris pushes his car safely into the side of the road, calls the AA and waits for them to attend to restart his car. Norman, who is driving well above the speed limit, loses control of his car, skids violently across the road and crashes into Chris's car. Chris's car is a write off and Chris is killed in the collision.

4.5 Causation in law and testing remoteness of damage

4.5.1 The tests of remoteness

The final element of proof in negligence is whether there is causation in law, otherwise known as remoteness of damage. Even though a causal link can be proved factually according to the but for test the claimant may still be prevented from winning the case if the damage suffered is too remote a consequence of the defendant's breach of duty.

The test is a matter of law rather than fact and like other aspects of negligence is much influenced by policy considerations. The principal justification for the rule is that the defendant should not be overburdened by compensating for damage linked to the breach that is of a kind that is unlikely or unforeseeable.

The original test of remoteness, however, was that the claimant could recover in respect of a loss that was a direct consequence of the defendant's breach regardless of how foreseeable this loss was.

CASE EXAMPLE

Re Polemis and Furness, Withy & Co [1921] 3 KB 560

Charterers of a ship filled the hold with containers of benzene that then leaked during the voyage, filling the hold with vapour. In port the ship was being unloaded when a stevedore negligently dropped a plank into the hold. A spark then ignited the vapours and the ship was destroyed. The arbitrator held that this was too unlikely a consequence of dropping the plank, though some damage was of course foreseeable. The Court of Appeal held that the charterers, as employers of the stevedores, were liable.

Scrutton LJ stated at 577:

JUDGMENT

'if the act would or might probably cause damage, the fact that the damage it in fact causes is not the exact kind of damage one would expect is immaterial, so long as the damage is in fact directly traceable to the negligent act'.

The test was not without its difficulties and it was criticised for its failure to distinguish between degrees of negligence.

In *Overseas Tankship (UK) Ltd v Morts Dock & Engineering Co (The Wagon Mound (No 1))* [1961] AC 388 Viscount Simmonds explained the deficiencies in the traditional 'direct consequence' rule, at 389:

JUDGMENT

'It does not seem consonant with current ideas of justice or morality, that for an act of negligence, however slight or venial, which results in some trivial foreseeable damage, the actor should be liable for all the consequences, however unforeseeable and however grave, so long as they can be said to be direct.'

As a result the test was later changed to one of liability for damage only that was a reasonably foreseeable consequence of the breach.

CASE EXAMPLE

Overseas Tankship (UK) Ltd v Morts Dock & Engineering Co (The Wagon Mound (No 1)) [1961] AC 388

Due to the defendant's negligence, bunkering oil was leaked into Sydney harbour from a tanker. The oil floated on the water to the claimant's wharf, mixing with various flotsam and jetsam, including patches of cotton wadding. Welding was taking place in the wharf and the claimant's manager enquired whether there was a risk of the oil igniting. This was considered unlikely since the oil had an extremely high flash point. Welding then continued and sparks did in fact ignite the oil-soaked wadding and then set fire to ships being repaired in the wharf. The oil also caused fouling to the wharf. The trial judge held that since some damage, the fouling, was foreseeable, the defendants were liable also for the fire damage which was a direct consequence of their breach of duty in allowing the spillage. The Privy Council reversed this decision, holding that the defendant could not be liable for the fire damage since the correct test for remoteness was reasonable foreseeability and, because of the improbability of the oil igniting, the fire damage was unforeseeable.

Viscount Simonds explained the principle and the reason for the change to the former test in *Re Polemis and Furness, Withy & Co* [1921] 3 KB 560, at 423:

JUDGMENT

'if it is asked why a man should be responsible for the natural or necessary or probable consequences of his act the answer is that it is not because they are natural or necessary or probable, but because, since they have this quality, it is judged by the standard of the reasonable man that he ought to have foreseen them'.

4.5.2 Applying the reasonable foreseeability test

Foreseeability of the kind of damage

The critical element of the test in *The Wagon Mound* is foreseeability of the general rather than the specific type of damage. It is not therefore necessary for the full extent of the damage to be foreseen in order for there to be liability.

CASE EXAMPLE

Bradford v Robinson Rentals [1967] 1 All ER 267

The claimant suffered frostbite when sent on a long journey from Exeter to Bedford by his employers in severe winter weather, being sent in a van without a working heater. The defendants argued that in England this type of damage was too remote and unforeseeable for them to be held liable. The court, however, disagreed. The court identified that it was certainly foreseeable that some cold-related illness was a possibility in the circumstances. As a result the court felt that it was immaterial that the actual damage was frostbite, and the defendant was held liable.

It is not therefore necessary for the defendant to have contemplated or to have foreseen the precise consequences of the negligent act or omission, provided that he is aware of the possibility of damage resulting.

CASE EXAMPLE

Margereson v J W Roberts Ltd [1996] PIQR P358

The court in this case considered that the owner of an asbestos works should have been aware of the dangers of people inhaling the asbestos dust, even in 1933. In consequence the court was prepared to impose liability on the defendant in respect of mesothelioma contracted by children who played in dust from the factory that collected in the streets around the entrance to the factory and the surrounding area.

If damage is foreseeable then neither is it necessary, when the defendant is negligent, for the precise consequences of the act or omission to be foreseen when some damage is a foreseeable consequence.

CASE EXAMPLE

Hughes v The Lord Advocate [1963] AC 837

Post Office employees working in a hole in the road negligently left a manhole uncovered inside a tent and then left the tent unattended. As a safety precaution the workmen left four lit paraffin lamps at the corners of the tent at night. A boy entered the tent with one of the lamps and when it fell into the hole there was an explosion, the boy fell in also and was burnt. This was an unlikely chain of events but the court nevertheless held the defendants liable since some fire-related damage was a foreseeable consequence of leaving the scene unattended.

The test of reasonable foreseeability and claims for personal injury

In general, the cases above seem to indicate that the courts will take a fairly broad view of what is reasonably foreseeable in the event that the damage suffered is personal injury.

CASE EXAMPLE

Jolley v London Borough of Sutton [2000] 3 All ER 409, HL

A council failed to move an abandoned boat for two years. It was well known that children played in the boat and it was a clear danger. A boy of 14 was then hurt when he and a friend jacked up the boat in order to try to repair it. The Court of Appeal felt that the activities engaged in by the boys and therefore the specific type of damage caused were not at all foreseeable. The House of Lords, however, disagreed with this reasoning. The House acknowledged that the boat was dangerous, and as a result that it was quite foreseeable that children coming into contact with the boat might suffer some kind of harm. The precise manner in which the injuries occurred was not important. It was sufficient that some harm was foreseeable for the defendant council to be liable for its negligence.

Nevertheless, there have been occasions on which courts have taken a much narrower view of what is foreseeable. As a result the decisions appear on the surface to work unfairly on the claimant.

CASE EXAMPLE

Tremain v Pike [1969] 3 All ER 1303

The claimant was a herdsman who contracted Weil's disease during the course of his work. This is a rare disease and is only contracted through contact with rats' urine. The claimant argued that this in fact happened when he worked with hay and washed with water that was contaminated with rats' urine. The court did accept that the defendant had negligently allowed the rat population on his farm to grow too large and that there was some inevitable risk of damage from rats. Nevertheless, the court held that the defendant was not liable since the court considered that the disease was so rare in humans that it was an unforeseeable consequence of the negligence.

The test of reasonable foreseeability and claims for property damage

With few exceptions the courts in general appear to adopt a much narrower approach to what might be considered foreseeable when the damage in question is to property rather than personal injury.

CASE EXAMPLE

Overseas Tankship (UK) Ltd v Morts Dock & Engineering Co (The Wagon Mound (No 1)) [1961] AC 388

The trial judge acknowledged that some damage was foreseeable in the circumstances. The judge, however, felt that the type of damage that was foreseeable would be fouling of the harbour and ships moored in it by the oil. He did not feel that fire damage was foreseeable in the circumstances. But since he believed fouling was foreseeable he held that the fire damage was also a direct consequence of the defendant's negligence. Inevitably the Privy Council could only consider the appeal on this basis.

Even the degree of risk of the type of damage actually caused has been considered narrowly thus avoiding imposing liability.

CASE EXAMPLE

Overseas Tankship (UK) Ltd v Miller Steamship Co Pty (The Wagon Mound (No 2)) [1967] 1 AC 617

The owners of the two ships that were being repaired in the wharf and were damaged in the fire brought this case. The trial judge showed a very narrow approach to foreseeability in relation to an action for property damage. While he accepted, unlike the trial judge in *Wagon Mound (No 1)*, that fire was a foreseeable consequence of the defendant's negligence, he nevertheless felt that it was so remote as to not give rise to any liability. He was reversed by the Privy Council which held that provided the type of damage was foreseeable, then liability must result and the degree of likelihood was irrelevant. The Privy Council was able to reach this result in the appeal because the trial judge had actually accepted fire damage as a remote but foreseeable consequence of the negligence.

Foreseeability of the way damage is caused

On occasions it also appears that the test in *Hughes v Lord Advocate* [1963] AC 837 can be contradicted if the court focuses too closely on the circumstances in which the damage occurs, rather than on the mere fact that some damage is foreseeable.

CASE EXAMPLE

Doughty v Turner Manufacturing Co Ltd [1964] 1 QB 518

Here, due to negligence, a cover over a cauldron of heated sodium cyanide was allowed to slide into the liquid in the tank. The cover was made of asbestos compound. There was a chemical explosion and the claimant who was working on the tank was badly burned. The Court of Appeal accepted that it was previously unknown that there would be such a chemical reaction between the asbestos and the sodium cyanide and the court held that the defendants were not liable as a result. The chemical reaction was unforeseeable and the damage was thus too remote. However, there certainly seems to be merit in the claimant's argument that damage from the liquid if splashed would be foreseeable. In deciding the case the Court of Appeal chose to apply the persuasive precedent of the Privy Council in *The Wagon Mound* rather than its own previous precedent in *Re Polemis*.

The judges will also apply policy reasons in determining whether an outcome is reasonably foreseeable.

CASE EXAMPLE

Corr v IBC Vehicles Ltd [2008] UKHL 13

An employee was badly injured as a result of his employer's negligence. He also developed post-traumatic stress disorder as a result and eventually committed suicide. The Court of Appeal accepted that depression was a foreseeable consequence of the original negligence. On this basis, since suicide is not uncommon in cases of depression, unless any evidence was introduced to the contrary, there was nothing to prevent recovery. The Court commented that to treat the chain of causation as being broken by the suicide would be unjustified and awarded the man's widow damages under the Fatal Accidents Act 1976. The House of Lords subsequently upheld this ruling. The view had already been confirmed in *Rothwell v Chemical and Insulating Co Ltd* [2007] UKHL 39 where the House of Lords rejected a similar claim because the employee could not show that his employer should have foreseen the risk of psychiatric injury and the claim did not fall within the exception identified in *Page v Smith* [1996] AC 155.

In contrast in *Grieves v FT Everard and Sons Ltd* [2006] EWCA Civ 27 the Court of Appeal was not prepared to accept a causal link between asbestos exposure and the development of pleural plaques (which could lead to subsequent asbestos-related diseases) and a depressive illness based on the fear of contracting such an illness.

Foreseeability of the extent of harm

If damage is foreseeable it will not matter that the damage is actually more extensive than might have been foreseeable, provided that the kind of damage itself is foreseeable.

CASE EXAMPLE

Vacwell Engineering Co Ltd v BDH Chemicals Ltd [1971] 1 QB 88

Here the defendants were the suppliers of a chemical product to the claimants. The defendants negligently failed to warn the claimants that the chemical would explode if it came into contact with water. When one of the claimant's scientists did expose the chemical to water there was an alarming explosion, causing very extensive damage. The court held that the defendants were liable even though the resultant damage to property was far more severe than might have been foreseen.

The court will not only be concerned with the likelihood of harm resulting from the defendant's negligence. It will also take account of the risk that the harm will be greater if it involves a claimant with a particular sensitivity. In this way the defendant is said to have to 'take the claimant how he finds him'. This is the so-called thin skull rule.

CRITIQUING THE LAW

It is difficult in some ways to see a real difference between the test based on direct consequences and the test based on reasonable foreseeability. In many instances certainly, damage that is reasonably foreseeable will also be a direct consequence of the defendant's negligent acts or omissions. It is similarly difficult to contemplate situations that are totally unforeseeable and yet are still a direct consequence. Besides this the difference may well be unimportant for a number of reasons.

Do you think that the consequences are fair in the following scenarios:

- The effect of the 'thin skull' rule is that many victims may be compensated for damage that the defendant will probably not have contemplated at all. Do you think that this is fair?

Many areas of quite remote damage are in any case within the scope of insurance and so a claimant may still gain some form of compensation even though this cannot be gained from the potential defendant. Should the defendant be liable for such damage?

ACTIVITY

Self-assessment questions

1 What are judges trying to achieve with the rule on remoteness of damage?
2 When precisely will damage be too remote to be compensated?
3 How does ***The Wagon Mound*** test differ from that in ***Re Polemis***?
4 How exactly is reasonable foreseeability measured, in other words what has to be foreseen?
5 Do the attitudes of the courts generally vary according to the type of damage caused?
6 To what extent are the judgments in ***Doughty v Turner Manufacturing*** and ***Hughes v Lord Advocate*** consistent?
7 What is the effect of a claimant's peculiar sensitivities on the issue of remoteness of damage?
8 Is there any justification for adopting a narrower approach to remoteness in cases involving property damage than in those involving personal injury?

KEY FACTS

Remoteness of damage	Case
At one time a defendant was liable for all damage that was a direct consequence of his negligent act or omission.	*Re Polemis and Furness, Withy & Co* [1921]
Now the modern test is one of liability for reasonably foreseeable damage.	*The Wagon Mound (No 2)* [1967]
Only the general, not the actual type of damage needs to be foreseen.	*Bradford v Robinson Rentals* [1967]
Nor do the precise consequences of the negligent act or omission have to be foreseen.	*Hughes v Lord Advocate* [1963]
The 'thin skull' rule means that the defendant will be liable for the full extent of injuries suffered by a claimant with particular sensitivities.	*Smith v Leech Brain* [1962]
The courts generally, but not always, seem to take a broader view of remoteness in personal injury cases than they do with property damage.	Compare *The Wagon Mound (No 1)* [1961] with *Bradford* [1967] or *Doughty* [1964]

thin skull rule
Also known as the 'eggshell skull rule' – means that the defendant has to take extra care of a claimant who is susceptible to a certain type of harm

4.6 Eggshell skull rule

The court will not only be concerned with the likelihood that harm will occur but the risk that the harm will be great if it does occur. In this sense the defendant must 'take the claimant how he finds him', the so-called **thin skull rule**.

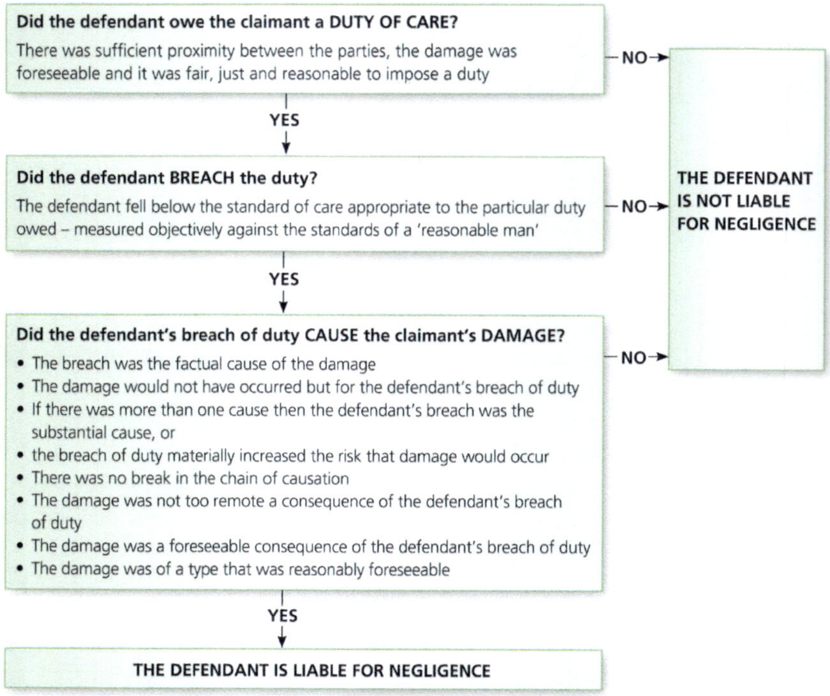

Figure 4.2 The essential elements for proof of negligence with particular emphasis on the cause of damage.

CASE EXAMPLE

Paris v Stepney Borough Council [1951] AC 367

The claimant was a mechanic who was already blind in one eye. He was working under a vehicle and trying to undo a tight nut but had not been supplied with safety goggles by his employer, the defendants, as they were legally required to do. The claimant was then injured in his good eye, causing him total blindness. The court held that the defendants were liable for the full extent of the claimant's blindness, rather than for causing blindness in one eye. The court identified that the claimant's condition meant that the defendants owed him a higher duty of care than would normally be the case and were in effect responsible for and therefore liable for his total blindness.

The 'thin skull' rule operates then so that the defendant will be liable for the full extent of the damage if damage of the type caused is in fact foreseeable.

CASE EXAMPLE

Smith v Leech Brain & Co Ltd [1962] 2 QB 405

Mr Smith worked as a galvaniser which involved dipping items into tanks containing molten metal. He suffered a burnt lip as a result of being splashed by molten metal following his employers' negligence. The burn activated a cancer from which the claimant later died. Mr Smith however, had a pre-disposition to developing cancer in any event Some form of harm from the burn was foreseeable. The court held at paragraph 415 that even though the death from cancer was not immediately foreseeable, harm resulting from the negligence was, and the defendants were held liable as a result.

JUDGMENT

'The test is not whether these employers could reasonably have foreseen that a burn would cause cancer and that he would die. The question is whether these employers could reasonably foresee the type of injury he suffered, namely, the burn. What, in the particular case, is the amount of damage which he suffers as a result of that burn, depends upon the characteristics and constitution of the victim.'

This is to say, the company take their victim as they find him with a premalignant condition and were responsible for Mr Smith's death as but for the burn, he would not have developed cancer and therefore would not have died.

The same principle can apply even where the harm is psychiatric damage and this is particularly important in employment relationships where employers subject employees to unnecessary stress.

CASE EXAMPLE

Walker v Northumberland CC [1995] 1 All ER 737

A senior social worker had already suffered one nervous breakdown and was allowed to return to work by his doctor on the understanding that his work schedule would not be too excessive or stressful. When in fact the employer subjected the claimant to even more stress this resulted in a second nervous breakdown. The court held that the employer was liable. This was because after the first breakdown they were aware of his susceptibility to stress and did nothing to reduce his workload or the pressure associated with it.

The principle can also apply where the expected damage is physical injury but the claimant suffers shock instead and has a particular sensitivity.

SAMPLE ESSAY QUESTION

'The two main aims of tort are to compensate the victims of wrongdoing and to deter wrongdoing.' Discuss whether the rules on causation and remoteness of damage achieve these aims.

Explain the basic rules on causation in fact and remoteness of damage

- The 'but for' test generally applies – but for the defendant's negligence the damage would not have occurred
- Courts will not compensate for loss that is too remote a consequence of the defendant's breach – so will only compensate foreseeable loss

Discuss the problems associated with multiple causes and how the courts have overcome them

- The 'but for' test generally applies – but for the defendant's negligence the damage would not have occurred
- Courts will not compensate for loss that is too remote a consequence of the defendant's breach – so will only compensate foreseeable loss
- With concurrent multiple causes – can be harsh and not deter if 'but for' test is applied where there are many possible causes
- But if there is a single cause but more than one defendant courts may accept that that cause materially increased the risk of harm or was a material contribution to the harm – ensures the claimant is compensated and is a deterrent but may be unfair on defendant
- Problem, too, of overcompensating or undercompensating victim

Discuss the problems associated with loss of a chance

- Defendant not liable on a balance of probabilities
- So defendant goes uncompensated
- And no deterrent to a defendant who has breached his duty

Discuss the problems associated with *novus actus interveniens*

- Three types – act of claimant, of nature, of a third party
- Breaks chain of causation – so usually no compensation and no much deterrence

Explain the problems associated with remoteness of damage

- Legal test based on foreseeable harm
- There has been inconsistent application
- If court tests against precise circumstances and damage then little chance of compensation or deterrent
- But if takes more liberal view then provides compensation and deterrent
- Different approach – direct consequences rule – when 'thin skull' rule applies

SUMMARY

- There are two types of causation: causation in fact and causation in law (remoteness of damage).
- Causation in fact is usually measured by the but for test – damage would not have occurred but for the defendant's breach of duty.
- But different approaches are taken when there are multiple causes: possibly no liability where there is a pre-existing condition – if there are several different concurrent causes then but for test applies – but if defendant materially increases the risk of harm or materially contributes then any defendant may be liable – but sometimes judges prefer to apportion damages.
- A *novus actus interveniens* by the claimant or an act of nature or an act of a third party breaks the chain of causation and the first defendant is not liable.
- Remoteness of damage, causation in law is a legal test – the defendant is only liable for foreseeable damage.
- Judges sometimes take a broad application where there is personal injury so it is the general circumstances and general type of damage rather than precise circumstances and specific damage that must be foreseen.
- Often judges take a narrow application where there is property damage.

Further reading

Hill, T, 'A lost chance for compensation in the tort of negligence by the House of Lords' (1991) *54 MLR* 511.

Lam, CM, 'Revisiting loss of chance in medical negligence: Employing public policy positively as justification' (2020) *36 PN* 105.

Morgan, A, 'Inference, principle and the proof of causation' (2002) *152 NLJ* 1060.

Owen, RF, 'Causation and apportionment' (2000) *152 NLJ* 1116.

Steel, S, 'Justifying exceptions to proof of causation in tort law' (2015) *78 MLR* 729.

5

Negligence: Defences

AIMS AND OBJECTIVES

After reading this chapter you should be able to:

- Understand the essential elements of the general defences
- Identify the criteria for establishing the defences of *volenti non fit injuria* (voluntary assumption of risk), illegality (*ex turpi causa non oritur actio*) and contributory negligence
- Recognise that *volenti* and illegality are complete defences removing liability while contributory negligence is only a partial defence with the effect of reducing damages
- Critically analyse the defences
- Apply the defences to factual situations

5.1 Introduction

This chapter will examine the defences available to a claim in negligence. Defences which are of particular importance to a tort have been highlighted in their relevant chapters and those which are applicable only to a particular tort have likewise been discussed in their respective chapters.

Generally, the defendant is responsible for establishing a defence on the balance of probabilities and the claimant may have to disprove it.

5.2 Defences and the relationship with causation

Causation also needs to be considered when determining whether the claimant has either accepted a risk of harm and voluntarily taken it, or indeed has otherwise contributed to his own damage by taking insufficient care for his own safety. In this way a claimant who takes part in

DOI: 10.4324/9781003202417-5

sporting activities, particularly in the case of a contact sport, may have voluntarily assumed the risk of injury by taking part and being aware of the nature of the sport. Similarly in the case of road traffic accidents there may be contributory negligence, for instance where the claimant has failed to wear a seat belt, or in the case of an accident involving a motorbike where the claimant failed to wear a crash helmet.

If on the other hand the claimant has contributed so much to the damage suffered as to be entirely responsible, then this will probably result in a successful plea of *novus actus interveniens*.

There are two specific defences that are particularly appropriate here: *volenti non fit injuria* (voluntary assumption of a risk) and contributory negligence. The distinction between *volenti* and contributory negligence is clearly important. *Volenti* is a complete defence and so defeats the claim, whereas contributory negligence is a partial defence only reducing the claimant's damages.

However, it is not easy to succeed in a defence of *volenti* since use of contributory negligence and apportionment of responsibility is fairer than denying any redress to a claimant where a defendant has been in breach of a duty of care.

5.3 Voluntary assumption of risk (*volenti non fit injuria*)

volenti non fit injuria

This literally means 'no injury can be done to a willing person' – so is a defence where the claimant understands the risk of harm and willingly accepts it

Volenti non fit injuria is a complete defence, unlike contributory negligence which only reduces damages, and if it is successful then a claimant will recover no damages. The defence succeeds because there is a voluntary assumption of the risk of harm by the claimant and a simple translation would be that no injury is done to one who freely consents to the risk. This defence is discussed in detail in Chapter 14 relating to trespass to the person and this defence is relevant to other torts, for example, in relation to claims under the Animals Act 1971. It is also specifically referred to in the Occupiers' Liability Acts 1957 and 1984.

Distinction must be drawn between:

- an intentional infliction of harm – which is negated by consent, for example where a patient signs a consent form in respect of an operation there is no battery, and
- a negligent infliction of harm – in which for the defendant to avoid liability for his otherwise negligent act the claimant must voluntarily accept the risk of injury.

A person who consents to damage or injury or to the risk that either may occur, cannot later complain and make the defendant liable for what has happened. Consent may be express, for example, where a person signs a consent form for a surgical procedure, or implied, for example, taking part in a contact sport.

The principal issue is whether or not the claimant has in fact consented. To decide this it must be shown that the claimant:

a was aware of the risk; and

b accepted it freely.

It must be remembered of course that before the defence can be applied successfully it must be shown that the defendant did in fact commit a tort.

CASE EXAMPLE

Wooldridge v Sumner [1963] 2 QB 43

The claimant attended a horse show as a professional photographer. A rider who was riding too fast lost control of his horse which then injured the claimant. The Court of Appeal recognised that the rider owed spectators a duty of care. Nevertheless, they considered that he had been guilty of an error of judgment in his riding of the horse but not negligence. He had not breached his duty so *volenti* was not an issue.

Some judges take the view that the defence succeeds because there is an express or implied agreement between the defendant and the claimant. However, certain judges believe that the defence can still succeed where the claimant has come upon a danger that has already been created by the defendant.

Defence of *Volenti*: the defendant will have to show three things:

- knowledge of the precise risk involved;
- exercise of free choice by the claimant; and
- a voluntary acceptance of the risk.

5.3.1 Knowledge of the precise risk

The test of *volenti* is a subjective one, not an objective one. It will not help the defendant to argue that the claimant ought to have been aware of the risk. The defence only applies where the claimant does actually know of the risk and freely accepts it.

Nevertheless, where a defence of *volenti* may fail for just such a reason, the defendant may still be able to successfully claim contributory negligence and at least reduce the amount of damages that are payable.

Claimants must be aware of the broad nature of the risk which they are taking, in other words they must know what they are doing and what the possible outcomes may be. It is not sufficient then merely that the claimant has knowledge of the existence of the risk. The defence is *volenti non fit injuria* and not *scienti non fit injuria*. The claimant must fully understand the precise nature of the actual risk and be prepared to run it. As has been seen, in the context of consent to medical treatment, this does not mean that they need to understand all the detail of the treatment but they must understand why the treatment is advisable, what it involves, what any side effects may be and the intended outcome. Failure to ensure such understanding may amount to negligence on the part of the health practitioner involved. In medical cases consent is usually express.

In the context of sport, the claimant consents to the risk of injury which is inherent in the game played according to the rules. This is an example of implied consent. An action may lie for trespass to the person if injury occurs as a result of something which is against the rules of the game.

What both examples have in common is the knowledge by the claimant of the nature of the risk which is being taken.

CASE EXAMPLE

Stermer v Lawson [1977] 79 DLR (3d) 366

The claimant borrowed the defendant's motorbike but was not shown how to use it so he could not and did not appreciate the risks involved. The defendant's claim of *volenti* failed as a result. The court held that he was unaware of the precise risk and therefore was not personally responsible.

5.3.2 Exercise of free choice by the claimant

Similarly, the risk must be freely taken for the defence to succeed. There will be no defence where the claimant had no choice but to accept the risk.

CASE EXAMPLE

Smith v Baker [1891] AC 325

The claimant drilled rock in a quarry bottom. He was injured when a crane moved rocks over his head and some fell on him. *Volenti* failed in the case because, as the court explained, the worker was given no proper warning of when the crane was in use and so was unaware of the danger. He was aware of the risk of stones falling but there was no voluntary assumption of risk in the circumstances.

Lord Halsbury LC explained why the defence could not apply at 336:

JUDGMENT

'I think that a person who relies on the maxim must shew a consent to the particular thing done . . . in order to defeat a plaintiff's right by the maxim relied on . . . the jury ought to be able to affirm that he consented to the particular thing being done which would involve the risk, and consented to take the risk upon himself.'

If the claimant's behaviour is such that he need not have been in any danger but for his own actions then *volenti* is clearly a possibility.

CASE EXAMPLE

ICI Ltd v Shatwell [1965] AC 656

The claimant and his brother were working in the defendants' quarry. They disregarded the defendants' orders and also statutory regulations by testing detonators without taking appropriate precautions. The claimant was injured in an explosion and maintained that the defendants were vicariously liable on the basis of the claimant's brother, who instructed him not to follow the instructions, having been negligent and in breach of statutory duty. The court held against him. By ignoring his employers and listening to his brother's unauthorised comments he had assumed the risk of injury by exercising his own free choice.

5.3.3 A voluntary acceptance of the risk

For a defendant to successfully raise the defence, the claimant must have had a genuine free choice, freedom of will and no feeling of constraint.

As Scott LJ put it in *Bowater v Rowley Regis Corporation* [1944] KB 476 at 479:

JUDGMENT

'A man cannot be said to be truly willing unless he is in a position to choose freely.'

CASE EXAMPLE

Smith v Baker [1891] AC 325

Here while the employers pleaded *volenti* it could not apply because there had been no warning of the moment of a recurring danger. Although the claimant knew of the risk, there was no evidence that he had voluntarily accepted the risk. Merely continuing to work in the circumstances was not voluntary acceptance of the risk.

This defence can be further examined in the context of various categories of claimants:

- employees
- rescuers
- sporting events
- passengers in vehicles.

5.3.4 Employees

The defence is often important in cases where an employee has been injured during the course of employment. The courts take a realistic view that an employee may be under pressure for all sorts of reasons to keep the job. Saying that there is always a right to leave the employment is certainly true but would be impractical for most people.

The position of many employees was explained in *Smith v Baker* [1891] AC 325 when Lord Herschell, while acknowledging that an employee 'no doubt voluntarily subjects himself to the risks inevitably accompanying the job' said that 'mere continuance in service, with knowledge of the risk' cannot amount to consent to the risk.

Employees may also feel that they put their jobs at risk if they make a complaint. The latter problem has in theory been dealt with by the Employment Rights Act 1996 which gives protection to employees who complain about unsafe practices. Although the Employment Tribunal could order reinstatement should the employee have been dismissed, there is no guarantee that the employer will comply. In times of high unemployment, the protection may appear to be flimsy to say the least.

While it is not denied that the defence can apply in employment situations, it only exceptionally does so. If an employee is not in a predicament actually imposed upon him by the defendant, but instead by pursuing a dangerous method of work through personal choice he injures himself, then *volenti* may well apply and the defence might succeed. An example of this type of case is found in *Imperial Chemical Industries Ltd v Shatwell* [1964] 3 WLR 329 (as discussed above and see section 17.4). Here the court held that if the claimant had sued his brother, the action would have failed on the basis of *volenti* and, as a result, the defendants were not vicariously liable. The claimant had consented to the conduct that had caused his injury. He had voluntarily accepted the risk of harm and was responsible for his own injury.

5.3.5 Rescuers

The courts have been reluctant to find that a rescuer has consented to the risks inherent in the rescue.

CASE EXAMPLE

***Baker v T E Hopkins & Sons Ltd* [1959] 1 WLR 966**

Two workmen had been overcome by fumes from a pump while trying to repair a well. Dr Baker had himself lowered by rope to try to rescue the men but was himself overcome when the rope jammed and he also became trapped. He died.

The Court of Appeal found that the defendants owed the doctor a duty of care, thus the issue of whether Dr Baker had voluntarily consented to the risk was irrelevant. Holding that the act of a rescuer in the circumstances was a foreseeable consequence of the breach of duty owed to the workmen, Lord Justice Willmer said at 983:

JUDGMENT

'it would certainly be a strange result if the law were held to penalise the courage of the rescuer by depriving him of any remedy'.

This case appears to say that a duty of care will be owed to a rescuer. This has been refined in *White v Chief Constable of South Yorkshire Police* [1999] 2 AC 455 which says that where the injury amounts to nervous shock, a rescuer must satisfy the same tests as any other primary victim (discussed in section 6.1.4).

The fact that the claimant has engaged in or attempted a rescue does not mean that he has voluntarily accepted the risk.

CASE EXAMPLE

Haynes v Harwood [1935] 1 KB 146

Here the claimant, a policeman, was injured when he attempted to stop a runaway horse. He was under a duty because of his employment to try to stop the horse and protect the public so he had not acted voluntarily. The court would not accept the defence.

However, if there is no actual danger then a claimant in such circumstances may indeed have voluntarily accepted the risk of harm.

CASE EXAMPLE

Cutler v United Dairies [1933] 2 KB 297

A horse bolted into an empty field. Nobody was in actual danger. The claimant tried to calm the horse but was injured. The court held that the claimant was indeed *volenti* and had exercised free choice. The defence succeeded.

5.3.6 Sporting events

There are two perspectives to consider here. The first is that of the spectator and the second, is that of the participants.

Considering spectators first, some sports, for example motor racing, are inherently dangerous and spectators may be injured by accidents.

The issue has been discussed by the Court of Appeal.

CASE EXAMPLE

Wooldridge v Sumner [1963] 2 QB 43

The claimant attended a horse show as a professional photographer. A rider who was riding too fast lost control of his horse which then injured the claimant. The Court of Appeal recognised that the rider owed spectators a duty of care. Nevertheless, they considered that he had been guilty of an error of judgment in his riding of the horse but not negligence. He had not breached his duty so *volenti* was not an issue.

Lord Justice Diplock explained the position at 68:

JUDGMENT

'A person attending a game or competition takes the risk of any damage caused to him by any act of a participant done in the course of and for the purposes of the game or competition notwithstanding that such an act may involve an error of judgement or a lapse of skill, unless the participant's conduct is such as to evince a reckless disregard for the spectator's safety.'

Nevertheless, a spectator does not consent to the negligence of a competitor merely by being present at the sporting event. The rule seems therefore to be that provided the cause of the incident was not due to negligence, the spectator will have consented to the risks which are inherent to watching the sport.

From the perspective of participants in sport, they generally freely consent to the risks involved in sport. In the case of sporting events as Barwick CJ identified in *Rootes v Shelton* [1968] ALR 33:

JUDGMENT

'By engaging in a sport . . . the participants may be held to have accepted risks which are inherent in that sport . . . but this does not eliminate all duty of care of the one participant to the other.'

Indeed, this does not absolve the organisers from ensuring the safety of participants either.

CASE EXAMPLE

***Shane Byrne v Motorsport Vision Racing Limited, Motorsport Vision Limited, Motorcycle Circuit Racing Control Board Limited* [2024] EWHC 2966 (KB)**

The claimant was a professional motorbike racer and at the height of his career having won numerous races. He was testing his superbike at the racing circuit prior to the race when he came off his bike crashing into a safety barrier. The claimant brought a claim against the track owners, event organisers and the governing body for competitive motorcycle racing.

It was held that defendants were negligent in their inspections of the barriers and that the barriers were suitable for a collision by a motor car but not for a motorcyclist.

The defendants argued that the claimant had willingly accepted the risk of injuries and possibly death not least because he had signed a 'signing on' form to that effect. However, these clauses are rendered ineffective pursuant to ss1.(3)(b) and 2 of the Unfair Contract Terms Act 1977. The defendants further argued that the principles of *volenti* absolved them of liability as the claimant had walked the track before riding around it and chose to use it – thus accepting the track's features and physical layout. The court held that whilst the claimant may have walked around the track, he was not an expert in track design, safety and construction and therefore rejected the notion that he willingly accepted the risk of colliding with the barrier or that he accepted that the barrier that he collided with provided him with a sufficient level of protection.

5.3.7 Passengers

Anyone who is a passenger in a motor vehicle driven by someone they know to be drunk or otherwise incapable is factually likely to have assumed the risk that they might be injured by the driver's negligence.

CASE EXAMPLE

Dann v Hamilton [1939] 1 KB 509

Hamilton drove the claimant and her mother to London to see the Coronation decorations. Hamilton drank alcohol during the evening. They met a man who was given a lift but who left the car shortly before it was involved in an accident when the claimant was injured and Hamilton was killed. The man had said to the claimant and her mother 'You two have more pluck than I have.' The claimant said, 'You should be like me. If anything is going to happen, it will happen.' The court held that *volenti* could not apply. The claimant had not consented to the defendant's negligence.

Mr Justice Asquith, while finding in the particular case that the defence did not apply, nonetheless acknowledged the possibility that in extreme cases it might be successfully pleaded at 518:

JUDGMENT

'There may be cases where the drunkenness of the driver . . . is so extreme and so glaring that to accept a lift is like . . . inter-meddling with an unexploded bomb or walking on the edge of an unfenced cliff.'

The position of passengers in a motor vehicle has been settled by the Road Traffic Act 1988, s149(3). Where a person is carried in a vehicle in circumstances such that compulsory third party insurance is required:

SECTION

'The fact that a person so carried has willingly accepted as his the risk of negligence on the part of the [insured] shall not be treated as negativing any . . . liability on the part of the [insured].'

Although the defence of voluntary assumption of risk cannot be used, the defence of contributory negligence remains open when a passenger can be seen to be aware of the risk and to have consented to it.

While passengers in motor vehicles are not vulnerable to the defence, passengers in other forms of transport may find that the defence can be successfully used against them.

CASE EXAMPLE

Morris v Murray and Another [1991] 3 QB 6

The claim was brought against the estate of a deceased person. The claimant and the deceased met at a pub and later, after several drinks, the claimant accepted the deceased's invitation to go for a ride in the deceased's plane. Flying from the aerodrome had been suspended because of bad weather but nonetheless they took off. The plane crashed, seriously injuring the claimant.

The Court of Appeal found that the claimant had been fully aware of the risk that he was taking. Fox LJ held at 16:

JUDGMENT

'He knowingly and willingly embarked on a flight with a drunken pilot.'

It was held that the claimant voluntarily assumed the risks inherent in the flight due to the condition of the pilot.

5.3.8 Agreement

In some cases judges have indicated that for the defence to succeed there must be either an express or implied agreement that the claimant would waive any claim against the defendant. This may for instance be as a result of an exclusion clause. Even then it would be subject to s2(1) of the Unfair Contract Terms Act 1977.

The courts are more reluctant to imply that there is an agreement that a claimant will accept the risk of injury.

CASE EXAMPLE

Dann v Hamilton [1939] 1 KB 509

Hamilton drove the claimant and her mother to London to see the Coronation decorations. Hamilton drank alcohol during the evening. They met a man who was given a lift but who left the car shortly before it was involved in an accident when the claimant was injured and Hamilton was killed. The man had said to the claimant and her mother 'You two have more pluck than I have.' The claimant said, 'You should be like me. If anything is going to happen, it will happen.' The court held that *volenti* could not apply. The claimant had not consented to the defendant's negligence.

Asquith J indicated that the defence was only applicable when the claimant came to a situation where the defendant's negligence had already created the danger. He also stated at 518:

JUDGMENT

'There may be cases in which the drunkenness of the driver at the material time is so extreme and so glaring that to accept a lift from him is like engaging in an intrinsically and obviously dangerous occupation, intermeddling with an unexploded bomb or walking on the edge of an unfenced cliff.'

In *Nettleship v Weston* [1971] 2 QB 691 Lord Denning commented at 701:

JUDGMENT

'Nothing will suffice short of an agreement to waive any claim for negligence. The claimant must agree, expressly or impliedly, to waive any claim for any injury that may befall him due to the lack of reasonable care by the defendant.'

Where a defendant tries to rely on an exclusion clause if the damage is death or personal injury the defence of *volenti* may fail because of s2(1) Unfair Contract Terms Act 1977, which states:

SECTION

's2(1) A person cannot by reference to any contract term or to a notice given to persons generally or to particular persons exclude or restrict his liability for death or personal injury resulting from negligence.'

In the case of other damage s2(2) may apply. This states:

SECTION

's2(2) In the case of other loss or damage, a person cannot so exclude or restrict his liability for negligence except in so far as the term or notice satisfies the requirement of reasonableness.'

In cases where there is no agreement and the claimant comes upon an already existing risk then s2(3) may apply:

SECTION

's2(3) Where a contract term or notice purports to exclude or restrict liability for negligence a person's agreement to or awareness of it is not of itself to be taken as indicating his voluntary acceptance of any risk.'

5.4 Contributory negligence

In cases where a claimant suffers damage partly through his own negligence as well as through the negligence of the defendant then contributory negligence may be used to reduce damages by the extent to which the claimant was responsible for his own loss or injury.

Unlike voluntary assumption of risk which is a total defence, contributory negligence is a partial defence which allows the court to apportion blame between the claimant and the other parties. This defence has proved particularly effective in cases involving negligence but it is, however, a general defence and can be used in the context of most torts. Contributory negligence was originally a complete defence so that no damages at all were payable if the defence succeeded.

CASE EXAMPLE

Butterfield v Forester [1809] 11 East 60

Here the defendant obstructed a road by placing a pole across it. The claimant was injured when his horse collided with the pole while he was violently riding the horse. It was held that the claimant had contributed to his own harm. Taking proper care would have avoided the accident and he was unable to claim any damages.

In the nineteenth century this was particularly harsh on people sustaining injuries while at work. Such a rule was hardly fair where a claimant's negligence was only slight in comparison to the defendant's negligence.

Now, the defence of contributory negligence enables the court to apportion blame between the claimant and the defendant to the extent that the facts suggest that each has some part to play in the events leading to the injury.

Defence of contributory negligence: the defendant will have to show three things:

- has the claimant failed to exercise reasonable care for their own safety;
- has that failure contributed to the claimant's harm – is there a causal link between the claimant's negligence and the harm suffered; and
- damages should be reduced in proportion to relative responsibility.

Considering the relationship between the defence of contributory negligence and voluntary assumption of risk, common sense suggests that a person would be unlikely to consent to the risk that another person would be negligent. Although in *Dann v Hamilton* the door was left open to the use of the defence in cases involving negligence, it seems clear that where negligence is involved the defence will rarely be successful. A hint of this was given by Lord Denning MR when he said in *Nettleship v Weston* [1971] 2 QB 691, at 701:

JUDGMENT

'Now that contributory negligence is not a complete defence . . . the defence of [voluntary assumption of risk] has been closely considered and, in consequence, it has been severely limited . . . Nothing will suffice short of an agreement to waive any claim for negligence.'

Although the defence was successfully used in *Morris v Murray* [1990] 3 All ER 801, both that case and the later case of *Pitts v Hunt* [1991] 1 QB 24 make it clear that the defence will only apply in the most extreme case of lack of care by the claimant.

CASE EXAMPLE

Pitts v Hunt [1991] 1 QB 24

The claimant was seriously injured when he was a passenger on a motorbike driven by Hunt. Both the claimant and Hunt were very much the worse for drink. The evidence showed that the claimant had actively encouraged Hunt to drive in a dangerous manner, to frighten other road users and that he knew that Hunt was underage, drunk and uninsured. The effect of the Road Traffic Act 1988 meant that the defence was unsuccessful but Lord Justice Beldam in the Court of Appeal said that the defence would have applied were it not for the statute.

A claimant might also place himself in a position that is not dangerous but which involves circumstances making it more likely that he will suffer harm. An example is where a claimant knows that a driver is drunk but nevertheless accepts a lift. *Volenti* will not apply but there will be contributory negligence as in *Owens v Brimmell* [1977] 2 WLR 943.

The Law Reform (Contributory Negligence) Act 1945 codified the rule that damages could be altered according to the extent to which the claimant had contributed to his own harm. Damages will then be reduced proportionately accordingly.

CASE EXAMPLE

***Sayers v Harlow Urban District Council* [1958] 1 WLR 623**

A lady became trapped in a public lavatory when through negligent maintenance the door lock became jammed. She then stood on the toilet roll holder in an effort to climb out of the cubicle. She had to catch a bus so it was reasonable for her to try to get out in the circumstances, and so her act did not break the chain of causation. The council was liable but the damages were reduced by 25 per cent because of the careless manner in which she tried to get out.

The Act states at s1(1):

SECTION

's1(1) Where any person suffers damage as the result partly of his own fault and partly of the fault of any other person or persons, a claim in respect of that damage shall not be defeated by reason of the fault of the person suffering the damage, but the damage recoverable in respect thereof shall be reduced to such extent as the court thinks just and equitable having regard to the claimant's share in the responsibility for the damage.'

The Act only applies where the damage was caused partly by the fault of the defendant and partly by the fault of the claimant.

The Act makes it clear in s4 that the defence does not apply only to a case where the claimant alleges negligence by the defendant. The effect of the provisions is to give the court true flexibility. Once the defendant's liability for the tort is established, the judge is then free to decide whether, and if so to what extent, the claimant must bear some part of the blame. In deciding the extent of the claimant's responsibility, the court will compare the claimant's behaviour with the way in which a reasonable person having regard for their own well-being would behave.

Section 4 – 'Damage' includes 'loss of life and personal injury' and also, it seems, property damage. Also by s4:

SECTION

's4 "Fault" means "negligence, breach of statutory duty or other act or omission which gives rise to liability in tort or would, apart from this Act, give rise to the defence of contributory negligence".'

The defence has become a common aspect of claims for injuries or damage sustained in road traffic accidents, so that damages can be reduced where a motorcycle passenger fails to take the precaution of wearing a crash helmet.

CASE EXAMPLE

O'Connell v Jackson [1972] 1 QB 270

Here it was acknowledged that the passenger received much greater injuries because of not wearing a crash helmet. So damages were reduced accordingly.

The defence is also commonly applied to passengers of motor cars who fail to wear seat belts as required by law.

CASE EXAMPLE

Froom v Butcher [1976] QB 286

Mr Froom suffered a broken rib and bruises on his chest when he was involved in a car accident. He would probably have been saved from these injuries if he had worn a seat belt. He also had a broken finger, but the seat belt would not have saved that. The court reduced the damages award to him as a result of his own negligence in failing to wear a seatbelt. The court applied an objective standard of care. A prudent person would have worn a seat belt, so damages were reduced by 20 per cent.

As Lord Denning explained in the Court of Appeal at 291:

JUDGMENT

'Contributory negligence is a man's carelessness in looking after his own safety. He is guilty of contributory negligence if he ought reasonably to have foreseen that, if he did not act as a reasonable prudent man, he might hurt himself.'

The reduction of damages when the claimant fails to wear a seatbelt can be depicted as follows:

Table 5.1 Contributory negligence: failure to wear seatbelt.

Impact of claimant's negligence	*Reduction in damages*
Failure to wear seatbelt could have prevented the claimant's injuries altogether	25 per cent
Failure to wear seatbelt could have prevented the claimant's injuries almost altogether.	20 per cent
Failure to wear a seatbelt had a considerable impact on the injuries sustained by the claimant	15 per cent
Failure to wear seatbelt would have made no difference to the injuries sustained by the claimant	0 per cent

A successful claim of contributory negligence depends on the defendant showing that the claimant has been negligent himself and is therefore partly to blame. This will mean that use of the defence, just as in negligence, depends on showing that the behaviour of the claimant meant that harm was foreseeable.

CASE EXAMPLE

Jones v Livox Quarries Ltd **[1952] 2 QB 608**

The claimant was employed in a quarry and, in defiance of his employer's express instructions, rode on the rear tow bar of a 'traxcavator'. The driver was unaware of the claimant and when another vehicle collided with the traxcavator the claimant was injured. It was however held that as he had exposed himself to the risk of injury from the traxcavator being run into from behind, that his damages should be reduced because of his contributory negligence. The court reduced his damages by 5 per cent.

Lord Denning stated at 615:

JUDGMENT

'A person is guilty of contributory negligence if he ought reasonably to have foreseen that, if he did not act as a reasonable, prudent man, he might be hurt himself; and in his reckonings he must take into account the possibility of others being careless.'

So for a successful claim a defendant must prove:

- fault on the part of the claimant (that he failed to take reasonable care for his own safety); and
- that negligence by the claimant (i.e. a failure to take reasonable care) was a cause of the damage suffered.

5.4.1 Fault on the part of the claimant

A claimant is under a duty to take care for himself. The appropriate standard of care is the same as that generally applied in negligence and is basically objective.

A failure, by the claimant, to take care for his own safety may be a cause of the damage. For example, where the claimant is injured in an accident but both the claimant and defendant are equally to blame.

Alternatively, a claimant may be injured in an accident where he has placed himself in a dangerous position and therefore at risk of injury.

CASE EXAMPLE

Davies v Swan Motor Co (Swansea) Ltd [1949] 2 KB 291

The claimant's husband had ridden on the step of a dustcart and was well aware of the dangers involved in doing so. One of the defendant's buses overtook the dustcart and the husband was killed in a collision. Both drivers were held to be negligent by the court but there was contributory negligence by the husband because of the dangerous manner in which he had ridden on the dustcart.

This inevitably applies even though the defendant has been negligent because the claimant has increased the risk of injury or suffered a worse injury as a result.

Also a claimant might place himself in a position which is not dangerous in itself but then fails to take precautions to avoid danger and in doing so increases the amount of harm suffered.

Contributory negligence can also be applied to children even though we would expect a child to be less careful than an adult. However, it would be very difficult to show that a very young child was guilty of contributory negligence.

CASE EXAMPLE

Gough v Thorne [1966] 1 WLR 1387

A lorry driver signalled to the claimant, who was 13 years old, to cross a road. She did so but did not stop to see if the road was clear. A car, being driven negligently, injured the claimant, who was held not to be guilty of contributory negligence. The outcome would have been different if she had been an adult (see Lord Denning's explanation in the judgment).

In the case of people at work there is legislation for their general protection and it appears that the courts consider that the prevention or reduction of an employee's damages due to contributory negligence should not undermine such protection.

The courts are reluctant in any case to find contributory negligence where an employee pursues an action for breach of statutory duty and possibly where there is an action for negligence.

In assessing contributory negligence the court will take into account the influence, upon an employee, of long hours and fatigue, repetition leading to a slackening of attention, noise and pre-occupation in a task sometimes at the expense of personal safety.

Nevertheless it is possible to succeed in claiming contributory negligence against employees.

CASE EXAMPLE

Jayes v IMI (Kynoch) Ltd [1985] ICR 155

The claimant, who was an experienced workman, lost the tip of a finger when his hand was pulled into a machine while he was cleaning it after removing the safety guard. He accepted that what he had done was very foolish and, because of the claimant's failure to take care of his own safety, the court held that he was 100 per cent contributorily negligent.

Where a rescuer is negligent in carrying out a rescue, then damages may also be reduced on the basis of contributory negligence.

CASE EXAMPLE

Harrison v British Railways Board [1981] 3 All ER 679

The defendant tried to board a moving train. The claimant guard saw the defendant but gave an incorrect signal to the train driver, to accelerate rather than to stop. The claimant guard then tried to pull the defendant onto the train but both fell and the claimant was injured. The court held that where someone places himself in danger and it is foreseeable that someone else will attempt a rescue then the rescued person owes a duty of care to the rescuer. As a result of the wrong signal the claimant was contributorily negligent and the court reduced his damages by 20 per cent. However, the court did point out that it would be rare for contributory negligence to be used against a rescuer.

Sometimes the defendant's negligence causes a claimant to be in imminent danger. If the claimant acts to avoid a reasonably perceived greater danger but makes a wrong decision, then the court may well have sympathy.

CASE EXAMPLE

Jones v Boyce [1816] 1 Stark 492

The claimant thought that the defendant's coach was going to crash and so he jumped out of it and in doing so broke his leg. As the coach did not crash he would have suffered no harm if he had remained where he was. However, the court accepted that he acted as a prudent and reasonable person would in the circumstances and so there was no contributory negligence.

5.4.2 Negligence by the claimant contributing to the damage

A claimant's contributory negligence must be a legal and factual cause of the harm to the claimant although it does not have to be a cause of the accident itself. An example of this is not wearing a seatbelt which may well cause more damage but not have been the cause of the accident itself, as in *Froom v Butcher* [1976] QB 286.

Factual causation involves the 'but for' test – would the alleged consequence have occurred but for the negligent cause?

CASE EXAMPLE

Jones v Livox Quarries Ltd [1952] 2 QB 608

Here the claimant riding on the towbar was one of the causes of his injury. Factual causation was established and the damage was not too remote. The court rejected an argument that the claimant's negligence had not caused damage to himself because the only foreseeable injury was by falling off the traxcavator, as opposed to being struck from behind.

It should also be remembered that proving a claimant has contributed to his harm is not the same as proving fault but is to do with his relative blameworthiness.

CASE EXAMPLE

Badger v Ministry of Defence [2005] EWHC 2941 (QB); [2005] All ER (D) 248

The claimant died of lung cancer at age 63. The defendant admitted that it had breached a statutory duty in exposing the claimant to asbestos dust but argued that damages should be reduced because if the claimant had not smoked cigarettes he would also have been unlikely to die of lung cancer at such a young age. The facts were complex since the claimant died of lung cancer, attributable both to exposure to asbestos and to smoking, but also had asbestosis, attributable to the exposure and also had heart disease and emphysema, attributable in part at least to his smoking. The claimant should have been aware by 1971 when the first health warnings appeared on cigarette packets of the risk of smoking to his health. He was also warned by doctors in 1968, 1991, 1992 and 1995 and advised to give up smoking. The court was satisfied that the claimant contributed to his harm and reduced damages by 20 per cent.

5.4.3 Apportioning damages

In deciding what apportionment is 'just and equitable' the courts consider the extent to which the claimant's and defendant's respective negligence caused the damage to the claimant and will also determine where blame lies.

On causation the courts will generally adopt a commonsense approach in order to reach an apportionment.

CASE EXAMPLE

Stapley v Gypsum Mines Ltd [1953] AC 663

Two miners disobeyed instructions and continued to work when they should have dealt with an unsafe part of the roof which was a danger to them. One of the miners died when the roof collapsed and his widow sued the defendants for negligence. The House of Lords took a commonsense approach and held that both miners were causes of the harm. The claimant's action succeeded but damages were reduced by 80 per cent because of the contributory negligence.

In the case of blameworthiness the test is objective and is measured against the standard of behaviour of the reasonable man.

In claims where there are multiple defendants and the claimant is not at fault then the loss may be recovered from any of the defendants. That defendant will then seek a contribution from the others under the Civil Liability (Contribution) Act 1978. However, if there was contributory negligence by the claimant then the court must consider:

- the amount by which the claimant's damages should be reduced as a result of his own contributory negligence; but also
- the amount of contribution recoverable from each defendant.

CASE EXAMPLE

Fitzgerald v Lane and Patel [1988] 2 All ER 961

The claimant stepped out on to a busy road and was then struck by the first defendant's vehicle. This impact pushed the claimant into the path of the second defendant's vehicle. Both defendants were found to be negligent but there was also contributory negligence by the claimant. Initially all three parties were held equally to blame and damages were reduced by one-third. However, the House of Lords indicated that this was the wrong approach. They suggested that there was a direct comparison between the negligence of both defendants and the negligence in the claimant's conduct. As a result damages were reduced by 50 per cent because the claimant's blame was equal to that of the defendants.

CRITIQUING THE LAW

Do you think that the defence of contributory negligence achieves the right balance in terms of apportioning blame or do you think that the defendant should be liable for all of the damage regardless of the claimant's own actions?

5.5 Illegality (*ex turpi causa non oritur actio*)

The Latin phrase translates as 'an action cannot be founded on a base cause'. This is clearly demonstrated in the rules governing illegal contracts,

ex turpi causa non oritur actio

A defence that may be raised against a claimant whose claim arises from their own criminal actions

which are unenforceable as a matter of public policy. The essential rationale of the illegality doctrine is that it would be contrary to the public interest to enforce a claim if to do so would be harmful to the integrity of the legal system.

It would be reasonable to suppose that a person who suffers a tort while engaged in illegal or unlawful activity would, for the same reason, be unable to bring a successful claim. Such a blanket rule would, however, cause injustice and the courts have tended to decide whether or not the illegality should have the effect of barring a claim looking very carefully at the particular circumstances of the case. Nevertheless, the elements to establishing the defence of illegality are as follows:

DEFENCE OF *ILLEGALITY*: THE DEFENDANT WILL HAVE TO SHOW THREE THINGS:

- the claimant has engaged in illegal activity;
- there is a link between the claimant's illegality activity and the tort; and
- the defence is not barred by another reason such as policy.

It might seem obvious that a crime should be regarded as disallowing any claim but this is not always the case.

In *Revill v Newbery* [1996] QB 567 the claimant succeeded although he had been injured while attempting to commit burglary. The defence of illegality was rejected, Lord Justice Evans saying at 579:

JUDGMENT

'It is one thing to deny a [claimant] any fruits from his illegal conduct, but different and far more far-reaching to deprive him even of compensation for injury which he suffers and which otherwise he is entitled to recover at law.'

CASE EXAMPLE

Stone & Rolls v Moore Stephens [2009] UKHL 39

Moore Stephens were the auditors for Stone & Rolls. Stone & Rolls was managed by Mr Stojevic who was actually using the company as a vehicle for defrauding banks. The banks then sought to bring a claim for their losses against the defendants as the better party to sue, on the basis that they should have identified the enormous fraudulent activity that was going on in Stone & Rolls given their position. The defendants however made it plain that actually public policy would militate against the imposition of liability given that although it was the actions of Mr Stojevic, these actions can be attributable to the company and as such they could not rely on its own illegal actions to bring the claim.

This decision has been widely welcomed by auditors given the liability that they could face if the decision were otherwise.

In the case of *Vellino v Chief Constable of Greater Manchester* [2002] 3 All ER 78 the question for the Court of Appeal was whether the police owe to an arrested person, a duty to take care that he is not injured in a foreseeable attempt by him to escape from police custody. It was known to the police that the claimant frequently would seek to evade arrest by jumping from the windows of his second floor flat to the ground floor sometimes with the aid of the balcony and sometimes without. One occasion when the police sought to arrest him, he tried to escape through the window but on this occasion he fell and suffered catastrophic injuries rendering him tetraplegic. The Court of Appeal concluded that the police owed no such duty not least because following *Clunis*, escaping from custody was a sufficiently serious criminal offence to attract the operation of the *ex turpi causa* principle and that in those circumstances the police owed to an arrested person no duty to take care that he was not injured in a foreseeable attempt by him to escape from police custody at 989.

JUDGMENT

'To suggest that the police owe a criminal the duty to prevent the criminal from escaping, and that the criminal who hurts himself while escaping can sue the police for the breach of that duty, seems to me self-evidently absurd. No policy reason has been suggested for the law adopting such a course.'

Such cases also overlap with other defences such as contributory negligence. So the decision of *Pitts v Hunt* which was discussed earlier in the chapter, is an example of where the actions of the claimant could not successfully be considered under contributory negligence but such an action nevertheless was destined to fail because by actively encouraging a driver whom you know is uninsured to drive recklessly will always fail as being directly *ex turpi causa*. That said, for the defence to apply, the tortious act that the defendant is engaged in has to be directly in pursuance of the criminal activity. The crucial question as highlighted in *Delaney v Pickett* is whether the injury is truly a consequence of the claimant's unlawful act or was it a consequence of the unlawful act only in the sense that it would not have happened if he had not been committing an unlawful act. So is the claim inextricably linked with the criminal activity or does the criminal activity merely give occasion for tortious conduct of the defendant? Consider these questions in the context of the following case:

CASE EXAMPLE

Delaney v Pickett [2011] EWCA Civ 1532

The claimant and defendant went out in an expensive Mercedes sports car which the defendant drove at considerable speed and unfortunately collided with another vehicle causing the claimant significant injuries. It transpires that both parties were in possession of a controlled drug. There was considerable discussion in this case about whether the amount of drugs found on their persons meant that it was for the purposes of supplying. If it were to be supplied then certainly the defence of illegality would apply. If however, it were not for supply then the accident was unrelated to the illegal enterprise and has no role in this case, and the claimant's claim must succeed as it was explained at paragraph 28:

JUDGMENT

'. . . the insurer cannot and therefore does not satisfy the burden of proof which lies on it to establish the degree of criminality they seek to fix upon the appellant. If that is correct, the defence fails. Simple possession could not possibly have any causative effect on the defendant's driving. Nor could it possibly be said that simply because the driver and passengers were in possession of drugs the vehicle was being used in the course or furtherance of a crime.'

By contrast, in *Joyce v O'Brien* [2013] EWCA Civ 546, the claimant and the defendant stole some ladders and were escaping from the scene in a van but the claimant suffered personal injury as a result of the defendant's negligent driving. In such a circumstance it can be said that the defendant's negligent driving caused the harm and that this was all part of the illegal enterprise that the parties were engaged in.

In *Clunis v Camden* and *Islington Area Health Authority* [1998] QB 978 the court rejected the claim on the basis that it was based essentially on the claimant's own illegal act, and he must be taken to have known what he was doing and that it was wrong.

CASE EXAMPLE

Clunis v Camden and Islington Area Health Authority [1998] QB 978

The claimant had been convicted of manslaughter on the ground of diminished responsibility. He sued the defendants for negligence in failing to make a proper assessment of his mental condition. Had this been done, he argued, he would not have been released from detention in a psychiatric hospital and the killing would not have taken place.

The essential difference between the two cases seems to be that in *Revill* the injury was in a sense separate from the claimant's criminal activity. Had he been a lawful visitor a claim would certainly have succeeded. In *Clunis*, however, the injury suffered by the claimant was the fact that he had committed a crime. Admitting the claim could perhaps have been seen as profiting from the crime.

The courts have sometimes argued that 'it would be an affront to the public conscience' to allow a criminal to recover damages. This approach was explained in the judgment in the case of *Euro-Diam Ltd v Bathurst* [1990] 1 QB 1, at 35 where Lord Justice Kerr said the defence will not apply:

JUDGMENT

'if, in all the circumstances, it would be an affront to the public conscience to grant the [claimant] the relief which he seeks because the courts would thereby appear to assist or encourage the [claimant] in his illegal conduct or to encourage others in similar acts'.

Lord Justice Kerr's approach in *Euro-Diam Ltd v Bathurst* when read alongside Lord Justice Evans' approach in *Revill* encapsulates the confusion in this part of tort law.

The defence of illegality has received a great deal of attention in recent years. It is based on a number of factors including the seriousness of the illegality, a potential deterrent impact the decision could have, how the decision could impact the illegal act itself. In 2001, the Law Commission published its consultation paper, 'The Illegality Defence in Tort', which reviewed the defence and decided that legislative intervention in this area would not be of assistance. This was largely due to two very prominent decisions before the House of Lords, *Stone & Rolls v Moore Stephens* and *Gray v Thames Trains* [2009] UKHL 33.

CASE EXAMPLE

Gray v Thames Trains [2009] UKHL 33

Thames Trains were responsible for the Ladbroke rail crash in which Gray suffered some minor physical injuries but more significantly, he suffered from post-traumatic stress disorder. One day, Gray became involved in an altercation with a drunk pedestrian who stepped out in front of Gray's car, and Gray became so enraged that he drove to the nearby house of his girlfriend's parents, took a knife from a drawer, drove off in pursuit of the pedestrian, found him and stabbed him to death. Gray claimed that his personality had changed since the rail crash and pleaded guilty to manslaughter on the ground of diminished responsibility and was detained under the Mental Health Act. Thames Trains accepted that they were responsible for Gray's mental state but that their liability effectively came to an end when Gray engaged in the criminal act of manslaughter. Gray argued that he should be allowed to recover loss of earnings for the period for which he was detained under the Mental Health Act since he felt that but for Thames Trains' negligence he would not have been in this state which caused him to kill. Thames Trains argued that the defence of illegality precluded any such claim. Gray's claim was inextricably linked with his own criminal acts.

Lord Hoffmann explained the interplay between the objectives of criminal law and tort law as follows at 29:

JUDGMENT

'Their principal argument invokes a special rule of public policy. In its wider form, it is that you cannot recover compensation for loss which you have suffered in consequence of your own criminal act. In its narrower and more specific form, it is

> that you cannot recover for damage which flows from loss of liberty, a fine or other punishment lawfully imposed upon you in consequence of your own unlawful act. In such a case it is the law which, as a matter of penal policy, causes the damage and it would be inconsistent for the law to require you to be compensated for that damage.'

Affirmation of the principle in *Gray v Thames Trains* can be found in *Henderson v Dorset Healthcare University NHS Foundation Trust* [2020] UKSC 43. Here the claimant killed her mother in a psychotic episode which she argued would not have happened but for the negligent care that she received from the defendants. The defendants admitted liability but successfully argued that their liability stopped there and could not be extended to illegal acts carried out by the claimant. As per *Gray v Thames Trains* and the other cases within this line of authority, public policy precluded such liability. The most recent statement of how the defence of illegality is to be applied moving forward comes in the following decision which provides the framework to be used when applying the defence of illegality.

CASE EXAMPLE

Lewis-Ranwell v G4S Health Services (UK) Ltd, Devon Partnership NHS Trust, Devon County Council [2026] UKSC 2

The claimant suffered from schizophrenia and during a serious psychosis episode, he killed three elderly men in their homes. He was charged with murder but found not guilty by reason of insanity. He was ordered to be detained under the Mental Health Act 1983. Two days prior to the killings, the claimant had been twice arrested by the police and released on both occasions after having been seen by mental health professionals. The claimant argued that the defendants were negligent in releasing him given that it was clear that there was a real risk that he would injure others if he were released. The defendants argue that the case should be struck out on the grounds that the claimant is basing his claim on his own illegal acts. The Court of Appeal held that the defence could only apply where the claimant had *known* that he was acting unlawfully, the defence could not be invoked here because the claimant did not know that the killings were unlawful because of his mental health. The defendants appealed to the Supreme Court. The Supreme Court unanimously allowed the appeal. It held that the claimant is barred by the doctrine of illegality from bringing civil proceedings in negligence to recover compensation for the consequences of the killings.

The Supreme Court used the analytical template for assessment of whether to uphold the defence of illegality developed in the case of *Patel v Mirza* [2016] UKSC 42 which was heard by an enlarged panel of nine Justices. Before turning to this assessment, the threshold question had to be answered: in what circumstances is the illegality defence engaged? It is the case that not every act by a claimant which involved some unlawfulness however trivial is to be a bar to their claim. The question is whether conduct is unlawful in the sense required for the application of the principle. Or in other words, the actions of the claimant do not have to carry criminal responsibility to cross the threshold for the defence of illegality. In this case the claimant was found not guilty by reason of insanity. However, that in of itself does not mean that the conduct is not illegal.

Lord Hodge and Lord Lloyd-Jones explain at paragraph 134:

JUDGMENT

'His actions are sufficient to engage and have engaged the interests of the State or the public interest. It is in the public interest that he was made the subject of a hospital order and a restriction order. We therefore conclude that the claimant's killing of the three men is unlawful conduct for the purpose of engaging the illegality defence.'

Having determined the threshold issue, the three-stage framework analysis developed in *Patel v Mirza* had to be considered and applied:

a consider the underlying purpose of the prohibition which has been transgressed and whether that purpose will be enhanced by denial of the claim:
   - The prohibition transgressed is that most fundamental injunction against the taking of human life: you shall not kill. Its purpose is the preservation of life and the promotion of respect for the sanctity of life.
   - The law seeks to protect the public and to deter unlawful killing. There is also a public interest in the public condemnation of unlawful killing and the punishment of those who behave in that way. His conduct is unlawful and deserves to be condemned.
   - This prohibition applies with equal force to an individual found not guilty of murder by reason of insanity. The claimant's conduct is not justified or excused because he is spared criminal responsibility Allowing the civil claim to proceed would give rise to a series of inconsistencies which would damage the integrity of the legal system.

b consider conversely any other relevant public policies which may be rendered ineffective or less effective by denial of the claim:
   - In general, it is in the public interest that the courts should adjudicate civil wrongs.
   - Allowing the civil claim would enable examination of what may have gone wrong there exist, however, alternative procedures, such as inquests and public inquiries, which are better suited for these purposes. The policy considerations in favour of maintaining the integrity of the legal system greatly outweigh those in favour of permitting a claim.

c consider whether denial of the claim would be a proportionate response to the illegality, bearing in mind that punishment is a matter for the criminal courts.
   - Considering the following factors as potentially relevant to the proportionality assessment: the seriousness of the conduct, its centrality, whether it was intentional and whether there was marked disparity in the parties' respective culpability.
   - Killing three men is of the utmost seriousness and central to all heads of loss claimant in the civil claim.
   - Denying the civil claim is a proportionate response to the illegality.

Importantly, the Supreme Court highlighted that the availability of the plea of illegality should not be fettered by the distinction drawn by the criminal law between diminished responsibility and insanity but should depend on a wider assessment of public policy considerations. *Patel* provides the framework within which that assessment can be conducted.

In summary, when arguing the defence of illegality the following framework should be used to determine whether the defence can be invoked having determined the threshold question:

- consider the underlying purpose of the prohibition which has been transgressed and whether that purpose will be enhanced by denial of the claim:
- consider conversely any other relevant public policies which may be rendered ineffective or less effective by denial of the claim:
- consider whether denial of the claim would be a proportionate response to the illegality, bearing in mind that punishment is a matter for the criminal courts.

CRITIQUING THE LAW

Consider the role of policy and the defence of illegality. What do you think would happen if the defence of illegality failed in the case of *Lewis-Ranwell*?

5.6 Inevitable accident

This defence is available where the defendant can show that despite exercising all reasonable care and taking all reasonable precautions, the accident could not have been avoided.

CASE EXAMPLE

Stanley v Powell [1891] 1 QB 86

The defendant 'accidentally' shot a beater while shooting pheasants. He was able to claim inevitable accident successfully because he showed that the injury was as a result of the pellet ricocheting off trees at unusual angles.

In *Fardon v Harcourt Rivington* [1932] 146 LT 391 (for facts see Chapter 12) Lord Dunedin said:

JUDGMENT

'People must guard against reasonable possibilities, but they are not bound to guard against fantastic possibilities.'

The defence exists but its usefulness is very limited.

5.7 Act of God

This defence is available only to the tort of *Rylands v Fletcher* [1868] LR 1 Exch 265. For full discussion see Chapter 11.

CASE EXAMPLE

Nicholls v Marsland [1876] 2 ExD 1

Here exceptionally heavy rainfall caused artificial lakes to burst their banks flooding neighbouring land. This defence in reality refers to extreme and unusual weather conditions. As a result of this the events leading to the loss or damage are said to be beyond the defendant's control. For the defence to succeed therefore the weather must be both extreme and unforeseeable. Since the defendant could not have anticipated the extreme weather at the time there was no liability.

5.8 Necessity

Necessity may justify what would otherwise amount to a tort. The defendant's actions must be for the purpose of protecting:

- the public,
- a third party, or
- himself

from what is perceived to be a greater danger.

CASE EXAMPLE

Leigh v Gladstone [1909] 26 TLR 169

During the early years of the twentieth century a movement developed to press for votes for women. The women called themselves suffragettes and engaged in many acts of protest, including illegal ones, to gain publicity for their cause. When many of them were imprisoned they embarked on hunger strikes, again to gain publicity for their cause. Because their deaths might have proved politically embarrassing they were subjected to force feeding. In an action for battery it was held that force feeding of suffragettes on hunger strike while in prison was not a trespass to the person. It was necessary to save their lives.

The essence of the defence is that the action was prompted by a reasonable perception that it was required to avoid an immediate and imminent danger judged by the circumstances at the time. There is no room for hindsight so that if the perception of the risk is reasonable, it does not matter that the danger never in fact materialises. The defence has been discussed in some detail in relation to trespass to the person where it may be used to justify medical treatment and trespass to land where it may justify commission of the tort (see Chapters 8 and 13).

5.9 Statutory authority

We have seen that statutory authority may be a defence in several contexts, in particular in relation to:

- nuisance,
- *Rylands v Fletcher*,
- breach of statutory duty,

and reference should be made to Chapters 9, 10 and 16 for discussion of the defence.

A good example of statutory authority being applied as a defence is the development of the railways and the potential nuisance they caused.

CASE EXAMPLE

Hammersmith and City Railway Co v Brand **[1869] LR 4 HL 171(HL)**

Vibrations from trains were an inevitable consequence of the existence of the railway. As Lord Cairns said it would be a *reductio ad absurdum* to grant injunctive relief since this would prevent the railway from operating.

5.10 Self-help

This generally takes one of three forms:

1. self-defence, which has been discussed fully in Chapter 13 in relation to trespass to the person;
2. ejectment in relation to trespass to land, discussed in Chapter 8;
3. abatement, which is relevant to nuisance and discussed in Chapter 9.

ACTIVITY

Self-assessment questions

1. What would a defendant have to prove about a claimant for a defence of *volenti* to succeed?
2. Why was the case of *ICI v Shatwell* decided how it was?
3. Is the test for *volenti* to succeed objective or subjective?
4. When will a claimant injured during a sporting event be deemed to have consented to the risk of injury?
5. What are the basic differences between the defences of *volenti* and contributory negligence?
6. What is the effect of a successful plea of contributory negligence?
7. What is the claimant's standard of care in relation to contributory negligence?
8. Why exactly did the claimant fail in *Livox*?
9. Why is the defence of contributory negligence so commonplace in road traffic accidents?

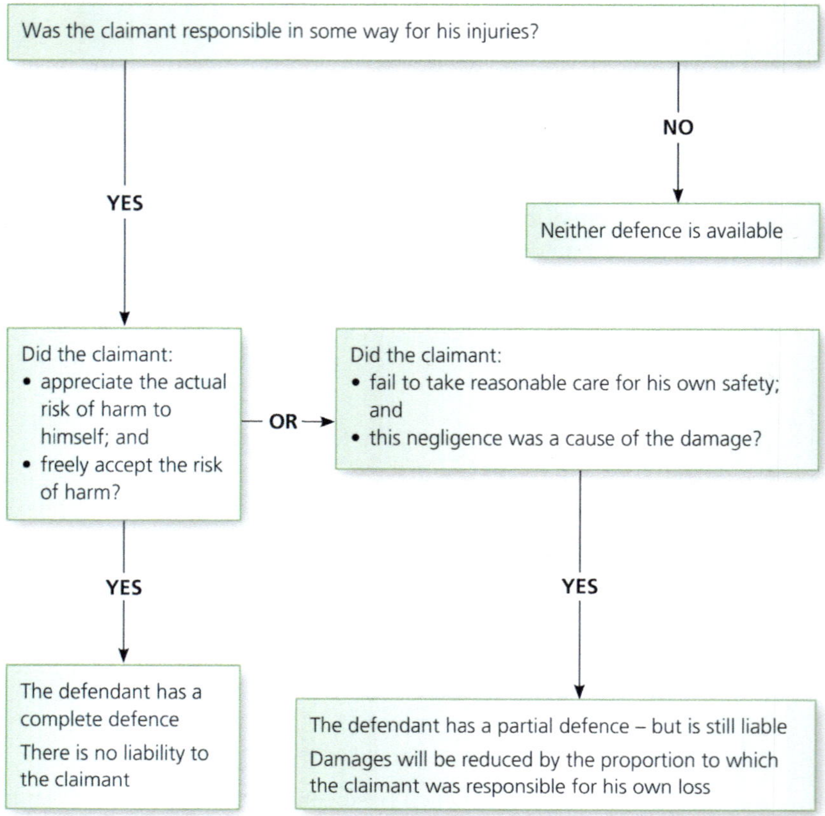

Figure 5.1 The availability of defences of *volenti non fit injuria* and contributory negligence and contrasting their effects.

ACTIVITY

Quick quiz

In the following situations say which defence a defendant might seek to apply, if at all, and why, and comment on the chances of using the defence successfully.

1. Morris was injured when he went for a flight in a light aeroplane with Peter, who Morris knows does not have a pilot's licence.
2. Lee was injured when he was elbowed in the face by Danny during a professional football match.
3. Manjit lost a hand while trying to free a blockage in the machine that he works on. His foreman had told him not to turn the machine off at any time.
4. Marion fell off a horse and was badly injured during a show jumping contest when the horse pulled up at a large fence.
5. Derek was injured when he was a passenger in his friend Ali's open top sports car. Derek was thrown out of the car when Ali, who Derek knew was almost too drunk to stand up, skidded and collided with a lamp post.

SAMPLE ESSAY QUESTION

'There is very little difference in the defences of *volenti non fit injuria* and contributory negligence when applied to a claim in negligence so that at least one of them is superfluous and unnecessary.' Discuss the accuracy of the above statement.

Explain the defence of *volenti non fit injuria*

It is a complete defence when

- defendant is negligent and causes damage to the claimant
- but the claimant has voluntarily exposed himself to the risk of harm

Explain the essential elements of the defence

- The claimant exercised free choice in accepting the risk
- The claimant understood the exact nature of the risk
- The claimant voluntarily accepted the risk

Explain the application of the defence to sport and medical treatment

- In sport the injury must have occurred within the rules of the game
- In medicine the patient must consent to all treatment
- And must be made aware of risk in broad terms
- Although emergency treatment may be an exception

Explain the defence of contributory negligence

- A partial defence under Law Reform (Contributory Negligence) Act 1945
- Damages are reduced to the extent to which the claimant is responsible for his own harm

Explain the essential elements of the defence

- The claimant failed to take reasonable care for his own safety
- This failure to take care was a cause of the harm suffered

Compare the effects of the defences

- *Volenti* is a complete defence, contributory negligence is only partial
- *Volenti* removes liability, contributory negligence reduces damages
- Before the 1945 Act the effects were the same
- *Volenti* is the free acceptance of a known risk,whereas contributory negligence merely means that the claimant failed to take care of his own safety and partially caused the harm
- Similar approach when claimant is a child
- But existence of two defences has caused confusion, e.g. sometimes both defences are referred to as consent to harm
- Harder to succeed under *volenti* than under contributory negligence
- In contributory negligence there is an apportioning of blame, whereas with *volenti* no blame is attached to the defendant
- There are obvious difficulties in accurately apportioning blame, so *volenti* simpler
- *Volenti* not available under the Road Traffic Act because of the availability of compulsory third party insurance, whereas contributory negligence is commonly used in road traffic accidents

KEY FACTS

***Volenti non fit injuria* (voluntary acceptance of risk)**	**Case**
A defendant will not be liable where there is a voluntary assumption of risk.	
So for the defence to succeed there must be: • knowledge of the precise risk involved • exercise of free choice by claimant • voluntary acceptance of the risk.	*Stermer v Lawson* [1977] *Smith v Baker* [1891] *ICI v Shatwell* [1965]
Engaging in a rescue need not mean that there is voluntary conduct.	*Haynes v Harwood* [1935]
A lack of actual danger may lead to a successful claim.	*Cutler v United Dairies* [1933]
Contributory negligence	**Case**
Originally a complete defence removing all liability. Now the Law Reform (Contributory Negligence) Act 1945 means that damages may be reduced where there is contributory negligence.	*Butterfield v Forester* [1809]
The defendant must show that: • the claimant has failed to take reasonable care of himself; and • this caused the injury or damage.	*Sayers v Harlow UDC* [1958] *Jones v Livox Quarries* [1952]
The defence is common in motoring accidents where claimants fail to wear seat belts.	*Froom v Butcher* [1976]
Or where motor cycle passengers fail to wear crash helmets.	*O'Connell v Jackson* [1972]
Even 100 per cent reduction is possible in the case of breaches of statutory duties.	*Jayes v IMI (Kynoch) Ltd* [1985]
Illegality *(ex turpi causa non oritur actio)*	**Case/statute**
General principle that a person should bear the consequences of acting illegally.	*Lewis-Ranwell v G4S Health Services (UK) Ltd, Devon Partnership NHS Trust, Devon County Council*, [2026] UKSC 3 *Gray v Thames Train UKHL* [2009] 33 *Henderson v Dorset Healthcare University NHS Foundation Trust* [2020] UKSC 43

(Continued)

(Continued)

Courts aware of potential for injustice. Illegality and driving.	*Revill v Newbery* [1996] *Pitts v Hunt* [1990] 3 ALL ER 344 *Delaney v Pickett* [2011] EWCA Civ 1532
Cases decided on circumstances relevant to the particular case.	*Lewis-Ranwell v G4S Health Services (UK) Ltd, Devon Partnership NHS Trust, Devon County Council* [2026] UKSC 2 *Clunis v Camden & Islington AHA* [1998]; *Euro-Diam v Bathurst* [1988]
Inevitable accident	**Case**
Rarely used.	
Defendant must show that despite taking all precautions the accident could not have been avoided.	*Fardon v Harcourt-Rivington* [1932]
Act of God	**Case**
Only relevant to –	*Rylands v Fletcher* [1868]
Necessity	**Case**
Tortious act will be excused provided defendant acted for the protection of himself or others – can extend to protection of property.	
Action must be prompted by reasonable perception of immediate and imminent danger.	
Statutory authority	**Case**
See discussion in relation to nuisance, breach of statutory duty and *Rylands v Fletcher*.	
Self-help	**Case**
Self-defence (see Chapter 13).	
Ejectment (see Chapter 8).	
Abatement (see Chapter 9).	

SUMMARY

There are many defences that are specific to individual torts – but there are also many general defences that could be applied to any torts:

- *Volenti non fit injuria* – means that there will be no liability to a person who voluntarily accepts a risk of harm – so must understand nature of risk and freely accept it.

- *Volenti* is a complete defence when the defendant is negligent and causes damage to the claimant but the claimant has voluntarily exposed himself to the risk of harm.
- The claimant must have understood the exact nature of the risk and voluntarily accepted the risk.
- The defence is particularly appropriate in the case of sport and medical treatment.
- Contributory negligence under the Law Reform (Contributory Negligence) Act 1945 – reduces damages to the extent that the claimant is responsible for his own harm – so claimant must fail to take proper care of himself and this is partly the cause of the damage suffered.
- Contributory negligence is a partial defence under Law Reform (Contributory Negligence) Act 1945 where damages are reduced to the extent to which the claimant is responsible for his own harm.
- The claimant must have failed to take reasonable care for his own safety and his failure to take care was a cause of the harm suffered.
- Illegality (*ex turpi causa no oritur actio*) – no claim possible where the damage occurs in a criminal venture to which the claimant is a party.
- Inevitable accident – no liability where the incident could not have been avoided and is pure accident.
- Act of God – basically involves the damage being caused by extreme weather conditions beyond the control of the claimant.
- Necessity – where the defendant's actions are prompted by imminent danger to himself or others.
- Statutory authority – if the activity is authorised by Parliament then it cannot lead to tortious liability.

Further reading

Gardner, J, 'Rethinking risk-taking: The death of volenti?' (2023) *82(1) The Cambridge Law Journal* 110–137.

Harvey, B, and Marston, J, 'Intoxication and claimants in negligence' (1999) *149 NLJ* 1004.

Lord Burrows the Illegality Defence after *Patel v Mirza*, The Professor Jill Poole Memorial Lecture 2022, Aston University, 24 October 2022.

Murray, J, *Street on Torts* (11th edn, Butterworths, 2003), Chapter 15.

Stark, F, and Tofaris, S, 'Illegality and insanity in tort law' (2024) *83(3) The Cambridge Law Journal* 429–432.

6

Negligence: Specific duty situations

AIMS AND OBJECTIVES

After reading this chapter you should be able to:

- Apply the criteria for establishing the existence of a duty of care in relation to nervous shock (psychiatric damage)
- Illustrate the restrictions on the scope of the duty
- Identify the criteria for imposing liability for pure economic loss
- Explain the reasons for the reluctance for imposing liability for pure economic loss
- Illustrate the criteria for imposing liability for economic loss caused by a negligent misstatement
- Distinguish the limited circumstances in which the law is prepared to impose liability for a failure to act
- Critically analyse each of these novel duty situations
- Apply the law on each duty to factual situations and reach conclusions as to liability

We have already seen how the tort of negligence is based on the existence of a duty of care owed by the defendant to the claimant. The law has developed over time to include many instances where a duty of care exists.

There are numerous straightforward relationships where we might naturally expect a duty of care to exist. These would include such relationships as those between fellow motorists, between doctor and patient, between employer and employee, between manufacturers of products and their consumers and, of course, there are many others. We have already seen examples in the case law of all of these.

However, there are also certain situations that are less obvious that have had to be considered by the courts where the duty arises more from specific circumstances than because of the relationship between the parties. They have proved to be more controversial but in some of them the

DOI: 10.4324/9781003202417-6

courts have held that a duty of care does in fact exist. For these situations, the test for establishing a duty of care cannot be determined by using the general test for establishing a duty as now restated in *Robinson*. Rather, specific tests have to be used in these specific scenarios to determine whether a duty of care exists. Once it is determined that a duty of care does exist, the analysis will continue it will need to be determined whether there has been breach of that duty and whether that breach caused the loss complained of.

The specific duty situations include the following examples.

6.1 Nervous shock (psychiatric injury)

6.1.1 The historical background

Psychiatric harm is a form of personal injury but because it impacts one's mental well-being rather than physical, it has been an area of negligence subject to uncertain development. The extent to which liability has been imposed has expanded or contracted according to:

- The state of medical knowledge, i.e. psychiatric medicine and the recognition of psychiatric disorders, has developed dramatically over the past 100 years.
- Policy considerations on the part of judges, particularly the 'floodgates' argument, that to impose liability in a particular situation may lead to a rush of claims and so should be avoided whatever the justice of the case; this has had the effect of operating particularly harshly on secondary victims.

Actions failed in the last century for three specific reasons:

- Because of the state of medical knowledge, psychiatric illness or injury was not properly recognised so there could be no duty if the type of damage concerned was not recognised.
- Another problem of course was the fear that a person making such a claim could actually be faking the symptoms.
- Finally, there was the 'floodgates' argument, that once one claim was accepted it would lead to a multitude of claims.

CASE EXAMPLE

Victoria Railway Commissioners v Coultas [1888] 13 App Cas 222

Nervous shock resulting from involvement in a train crash did not give rise to liability, not least because of the 'floodgates' argument.

Even from the start there were two aspects to determining whether liability should be imposed:

- First, the injury alleged must conform to judicial attitudes of what constitutes nervous shock, a recognised psychiatric disorder.
- Second, the person claiming to have suffered nervous shock must fall into a category accepted by the courts as being entitled to claim.

6.1.2 Recognised psychiatric illness

The duty is to avoid causing psychiatric harm. In what circumstances will a duty of care be imposed to avoid causing psychiatric harm?

First, the claim must involve an actual, recognised psychiatric condition capable of resulting from the shock of the incident and recognised as having long-term effects. It is sometimes referred to as a 'medically recognised psychiatric illness' that the claimant has to establish. There needs to be some threshold level of psychological harm that must be exceeded to justify an award of damages. This is to say, mere grief, sorrow, distress, nightmares or upset, will not suffice and the claim cannot progress. Examples of medically recognised illness include post-traumatic stress disorder or depression.

CASE EXAMPLE

Reilly v Merseyside Regional Health Authority [1994] 23 BMLR 26

The court would not impose liability when a couple became trapped in a lift as the result of negligence and suffered insomnia and claustrophobia after they were rescued. These could not be classed as recognised psychiatric illnesses.

Psychiatry is now well advanced and in modern times conditions such as post-traumatic stress disorder, depression and acute anxiety syndrome would be recognised. However, the courts would be reluctant to allow a claim purely for a temporary upset such as grief or distress or fright because it is accepted that these are common problems that periodically we all suffer from.

CASE EXAMPLE

Tredget v Bexley Health Authority [1994] 5 Med LR 178

The parents of a child born with serious injuries following medical negligence and then dying two days later successfully claimed for nervous shock. The result of the case is perhaps surprising but the court held that they did indeed suffer from psychiatric injuries despite the defendants' argument that their condition was no more than profound grief.

The courts in recent times have been prepared to accept a claim that is partly caused by grief and partly by the severe shock of the event.

CASE EXAMPLE

Vernon v Bosely (No. 1) [1997] 1 All ER 577

Here a father had witnessed his children being drowned in a car negligently driven by their nanny. His claim was successful and he recovered damages for nervous shock that was held to be partly the result of pathological grief and bereavement, but partly also the consequence of the trauma of witnessing the events.

6.1.3 The development of a test of liability

Originally claims were first allowed purely on the basis of foreseeability of a real and immediate fear of personal danger (the so-called *Kennedy* test) so that the class of possible claimants was at first very limited.

CASE EXAMPLE

Dulieu v White & Sons [1901] 2 KB 669

The court accepted a claim when a woman suffered nervous shock after a horse and van that had been negligently driven burst through the window of a pub where she was washing glasses. She was able to recover damages because she had been put in fear for her own safety.

This limitation was later extended to include a claim for nervous shock suffered as the result of witnessing traumatic events involving close family members and therefore fearing for their safety.

CASE EXAMPLE

Hambrook v Stokes Bros [1925] 1 KB 141

A woman recovered damages for nervous shock when she saw a runaway lorry going downhill towards where she had left her three children and then heard that there had indeed been an accident involving a child. The court disapproved the *Kennedy* test and considered that it would be unfair not to compensate a mother who had feared for the safety of her children when she could have claimed if she only feared for her own safety.

This principle was even extended at one point to include shock suffered from witnessing events involving close but not related people and fearing for the safety of the victim.

CASE EXAMPLE

Dooley v Cammell Laird & Co [1951] 1 Lloyd's Rep 271

A crane driver claimed successfully for nervous shock when he saw a load fall and thought that workmates underneath would have been injured.

Indeed claims have even been allowed where harm to the person with whom the close tie exists would be impossible.

CASE EXAMPLE

Owens v Liverpool Corporation [1933] 1 KB 394

Here relatives of a deceased person recovered damages for nervous shock when the coffin fell out of the hearse that they were following.

One restriction on this development was to prevent a party from recovering who was not within the 'area of impact' of the event.

CASE EXAMPLE

King v Phillips [1953] 1 QB 429

A mother suffered nervous shock when from 70 yards away she saw a taxi reverse into her small child's bicycle and presumed him to be injured. Her claim failed because the court said she was too far away from the incident and outside the range of foresight of the defendant.

An alternative measure to the area of impact test is whether the claimant falls within the 'area of shock'.

CASE EXAMPLE

Bourhill v Young [1943] AC 92

A pregnant Edinburgh fishwife claimed to have suffered nervous shock after getting off a tram, hearing the impact of a crash involving a motorcyclist, and later seeing blood on the road, after which she gave birth to a stillborn child. The House of Lords held that, as a stranger to the motorcyclist, she was outside the area of foreseeable shock or the zone of danger and her claim failed.

Successful claims for nervous shock have also been made even where the traumatic event is not an accident of some kind, as is usually the case in such claims. The same principle of reasonable foresight has therefore allowed for recovery in nervous shock claims even where the principal damage was to property rather than involving injury to or the safety of a person.

CASE EXAMPLE

Attia v British Gas [1987] 3 All ER 455

A woman who witnessed her house burning down when she arrived home was able to claim successfully for nervous shock. She was within the area of impact. The claim was said to be within the reasonable foresight of the contractors who negligently installed her central heating, causing the fire.

6.1.4 The duty of care and type of claimant

In the very important and controversial case following the Hillsborough disaster the House of Lords reviewed all aspects of the duty. The 'floodgates argument' was clearly an important feature of their deliberations and the House identified a fairly restrictive set of circumstances in which a claim for nervous shock might succeed.

CASE EXAMPLE

Alcock v Chief Constable of South Yorkshire **[1992] 1 AC 310**

At the start of a football match police allowed a large crowd of supporters into a caged pen as the result of which 96 people in the stand suffered crush injuries and were killed. Since the match was being televised much of the disaster was shown on live television. A number of claims for nervous shock were made. These varied between those present or not present at the scene, those with close family ties to the dead and those who were merely friends. The House of Lords refused all of the claims and identified the factors important to consider in determining whether a party might recover. These were:

- The proximity of the relationship with a party who was a victim of the incident – a successful claim would depend on the existence of a close tie of love and affection with the victim, or presence at the scene as a rescuer.
- The proximity in time and space to the negligent incident – there could be a claim in respect of an incident or the immediate aftermath that was witnessed or experienced directly, there could be none where the incident was merely reported.
- The proximity of perception of the cause of the nervous shock – the court accepted that this must be the result of witnessing or hearing the horrifying event or the immediate aftermath.

Lord Ackner at 369 identified these restrictions as follows, although see *Paul v Wolverhampton* [2024] UKSC 1 below on the requirement of sudden shock which is no longer required:

JUDGMENT

'Because "shock" in its nature is capable of affecting such a wide range of persons, Lord Wilberforce in *McLoughlin v O'Brian* [1983] concluded that there was a real need for the law to place some limitation upon the extent of admissible claims and in this context he considered that there were three elements inherent in any claim.

1 The class of persons whose claims should be recognised.
Lord Wilberforce . . . contrasted the closest of family ties – parent and child and husband and wife – with that of the ordinary bystander. As regards [the former] the justifications for admitting such claims is the presumption, which I would accept as being rebuttable, that the love and affection normally associated with persons in those relationships is such that a defendant ought reasonably

contemplate that they may be so closely and directly affected by his conduct as to suffer shock resulting in psychiatric illness. While as a generalisation more remote relatives and friends can reasonably be expected not to suffer illness from the shock, there can well be relatives and friends whose relationship is so close and intimate that their love and affection for the victim is comparable . . .

2 The proximity of the plaintiff to the accident.
It is accepted that the proximity to the accident must be close both in time and space. Direct and immediate sight or hearing of the accident is not required. It is reasonably foreseeable that injury by shock can be caused to a plaintiff, not only through the sight or hearing of the event, but of its immediate aftermath.

3 The means by which the shock is caused.
Lord Wilberforce concluded that the shock must come through sight or hearing of the event or its immediate aftermath.'

The case then identifies the following classes of claimants who will be successful and those who will not:

- Primary victims – those who suffer psychiatric harm because they were physically injured because of the defendant's negligence.
- Primary victims – those who suffer psychiatric harm because they were at risk of being injured because of the defendant's negligence but are physically unharmed.
- Secondary victims – those who do not suffer any physical injury themselves but witness injury to others with whom they have a close tie of love and affection, caused by the defendant's negligence.

6.1.5 Duty of care owed to primary victims

Primary victims include those who are directly involved in the event so are present at the scene and may suffer physical injury or fear for their own personal safety. It was explained further in *Alock* by Lord Oliver that primary victims fall into those cases in which the injured claimant is involved, either mediately or immediately, as a participant. The following are examples of such participants.

Someone who fears for their own safety

A primary victim may be a participant as someone who fears for their own safety. This was the situation in the case of *Dulieu v White* [1901] 2 KB 669 where the woman could have been hurt by the horse coming through the glass window, and did in fact suffer a miscarriage as a result of the defendant's negligence.

The primary victim need not suffer any physical injury. It is sufficient that they are present at the event causing the shock and are at risk of harm. Neither will it matter that the primary victim is more susceptible to shock. This contrasts with secondary victims who are compared with 'a man of ordinary phlegm' and will not be compensated if they are more likely to suffer psychiatric illness. The rules on both were considered in *Page v Smith* [1996] 3 All ER 272 considered below.

Rescuers

A defendant will owe a duty of care to those who are induced to go to the rescue of those directly injured or threated by the defendant's negligence and are injured as a result. Rescuers may well of course be primary victims and at risk in the circumstances of the incident causing the nervous shock. Traditionally, in any case courts tended to treat professional rescuers as primary victims. That a rescuer is able to recover when suffering nervous shock can be seen in the following case.

CASE EXAMPLE

***Chadwick v British Railways Board* [1967] 1 WLR 912**

When two trains crashed in a tunnel a man who lived nearby was asked because of his small size to crawl into the wreckage to give injections to trapped passengers. He was able to claim successfully for the anxiety neurosis he suffered as a result. This was largely explained on the basis that he was a primary victim, at risk himself in the circumstances.

Usually only professional rescuers will be able to claim or those present at the scene or the immediate aftermath.

CASE EXAMPLE

***Hale v London Underground* [1992] 11 BMLR 81**

A fireman who had been involved in the rescue of victims at the King's Cross fire, successfully claimed for post-traumatic stress disorder that he suffered.

However, claims for shock suffered at the scene of disasters will not be successful in the case of those people considered only to be bystanders.

CASE EXAMPLE

***McFarlane v E E Caledonia* [1994] 2 All ER 1**

A person who was helping to receive casualties from the *Piper Alpha* oil rig failed in his claim because he was classed as a mere bystander rather than a rescuer at the scene.

The law has always made a distinction between rescuers or people who are at risk in the incident and those who are merely bystanders and have no claim. This point goes back as far as *Bourhill v Young* [1943] AC 92.

There has been a more restrictive attitude to claims by members of the emergency services for psychiatric injury suffered while dealing with the aftermath of a disaster in the course of their duties. A rescuer will only be able to claim where he is a genuine 'primary victim'.

CASE EXAMPLE

White v Chief Constable of South Yorkshire [1998] 1 All ER 1, HL

Police officers who claimed to have suffered post-traumatic stress disorder following their part in the rescue operation at the Hillsborough disaster were denied a remedy by the House of Lords. The reasoning seems to be that they did not actually put themselves at risk, and that public policy prevented them from recovering when the relatives of the deceased in the disaster could not.

An alternative the courts have been willing to consider is that a rescuer can also claim as a secondary victim. However, this will only be possible where the rescuer conforms to all of the requirements for secondary victims laid out in *Alcock*. So, the fact that a person can prove that they are a rescuer is insufficient on its own to claim unless they can also prove that they are either a genuine primary victim or a genuine secondary victim.

CASE EXAMPLE

Greatorex v Greatorex [2000] 4 All ER 769

Here a fire officer attended the scene of an accident caused by the negligence of his son. When he was required to attend to his son he claimed afterwards to suffer nervous shock. The court would not accept the claim because of the conflict that it would cause between family members, but had the son not been the cause of the accident a claim may have been possible in the circumstances.

Involuntary participants

This is where the negligent act of the defendant has put the claimant in the position of being, or of thinking that they are the involuntary cause of another's death or injury and the illness complained of stems from the shock to the claimant of the consciousness of this supposed fact. The question in these scenarios is whether, the injury of that type to that claimant was or was not reasonably foreseeable.

One such example has already been discussed above in the case of *Dooley v Cammell Laird & Co.* A further example can be seen in the next case:

CASE EXAMPLE

Stephen Monk v PC Harrington UK Ltd [2008] EWHC 1879 (QB)

The claimant helped two workers who were injured when a platform fell on them during the building of Wembley Stadium. The court denied him damages for psychiatric injury. While the court accepted that the man did act as a rescuer, it would not accept his argument that he was a primary victim because he felt that he had caused the accident as he was responsible for supervision of the platform that fell. The court felt that he was unlikely to have believed at any time that he was in danger.

However, the question of who qualifies as a rescuer and will be able to recover damages over who is an involuntary participant has some overlap as demonstrated in the following case.

CASE EXAMPLE

Duncan v British Coal [1990] 1 All ER 540

There was surprisingly no liability where a miner saw a close colleague crushed in a roof fall that was the fault of the employers, and tried unsuccessfully to resuscitate him.

CASE EXTRACT

In the case extract below a significant section of the judgment has been reproduced in the left-hand column. Individual points arising from the judgment are briefly explained in the right-hand column. Read the extract including the commentary in the right-hand column and complete the exercise that follows this section.

Extract adapted from the judgment in *Page v Smith* [1995] 2 All ER 736	
Facts	
The claimant was involved in a minor car collision which was through the defendant's negligence. While the claimant suffered no physical injury, he suffered in consequence of the accident a recurrence of myalgic encephalomyelitis (ME). The House of Lords held that the defendant did owe the claimant a duty of care to avoid this injury.	*The significant facts were: the defendant was negligent while no physical injury was suffered the claimant suffered a recurrence of a psychiatric injury.*
Judgment	
LORD LLOYD	
This is the fourth occasion on which the House has been called on to consider 'nervous shock'. On the three previous occasions, *Bourhill v Young* [1943] AC 92, *McLoughlin v O'Brian* [1983] 1 AC 410 and *Alcock v Chief Constable of South Yorkshire Police* [1992] 1 AC 310, the [claimants] were, in each case, outside the range of foreseeable physical injury . . .	*Lord Lloyd recognises the significance of foreseeable physical injury to a successful claim.*
In all these cases the [claimant] was the secondary victim of the defendant's negligence. He or she was in the position of a spectator or bystander. In the present case, by contrast, the [claimant] was a participant. He was himself directly involved in the accident, and well within the range of foreseeable physical injury. He was the primary victim. This is thus the first occasion on which your Lordships have had to decide whether, in such a case, the foreseeability of physical injury is enough to enable the [claimant] to recover damages for nervous shock . . .	*Previous House of Lords appeals failed because they involved secondary victims – but who ranked as mere bystanders.* Page *is first House of Lords case involving a primary victim.*

(*Continued*)

Though the distinction between primary and secondary victims is a factual one, it has, as will be seen, important legal consequences. So the classification of all nervous shock cases under the same head may be a misleading one . . .	*Question is whether foreseeability of physical injury is enough for claim for psychiatric injury only.*
[T]he peculiarity of the present case is that [the claimant] suffered no . . . physical injury of any kind. But as a direct result of the accident he suffered a [recurrence] of an illness or condition known variously as ME, CFS or PVFS, from which he had previously suffered in mild form on occasions, but which, since the accident, has become an illness of 'chronic intensity and permanency' . . .	*Important to distinguish between primary victims and secondary victims because consequences are different.*
We now know that the [claimant] escaped without external injury. Can it be the law that this makes all the difference? Can it be the law that the fortuitous absence of foreseeable physical injury means that a different test has to be applied? Is it to become necessary, in ordinary personal injury claims, where the [claimant] is the primary victim, for the court to concern itself with different 'kinds' of injury?	*Critical fact is that Page suffered no physical injury – and only a* recurrence *of a psychiatric injury.*
Suppose in the present case, the [claimant] had been accompanied by his wife, just recovering from a depressive illness, and that she had suffered a cracked rib, followed by an onset of psychiatric illness. Clearly, she would have recovered damages for her illness, since it is conceded that the defendant owed the occupants of the car a duty not to cause physical harm. Why should it be that necessary to ask a different question, or apply a different test, in the case of the [claimant]? Why should it make any difference that the physical illness that the [claimant] undoubtedly suffered as a result of the accident operated through the medium of the mind, or of the nervous system, without physical injury? If he had suffered a heart attack, it cannot be doubted that he would have recovered damages for pain and suffering, even though he suffered no broken bones. It would have been no answer that he had a weak heart.	*For primary victims the type of injury suffered does not matter as long as some type of injury is foreseen.*
Foreseeability of psychiatric injury remains a crucial ingredient when the [claimant] is a secondary victim, for the very reason that the secondary victim is almost always outside the area of physical impact, and therefore outside the range of foreseeable physical injury. But where the [claimant] is the primary victim of the defendant's negligence, the nervous shock cases, by which I mean the cases following on from *Bourhill v Young,* are not in point. Since the defendant was admittedly under a duty of care not to cause the [claimant] foreseeable physical injury, it was unnecessary to ask whether he was under a separate duty of care not to cause foreseeable psychiatric injury.	*But psychiatric injury must be foreseeable for secondary victims.*

(*Continued*)

[I]n claims by secondary victims . . . the courts have, as a matter of policy, rightly insisted on a number of control mechanisms. Otherwise, a negligent defendant might find himself being made liable to all the world . . . foreseeability of injury by shock is not enough. The law also requires a degree of proximity . . . not only . . . to the event in time and space, but also proximity of relationship [with] the primary victim . . . A further control mechanism is that the secondary victim will only recover damages for nervous shock if the defendant should have foreseen injury by shock to a person of normal fortitude or 'ordinary phlegm'.	*Claims by secondary victims have extra controls because of policy considerations.*
None of these mechanisms are required in the case of primary victims. Since liability depends on foreseeability of physical injury, there could be no question of the defendant finding himself liable to all the world. Proximity of relationship cannot arise, and proximity in time and space goes without saying. Nor in the case of a primary victim is it appropriate to ask whether he is a person of 'ordinary phlegm'. In the case of physical injury there is no such requirement. The negligent defendant, or more usually his insurer, takes his victim as he finds him. The same should apply in the case of psychiatric injury. There is no difference in principle . . . between an eggshell skull and an eggshell personality. Since the number of potential claims is limited by the nature of the case, there is no need to impose any further limit by reference to a person of ordinary phlegm. Nor can I see any justification for doing so.	Alcock *criteria.* *Also must be of normal phlegm and fortitude.* *But no such controls for primary victims.* *And eggshell skull rule applies to primary victims.*

KEY POINTS FROM *PAGE V SMITH*

- Lord Lloyd identifies and confirms that it is essential first to distinguish between primary and secondary victims because different rules apply.
- The case confirms the existing definition of primary victims:
  - that there is liability to a person present at the scene and suffering physical injury as well as psychiatric injury;
  - there is also liability to a person present at the scene and fearing for his own safety;
  - but only if suffering from a recognised psychiatric injury;
  - the definition of foreseeable harm for a primary victim needs only foresight of some injury.
- The case also represents a development in the law because:
  - it does not have to be physical harm – and there is no reason to separate out physical and psychiatric harm;
  - the application of the 'thin skull' rule to nervous shock in the case of primary victims;

- this contrasts with the requirement of 'reasonable phlegm and fortitude' for secondary victims;
- and there is no application of hindsight in assessing claims for primary victims.

ACTIVITY

Apply the above principles in the following factual situation to determine in each case whether the claimant is a primary victim or a secondary victim or a mere bystander and how likely they are to succeed in the circumstances:

Through the negligent maintenance of its premises by his employer's, Witless Engineering, Victor is badly injured when a section of steel staircase and walkway collapses on him. He dies two hours later in hospital from his very serious crush injuries.

Consider the possibility of each of the following succeeding if they claim against Witless Engineering for psychiatric damage (nervous shock):

a Ali, Victor's closest friend, who is present in the factory at the time of the accident, and sees the staircase and walkway collapse on to Victor from his machine on the other side of the factory. Ali suffers post-traumatic stress disorder as a result.

b Bernard, Victor's son, who also works in the factory on the machine next to Ali and who suffers grief after seeing the extent of Victor's injuries.

c Cath, Victor's mother, who is on holiday at the time of the accident, and is told about her son's death ten days later on her return to England, and who suffers severe depression as a result.

d Denzil, a fire officer who cut Victor from the wreckage. At all times there was a danger that more of the walkway would collapse and so it was vital that Denzil cut Victor from the wreckage as quickly as possible for Victor to have any chance of surviving. Denzil suffers post-traumatic stress disorder as a result.

One consequence of the application of the 'thin skull' rule in *Page v Smith* is that a psychiatric injury that follows a physical injury will rarely be considered unforeseeable and therefore too remote a consequence of the breach.

CASE EXAMPLE

Simmons v British Steel [2004] UKHL 20

Following an industrial injury caused by his employer's negligence the claimant suffered a worsening of his psoriasis, a stress-related skin disease, and of a depressive illness, also leading to a personality change. This resulted from his anger at his employer's lack of apology and lack of support, rather than from the injury itself. However, the court imposed liability for both types of injury even though, as the court admitted, the psychological injuries were not reasonably foreseeable, because the claimant was a primary victim.

The following case demonstrates the significance of whether a claimant is classified as a primary or secondary victim as there are a greater number of hurdles to overcome as a secondary victim.

CASE EXAMPLE

YAH v Medway NHS Foundation Trust [2018] EWHC 2964

The claimant's daughter was born brain damaged after a traumatic birth as a result of the defendant's negligence. The baby required an emergency C-section, intubation and resuscitation amongst other help. The claimant claimed for psychiatric injury but was met with the challenge that she had not suffered shock as a result of the event or its immediate aftermath.

The trouble with this claim was that as a secondary victim, the claimant has to satisfy the *Alcock* criteria and as this case was decided well before *Paul*, the claimant also had to show that she suffered psychiatric harm caused by shock. As a primary victim, she did not have to satisfy these criteria. So the claimant argued that she is a primary victim and since the baby was unborn at the time of the event, the mother and baby were one and the same legal person. The claimant therefore suffered personal injury which caused the psychiatric harm as a primary victim. It was considered whether shock needs to be established in the same way that it needs to for secondary victims, this was dealt with swiftly by applying the decision of *Page v Smith*, namely that there is no requirement for a primary victim to show that the psychiatric injury they have suffered was caused by shock. This case further reiterates that it is far easier to establish a claim as a primary victim than it is as a secondary victim where the criteria are more stringent and numerous by comparison.

6.1.6 Duty of care owed to secondary victims

These are people who are not primary victims of the incident but who are passive and unwilling witnesses of injury caused to the primary victims. Those who fall into this category are referred to as secondary victims. For secondary victims to bring a claim they need to meet the criteria set out in *Alcock* often referred to as the control mechanisms or proximity criteria:

- Proximity of relationship with the primary victim;
- Proximity in time and space to the scene of the event;
- Proximity of perception (or its immediate aftermath) of the death or extreme danger, or injury to the primary victim.

A further requirement set in *Alcock* in addition to the above was that the injury for which damages were claimant arose from the sudden and unexpected shock to the claimant's nervous system. However, since the Supreme Court decision in *Paul* this is no longer needed.

Proximity of relationship

Lord Justice Parker in *Alcock* explained at 359, that:

JUDGMENT

'It can in my view only be on the basis that, normally, the parent-child and the husband-wife relationship can be presumed to be so close that fear for the child or spouse can be reasonably foreseen by the wrongdoer as likely to result in nervous shock to a parent or spouse of ordinary phlegm who witnesses or comes upon the immediate aftermath of catastrophe involving, or which appears likely to involve, the child or other spouse. This however is a presumption and is not based on expert evidence as to the susceptibility of parents or spouses of ordinary phlegm to suffer shock followed by psychiatric illness from such situations.'

This is to say that a close tie of love and affection can be presumed to exist in the case of spouses, a fiancée, parents and children but not so in the case of siblings. In all other cases such as grandparents, aunts, uncles and siblings, a claimant would need to prove a tie of close love and affection; failure to prove this is what led to claims failing in *Alcock* even where the primary victim was a close relation.

In *Alcock* itself Ackner LJ at 406 held:

JUDGMENT

'The quality of brotherly love is well known to differ widely – from Cain and Abel to David and Jonathan . . . [the] claim was not presented upon the basis that there was such a close and intimate relationship between them, as gave rise to that very special bond of affection which would make his shock-induced psychiatric illness reasonably foreseeable by the defendant . . . there was no evidence to establish the necessary proximity which would make his claim reasonably foreseeable . . .'

Lord Justice Ackner at 402 explored why there is a difference in treatment between these relations and considers the position of bystanders who are completely unrelated to the primary victim but witness an exceptionally horrifying event.

JUDGMENT

'I respectfully share the difficulty expressed by Atkin LJ in *Hambrook v Stokes Brothers* [1925] 1 KB 141, 158–159 – how do you explain why the duty is confined to the case of parent or guardian and child and does not extend to other relations of life also involving intimate associations; and why does it not eventually extend to bystanders? As regards the latter category, while it may be very difficult to envisage a case of a stranger, who is not actively and foreseeably involved in a disaster or its aftermath,

> other than in the role of rescuer, suffering shock-induced psychiatric injury by the mere observation of apprehended or actual injury of a third person in circumstances that could be considered reasonably foreseeable, I see no reason in principle why he should not, if in the circumstances, a reasonably strong-nerved person would have been so shocked. In the course of argument your Lordships were given, by way of an example, that of a petrol tanker careering out of control into a school in session and bursting into flames. I would not be prepared to rule out a potential claim by a passer-by so shocked by the scene as to suffer psychiatric illness.'

In *Bourhill v Young* [1943] AC 92 it will be recalled that the claimant who was alighting from a tram was not proximate to the motorcyclist. Of course if she had been crossing the road and was either struck by the motorcyclist or narrowly missed by him which caused her to fear for her personal safety, she may have fallen into the category of a primary victim.

Likewise in *McFarlane v E E Caledonia Ltd* [1994] 2 All ER 1, it was not reasonably foreseeable that a mere 'bystander' would suffer psychiatric illness in such circumstances and that a mere bystander by definition is not proximate to the primary victims.

Workmates who witness accidents involving their colleagues will not be able to claim because any ties are not close enough to involve foreseeable harm.

CASE EXAMPLE

Robertson and Rough v Forth Road Bridge Joint Board [1995] IRLR 251

Three workmates had been repairing the Forth Road Bridge during a gale. One of them was sitting on a piece of metal on a truck when a gust of wind blew him off the bridge and he was killed. His colleagues who witnessed this were unable to claim even though they were friends outside of work. They were held not to be primary victims and had insufficient ties of love and affection with the dead worker for injury to be foreseeable.

Proximity in time and space to the scene of the event

In *Alcock* which referenced *McLoughlin*, it was explained that the claimant must have witnessed injury to their loved one in close proximity both physically and temporally so that the shock come through sight or hearing the event or of its immediate aftermath.

As is explained further below in the context of the immediate aftermath, the shock must result from being present at the scene of the event or its immediate aftermath. So, for instance in *Alcock*, those who may have arrived on the scene of the incident were classified as lacking the necessary proximity of time and space. This is because there would have been time to absorb the shock of the situation and therefore they were not deemed to have been suffering sudden shock that would be generated by actually being there. This criterion is extended to take into account those arriving within the accepted immediate aftermath which accepts that in some exceptional cases, secondary victims can witness sudden shock when seeing the incident sometime after it occurred but the incident is sufficiently alike to when it first happened.

Indeed the courts have engaged in some fairly fine distinctions as to what can acceptably be called 'the immediate aftermath' in later cases. The widest point of expansion of liability came when the claimant was not present at the scene but was at the 'immediate aftermath'. Inevitably 'the meaning of immediate aftermath' has been open to an interpretation based on policy.

CASE EXAMPLE

McLoughlin v O'Brian [1982] 2 All ER 298, HL

A woman was summoned to a hospital about an hour after her children and husband were involved in a car crash. One child was dead, two were badly injured, all were in shock and they had not yet been cleaned up. The House of Lords held that since the relationship with the victims was sufficiently close and the woman was present at the 'immediate aftermath' she could claim. Lord Wilberforce identified a three-part test for secondary victims that was approved later in *Alcock v Chief Constable of South Yorkshire* [1992] 4 All ER 907.

CASE EXAMPLE

Taylor v Somerset HA [1993] 4 Med LR 34

The claimant's husband suffered a fatal heart attack while at work. She was told only that he had been taken to hospital and when she arrived at the hospital she was told that he was dead. She was so shocked that she would not believe he was dead until she identified his body in the mortuary. She later suffered a psychiatric illness and claimed against the hospital. Even though she was at the hospital within an hour her action failed. The court held that the actual purpose for her visit was to identify the body so that it was not to do with the cause of his death.

Essentially, the secondary victim has to show a close enough tie of love and affection to a victim of the incident, they must have witnessed the incident or its 'immediate aftermath' at close hand. The probable limit of this is in *McLoughlin v O'Brian* in relation to the immediate aftermath. In *Alcock* the judges were reluctant to allow claims where there was a of lack of proximity both in time and space to the incidents at Hillsborough and turned down claims from people who had identified bodies in the morgue sometime after the events of the match. The Court of Appeal decision in *Walters* which extended the remit of the immediate aftermath has now been overturned by the Supreme Court in *Paul* confirming that a secondary victim must have witnessed the accident or its immediate. Witnessing a medical crisis does not fall within the scope of the immediate aftermath.

CASE EXAMPLE

North Glamorgan NHS Trust v Walters [2002] EWCA Civ 1792

Doctors negligently failed to diagnose that a ten-month-old baby suffering from hepatitis required a liver transplant. His mother was reassured that he would be unlucky not to recover; however, he suffered a major fit in front of her. They were both then taken to a London hospital for the child to have a liver transplant and on arrival it was discovered that the child had irreversible and severe brain damage. The parents' permission was gained to switch off life support and the baby died minutes later in its mother's arms. The whole episode took 36 hours and the mother suffered pathological grief, recognised as a psychiatric illness, as a result, and sued successfully. The defendants appealed on the grounds that the psychiatric injury was not brought about as a result of witnessing a single shocking event. The Court of Appeal rejected this argument and held that the whole period from when the baby suffered the fit to when it died was 'a single horrifying event'. The trial judge was correct to conclude that the appreciation of the horror was sudden because seeing the fit, hearing that the baby was irreversibly brain damaged and the recommendation to end life support all had an immediate impact and were part of a continuous chain of events. The case could therefore be distinguished from those cases involving a gradual realisation of shocking consequences over a period of time.

Walters was decided on the basis that the claimant's experience was to be regarded as one entire event. This decision was also referred to in *Atkins v Seghal* [2003] EWCA Civ 697 where a mother was told of her daughter's death by a police officer but did not see the body until two hours later. The Court of Appeal accepted that this still represented the immediate aftermath.

In *Paul* on the question of whether the events in each of the cases could be regarded as one single event, the Supreme Court overturned the decision in *Walters* giving the following explanation at 120 and 121:

JUDGMENT

'It is clear that on the facts of *Walters* the brain damage and death of Mrs Walters' baby were not caused by an accident. It follows from our conclusion that a claimant cannot recover damages for personal injury as a secondary victim unless the claimant witnessed an accident (or its immediate aftermath) that, had this defence been raised in *Walters*, the claim should have failed. As the defence was not raised and in consequence was not considered either by the trial judge or by the Court of Appeal, *Walters* cannot be regarded as an authority which weighs against our conclusion . . . [T]he argument in *Walters* was preoccupied with whether Mrs Walters' experience was to be regarded as "a sudden appreciation by sight or sound of a horrifying event". We have explained why we do not consider that an appropriate test. We would therefore hold that *Walters* was wrongly decided on its facts and should not be followed.'

In an anomalous case the House of Lords was prepared to accept a claim for negligence causing nervous shock in circumstances where the claimant is a secondary victim, but the last two controls under *Alcock*, present at the event or its immediate aftermath and witnessing the event with own unaided senses, are arguably not satisfied.

CASE EXAMPLE

W v Essex and Another [2000] 2 All ER 237

The claimants were parents who also acted as specialist foster parents for a local authority. They agreed to foster a 15-year-old boy, having stated beforehand that they were not prepared to take a child with a record of or suspected of being a child abuser. In fact the boy had been cautioned in the past for indecent assault and was currently under investigation for rape. The boy then committed serious acts of sexual abuse against the claimants' children. The children brought negligence claims and the parents brought claims for psychiatric injury caused through the shock of discovering the abuse. The marriage eventually broke up and both parents suffered from depression. The Court of Appeal struck out the parents' claim on the ground that it would not be fair and reasonable on policy grounds to impose such a duty on the authority because of its implication for fostering arrangements. On eventual appeal, the House of Lords rejected the council's arguments that the parents were secondary victims who were neither near in time or space nor witnessed the shocking event, the abuse of their children. Lord Slynn left open the question of whether the parents could be classed as primary victims. He also considered that it was arguable whether or not the shock of learning of the abuse fell within the immediate aftermath or not, and that it was impossible to say that the psychiatric injuries in question fell outside of that which the law considers deserving of compensation. As a result the House of Lords was not prepared to strike out the claims of the parents.

No requirement to demonstrate sudden shock or horrifying event

A major control mechanism from both *McLoughlin* and *Alcock* in restricting claims by secondary victims, was that secondary victims had to establish that they experienced sudden shock of seeing their loved one in distress which caused the recognised psychiatric illness to develop. Whether a secondary victim must experience a sudden shock was explored in detail by the Supreme Court in *Paul* discussed further below. The Supreme Court held that a secondary victim does not need to demonstrate that their injury must have been caused by the a 'sudden shock' to the nervous system. Nor do they need to prove that the event perceived was 'horrifying'. Over time, both elements, sudden shock and appreciation of a horrifying event that causes the recognised psychiatric harm, had become intertwined with the proximity requirements and were given an elevated status in the *Liverpool Women's Hospital NHS Foundation Trust v Ronayne* [2015] EWCA Civ 588. In this case the victim underwent a hysterectomy at the appellant's hospital. Unfortunately, it was performed negligently which meant that the victim's health deteriorated rapidly and significantly in the days following the operation. Fortunately, the victim went on to make a full recovery even though this took some weeks. The respondent in this case was the victim's husband who watched his wife becoming extraordinarily ill. He claimed that he suffered PTSD consequent on the shock of seeing his wife's sudden deterioration. Initially the respondent was successful but the appellant appealed on two grounds:

a whether the events concerned were of a nature capable of founding a secondary victim case, i.e. were they in the necessary sense "horrifying"; and b whether the sudden appreciation of that event or those events, i.e. shock, caused the claimant's psychiatric illness.

The key question for the Court of Appeal was whether the event or events said were to be of a sufficiently horrifying character? Whether something is horrifying in this context must be assessed by objective standards and according to persons of ordinary fortitude or phlegm.

Lord Justice Tomlinson at 41:

JUDGMENT

'Furthermore what the Claimant saw on these two occasions was not in my judgment horrifying by objective standards. Both on the first occasion and on the second the appearance of the Claimant's wife was as would ordinarily be expected of a person in hospital in the circumstances in which she found herself. What is required in order to found liability is something which is exceptional in nature.'

The victim's husband upon seeing his wife in this distressed state did not suffer the requisite level of sudden shock in this case. Nor were there exceptional horrifying events that would cause sudden shock. Rather he suffered an accumulation over a period of time of more gradual assaults on the nervous system. These two points were reviewed in detail by the Supreme Court in *Paul* together with whether the event on which the secondary victim bases their claim has to be the first manifestation of injury.

Lord Leggatt and Lady Rose of the Supreme Court clarified the points on the requirements of sudden shock and horrifying events as follows at 78:

JUDGMENT

'Again, [the horrifying event] test is not one of the requirements established by *Alcock* and confirmed in *Frost*. In engrafting onto those requirements additional requirements of needing to prove that the claimant's injury was caused by the mechanism of a "sudden shock to the nervous system" and was a sufficiently "horrifying event", the law has in our opinion taken an unfortunate wrong turn which these appeals enable us to correct.'

Regarding the third point, this was considered in *Paul* at paragraph 113 where it was held that:

JUDGMENT

'We have discussed above three such criteria which have been applied or proposed: the "sudden shock", "horrifying event" and "first manifestation of damage" tests. For the reasons indicated, none of these, in our view, is an acceptable test. We have not been shown any cases in which comparable difficulties have arisen where the claim is based on presence at, and direct perception of, an accident.'

In *Paul*, the Supreme Court convened a panel of seven judges to deliver the landmark decision. This is the leading case on the position of secondary victims and provides clarity on the limits of the immediate aftermath doctrine as well as distinguishing between those cases which involved accidents and those which involve a medical crisis. If a claimant does not witness the accident but witnesses the medical crisis, e.g. if the claimant witnesses their loved one suffer a heart attack which was due to negligent medical care, are they able to claim as secondary victims? The answer given by the Supreme Court is no.

Paul involved three conjoined appeals. Each appeal had in common a negligent failure to diagnose and treat a life-threatening medical condition to which the primary victim in each appeal succumbed. The deterioration in health and ultimate death of the primary victim in shocking circumstances was witnessed by a close relative(s) who satisfied the requirement of having a close tie of love and affection but there was a considerable time lag between the alleged negligence and the deaths. The Supreme Court considered whether such a time lag could fall within the 'immediate aftermath' after reviewing in detail, the decision in *Taylor v A Novo (UK) Ltd* [2013] EWCA Civ 194. In *Taylor*, the claimant's mother was injured at work caused by her employer, the defendant. The claimant was recovering but three weeks later, she collapsed and died at home due to the injuries she had sustained in the accident at work. The claimant witnessed her mother die and as a result developed post-traumatic stress disorder. The claimant satisfied all but one of the *Alcock* criteria, namely she was not physically present at the scene of the accident nor involved in its immediate aftermath. The Court of Appeal explored whether this scenario would qualify as falling within the 'immediate aftermath'. The Court of Appeal decided that the relevant event was the original accident at work to which the claimant needed to be proximate and not, her mother's eventual death. There were two reasons given for this decision. First, if the decision were otherwise, and the mother had died some months or years after the original accident, and the claim were allowed, it would stretch the concept of immediate aftermath too far. Second, there was a reluctance to extend the scope of liability to secondary victims considerably beyond what was intended, and that is only something that would be undertaken by Parliament.

In *Paul*, common to all three cases is that the secondary victims witnessed a 'medical crisis' such as witnessing a death or injury of their loved one who were not involved in an accident. The Supreme Court had to determine whether witnessing a negligently caused medical crisis (or its aftermath) can in principle found a claim for damages by a secondary victim or whether such a claim can lie *only* where the triggering event is an accident (i.e. an unexpected event).

CASE EXAMPLE

Paul and another v Royal Wolverhampton NHS Trust [2024] UKSC 1

Paul v Wolverhampton

The claimants are the daughters of the deceased who were out shopping when they witnessed him collapse, hit his head and die. Some 14 months prior to this, the deceased was admitted to the defendant's hospital complaining of chest and jaw pain. He was given treatment by a cardiology registrar for acute coronary syndrome and it was recommended that he undergo echocardiography as an inpatient but he was discharged as echocardiography was not available. The claimants argued the defendants were negligent in failing to recognise their father's heart condition and failed to conduct an echocardiography which would have prevented him from suffering a fatal heart attack, which in turn would have prevented the claimants developing psychiatric illnesses from watching their father die in horrific and shocking circumstances.

Polmear v Royal Cornwall Hospital NHS Trust

The claimants' daughter Esmee had suffered from various episodes of difficulty in breathing and turning blue and had been monitored by a paediatrician who concluded that there was nothing to suggest an underlying abnormality. The day that Esmee died, she returned to school after a school trip during which she felt very unwell. When her father was called to the school he saw Esmee lying on the floor while a teacher was providing first aid which he also did. Esmee's mother arrived and saw members of staff attempting resuscitation but Esmee did not survive.

Both claimants developed post-traumatic stress disorder and major depression as a result of witnessing their daughter die in these circumstances. The defendant conceded that Esmee's condition (pulmonary veno-occlusive disease) should have been diagnosed earlier and that with proper diagnosis and management, she would not have died when she did.

Purchase v Dr Ahmed

The claimant is the mother of Evelyn Purchase so who died from extensive bilateral pneumonia with pulmonary abscesses. In January 2013, Evelyn visited her GP with acute sinusitis although she continued to feel unwell. Evelyn visited the GP again in March and was taken to an out-of-hours doctor by the claimant in April as Evelyn was struggling to walk and had trouble breathing. It is the claimant's case that Evelyn had severe pneumonia when seen by the defendant on 4 April 2013. A few days later when the claimant returned home, she found Evelyn lying motionless. When the claimant attempted resuscitation, blood and fluid came out of her mouth and nose. Evelyn had died. The claimant developed post-traumatic stress disorder, severe chronic anxiety and depression. The claimant argued that Evelyn had severe pneumonia when seen by the defendant in April and that there was a negligent failure properly to assess and treat Evelyn's symptoms and that, but for the alleged breaches, the events that the claimant witnessed, and which it is alleged caused her psychiatric illness, would have been avoided.

The Supreme Court held that the duty of care cannot be extended to include medical crises. The occurrence of an accident is integral to identify the category of claims by secondary victims arising from the accident and in defining the limits of such claims. Three reasons were given:

i An accident is a discrete event meaning that something happens at a particular time, at a particular place, in a particular way allowing there to be a level of certainty;

ii Witnessing an accident is likely to be a disturbing an upsetting event by comparison to witnessing an injury or illness of a family member which would be traumatic but variable;

iii It would be difficult to distinguish between primary and secondary victims in accident cases because it would be unclear whether the primary victim's psychiatric illness was caused by the fear of their own safety or that of others.

The Supreme Court's decision was undoubtedly driven by keeping the remit of such claims within limits and to avoid overexposure of liability of medical practitioners. This is explained further per Lord Leggatt and Lady Rose at 137 and 138:

JUDGMENT

Paul and another v Royal Wolverhampton NHS Trust [2024] UKSC 1

'It cannot be said that a doctor who treats a patient thereby enters into a doctor-patient relationship with any member of the patient's family and thereby assumes responsibility for their health. As regards other factors relevant to whether the necessary relationship of proximity exists, the extent of the control which a doctor may be seen as having over the risk of injury to members of the patient's family and the directness of the causal link between the doctor's negligence and the materialisation of that risk will depend upon the particular facts of the case. In a case such as *Paul*, it may be happenstance whether, if the patient's untreated coronary artery disease leads at some unpredictable future time to a cardiac arrest, this happens to occur in the presence of close family members or elsewhere, such as at the person's workplace . . . Common to all cases of this kind, however, is a fundamental question about the nature of the doctor's role and the purposes for which medical care is provided to a patient. We are not able to accept that the responsibilities of a medical practitioner, and the purposes for which care is provided, extend to protecting members of the patient's close family from exposure to the traumatic experience of witnessing the death or manifestation of disease or injury in their relative. To impose such a responsibility on hospitals and doctors would go beyond what, in the current state of our society, is reasonably regarded as the nature and scope of their role.'

Proximity of perception

The proximity of perception of the cause of the nervous shock – the court accepted that this must be the result of witnessing or hearing the horrifying event or the immediate aftermath.

It is helpful to read the Court of Appeal judgment in *Alcock* to understand this criterion in further detail [1991] 3 All ER 88.

Nolan LJ, at 122 expressed that he

JUDGMENT

'would not exclude the possibility in principle of a duty of care extending to the watchers of a television programme. For example, if a publicity seeking organisation made arrangements for a party of children to go up in a balloon, and for the event to be televised so that their parents could watch, it would be hard to deny that the organisers were under a duty to avoid mental injury to the parents as well as physical injury to the children, and that there would be a breach of that duty if through some careless act or omission the balloon crashed. But that would be a different case.'

Alcock claims were defeated because they exceeded the two hours accepted as immediate aftermath in *McLoughlin*.

Summary

Primary Victim	*Secondary Victim*
Recognised psychiatric harm	Recognised psychiatric harm
Foreseeability – foreseeable harm for a primary victim needs only foresight of some injury – normal fortitude rule does not apply – thin skull rule applies.	Foreseeability – the psychiatric illness must be reasonably foreseeable to a person of ordinary fortitude.
Claimant must be within the zone of danger.	There must be an 'accident' or external event.
No requirement of sudden shock	*Alcock* criteria: • Proximity of relationship • Proximity in time and space/immediate aftermath • Proximity of perception/immediate aftermath
	No requirement for sudden shock or horrifying event

CRITIQUING THE LAW

Consider whether the duty of care should be extended to include medical crises. Does the drive to protect medical professionals override the true victims who suffer trauma as a result of witnessing a medical crisis?

6.1.7 The problem of policy

From the foregoing it is apparent that the proximity requirements as expounded in *Alcock* are designed to control the type of claims that can successfully be put forward by secondary victims. This is further reinforced by the decision in *Paul*. This approach is largely due to policy reasons such as controlling the volume of cases. Unless it is a very clear case, the requirements for bringing a claim as a secondary victim are very strict and so the chances of successfully bringing a claim are very slim. Whether this should be changed is a point that is often mooted.

Clearly the area of recovery for psychiatric injury (nervous shock) has been subject to an erratic development. There is no doubt that secondary victims have been treated harshly by comparison to primary victims, although, taken the kind of harm suffered, they are just as likely to suffer harm. Even in the case of bystanders it seems that it is policy reasons rather than the foreseeability of harm that has led to a denial of liability.

Trindade comments that: '[I]t is generally recognised that the rules governing recovery for damages for nervous shock lack coherence, logic, justice and even plain common sense.' (*F A Trindade, 'Reformulation of the nervous shock rules' (2003) 179 LQR 204).*

6.1.8 Reform

The need for reform in the area has been identified by the Law Commission in its Report, Liability for Psychiatric Illness (Law Com. No. 249) in 1998. Its chief recommendations are:

- to retain the requirement of a close tie of love and affection to the primary victim in the case of secondary victims;
- to remove the requirements for secondary victims to show proximity in time and space, and that the event has been witnessed by the claimant's own unaided senses;
- that the injury should be accepted even where not caused by a sudden traumatic event.

The proposals seem to be much fairer. However, it was decided that there was no need to proceed with these recommendations as it was felt that any such changes should be left to the judiciary to develop through case law rather than the law in this area being codified. This is a tricky outcome as on the one hand, the judiciary seem to take a particularly stringent view of secondary victims and as it can be seen from the foregoing, it is notoriously difficult to

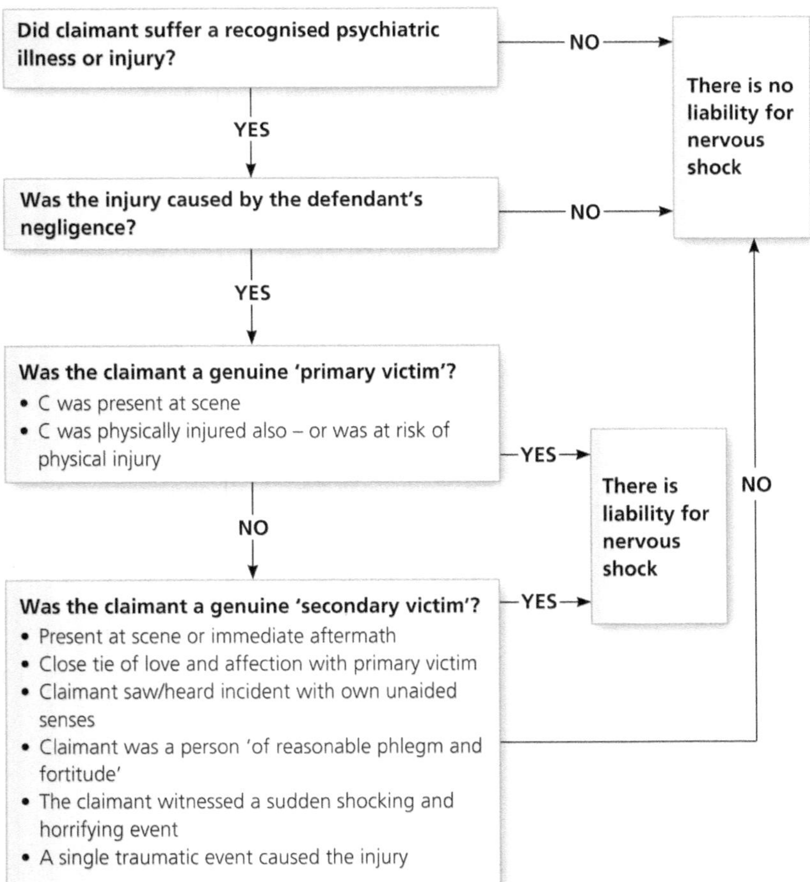

Figure 6.1 The means of determining liability for nervous shock.

bring about a successful claim as a secondary victim, but on the other hand there is a need to ensure that only claims that merit compensation for psychiatric harm are recognised otherwise there may be a flood of claims.

6.1.9 Rest of the action

Once it has been established that the claimant was owed a duty of care either as a primary or secondary victim, they must go on to establish whether the duty was breached and whether the breach caused the psychiatric illness. Whether the illness is too remote will be subject to *Page* if the claimant is a primary victim, otherwise the normal rules will apply. Finally, any valid defences should be considered.

ACTIVITY

Self-assessment questions

1 What exactly is meant by the term 'nervous shock'?
2 Why were courts originally reluctant to allow a claimant to recover for nervous shock, and why has this changed?
3 How broad is the definition of 'psychiatric injury'?
4 Has there been any logical kind of development to nervous shock?
5 What is the 'area of impact' and what is the 'area of shock'?
6 What is the difference between a 'primary victim' and a 'secondary victim'?
7 In what specific ways is a primary victim in a better position to claim than a secondary victim?
8 What are the three essential features of a successful claim by a secondary victim?
9 How did the courts originally define the meaning of 'immediate aftermath' in the decisions of cases?
10 To what extent is policy a determining factor in deciding whether or not a claim will succeed?
11 To what extent does *McLoughlin v O'Brian* fit in with other cases?
12 In what way is *Attia v British Gas* such a strange case?
13 In what ways does the case of *Paul v Wolverhampton* demonstrate major developments in the law on nervous shock?
14 What improvements would the Law Commission proposals have made to the law?

ACTIVITY

Multiple choice questions

In the following series of situations, in each case suggest which of the statements may raise a successful claim of nervous shock.

1

a Rajinder is present when his dog is run over by Andrew's negligent driving and suffers nervous shock.

b Rajinder hears his mother has been run over by Andrew's negligent driving three weeks ago and he suffers nervous shock.
c Rajinder is a passenger in a car when his friend Parminder, the driver, is killed by Andrew's negligent driving and Rajinder suffers nervous shock.
d Rajinder hears screams when Andrew crashes his car and Rajinder suffers nervous shock.

2

a Sally hears that a friend has died in a car crash caused by negligence and suffers from profound grief.
b Sally sees her friend killed in an accident at work caused by the employer's negligence and cannot sleep.
c Sally is called to the hospital to identify her mother's body after a car driver has negligently run her over and it makes her very angry.
d Sally is with her father when he drowns as a result of negligence when a ferry sinks and she suffers post-traumatic stress disorder.

KEY FACTS

The development of a claim for psychiatric injury	Case
Originally courts were unwilling to allow actions for nervous shock. This was because of the primitive state of psychiatric medicine. So the key requirement is always that the illness amounts to a recognised psychiatric disorder. An action was at first only possible if the claimant was also in physical danger. But this was then extended to include a person who was in the area of shock, i.e. witnessed the accident and had some close tie with the victim. The widest extent of the duty was to include witnessing the immediate aftermath of the accident. The event causing shock may be made up of a series of events lasting over quite a prolonged period of time but cannot include medical crises. A claim has even been allowed for nervous shock on witnessing property damage.	*Victoria Railway Commissioners v Coultas* [1888] *Vernon v Bosely* [1997] *Dulieu v White* [1901] *Hambrook v Stokes* [1925] *McLoughlin v O'Brian* [1982] *North Glamorgan NHS Trust v Walters* [2002] *Attia v British Gas* [1987]

(*Continued*)

(Continued)

Those who can claim for nervous shock	Case
Now basic rules identify a restricted range of people who can claim – which include: • primary victims – present and either injured or at risk • secondary victims – there must be a close tie of love and affection to the victim, and a witness of the incident or its immediate aftermath – here the meaning of immediate aftermath – there must be an accident and medical crisis will not suffice • rescuers – where the rescuer is either a genuine primary victim; or a genuine secondary victim – but there is now no general category of liability to a rescuer. (Those witnessing it on live TV in contravention of broadcasting requirements – possibly.)	*Alcock v Chief Constable of South Yorkshire* [1992] *Page v Smith* [1996] *Liverpool Women's Hospital v Ronayne* [2015] *McLoughlin v O'Brian* [1982] *White v Chief Constable of South Yorkshire* [1998] *Paul v Wolverhampton* [2024] *Greatorex v Greatorex* [2000]
Those who cannot claim for nervous shock	**Case**
There are a number of classes of people who could not claim: • mere bystanders • secondary victims without close ties to the victim • secondary victims not present at the scene or the immediate aftermath – but see the decision in • those not suffering a recognised psychiatric injury • those outside the area of foreseeable shock of the accident The Law Commission has suggested relaxing the rules for claims by secondary victims, so that they should only need to prove the close tie of love and affection with the primary victim.	*McFarlane v E E Caledonia* [1994] *Robertson and Rough v Forth Road Bridge Joint Board* [1995] *Alcock v Chief Constable of South Yorkshire* [1992] *W v Essex CC* [2000] *Reilly v Merseyside Regional Health Authority* [1994] *Bourhill v Young* [1943]

6.2 Pure economic loss

6.2.1 The traditional position

The question in relation to recovery for economic loss is neatly summed up in the decision in *Steel v NRAM* [2018] UKSC 13 by Lord Wilson: 'A makes a careless misrepresentation which causes economic loss to B. There was no contract between them. But did A owe a duty of care to B?'

The case of *Hedley Byrne v Heller and Partners Ltd* [1964] AC 465 introduced the concept that a claimant could recover for economic loss arising from negligently made statements only if certain circumstances exist. However, the courts have always distinguished such an action from 'pure economic loss' arising out of negligent acts. The position here was traditionally very clear; there was no liability for a 'pure economic loss'.

In the past this was based on policy and the idea that 'economic loss', for instance a loss of profit, was a concept applicable to contract law rather than tort. The principle has been quite clearly stated and illustrated in past cases.

CASE EXAMPLE

***Spartan Steel v Martin & Co (Contractors) Ltd* [1973] 1 QB 27**

An electric power cable was negligently cut by the defendants, resulting in loss of power to the claimants, who manufactured steel alloys. A 'melt' in the claimant's furnace at the time of the power cuts had to be destroyed to stop it from solidifying and wrecking the furnace. The claimants were able to claim for physical damage and the loss of profit on the 'melt' in the furnace. The court refused to allow their claim for lost profits for four further 'melts' they argued they could have completed while the power was still off. The loss was foreseeable. Nevertheless, Lord Denning held that a line must be drawn as a matter of policy, and that the loss was better borne by the insurers than by the defendants alone.

In the case Lord Denning explained the basis of the rule as follows at 37:

JUDGMENT

'It seems to me better to consider the particular relationship in hand, and see whether or not, as a matter of policy, economic loss should be recoverable or not.'

There appears to be an artificial distinction here created for policy reasons purely for the purpose of restricting any extension of liability. The distinction has the obvious potential to create unfair anomalies in the law. For instance it might mean that an architect giving negligent advice leading to the construction of a defective building could be liable where the builder whose negligence leads to a defect in a building may not be.

Nevertheless other cases have confirmed the principle that a pure economic loss arising from a negligent act is unrecoverable.

CASE EXAMPLE

***Weller & Co v Foot and Mouth Disease Research Institute* [1966] 1 QB 569**

Auctioneers' regular income from sale of cattle was disrupted as the result of a ban on the movement of livestock following an escape of a virus from the defendant's premises. No liability could be accepted for their loss of profit.

However, there have also been situations where an economic loss was recovered, although in less clear-cut situations where the difference between a negligent statement and a negligent act was less obvious.

CASE EXAMPLE

Dutton v Bognor Regis Urban District Council [1972] 1 QB 373

A local authority was responsible for a negligently carried out building inspection that resulted in defective foundations having to be repaired at great financial cost to the owner of the building. The Court of Appeal held that, since a local authority was under no duty to carry out an inspection then it could not be held liable for a negligent inspection. Nevertheless it was prepared to impose liability on the basis of physical damage, that the defective foundations were a risk to the health and safety of the occupants. The claimant as a result was awarded damages to restore the building to a state where it was no longer a danger. Clearly it is difficult to distinguish between a negligent inspection (an act) and a satisfactory report based on the inspection (a statement). The case did not fit easily under either *Hedley Byrne* or *Donoghue v Stevenson* [1932] AC 562, which perhaps explains the court's reasoning.

6.2.2 Pure economic loss under *Anns*

Further erosion of the basic principle that pure economic loss is unrecoverable came as a result of Lord Wilberforce's 'two-part' test.

CASE EXAMPLE

Anns v Merton London Borough Council [1978] AC 728

Here the negligent building inspection had failed to reveal that the foundations were too shallow. On the basis of the two-part test and that there were no policy grounds to avoid imposing a duty, the tenant was able to recover the cost of making the flat safe: economic loss in other words.

Because of the availability of the *Anns* two-part test, the so-called high water mark was then reached in respect of recovery for a pure economic loss.

CASE EXAMPLE

Junior Books Ltd v Veitchi Co Ltd [1983] 1 AC 520

The claimants' architects nominated the defendants to lay the floor in the claimants' new print works. As a result they sub-contracted to the main builders to complete the work. In the event the defendants laid a thoroughly unusable floor which then had to be re-laid. The claimants could not sue the builders who had hired the floor layers at the claimant's request, and they had no contractual relationship with the floor layers. Nevertheless they succeeded in winning damages not just for the cost of re-laying the floor, but also for their loss of profit during the delay. There were said to be three key issues:

- The claimant had nominated the defendants and so they relied on the defendants' skill and judgment.
- The defendants were aware of this reliance at all material times.
- The damage caused was a direct and foreseeable consequence of the defendants' negligence.

Lord Fraser's explanation of the reasons for liability was at 548:

JUDGMENT

'The proximity of the parties is extremely close, falling only just short of a direct contractual relationship.'

Lord Brandon dissented and criticised the other judges for creating obligations in a non-contractual relationship only appropriate as between contracting parties.

6.2.3 Pure economic loss after *Anns*

Almost immediately judges considered that the relaxation of the principle concerning recovery for economic loss had now gone too far. A long line of cases followed which tried to limit the scope of the above cases.

CASE EXAMPLE

Governors of the Peabody Donation Fund v Sir Lindsay Parkinson & Co Ltd [1985] 3 All ER 529

The court would not accept that there was liability owed for a negligent council inspection that resulted in a drain having to be re-laid because it did not conform to regulations. The council's duty in inspecting was to protect the health and safety of the public.

The cases had often arisen because an action in contract was not available and the reliance test from *Junior Books Ltd v Veitchi Co Ltd* [1983] 1 AC 520 was argued.

CASE EXAMPLE

Muirhead v Industrial Tank Specialists Ltd [1985] 3 All ER 705

Fish merchandisers bought lobsters while they were cheap, to sell on when their price increased. They bought storage tanks in which to hold the lobsters and lost money when the French-built pumps in the tanks were defective and the lobsters could not be stored. They originally succeeded against the supplier of the tanks in contract but when they went into liquidation brought an action in tort against the manufacturers of the pumps. Their claim that the test of proximity and reliance in *Junior Books* applied failed. The court held that reliance had only been possible in that case because the claimants nominated the defendants. The case was therefore distinguished.

The argument that costs of repairing defects in property that could lead to a danger to health or safety, approved in *Anns,* was also gradually rejected.

CASE EXAMPLE

D & F Estates v Church Commissioners [1989] 2 All ER 992

Liability against builders was rejected when plaster cracked, fell off walls and had to be replaced as the result of the negligence of sub-contractors. The builders had satisfied their duty by hiring competent tradesmen and, in the absence of injury or an actual risk to health, any loss was purely economic and not recoverable.

These represent only a few of the cases where *Anns* was argued to allow economic loss and was rejected or the case distinguished. The general unease that was felt at Lord Wilberforce's test in *Anns* and at the extension of liability for economic loss led eventually to the overruling of *Anns,* and thus back to a more restrictive attitude towards economic loss.

CASE EXAMPLE

Murphy v Brentwood District Council [1991] 1 AC 398

The House of Lords would not impose liability on a council that had approved plans for a concrete raft on which properties were built and which then moved causing cracks in the walls. The claimant was forced to sell the house for £35,000 under the value if there had been no defects, but in the absence of any injury, loss was purely economic. So the ratio in *Anns* was overruled and the principle of law now is that a local authority will not be liable for the cost of repairing dangerous defects (in the case gas pipes had broken during the settlement of the property) until physical injury is actually caused. *Junior Books v Veitchi* was not overruled but was allowed to stand on its own facts. It is unlikely, however, to have much impact on future cases.

In his judgment Lord Bridge explained the basis for denying liability at 475:

JUDGMENT

'If a dangerous defect in a chattel is discovered before it causes any personal injury or damage to property, because the danger is now known and the chattel cannot safely be used unless the defect is repaired, the defect becomes merely a defect in quality. The chattel is either capable of repair at economic cost or it is worthless and must be scrapped. In either case the loss sustained by the owner or hirer of the chattel is purely economic. It is recoverable against any party who owes the loser a relevant contractual duty. But it is not recoverable in tort in the absence of a special relationship of proximity imposing on the tortfeasor a duty of care to safeguard the plaintiff from economic loss.'

The principles in *Murphy v Brentwood DC* [1990] 2 All ER 908 have subsequently been accepted and followed by the courts.

CASE EXAMPLE

Department of the Environment v Thomas Bates & Sons Ltd [1990] 2 All ER 943

Here the claimant failed to recover the cost of repairing a building that had been built of concrete that was of insufficient strength to support its intended load, although it was not dangerous to carry its existing load. The court held that such cost was purely economic and thus unrecoverable.

As a result it would appear that the present policy of the courts in relation to economic loss is that recovery for such loss should be through the normal insurance of the injured party rather than through the courts by using an action for negligence.

CASE EXAMPLE

Marc Rich & Co v Bishop Rock Marine Co Ltd [1995] 1 WLR 1071

A vessel was negligently classed as seaworthy, and then sank. The classification society did not owe a duty of care to the owners of a cargo that sank with the ship. This was economic loss. The House of Lords applied the three-part test from *Caparo v Dickman* [1990] 1 All ER 568 (see section 6.3.2) and determined that it was not just and reasonable in the circumstances of the case to impose a duty.

Arguments that losses should be seen as physical rather than purely economic have also been rejected in order to limit the extent of liability.

CASE EXAMPLE

D Pride & Partners v Institute for Animal Health [2009] EWHC 685

The case followed the inadvertent escape of foot and mouth disease from a research institute in 2007. Restrictions were placed on the movement of cattle and farmers suffered significant losses as a result. The court rejected the arguments put by farmers, first, that the damage suffered was physical rather than merely economic and, second, that the farmers had a special relationship with the institute. The court held that this would be to create limitless liability. The case mirrors the earlier *Weller v Foot and Mouth Disease Research Institute* (see section 6.2.1).

ACTIVITY

Self-assessment questions

1. What exactly is a 'pure economic loss'?
2. Why are the courts more willing to accept an economic loss caused by a negligently made statement than one resulting from a negligent act or omission?
3. Why were judges in later cases nervous about the judgment in *Junior Books*?
4. What is the difference between physical damage to property and the cost of repairing defects in property?
5. How would the courts now prefer a claimant to recover compensation for an economic loss?
6. Why did the judges in *Murphy* decide not to overrule *Junior Books*?

KEY FACTS

Pure economic loss	**Case**
The courts have always been reluctant to allow liability for 'pure economic loss', since it is felt that it is more to do with contract.	*Spartan Steel v Martin* [1973]
Although claims have been successful where there has been a risk also to health.	*Dutton v Bognor Regis UDC* [1972]
And the position on economic loss was drastically relaxed as the result of Lord Wilberforce's two-part test.	*Anns v Merton LBC* [1978]
And in a 'near contractual' relationship between the two parties.	*Junior Books v Veitchi* [1983]
Later judges were unhappy with *Anns* and the two-part test and these were eventually overruled (but not *Junior Books*).	*Murphy v Brentwood DC* [1990]
The principle in *Murphy* has been followed in subsequent cases.	*Department of the Environment v Thomas Bates & Sons Ltd* [1990]
It appears that the more appropriate remedy for the damage is a claim against the claimant's own insurance.	*Marc Rich & Co v Bishop Rock Marine Co Ltd* [1995]

6.3 Negligent misstatement

6.3.1 The origins of liability

The law of torts is concerned mainly with compensating for physical damage or personal injury, not for loss that is only economic. The obvious justification for this stance is that economic loss, or for instance loss of a profit or bargain, is more traditionally associated with contract law and the judges have always been eager to separate out the two.

An action for an economic loss caused by a statement was traditionally available in tort, but in the tort of deceit and only in the case of fraudulently made statements.

CASE EXAMPLE

Derry v Peek [1889] 14 App Cas 337

A representation in a share prospectus that a tram company could use motive power led to loss when the Board of Trade refused the company a licence to use motorised trams. The company had fully expected to be granted the licence, so their misstatement was not considered to be fraudulent.

That action for economic loss caused by reliance on a negligently made statement should be available was reaffirmed even more recently, although not without some fundamental disagreement being expressed.

CASE EXAMPLE

Candler v Crane Christmas & Co [1951] 2 KB 164

Accountants negligently prepared a company's accounts and investors then lost money. In the absence of a contractual relationship or fraud the court was not prepared to declare the existence of a duty of care.

Lord Denning, dissenting, felt that there should be a duty of care to the investor and to at 165:

JUDGMENT

'any third party to whom they themselves show the accounts, or to whom they know their employer is going to show the accounts so as to induce them to invest money'.

The House of Lords eventually accepted this dissenting judgment a long time afterwards, and initially only *in obiter.*

CASE EXAMPLE

***Hedley Byrne v Heller and Partners Ltd* [1964] AC 465**

An advertising company was approached with a view to preparing a campaign for a small company, Easipower, with whom they had not previously dealt. The advertisers then did the most sensible thing in the circumstances and approached Easipower's bank for a credit reference. The bank gave a satisfactory reference without checking on their current financial standing and the advertisers produced the campaign. They then lost money when Easipower went into liquidation. They sued the bank for their negligently prepared advice. They failed, because the bank had included a disclaimer of liability in the credit reference. Nevertheless, the House of Lords, approving Lord Denning's dissenting judgment in the last case, held that such an action should be possible, and this has subsequently been accepted as law.

Lord Reid explained the basis for imposing liability at 486:

JUDGMENT

'A reasonable man, knowing that he was being trusted or that his skill and judgement were being relied on, would, I think, have three courses open to him. He could keep silent or decline to give the information or advice sought: or he could give an answer with a clear qualification that he accepted no responsibility for it or that it was given without that reflection or inquiry which a careful answer would require: or he could simply answer without any such qualification. If he chooses to adopt the last course he must, I think, be held to have accepted some responsibility for his answer being given carefully, or to have accepted a relationship with the inquirer which requires him to exercise such care as the circumstances require.'

The interesting point of the court's approval of the principle in the case is that they were holding that such a duty could apply despite there being no contractual relationship, and despite the fact that, in effect, they were accepting that they could impose liability for an economic loss.

As a result the House of Lords laid down strict guidelines for when the principle could apply.

i There must be a special relationship between the two parties – based on the skill and judgment of the defendant and the reliance placed upon it.

ii The person giving the advice must be possessed of special skill relating to the type of advice given – so the defendant ought to have realised that the claimant would rely on that skill.

iii The party receiving the advice has acted in reliance on it – and in the circumstances it was reasonable for the claimant to rely on the advice.

The subsequent case law has in general followed, but also in some cases added to, these requirements.

The basis of the specific duty has also been identified in the case law.

In *Smith v Eric S Bush* [1990] 1 AC 831 HL Lord Templeman identified at 845:

JUDGMENT

'The duty of professional men "is not merely a duty to use care in their reports. They have also a duty to use care in their work which results in their reports."'

6.3.2 The criteria for imposing liability

A special relationship

The precise meaning of 'special relationship' was never really examined in *Hedley Byrne* and so it has become an area for judicial policy making. The original leaning was towards a narrow interpretation that would then only include a relationship where the party giving the advice was in the business of giving advice of the sort in question.

However, it has since been suggested that a business or professional relationship might in general give rise to the duty if the claimant is genuinely seeking professional advice.

CASE EXAMPLE

Howard Marine & Dredging Co Ltd v Ogden & Sons Ltd [1978] QB 574

Dredging took a lot longer because the hirers of the barges had misstated the payload weight to the party hiring them. It was accepted that the relationship, while a standard business one, could give rise to a special relationship for the purposes of imposing a duty.

A purely social relationship should not normally give rise to a duty of care, but has done when it has been established that carefully considered advice was being sought from a party with some expertise.

CASE EXAMPLE

Chaudry v Prabhaker [1988] 3 All ER 718

A woman asked her friend, who, while not a mechanic, had some experience of cars, to find her a good second-hand car that had not been in an accident. When it was later discovered that the car advised on had been in an accident and was not completely roadworthy, the friend advising on its purchase was successfully sued.

Common relationships where a duty will be identified though are those where valuers or accountants are providing the advice. Even though there may not be a contractual relationship between a building society surveyor and the house purchaser, it might still be possible to identify a special relationship.

CASE EXAMPLE

Yianni v Edwin Evans & Sons [1982] 2 QB 438

A building society surveyor was held to owe a duty to purchasers of a property valued at £12,000 where it was later discovered that repairs worth £18,000 were required. The court was prepared to impose the duty here because it was shown that at the time less than 15 per cent of purchasers would have their own independent survey carried out, and therefore it was foreseeable that they would rely on the standard building society survey.

The test is whether there is sufficient proximity between the parties for there to be the possibility of reliance and therefore for the duty to arise.

CASE EXAMPLE

Raja v Gray [2002] 33 EG 98 (CS)

Here the question was whether there was a duty of care owed by valuers appointed by receivers. The Court of Appeal accepted that the case law showed that there was a duty owed by valuers to parties with an interest in mortgaged property. Nevertheless, it was not prepared to accept that the same duty was owed where a receiver appointed the valuer because there would be insufficient proximity between the parties. The valuers would be purely acting for the receivers and it would be unfair to hold that their advice could be generally relied upon.

Simple policy reasons can be used to determine that there is insufficient proximity between parties to impose liability.

CASE EXAMPLE

West Bromwich Albion Football Club Ltd v El-Safty [2005] EWHC 2866 (QB)

A professional footballer suffered a knee injury and, on the advice of the club physiotherapist, was sent for consultation with the defendant specialist. The defendant advised reconstructive surgery which failed and the player had to retire. It was later accepted that the advice was negligent and that other treatment should have been considered first. The football club then sued the doctor for the economic loss that it had suffered as a result of the player's premature retirement from the game, arguing that because the club had referred the player and had paid for his treatment there was a special relationship over and above that normally relating to employers. The court held that there was insufficient proximity between the club and the doctor, the person really taking the advice was the player and it would be unfair to impose a duty in the circumstances. It is easy to see why. If such a duty was imposed then there could be a flood of claims by employers in general in respect of the costs of replacing workers injured in negligent events.

The issue of exactly who is owed a duty of care by an accountant has proved to add its own complexities in determining the existence of a special relationship. Originally, for instance, it was held that there was no duty held to persons who might in general terms rely on the accounts since there was no contractual relationship. This was precisely the position taken in *Candler v Crane Christmas & Co* [1951] 2 KB 164.

Nevertheless, following *Hedley Byrne* the possibility of such a duty arising has been considered by the courts. In *JEB Fasteners v Marks Bloom & Co* [1983] 3 All ER 289 the court accepted this possibility in certain circumstances even though it did not apply in the case because the accounts had no actual effect on the take-over since that had been undergone for other more specific reasons (see later).

More recently, the courts have examined in detail the reasons why a duty will not be imposed upon an accountant in relation to the audited accounts of companies.

CASE EXAMPLE

Caparo Industries plc v Dickman [1990] 1 All ER 568

The case concerned the annual audit of a company required under the Companies Act 1985. The House of Lords held that the purpose of such audits was to enable the members of the company to exercise control over the officers in the administration of the company. As a result there could be no duty owed to the claimant in the case who was a shareholder purchasing further shares and who claimed to have suffered economic loss as a result of the negligently prepared accounts.

The possession of special skill or expertise

Ordinarily, then, a claim is only possible if the party giving the advice is a specialist in the field which the advice concerns.

CASE EXAMPLE

Mutual Life and Citizens Assurance Co Ltd v Evatt [1971] AC 793

A representative of an insurance company gave advice about the products of another company. The court held that there could only be a duty in such circumstances if the party giving the advice had held himself out as being in the business of giving the advice in question.

So, advice given in a purely social context could not usually give rise to liability. In this way the defendant in *Chaudry v Prabhaker* might be considered unfortunate, although the result was justified since he should have applied the same caution in advising that he would have if he had been buying it himself.

Reasonable reliance on the advice

It is only fair and logical that if there has been no reliance placed on the advice given then there cannot be liability on the defendant for giving it.

CASE EXAMPLE

JEB Fasteners Ltd v Marks Bloom & Co [1983] 3 All ER 289

A negligent statement of the value of a company's stock did not give rise to a duty. This was because the party buying the company was doing so only to secure the services of two directors, and so placed no reliance on the stock.

In consequence it will not be foreseeable reliance if the claimant belongs to a group of potential claimants that is too large for the claimant to have fairly within his contemplation when giving the advice.

Although it is much more likely that there will be genuine reliance in contractual situations or those that are near contractual such as pre-contractual arrangements. In *Commissioner of Police for the Metropolis v Lennon* [2004] EWCA Civ 130, for instance, acting on advice the claimant took time off before moving to a new force and as a result lost his housing allowance. The police were held liable under *Hedley Byrne*.

However, whenever there is foreseeable reliance on advice that has been given then there will be a duty of care owed.

CASE EXAMPLE

Smith v Eric S Bush [1990] 2 WLR 790

A building society valuation had identified that chimney breasts had been removed, but the valuer had failed to check whether the brickwork above was properly secured. It was not, and after the purchase it collapsed. The court determined that there was a duty of care because, as in *Yianni v Edwin Evans and Sons* [1982] 2 QB 438, even though the contract was between building society and valuer, it was reasonably foreseeable that the purchaser would rely on it.

Inevitably for a claim to succeed it must be shown that reliance on the negligently given advice was indeed reasonable.

CASE EXAMPLE

Lambert v West Devon BC [1997] 96 LGR 45

The council was held liable when the claimant relied on its advice that he could begin building even though planning permission had not yet been obtained. Since the defendant was the body from which permission was being sought, it was perfectly reasonable that the claimant would rely on the advice given as being accurate.

The test is obviously whether the defendant knew or ought reasonably to be expected to know of the reliance on the advice given (see *Yianni v Edwin Evans & Sons*). In this way foreseeable reliance by the party seeking the advice might also prevent an exclusion of liability clause in a contract from operating successfully.

CASE EXAMPLE

Harris v Wyre Forest District Council **[1989] 1 All ER 691**

Here in the sale of a council house a negligent survey had been carried out for the local authority. Even though the purchaser did not see the valuation he could rely on it and a disclaimer of liability inserted in the valuation was ineffective because it was not reasonable within the terms of the Unfair Contract Terms Act 1977.

Policy considerations have been as important in identifying when reasonable reliance occurs as in determining when a special relationship exists between the parties. This was clear in *Caparo*. As a result the range of claimants that might be covered by *Hedley Byrne* principles is limited. The courts are not prepared to extend the range at the expense of holding to the principle that it is fair, just and reasonable to impose a duty as is required by the *Caparo* three-part test for liability in negligence.

CASE EXAMPLE

Newell v Ministry of Defence **[2002] EWHC 1006 (QB)**

An army officer made an application for early release and then waited for what he alleged was an unreasonable time for a reply and claimed negligence on the part of his employers. While waiting to hear, he had turned down a civilian job and claimed to have lost financially as a result. The court was not prepared to accept that the employer had undertaken any responsibility for his affairs in seeking civilian employment and rejected the argument that he could bring himself within the scope of the duty. It would not be fair to impose a duty in circumstances where the employer was in no way involved in the officer's applications for civilian employment.

Where a duty to act is imposed by statute a civil action is only usually available to a party when the type of harm suffered was that anticipated by the statute. This was one of the reasons why the action failed in *Caparo v Dickman*. However, a duty may apply where the public would generally benefit.

CASE EXAMPLE

Law Society v KPMG Peat Marwick **[2000] 4 All ER 540**

Here the Law Society was owed a duty of care by a firm of accountants hired by solicitors to prepare annual accounts for the Law Society because Law Society compensation to clients of firms would be possible on a bad report.

6.3.3 The current state of the law

In *Caparo v Dickman* the House of Lords had the opportunity to consider the principles involved in liability under *Hedley Byrne*. The financial booms and rapid development in property markets had not only led to a greater increase in home ownership and share ownership, it had also led on to a great number of claims for negligent misstatement, particularly against property surveyors and accountants.

The House of Lords preferred an incremental approach to establishing the duty of care, as we have already seen. They also made a number of observations regarding the circumstances in which the *Hedley Byrne* type duty will be owed.

- The advice must be required for a purpose described at the time to the defendant at least in general terms.
- This purpose must be made known actually or by inference to the party giving the advice at the time it is given.
- If the advice will subsequently be communicated to the party relying on it, this fact must be known by the adviser.
- The adviser must be aware that the advice will be acted upon without benefit of any further independent advice.
- The person alleging to have relied on the advice must show actual reliance and consequent detriment suffered.

So the significant feature of this development of the duty is the express or implied knowledge of the purpose for which the claimant acted in reliance of the statement.

This is yet further refined in the decision of *Steele v NRAM* [2018] UKSC 13 where the Supreme Court confirms that, following on from *Robinson*, an incremental approach to establishing a duty of care must be adopted and that the central question in *Caparo* was at 23:

JUDGMENT

'. . . the need for a representee to establish that it was reasonable for him to have relied on the representation and that the representor should reasonably have foreseen that he would do so.'

In *Steele*, Ms Steele prepared a document for benefit for her client but this was subsequently relied upon by NRAM. It transpired that the document that she prepared was done so negligently. The central question here was whether it was reasonable for NRAM to have relied on this information and indeed whether Steele could foresee that they would rely on this information. In other words, did she assume responsibility towards NRAM? The Supreme Court held that it was not reasonable for NRAM to have relied on this advice prepared by Steele and nor was it foreseeable by Steele that NRAM would rely on it.

The Supreme Court in NRAM further endorsed the following decision in the case of *James McNaughten Paper Group Ltd v Hicks Anderson*, which asserts the importance of foreseeability and reliance.

CASE EXAMPLE

James McNaughten Paper Group Ltd v Hicks Anderson & Co [1991] 1 All ER 134

Here accountants who drew up accounts at very short notice for the Chairman of a company had no duty of care to the person who acquired the company in a take-over bid, having inspected the accounts. The Court of Appeal identified the factors that should be taken into account in establishing a duty of care as follows:

1 the purpose for which the statement was made;
2 the purpose for which the statement was communicated;
3 the relationship between the person giving the advice, the person receiving the advice and any relevant third party;
4 the size of any class that the person receiving the advice belonged to;
5 the degree of knowledge of the person giving the advice.

This is a very narrow approach to the duty and subsequent cases have tended to take a more relaxed view. In *Henderson v Merrett Syndicates* [1994] 3 All ER 506, for instance, the court added a fifth factor for determining that a duty exists under *Hedley Byrne* principles. The requirement is that there is an assumption of responsibility by the party giving the advice.

Some cases certainly seem to be at odds with the general principle and liability has been imposed apparently to prevent a party being without any remedy.

CASE EXAMPLE

White v Jones [1995] 1 All ER 691

Solicitors who negligently failed to draw up a will before the testator's death were held to owe a duty to the intended beneficiaries who consequently lost their inheritance. Any contractual relationship was with the testator, and since a will can be changed a beneficiary is not necessarily ensured the inheritance. Nevertheless, the House of Lords was prepared to identify both a special relationship in the circumstances and reliance.

Certain cases appear not to fit easily within the *Hedley Byrne* principle because the person relying on the advice is not the person who actually suffers the loss.

CASE EXAMPLE

Ross v Caunters [1980] Ch 297

Here solicitors were held to be liable to the beneficiaries under a will for failing to warn the testator not to allow the spouse of a beneficiary to witness the will. The court decided that the duty existed because there was sufficient proximity between the defendant and the beneficiaries who in effect relied on their expertise.

As a result it sometimes appears that a court will impose liability simply because it is foreseeable that a party will rely on the negligent advice.

CASE EXAMPLE

Ministry of Housing and Local Government v Sharp [1971] 2 QB 223

The court held the ministry liable when a land registry clerk negligently gave a clean certificate to land that was actually subject to a charge, as a result of which

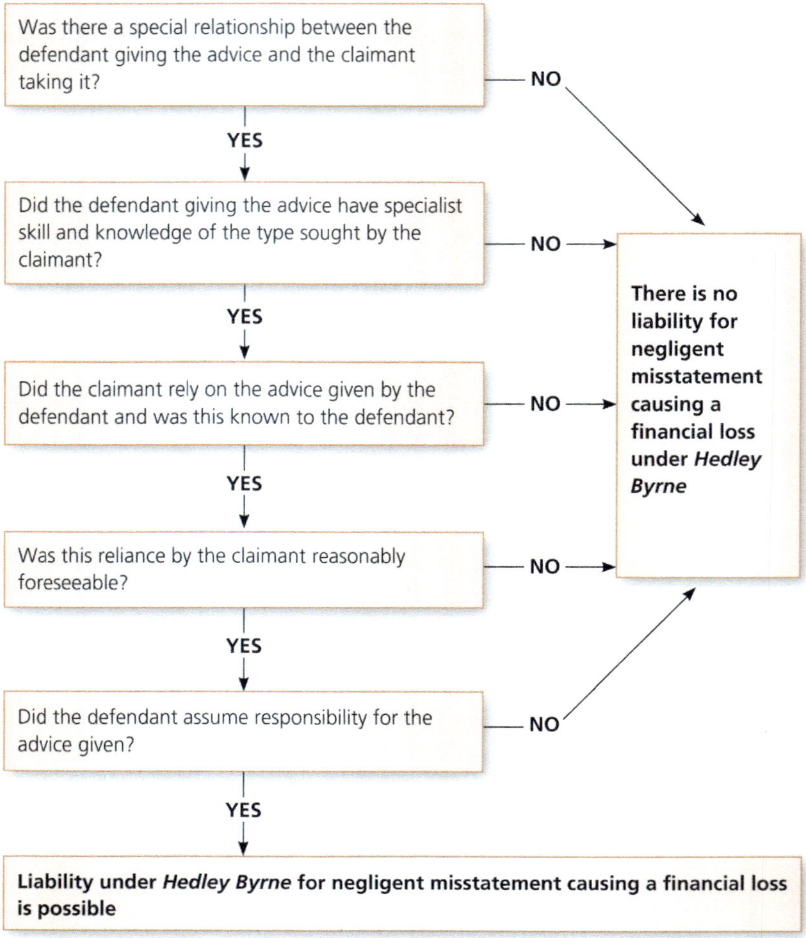

Figure 6.2 The essential elements for a successful claim under *Hedley Byrne*.

the ministry lost compensation that it would otherwise have been entitled to. Any reliance, and indeed any special relationship, was by the purchaser of the property. Nevertheless this reliance in effect led only to a loss by the ministry.

However, in some instances the case seems out of context because the court is uncertain whether it is the principle in *Hedley Byrne* or that in *Donoghue v Stevenson* which is the appropriate one to apply. The latter is certainly less restrictive.

CASE EXAMPLE

Spring v Guardian Assurance plc [1995] 3 WLR 354

An employee of an insurance company was dismissed and then prevented from gaining a position with another company because of a negligently prepared and highly unfavourable reference provided by the first company. The House of Lords held that the first employers were liable because of the reference, but the House was split on whether *Hedley Byrne* should apply.

The approach to dealing with negligently prepared references has since been developed by the Court of Appeal. In *Bartholomew v London Borough of Hackney* [1999] IRLR 246 the Court increased the duty to ensuring that information provided is accurate and that the reference does not create any unfair impression.

This test has now been developed further.

CASE EXAMPLE

Cox v Sun Alliance Life Ltd [2001] IRLR 448

The claimant was a branch manager who was suspended for reasons not related to dishonesty. An allegation of dishonesty was made during negotiations for a termination agreement. However, the investigation that followed was abandoned and Sun Alliance Life agreed that in any references they would make no mention of the allegation. However, they did so in one reference which cost the claimant a job and he sued successfully for negligence. Lord Justice Mummery stated that before divulging information that is unfavourable to an ex-employee in a reference, the employer must believe in the truth of the information, have reasonable grounds for that belief and make a reasonably thorough investigation before making the statement.

What is clear is that policy remains an important fact in determining whether or not a duty is imposed in particular circumstances.

CASE EXAMPLE

Gorham v British Telecommunications plc [2000] 1 WLR 2129

The claimant had asked the defendants to sell him a pension that would provide benefits not only for himself but also for his dependants in the event of his death. Standard Life sold him a pension, but one which did not fulfil this requirement. In fact the company should have advised him to remain with his existing employee pension scheme in the circumstances. The court held that the claimant was owed a duty to be advised in a way that would achieve his stated purpose. This duty had been breached because the pension that he was sold on the contrary affected him detrimentally.

ACTIVITY

Self-assessment questions

1 Why did the House of Lords in *Hedley Byrne* alter the previous rule in *Candler v Crane Christmas & Co*?
2 What exactly is a special relationship?
3 How can the decision in *Chaudry v Prabhaker* be justified?
4 What level of specialist expertise is required for liability under *Hedley Byrne*?
5 Against what standards is reasonable reliance measured?
6 How can the *Goodwill v British Pregnancy Advisory Service* case be distinguished from other cases on reasonable reliance?

7 Why was the decision in *Yianni v Edwin Evans* greeted with such shock by building society surveyors?
8 To what extent does the case of *Caparo v Dickman* limit liability under *Hedley Byrne*?
9 What elements have been added to the test for liability by *Caparo*?
10 What further aspect of the test has been added by the case of *Henderson v Merrett Syndicates*?
11 How do cases like *White v Jones* and *Spring v Guardian Assurance* fit in with the normal rule?

KEY FACTS

The origins of the duty	Case
Originally there was only an action available for misrepresentations if they were made fraudulently. And an action for negligence was originally specifically rejected. But the House of Lords eventually accepted *in obiter* that such an action was possible.	*Derry v Peek* [1889] *Candler v Crane, Christmas & Co* [1951] *Hedley Byrne v Heller & Partners* [1964]
The essential elements of the duty	**Case**
But only subject to certain requirements: • the existence of a special relationship • where the party giving the advice has specialist skill and knowledge of the type sought • the other party acts in reliance of the advice which is known to the other party • limitations on these requirements have since been made – the principal one being that the reliance is reasonable and foreseeable to the defendant • a list of import factors to be considered has been identified including: • the purpose for which the statement was made and communicated • the relationship between all relevant parties • the degree of knowledge of the defendant • a requirement that the defendant has assumed responsibility for the advice has been added. But there are also cases that do not fit the principle neatly.	*Yianni v Edwin Evans* [1982] *Mutual Life & Citizens Assurance v Evatt* [1971] *Smith v Eric S Bush* [1990] *Caparo v Dickman* [1990] *Steele v NRAM* [2018] *James McNaughten Paper Group v Hicks Anderson* [1991] *Henderson v Merrett Syndicates* [1994] *White v Jones* [1995]; *Spring v Guardian Assurance* [1995]

6.3.4 Rest of the action

Once it has been established that the claimant was owed a duty of care for a negligence misstatement, they must go on to establish whether the duty was breached and whether the breach caused the loss suffered. Whether the financial loss is too remote will also have to be analysed as will any relevant applicable defences.

SAMPLE ESSAY QUESTION

Discuss the extent to which the way that rules on liability for a financial loss caused by a negligent misstatement have been developed so as to produce a just solution to a dispute.

Explain the basis of a claim in negligence

- Defendant owes claimant a duty of care
- Defendant breaches the duty
- And causes foreseeable harm

Discuss the original attitude of the courts

- Unwilling to allow recovery for pure economic loss
- Also applied same principles to negligent advice
- But Lord Denning thought there should be liability
- Consider that this reluctance was based on policy grounds so was probably unjust to potential claimants
- Explain that originally there was only an action available for misrepresentations that were made fraudulently

Explain the original basis of a claim for negligent misstatement causing a pecuniary loss

- Existence of a special relationship
- Possession of specialist skill by the person giving the advice
- Reasonable reliance on the defendant's skill and judgement

Discuss the later developments of the tort

- The widest point of liability came with liability owed for advice given by a friend – potentially unfair to possible defendants
- And the tort has impacted upon valuers and auditors particularly
- But courts have since rejected a test of foreseeability and the narrower test of knowledge of the purpose for which the advice is now needed – harder to bring an action
- The test of knowledge includes the purpose for which the statement was made and communicated, the relationship between all relevant parties and the degree of knowledge of the defendant
- A later development requires assumption of responsibility for the advice given – so again makes an action harder to bring

Discuss potential future development

- Courts have gradually rejected the early expansion and have narrowed the basis for the test clearly aiming to be fair to defendants, but comes at the expense of claimants
- Further expansion is unlikely

SUMMARY

Pure economic loss

- Courts have always been unwilling to allow recovery for 'pure economic loss'.
- This is because contract law is more appropriate for loss of profit.
- Some claims have been successful where there has been a risk also to health.
- And also in a 'near contractual' relationship between the two parties.

Negligent misstatement

- Originally an action was only available for advice given fraudulently.
- Then it was accepted that an action was possible if:
  - there was a special relationship between the parties;
  - the party giving the advice had specialist knowledge of the type needed by the other party; and
  - there was reasonable reliance on the advice.

- These requirements have since been limited to include:
  - that the reliance is reasonably foreseeable to the defendant;
  - that the defendant has knowledge of the purpose for which the advice is needed; and
  - that the defendant has assumed responsibility for the advice given.
- There are also some anomalous cases.

Further reading

Brooman, S, 'Back to basics' [1995] *LEJ* 23.

Denning, L, *The Discipline of Law* (Butterworths, 1979), Part 6, Chapters 3 and 4.

Goold, I, and Kelly, C, 'Time to start de Novo: the Paul, Purchase and Polmear litigation and the temporal gap problem in secondary victim claims for psychiatric injury' (2023) *39(1) PN* 24–40.

Tofaris, S, 'Limping into the future: Negligence liability for mental injury to secondary victims' (2022) *81(3) CLJ* 452–456.

Trindade, FA, 'Reformulation of the nervous shock rules' (2003) *119 LQR* 204.

7

Occupiers' liability and liability for defective premises

AIMS AND OBJECTIVES

After reading this chapter you should be able to:

- Recognise and distinguish the nature of liability under the Occupiers' Liability Acts
- Explain the meaning of occupier and premises
- Distinguish the different types of visitor and the Act appropriate to each
- Identify the different duties under the two Acts
- Identify and apply the different standard of care appropriate to children
- Explain how occupiers can discharge liability in respect of tradesmen, where independent contractors have caused the harm, and explain the effect of warnings, exclusion clauses and defences
- Critically analyse the Acts
- Apply the law to factual situations and reach conclusions as to liability

7.1 Origins and general character

7.1.1 Introduction and origins

Occupiers' liability concerns the liability of an 'occupier' of land or premises for the injury or loss or damage to property suffered by claimants while on the occupier's 'premises'. It must immediately be distinguished from damage caused by the defendant's use of his land, which is suffered by the claimant outside of the occupier's land. If this were on the claimant's own land then it might lead to an action in nuisance (see Chapter 9) or possibly *Rylands v Fletcher* [1868] LR 1 Exch 265 (see Chapter 10), or there may in any case be an action in negligence available.

DOI: 10.4324/9781003202417-7

Liability for land and premises falls into two distinct areas:

- Liability by an occupier of premises for loss or injury caused by the state of the premises – such liability can also be divided according to whom has suffered the loss or injury.
- Liability by a person other than an occupier of land for defects in the premises themselves – this involves landlords and builders.

Occupiers' liability is a fairly recent tort and is found in two statutes:

- the Occupiers' Liability Act 1957 – which is concerned with the duty of care owed to all lawful visitors; and
- the Occupiers' Liability Act 1984 – which is concerned with the duty owed to people other than lawful visitors, the major group here being **trespassers**.

trespasser
A person who enters premises without permission or who exceeds the permission they are given

Both areas then are statutory in form, but certainly in the case of occupiers' liability have developed out of negligence. As a result much of the terminology and many of the principles are the same or similar to basic negligence principles. Indeed, though the Acts do contain extensive definition, where definitions are not supplied in the Acts these are to be found in the common law.

Inevitably there is some overlap with negligence. The basic liability arises from the loss or injury caused by the 'state of the premises'. Loss or damage that arises other than because of the state of the premises then should be claimed for under negligence where this is possible.

CASE EXAMPLE

Ogwo v Taylor [1987] 2 WLR 988

Here there was no liability under the Act when a fireman was injured in a fire on the defendant's premises. As Brown LJ commented in the case the fire did not result from defects in the state of the premises, so liability was in negligence.

Nevertheless academics have argued that the Act should still apply in the case of damage caused other than by the state of the premises since s1(1) of the 1957 Act states that the Act should apply 'in respect of dangers due to the state of the premises or to things done or omitted to be done on them'.

The law on occupiers' liability is generally accepted as being very straightforward. *V Harpwood, Principles of Tort (Cavendish Publishing, 2000)* explains that the '1957 Occupiers' Liability Act . . . has always been regarded as a particularly well drafted statute, partly because it is one of the few statutes which attempts to give illustrations and examples of the way in which it is to operate, and partly because there has been little litigation which involves its interpretation'.

On the other hand, the law on defective premises has never been considered to be particularly straightforward with *W Rogers, The Law of Tort (Sweet & Maxwell, 1989)* stating that "few areas of tort have fallen into greater confusion than the liability of those who build and sell premises'.

Although the 1957 Act has been described as a particularly well-drafted statute it still suffers from under-use. The Pearson Report in 1978 for instance recognised that as many as 27 per cent of reported accidents occur in the home. Nevertheless, apparently very few claims are made following domestic accidents. There can obviously be many reasons for this. These include ignorance of the possibility of making a claim, a natural reluctance to sue friends or family and sometimes even a lack of household insurance might prevent a claim.

7.1.2 Definition of occupier – potential defendants

In the case of both the 1957 Act and the 1984 Act potential defendants are identified as being occupiers of premises.

There is in fact no statutory definition of 'occupier' in either Act. Section 1(2) of the 1957 Act merely states that the rules apply 'in consequence of a person's occupation or control of premises'. In the absence of a statutory test the established test for determining occupation then is found in the common law.

CASE EXAMPLE

Wheat v E Lacon & Co Ltd [1966] AC 552

A manager of a public house was given the right to rent out rooms in his private quarters even though he had no proprietary interest in the premises. When a paying guest fell on an unlit staircase, the House of Lords held that both the manager and his employers could be occupiers for the purposes of the Act. In the event neither had actually breached their duty since it was a stranger who had removed the light bulb and therefore there was no liability to the manager.

Earlier in the House of Lords, Lord Denning at 578 explains that:

JUDGMENT

'. . . wherever a person has a sufficient degree of control over premises that he ought to realise that any failure on his part to use care may result in injury to a person coming lawfully there, then he is an "occupier" and the person coming lawfully there is his "visitor": and the "occupier" is under a duty to his "visitor" to use reasonable care. In order to be an "occupier" it is not necessary for a person to have entire control over the premises. He need not have exclusive occupation. Suffice it that he has some degree of control. He may share the control with others. Two or more may be "occupiers." and whenever this happens, each is under a duty to use care towards persons coming lawfully on to the premises, dependent on his degree of control.'

Identifying the occupier will depend then on various considerations, including the nature of the interest held and therefore the particular duty owed. For instance, in a case like the above the brewery might very obviously be responsible for ensuring that there were no defects in the wiring, while the publican might be responsible for ensuring that light bulbs were changed.

So there can be dual or multiple simultaneous occupation of premises and the identity of the defendant, which party was in control of the premises, may depend on the circumstances in which the damage or injury was suffered.

CASE EXAMPLE

Collier v Anglian Water Authority, The Times, 26 March 1983

Here a promenade formed part of the sea defences for which the water authority was responsible. The local authority owned the land, and was responsible for cleaning the promenade. Both could therefore be classed as occupiers for the purposes of the Act. When the claimant was injured as a result of disrepair to the promenade, it was the water authority rather than the local authority which was liable, though both were occupiers.

Control and therefore occupation of premises does not require either proprietary interest or possession, so the position is quite different from trespass to land (see Chapter 8). All that is required for liability is that the defendant has sufficient control of the premises at the time that the damage was caused to be responsible for it.

CASE EXAMPLE

Harris v Birkenhead Corporation [1976] 1 All ER 341

Here a four-year-old child had been injured in an empty house which was not boarded up or secured in any way. The child had entered the premises and fallen from a second floor window. Even though the council had not yet taken possession of the house they were liable since they had served notice of a compulsory purchase order and were effectively in control of the premises. They were held to be occupiers and liable even though they had not yet taken physical control because in effect they had legal control of the premises and were the best placed in that sense to avoid accidents of the sort that occurred.

In the final analysis the court in applying the control test to determine the identity of the defendant will be influenced by the ability of the party to meet a successful claim, whether through insurance or by other means.

7.1.3 Definition of 'premises'

The Acts are again relatively silent on the meaning of premises and there is no fixed definition. Some limited reference is given in s1(3)(a) of the 1957 Act which refers to a person having occupation or control of any 'fixed or moveable structure, including any vessel, vehicle and aircraft'.

As a result the common law again applies and besides the obvious, such as houses, buildings and the land itself, premises have also been held to include:

- ships in dry dock – *London Graving Dock v Horton* [1951] AC 737;
- vehicles – *Hartwell v Grayson* [1947] KB 901;
- aircraft – *Fosbroke-Hobbes v Airwork Ltd* [1937] 1 All ER 108;
- lifts – *Haseldine v Daw & Son Ltd* [1941] 2 KB 343;
- and even a ladder – *Wheeler v Copas* [1981] 3 All ER 405.

7.2 Liability to lawful visitors under the 1957 Act

7.2.1 Potential claimants

The 1957 Act was passed in order to simplify a fairly complex common law, whereby the duty owed to a person entering premises varied according to the capacity in which that person entered. The Act introduced a common duty to be applied to all lawful visitors.

By s1(2) the classes of people to whom the occupier owes a duty remains as it was under common law. These are called visitors under the Act and as a result of s1(2) will include:

- Invitees – these are people who not only have permission to enter but whose entry is in the material interest of the occupier – it can include, for example, friends making a social call, but also people invited onto land for a specific purpose, for example to give a quote for work.
- Licensees – these are people whose entry is to the material interest of the occupier, for example customers, they can include anyone with permission to be on the premises for whatever purpose (there was a very unfair distinction drawn between invitees and licensees at common law – the latter were treated somewhat harshly by the common law, being entitled to no more than warnings of danger of which the occupier was aware – it was indeed criticism of this unfairness by the Law Reform Committee in 1954 that in part led to the passing of the 1957 Act) – visitors under an implied licence will need to prove that the conduct of the occupier amounted to a grant of a licence.

CASE EXAMPLE

Lowery v Walker [1911] AC 10

Ten members of the public had used a short cut across the defendant's land for many years. While the defendant objected, he took no legal steps to stop it. When he set loose a wild horse on to the land, which savaged the claimant, he was liable. The House of Lords concluded that the defendant's conduct had created an implied licence in favour of the claimant.

CASE EXAMPLE

Harvey v Plymouth City Council [2010] EWCA Civ 860

The Council owned open land which it was aware was used by children and teenagers for a variety of recreational purposes. The claimant was injured one evening when he fell about five metres down a sheer drop after running away from a taxi having not paid the fare. The drop was actually bordered by a chain link fence but this had been pushed down. The trial judge held that the claimant had an implied licence to use the land and the council was liable, although it did reduce damages significantly for the claimant's contributory negligence in running in the dark. The Court of Appeal held that on the contrary the implied licence would only cover reasonable recreational activities and there was no liability on the council to compensate the claimant for injuries that resulted from reckless behaviour, running in the dark.

An implied licence can be created in the following situations, for example:

- Those entering under a contractual agreement which could occur in one of two situations:
- where the person has a direct contract with the occupier, for example a painter and decorator, plumber – in this case the express terms of the contract will determine the extent of the duty or there may be an implied duty to keep the premises safe – by s5(1) the common duty of care will apply unless the contract actually provides for a greater level of care;
- where the person entering has a contract with a third party, for example a sub-contractor – in this case that person ranks as a licensee and the question is whether or not they could be subject to the exclusion clauses imposed by the occupier.
- Those not requiring any permission to enter because of a legal right to enter, for example meter readers, police officers in execution of a warrant – s6(2) provides that such persons are 'visitors for that purpose whether or not the occupier has given permission'. Persons entering under this category traditionally would have included those exercising either public or private rights of way – specific rules covered these parties at common law but neither is covered by the 1957 Act.

The 1957 Act imposes no duty of care towards trespassers. A more limited duty is owed to trespassers under the Occupiers' Liability Act 1984. Certain other categories of entrants are also not covered by the 1957 Act. These include:

- Those using a private right of way – here the 1984 Act now applies but prior to that there would have been no liability.

CASE EXAMPLE

Holden v White [1982] 2 WLR 1030

Here a milkman was injured because of a defective manhole cover on the defendant's premises while using a private right of way. It was held that he was not a visitor for the purposes of the 1957 Act and his claim was unsuccessful.

- Those entering under an access agreement or order under the National Parks and Access to the Countryside Act 1949 (which is specifically excluded by s1(4) of the 1957 Act but is also now dealt with under the 1984 Act).
- Those using a public right of way – these are excluded by both the 1957 Act and the 1984 Act and will fall under common law with the tortfeasor being liable for misfeasance but not non-feasance unlike either Act.

CASE EXAMPLE

McGeown v Northern Ireland Housing Executive [1994] 3 All ER 53

The claimant lived in a cul-de-sac on a housing estate owned by the defendants. She was injured on a footpath belonging to the defendants but which had become a public right of way. The reason for the injury was a failure to maintain the footpath and her action failed.

ACTIVITY

Quick quiz

Consider which of the following potential claimants would be able to class themselves as visitors for the purposes of the 1957 Act and why.

1 Trevor is a milkman delivering milk to Archie's door.
2 Kurt is a milkman who picks flowers in Archie's garden after delivering the milk.
3 Gordon, a football fan with a season ticket for the Wanderers, arrives at the ground on Wednesday night for the match with United.
4 Hannah regularly crosses Farmer Giles' field using a well-known public path.
5 Greg is at Mavis's house on Monday morning as agreed to paint the outside.
6 Ali is a police officer who has called at Brian's house for some routine enquiries.
7 Tom regularly climbs over his neighbour's back fence and comes through his back garden on his way home, knowing that his neighbour works later so will be out.
8 Parminder calls at her friend Baljinder's house as arranged to enjoy a meal together.
9 Baljinder is at her friend Parminder's house for a meal and enters Parminder's bedroom and takes a valuable ring.
10 Yuri is an employee of British Gas and has called at Ojukwu's house to read the gas meter.

7.2.2 The scope of the Act – the common duty of care

The extent of the duty of care is set out in s2(1) of the 1957 Act:

SECTION

's2(1) An occupier owes the same duty, the common duty of care, to all his visitors except insofar as he is free to do and does extend, restrict, modify or exclude his duty to any visitors by agreement or otherwise.'

'Common' here is obviously used to signify that the Act applies to all types of lawful visitors by comparison with the more disparate range of duties that were formerly held under the common law.

The nature of the duty is found in s2(2). The duty is to:

SECTION

'*s2(2)* The common duty of care is a duty to take such care as in all the circumstances of the case is reasonable to see that the visitor will be reasonably safe for the purpose for which he is invited or permitted by the occupier to be there'.

Two key points can be made here:

- First, the duty is to keep the visitor safe, and not necessarily to maintain safe premises. So if the visitor is blind or partially sighted, the occupier needs to take greater care to ensure that that visitor is safe than would be the case in relation to a sighted person.

CASE EXAMPLE

Atkins v Butlins Skyline Ltd [2005] 5 WLUK 739

The defendant occupier was liable under the 1957 Act to the blind claimant who had been staying at one of the defendant's holiday camps with his wife and daughter. Upon exiting from a lift, the door of the lift closed, trapping him by his upper arm and shoulder. The contractor engaged to inspect and maintain the lift had recommended, some nine months before the accident occurred, that an enhanced safety device called a full screen sensor edge, designed to identify any obstruction, should be installed; however, such a device was not fitted until after claimant's accident.

An occupier will not have to go to extraordinary lengths to protect a visitor from harm but the duty is to ensure that the visitor rather than simply the premises are safe.

CASE EXAMPLE

Cole v Davis-Gilbert and the Royal British Legion [2007] All ER (D) 20 (Mar)

A woman broke her leg when she stepped on a hole hidden by grass while she was crossing a village green. The hole was used for inserting a maypole during annual fetes. She sued the owner of the village green arguing that, as an occupier, he had a duty to keep visitors safe. She also sued the British Legion which had erected the maypole and filled the hole after the fete, some 21 months before the woman's injuries. At first instance she failed against the owner but succeeded against the

Royal British Legion. The Court of Appeal held that there could be no duty on the owner to inspect the green for holes. Even a daily inspection could not guarantee that there would be no holes as the green was used by many people for many different purposes. Even if the British Legion owed a duty to see that the hole was properly filled in, this duty could not last indefinitely, and certainly not for 21 months after it last filled it. As Lord Justice Scott Baker observed in his judgment, sometimes accidents are just pure accidents.

It is important that the safety of the visitor is prioritised rather than just the premises. If this were not the case, it would make industry unworkable, so it is possible to cordon off unsafe parts as long as the visitor is still made safe in those parts to which he lawfully has access.

Second, the duty in the 1957 Act only applies so long as the visitor is carrying out activities that are authorised within the terms of the visit. So if the visitor strays he may lose protection under the 1957 Act, although an action might still be possible since the 1984 Act might still apply. However, whether the visitor strays must be examined in the context of the premises and the purpose of the visit. This is further illustrated in the following case.

Spearman v Royal United Bath Hospitals NHS Foundation Trust [2017] EWHC 3027 (QB)

The claimant was taken to hospital following a severe hypoglycaemic attack. Shortly after he arrived, he went through a number of doors and accessed a flat roof which was surrounded on all sides by safety fencing. He used furniture that was on the roof to climb over the fence. He fell into the courtyard below suffering from severe brain injury and multiple fractures. A question for the court was whether the claimant was a visitor under the 1957 Act or a trespasser under the 1984 Act. It was held that the claimant was a visitor. Whether a person is a visitor or trespasser was not solely determined by whether the person was in an authorised place but rather their state of mind and intention was an important additional factor. For example, if a patient made a mistake and went the wrong way, it could not be suggested that they became a trespasser. Here the claimant in his confused state of mind, believed that he had to go upstairs to get out of the hospital. His belief meant that he remained a lawful visitor and did not become a trespasser at any material time. The court emphasised that the duty of the hospital was to ensure that the premises were reasonably safe for the claimant as a vulnerable patient who was confused and mentally unstable at the time.

In *Spearman*, the court considered that the hospital owed the claimant a superimposed duty which encompassed his reasonable safety not merely by reference to the state of the premises but also by reference to the overall operation of the hospital which included supervision of patients, flow and management of patients and restriction of access to areas where patients did not need to go.

7.3 Discharging the common duty of care and the standard of care

The standard of care is that generally applied in negligence, the standard of the 'reasonable man'. As a result the occupier is merely obliged to guard against foreseeable risks, not unexpected risks.

The standard of care is measured objectively by the court so it is what is reasonable in the circumstances.

CASE EXAMPLE

Esdale v Dover District Council [2010] EWCA Civ 409

The council owned a block of flats in which the claimant lived. She was injured when she tripped on a path leading to the flats. The path was made partly of concrete and partly of tarmac and the path was uneven where the two materials joined which the claimant argued had caused her injury. Although the trial judge rejected the claim an appeal was lodged on the basis that the council generally repaired defects in paths which were uneven by three-quarters of an inch. Here the unevenness was between three-quarters of an inch and an inch. The Court of Appeal rejected the argument that this policy of the council meant that it had not acted reasonably in the circumstances by not remedying the defect.

CASE EXAMPLE

Laverton v Kiapasha (t/as Takeaway Supreme) [2022] EWCA Civ 1656

The claimant slipped at the defendant's takeaway food shop and broke her ankle. The claimant had been out drinking before going to the takeaway shop. It had also been raining, and the floor was wet and slippery. The defendant had taken precautions for the safety of his customers laying non-slip floor tiles, having a doormat to limit the water brought in by customers, and using a mop to clean up excess water several times a day on days that it rained. On the night in question, it was busy night and it was conceded that the doormat may have been kicked out of the way but it was argued by the defendant that on busy nights with a large number of customers coming and going in a confined space it was not reasonable to expect such a business to remove all water from the floor so that no-one, whatever the circumstances, will slip. It was held that the defendant was not liable. The Court of Appeal explained that at busy times in a business such as this, the defendant must be right that it is simply not practicable to mop up the water as it arrives. The only solution would be to close the shop, which he can only be expected to do if the customers cannot otherwise be reasonably safe. If the defendant were to be held liable in such circumstances, is to suggest a level of perfection imposing a near strict liability which the law does not at present do.

From the above case it can be seen that the courts exercise some caution to avoid imposing an unrealistic standard of care and that the standard of care is reasonable in the circumstances.

The circumstances relevant in determining whether the defendant has fallen below the standard of care required or in other words breached the duty of care is set out in s2(3) of the Act:

SECTION

'The circumstances relevant for the present purpose include the degree of care, and of want of care, which would ordinarily be looked for in such a visitor.'

The general factors considered in determining whether the defendant has breached their duty of care in a claim for general negligence are equally applicable here (see Chapter 3) but there are some specific examples which help to determine the court's approach in this area. For example, an occupier will not always be able to control and check every aspect of their premises 24 hours a day but they can and should implement a reasonably safe system in place to ensure that checks are made at regular intervals. Evidence of this will demonstrate that the occupier has been reasonable together with consideration of the purpose of the claimant's visit.

CASE EXAMPLE

Tedstone v Bourne Leisure Ltd [2008] EWCA Civ 654

In this case the claimant was injured when she slipped on a pool of water in the vicinity of a Jacuzzi on an area of non-slip tiles at the swimming pool of the defendants' hotel. The question was whether the defendant had exercised the requisite standard of care in the circumstances, namely did they have a system in place to inspect and clean. Five minutes prior to the accident occurring there was no water present in the area in question. It was held that no reasonable system would have prevented this accident from occurring as it arose out of unusual spillage of water from the Jacuzzi and the spillage probably arrived within a minute or two before the accident. No reasonable system would, on the balance of probabilities, have dealt with this unusual occurrence in the short time available. The spillage had not been on the floor long enough for it to have been cleaned up. The accident did not occur from want of due care on the part of the defendants.

This is to say that had the spillage been on the floor for a long period of time and the defendants made no attempt to clean it up, on the balance of probabilities would be in breach of their duty of care. By comparison, a duty was established in the following case:

CASE EXAMPLE

Butcher v Southend-on-Sea BC [2014] EWCA Civ 1556

The hazard on which the claimant slipped which was an uneven tarmac, was apparent for such a length of time, that it was reasonably foreseeable that someone could slip. The defendants failed to take care in all the circumstances to ensure that their visitors would be reasonably safe in using the premises.

Due to the scope and potential limitations of the duty the Act sensibly makes some different rules for particular classes of visitor.

7.3.1 Liability to children

Under s2(3)(a) the occupier:

SECTION

'. . . must be prepared for children to be less careful than adults . . . the premises must be reasonably safe for a child of that age.'

This demonstrates again that it is the visitor that must be kept safe and that in the case of children the standard of care is measured subjectively rather than objectively.

The reasoning is perfectly logical, what may pose no threat to an adult may nevertheless be very dangerous to a child.

CASE EXAMPLE

Moloney v Lambeth LBC [1966] 64 LGR 440

Here a four-year-old fell through a gap in railings guarding a stairwell and was injured. An adult could not have fallen through the gap so such an injury would have been impossible. Nevertheless it was dangerous to a child, and a child in any case may have been incapable of appreciating the risk involved. The occupier was held to be liable by the court.

Children in any case are taken to be unlikely to appreciate risks in a way that an adult would and indeed might even be attracted to the danger. As a result an occupier should do nothing to attract the child to the danger and must guard against any kind of 'allurement' which places a child visitor at risk of harm.

CASE EXAMPLE

Glasgow Corporation v Taylor [1922] 1 AC 44

Here a seven-year-old child ate poisonous berries in a botanical garden and died as a result. The shrub on which the berries grew was not fenced off in any way. The court held that the occupier should have expected that the berries might naturally attract a young child's interest and the occupier was liable.

Nevertheless, the mere existence of an allurement on its own is not sufficient ground for liability.

CASE EXAMPLE

Liddle v Yorkshire (North Riding) CC [1944] 2 KB 101

A child was injured when he jumped off a soil bank while showing off to his friends. The court held that, despite the obvious allurement, the defendant was not liable since the occupier had warned the child away from the bank on numerous previous occasions.

In fact, even though an allurement exists there will be no liability on the occupier if the damage or injury suffered is not foreseeable. As with negligence generally it is the general type of damage that must be foreseen rather than the specific circumstances in which the damage occurs.

CASE EXAMPLE

Jolley v London Borough of Sutton [2000] 1 WLR 1082

The council failed to move an abandoned boat from an estuary shore for two years. Children regularly played in the boat and it was clearly a potential danger. When two young boys of 14 jacked the boat up to repair it, the boat fell on one, injuring him. In the Court of Appeal the action for compensation failed, since it was held that, while the boat was an obvious allurement, the course of action taken by the boys and therefore the specific type of damage were not foreseeable. The House of Lords reversed this. The House of Lords felt that it was an obvious risk that children playing on or near the boat might be injured. It was sufficient for liability that some injury was foreseeable.

As Lord Hoffmann said in the House of Lords at 1093:

JUDGMENT

'the [trial] judge's broad description of the risk as being that children would "meddle with the boat at the risk of some physical injury" was the correct one to adopt'.

So the House of Lords applied the principle of causation from *The Wagon Mound.*

Obviously the decision can seem harsh since it would be quite difficult to argue that the council could in fact have foreseen the very unusual way in which the injuries occurred. Nevertheless, the Act imposes a duty on an occupier to recognise that children may behave in very different ways from adults. It is possible therefore to see the judgment as a very practical application of the law. *S Brooman, 'Expect the Unexpected' (November 2000) L Ex, p. 34* comments that: 'In essence, the House of Lords has confirmed in case law what all parents knew already: the only predictable attribute of children is that they are unpredictable, and society (including councils) should protect them accordingly.'

In any case the courts will sometimes take the view that very young children should be under the supervision of a parent or other adult. In this case the occupier might find that he is relieved of liability.

CASE EXAMPLE

Phipps v Rochester Corporation [1955] 1 QB 450

A five-year-old child was injured having fallen down a trench dug by the defendant council where the child frequently played. The defendant was not liable because the court concluded that the parents should have had a child of that age under proper control.

In his judgment Devlin J explained the position at 472:

JUDGMENT

'the responsibility for the safety of little children must rest primarily upon the parents; it is their duty to see that such children are not allowed to wander about by themselves, or at the least to satisfy themselves that the places to which they do allow their children to go unaccompanied are safe for them to go. It would not be socially desirable if parents were, as a matter of course, able to shift the burden of looking after their children from their own shoulders to those persons who happen to have accessible bits of land.'

CASE EXAMPLE

Marsden v Bourne Leisure [2009] EWCA Civ 671

The claimant family had been staying at the defendant's holiday park. The mother was speaking with another visitor when Matthew, her 2.5 year old son, and his younger brother disappeared. At the holiday park there were three ponds, and tragically, Matthew was found drowned in one of these lakes. Matthew had gone down a surfaced pathway bounded by wooden rails which led between two caravans onto a roadway, passed static caravans to the edge of the pond. This was a small pond surrounded by wooden horizontal rails approximately two feet high, several feet from the edge of the water, and fenced with wire mesh below the rails. He must have climbed over. His father found him drowned in the pond. Less than a year previous to this, another boy age 4 had to be rescued from that same pond and further safety precautions had been taken by the occupier. Taking into account the occupier's obligation under s2(2) and (3) of the 1957 Act as well as the proposition set out by Devlin J in *Phipps v Rochester*, the Court of Appeal held that there was no basis upon which it could be said that, in the exercise of reasonable care, the occupiers should have underlined or emphasised so obvious a danger. Mr and Mrs Marsden knew, as any conscientious parent would have known, that the site as a whole was dangerous to small unaccompanied children for many reasons. As conscientious parents, they did not need to be told that.

7.3.2 Liability to persons entering to exercise a calling

Sensibly the Act also has a more particular attitude to professional visitors, taking the view that, by s2(3)(b), in relation to activities carried on within their trade, the occupier is entitled to expect that 'a person in the exercise of his calling, will appreciate and guard against any special risks ordinarily incident to it'.

So whereas an occupier must accept child visitors to be less capable, in the case of visitors exercising their calling the occupier will not be liable where tradesmen fail to guard against risks which they should know about.

There are three stages to consider in the application of s2(3)(b):

i. The specialist visitor has a special skill/calling;
ii. The risk of danger is one that is ordinarily incidental to that skill or calling; and
iii. The danger that caused the harm is one that the specialist could have taken steps to avoid.

CASE EXAMPLE

Roles v Nathan [1963] 1 WLR 1117

The Court of Appeal refused to impose liability on the occupiers when chimney sweeps died after inhaling carbon monoxide fumes while cleaning flues in an industrial chimney. The sweeps should have accepted the advice of the occupiers to complete the work with the boilers off rather than leaving them lit.

However, the existence of a skill is not proof *per se* that the occupier is not liable to the skilled visitor. It depends on whether the normal safeguards associated with the trade would have been sufficient to avert the loss or injury.

CASE EXAMPLE

Salmon v Seafarers Restaurants Ltd [1983] 1 WLR 1264

Owners of a chip shop were liable for the injuries caused to a fireman which were unavoidable because of the character of the fire. The fireman was obviously bound to take the normal risks associated with firefighting. However, he had exercised all of the normal skills of a fireman and it was only the character of the fire that caused his injuries, not anything that he could have guarded against himself. As a result of this the court held the occupier liable.

7.3.3 Liability for the torts of independent contractors

Generally the occupier will be able to avoid liability for loss or injuries suffered by his visitors when the cause of damage is the negligence of an independent contractor hired by the occupier. Under s2(4)(b) the occupier is not liable for 'damage caused to a visitor by a danger due to the faulty execution of any work or construction, maintenance or repair by an independent contractor employed by the occupier'.

It is a sensible rule because reputable contractors will in any case be covered by their own insurance and so the claimant will still be able to recover compensation.

However, three requirements will apply.

i. it must be reasonable for the occupier to have entrusted the work to the independent contractor;
ii. the contractor hired must be competent to carry out the task; and
iii. if possible the occupier must inspect the work.

It is reasonable to hire a contractor

It must be reasonable for the occupier to have entrusted the work to the independent contractor in the first place. This in itself depends on the character of the occupier and also on the nature of the work done. For example, much less might be expected of a private householder than of a business which might already employ its own specialists.

CASE EXAMPLE

Haseldine v Daw & Son Ltd [1941] 2 KB 343

Here the issue was the death of the claimant following the negligent repair of a lift by the independent contractors. The occupier was not liable because repair of a lift is a highly specialist activity and could not be expected of the occupier. The court accepted that the occupier had discharged his duty by hiring a supposedly competent contractor to carry out the work.

The contractor must be competent to carry out the work

For the occupier to avoid liability, the contractor that he hired must be competent to carry out the actual task required. Again there is little adequate check that somebody like a householder can make. They might improve their chance of avoiding liability as an occupier by using contractors recommended by a trade association etc.

CASE EXAMPLE

Ferguson v Welsh [1987] 1 WLR 1553

Demolition contractors were hired by the local authority and also employed the claimant to complete the work. When the claimant was injured as a result of their unsafe working systems the court held that the local authority was liable.

As Goff LJ explained (at 1561) the local authority has a duty not to 'countenance the unsafe working methods of cowboy operators'.

The fact that the contractor fails to carry insurance for the activity should be a fair indication to the occupier that the contractor is not competent.

CASE EXAMPLE

Bottomley v Todmorden Cricket Club [2003] EWCA Civ 1575

The club hired a stunt team to carry out a 'firework display'. The team chose to use ordinary gunpowder, petrol and propane gas rather than the more traditional fireworks and also then enlisted the help of the claimant, an unpaid amateur with no experience of pyrotechnics, for the stunt. The claimant was burnt and broke an arm when the stunt went wrong. The stunt team had no insurance and the court held that this was sufficient to impose liability on the cricket club.

Although this will not always apply if there are other accepted means of assessing the independent contractor's competence to carry out the work.

CASE EXAMPLE

Naylor (t/a Mainstream) v Payling [2004] EWCA Civ 560

The claimant was injured while being thrown out of a nightclub owing to the negligence of the door attendant. The door attendant was supplied by an independent contractor. The claimant successfully sued on the basis that the nightclub had negligently failed to check whether the independent contractor had insurance and for negligently failing to ascertain whether the independent contractor was competent. The nightclub appealed and the Court of Appeal upheld that appeal. It held that there was no obligation to check whether the independent contractor was insured since the nightclub had complied with a local scheme supported by both the local authority and the police for establishing whether door attendants were suitably qualified for the work.

The occupier may be expected to inspect the work

Third, and only if it is in fact possible, the occupier must inspect the work to ensure that it has been carried out to an appropriate standard.

Inevitably the more complex and technical the work and the less expert the occupier, then the less reasonable it is to impose this obligation. It may be sufficient that a competent contractor was hired. Although where an inspection is straightforward, the requirement still exists.

CASE EXAMPLE

Woodward v Mayor of Hastings **[1945] KB 174**

Occupiers were liable when a child was injured on school steps which were negligently left in an icy state after they had been cleared of snow. The danger should have been obvious to the occupiers and the court held them liable. It was identified (at 183) that there was: 'no esoteric quality in the nature of the work which the cleaning of a snow covered step demands'.

However, it may be that in certain circumstances the occupier is obliged to delegate supervision of the work to a suitable professional, for example an architect, in order to ultimately avoid liability for any damage or injury.

CASE EXAMPLE

AMF International Ltd v Magnet Bowling Ltd **[1968] 2 All ER 789**

The company AMF International was contracted to install bowling equipment in a centre that was being built by contractors hired by Magnet. The contractors gave the go-ahead for the equipment to be installed but then AMF's equipment was destroyed when the partially built building was flooded during torrential rainfall. Magnet was held to be liable for failing to check on the state that the contractors had left the building in before AMF were instructed to enter it.

One interesting aspect of the occupier's duty to inspect is the duty to inspect also that the independent contractor is insured so that he may stand the loss if found liable. This in itself is also another example of the occupier's duty to ensure that a competent contractor is chosen, since it can be assumed that a competent contractor would not engage in work without public liability insurance cover.

CASE EXAMPLE

Gwillam v West Hertfordshire NHS Trust **[2002] 3 WLR 1425**

The hospital trust was responsible for a fund-raising fair held on its premises for which it hired a 'splat wall' from a firm called Club Entertainments who were also responsible for operating it. (A 'splat wall' is a wall that a person wearing a Velcro suit will stick to after bouncing from a trampoline.) The claimant was injured when she fell because the wall had been negligently assembled. As part of the contract between the trust and Club Entertainments the wall was to be covered by the latter's public liability insurance. However, this had expired four days before the fair and the claimant sought damages from the trust. Both Lord Woolf CJ and Lord Justice Waller in the Court of Appeal held that there was a duty to ensure that the contractor had insurance cover, but that the trust had not breached this duty. Lord Woolf CJ in any case felt that the trust had not breached the duty to keep the woman safe while on its premises.

ACTIVITY

Quick quiz

Consider whether or not a duty would be owed under the Occupiers' Liability Act 1957 in the following circumstances and suggest whether an action is likely to succeed.

1 Ted, a burglar, has been injured when he broke into Melanie's house and fell downstairs in the dark because the handrail was broken and had not been repaired.
2 Ted, a postman, was injured while delivering letters to Melanie's house when the chimney pot fell on him.
3 Ted, an electrician, was injured when he was electrocuted by a live wire while he was fitting new lights for Melanie.
4 Ted, a four-year-old child, was very ill after he ate berries from a bush overhanging from Melanie's garden. Ted was on his own on the pavement outside Melanie's house at 7 p.m. at night when he ate the berries. Melanie had shouted to Ted on several occasions before when she had seen him going to pick the berries.

7.3.4 Avoiding the duty

As we have already seen, according to s2(1) the occupier is free to extend, restrict, modify or exclude his duty to visitors. This can be achieved by the occupier in one of three ways.

Warnings

Under s2(4)(a) a warning will not absolve the occupier of liability unless 'in all the circumstances it was enough to enable the visitor to be reasonably safe'.

There are two aspects to this provision.

i. There was a warning; and
ii. The warning must enable the visitor to be reasonably safe.

What amounts to a sufficient warning then will be a question of fact in each case. In *Roles v Nathan* [1963] 1 WLR 1117, for instance, Lord Denning used the example of a warning that the only access to the premises over a rotting footbridge was unsafe. This he said could not absolve the occupier because the visitor had no other means of access and so would have no choice but to use the unsafe bridge. Presumably this means that if there were another means of access which was safe, then the warning not to use the footbridge may well be sufficient.

Sometimes in any case even a very precise warning may be insufficient to safeguard the visitor and the occupier may be obliged to set up barriers instead to ensure the visitor's safety.

CASE EXAMPLE

Rae v Mars (UK) Ltd [1990] 3 EG 80

Here a warning notice was used in respect of a deep pit inside the entrance of a dark shed with no artificial lighting. The occupier was held liable because the pit was immediately inside the entrance and so the warning was insufficient to safeguard the visitor from the danger.

However, the occupier will not be obliged to take excessive steps to avoid danger when the danger is obvious and sufficient steps have been taken to prevent harm.

CASE EXAMPLE

Beaton v Devon County Council [2002] EWCA Civ 1675

The claimant was injured while riding through a cycle tunnel. The tunnel was in good condition and the defendant council had supplied good lighting throughout it. There were two gullies in the tunnel but this was well known. The Court of Appeal held that the council had done everything practicable to keep cyclists safe.

The actual wording of warning signs can be critical in determining whether liability is avoided. A distinction must be made between a proper warning, for example 'Danger: steps slippery when wet' and mere attempts to set up a defence of *volenti*, for example 'Persons enter at their own risk', which will not absolve liability; and even ones that are attempts to exclude liability, for example 'No liability will be accepted for any injury howsoever caused' will be subject to the limitations in the Unfair Contracts Terms Act 1977, particularly s2(1) in this case.

Nevertheless, there are certain risks that are possibly so obvious to all that a court will decide that no additional warning is needed in the circumstances.

CASE EXAMPLE

Staples v West Dorset DC [1995] 93 LGR 536

Danger of wet algae on a high wall at Lyme Regis should have been obvious. Therefore, there was no additional duty to warn of the danger and no liability on the council when a visitor slipped on the wall and was injured.

Exclusion clauses

Section 2(1) of the 1957 Act specifically refers to the right of the occupier to exclude liability 'by agreement or otherwise'. Exclusion clauses can be included as a term in a contractual licence and may be alternatively communicated in an effective notice. Whilst the Unfair Contract Terms Act 1977 (UCTA) (ss1 and 2) deal with actions relating to occupation of premises used for business purposes, the Consumer Rights Act 2015 (CRA) s64 deals with exclusion clauses in consumer contracts i.e. between trader and consumer.

CASE EXAMPLE

Ashdown v Samuel Williams & Sons Ltd [1957] 1 QB 409

The claimant was injured by the negligent shunting of railway trucks while on the occupier's land. She was unable to recover for injuries sustained in a shunting yard because notices excluding liability were sufficiently brought to her attention and she was no more than a contractual licensee when she entered.

The use of exclusion clauses, however, will be subject to various restrictions.

- They are apparently unavailable in the case of persons entering under a legal right.
- They will not apply in the case of strangers, for example a tenant's visitors, because they will not have had any chance in advance to agree to the exclusion – this is under s3(1) UCTA – however, such visitors will be able to take advantage of any additional protections identified in the contract.
- They will most probably fail against children, who may be unable to read and who may not fully understand their implications.
- They will not be allowed in respect of death or personal injury caused by the occupier's negligence because this will be prevented by s2(1) UCTA.
- There is also an additional argument that, since the Occupiers' Liability Act 1984 imposes a minimum standard of care owed to trespassers, then this minimum standard should be beyond exclusion, or trespassers would have better rights than lawful visitors.

Causation and remoteness

The usual rules on causation and remoteness discussed in relation to general negligence apply here.

CRITIQUING THE LAW

How successful is the law on occupiers' liability in preventing the development of a compensation culture?

General defences

There are two possible defences.

a The claimant's contributory negligence. Under the Law Reform (Contributory Negligence) Act 1945 this has the effect of reducing awards of damages according to the extent to which the court believes that the visitor is responsible for his own injuries or loss.

b *Volenti non fit injuria* – consent. Section 2(5) allows that the occupier 'has no liability to a visitor in respect of risks willingly accepted as his by the visitor'. However, a number of basic requirements apply.

The risk must be fully understood by the visitor.

CASE EXAMPLE

Simms v Leigh RFC **[1960] 2 All ER 923**

There was no liability to a rugby football player when the injury was sustained within the normal rules of the game.

The visitor must have also have freely and voluntarily accepted the risk. In such circumstances an occupier will not be liable for accidents caused to adults who are fully warned and ought to take responsibility for their own safety when they engage in obvious risks.

CASE EXAMPLE

Evans v Kosmar Villa Holidays plc **[2008] 1 WLR 297**

The claimant, who was 18 at the time, was injured when, in the early hours of the morning, he dived into the shallow end of a swimming pool in a holiday complex in Corfu in which he was staying. The claimant hit his head on the bottom as he dived and suffered tetraplegia as a result of his injuries. There were two small 'no diving signs' although it was accepted that these were probably not visible at night. The trial judge found Kosmar liable with 50 per cent reduction in damages for contributory negligence. The Court of Appeal held that there was no breach of duty and the defendant had not caused the injury, which was caused by the claimant's voluntary action in diving into the shallow end.

Lord Justice Richards stated at 41:

JUDGMENT

'[the defendant's] duty of care did not extend, in my judgment, to a duty to guard the claimant against the risk of his diving into the pool and injuring himself. That was an obvious risk, of which he was well aware. Although just under 18 years of age, he was of full capacity and was able to make a genuine and informed choice. He was not even seriously affected by drink.'

- Mere knowledge of the risk is also insufficient, it must actually be accepted by the visitor and the knowledge must be sufficient to make the visitor safe.

CASE EXAMPLE

White v Blackmore [1972] 2 QB 651

General knowledge that 'jalopy racing' was a dangerous activity did not mean that the claimant had accepted inadequate safety arrangements. The court held the occupier liable.

- If the claimant has no choice but to enter the premises then he cannot be taken to have accepted the risk and the defence will be unavailable.

CASE EXAMPLE

Burnett v British Waterways Board [1973] 2 All ER 631

A claimant entering the defendant's dry dock on a barge had no choice but to be there and so *volenti* was unavailable as a defence.

- Express warnings that the claimant enters at his own risk may well be caught by the Unfair Contract Terms Act 1977.

ACTIVITY

Self-assessment questions

1. Who exactly is a visitor?
2. What sorts of people are non-visitors?
3. What decides whether a person is an occupier?
4. Why is the duty called 'the common duty of care'?
5. What exactly is the duty owed by the occupier?
6. Why should children have a different duty of care applied to them?
7. What exactly is 'allurement'?
8. What protection does the case of *Phipps v Rochester Corporation* give to an occupier?
9. When will a tradesman be able to successfully sue an occupier?
10. When will an occupier be liable for the negligent acts or omissions of people who have carried out work on his premises?
11. How can an occupier avoid being liable to a lawful visitor?
12. When will a warning sign protect an occupier from liability and when will it not?
13. When is an exclusion clause likely to be used and what will prevent it from succeeding?

KEY FACTS

Occupiers' liability – general	**Case**
Occupiers' liability is covered by two Acts: the Occupiers' Liability Act 1957 in the case of lawful 'visitors', and the Occupiers' Liability Act 1984 in the case of trespassers.	
An 'occupier' is anybody in actual control of the land.	*Wheat v Lacon* [1966]
Premises is widely defined and has included even a ladder.	***Wheeler v Copas* [1981]**
The duty and the standard of care in the 1957 Act	Case/statute
A 'common duty of care' is owed to all lawful visitors.	s2(1)
The duty is to ensure that the visitor is safe for the purposes of the visit.	s2(2)
Must take extra care for children, who are less careful than adults, and not put extra danger or 'allurements' in their path.	s2(3) *Glasgow Corporation v Taylor* [1922]
Applies to any foreseeable danger to the child regardless of what injury is actually caused.	*Jolley v London Borough of Sutton* [2000]
Although it is assumed that parents should keep control of young children.	*Phipps v Rochester Corporation* [1955]
A person carrying out a trade or calling on the occupier's premises must prepare for the risks associated with the trade.	*Roles v Nathan* [1963]
The occupier will not be liable for damage that is the result of work done by independent contractors if: • it is reasonable to entrust the work • a reputable contractor is chosen • the occupier is not obliged to inspect the work.	*Haseldine v Daw* [1941] *Ferguson v Welsh* [1987] *Woodward v Mayor of Hastings* [1945]
Avoiding the duty	**Case**
Possible to avoid liability where: • adequate warnings are given • exclusion clauses can be relied on – subject to the Unfair Contract Terms Act • defences of consent or contributory negligence apply.	*Rae v Mars* [1990]

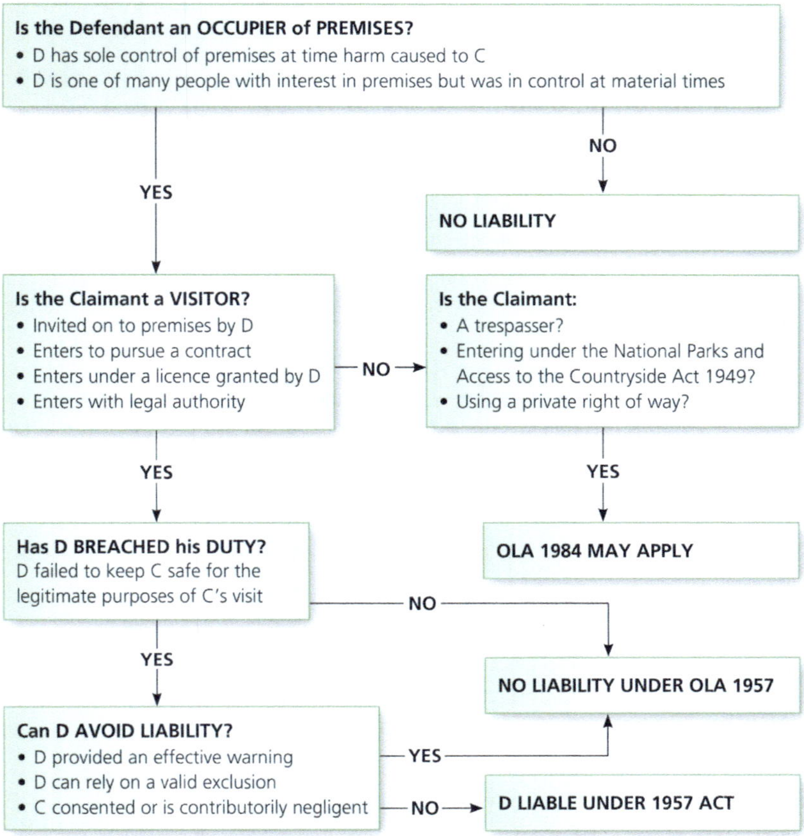

Figure 7.1 The assessment of liability under the Occupiers' Liability Act 1957.

7.4 Liability to trespassers and non-visitors under the 1984 Act

7.4.1 Common law and the duty of common humanity

The 1984 Act was introduced to provide a limited duty of care mainly towards trespassers. The Act came about because traditionally at common law trespassers were treated rather harshly and an occupier owed such entrants no duty at all, other than possibly to refrain from deliberately or recklessly inflicting damage or injury.

CASE EXAMPLE

Bird v Holbreck [1828] 4 Bing 628

This case did not particularly create any duty to protect a trespasser from harm but it finally made the use of mantraps illegal.

However, an occupier was still entitled to take reasonable steps in his own protection or in the protection of his property.

CASE EXAMPLE

Clayton v Deane [1817] Taunt 489

The court here accepted that an occupier was entitled to use reasonable deterrents to keep trespassers out, in this case broken glass on top of a wall. The requirement was that the deterrent should be reasonably visible to the trespasser.

The common law could be particularly harsh when it was applied to child trespassers who might have limited understanding, either of the risks confronting them, or indeed the nature of trespass itself.

CASE EXAMPLE

Addie v Dumbreck [1929] AC 358

Children frequently played on colliery premises and near to dangerous machinery and were turned away by the owners. When one child was injured the court held that there was no liability on the occupier since the child was a trespasser.

Because of the growth of more dangerous premises and taking into account the difficulties of making children appreciate danger many attempts were made to change the law, and this was finally achieved with the establishment of the so-called common duty of humanity.

CASE EXAMPLE

British Railways Board v Herrington [1972] AC 877

A six-year-old was badly burned when straying onto an electrified railway line, through vandalised fencing. It was well known that the fences were often broken and that small children played near the line and the railway board regularly repaired it. The House of Lords, using the *Practice Statement*, established the 'common duty of humanity'. This was a limited duty owed to child trespassers when the occupier knew of the danger and of the likelihood of the trespass, and had the skill, knowledge and resources to avoid an accident.

This duty would obviously operate in fairly limited circumstances and was not without criticism or difficulties. Because of some of the impracticalities of the rule the 1984 Act was passed.

7.4.2 When the Act applies

By s1(1)(a) a duty applies in respect of people other than visitors (who are covered by the 1957 Act) for:

SECTION

's1(1)(a). . . injury on the premises by reason of any danger due to the state of the premises or things done or omitted to be done on them'.

CASE EXAMPLE

Keown v Coventry Healthcare NHS Trust [2006] 1 WLR 953

The 11-year-old claimant climbed the underside of an external metal fire escape at the defendant's hospital. Unfortunately, the claimant fell 30 feet, which resulted in him fracturing his arm and suffering from brain injury. It was argued on behalf of the claimant that as that area of the hospital grounds was used by the public and was known as a place where children liked to play, the hospital owed a duty under the 1984 Act to take such care as was reasonable in all the circumstances to see that the he did not suffer injury by reason of a material danger on the premises, specifically that the fire escape constituted an allurement to children, and that the hospital was aware of the danger. It was accepted that the claimant should be treated as a trespasser while climbing the fire escape. It was argued on behalf of the defendant that the fire escape was not itself dangerous but rather that the danger was due to the claimant's activity on the premises. This question here is whether this was an obvious risk. Moreover, a risk that may be obvious to an adult, may not be so to a child. It was held that as an 11-year-old, the claimant could appreciate the dangers involved in climbing the fire escape and so the danger was caused not by the state of the premises but rather the claimant's activity. As such, the claimant did not satisfy s1(1)a of the 1984 Act.

The occupier will only owe a duty under s1(3) if:

SECTION

s1(3)(a) he is aware of the danger or has reasonable grounds to believe it exists;

s1(3)(b) he knows or has reasonable grounds to believe that the other is in the vicinity of the danger (in either case whether the other has lawful authority for being in that vicinity or not); and

s1(3)(c) the risk is one against which, in all the circumstances of the case, he may reasonably be expected to offer the other some protection.

So the first part of the test is subjective and based on the occupier's actual knowledge, but the final part is objective and based on what a reasonable occupier should do.

7.4.3 The nature of the duty

The character of the duty is identified in the Act. According to s1(4) the duty is to 'take such care as is reasonable in all the circumstances' to prevent injury to the non-visitor 'by reason of the danger concerned'.

So the standard of care is clearly an objective standard based on negligence. What is required of the occupier depends on the circumstances of each case. The greater the degree of risk the more precautions the occupier will have to take. Factors to be taken into account include the nature of the premises, the degree of danger, the practicality of taking precautions and of course the age of the trespasser.

CASE EXAMPLE

Tomlinson v Congleton Borough Council [2003] 3 WLR 705

The local authority owned a park including a lake. Warning signs were posted prohibiting swimming and diving because the water was dangerous, but the council knew that these were generally ignored. The council decided to make the lake inaccessible to the public but delayed start on this work because of lack of funds. The claimant, aged 18, dived into the lake, struck his head and suffered paralysis as a result of a severe spinal injury. His claim under the 1984 Act was initially rejected by the trial judge but succeeded in the Court of Appeal. The Court of Appeal was satisfied that all three aspects of s1(3) were satisfied. The Court felt that the gravity of the risk of injury, the frequency with which people were exposed to the risk and the fact that the lake acted as an allurement, all meant that the scheme to make the lake inaccessible should have been completed with greater urgency. However, the Court reduced damages by two-thirds because of the contributory negligence of the claimant. The House of Lords, however, accepted the council's appeal. It based its decision on three reasons. First, that the danger was not due to the state of the premises (although Lord Hutton felt that because the water was so dark and murky it was). Second, the House of Lords felt that it was not the sort of risk that a defendant should have to guard against but one that the trespasser in fact chose to run. Finally, the House felt that the council would not have breached its duty even in the case of a lawful visitor since the practicality and financial cost of avoiding the danger was not such that a reasonable occupier ought to be obliged to go to such ends.

The mere fact that the occupier has taken precautions or fenced the premises does not in itself indicate that the occupier knew or ought to have known of the existence of a danger.

CASE EXAMPLE

White v St Albans City Council, The Times, 12 March 1990

Here the claimant had taken an unauthorised short cut over the council's land. He fell from a narrow bridge that had been fenced. The court did not feel that this was sufficient to make the council liable.

In assessing whether s1(3) applies the court must take into account all of the circumstances at the time the injury occurred.

CASE EXAMPLE

Donoghue v Folkestone Properties [2003] EWCA Civ 231

The claimant was injured when he was trespassing on a slipway in a harbour and dived into the harbour after midnight in mid-winter. The claimant struck his head on an underwater pile. The Court of Appeal held that the occupier did not owe a duty of care. A reasonable occupier would not expect that a trespasser might be present or engage in such a foolhardy escapade. It is not the case that a person carrying on such an activity can ascribe to the "state of the premises" an injury sustained as a result of a mishap in the course of carrying on the activity-provided of course that the mishap is not caused by an unusual or latent feature of the landscape. The 1984 Act does not impose any duty on an occupier to protect a trespasser from making use of a particular feature of the premises in order to carry on an activity simply because that activity carries with it an inherent risk of injury.

So there can be no liability if the occupier had no reason to suspect the presence of a trespasser.

CASE EXAMPLE

Higgs v Foster [2004] EWCA Civ 843

A police officer investigating a crime entered the occupier's premises for surveillance purposes and fell into an uncovered inspection pit behind some coaches and suffered severe injuries causing him to retire from the police force. The police officer was a trespasser and the occupier could not have anticipated the presence of the trespasser or that he would have gone behind the coaches for any reason so there was no liability.

Similarly there can be no liability if the occupier was unaware of the danger or had no reason to suspect the danger.

CASE EXAMPLE

Rhind v Astbury Water Park [2004] EWCA Civ 756

The claimant had ignored a notice stating 'Private Property. Strictly no Swimming' and jumped into a lake, being injured by objects below the surface of the water. The claimant was a trespasser and the occupier had no reason to know that there were dangerous objects below the surface so there was no liability.

7.4.4 Avoiding liability under the 1984 Act

Again, as with the 1957 Act, it is possible for the occupier to avoid liability and warnings. The defence of *volenti* and the possibility of exclusion of liability also need to be considered.

Warnings

Under s1(5) in an appropriate case the occupier could do so by taking 'such steps as are reasonable in all the circumstances'. This might, in the case of adult trespassers, be achieved by use of effective warnings or by discouraging people from entering.

CASE EXAMPLE

Westwood v The Post Office [1973] 1 QB 591

A notice posted on a motor room door that 'Only the authorised attendant is permitted to enter' was held as sufficient warning for an intelligent adult. The occupier was not liable.

However, once again, it is unlikely that such warnings will succeed in the case of children, who may not be able to read or may not understand the warning. It is possible that in certain circumstances even physical barriers may be insufficient to discharge the occupier's duty.

Volenti

Section 1(6) also preserves the defence of *volenti*. Again the claimant must appreciate the nature and degree of the risk, not merely be aware of its existence for the defence to apply.

CASE EXAMPLE

Ratcliffe v McConnell [1999] 1 WLR 670

A warning notice at the shallow end of a swimming pool read: 'Deep end shallow dive'. The pool was always kept locked after hours and the claimant knew that entry was prohibited at this time. He was a trespasser and when he was injured while diving into the shallow end his claim failed. The court held that he was aware of the risk and had freely accepted it.

The facts of this next case can be found in Chapter 2 where it is discussed in relation to establishing a duty of care. Here we consider this case in the context of the defences raised.

CASE EXAMPLE

Geary v JD Wetherspoon plc [2011] EWHC 1506 (QB)

It was held that sliding down bannisters carries an obvious risk and one that falls squarely within the principle of voluntary assumption of risk. The claimant freely chose to do something which she knew to be dangerous. She knew that sliding down the banisters was not permitted, but she chose to do it anyway. She was therefore the author of her own misfortune. The defendant owed no duty to protect her from such an obvious and inherent risk.

Exclusion of liability

There is no reference to exclusion clauses in the Act unlike the 1957 Act. It has been argued that exclusion should be impossible since the Act creates a minimum standard of care that would then be thwarted. However, this does then create the uneasy situation where a trespasser may well be entitled to more care than a lawful visitor.

Remedies

The 1984 Act provides compensation for personal injuries only and not property damage. Section 1(8) explains that damage to property is not covered, reflecting an understandable view that trespassers are deserving of less protection than are lawful visitors.

ACTIVITY

Self-assessment questions

1 What protections, if any, did the law traditionally offer to trespassers?
2 Is it possible for an occupier to legitimately protect against intruders?
3 What type of damage is compensated under the 1984 Act?
4 Do the 'duty of common humanity' and the duty owed to trespassers under the 1984 Act differ at all?
5 What factors must be present in order to impose a duty on the occupier under the 1984 Act?
6 What difficulties are created by the minimum standard of care in the 1984 Act?

ACTIVITY

Quick quiz

Consider the following problem on occupiers' liability.

Alsopp Towers is a large pleasure theme park. At the entrance gate there is a sign which reads 'All of the rides are dangerous and customers enter entirely at their own risk'. Consider any liability that Alsopp Towers may incur for the following customers.

a Jasbir catches her heel in a gap between the boards while getting off 'The Screw', falls several feet and injures herself badly.

b Sean, who is a delivery driver, leaves his lorry to pick flowers from one of the ornamental borders and tears his shoe and sock and cuts his foot quite badly on broken glass.

c Pedro, an electrical contractor who is repairing one of the rides, is electrocuted and badly burnt when Daisy, who operates the ride, carelessly plugs it in.

d Tom and Jerry, two ten-year-old boys, have sneaked in by climbing over a fence. They are both injured when they walk across the rails on one of the rides and are hit by one of the cars.

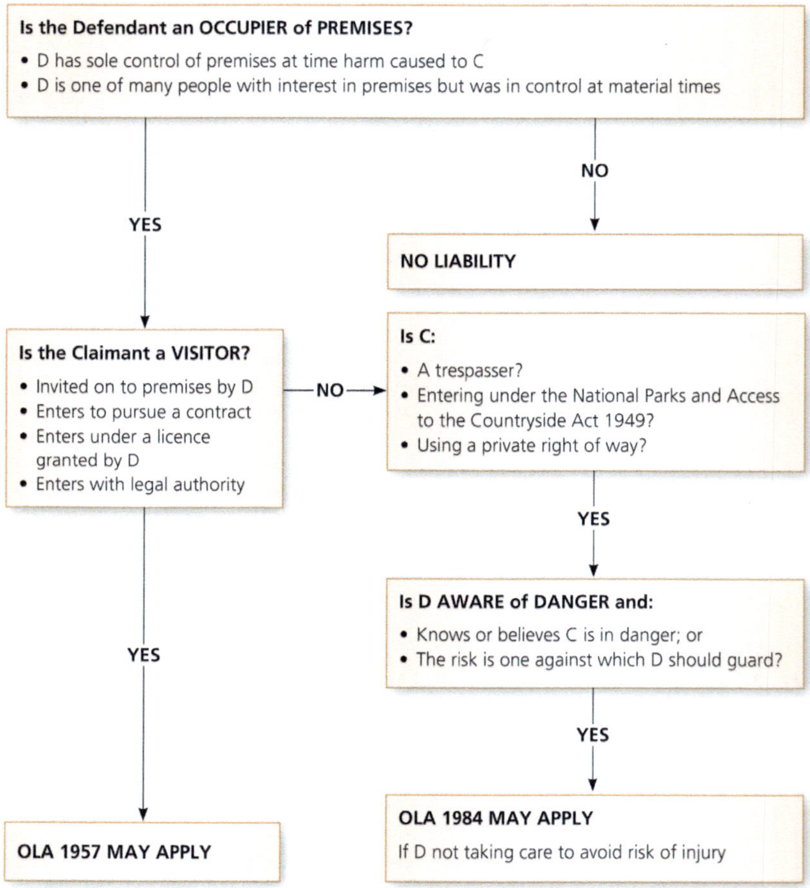

Figure 7.2 The assessment of liability under the Occupiers' Liability Act 1984.

KEY FACTS

The common law	**Case**
The law was originally merely not to deliberately cause harm.	*Bird v Holbreck* [1828]
Because of the harshness of the rule as it applied to children a common duty of humanity to trespassers was introduced.	*BR Board v Herrington* [1972]
The scope of the duty under the 1984 Act	**Case/statute**
This was given statutory force in the 1984 Act.	
The occupier only owes a duty if he: • is aware of the danger or has reasonable grounds to believe it exists • knows or believes the other is in the vicinity of the danger and • the risk is one against which he may be expected to offer some protection.	s1(3)
Compensation is only available in respect of personal injury or death, not personal property.	*Tomlinson v Congleton Borough Council* [2003]
The greater the risk the more precautions must be taken.	
Avoiding the duty	**Case/statute**
The occupier can defend if he has taken reasonable steps to avoid harm.	s1(5)
So warnings may succeed – but not against children.	*Westwood v The Post Office* [1973]
Volenti is also possible if the trespasser is fully aware of the risk.	s1(6) *Ratcliffe v McConnell* [1999]

7.5 Liability for defective premises and the Defective Premises Act 1972

We have already seen that it is possible for persons other than the occupier of land to be responsible for damage that is caused by the state of the premises. The obvious example of this is that identified in section 7.3.5 regarding independent contractors. If the usual occupier of the land can satisfy the tests in s2(4) of the 1957 Act and show that an independent contractor who has worked on the land was in fact the cause of the damage then, provided the independent contractor can also be shown to have control of the premises for those purposes, the independent contractor may be liable. If, however, this last test fails, the independent contractor may still be liable under the normal rules of negligence.

There are, however, other categories of people who may be fixed with liability for the state of the premises and damages that occur as a result of the defective state of the premises. There are generally two classes of person to whom this will apply and such liability falls under the Defective Premises Act 1972. The two classes are landlords and builders.

7.5.1 Landlords

It is possible that a landlord might retain control of certain parts of premises. If the test in *Wheat v Lacon* is satisfied then the landlord may be classed as an occupier and may be subject to the duties in either the 1957 or the 1984 Acts.

In other cases where the landlord no longer has control over the premises then liability may still be possible either under the Defective Premises Act 1972 or under some often inconsistent common law.

The early common law was based on the contract between landlord and tenant and the maxim *caveat emptor* was applied so that there was general immunity from negligence actions. This has been reaffirmed.

CASE EXAMPLE

Rimmer v Liverpool Corporation [1984] 2 WLR 426

Here there was held to be no duty of care owed by a landlord to ensure the safety of the premises at the time of letting. The claimant was injured when he put his hand through a glass panel but there was no liability on the landlord.

The Act was passed at a time when it was generally felt that tenants were badly treated not just by their landlords but also by the existing law.

The basic duty is found in s4 of the Act.

- By s4(1) where the landlord has the obligation of maintenance and repair then he has a duty to all those likely to be affected 'to take such care as is reasonable in all the circumstances [to prevent] personal injury or damage . . . caused by a relevant defect'.
- By s4(2) the duty is owed if the landlord knows or ought to know of the defect.
- By s4(3) a relevant defect is identified as 'one arising from or continuing from an act or omission . . . which constituted . . . a failure to carry out the obligation of "maintenance or repair"'.

The duties can neither be restricted nor excluded by virtue of the Act.

Further duties also exist in the Landlord and Tenant Act 1985, in respect of the structure, the exterior and services in leases under seven years; and in the Housing Act 1988 in respect of basements and roofs.

7.5.2 Builders

The expression 'builder' has been used in the widest sense to include all persons involved in the construction or sale of a building. In this way the term might arguably include surveyors, architects and others. However, it is not certain whether this would actually apply in the case of the Defective Premises Act 1972.

Obviously one of the major problems facing potential claimants will usually involve latent defects in the property. With modern properties this may in part be covered by the NHBC scheme where builders are covered by it. Where a builder merely worked on premises he may in any case face liability under straightforward *Donoghue v Stevenson* [1932] AC 562 principles. However, where the builder was also owner and sold on, then traditionally there was no liability because of the doctrine of privity of contract.

The Defective Premises Act 1972 removed this anomaly by s3 and allowed that there would be no reduction or removal of liability merely because of the 'subsequent disposal of the premises'.

A number of cases in the 1970s, *Dutton v Bognor Regis UDC* [1972] 1 QB 373 and *Anns v Merton LBC* [1978] AC 728 included, attempted to remove various of the builders' immunities. However, these were for the most part overruled in *Murphy v Brentwood DC* [1990] 2 All ER 908. This case accepted that 'In the case of a building . . . a careless builder is liable on the principle in *Donoghue v Stevenson* where a latent defect results in physical injury to anyone, or damage to the property of any such person.' The builder will not, however, be liable for damage to the building itself because this is pure economic loss (the case has been criticised).

For the claimant who wishes to recover for damage to the building itself the appropriate action is through the Defective Premises Act 1972.

The duty is identified in s1 and this imposes three obligations:

- that the work is carried out in workmanlike manner;
- that proper materials are used;
- that the house is fit for human habitation.

The Act does have a number of limitations:

- it only applies to dwellings, not commercial premises;
- the limitation period is only six years from completion;
- it excludes approved schemes such as the NHBC scheme;
- the definition of pure economic loss is uncertain – and it is possible that the Act goes no further than the common law;
- it is also uncertain to whom the Act applies.

SAMPLE ESSAY QUESTION

'The Occupiers' Liability Act 1957 modifies the common law to the extent that the safety of lawful visitors is ensured.' Discuss how the law on occupiers' liability has developed in the light of the above statement.

Explain the basis of the 1957 Act

- The Act is a statutory form of negligence
- But was introduced to create a common duty of care where different visitors were formerly owed a different duty
- But breach and causation still apply

Explain the scope of the duty under the Act

- Basic duty in s2(1) – the common duty of care owed to all lawful visitors
- But s2(1) also allows the occupier to extend, restrict, modify or exclude his duty
- Duty under s2(2) is to take reasonable care to keep the visitor safe for the purposes for which the visitor is permitted entry on to the premises

Discuss how many aspects of the common law are incorporated in the Act, e.g.:

- Definitions of occupier and premises
- Extra care taken over children – but allurement and parental responsibility for young children is common law
- The position on those entering to exercise a trade

Discuss how an occupier can avoid liability

- Where the damage is caused by the negligence of an independent contractor and it is appropriate to hire one
- Where appropriate warning notices are used, sometimes exclusion clauses are possible, and where consent or contributory negligence apply
- These are more extensive than under common law so possibly fail to ensure safety of visitor
- Discuss the common features of the common law and the Act
- Discuss the ways in which the Act improves upon the common law – if any – the Act was mainly introduced to standardise the duty owed to different types of lawful visitor

SUMMARY

- Occupiers' liability is covered by two Acts: the Occupiers' Liability Act 1957 for lawful 'visitors', and the Occupiers' Liability Act 1984 for trespassers.
- An 'occupier' is anybody in actual control of the land and premises is broadly defined.
- By s2(1) of the 1957 Act a 'common duty of care' is owed to all lawful visitors.

- By s2(2) the duty is to ensure that the visitor is safe for the purposes of the visit.
- Under s2(3) an occupier must take extra care for children, who are less cautious, and not allure them – although parents are responsible for young children.
- A person carrying out a trade or calling on the occupier's premises must guard against the risks associated with the trade.
- The occupier is not liable for damage which is the result of work done by independent contractors if:
  - it is reasonable to entrust the work;
  - a reputable contractor is chosen; and
  - the occupier inspects the work if necessary.
- Adequate warnings; exclusion clauses and the defences of consent or contributory negligence can also be used to avoid liability.
- Trespassers are protected by the 1984 Act under s1(3) if the occupier:
  - is aware of the danger;
  - knows of the trespass; and
  - the risk is one against which he may be expected to offer some protection but only covers personal injury.

Further reading

Farrelly, M, 'Dangerous premises and liability to trespassers' (2001) *151 NLJ* 309.

Harvey, B, and Marston, J, *Cases and Commentary on Tort* (4th edn, Longman, 2000), Chapter 7.

Wilkinson, H, 'Boys will be boys' (2000) *150 NLJ* 870.

8

Trespass to land

AIMS AND OBJECTIVES

After reading this chapter you should be able to:

- Illustrate and understand the definition of land
- Explain the nature of trespass and distinguish it from other torts
- Identify who can be a party to an action in trespass
- Apply the available defences and remedies
- Apply the law to factual situations and reach conclusions as to liability

8.1 The origins and character of trespass to land

'Trespassers will be prosecuted' is a phrase which appears on notices throughout England. Most people do not realise that it is rarely possible to prosecute. Originally trespass to land was a crime as well as a civil offence. This is generally no longer the case, the only remedy being available through the civil courts. Trespass to land is one of the oldest torts originating from the old action for trespass (see Chapter 1).

English common law has always gone to great lengths to protect interests in land. In the early days, a landowner was entitled to place mantraps or other devices on his land and would not be liable for any injury caused. This is no longer the case. People are entitled to say who can come on to their land and to take steps to keep unwanted visitors (trespassers) out, but the steps should not cause injury. As has been seen, in Chapter 7, in certain circumstances landowners can be liable for injuries caused to unlawful visitors resulting from a danger on the land (Occupiers' Liability Act 1984).

The tort retains some original characteristics. It is actionable *per se*, so that no actual damage need be caused. It is enough that the trespasser has

DOI: 10.4324/9781003202417-8

crossed the boundary intentionally for liability to arise. Trespass will occur when even a small part of the trespasser's anatomy has crossed the boundary. Thus in *Franklin v Jeffries, The Times*, 11 March 1985 there was a trespass when an unwanted arm came through an open window. Obviously the level of compensation where no actual damage has occurred will in most cases be limited. It will be seen, however, that it is not unusual for the remedy of choice to be an injunction, preventing a repeat of the tort.

The interference with the owner's rights must be direct and intentional. Indirect interference may give rise to a cause of action in nuisance (see Chapter 9). The issue of intention can cause some problems. The action itself must be deliberate but there is no requirement that there should be any intention to trespass. A drunkard who staggers up the path to what he mistakenly believes to be his own front door intentionally trespasses on the neighbour's land. They intended to go along that path although they did not intend to trespass. In *Conway v George Wimpey & Co Ltd* [1951] 2 KB 266 it was held that it was irrelevant that the person was unaware that they were trespassing or even honestly believed that the land was theirs. Conversely, a parachutist who gets blown on to land by the wind does not commit trespass as the entry was not intended. In *Smith v Stone* (1647) Style 65; 82 ER 533 a person who was pushed on to land by someone else was not liable for trespass.

It is sometimes argued that the tort protects a right of privacy. As will be seen, this is unlikely to happen in most cases. Photographs taken with a long lens may infringe privacy and be actionable as breach of confidentiality or nuisance, but without the crossing of the boundary there is no trespass.

8.2 Definition

A simple definition is: a direct physical and unlawful interference with land which is in the possession of another person.

Trespass to land can occur in a number of ways, the most common being by way of entry on to land. It can also occur by remaining on land having been asked to leave and after a reasonable time has been allowed for that purpose.

CASE EXAMPLE

Robson v Hallett [1967] 2 QB 939

A police officer was invited into a house to pursue enquiries. The consent to him being there was withdrawn and he tried to leave. Before he could do so he was assaulted. The issue was whether or not at the time of the assault he was a lawful or unlawful visitor.

Once permission is withdrawn a reasonable time must be allowed for the visitor to leave and Lord Diplock at 954 explained that: 'provided he did so with reasonable expedition, he would not be a trespasser while he was doing so'.

Placing an object on or against land will also amount to trespass. This can extend to the placing of a human being on land. In *Smith v Stone* (1647) Style 65 it was held:

JUDGMENT

'that it is the trespass of the party that carried the defendant upon the land, and not the trespasses of the defendant: as he that drives my cattle into another man's land is the trespasser against him, and not I who am the owner of the cattle'.

More usually cases are concerned with objects. An example of the more usual case is found in *Westripp v Baldock* [1938] 2 All ER 799 when it was held that a ladder leaning against the claimant's wall was a trespass.

8.3 What is 'land'?

The word 'land' sounds simple – we all know what it means but for legal purposes it can mean vastly more than the soil itself. The term includes the surface of the soil, any buildings erected on it, the airspace above it and the subsoil beneath it. In theory therefore 'land' includes airspace out to infinity and the subsoil through to Australia! Clearly in the modern world this is nonsense. Limits have to be drawn.

In *Bernstein v Skyviews and General Ltd* [1978] QB 479 Mr Justice Griffiths said that he could find 'no support in authority for the view that a landowner's rights in the air space above his property extend to an unlimited height'. It was observed, this would mean that every time an aircraft or a satellite passed over the land a trespass would be committed. In trying to balance the rights of the landowner with those of the general public to take advantage of modern technology, it was held (at 488):

JUDGMENT

'The balance is in my judgment best struck in our present society by restricting the rights of an owner in the air space . . . to such height as is necessary for the ordinary use and enjoyment of his land and the structures on it, and declaring that above that height he has no greater rights in the air space than any other member of the public.'

CASE EXAMPLE

Bernstein v Skyviews and General Ltd [1977] 2 All ER 902

The defendants' business was taking aerial photographs of premises which were then sold to the owners of the premises. They took pictures of the claimant's house. He claimed that the defendants were liable for trespass. Mr Justice Griffiths found that the defendants had flown over the land without permission but, in the light of the reasoning set out above, held that there had been no trespass.

Bernstein is in reality more concerned with the issue of privacy. The position of commercial airlines has been dealt with by the Civil Aviation Act 1982 which provides:

SECTION

's76(1) No action shall lie in respect of trespass . . . by reason of the flight of an aircraft over any property at a height . . . which, having regard to wind, weather and all the circumstances of the case is reasonable, or the ordinary incidents of such flight.'

Section 76(2) identifies that 'damages in respect of the loss or damage shall be recoverable without proof of negligence or intention' – so this is strict liability.

An owner's rights in relation to the subsoil are restricted in various ways but the fact that ownership vests in him has been used to advantage in the context of problems arising from the use of the highway (see section 8.5.2).

8.4 Parties to the action

8.4.1 Who can sue?

So far, the person whose rights have allegedly been infringed has been referred to as the owner of the land. This implies that ownership is necessary to maintain an action for trespass. This is not in fact the case. As a general rule, the person in possession of land has the right to sue, thus proving that there is some truth in the saying that 'possession is nine-tenths of the law'. Rejecting the proposition that legal title is necessary before an action can be brought, Lord Kenyon CJ in *Graham v Peat* [1801] 1 East 244 said 'Any possession is a legal possession against a wrongdoer'. As a consequence, even a squatter has enforceable rights against anyone who enters that land other than a person with a better legal title.

In contrast an action attempted against a party with superior rights of occupation is bound to fail.

CASE EXAMPLE

Delaney v T P Smith & Co [1946] KB 393

The claimant and the defendant had reached an oral agreement under which the claimant would acquire a tenancy of the defendant's property. However, the claimant then secretly entered the property before the lease was actually executed. When the defendant then ejected the claimant he sued in trespass but failed. The agreement on the lease had not been put in writing as required, as a result of which the defendant still had superior rights of occupation and was entitled to eject the claimant.

It would also of course be possible for a tenant to bring an action in trespass against the freehold owner of the property because a leaseholder has rights of exclusive possession. However, it would not be possible for a lodger to sue in trespass against a landlord because a lodger only has a licence.

CASE EXAMPLE

White v Bayley [1861] 142 ER 438

The claimant was paid £75 a year for managing and living in premises rented by his employers. When the defendants gave the claimant notice to quit and took possession the claimant forcibly re-entered. The defendants sought an injunction. The claimant then brought a counter claim in trespass but failed. As the court identified he was entitled to 'the use but not the occupation of the premises'.

8.4.2 Who can be sued?

The general and obvious rule is that the person who commits a trespass will be liable for it. This simple statement is modified in some ways.

A person with a better legal title is able to enter land and eject the trespasser from it without being liable in their turn for trespass. It should be noted that where there is an issue of residential occupancy, even a better legal title will not protect the person from liability under the Protection from Eviction Act 1977 which requires that a court order for possession be obtained prior to any eviction.

It will be seen that certain defences will protect someone who clearly enters land without authority to do so in order to deal with an emergency (see section 8.6.3).

8.5 Actions amounting to trespass

The various ways in which a trespass may occur have already been discussed but it is useful to consider the principles which have emerged from case law in order to 'put flesh on the bones' of the basic rules.

8.5.1 Airspace

It has already been seen that claimants are only entitled to limited protection against infringement of the airspace above their land (*Bernstein v Skyways and General Ltd*). Protection will be given by the courts against something which occurs at a lower level and has a more immediate impact than an over-flying aircraft. In *Kelson v Imperial Tobacco Co* [1957] 2 QB 334 it was held that an advertising sign which overhung the claimant's land amounted to a trespass.

The construction industry is particularly vulnerable in this regard as the use of very tall cranes is common. Such cranes have wide booms which are likely to travel through another's airspace. In *Woolerton & Wilson v Richard Costain Ltd* [1970] 1 WLR 411 the defendants' crane swung over the claimant's land. The defendants were liable for trespass. More recently, in

Anchor Brewhouse Developments Ltd and Others v Berkley House (Docklands Developments) Ltd [1987] 38 BLR 82 the matter was further considered.

CASE EXAMPLE

***Anchor Brewhouse Developments Ltd and Others v Berkley House (Docklands Developments) Ltd* [1988] 4 Const LJ 29**

A site was being developed which involved the use of very tall cranes. When the cranes were not being used they were left so that the booms were free to swing with the wind to avoid them being blown over. As they swung, the cranes travelled over adjoining property.

The over-swinging cranes amounted to a trespass. Drawing a distinction with over-flying aircraft Mr Justice Scott rejected the concept of the balancing of rights propounded in *Bernstein*. He took the view that by erecting a structure on land, the landowner takes the airspace into his possession. Justice Scott at 32 explains the following:

JUDGMENT

'If an adjoining owner places a structure on his (the adjoining owner's) land that overhangs his neighbour's land, he thereby takes into his possession air space to which his neighbour is entitled.'

8.5.2 Highways

It has been accepted for many years that the public has a right of passage along a highway. This includes other activities as explained by *Lord Irvine LC in DPP v Jones* [1999] 2 AC 240, at 254:

JUDGMENT

'[p]rovided these activities are reasonable, do not involve the commission of a public or private nuisance, and do not amount to an obstruction of the highway unreasonably impeding the primary right of the general public to pass and repass'.

In *DPP v Jones* the House of Lords accepted that reasonable activity could include a peaceful non-obstructive assembly of people.

The soil of the highway is deemed to belong up to the mid-point to those who own the land on either side. By the Highways Act 1980 a highways authority is the owner of the surface of a public highway to the depth of two spits, that is the depth of two spades, and is responsible for maintenance and operation of the highway. The subsoil remains vested in the adjoining owners. This can have some odd consequences. In *Harrison v Duke of Rutland*

[1893] 1 QB 142 it was held to be a trespass to the adjoining owner's land when the defendant used the road for the purpose of disturbing the claimant's exercise of shooting rights over his land. In *Hickman v Maisey* [1900] 1 QB 752 the defendant was a racing tout who had used a public highway passing across the claimant's land to observe the progress of race horses being trained on that land. The defendant was liable in trespass. In both these cases, the defendant was held to have abused the general public right of passage and thus to have committed an unlawful act.

8.5.3 Subsoil

Since the onset of industrialisation rights over subsoil also raise issues in relation to excavation for minerals or fossil fuels.

CASE EXAMPLE

Bocardo SA v Star Energy Weald Basin Ltd & Another [2010] UKSC 35

Star Energy held a licence to drill for and to extract oil from an oilfield that extended under Bocardo's land. In fact it had to drill diagonally from as close to Bocardo's land as possible to get as close to the apex of the oilfield as possible which was under Bocardo's land, otherwise drilling under the apex could lead to a loss of a substantial amount of the oil. This would have been legitimate because Star Energy had a licence to carry out such work under the Petroleum Act 1988. However, what it had not done was to negotiate a contractual licence with Bocardo. Nor had it applied for any statutory right to do this under the Mines (Working Facilities and Support) Act 1966 or the Pipelines Act 1962. The oil well and pipeline were at depths varying between 800 feet and 2,900 feet below the surface of Bocardo's land and Bocardo had suffered no loss. The question for the court then was whether an oil company which had been granted a licence to search for and extract petrol or gas under land belonging to another without obtaining the landholder's agreement or any statutory right under the Mines (Working Facilities and Support) Act 1966 to do so, is committing an actionable trespass. It was held that Bocardo did own the strata at the depth of the oil well and there was therefore a trespass.

As Lord Hope identified at 27:

JUDGMENT

'There must obviously be some stopping point, as one reaches the point at which physical features such as pressure and temperature render the concept of the strata belonging to anybody so absurd as to be not worth arguing about. But the wells that are at issue in this case, extending from about 800 feet to 2,800 feet below the surface, are far from being so deep as to reach the point of absurdity. Indeed the fact that the strata can be worked upon at those depths points to the opposite conclusion.'

8.5.4 Trespass *ab initio*

trespass *ab initio*

In the case of people who have a legal right to enter land such as a meter reader if they commit wrong while on the land they are said to be trespassers from when they entered

The old rule of **trespass *ab initio*** states that a person who enters land lawfully but subsequently abuses that right of entry will be liable for the entire transaction, not merely that portion of it which follows the abuse. The rule is illustrated by *The Six Carpenters' Case* [1610] 8 Co Rep 146a.

CASE EXAMPLE

***The Six Carpenters' Case* [1610] 8 Co Rep 146a**

Six carpenters entered a public house, the Queen's Head, Cripplegate, where they consumed a quart of wine worth 7d and bread worth 1d. They refused to pay. The issue was whether the refusal to pay made their entry into the public house tortious.

It was held that when a person has permission or authority to enter premises, he will be a trespasser *ab initio* if that purpose is abused, for example by a theft. The courts deem that the entry was in fact for that unlawful purpose and therefore a trespass. However, refusing to pay for wine and bread does not make the original entry tortious; it does not take away the entire reason for the entry.

It all seems very complicated but a more recent case has helped to shed some light on how the principle might be applied today. In *Elias v Passmore* [1934] 2 KB 164 documents were seized by police officers executing a warrant. Some documents were seized unlawfully. It was held that they were trespassers as to the documents unlawfully seized. They were not trespassers *ab initio*, which would have made them liable for damage done to the front door when entry was effected, as the entry was by virtue of an independent ground, namely the warrant.

More recently still, Lord Denning MR described the doctrine as 'a by-product of the old forms of action. Now that they are buried, it can be interred with their bones' (*Chic Fashions (West Wales) Ltd v Jones* [1968] 1 All ER 229). Lord Denning was not, however, entirely consistent. In *Cinnamond v British Airports Authority* [1980] 2 All ER 368 he referred to the doctrine without criticism and indeed commenting on its potential usefulness.

The doctrine is unusual in that the legality of an act is judged by what happens subsequently. The entry may become unlawful by virtue of what the defendant has done after the entry. It can be argued that it is still important that this can happen in the area of the protection of one's person, goods and land against abuse of official power (W V H Rogers, *Winfield and Jolowicz on Tort* (16th edn, Sweet & Maxwell, 2002), p. 498).

8.6 Defences

8.6.1 Consent

A person who enters land with consent of the person in possession is not liable for trespass.

Consent may be express, for example an invitation to 'Come in' when a caller knocks at the door. Express consent may be more formally granted by the creation of a legal agreement granting a licence, for example a theatre ticket grants a licence to enter the theatre on that occasion. In the realms of land law licences granting rights over land are of crucial importance but these are not considered here.

Consent may also be implied. A shopping centre gives implied consent to shoppers to enter the centre; a householder gives implied consent to those delivering post. An unlocked front gate allows anyone to go as far as the front door to enquire whether or not the householder is interested in whatever the caller is peddling, for example religion or a political party.

Withdrawal of consent can occur at any time although in the case of property licences notice is usually required. Shopping centres plagued by persistent shoplifters are more frequently turning to the civil law of trespass for assistance. Provided the civil action is successful, the centre can hope to obtain an injunction to restrain the shoplifter from returning with an effective sanction should they in fact do so. Breach of injunction is of course punishable as a contempt of court and can lead to imprisonment. A householder can withdraw implied consent to callers by simply locking the gate.

8.6.2 Lawful authority

The police and others may have authority to enter property by virtue of statute. The provisions of the relevant Act must be fully adhered to. The police are governed by the provisions of the Police and Criminal Evidence Act 1984. Other statutes also grant powers of entry. Examples include:

- the Children Act 1989, which gives social workers the right to enter premises to seek a child at risk provided a warrant has been granted by a magistrate;
- the Environment Act 1995, which gives the Environment Agency and local authorities power to enter premises to deal with environmental protection issues.

8.6.3 Necessity

A trespass to land may be excused if it occurs as a result of necessity. Necessity is a defence if action is taken in an emergency to deal with a genuinely perceived danger. The fact that with hindsight the danger did not in fact materialise is irrelevant.

The danger may be to property as well as people.

CASE EXAMPLE

Cope v Sharp (No 2) [1912] 1 KB 496

The defendant entered the claimant's land and burned a strip of heather in order to protect the defendant's own land. Although the action proved to have been unnecessary, the fire not spreading as feared, the court held that the action was motivated by a genuine perception of danger and was therefore necessary.

This has been subjected to some comment in later cases. In *Esso Petroleum Co Ltd v Southport Corporation* [1956] AC 218 (a case involving the discharge of oil from a stricken tanker to save not just the ship but also the crew) Mr Justice Devlin (as he then was) said (at 228) at first instance:

JUDGMENT

'The safety of human lives belongs to a different scale of values from the safety of property. The two are beyond comparison and the necessity for saving life has at all times been considered a proper ground for inflicting such damage as may be necessary upon another's property.'

The courts have been concerned to limit the defence. In *London Borough of Southwark v Williams* [1971] Ch 734 the issue was whether homeless squatters could use the defence when they had taken possession of empty property belonging to the claimant. Lord Denning MR commented at 744:

JUDGMENT

'If homelessness were once admitted as a defence to trespass, no one's house would be safe. Necessity would open a door which no man could shut.'

While the decision in *London Borough of Southwark v Williams* may be questioned on moral grounds, the law apparently putting property rights before the needs of people, the reasoning can be understood. It is difficult not to agree with the sentiments expressed by Lord Denning that to hold otherwise would be to open the floodgates, which the courts try to avoid doing.

The defence was, however, held to apply to damage to property in *Rigby v Chief Constable of Northamptonshire* [1985] 2 All ER 985.

CASE EXAMPLE

Rigby v Chief Constable of Northamptonshire
[1985] 1 WLR 1242

During a strike by the fire service there was a siege of a gun shop in which a dangerous armed psychopath was hiding. The police fired a tear-gas canister into the shop which ignited powder causing a serious fire. The shop-owners claimed damages for trespass to land.

Justice Taylor at 1254 comments that:

JUDGMENT

'a defence of necessity is available in the absence of negligence on the part of the defendant creating or contributing to the necessity. In this case there was a dangerous armed psychopath whom it was urgently necessary to arrest.'

The defence of necessity was upheld. Had the defendant been negligent, that tort would have provided an appropriate remedy.

8.7 Remedies

8.7.1 Damages or injunction?

In a simple case the claimant may seek compensation for the injury done to his land, whether this relates to physical damage or the sum lost by reason of being out of possession. The latter takes the form of *mesne profits* equating to the rent that would have been recoverable had there been a proper letting. Where there is a likelihood that a trespass will be repeated, an injunction will usually be the remedy of choice.

Difficulties arise when the trespass is a continuing problem as with the erection of a building which encroaches on to the claimant's land. An injunction could be granted whereby the encroaching building would be demolished, or the defendant can, in effect, purchase the right to continue the trespass by payment of damages. The latter will not always be sufficient to convince the claimant that they have received justice. The courts are reluctant to allow the defendant to 'get away with it' in this way.

In *Shelfer v City of London Electric Lighting Co* [1895] 1 Ch 287 it was held that where the appropriate remedy would usually be the grant of an injunction, damages could be awarded in lieu only:

i. if the injury to the claimant's rights is small;
ii. is capable of being estimated in money;
iii. can be adequately compensated by a small money payment; and
iv. the case is one in which it would be oppressive to the defendant to grant an injunction.

The rules as regards damages in lieu of an injunction have been reconsidered in the case of *Coventry v Lawrence* (see Chapter 9 on nuisance) in which the Supreme Court states that the guidelines in *Shelfer* have become too restrictive and that an award of an injunction is a discretionary remedy and that a court should be prepared to award an injunction and not allow someone to effectively buy the right to commit a tort. These rules were considered in a case where the defendant had built a house in breach of a restrictive covenant prohibiting any building on that part of the land.

CASE EXAMPLE

Jaggard v Sawyer [1995] 1 WLR 269

At first instance, the judge refused an injunction, granting damages in lieu. The claimant appealed. Holding that the decision at first instance was correct, Sir Thomas Bingham LJ accepted that the first three requirements of Shelfer were satisfied. He then turned to consider the issue of oppression of the defendant at 283:

JUDGMENT

'The oppression must be judged as at the date the court is asked to grant an injunction and . . . the court cannot ignore the reality with which it is then confronted.'

On the facts the grant of an injunction to demolish the house would be oppressive and the award of damages in lieu was appropriate.

The Court of Appeal was undoubtedly influenced by the fact that no application to the court was made until the building work was at an advanced stage. In the absence of blatant and calculated disregard for the law by the defendant the courts are reluctant to order the demolition of a building. This approach would perhaps remain unaffected by the decision in *Coventry v Lawrence* as such concerns should be addressed at the planning stage rather than the building stage. In such circumstances damages may be appropriate.

In other cases, the situation is easier to deal with. For example, a trespass into airspace may well be remedied by injunction, as will a frequent incursion on foot or by car into the claimant's land.

In *Secretary of State for the Environment, Food and Rural Affairs v Meier* [2009] UKSC 11 the Supreme Court had to consider the extent of possible remedies. Travellers were constantly being moved off land owned by the Forestry Commission and then had to be moved off other land in the same ownership by possession orders and injunctions and at great cost. So the Forestry Commission sought a wider possession order for land that the travellers might move on to and an injunction to restrain it. The Supreme Court held that it had no power to grant an order for possession of land on which the defendant had not yet trespassed because it would deny the trespasser the right of due process.

8.7.2 Re-entry

By the Criminal Law Act 1977 it is an offence for anyone other than a displaced residential occupier, to use or threaten violence for the purpose of securing entry to land occupied by another. Peaceable re-entry is lawful. Case law indicates that a landowner may not have civil liability if no more force than is necessary is used to remove a trespasser (*Hemmings v Stoke Poges Golf Club* [1920] 1 KB 720). It is not clear whether this rule survives the Criminal Law Act 1977. Lord Clarke in *Ropaigealach v Barclays Bank plc* [2000] 1 QB 263 took the view that the rule does survive but as yet there is no case law on the specific point.

A displaced residential occupier may not be prosecuted pursuant to the Criminal Law Act 1977 but needs to be wary of the Protection from Eviction Act 1977 (see the next section) and the Protection from Harassment Act 1997 (discussed in section 13.6.2).

8.7.3 Action for the recovery of land

A person may bring an action to recover possession of land (formerly known as an action for ejectment). The action can be brought against any person without a better legal title than the claimant. Thus someone who has been 'squatting' on land for six months would be able to bring an action against a later squatter.

Someone seeking to recover possession from a residential occupier, even if the occupier is a squatter, will generally require a court order before eviction can take place. Unlawful eviction or other conduct calculated to 'persuade' an occupier to leave a dwelling is punishable as a crime (Protection from Eviction Act 1977).

Anyone seeking to recover possession of land should also be wary of the provisions of the Protection from Harassment Act 1997 the terms of which are broad enough to encompass behaviour which might not fall within the definitions to be found in the Protection from Eviction Act.

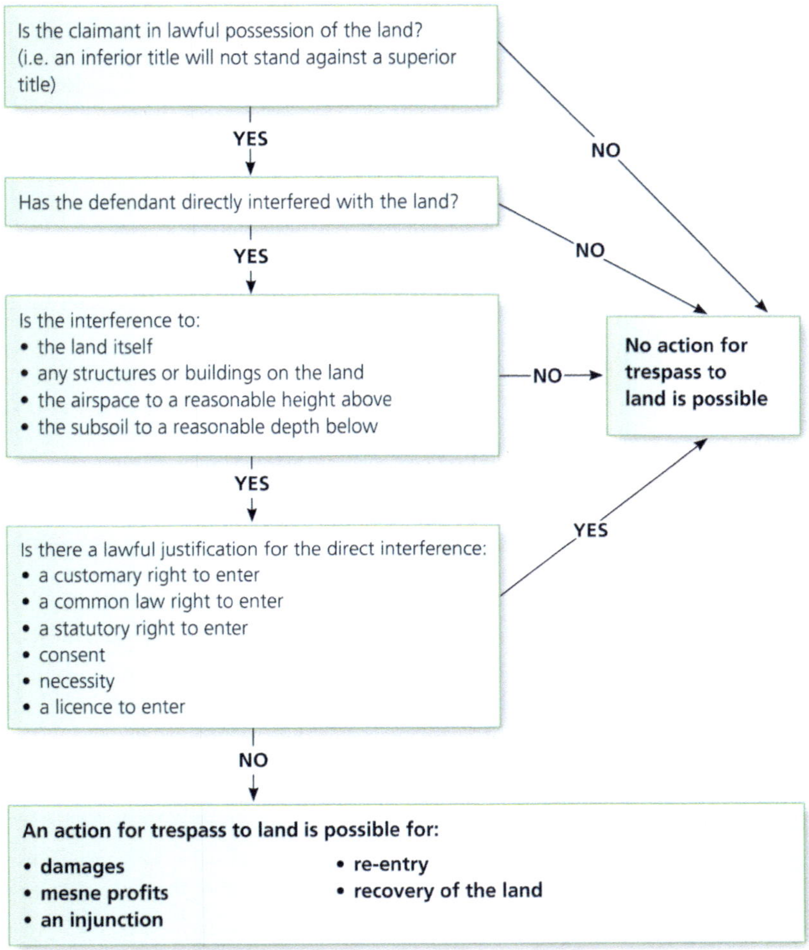

Figure 8.1 The essential elements for a claim in trespass to land, including the possible remedies.

ACTIVITY

Self-assessment questions

1 What is meant by the word 'land' for the purposes of this tort?
2 In what circumstances can a person who does not have legal title to land bring an action for trespass to land?
3 Explain the essential difference between *Bernstein v Skyways and General Ltd* and *AnchorBrewhouse Developments Ltd v Berkeley House (Docklands Developments) Ltd*.
4 What, exactly, is trespass *ab initio*? Is the concept still relevant in the twenty-first century?
5 How does *Coventry v Lawrence* assist the courts to decide whether or not the grant of an injunction is an appropriate remedy?

SAMPLE ESSAY QUESTION

'The two principal aims of tort law are to compensate the victims of wrongs and to deter wrongdoing.' Discuss the extent to which the tort of trespass to land succeeds in achieving these aims.

Define the tort of trespass to land

- Any intentional and direct entry on to land in another person's possession
- Can involve entering land voluntarily and intentionally or remaining on the land after permission is withdrawn
- Could also be placing things on the land or taking things away from the land
- And can include even the merest contact

Discuss how land is defined and the effect on compensation

- Obviously covers the land itself and anything built on it – so possibly is effective
- But extends to the airspace above – but only to a reasonable extent and is regulated by the Civil Aviation Act 1982 so may limit the effectiveness of protection of the tort as a deterrent
- Also extends to subsoil with similar problems

Discuss some of the problems associated with bringing an action

- The distinction between lawful and unlawful entry and express and implied consent
- The concept of trespass *ab initio* where a lawful visitor abuses the proper limits on their right to enter
- The need to show an interest in land to claim and the need to have a superior right of possession to the defendant

Discuss the available remedies and whether they adequately remedy or deter

- Damages – but only if some damage to the land – and mesne profits possible
- Injunctions
- Removal of trespasser by reasonable force

Discuss the effectiveness as a deterrent or means of compensation

- The tort is actionable per se so may act as a deterrent
- Compensation is only relevant if damage has been caused
- Entry by mistake will not necessarily remove liability increasing the possibility of both compensation and deterrence
- Only available to people with a superior interest in land so does not protect lodgers or deter bad behaviour by landlords
- Statutory right to enter may deny compensation for harm
- Damages are difficult to assess, limits on granting injunctions, requirement of reasonable force in removing trespassers – so limits effectiveness of both compensation and deterrence

KEY FACTS

Definition	Case
Actionable per se.	
Direct and unlawful interference with land in possession of another.	*Franklin v Jeffries* [1985]; *Conway v George Wimpey & Co Ltd* [1951]
Must be intentional.	
'Land' includes surface and everything on the surface, the subsoil and airspace.	
'Subsoil' can extend beneath highway.	*Harrison v Duke of Rutland* [1893]; *Hickman v Maisey* [1900]
'Airspace' extends only to height necessary for ordinary use and enjoyment of land.	*Kelson v Imperial Tobacco* [1957]; *Bernstein v Skyviews* [1977]
Usually occurs with entry but can include placing object on to land: • a person • a ladder against a wall Can include remaining on land after permission to be there is withdrawn.	*Anchor Brewhouse Development v Berkley House (Docklands Developments)* [1987] *Smith v Stone* (1647) *Westripp v Baldock* [1938]
Claimant	**Case**
Must be in possession of the land.	
Possession does not necessarily mean legal right – in some circumstances a squatter can sue.	*Graham v Peat* [1801]
Trespass *ab initio*	**Case**
Subsequent actions can cause lawful entry to be regarded as unlawful making entry a trespass.	*Six Carpenters' Case* [1610]
For modern potential see –	*Elias v Passmore* [1934]
Defences	**Case/statute**
Consent – can be express, for example by invitation, or implied, for example delivery of mail – can be withdrawn.	
Lawful authority – statutory examples include –	Police and Criminal Evidence Act 1984; Children Act 1989; Environment Act 1995
Necessity – limited to entry to deal with genuinely perceived danger.	*Cope v Sharp (No 2)* [1912]; *Esso Petroleum v Southport Corp* [1956]

(Continued)

(Continued)

Remedies	Case/statute
Damages – for actual damage but can extend to compensation for loss caused by being out of possession (*mesne profits*).	
Injunction – where trespass is continuing problem or likely to recur unless damages would adequately compensate claimant or injunction would be unduly oppressive to defendant.	*Shelfer v City of London Electric Lighting* [1895]; *Coventry v Lawrence UKSC* [2014] 13s; *Jaggard v Sawyer* [1995]
Re-entry – must be peaceable – note special rules relating to eviction of residential occupier.	
Action for recovery of land – can be used by anyone with better legal title than defendant – note importance where residential premises involved.	Protection from Eviction Act 1977

SUMMARY

- Trespass involves direct interference with another person's land.
- A person with an interest in the land can sue anyone with a lesser interest in the land but not someone with a superior interest.
- Must involve direct entry on to the land although can be merely temporary.
- Trespass is actionable *per se* so no damage has to be caused.
- Land includes the subsoil below and the airspace above to some extent.
- A legal entry can become a trespass where the legitimate purpose of the visit is exceeded.
- Defences include: a customary or a common law or a statutory right to enter, consent, necessity and licenses.
- And remedies include: ejectment, repossession and damages.

9

Nuisance

AIMS AND OBJECTIVES

After reading this chapter you should be able to:

- Illustrate the differences between private nuisance, public nuisance and statutory nuisance
- Explain what determines who the potential parties are in each action
- Identify elements for proving private nuisance
- Explain the requirements for proving public nuisance
- Define the scope of statutory nuisance
- Apply the defences available to a claim of nuisance
- Critically analyse the tort of nuisance
- Apply the law to factual situations and reach conclusions as to liability

9.1 Nuisance generally

Nuisance is perhaps the part of tort law which is most closely connected to protection of the environment. As will be seen, action in nuisance can lie for oil spills, nasty smells, noise and anything else which affects nearby land or the comfort and convenience of the occupiers of that land.

The recent Supreme Court decision in *Fearn v Tate Gallery* [2023] UKSC 4 reminds us that the purpose of the law of private nuisance is to protect one's enjoyment of their land which should be free from interference which can take the form of a tangible intrusion such as tree branches over hanging over into your garden but also, intangible intrusions such as smells as well as a visual intrusion which impacts on one's privacy.

DOI: 10.4324/9781003202417-9

CASE EXAMPLE

Fearn v Tate Gallery [2No i 023] UKSC 4

In this case, the Tate Modern opened a new extension called the Blavatnik Building. This building on its top floor has a viewing platform which offers panoramic views of London. At the time of the trial, the viewing platform was visited by an estimated 500,000–600,000 people each year. The claimants live in a block of flats next to the Tate Modern. These flats have floor-to-ceiling glass windows, and visitors to the viewing platform can see straight into their flats and clear and uninterrupted views of how the claimants seek to conduct their lives. Visitors took an interest in the interior of the claimants' flats, some would wave at the claimants, some used binoculars to take a closer look, some took photographs with some of these photographs being posted on social media. The claimants sought an injunction to prevent members of the public from viewing their flats in this way. The question for the courts was whether a viewing into the claimants' flats could be considered a material intrusion into the privacy of the lives of the claimants. In other words, could an invasion of privacy in this way, be considered a nuisance? The Supreme Court held that it could.

It is important for students to read this decision in full as a number of references to the reasoning in this case will be made throughout this chapter.

Nuisance can take many forms, but what is a legal nuisance is distinct from what we may describe as a nuisance in everyday life *Andrews v Kronospan Limited* [2025] EWHC 2429 (TCC), at 2:

JUDGMENT

'. . . a state of affairs which people might describe in general speech as a nuisance is a different thing from something which is a nuisance as a matter of law.'

Nuisance may take three forms:

- private nuisance;
- public nuisance;
- statutory nuisance.

As will be seen these are not necessarily mutually exclusive of each other but the traditional method of discussing each separately will be followed.

Nuisance is concerned with the use of land as was highlighted in *Fearn* by Lord Leggatt at 9:

JUDGMENT

'. . . in the law of property, the legal concept of land includes here not only the earth itself but also buildings and other things which are physically attached to it and rights, for example easements, which attach in law to the land.'

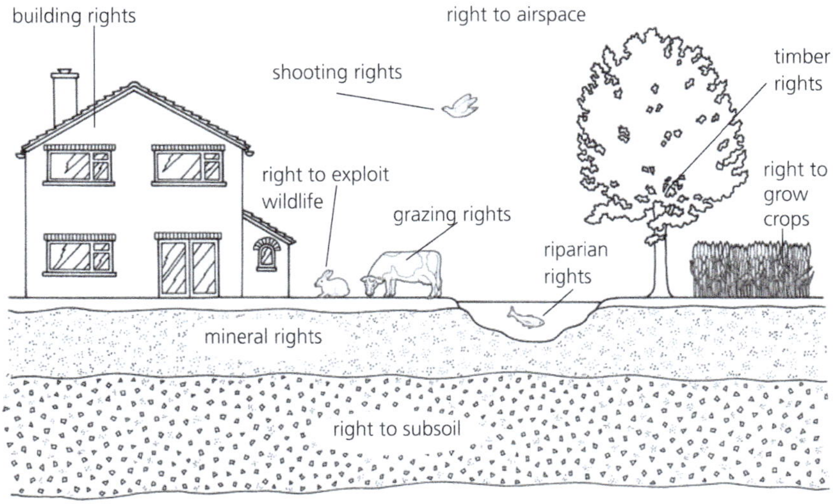

Figure 9.1 Land.

The law on private nuisance seeks to protect the diminution in the utility and amenity value of the claimant's land. In other words, the injury is to the property not the person. Nuisance is concerned with all aspects of land use. This can include:

- the right to grow crops and graze animals;
- shooting rights;
- riparian rights;
- rights of support from neighbouring land;
- timber rights;
- leisure and domestic activity;
- mineral rights;
- invasion of privacy.

It is essential that the interest being interfered with is one recognised by law. In *Fearn* the Supreme Court confirmed that despite the Court of Appeal in the same case taking a different view, that there is no legal reason why the invasion of privacy could not be actionable. The key point is that any activity that substantially interferes with the ordinary use and enjoyment of the neighbour's land, may constitute an actionable nuisance. In *Hunter and Others v Canary Wharf* [1997] 2 WLR 684 the Canary Wharf tower block in London interfered with television signals. The House of Lords held that this amounted to interference with a 'purely recreational facility as opposed to interference with the health or physical comfort or well-being' of the claimant. This may seem odd in the twenty-first century but the judges did take into account the widespread availability of cable and satellite television. (Imagine if there was an interruption to our broadband connection in this day and age). The judges also considered whether the fact that a building blocking television signals was capable of amounting to a nuisance. Referring to an old principle Goff LJ said at 685:

JUDGMENT

'[I]n the absence of an easement, more is required than the mere presence of a neighbouring building to give rise to an actionable private nuisance . . . . [I]t will generally arise from something emanating from the defendant's land.'

A building clearly cannot 'emanate' from land and is therefore unlikely to amount to an actionable nuisance. The defendant has a legal right to use the airspace above his land provided such use is reasonable. Building on that land is a reasonable use in the absence of malice. It is difficult to see how a building can be a malicious use of land but perhaps a hoarding or a screen would suffice.

9.2 Private nuisance

9.2.1 Definition

An actionable private nuisance occurs where a person's use or enjoyment of their land is unlawfully interfered with by activities carried on by another person on their land. In most cases, the two areas of land are likely to be close together. The activities complained of must generally be continuous but it is possible, in rare circumstances, for a 'one-off' activity to amount to a nuisance.

9.2.2 Interference

Generally, nuisance claims will involve some interference resulting from a physical emanation of the neighbour's land although it need not always be physical as can be seen in *Fearn* which involved people looking into the homes of others.

An example of an interference of a physical emanation of the neighbour's land can be illustrated by thinking about a garden bonfire. The bonfire itself is not a nuisance but the smoke arising from it can mean that neighbours have to take in washing and shut windows. The activity is lighting the bonfire, the indirect consequence of that activity is the smoke. Direct interference may amount to trespass to land (see Chapter 8).

In this way a variety of things which indirectly affect the claimant's land have been held to be actionable as nuisances including:

- fumes drifting over neighbouring land, *Bliss v Hall* [1838] 4 Bing NC 183;
- vibrations from industrial machinery, *Sturges v Bridgman* [1879] 11 CH D 852;
- smuts from factory chimneys, *Halsey v Esso Petroleum* [1961] 1 WLR 683;
- fire, *Spicer v Smee* [1946] 1 All ER 489;
- continuous interference from cricket balls, *Miller v Jackson* [1977] QB 976.

9.2.3 A balancing act between competing interests

The tort is essentially concerned with balancing the competing interests of neighbours to make lawful use of their own land. The difficulty is that what may be reasonable to the person carrying out the activity, may be perceived as wholly unreasonable by a neighbour because of the way it interferes with what the neighbours want to do on their land. The courts are left to conduct a balancing act. Only interference which is found by the court to be unreasonable can amount to a private nuisance. In considering whether or not the interference is reasonable, the courts will have regard to

- the extent of the harm;
- the nature of the use interfered with.

This balancing act and the interest protected by the law of nuisance was recently reiterated by Mr Justice Fancourt in *Cooper v Ludgate House Limited* [2025] EWHC 1724 (Ch), 43:

JUDGMENT

'It is the law of nuisance that maintains this balance, as it has always done, by focusing on the degree of harm done to the utility and amenity value of the claimant's land: see *Fearn v Tate Gallery* at [11], per Lord Leggatt. The interest protected by the law of nuisance is the utility of land, and whether there is or is no substantial interference is to be assessed objectively on that basis . . .'

Substantial interference

Before we engage in a detailed analysis of what factors are considered in determining whether there is an actionable nuisance, two points need to be noted. The first is whether the defendant's use of land has caused a substantial interference with the ordinary use of the claimant's land. This is an important requirement since it means that the interference with the claimant's land must exceed a minimum level of seriousness.

St Helen's Smelting Co v Tipping *[1865] 11 HL Cas 642, 653–654*

JUDGMENT

Per Lord Wensleydale:

'. . . the law does not regard trifling and small inconveniences, but only regards sensible inconveniences, injuries which sensibly diminish the comfort, enjoyment, or value of the property which is affected.'

The test is objective in that what is considered a substantial interference will be judged according to an average person in the claimant's position rather than what the claimant happens to find annoying. Knight Bruce V-C in *Walter v Selfe* (1851) 4 De G & Sm 315, at 322 summarises the point by stating that the question is whether the interference ought to be considered a material inconvenience 'not merely according to elegant or dainty modes and habits of living, but according to plain and sober and simple notions among the English people'.

Ordinary use of land

The use to which the claimant puts their land is often also relevant to whether he has suffered a nuisance. The extent of the harm is judged on the basis of the impact on the claimant. This is judged subjectively. A defendant who plays a loud instrument objectively causes a nuisance to a neighbour. It will not be perceived subjectively as a nuisance by a neighbour who is deaf and who is therefore unlikely to hear the noise.

CASE EXAMPLE

Smith v Giddy [1904] 2 KB 448

The defendant was liable in nuisance for the branches of trees on his property which overhung the claimant's land. While this would normally have been an unactionable blockage of light, the fact that the claimant ran a fruit orchard and the interference meant that the fruit trees did not grow properly was decisive in the decision that the defendant was liable.

9.3 The parties to an action in private nuisance

9.3.1 Who can sue?

Private nuisance protects interests in and the enjoyment of land. To bring an action, the claimant must have a legal interest in the land. This will normally mean a right to exclusive possession by way of freehold or leasehold title. A licensee, for example a lodger or a member of the owner's family, has no interest in land and cannot therefore bring an action.

CASE EXAMPLE

Malone v Laskey [1907] 2 KB 141

The claimant lived with her husband who occupied a house as licensee. Vibrations from the use of an engine on the defendant's adjoining land caused a bracket to fall onto the claimant causing her injury. Her claim in nuisance was dismissed by the Court of Appeal as she had no interest in the land on which to found a claim.

In 1993 it was believed that the apparent injustice suffered by a person in Mrs Malone's situation had been remedied. In *Khorasandjian v Bush* [1993] 3 WLR 476 a claim by a daughter living with her parents succeeded when the majority of the Court of Appeal recognised that an injunction on the ground of private nuisance could be granted despite the fact that she had no interest in the land. The case concerned harassment by way of telephone calls and was heard prior to the Protection from Harassment Act 1997 coming into force. It may be that the judges were influenced by the need to find a remedy for what was, on the facts, serious harassment.

The apparent easing of the requirement for the claimant to have a legal interest was later reversed by the House of Lords.

CASE EXAMPLE

Hunter and Others v Canary Wharf Ltd and Hunter and Others v London Docklands Corporation [1997] AC 655

Two joined appeals were heard together by the House of Lords.

The first case concerned interference with television reception, the second damage caused by dust during the construction of a road. The House of Lords certainly took the view that the Court of Appeal in *Khorasandjian* had been trying to create 'by the back door a tort of harassment'. Pointing out that the decision was inconsistent with that in *Malone v Laskey* [1907] 2 QB 141, Goff LJ stated very clearly at 692:

JUDGMENT

'an action in private nuisance will only lie at the suit of a person who has a right to the land affected. Ordinarily, such a person can only sue if he has the right of exclusive possession.'

Private nuisance protects the use and enjoyment of land so it is the case that only a person with a legal interest in the land can sue. The position now appears to be clear but the fact is that the injustice suffered by a lodger or some other person without a right to exclusive possession remains. The Protection from Harassment Act 1997 will help some claimants, for example the daughter in *Khorasandjian*, but not someone who cannot meet the criteria of the statute. It may be that in the future we may see an action under the Human Rights Act 1998 for breach of Article 8 of the European Convention on Human Rights.

A reversioner is the person to whom the land will return after the expiration of the current occupier's interest, for example at the end of a lease. Such a person can sue if it can be shown that the reversion, i.e. the value of the land after its return, will be diminished by the present nuisance. This tends to mean that the nuisance will be permanent. In *Tucker v Newman* [1839] 11 Ad & El 40 a reversioner was successful when a house had been built on adjoining land. The eaves of the house overhung his land and allowed rainwater to fall on to it.

9.3.2 Who can be sued?

The creator of the nuisance

The obvious answer, and the one which is usually correct, is the person who causes the nuisance. Unlike the claimant, it seems that the defendant need not have an interest in the land on which the activity takes place. In *Esso Petroleum Co Ltd v Southport Corporation* [1956] AC 218 (for facts see section 8.6.3) Mr Justice Devlin (as he then was) said at 225:

JUDGMENT

'I can see no reason why . . . if the defendant as licensee or trespasser misuses someone else's land, he should not be liable in nuisance in the same way as an adjoining occupier would be.'

This simple statement is not as straightforward as it might appear. In *Thomas v National Union of Mineworkers* [1985] 2 All ER 1 (for facts see section 13.2.2) it was said by Mr Justice Scott, at first instance, that an activity on the highway which unduly interferes with the right of citizens to enjoy the highway could amount to a 'species of private nuisance, namely unreasonable interferences with the claimant's right to use the highway'. However, the statement has apparently also been contradicted in another decision.

CASE EXAMPLE

***Hussain v Lancaster City Council* [2000] QB 1**

Here the claimants were the victims of extreme racial harassment by persons using the highway. It was held by the Court of Appeal that there was no nuisance because the wrongdoing did not involve the defendants' use of their land. The wrongdoers, who were not the defendants, had no legal interest in the highway.

The implications for the law relating to private nuisance are substantial as those in temporary possession of land but with no legal interest in that land, such as independent contractors, may be able to escape liability. The decision in *Hussain* may have resulted from policy influences. To hold a local authority liable in nuisance for the activities of those using the highway who are responsible for racial harassment would indeed be to open the floodgates.

9.3.3 The occupier

Generally the occupier of the premises from which the nuisance emanates will be liable for that nuisance. This is subject to qualification where the nuisance is caused by

- independent contractors;
- trespassers;
- an act of nature.

Independent contractors

An independent contractor's activities may be the cause of a nuisance. An obvious example is the problems caused to neighbours by building works. In such cases, there are certain 'non-delegable' duties which fall on the occupier notwithstanding that the nuisance arises from the activities of the contractor. Such duties relate to activities which carry with them particular danger. In *Bower v Peate* [1876] 1 QBD 321 the defendant employed a contractor to demolish his house. The adjoining house was damaged as a result of the work. The occupier was held liable.

The courts have refined this principle to cover only those activities by the contractor which are extra-hazardous, for instance those acts which 'in their very nature, involve in the eyes of the law special danger to others' (per Slesser LJ in *Honeywill and Stein v Larkin Brothers Ltd* [1934] 1 KB 191). The essence of 'special danger' seems to be that the activity carries with it a special risk that a nuisance may be caused to neighbours. (For a fuller discussion of the potential liability for the activities of an independent contractor see section 7.3.3.)

Trespassers

An occupier may well feel that if the nuisance is caused by a trespasser, then there ought to be no liability on their part for a resulting nuisance. Life is not that simple. The occupier will be liable if the 'nuisance' is adopted by using the state of affairs for the occupier's own purpose or where the nuisance is 'continued'. This point is illustrated by *Sedleigh-Denfield v O'Callagan (Trustees for St Joseph's Society for Foreign Missions)* [1940] AC 880.

CASE EXAMPLE

Sedleigh-Denfield v O'Callaghan (Trustees for St Joseph's Society for Foreign Missions) [1940] AC 880

A ditch on the boundary of the claimant's land belonged to the defendants. A trespasser laid a culvert in the ditch and no grid was put in place to prevent rubbish etc. from blocking it. A grid was in fact placed on top of the culvert where it served no useful purpose. This was known to the defendants. Thereafter, over a three-year period, the ditch was cleaned out twice a year by the defendants. After a heavy storm the culvert became blocked and the claimant's land was flooded.

JUDGMENT

Viscount Maugham LJ, at 896:

'After the lapse of nearly three years, [the defendants] must be taken to have suffered the nuisance to continue, for they neglected to take the very simple step of placing the grid in the proper place, which would have removed the danger to their neighbour's land. They adopted the nuisance, for they continued during all that time to use the artificial contrivance . . . for the purpose of getting rid of water from their property without taking the proper means for rendering it safe.'

It seems that an occupier who knows, or is deemed to know, that the potential for the creation of a nuisance exists, will be held liable even though the original act which created the nuisance was not the present occupier's act.

CASE EXAMPLE

Anthony and others v The Coal Authority [2005] EWHC 1654 (QB)

Between 1957 and 1995, first the National Coal Board and as it became the British Coal Corporation, tipped waste from mining on to a tip on its land. In 1995 the tip was partly landscaped and passed into private hands. In 1996 spontaneous combustion of the coal created a fire which continued for three years. The claimant sued the Coal Authority, the body taking over responsibility of the former two bodies, for the interference caused by the fumes and smoke. The defendant was held liable under the principle in *Sedleigh-Denfield v O'Callaghan* that it became aware of the problem while the tip was still under its control and failed to prevent the nuisance.

An act of nature

Until recently, a nuisance resulting from an act of nature, for example a severe storm which washed topsoil on to a neighbour's land, would not impose liability on the occupier of the land from which the soil had been washed. This, at first sight, appears to be very reasonable as it may well be impossible to foretell the consequences of an unusual and extreme event. But what about the situation where an occupier is aware, or ought to be aware, of the potential for the nuisance to occur? It would be unjust if the occupier could escape liability in such circumstances.

The matter was first considered by the Privy Council in *Goldman v Hargrave* [1967] 1 AC 645 when Lord Wilberforce explained that the occupier's duty is in reality more positive, resulting in liability for failure to take positive steps to abate a nuisance of which the occupier is aware.

CASE EXAMPLE

Goldman v Hargrave [1967] 1 AC 645

The defendant dealt with a fire caused by lightning hitting a gum-tree. The tree was felled, cut into sections and left to burn itself out. The weather deteriorated and the fire reignited causing damage to the claimant's land.

It was held that on the facts the defendant owed the claimant a duty to abate the nuisance which he was, or ought to have been, aware arose from the natural state of affairs on his land.

The principle set out in *Goldman v Hargrave* has been enshrined in English law in the case of *Leakey v National Trust* [1980] QB 485.

CASE EXAMPLE

Leakey v National Trust [1980] QB 485

The defendants owned a hill known as Barrow Mump; the claimants' homes were at the foot of the hill. The homes were threatened by the possibility that the hill would slip as a result of the action of the weather on the type of clay. From time to time small slips occurred on to the claimants' land. The defendants had been aware of the problem for more than eight years and had taken no steps to minimise the risk.

Developing the dicta from *Sedleigh-Denfield* Megaw LJ held that where a potential nuisance exists resulting from an act of nature and the defendant was aware of the danger, it would be an injustice were the occupier not to be under a duty to ameliorate the nuisance. Explaining the scope of the duty, the Judge went on to say at 486:

JUDGMENT

'the duty is a duty to do that which is reasonable in the circumstances . . . to prevent or minimise the known risk of damage or injury to one's neighbour or his property'.

In considering what can reasonably be done, the court should have regard to what the particular defendant could have reasonably been expected to do. This is not the standard of the 'reasonable man' whom we meet in the context of negligence. It takes account of matters such as cost in relation to the defendant's means; the need for physical exertion in the context of the defendant's age and state of health. Alongside this the court will have regard to what, if anything, the neighbour could reasonably have been expected to do to protect his own land.

The issue of what is reasonable was further considered in *Holbeck Hall Hotel Ltd v Scarborough Borough Council* [2000] 2 All ER 705.

CASE EXAMPLE

Holbeck Hall Hotel Ltd v Scarborough Borough Council [2000] 2 QB 836

The hotel stood at the top of a cliff. On 6 June 1993 the lawn between the hotel and the edge of the cliff fell into the sea and the land collapsed beneath the hotel so that it became unsafe and had to be demolished. The coastline was owned by the defendants. It had been known since 1893 that cliff falls occurred along that part of the coastline. Some remedial work was carried out in 1989 but was ineffective in preventing further erosion and collapse. At first instance it was held that the defendants were liable. The matter came before the Court of Appeal.

Holding that a duty to ameliorate the potential nuisance arises when 'the defect is known and the hazard or danger to the claimants' land is reasonably foreseeable'. Stuart-Smith LJ explained at 42:

JUDGMENT

'It is the existence of the defect coupled with the danger that constitutes the nuisance; it is knowledge or presumed knowledge of the nuisance that involves liability for continuing it when it could reasonably be abated.'

The important point at issue was what knowledge of the risk could be imputed to the defendants? It was clear that without further substantial geological investigation, the extent of the risk could not be anticipated although it was known that gradual erosion would be likely to continue. Lord Justice Stuart-Smith concluded that the scope of the defendants' duty was limited to what ought to have been foreseen without further investigation.

Pointing out that *Goldman* and *Leakey* were decided prior to *Caparo Industries Ltd v Dickman* [1990] 2 AC 605, Lord Justice Stuart-Smith reminded the Court that the three-stage test of:

- foreseeability;
- proximity; and
- the need for it to be fair just and reasonable

applies whatever the nature of the damage. He was of the view that it was not fair, just or reasonable in this case to impose liability for damage which was beyond that which could be foreseen.

So where does all this leave the potential for liability arising from natural causes? It seems that occupiers who know or ought to know of the potential for a nuisance arising from the state of affairs on their land owe what the judges have described as a 'measured duty of care' to do what can reasonably be done having regard to such matters as their resources etc. It is clear that imputed knowledge will not extend to knowledge which could only be obtained by further investigation.

The nuisance must be a foreseeable result of the activity, whether it arises from an activity or from natural causes. *The Wagon Mound (No 2) (Overseas Tankship (UK) Ltd v the Miller Steam Ship Co Pty Ltd)* [1967] 1 AC 617 involved allegations of nuisance as well as negligence. On the nuisance point, the rules as to foreseeability of damage were held to be the same in both negligence and nuisance. Lord Reid put it simply saying at 640:

JUDGMENT

'It is not sufficient that the injury suffered . . . was the direct consequence of the nuisance, if that injury was in the relevant sense unforeseeable.'

(For a full discussion of the principles of *The Wagon Mound* see section 4.5.1.)

The issue of foreseeability has been further considered by the House of Lords in *Cambridge Water Co Ltd v Eastern Counties Leather plc* [1994] 2 WLR 53. (For the facts of this case, see section 10.3.2.) Goff LJ explained that the fact that defendants have taken all reasonable care to avoid the nuisance will not exonerate them from liability, but he went on to say at 300:

JUDGMENT

'it by no means follows that the defendant should be held liable for damage of a type which he could not reasonably foresee . . . foreseeability of harm is indeed a prerequisite of the recovery of damages in . . . nuisance.'

Landlords

While a tenant who creates a nuisance will be liable, in certain circumstances the landlord may also have liability. A landlord who authorises the activity which creates the nuisance will be liable, if the nuisance is an inevitable result of the permitted activity.

CASE EXAMPLE

***Tetley and others v Chitty and others* [1986] 1 All ER 663**

Premises were leased for the purpose of a go-karting club. The landlord, a local authority, was well aware of the potential problems such use would cause in the way of noise. It was held that as noise was a natural and necessary consequence of the use of go-karts, the landlord was liable for the nuisance which had been authorised.

ACTIVITY

Self-assessment questions

1 What is the essential purpose of the judges when deciding a claim using the tort of private nuisance?
2 Does the decision in *Hunter v Canary Wharf* mean that some classes of occupiers may be unable to bring an action for private nuisance thereby suffering injustice?
3 When is a person liable for a nuisance arising from
   a the activities of someone else;
   b an act of nature?

9.4 Identifying private nuisance

9.4.1 Introduction

It is clear from the definition (section 9.2.1) that there are three elements which must be established to prove that there is an unreasonable user:

i. an unlawful, in the sense of unreasonable, use of land;
ii. which causes substantial interference;
iii. with another's land.

9.4.2 Unlawful use of land – reasonable user

Everyone has the right to use their land for their own purposes. While this may be subject to other parts of the law, for example town planning legislation, the general right exists and cannot be interfered with by others. Difficulties arise only when the use to which one person puts the land interferes with what a nearby occupier wishes to do on their land. It is always a question of fact but the general rule is that if the use causes interference which is unreasonable, then it is likely to be regarded by the courts as unlawful and a private nuisance.

The essence of unlawfulness for the purpose of this tort is therefore that the use is unreasonable. What neighbour A regards as perfectly reasonable use of *Blackacre* may be regarded as totally unreasonable by B when it interferes with B's use of *Whiteacre*. This is further explained by Lord Leggatt at paragraph 20 of *Fearn*:

JUDGMENT

'. . . the Court of Appeal rightly emphasised that liability for private nuisance "does not turn on some overriding and free-ranging assessment by the court of the respective reasonableness of each party in the light of all the facts and circumstances". . . the best the law can do is to ask an impartial judge to decide what he or she intuitively feels is reasonable or right between the parties in all the circumstances of the case . . . there are principles, settled since the nineteenth century, which run through the cases and govern whether interference with the use and enjoyment of land is "unlawful" or "undue" or (if the term is to be used) "unreasonable". These principles are not formulae or mechanical rules. They involve judgment in their application. But they provide clear standards rooted in values of reciprocity and equal justice.'

The activity complained of must result in interference which is more than the inevitable result of ordinary life.

CASE EXAMPLE

Southwark London Borough Council v Mills and Others, Baxter v Camden London Borough Council [1999] 2 WLR 742

Cases were brought by tenants who lived in blocks of flats owned by the councils. The flats were badly soundproofed and the tenants complained that their lives were made miserable by everyday noises coming from next door. As the noises complained of were part and parcel of everyday life, the behaviour of those causing the noise could not be unreasonable. It was not unreasonable activity which was causing the tenants' problems but lack of sound-proofing. It was held that the governing principle is good neighbourliness, and this involves reciprocity. A landowner must show the same consideration for his neighbour as he would expect his neighbour to show for him.

There are no hard and fast rules as to when use will be regarded as unreasonable but past cases give a good indication of how the courts will approach the task and the issues which will be taken into account. The correct test is whether a normal person would find it reasonable to have to put up with the effects of the defendant's activities.

CASE EXAMPLE

Barr v Biffa Waste Services Ltd [2012] EWCA Civ 312

This involved a landfill site near to residential housing in which the defendant tipped 'pre-treated' waste (from which recyclables had been extracted) so that it had spent longer before being tipped, had a higher level of organic matter than normal and so was very smelly. The Court of Appeal, allowing the appeal held that the trial judge was wrong to base the test on whether the activity was reasonable because it was under a permit from the Environment Agency and also wrong that this permit had transformed the nature of the locality for the purposes of private nuisance. The trial judge had also introduced a requirement of a threshold level of seriousness and the Court of Appeal felt that this was wrong also.

The basic question to ask is whether the defendant's act is foreseeably likely to cause the nuisance. If the answer to this question is in the affirmative, the defendant is liable. Matters which will be considered by the courts in determining whether the use of the law is reasonable include:

- locality;
- duration;
- malice;
- sensitivity of the claimant

but none of these matters is decisive nor is the list exhaustive.

Locality

No one reasonably expects the same levels of peace and quiet in urban and industrial areas which are to be found in rural areas. Each has its own characteristics. This means that where the activity occurs is important. As Thesiger LJ said in *Sturges v Bridgman* [1879] 11 Ch D 852:

JUDGMENT

'What would be a nuisance in Belgrave Square would not necessarily be so in Bermondsey.'

It is clear that where actual physical damage is caused as a result of the activity, the issue of locality is not relevant. In *St Helen's Smelting Co v Tipping* [1865] 11 HL Cas 642 the fact that the industrial use which caused physical damage occurred in an industrial area was held to be irrelevant.

Where, however, the interference is with a person's comfort, peace or personal freedom, locality is important. In *Laws v Florinplace Ltd* [1981] 1 All ER 659 an injunction was granted to prevent the use of a shop converted to a sex shop and cinema club in a residential area. In the seminal case of *Coventry v Lawrence* [2014] UKSC 13, the Supreme Court addressed a number of issues one of which was whether and to what extent, noise is open to a defendant to a nuisance claim to invoke the actual use of his premises, complained of by the claimant, when assessing the character of the locality. This is to say, in this case, the claimant complained that the defendant's motorbike track on which racing takes place was too noisy but the defendant argued that this track formed part of the locality and this needs to be taken into account when assessing the nature of the locality. By comparison, the claimants asserted that the locality was rural and included a small village and that it is counterintuitive to allow the defendant to rely on their own activities in defending a nuisance claim.

The Supreme Court held at 65, that:

JUDGMENT

'[The activities] should be notionally stripped out of the locality when assessing its character. Thus, in the present case, where the judge concluded that the activities at the Stadium and the Track were actually carried on in such a way as to constitute a nuisance, although they could be carried on so as not to cause a nuisance, the character of the locality should be assessed on the basis that (i) it includes the Stadium and the Track, and (ii) they could be used for speedway, stockcar, and banger racing and for motocross respectively, but (iii) only to an extent which would not cause a nuisance . . . a defendant, faced with a contention that his activities give rise to a nuisance, can rely on those activities as constituting part of the character of the locality, but only to the extent that those activities do not constitute a nuisance – and to avoid any misunderstanding, if the activities couldn't be carried out without creating a nuisance, then they would have to be entirely discounted when assessing the character of the neighbourhood.'

This conclusion must be right in that when addressing the nature of the locality, other activities that create noise in the neighbourhood are considered whether or not they are authorised and deemed to form part of the character of the neighbourhood. Therefore, the extent that the motorbike track does not emit so much noise so as to cause a nuisance, can be considered as forming part of the locality.

Duration

It is said that for an activity to amount to a nuisance, it must be continuous. This requirement may be satisfied by an activity which recurs regularly; there is no requirement that it should continue day and night over a period of time.

The fact that an activity is temporary does not mean that it cannot amount to a nuisance. Examples can be most easily found in the context of building work. Such work almost invariably causes annoyance and inconvenience to the neighbours but it would be wholly unreasonable to prevent such work taking place. It must, however, be carried out in a way which is sensitive to the needs of the neighbours.

The extent of the interference is very relevant.

CASE EXAMPLE

Andreae v Selfridge & Co Ltd [1937] 3 All ER 255

Demolition work created an excessive amount of noise and dust which interfered with the business of a hotel. No injunction was granted, as building work is not in itself an unreasonable use of land, but the excessive interference with the business meant that damages were payable.

An injunction will, however, be granted where the temporary interference can reasonably be avoided.

CASE EXAMPLE

De Keyser's Royal Hotel Ltd v Spicer Bros Ltd [1914] 30 TLR 257

Pile driving at night meant that the sleep of the owner of the next door hotel was disturbed. An injunction was granted to prevent the work at night.

A 'one-off' or isolated incident can be a nuisance. Thus, in *Spicer v Smee* [1946] 1 All ER 489 a fire was caused by defective wiring in the defendant's property resulting in the claimant's property being burned to the ground. The defendant was held liable in nuisance, the damage resulting from a dangerous state of affairs on the defendant's premises. The position was explained by Mr Justice Potter in *Crown River Cruises Ltd v Kimbolton Fireworks Ltd* [1996] CLC 1214 when debris from a 20-minute firework display set fire to one of the claimant's barges. The judge said at 1229:

JUDGMENT

'Where an activity creates a state of affairs which gives rise to risk of escape of physically dangerous or damaging material . . . then the law of nuisance is . . . available to give a remedy for that state of affairs, albeit brief in duration.'

Malice

It is rare for the motive behind a defendant's act to be relevant in the law of tort save in those torts based on intention. In nuisance, the defendant's motive, if it can be characterised as ill-will or spite, may well result in the court regarding what would otherwise be a reasonable activity as unreasonable and therefore a nuisance.

CASE EXAMPLE

Christie v Davey [1893] 1 Ch 316

The claimant taught music and had a musical family. Music was frequently played and could be heard by the defendant who lived in the adjoining house. In retaliation, the defendant banged trays and beat on the wall to disturb the claimant.

Finding that the defendant had acted deliberately and maliciously to interfere with the claimant, Mr Justice North explained that had the defendant not acted maliciously, he would have taken a different view of the case. The malicious nature of the behaviour meant that it 'was not a legitimate use of the defendant's house to use it for the purpose of vexing and annoying his neighbours'.

CASE EXAMPLE

Hollywood Silver Fox Farm Ltd v Emmett [1936] 2 KB 468

The claimant ran a farm on which silver foxes were bred for the fur trade. At the time this was morally acceptable. The defendant, who owned the next-door farm wanted to sell land for development and believed that the presence of the fox farm reduced the value of the site. He arranged for gun shots to be fired near to the fox enclosures so that their breeding would be interrupted. It was held that the defendant's motive amounted to malice and he was liable in nuisance.

These examples are easily understood but the rules are complicated by an apparently contradictory case heard in 1895.

CASE EXAMPLE

Bradford Corporation v Pickles [1895] AC 587

Water percolated under the defendant's land eventually reaching the claimant's land from beneath which it was extracted by the claimant to maintain the municipal water supply. The defendant began to pump out the water from his own land in order to reach mineral deposits. As a result, the quantity and quality of the water reaching the claimant's land was diminished. The claimant asked for an injunction to stop the defendant from damaging the water supply to their land.

Holding that a landowner had an absolute right to extract water from undefined channels beneath his own land, Lord Macnaghton said that an act which gives rise to no legal injury cannot be made tortious no matter what the defendant's motive. It had been suggested that the defendant's motive in the case was to force the claimant to purchase either his land or the water. Even if this was morally wrong, the motive could not make the lawful act unlawful.

This at first sight appears totally to contradict the later cases on malice. However, it must be borne in mind that the court found that the factual interference in *Bradford Corporation v Pickles* was minimal. It can be suggested that the decision was reached on the principle *de minimis non curat lex* (the law will not correct a trivial injury). Had the damage been substantial, the outcome may have been different.

Sensitivity of the claimant

Nuisance only operates to protect the claimant's reasonable use of their land. Where the use to which the claimant puts the land is unusually sensitive to things such as heat or fumes the defendant will not be liable.

CASE EXAMPLE

Robinson v Kilvert [1889] 41 Ch D 88

The claimant stored brown paper on the ground floor of a warehouse. The paper needed particular conditions for storage if it was not to deteriorate. Heat from the basement, used by the defendant, seeped into the ground floor and caused damage to the paper. It was held that there was no nuisance. The heating would not have caused problems for ordinary use of the premises. It was the particular character of the paper being stored that led to the damage.

Where, however, ordinary uses of land are also interfered with, there will be a remedy for that interference and for the interference with the sensitive use. This is understood if a simple example is used. If fumes cause damage to roses, a quintessentially English flower, then the claimant will be entitled to a remedy, not only for the damage to the rose bushes but also for any damage which has been caused to exotic and sensitive plants (*McKinnon Industries Ltd v Walker* [1951] 3 DLR 577).

In general the law is now moving away from the concept of 'abnormal sensitivity' and more towards a general test of foreseeability in line with negligence.

CASE EXAMPLE

Network Rail Infrastructure v Morris [2004] EWCA Civ 172

The claimant ran a recording studio close to a railway line. The defendant then installed new track circuits which interfered with the claimant's amplification system and caused the claimant to lose business as a result. The Court of Appeal held that the defendant was not liable, not because the recording studio represented an abnormally sensitive use of land, but because it was not foreseeable that the installation would interfere with the claimant's use of land in such a way.

The case also runs in line with the line of cases (e.g. *Hunter v Canary Wharf* and *Bridlington Relay Ltd v Yorkshire Electricity Board*) which prevent claims for interference with recreational activities.

In *Fearn* it was argued that the claimants may have been a sensitive user given that they chose to live in flats with floor-to-ceiling glass windows. It was considered that in an inner-city environment the occupier of a flat high above ground level must recognise the possibility that a building of similar height might be constructed nearby from which the occupants can see through their windows. Provided that the nearby building is used in an ordinary way the fact that the interiors of flats with glass walls can be seen is something the owners have to put up with in accordance with the rule of give and take. However, this is not the case here. It was held that the nature of and extent of the viewing of the claimants' flats goes far beyond anything that could reasonably be regarded as a necessary or natural consequence of the common and ordinary use and occupation of the Tate's land. Objecting to people peering into your flat, taking photographs and sometime using binoculars, is not seeking any special or unequal treatment.

9.4.3 Indirect interference

The cases referred to all demonstrate that the consequences suffered by the claimant are the indirect result of the defendant's activity or the state of affairs on the defendant's land.

9.4.4 The use and enjoyment of land

Nuisance is not actionable per se thus the claimant must prove damage. Where physical damage has been caused to the land itself, the claimant will not usually face undue difficulty in establishing a case. Interference with use and enjoyment of land is more complex. It has already been seen that the issue is judged subjectively, the courts asking the question 'What effect does this activity have on this claimant?' It is obviously not enough for a claimant living in a town to complain that a neighbour keeps chickens in the garden. Something more is needed. For example if a cockerel is also kept which welcomes the dawn (and wakes the neighbours) with a 'cock-a-doodle-doo' every morning, the neighbours are likely to have a valid cause of action. Simply taking a dislike to a neighbour's activity will not suffice.

The interference, although it is intangible, must still be substantial. Lord Knight Bruce VC explained that it must interfere with 'the ordinary comfort physically of human existence'. He discounted 'elegant or dainty modes and habits of living' preferring to judge comfort 'according to plain and simple notions' (*Walter v Selfe* [1851] 4 De G & Sm 315).

Interests which are regarded as aesthetic are not usually protected. Thus the courts have refused to recognise

- the right to a view (*A-G v Doughty* [1752] 2 Ves Sen 453);
- the right to an unrestricted flow of air in the absence of an easement (*Bland v Moseley* [1587] 9 Co Rep 58; *Chastey v Ackland* [1895] 2 Ch 389);
- in the absence of an easement, the right to light (*Dalton v Angus* [1881] 6 App Cas 740).

Reviewing these cases in *Hunter and Others v Canary Wharf Ltd*, the House of Lords held that there could be no right to freedom from interference with television reception. (For a fuller discussion of this case see section 9.1.)

CRITIQUING THE LAW

What is the main difference between the decision in *Hunter* and *Fearn*? In *Hunter* the claimants were upset over the interference with their TV signal whereas in *Fearn* the claimants were upset because of interference with their privacy because people could peer into their homes as they had floor-to-ceiling glass windows. Is one scenario of interference more deserving of protection than another?

9.5 Defences

This section deals with the accepted defences of:

- **prescription**;
- statutory authority;
- planning consent.

prescription
A defence in private nuisance where the thing complained of had been active for 20 years or more and the claimant had known about it and not complained before

It also deals with matters which are commonly thought of as defences but which are not in fact effective:

- coming to the nuisance;
- social utility;
- acts of others.

It can be argued that the last three matters could be morally justified as defences but the courts have not given any indication that the position may change.

9.5.1 Prescription

While the fact that the claimant moved to the nuisance is not a defence, it is possible for a person to obtain a prescriptive right to carry on an activity that in the eyes of some amounts to a private nuisance. The activity complained of must have been continuously carried on for at least 20 years. Throughout that time it must have been actionable as a private nuisance but nobody has in fact taken action.

Care should be taken in relation to this defence. It does not matter how long an activity has been carried on for unless, for the last 20 years at least, someone has been in occupation of nearby land and would have been able to establish a nuisance affecting that land. The occupiers of a new housing development built next to an isolated church in which bells have been rung for centuries may be able to silence the bells. The basis of this is that until the new houses were built no one had been in a position to establish a nuisance.

The leading case on this issue is *Sturges v Bridgman* [1879] 11 Ch D 852.

CASE EXAMPLE

Sturges v Bridgman [1879] 11 Ch D 852

For more than 20 years a confectioner had carried on his business which included the use of an industrial pestle and mortar to grind sugar. The premises abutted on to the garden of premises occupied by a doctor. The doctor built a new consulting room at the bottom of his garden but found that it could not be used because of the noise and vibration coming from the confectioner's premises. The doctor was able to obtain an injunction against the confectioner despite the fact that the business had been in operation for more than 20 years. It had only become an actionable nuisance once the new consulting room was built therefore no prescriptive right could exist.

This defence was given further consideration in *Coventry v Lawrence* which has already been considered above in relation to locality. The Supreme Court was asked to deal with the possibility of whether it is open to a defendant to contend that he has established a prescriptive right to commit what would otherwise be a nuisance by means of noise. The Supreme Court reminded us that, in order to establish a right by prescription, a person must show at least 20 years uninterrupted enjoyment as of right once it is known that the activity is causing a nuisance to another. On these facts, the defendant did not show that their activities amounted to a nuisance over the duration of 20 years. It is simply not enough to say that the activity has been carried on for 20 years or that a noise has been emitted for 20 years. What needs to be established for a successful application of this defence is that the activity has caused a nuisance over 20 years. This may not appear to be logical but the Supreme Court said that this helps those in the position of the claimant have a real chance to object to the nuisance. This makes it extraordinary difficult for a defendant to ever rely on this defence. But note this defence does not require the activity to be carried out every day over a period of 20 years.

This defence, if established, is a species of easement.

9.5.2 Statutory authority

In the modern world many activities are undertaken by public utilities and large commercial enterprises, some of which require the assistance of specific legislation to be established. Examples of recent projects requiring legislation include the redevelopment of Docklands, the construction of the Channel Tunnel and the creation of the high-speed rail link between the Tunnel and London.

Since many of the activities that are likely to be the cause of a nuisance are now regulated or licensed by environmental or other laws then statutory authority is likely to be one of the most effective defences. However, the defence may not be available where discretion to act is exercised improperly.

CASE EXAMPLE

***Metropolitan Asylum District Hospital v Hill* [1881] 6 App Cas 193**

Here a general power had been granted by statute to build a smallpox hospital. However, the defence was then unavailable when the hospital was sited in a place that would cause a nuisance (obviously owing to the highly contagious nature of the disease).

When an actionable nuisance arises as a result of the activity permitted by the statute, the statute must be interpreted by the courts to ascertain whether or not the nuisance itself has been authorised and what, if any, remedy may be available. (For a discussion on how the courts approach this task, see Chapter 16.) Some statutes contain a 'nuisance' clause which specifically states that the common law of nuisance shall continue to apply to the activity. In such a case the parties adversely affected need only satisfy the usual rules. Occasionally statutes make it explicitly clear that carrying out the permitted activity will not give rise to a civil claim. We have already seen that the Civil Aviation Act 1982 contains specific provision that over-flying aircraft cannot give rise to a claim in nuisance or trespass to land (see section 8.3).

Other statutes may prescribe a remedy while not specifically stating that there shall be no remedy in nuisance. An example of this is found in the Water Industry Act 1991 which gives individuals the right to complain to the Director-General of Water Services who has enforcement powers. In the recent case of *Marcic v Thames Water Utilities Ltd* [2003] UKHL 66 (for facts see section 1.5.6) it was held that the common law of nuisance could 'not impose on Thames Water obligations inconsistent with the statutory scheme' (per Lord Nicholls at para. 33), leaving the claimant no remedy for what was in reality a nuisance even if it was not one in law.

Other statutes are silent on the issue. The question then to be answered is whether the activity is within the scope of that authorised by the statute. If it is, and is the inevitable consequence of that activity, there will be no redress. It is for the organisation carrying out the activity to prove that it is within the scope of the statute and that all reasonable care has been taken to minimise the problems.

The basis of this approach was explained by Lord Wilberforce in *Allen v Gulf Oil Refining Ltd* [1981] 2 WLR 188 when he said at 1011:

JUDGMENT

'It is now well settled that where Parliament by express direction or by necessary implication has authorised [an activity], that carries with it an authority to do what is authorised with immunity from any action based on nuisance.'

It may be that the provisions of the Human Rights Act 1998 have altered the position somewhat. This is discussed in section 9.9.3.

9.5.3 Planning permission

Planning permission is granted by local authorities using delegated statutory powers. Those making the decisions are the elected representatives of the local community and among the issues they must take into account is the suitability of the proposals for the particular area. It can be argued therefore that the issue of locality has been considered by the local authority which has decided that the proposal is in fact likely to be a reasonable use of land in that locality. This would mean that the grant of planning permission should be regarded as a defence working in a similar way to statutory authority. This is not in fact the case although, as we shall see, there is some movement in the courts towards this idea and planning permission can be relevant.

In *Allen v Gulf Oil Refining Ltd* Lord Cumming-Bruce said:

JUDGMENT

'the planning authority has no jurisdiction to authorise nuisance save (if at all) in so far as it has . . . power to permit the change of the character of the neighbourhood'.

This comment proved to be important when *Gillingham Borough Council v Medway (Chatham) Dock Co Ltd* [1993] QB 343 came before the courts.

CASE EXAMPLE

Gillingham Borough Council v Medway (Chatham) Dock Co Ltd [1993] QB 343

The Council alleged a public nuisance was being caused by the operation of a former naval dockyard as a commercial enterprise. Heavy goods vehicles were using local residential roads by night disturbing the local population. Planning permission had been given for the development despite acknowledged concerns about the extensive use of one particular entrance to the area. It was this which caused the eventual problem.

Mr Justice Buckley stated that he must at 360:

JUDGMENT

'judge the present claim in nuisance by reference to the present character of the neighbourhood pursuant to the planning permission'. He took the view that 'The [defendant] could not operate a commercial port . . . without disturbing nearby residents'. It was that operation which was specifically authorised. In conclusion the Judge stated:

'where planning consent is given for a development or change of use, the question of nuisance will . . . fall to be decided by reference to a neighbourhood with that development or use and not as it was previously'.

These two cases seem to indicate that the grant of planning permission can indeed have the same effect as statutory authority. Following *Gillingham* the view was taken that the grant of planning permission of itself meant that no nuisance could arise from the authorised activity.

This proved to be inaccurate when the matter was considered further by the Court of Appeal in *Wheeler and Another v J J Saunders Ltd and Others* [1996] Ch 19.

CASE EXAMPLE

Wheeler and Another v J J Saunders Ltd and Others [1996] Ch 19

The claimants bought a farmhouse on land next to farmland and obtained planning permission to convert outbuildings into holiday homes. This was the only permitted use of the outbuildings by virtue of a restrictive covenant in the title deeds of the premises. The defendants obtained planning permission to build two pig housing units on the farmland but very close to the holiday homes. At first instance it was held that the smell coming from the pig units amounted to a nuisance. The defendants appealed arguing that as they had planning permission for the units, no nuisance could be actionable.

Considering the judgments in *Allen v Gulf Oil* and in *Gillingham v Medway*, Lord Justice Peter Gibson held that planning permission can only amount to a defence where as a result of the permitted activity.

JUDGMENT

'[T]he judge was entitled to conclude that the planning consents did not prevent the [claimants] from succeeding in their claim in nuisance.'

So where does this leave the law? The rules can be summarised as follows:

- Where planning consent is granted for a development which will inevitably mean a change in the nature of the locality, an actionable nuisance will not arise provided the operation is undertaken with reasonable care.
- In other cases, the grant of planning consent will simply be one of the factors taken into account by the court but will not of itself afford a defence to a nuisance.

A different problem occurs for instance where sporting venues are involved.

CASE EXAMPLE

Watson v Croft Promo-sport [2009] EWCA Civ 15

Planning permission was gained in 1963 to use a former aerodrome as a motor racing track. After a while racing ceased for a few years, but in 1995 new owners reopened it and it became a very popular circuit. The new owners reapplied for planning permission for 210 days per year and following a public inquiry this was again granted. The claimant who lived about 300 metres from the circuit brought an action in private nuisance. The planning authority had accepted that the planning permission in 1998 had changed the character of the area and so the defendant's use of the circuit was reasonable. However, the Court of Appeal granted an injunction restraining the defendant from using the race track for more than 40 days per year.

Clearly where planning permission has been granted that substantially alters the character of the locality then this may make it difficult to achieve a successful claim in nuisance. One question that the Supreme Court considered was the extent, if any, to which the grant of planning permission for a particular use can affect the question of whether that use is a nuisance or any other use in the locality can be taken into account when considering the character of the locality.

CASE EXAMPLE

Coventry v Lawrence [2014] UKSC 13

The claimants bought a house which was close to a motocross stadium and race track in 2006, although they claimed that they were unaware of this when they bought the house. They argued that the noise from the track was an actionable nuisance. In fact the local council had granted permanent planning permission for the motocross track in 2002 following a number of temporary permissions from 1992 and had given permission for stock car and banger racing in 1997 for 20 days each year. The trial judge granted the injunction and severely limited the use of the track for motor sport. However, the Court of Appeal, in granting the appeal by the stadium held that the planning permission had changed the nature of the locality so that noisy car racing for 20 days each year was the norm and by the time the claimants had bought their house this was well established and by the time of the house purchase there was also a prescriptive right. The Supreme Court however took a different approach. It proclaimed that the Court of Appeal had decided this point wrongly. The clear reason for this was that it was wrong in principle that, through the grant of a planning permission, a planning authority should be able to deprive a property-owner of a right to object to what would otherwise be a nuisance, without providing her with compensation. Lord Neuberger explains this at paragraphs 94 and 193:

JUDGMENT

'. . . the mere fact that the activity which is said to give rise to the nuisance has the benefit of a planning permission is normally of no assistance to the defendant in a claim brought by a neighbour who contends that the activity cause a nuisance to her land in the form of noise or other loss of amenity. . . . The law of private nuisance, of far greater antiquity than modern planning legislation, also fulfils the function of protecting the interests of property owners. There is, however, a fundamental difference between planning law and the law of nuisance. The former exists to protect and promote the public interest, whereas the latter protects the rights of particular individuals. Planning decisions may require individuals to bear burdens for the benefit of others, the local community or the public as a whole. But, as the law stands, it is generally no defence to a claim of nuisance that the activity in question is of benefit to the public.'

This is to say that a planning authority cannot override the private rights of another individual otherwise such common law rights will be meaningless and unenforceable. Planning permissions must co-exist with the private law of nuisance but cannot cut down such private law rights. Planning permissions and the like are after all, administrative in nature. So the mere granting of planning permission is not to be treated as saying that there is not a nuisance; this must be determined by the court and not a planning authority although the planning permission may be helpful in the court's determination.

9.5.4 Coming to the nuisance

This section considers the first of three issues which are commonly thought to raise a defence but which do not in fact do so!

Unless the defence of prescription applies (see section 9.5.1) the fact that an activity has continued for some time without anyone complaining about it will make no difference to the validity of a claim.

CASE EXAMPLE

Bliss v Hall [1838] 4 Bing NC 183

The claimant who had just moved to the area was granted an injunction to prevent a nuisance caused by a tallow-chandlery. The chandlery had been emitting 'divers noisome, noxious, and offensive vapours, fumes, smells and stenches' for three years prior to the claimant's action but this could not be a defence.

Cases such as *Miller v Jackson* [1977] QB 966 and *Kennaway v Thompson* [1980] 3 WLR 361 make it clear that the issue may be relevant to the remedy granted to the claimant. It will not, however, enable the court to conclude that a nuisance does not exist where the relevant criteria are satisfied (see section 9.6 for full discussion of remedies).

Coming to the nuisance was given some consideration in the decision of *Coventry v Lawrence* already referenced extensively in this chapter. The issue in this case was the extent, if any, to which a defendant to a nuisance claim can rely on the fact that the claimant 'came to the nuisance'. Lord Neuberger reiterated at paragraph 52:

JUDGMENT

'Furthermore, the notion that coming to the nuisance is no defence is consistent with the fact that nuisance is a property-based tort, so that the right to allege a nuisance should, as it were, run with the land. It would also seem odd if a defendant was no longer liable for nuisance owing to the fact that the identity of his neighbour had changed, even though the use of his neighbour's property remained unchanged. . . . There is much more room for argument that a claimant who builds on, or changes the use of, her property, after the defendant has started the activity alleged to cause a nuisance by noise, or any other emission offensive to the senses, should not have the same rights to complain about that activity as she would have had if her building work or change of use had occurred before the defendant's activity had started. That raises a rather different point from the issue of coming to the nuisance, namely whether an alteration in the claimant's property after the activity in question has started can give rise to a claim in nuisance if the activity would not have been a nuisance had the alteration not occurred.'

It was therefore not a defence to argue that the claimant came to the nuisance.

9.5.5 Social utility

The fact that the defendant's activity is of social utility and benefit to the general community does not amount to a defence. This can have some results which may be devastating for the local community and the economy.

CASE EXAMPLE

Adams v Ursell [1913] 1 Ch 269

A fried-fish shop was closed as it was claimed that it was a nuisance to the residents in the part of the street where it was situated. The fact that its closure would cause great hardship to the defendant and the poor people who were his customers was irrelevant.

Similarly in *Bellew v Cement Co* [1948] Ir R 61 the only cement factory in Ireland was closed despite the urgent need for building at that time.

The modern cases indicate that social utility may be taken into account in considering the remedy but it will not be regarded as a defence.

9.5.6 Freedom to build

The general rule at common law is that anyone whatever they like on their land unless there are certain restrictions in place. So, can a building that causes interference with for example television reception as in *Hunter*, give rise to a claim for nuisance? On the facts it did not. In a similar vein, in *Fearn*, would the building and provision of a viewing platform give rise to a claim in nuisance? The Supreme Court held that it would not because as explained at paragraph 98:

JUDGMENT

'The claimants cannot be obliged to live behind net curtains or with their blinds drawn all day every day to protect themselves from the consequences of intrusion caused by the abnormal use which the Tate makes of its land. In circumstances where the claimants are doing no more than occupying and using their flats in an ordinary way and in accordance with the ordinary habits of a reasonable person, it is no answer for someone who interferes with that use by making an exceptional use of their own land to say that the claimants could protect themselves in their own homes by taking remedial measures.'

9.5.7 The nuisance results from the acts of many people

Defendants may well feel very hard done by when they are found liable for a nuisance emanating from their land which results from the actions of others. It has already been seen that a defendant can be liable for the acts of a trespasser (*Sedleigh-Denfield v O'Callagan*). Where the nuisance is caused by many individuals each doing something which is not in itself unlawful, the occupier may well find that they are liable because of the cumulative effect (*Thorpe v Brumfitt* [1873] LR 8 Ch App 650).

This may perhaps be relevant where a landowner permits discarded goods to be placed on land. The situation would be partly governed by environmental protection legislation but the potential for civil liability for nuisance remains.

9.6 Remedies

9.6.1 Injunction

An injunction is the remedy of choice where a nuisance is continuing or is likely to recur. The principles which govern injunctions generally are discussed in Chapter 19. It has usually been asserted that an injunction should be granted unless the injury suffered by the claimant is trivial or temporary in nature or the activity is an isolated incident or so irregular that any injury can be compensated with damages. However, this position was considered in *Fearn* at paragraphs 122 and 126:

JUDGMENT

'. . . it is fundamental to the integrity of any system of property rights that, in any such case, the individuals whose rights are infringed or overridden receive compensation for the violation of their rights. In other words, the public interest may sometimes justify awarding damages rather than granting an injunction to restrain the defendant's harmful activity, but it cannot justify denying the victim any remedy at all. . . .

The real issue, therefore, in a case where it is said that a continuing activity which causes a nuisance is for the public benefit is not whether the individuals harmed by the activity should have to bear the loss – which on any view would be unjust. It is whether it is sufficient to compensate the loss by awarding damages or whether the activity should be stopped by an injunction.'

Clearly, by offering compensation to the claimants in *Fearn*, this avoided the closure of part of a building in a famous landmark which attracts thousands of visitors a year and has public utility. The offer of compensation in this way protects the claimant against a diminution in the utility and amenity value of their land. This reasoning is in line with some of the older authorities.

CASE EXAMPLE

Miller v Jackson [1977] QB 966

A cricket ground had been used for more than 70 years when a new housing estate was built. The houses were so close to the ground that balls regularly came into the garden meaning that using the garden during a match was dangerous. The claimants alleged nuisance and negligence. The majority of the Court of Appeal held that both torts were established (Lord Denning dissenting) and the majority also held that no injunction should be granted (Lord Lane dissenting).

Lord Denning's judgment is interesting in the view he took as to whether or not the use of the cricket ground could be regarded as unreasonable use of that land. Rejecting the precedent set by *Sturges v Bridgman* he argued that the case should be approached 'on principles applicable to modern conditions'. There was a conflict between the interest of the public at large and the private interest. The public interest would be served by preservation of playing fields in the face of mounting development and thus allow people to enjoy the benefit of outdoor games. The private interest is to secure privacy of home and garden without interference.

Taking account of the fact that the claimants bought the house in midsummer when the cricket season was at its height, Lord Denning took the view that the risk of balls coming into the property should have been obvious. On this basis, he held at 982:

JUDGMENT

'As between [these] conflicting interests, I am of the opinion that the public interest should prevail over the private interest.'

The majority of the court having found a nuisance, an injunction was refused although damages were awarded.

The case has since been criticised but not overruled. The judgment seems to have contributed to the more recent tendency to tailor an injunction to try to give a fair balance between competing interests. A good example of this is found in *Kennaway v Thompson* [1980] 3 WLR 361.

CASE EXAMPLE

Kennaway v Thompson [1980] 3 WLR 361

The claimant had built and occupied a house next to a lake on which, as she knew at that time, there had been water sports for the last ten years. Over the years the use of the lake increased as it became a centre for world-class events involving much larger and noisier boats. The court found that the increased use, which attracted large numbers of spectators, had gone beyond the point at which the claimant could reasonably be expected to tolerate it. At first instance the claimant was refused an injunction but the Court of Appeal took a different view.

The Court held that it was bound by the principles expounded in *Shelfer v City of London Electric Lighting Co* [1895] 1 Ch 287 in which the principle was laid down that unless the injury to the claimant was small, an injunction should be the appropriate remedy. In this case, the injury was not small and the claimant was entitled to an injunction. The judges were concerned to balance the interests of claimant and defendant. They concluded that an injunction allowing one annual international event over three days plus three club events each year of one day each but separated by at least four weeks would achieve this. A limit was also imposed on the power of the boats used and the number of water-skiing boats at other times.

While it is likely that neither of the parties was completely happy with the outcome, the case illustrates the extent to which the courts were prepared to go to try to achieve a true balance between the competing interests of neighbours.

In the seminal decision of *Coventry v Lawrence* the Supreme Court considered the approach to be adopted by a court when deciding whether to grant an injunction to restrain a nuisance being committed, or whether to award damages instead, and the relevance of planning permission to that issue.

The defendants were aggrieved by the earlier court's decision to award an injunction as they were of the view that damages should have been awarded in lieu of an injunction which was the practice following the decision in *Kennaway*. The argument here being that damages would have compensated the claimants to the extent that their property had been devalued and perhaps to cover the inconvenience suffered but that they could then continue with the activities causing the nuisance. The flip side of this argument and one that has long been recognised, is that for the law of nuisance to provide adequate protection, one cannot be allowed to effectively purchase their neighbour's rights which would be the case if damages were awarded to the claimant as opposed to imposing an injunction against the defendant. The goal must always be to protect the claimant's legal right to enjoy their property with due regard to others' ability to enjoy their property.

In *Shelfer* it was determined that:

1. if the injury to the plaintiff's legal rights is small,
2. and is one which is capable of being estimated in money,

3. and is one which can be adequately compensated by a small money payment,
4. and the case is one in which it would be oppressive to the defendant to grant an injunction – then damages in substitution for an injunction may be given.

An injunction is an equitable remedy granted at the discretion of the court. This is to say that it is important that a court's discretion is not fettered by this guidance from *Shelfer* and that it is treated as just that, guidance. However, the guidance had been treated as the law in that the four criteria are normally to be applied, so that if all four tests are satisfied, there is little jurisdiction to award an injunction but if they are not satisfied then an injunction may be awarded. This is not in keeping with this remedy being a discretionary remedy involving necessary flexibility and account of all of the facts of the case or indeed the conduct of the parties.

Lord Neuberger took this as an opportunity to comprehensively review the law in this area. He said at paragraphs 116–119 and 149:

JUDGMENT

'It seems to me that there are two problems about the current state of the authorities on this question of the proper approach for a court to adopt on the question whether to award damages instead of an injunction. The first . . . [does the] approach in *Shelfer* . . . require an exceptional case before damages should be awarded in lieu of an injunction, . . . [or should we take] into account the conduct of the parties . . . [A]n approach which involves damages being awarded only in "very exceptional circumstances", are each simply wrong in principle, and give rise to a serious risk of going wrong in practice. The court's power to award damages in lieu of an injunction involves a classic exercise of discretion, which should not, as a matter of principle, be fettered . . . it would, in the absence of additional relevant circumstances pointing the other way, normally be right to refuse an injunction if those four tests were satisfied . . . the fact that those tests are not all satisfied does not mean that an injunction should be granted . . . The decision whether to award damages instead of an injunction can be dependent on a number of issues, including the behaviour and attitude of the parties . . .'

Lord Neuberger has made clear that where a claimant establishes a nuisance, they are entitled to an injunction to restrain the defendant from continuing with the nuisance. That said, the court may wish to award damages in lieu of an injunction with due consideration being given to the guidance given in *Shelfer* highlighting that even if all four criteria are met, that is not in itself sufficient justification to refuse to award an injunction as other factors such as the behaviour and attitude of the parties and public benefit (i.e. job losses) must be considered just as much as it is necessary to consider that if all four criteria are not met, that in itself is not sufficient to deny the award of damages and award an injunction instead. The careful balancing exercise of relevant factors as they are applicable to each case must be conducted.

9.6.2 Damages

The claimant will be able to recover damages for any loss which has occurred to the value of the land and for any physical consequences of the nuisance or business loss. There has been some doubt about whether damages for personal injury which has resulted from the nuisance can be recovered. The doubt has been raised by the judgment in *Hunter v Canary Wharf* where it was held by three of the judges that damages for personal injury could not be recovered in the tort of private nuisance. The view that such damages cannot be awarded has been confirmed *obiter* in *Transco plc v Stockport Metropolitan Borough Council* [2003] UKHL 61, a case about *Rylands v Fletcher* [1868] LR 1 Exch 265, which is discussed in detail in Chapter 10.

9.6.3 Abatement

A person affected by a nuisance has the right to take action to reduce or eliminate the nuisance. This self-help remedy is not as straightforward as it would seem. Where tree branches overhang the claimant's land, for example, the offending branches can be lopped without entering the defendant's land. Care must be taken not to cause unnecessary damage to the trees and the branches must be returned to the defendant.

Where entry on to the defendant's land is necessary the claimant needs to alert the defendant to the problem and give enough time for the necessary remedial action to be taken. If the claimant then needs to take action, care must be taken to do only that which is necessary and not to cause unnecessary damage.

Where the situation is such that there is a serious risk of damage to people or property, action can be taken without notice.

The remedy looks attractive at first sight but has one major drawback. In many cases the existence of the nuisance may well have caused a deterioration of the relationship between neighbours. It is unlikely that exercising the right to abate the nuisance will improve the relationship!

ACTIVITY

Self-assessment questions

1. What is meant by the word 'unlawful' in the context of private nuisance?
2. Explain the matters which may be relevant to the court's decision.
3. Consider the extent to which the defendant's motive for the activity may be relevant.
4. How does the defence of prescription contradict the principle that coming to the nuisance is no defence?
5. Explain the circumstances in which the grant of planning consent by a local planning authority may serve as a defence.

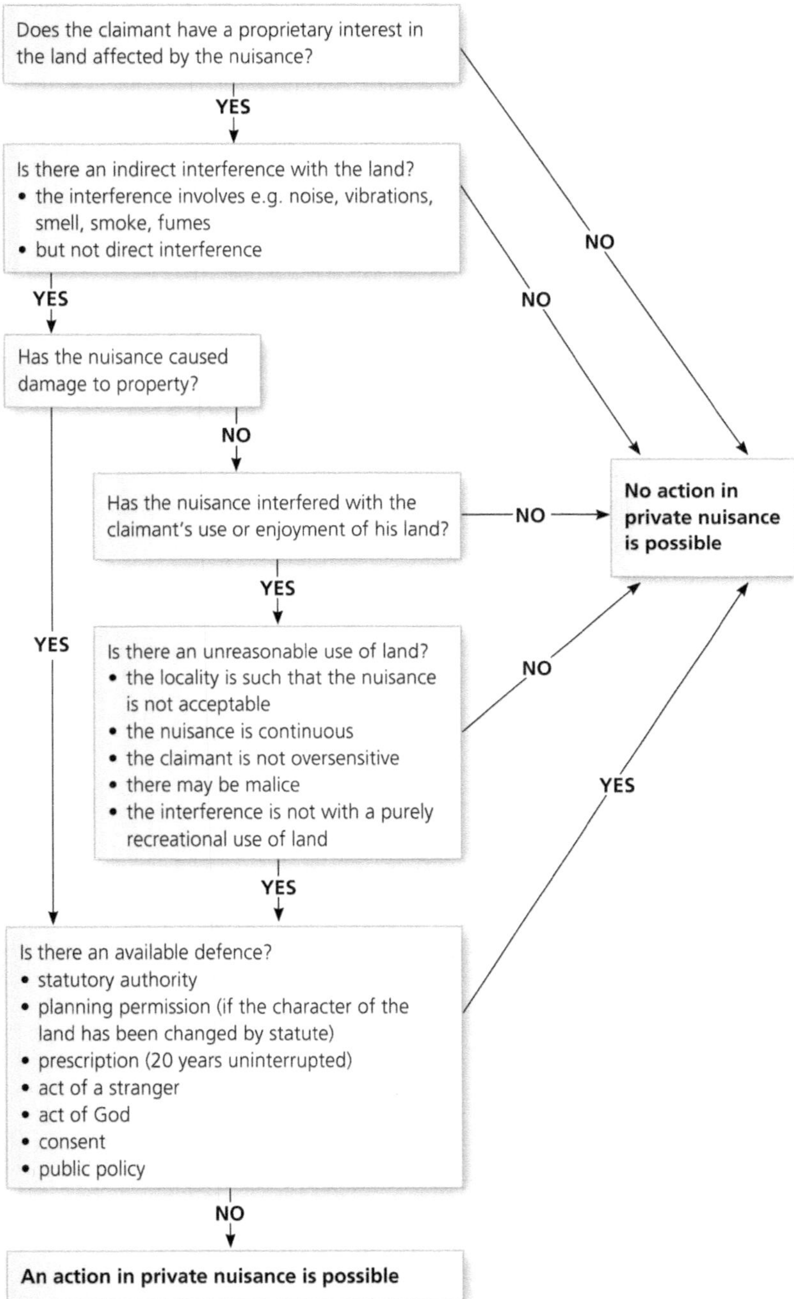

Figure 9.2 The essential elements for a claim of private nuisance.

KEY FACTS

Key facts on private nuisance

Definition	**Case**
One person's use of their land unlawfully interferes with another's use of their land.	
The law on private nuisance seeks to protect the diminution in the utility and amenity value of the claimant's land. In other words, the injury is to the property not the person. Requires balancing of interests of parties concerned.	*Fearn v Tate Gallery* [2023] UKSC 4
Interference is unlawful if it is unreasonable.	
Claimant	**Case**
Must have a legal interest – usually right to exclusive possession.	
Others, e.g. lodgers, have no remedy. Note – HL overruling CA attempt to widen categories of claimant in	*Malone v Laskey* [1907] *Hunter v Canary Wharf* [1997] *Khorasandjian v Bush* [1993]
Defendant	**Case**
Person who creates nuisance usually occupier.	
Independent contractors liable for their activities unless extra-hazardous when occupier remains liable. Occupier who 'adopts' nuisance created by trespasser liable for that nuisance. Occupier liable for act of nature where they are or ought to be aware of the potential for nuisance but note requirement of reasonable foreseeability.	*Honeywill and Stein v Larkin Brothers* [1934] *Sedleigh-Denfield v O'Callaghan* [1940] *Goldman v Hargrave* [1967]; *Leakey v National Trust* [1980] *Cambridge Water v Eastern Counties Leather* [1994]; *Holbeck Hall Hotel v Scarborough BC* [2000]
Landlords not generally liable unless nuisance inevitable result of activity permitted by terms of letting.	*Tetley v Chitty* [1986]
Unlawful	**Case**
If interference is unreasonable it is likely to be unlawful.	
Problem for courts as 'unreasonable' cannot be defined.	
Ordinary everyday activities cannot be unreasonable.	*Southwark LBC v Mills* [1999]

(Continued)

(Continued)

Unlawful	Case
Relevant factors depend on facts of particular case but include: Locality. Note locality is irrelevant where physical damage is caused. The activities complained of should be notionally stripped out of the locality when assessing its character. Duration in sense of continuous or regular – can be temporary as in case of building work which is insensitive to needs of neighbours.	*Sturges v Bridgman* [1879] *Laws v Florinplace Ltd* [1981] *Coventry v Lawrence (No 2)* [2014] UKSC 46 *St Helen's v Tipping* [1865]; *Andreae v Selfridge* [1937]
Exceptionally can be 'one-off' incident.	*De Keyser's Royal Hotel v Spicer Bros* [1914]; *Spicer v Smee* [1946]; *Crown River Cruises v Kimbolton Fireworks* [1996]
Note effect of malice which can make activity unreasonable.	*Christie v Davey* [1893]; *Hollywood Silver Fox Farm v Emmett* [1936]
No remedy if only damage caused results from unusual sensitivity of claimant or claimant's property.	*Robinson v Kilvert* [1889]; *McKinnon Industries v Walker* [1951]
Damage	**Case**
Must be proved – not usually difficult in case of physical damage. Court must consider effect of the particular activity on the particular claimant – subjective assessment.	
Interference must be with interest recognised thus, e.g. no right to a view.	*A-G v Doughty* [1752]
Intrusion of privacy can be a nuisance	*Fearn v Tate Gallery* [2023] UKSC 4
nor to freedom of interference with TV reception.	*Hunter v Canary Wharf* [1997]
Must be reasonably foreseeable.	*Cambridge Water v Eastern Counties Leather* [1994]
Defences	**Case**
Prescription – activity has amounted to actionable nuisance for at least 20 years without anyone in position to do so taking action.	*Sturges v Bridgman* [1879] *Coventry v Lawrence (No 2)* [2014] UKSC 46
Statutory authority – statute may give remedy or specifically provide that the common law shall not apply – possible action for breach of statutory duty – if statute does not say no remedy for activity permitted by statute which inevitably creates nuisance.	*Allen v Gulf Oil* [1980]

(Continued)

(Continued)

Defences	Case
Planning consent full defence if nuisance inevitable consequence of change in nature of locality authorised by the consent.	*Gillingham BC v Medway (Chatham) Dock* [1993]
It is however, not permissible for planning consent to deprive a person of their private law rights to enjoy their property free of a nuisance.	*Coventry v Lawrence (No 2)* [2014] UKSC 46
No defence in other circumstances.	*Wheeler v J J Saunders* [1996]
Oddities	**Case**
Fact that claimant moved to the area of the nuisance and even knew about it is no defence.	*Bliss v Hall* [1838]
but see Lord Denning's comments in –	*Miller v Jackson* [1977]
Activity which has social utility may be prohibited.	*Adams v Ursell* [1913]; *Bellew v Cement Co* [1948]
Nuisance can result from acts of many people none of which is in itself unlawful.	*Thorpe v Brumfitt* [1873]
Remedies	**Case**
Injunction – may be granted unless injury is trivial or can be adequately compensated by damages taking public utility into account. This is a discretionary remedy and the court's discretion must not be fettered. This remedy should be tailored to strike balance between interests of claimant and defendant. Damages – recoverable for loss to value of the land and any physical damage to land – not available for personal injury. Abatement or self-help.	*Fearn v Tate Gallery* [2023] UKSC *Kennaway v Thompson* [1980] *Coventry v Lawrence (No 2)* [2014] UKSC 46 *Hunter v Canary Wharf* [1997]; *Transco v Stockport MBC* [2003]

9.7 Public nuisance

9.7.1 Definition

The most commonly used definition is that given by Lord Justice Romer in *Attorney-General (on the relation of Glamorgan County Council and Pontardawe Rural District Council) v PYA Quarries Ltd* [1957] 2 QB 169, at 184:

JUDGMENT

'Any nuisance is "public" which materially affects the reasonable comfort and convenience of life of a class of Her Majesty's subjects.'

It is clear from this definition that in reality it is impossible to state precisely what a public nuisance is! Some things are, however, certain.

Public nuisance is a crime as well as a tort and can lead to prosecution and punishment. Apart from noting this fact, this book does not concern itself with the criminal aspect.

An action for public nuisance is brought by the Attorney-General on behalf of all those affected. The civil action is known as a 'relator action'. This enables an injunction to be obtained prohibiting nuisance behaviour when it would be unreasonable to expect each individual affected to bring their own separate action, saving time and costs. Local authorities may also apply on behalf of the local community (Local Government Act 1972 s222).

Damages cannot be awarded to any individual for injuries caused by a public nuisance unless that individual can prove that they have suffered special damage beyond that generally arising from the nuisance. Where an individual has suffered such additional injury, the action may be brought by the Attorney-General or by the individual.

9.7.2 Elements of the tort

A class of people

The question can be asked – what is a class of people? How many people need to be affected before an action can be brought? This is in reality simply a question of fact in each case.

CASE EXAMPLE

Attorney-General (on the relation of Glamorgan County Council and Pontardawe Rural District Council) v PYA Quarries Ltd [1957] 2 QB 169

Here the nuisance complained of was the noise and vibrations caused by quarrying near to neighbouring properties. The defendant's argument that too few people were affected failed. It was sufficient that a representative class was affected. It is always, however, essential that a substantial 'class of people' are affected by the nuisance.

Special damage

If an individual is to succeed, damage which is 'particular, direct and substantial' beyond that suffered by others affected must be proved (per Brett J in *Benjamin v Storr* [1874] LR 9 CP 400).

CASE EXAMPLE

Benjamin v Storr [1874] LR 9 CP 400

The claimant ran a coffee house. The light to the windows was obstructed by the defendant's horse-drawn vans which stood outside the coffee house. As a result the claimant had to use gas lamps all day, his customers had problems reaching the coffee house and they complained about the smell from the horses. The court had little difficulty in finding that the claimant had suffered in excess of others affected by the defendant's actions.

special damage
This occurs in slander where the claimant usually has to prove that he has suffered damage as a result – also occurs in public nuisance where the claimant has to show that he has suffered damage over that suffered by the public generally

Unless **special damage** can be established, there is no cause of action available to individuals. In *Thomas v National Union of Mineworkers* working miners claimed that they had suffered special damage by reason of the pickets who were obstructing the highway. As their entrance into the mine was not physically prevented, it was held that the obstruction of the highway did not cause the working miners special damage.

Where public nuisance is concerned, there is no requirement that the claimant has an interest in land. The following case example concerns rights of navigation over a river bed.

CASE EXAMPLE

Tate & Lyle Industries Ltd v Greater London Council and another [1983] 2 AC 509

The claimants operated a jetty that they had built on the bank of the Thames from which refined sugar could be loaded on to boats. They obtained a licence from the Port of London Authority (PLA) to build a new jetty for the off-loading of raw sugar. At the same time the PLA granted a licence to the GLC to build two ferry terminals. The new 'sugar' jetty was rendered very expensive to operate because of silting caused by the ferry terminals. The claimants sued the GLC and the PLA in public nuisance. The House of Lords held at 537:

JUDGMENT

'[The] interference with the public right of navigation caused particular damage to [the claimants] because vessels of the requisite dimensions were unable to pass and repass over the bed and foreshore between the main channel and the [jetties].'

A particular set of facts may give rise to claims in both public and private nuisance. *Halsey v Esso Petroleum Co Ltd* [1961] 1 WLR 683 illustrates this very clearly.

CASE EXAMPLE

Halsey v Esso Petroleum Co Ltd [1961] 1 WLR 683

The claimant lived on a house adjoining the Fulham Road in London, a very busy area, and near to a depot owned and operated by the defendants. The claimant and his neighbours all suffered from the use of the depot but the claimant alleged that he suffered more than most. Washing, hung out to dry, and his car, parked on the road outside his house, was damaged by acid smuts; the noise of tankers turning into and out of the depot kept him awake at night; finally there was a dreadful smell. The smuts were disgorged from the chimneys in the depot, the noise from the tankers came from the use of the highway.

It was held that the damage to the washing and the consequences of the smell interfered with the claimant's use and enjoyment of his land and arose from the defendant's use of their land. This gave rise to liability for private nuisance. The damage to the car occurred on the highway and did not affect the claimant's use and enjoyment of his land; the sleepless nights also resulted from use of the highway. These were held to give rise to liability in public nuisance and the claimant was able to recover damages as he had suffered more than other residents who were affected by the defendant's activities.

Highways

Many public nuisances occur as a result of abuse of the right of passage over a highway. A temporary obstruction is unlikely to amount to a public nuisance unless it is also unreasonable. This is illustrated by *Trevett v Lee* [1955] 1 All ER 406. Unlike in private nuisance it appears that a claimant can recover for personal injury *Corby Group Litigation v Corby BC* [2008] EWCA Civ 463.

CASE EXAMPLE

Trevett v Lee [1955] 1 All ER 406

The claimant tripped over a hosepipe laid across the highway by the defendant who had no mains connection to his premises. The claimant's action failed as the use by the defendant was regarded as reasonable.

Where premises adjoin the highway and damage is caused by something falling on to the highway there may be liability for public nuisance on the part of the land owner. The evidence must show that the owner knew or ought to have known of the danger. Thus in *Noble v Harrison* [1926] 2 KB 332 the defendant was not liable when a branch fell from a tree onto the claimant's vehicle. The defect which caused the fall of the branch was latent and could not have been found on reasonable examination of the tree.

Dangerous premises which collapse on to a highway will amount to a public nuisance if the collapse is caused by lack of maintenance. In *Wringe v Cohen* [1940] 1 KB 229 it was made clear that knowledge or imputed knowledge of the dangerous state of the premises is not required. It is enough that want of repair has led to the consequence which has occurred.

Local authorities and the Highways Authority face a never-ending battle to maintain the highway in a safe condition. Following the Highways Act 1980 s41(1) a highway authority is under a duty to maintain the highway and is liable for any damage resulting from lack of repair unless reasonable care has been taken to maintain the highway in a safe condition (s58). A person who trips over uneven paving stones will probably be able to obtain compensation. However, the duty has limitations. In *Sandhar v Department of Transport* [2004] EWCA Civ 1440 there was held to be no general common law duty to salt roads to prevent the build-up of ice.

9.7.3 Remedies

The individual who can establish a case will be entitled to damages. It was thought that these could include compensation for personal injury but doubt has now been cast on this by *Hunter v Canary Wharf* and *Transco v Stockport* (see section 9.6.2).

An injunction will usually be granted on the application of the Attorney-General or a local authority but there is theoretically no reason why an individual should not obtain such an order in an appropriate case.

KEY FACTS

Public nuisance	Case
Defined as something which affects the comfort and convenience of a class of people.	
Crime as well as tort.	
Action taken on behalf of those affected by Attorney-General or local authority.	
Individual can bring action only if they have suffered special damage above and beyond that suffered by the other members of the class.	*Benjamin v Storr* [1874]
Individual affected need not have any interest in land	*Tate & Lyle v GLC* [1983]
facts of particular case can amount to both public and private nuisance.	*Halsey v Esso Petroleum* [1961]
Abuse of right of passage over highway can be public nuisance – damage caused by something falling on to highway can be nuisance.	*Noble v Harrison* [1926]; *Wringe v Cohen* [1940]

ACTIVITY

Self-assessment questions

1 What are the significant differences between private nuisance and public nuisance?

2 Explain the extent to which an individual affected by public nuisance can hope to receive damages for special damage.

9.8 Statutory nuisance

9.8.1 Introduction

Statutory nuisance is not generally dealt with in a book on tort law. It is, however, useful to include some brief detail. A statutory nuisance will often also amount to a private nuisance. Where this is the case, the claimant has the choice of a simple, cheap and effective course of action available by virtue of powers vested in the local authority.

9.8.2 Definition

A statutory nuisance is defined by the Environmental Protection Act 1990 s79. The definition includes:

- premises prejudicial to health or a nuisance;
- smoke from premises prejudicial to health or a nuisance;
- fumes or gases from premises;
- dust, steam, smell or other effluvia arising on industrial, trade or business premises;
- accumulations or deposits;
- animals;
- noise emitted from premises or from or caused by a vehicle, machinery or equipment in a street;
- any other matter declared by statute to be a statutory nuisance, provided in each case the matter is prejudicial to health or a nuisance.

'Prejudicial to health' in this context means actually injurious or likely to cause injury to health. The reference appears to be to physical rather than mental health. 'Nuisance' has the same meaning as for the common law tort.

9.8.3 What action can be taken?

The local authority has a duty to investigate complaints from local inhabitants in respect of statutory nuisance. Once the authority is satisfied that a nuisance exists, or is likely to occur or to recur, an abatement notice must be served which tells the person on whom it is served what is wrong, what needs to be done to put matters right (abatement) and imposes a time limit for compliance.

There is a right of appeal to the magistrates' court against the notice. Non-compliance means that the local authority will take enforcement action through the magistrates' court which has power to require the work to be done within a specified time limit. Thereafter, for every day that the work remains outstanding, a fine will be imposed.

The advantage of local authority action is that it does not cost the complainant anything, beyond the usual payment of Council Tax, and the sanction available through the courts tends to mean that abatement notices are not ignored.

For a full discussion of statutory nuisance, reference should be made to a text on environmental law.

9.9 Nuisance in relation to other parts of the law

9.9.1 Nuisance in relation to negligence

It has been seen that nuisance and negligence have at least two things in common:

i. a duty of care;
ii. foreseeability of damage.

The duty of care is in fact dissimilar. In negligence the duty of care is to avoid acts or omissions which the reasonable person would foresee as likely to cause injury or damage. Provided reasonable care is taken to avoid those risks, the defendant will not be liable. In nuisance, the duty of care is to take reasonable care in carrying out the activity complained of. In *Sedleigh-Denfield v O'Callagan* the defendants failed to take reasonable care having 'adopted' a defective culvert; in *Goldman v Hargrave* and in *Leakey v National Trust* the defendants failed to take reasonable care to deal with the consequences of an act of nature. The fact that a defendant has taken all reasonable care to avoid a nuisance will not of itself mean that the defendant is not liable (*Cambridge Water v Eastern Counties Leather*).

In relation to damage, in both torts the rules in *The Wagon Mound* apply so that the defendant will be liable for damage which is of the type or kind which is a reasonably foreseeable consequence of the act.

9.9.2 Nuisance in relation to *Rylands v Fletcher*

In reality the torts have much in common. This is hardly surprising when it is remembered that *Rylands v Fletcher* is rooted in nuisance. As we have seen, nuisance will generally only be established where an activity has continued for some time. This leaves a gap where the claimant's land has been damaged as a result of a non-negligent escape of something from the defendant's land. As will be seen in Chapter 10, *Rylands v Fletcher* goes some way to fill the gap by setting out circumstances in which defendants will be liable for the escape of something dangerous from their land.

9.9.3 Nuisance in relation to human rights

The general issue of human rights is considered in Chapter 1 and reference should be made to that chapter for detail. We have seen that in a number of cases, notably in *Hatton and Others v UK* [2003] ECtHR 37 EHRR 28 and *Dennis and Dennis v Ministry of Defence* [2003] EWHC 793 (QB), that a nuisance which is not actionable, in both cases because of the wider public interest, may nonetheless be recognised as a breach of Article 8. In *Hatton* it was held that no compensation should be awarded, but in *Dennis* the High Court held that the claimants were entitled to compensation for the reduced value of their land.

This is a very recent development in English law. The true extent of the impact of human rights on the law of nuisance is not yet clear but it can be suggested that further developments are very likely to occur.

9.10 Other remedies for nuisance behaviour

It is easy to see that the tort of nuisance in all its various guises cannot deal with all forms of nuisance behaviour. Stories of the 'neighbours from hell' are common. Problems between neighbours can have a serious effect both on individuals and on their communities. People are not always reasonable nor are they always prepared to accept that their behaviour is causing problems for others. Nuisance does not provide a remedy where, for example, children are running riot or where abusive and aggressive behaviour regularly occurs.

In some cases the criminal law may be of some help. Vandalism, for example, may amount to criminal damage and the perpetrator can be punished. It is easy to see that this is not often a very effective remedy.

9.10.1 Anti-social behaviour orders

The anti-social behaviour order, introduced by the Crime and Disorder Act 1998, enables the magistrates' court to tailor an order to the particular circumstances. This can include imposing a curfew, excluding a person from a particular area or forbidding a person to contact named individuals. The order can only be made on the application of the police or a local authority. The basic requirements are:

- the person against whom the order is sought is aged ten or more;
- the behaviour complained of has caused or is likely to cause harassment, alarm or distress to one or more persons not in the same household.

The best indication of the type of behaviour with which the orders are intended to deal is found in a Consultation Paper published in 1995:

'Such behaviour manifests itself in many different ways and at varying levels of intensity. This can include vandalism, noise, verbal and physical abuse, threats of violence, racial harassment, damage to property, trespass, nuisance from dogs, car repairs on the street, joyriding, domestic violence, drugs and other criminal activities such as burglary.'

Consultation Paper on Probationary Tenancies, Department of the Environment (1995)

Examples of orders which have been imposed include one on teenagers who were prevented from entering a particular area following disturbances (see, for example, *R v Manchester Crown Court, ex p McCann* [2001] *Legal Action Group Journal*, February 2001, p. 27) and against tenants using their home for the purposes of drug-dealing and prostitution (see for example *Leicester CC v Lewis* [2000] *Legal Action Group Journal*, November 2000, p. 21).

Breach of the order is a criminal offence and can be punished by up to five years' imprisonment and/or an unlimited fine where the breach is serious enough to be tried in the Crown Court.

An Anti-social Behaviour, Crime and Policing Bill 2013–14 was passing through the various stages in the House of Commons and was going to the committee stage in June 2013. This introduces a Criminal Behaviour Order to replace 'ASBOs'.

9.10.2 Protection from Harassment Act 1997

This is discussed in some detail in section 13.6.2 in the context of trespass to the person. It will also be useful where nuisance fails to provide a remedy because the person subjected to the nuisance does not have the necessary interest in land.

9.10.3 Alternative dispute resolution, etc.

In many cases taking legal action is likely to exacerbate an already difficult situation. It is clear that lack of effective communication between neighbours can mean that nothing is said about the problem until matters have reached the point where there is a major argument or worse. Some local authorities have introduced mediation or conciliation schemes to try to take the confrontational aspect out of the situation and to reach an acceptable solution.

Given the drive to reduce the number of cases coming before the courts where an alternative way can be appropriately used, it is likely that such schemes will proliferate. Could it be that the use of such schemes where they are available may become a condition precedent to the taking of court action?

SAMPLE ESSAY QUESTION

'The torts of private and public nuisance achieve different ends but are equally effective.' Discuss the accuracy of this statement.

Outline the basic elements of a claim in private nuisance

- Defined as unlawful, indirect interference with another person's use or enjoyment of land
- Claimants have to show an interest in the land
- There is a difference between nuisance causing damage and one causing interference with comfort or the enjoyment of land
- Unlawful means unreasonable behaviour

Discuss factors courts use to determine whether there is unreasonable use of land

- Locality – what is a nuisance in one area may not be in another
- Duration – a nuisance must be continuous interference
- Abnormal sensitivity of the claimant may relieve liability
- The presence of malice by either party

Outline the basic elements of a claim in public nuisance

- Defined as something which affects the comfort and convenience of a class of people
- But a claimant must suffer special damage over that suffered by the class
- Most actions involve the highway, e.g. obstruction to the highway and condition of the highway

Discuss the effectiveness of private nuisance

- The limitation on potential claimants
- Difficult to establish use of land is unreasonable
- Easier to claim nuisance where damage occurs
- Liability dependent on locality is unfair
- Statutory authority makes it harder to claim
- The effect of the other defences

Discuss the effectiveness of public nuisance

- The definition lacks clarity
- Not having to show an interest in the land makes the action less restrictive than private nuisance
- The meaning of class of people may be uncertain
- Is a crime as well as a tort so may have more deterrent value
- Brought by the Attorney-General so may be harder to bring but more likely to be successful
- If special damage cannot be shown then no action is possible

SUMMARY

- There are three types of nuisance: private nuisance, public nuisance and now statutory nuisance also (e.g. Clean Air Act 1993, Environment Act 1995, Environmental Protection Act 1990).
- A private nuisance is defined as an unlawful indirect interference with a person's use or enjoyment of his land (but not a purely recreational use).
- Unlawful means unreasonable, and what is unreasonable can depend on locality, whether the nuisance is continuous, the sensitivity of the claimant, whether damage is caused or merely inconvenience, the presence of malice.
- The interference must be indirect; direct interference would be a trespass.
- Defences include: statutory authority, prescription, act of a stranger, consent and public policy.
- A public nuisance is one that interferes with the material comfort of a class of Her Majesty's subjects but involves damage to the claimant over and above that caused to the public generally.
- It usually involves the highway: i.e. damage caused by obstructions to the highway, projections over the highway and the condition of the highway.

Further reading

Chen, C, 'The unfinished architecture of private nuisance: Bridging the gap between Coventry v Lawrence and Fearn v Tate gallery' [2026] *CLJ* 1–32.
Lee, M, 'What is private nuisance' (2003) *11 LQR* 298.
Lee, M, 'Visual intrusion, public interests and private nuisance: Fearn v Tate' (2023) *82(2) CLJ* 208–211.

10

Strict liability and land – Rylands v Fletcher

AIMS AND OBJECTIVES

After reading this chapter you should be able to:

- Evaluate the reason for the creation of the rule
- Identify the essential elements that must be proved for a successful claim
- Explain what relevant defences may be available
- Identify the limitations on bringing a claim
- Illustrate and critically explain the wide range of difficulties associated with it
- Apply the law to factual situations and reach conclusions as to liability

10.1 Purpose and character of the tort

Trespass to land protects landowners from infringement of their boundaries. The tort of negligence gives a right of action where damage is caused as a result of a 'careless' act. We have also seen that the tort of nuisance comes to the assistance of a person whose use of land is interfered with indirectly by activities of the defendant on their land. It might appear that all possible eventualities have been catered for but this is not the case.

Trespass to land depends on direct and intentional interference while negligence will fail if it can be shown that the defendant did all that was reasonable to minimise the risk of damage. Nuisance will generally only be established if the activity is continuing over a period of time even though there can be liability for a 'one-off' incident in rare cases.

So it could traditionally be considered where this leaves occupiers whose land is damaged by a non-negligent escape of something from another's land?

DOI: 10.4324/9781003202417-10

This would be an indirect interference so might fail under trespass to land. A one-off escape might also fail the requirement of continuous interference in private nuisance.

The rule in *Rylands v Fletcher* [1865] 3 H & C 774 (Court of Exchequer) came about to fill this gap. It has its roots in nuisance and in reality most claimants are likely to plead nuisance as an alternative to *Rylands v Fletcher*. For many years it has been argued that *Rylands v Fletcher* is a tort of strict liability. It is questionable whether this has been an accurate view since the early part of the twentieth century. From that time, as will be seen, the judges have gradually changed the rules so that it has long been a favourite question of examiners – 'To what extent can the tort of *Rylands v Fletcher* be truly described as a tort of strict liability?' The issue will be returned to later in this chapter.

10.2 Definition

The definition most commonly used is found in the judgment of Mr Justice Blackburn in *Rylands v Fletcher* as modified in the House of Lords judgment in the same case by Lord Cairns LC [1868] LR 3 HL 330, at 339–340.

JUDGMENT

> 'A person who for his own purpose brings onto his land and collects and keeps there anything likely to do mischief if it escapes, must keep it in at his peril, and if he does not do so, is . . . answerable for all the damage which is the natural consequence of its escape.'

It was later added in the House of Lords in the case by Lord Cairns that the use of the land must amount to a non-natural use. So even at the very start the scope of the tort was being limited.

On the face of it, there is no requirement of fault on the part of the person who accumulates the thing, nor need the escape or the likelihood of damage be foreseeable. It is these facts which for many years led lawyers to argue that the tort imposed strict liability. As we shall see, the judges have refined these basic principles over the years. A useful guide to how the courts will approach liability under this rule can be found from the Court of Appeal's judgment in *Gore v Stannard (trading as Wyvern Tyres)* [2012] EWCA Civ 1248 at 22.

Approach to applying the rule in *Rylands v Fletcher*:

1 The defendant must be the owner or occupier of land.
2 He must bring or keep or collect an exceptionally dangerous or mischievous thing on his land.
3 He must have recognised or ought reasonably to have recognised, judged by the standards appropriate at the relevant place and time, that there is an exceptionally high risk of danger or mischief if that thing should escape, however unlikely an escape may have been thought to be.
4 His use of his land must, having regard to all the circumstances of time and place, be extraordinary and unusual.

5 The thing must escape from his property into or onto the property of another.

6 The escape must cause damage of a relevant kind to the rights and enjoyment of the claimant's land.

7 Damages for death or personal injury are not recoverable.

8 It is not necessary to establish the defendant's negligence but an Act of God or the act of a stranger will provide a defence.

10.3 Elements of the tort

10.3.1 Bringing the thing onto land and keeping it there

The first requirement is that the thing must be brought on to the land. Anything which is naturally there will not suffice.

CASE EXAMPLE

Giles v Walker [1890] 24 QBD 656

Here the defendant was not liable for the spread of thistledown from his land and could not be. He had not brought the weeds on to his land and accumulated them there. They had grown naturally.

Similarly this element is not made out where things accumulate on the land normally such as rainwater.

CASE EXAMPLE

Ellison v Ministry of Defence [1997] 81 BLR 101

It was held that at Greenham Common (the scene of a very long-running protest against nuclear weapons) a natural accumulation of rainwater which escaped and caused flooding to neighbouring land did not give rise to liability.

Although it is still possible for there to be an action in nuisance where the defendant is aware of the thing causing the nuisance and has in effect 'adopted it' by failing to do anything about it.

CASE EXAMPLE

Leakey v The National Trust [1980] QB 485

Here a mound of loose earth on a hill was particularly subject to cracking and slipping in bad weather. When the mound did in fact slip and cause damage to neighbouring land the defendants were liable because they knew of this possibility and yet failed to do anything to prevent it.

The fact that something naturally on the land has escaped will not suffice for liability under *Rylands v Fletcher* but we have already seen in section 9.3.3 there may be liability in nuisance (*Leakey v National Trust* [1980] QB 485).

It is not essential that the thing be brought on to the land by an owner or occupier.

CASE EXAMPLE

Charing Cross Electric Supply Co v Hydraulic Power Co **[1914] 3 KB 772, CA**

Water mains were placed above electric cables. When the water main burst, the cables were flooded and a large part of London was blacked out. The water company, a mere licensee with no interest in the land, was liable for the escape of the water.

The thing has to be accumulated for the purposes of the defendant but this does not necessarily mean that it is also for the defendant's benefit. For instance the accumulation of sewage by a local authority is done for the purpose of exercising statutory powers. It cannot be said that the local authority benefits from the accumulation.

CASE EXAMPLE

Smeaton v Ilford Corporation **[1954] Ch 450**

A local authority collected sewage under a statutory authority and some of this escaped on to the claimant's land. It was held that it was responsible for the sewage even though it was accepted that it derived no benefit from collecting the sewage but it did have a defence under the statute.

10.3.2 Something likely to do mischief if it escapes

The thing need not be dangerous in itself but it must be likely to cause damage should an escape occur. This point is illustrated by the facts of *Rylands v Fletcher*.

CASE EXAMPLE

Rylands v Fletcher **[1868] LR 1 Exch 265; LR 3 HL 330**

The defendants used reputable engineers to build a reservoir on their land to accumulate water. While the reservoir was under construction, the engineers came across old mine shafts which they failed to seal properly. When the reservoir became full of water, it escaped along the old shafts into the mine owned by the claimant. Water is not intrinsically dangerous but a large accumulation of water will be likely to cause damage if it escapes. The defendant was held liable and the tort of *Rylands v Fletcher* came into being.

It is important to recognise that there must be an 'escape' for this rule to apply. This may seem obvious but take for example the decision in *Gore v Stannard (trading as Wyvern Tyres)* [2012] EWCA Civ 1248.

CASE EXAMPLE

Gore v Stannard (trading as Wyvern Tyres) [2012] EWCA Civ 1248

The defendant carried on a tyre fitting business on which it was found that the defendant had stored tyres on the premises somewhat haphazardly wherever space could be found. A fire broke out on the defendant's premises which intensified and spread to the claimant's property. The claimant brought a claim on the basis of the rule in *Rylands v Fletcher*. On the basis that there was a dangerous and non-natural use of the land namely that the tyres were brought onto the land, stored there and if they were to catch on fire, be extremely dangerous given they are highly flammable which it was argued was foreseeable. Lord Justice Ward explains why there was no escape at paragraph 50:

JUDGMENT

Applying the principles set out in this area the Court of Appeal concluded that there was no escape:

1 The 'thing' brought onto defendant's premises was a large stock of tyres.
2 Tyres, as such, are not exceptionally dangerous or mischievous.
3 There is no evidence that the defendant recognised nor ought he reasonably to have recognised that there was an exceptionally high risk of danger or mischief if the tyres, as such, should escape.
4 The tyres did not escape. What escaped was the fire, the ferocity of which was stoked by the tyres which were burning on, and remained burning on, the defendant's premises. The Recorder was wrong to conclude it was the escape of fire that brought the case within *Rylands v Fletcher* principles.
5 In any event, keeping a stock of tyres on the premises of a tyre-fitting business, even a very large stock, was not for the time and place an extraordinary or unusual use of the land. Here again the Recorder erred.
6 Therefore *Rylands v Fletcher* liability is not established and, no negligence having been proved, the claim must fail.
7 The moral of the story is taken from the speech of Lord Hoffman (in *Transco v Stockport MDC* [2004] 2 AC 1): make sure you have insurance cover for losses occasioned by fire on your premises.

This is to say that since it was not the tyres that escaped, the claim must fail. This approach therefore restricts when the rule in *Rylands v Fletcher* can be invoked.

Over the years a wide variety of things have been held to be likely to cause damage if they escape and for this reason have been categorised as dangerous. Examples include:

- The owners of a cemetery were liable when branches from yew trees spread across the boundary into an adjoining field where they were eaten and poisoned animals pastured in the field (*Crowhurst v Amersham Burial Board* [1879] 4 Ex D 5).

- A motor car, which was then regarded as a 'new fangled thing', was stored in a garage with petrol in the tank. The car caught fire and a neighbour's house was damaged. The owner of the car was held liable under *Rylands v Fletcher* (*Musgrove v Pandelis* [1919] 2 KB 43).
- A flag pole 'escaped' from a building by falling and causing damage. It was held to be a dangerous thing (*Shiffman v Order of the Hospital of St John of Jerusalem* [1936] 1 All ER 557). (This also illustrates the point that the thing need not be dangerous in itself, but merely likely to become so if it escapes.)
- A fairground was liable when a chair flew from a 'chair-o-plane' roundabout causing injury to a neighbouring stallholder (*Hale v Jennings Bros* [1938] 1 All ER 579).
- Electricity stored in high voltage cables which 'leaked' from under the claimant's land and electrocuted his cows meant that the defendant was liable (*Hillier v Air Ministry* [1962] CLY 2084).

The list could go on but what is clear is that anything can be regarded as dangerous, or 'liable to cause a mischief', in particular circumstances. The courts have avoided giving a definition of 'dangerous' and have decided each case on its own particular facts.

Recent case law has added another dimension to what will be regarded as 'dangerous'. In *Cambridge Water v Eastern Counties Leather* [1994] 2 AC 264 Goff LJ explained at 306:

JUDGMENT

'foreseeability of damage of the relevant type should be regarded as a prerequisite of liability in damages under the rule'.

He added that it must be possible to foresee the potential for damage at the time the accumulation occurs. The facts of the case illustrate the point.

CASE EXAMPLE

Cambridge Water v Eastern Counties Leather [1994] 2 AC 264

Chemicals which were stored by the defendants seeped into the underground water supply used by the claimant. At the time the chemicals were accumulated the amount of contamination caused to the water supply was within acceptable standards. Some time later, the law was changed and the level of contamination could no longer be tolerated. The change in the law could not have been foreseen by the defendants who were found not to be liable.

The issue of foreseeability has been discussed in the later case of *Transco plc v Stockport Metropolitan Council* [2003] UKHL 61 which enabled the House of Lords to review the scope and application of the tort.

CASE EXAMPLE

Transco plc v Stockport Metropolitan Council [2003] UKHL 61

A multi-story block of flats, built by the defendants, was supplied with water for domestic use. A large pipe from the water mains led to tanks in the bottom of the buildings to supply the needs of 66 households. Without negligence, the pipe failed and water escaped. Without negligence the leak was undiscovered for some time by which time sufficient water had escaped to cause an embankment beneath the claimant's gas mains to collapse. As a result, the gas main posed an immediate and serious risk. The claimants took prompt action and sought to recover the cost from the defendants on the basis that the defendants were strictly liable under *Rylands v Fletcher*.

Lord Bingham having reviewed cases since *Rylands v Fletcher* itself, acknowledged and concluded at 10:

JUDGMENT

'. . . many things not ordinarily regarded as sources of mischief or danger may nonetheless prove to be such if they escape. 'It must be shown that the defendant has done something which he recognised, or judged by the standards appropriate at the relevant place and time, he ought reasonably to have recognised, as giving rise to an exceptionally high risk of danger or mischief if there should be an escape, however unlikely an escape may have been thought to be.'.

It is clear from this judgment that the issue of foreseeability is closely linked to the concept of 'non-natural user' discussed in section 10.3.4.

The rules for foreseeability of the type of damage are those which have previously been discussed coming from *The Wagon Mound (No 1)* (see *Overseas Tankship (UK) Ltd v Morts Dock & Engineering Co (The Wagon Mound)* [1961] AC 388).

When considering the nature of damage caused, it is clear that there will be other factors being satisfied as well as liability for damage to property. For many years it was not clear whether there could also be liability for personal injury. In *Read v Lyons* [1947] AC 156 the damage caused was personal injury. While the case was decided upon the issue of escape, the judges discussed, *obiter*, whether or not the tort could enable such damages to be paid. Lord Macmillan suggested that there could not be liability for personal injury in the absence of negligence, stating that the basis of *Rylands v Fletcher* is a mutual duty owed between landowners. 'It has nothing to do with personal injury.' Lord Simonds stated that he could not support the view that liability under the tort 'extends to purely personal injuries'. The point was discussed *obiter* and it should be remembered that damages had in fact already been awarded for personal injury.

CASE EXAMPLE

Hale v Jennings Bros [1948] 1 All ER 579

A car from a 'chair-o-plane' ride on a fairground became detached from the main assembly while it was in motion and injured a stallholder as it crashed to the ground. The owner of the ride was held liable. Risk of injury was foreseeable if the car came loose.

However, in *Hunter v Canary Wharf* [1997] 2 All ER 426 the judges, in holding that a claimant must have an interest in the land affected by the nuisance, appear to have ruled out the possibility of a claim for purely personal injury arising from nuisance.

In *Transco v Stockport*, two of the judges took the opportunity to debate this issue further. Although the comments are *obiter* as the case did not involve any claim for personal injury, they are informative. Lord Bingham stated at paragraph 9 that 'the claim cannot include a claim for death or personal injury, since such claim does not relate to any right in or enjoyment of land'.

Lord Bingham acknowledged that his view, given the close relationship between *Rylands v Fletcher* and nuisance, was based on *Hunter v Canary Wharf*. Lord Hoffmann referred to the fact that claims for personal injury had been admitted in the past but stated at 35:

JUDGMENT

'the point is now settled by [Cambridge Water] which decided that *Rylands v Fletcher* is a special form of nuisance and *Hunter v Canary Wharf*. . . which decided that nuisance is a tort against land. It must, I think, follow that damages for personal injuries are not recoverable under the rule.'

10.3.3 The thing must escape

This means precisely what it says – the thing must move from the land controlled by the defendant to land controlled by the claimant. This is clear from the facts of *Rylands v Fletcher* but it was explained in *Read v J Lyons & Co Ltd*.

CASE EXAMPLE

Read v J Lyons & Co Ltd [1947] AC 156

In 1942, munitions were manufactured by the defendants. The claimant was a munitions inspector in the shell-filling shop when an explosion occurred. One person was killed and the claimant was injured. There was no negligence involved in the explosion.

Viscount Simon LC held that the claimant could not succeed in her claim under *Rylands v Fletcher*, explaining:

JUDGMENT

'Escape, for the purpose of . . . *Rylands v Fletcher* means escape from a place which the defendant has occupation of, or control over, to a place which is outside his occupation or control.'

It is also clear that the 'thing' itself need not escape.

CASE EXAMPLE

***Miles v Forest Rock Granite Co (Leicestershire) Ltd* [1918] 34 TLR 500**

The claimant brought the action in respect of injuries suffered when rocks flew on to the highway from the defendants' land where they were blasting. It was the explosives that had been brought onto land that actually caused the rock to escape, but there was still liability. There had been an escape – the blast.

It is sometimes difficult to see how the courts have enforced this requirement. In *Hale v Jennings* both the roundabout and the injured stallholder were in fact on the same land while in *Crown River Cruises v Kimbolton Fireworks* [1996] 2 Lloyd's Rep 533 both parties occupied the same stretch of river.

10.3.4 Non-natural use

It is always difficult to decide where the discussion of non-natural use should appear. It is arguable that all the above essential elements of the tort are involved therefore it has been decided to include this very important issue at this point.

The House of Lords in *Rylands v Fletcher* stated that the escape must be of something which is brought on to the land and does not naturally occur there. This view is potentially extremely wide and the floodgates were at risk of being opened to extremes. Over the years the courts have guarded against this risk by refusing to give a specific definition of what will be regarded as 'non-natural use' preferring instead to deal with the issue on a case by case basis.

In *Read v J Lyons & Co Ltd* Viscount Simons LC said at 169 and 176 *obiter* that he would question "whether the making of munitions in a factory at the government's request in time of war for the purpose of helping to defeat the enemy' was a non-natural use of land. In the same case Lord Porter at 176 said that the court should take into account: 'all the circumstances of time and practice of mankind . . . so that what may be regarded as dangerous or non-natural may vary according to the circumstances'.

While Viscount Simon's view can be understood in the context of the times, it is Lord Porter's view which appears to have influenced later decisions.

Lord Porter's view appears to have been based in an earlier view expressed by the Privy Council *Rickards v Lothian* [1913] AC 280.

CASE EXAMPLE

Rickards v Lothian [1913] AC 280

Here the defendant was not liable when an unknown person turned on water taps and blocked plugholes on his premises so that damage was caused in the flat below. A domestic water supply was in any case considered to be a natural use of land.

In the case Lord Moulton held that the issue of non-natural use could be explained as follows at 280:

JUDGMENT

'It is not every use . . . that brings into play that principle . . . . It must be some special use bringing with it increased danger to others and must not merely be the ordinary use of the land or such a use as is proper for the benefit of the community.'

The issue of benefit to the community was an obvious element taken into account in *Read v Lyons*. It was also a factor in *British Celanese v Hunt* when the problem was caused by the manufacture of goods of a common type needed 'for the benefit of the community' (per Lawton J). Mr Justice Lawton was also influenced by the fact that the defendant's factory was an industrial use of premises which were situated on an industrial estate.

CASE EXAMPLE

British Celanese v A H Hunt (Capacitors) Ltd [1969] 1 WLR 959

The defendant stored strips of metal foil, which were used in the process of manufacturing electrical components. Some of these strips of foil blew off the defendant's land and on to an electricity substation causing power failures. The court held that the use of land was natural. This was partly because of the benefit derived from the manufacture by the public, and there was no liability under the rule as a result.

The use of the premises for a non-industrial use would have been non-natural in that locality.

The issue was considered by Goff LJ in his minority judgment in *Cambridge Water v Eastern Counties Leather*. Goff LJ argued that to accept the view stated by Lord Moulton (quoted above) would be to extend the concept of natural use beyond 'reasonable bounds'. In *Cambridge Water v Eastern Counties Leather* it had been accepted at first instance that the creation of employment was a proper consideration in deciding the issue of natural use. Goff LJ said that he could not accept that the creation of employment is enough to constitute a natural or ordinary use of land. While acknowledging that this issue was not relevant to the decision in the case, he went on to say at 267:

JUDGMENT

'the storage of substantial quantities of chemicals on industrial premises should be regarded as an almost classic case of non-natural use'.

The issue has apparently now been resolved in *Transco v Stockport*. Citing Lord Moulton's statement in *Rickards v Lothian*, Lord Bingham said at 11:

JUDGMENT

'I think it clear that ordinary user is a preferable test to natural user, making it clear that the rule in *Rylands v Fletcher* is engaged only where the defendant's use is shown to be extraordinary and unusual. . . . The question is whether the defendant has done something which he recognises, or ought to recognise, as being quite out of the ordinary in the place and at the time when he does it.'

This is to say, that foreseeability also has a role to play. On the facts in *Transco v Stockport* the judges were unanimous in finding that the supply of water for domestic purposes in large pipes which were not maintained at high pressure did not amount to non-natural use.

Lord Hoffmann suggested at paragraph 46:

JUDGMENT

'A useful guide in deciding whether the risk has been created by a "non-natural" user of land is . . . to ask whether the damage was something against which the occupier could reasonably be expected to have insured himself.'

CRITIQUING THE LAW

Consider the various approaches that the courts have taken with regard to what can be considered as a 'non-natural use of land'. How have the courts approached this when applying the rule in *Rylands v Fletcher* to changes in modern life?

10.4 Parties to the action

10.4.1 Potential claimants

Judges have expressed different views as to who can claim. In *Rylands v Fletcher* no indication is given that a claimant needs to have a proprietary interest in the land affected by the escape.

In *Read v Lyons* Lord Macmillan expressed the view at 173 that the tort 'derives from a conception of the mutual duties of adjoining or neighbouring landowners'.

When it is remembered that the tort has its roots in nuisance, decisions relating to that tort are seen to be relevant. In this context, *Hunter v Canary Wharf* is helpful. As we have seen, the House of Lords held that in order to bring an action in nuisance, the claimant must have a legal interest in the land affected by the nuisance.

There would be no reason to believe that a different approach would be taken in *Rylands v Fletcher* were it not for *Crown River Cruises v Kimbolton Fireworks*.

CASE EXAMPLE

Crown River Cruises Ltd v Kimbolton Fireworks Ltd [1996] 2 Lloyd's Rep 533

Here inflammable material from a firework display fell on to barges used as a jetty for pleasure cruisers causing fire damage The claimant in that case had no interest in land and, although claims in *Rylands v Fletcher* were rejected, the logical outcome of the 'control' approach stated in *British Celanese v Hunt* allowed the claimant to establish liability for nuisance.

The debate will no doubt continue but in the meantime it is likely that the close link to nuisance will be maintained and that the decision in *Hunter v Canary Wharf* will prevail. There is much other law which protects the environment and, as we shall see, the tort is likely to be restricted to situations where the problems are indeed concerned only with damage relating to an escape onto land in which the claimant has an interest.

10.4.2 Potential defendants

We have seen that in *Read v Lyons* the court took the view that the defendant would be the person, even if it were only as a mere licensee, from whose land the 'thing' had escaped on to another's land while in *British Celanese v Hunt* liability could lie on the person from whose control the 'thing' had escaped. The issue is still unclear.

CASE EXAMPLE

Rigby v Chief Constable of Northants [1985] 1 WLR 1242

The claimant alleged that the tear gas had 'escaped' from the defendant's control on to the claimant's property and therefore the defendant was liable under *Rylands v Fletcher*. The claim was rejected but in the course of his judgment Mr Justice Taylor appeared to accept the 'control' approach. He said at 1255:

JUDGMENT

'I can see no difference in principle between allowing a man-eating tiger to escape from your land on to that of another and allowing it to escape from the back of your wagon parked on the highway.'

10.5 Defences

10.5.1 Statutory authority

A statute may impose a duty on the defendant to accumulate the thing which has escaped. In such a case, the defendant will not be liable for the escape, in the absence of negligence, provided the damage is the inevitable consequence of any escape. This is illustrated by two contrasting cases.

CASE EXAMPLE

Charing Cross Electricity Co v Hydraulic Power Co [1914] 3 KB 772

The claimant's land was damaged by the escape of water maintained at high pressure in the defendant's mains. The statute enabling the provision of water for industrial purposes was permissive only. There was no duty to maintain water under high pressure. Had the water not been maintained under high pressure it would not have escaped. As the escape was not the inevitable consequence of the exercise of the statutory power, the defendants were liable.

CASE EXAMPLE

Green v Chelsea Waterworks Co [1894] 70 LT 547

The defendant was under a duty to maintain pressure in its water mains. Damage would inevitably be caused by any escape of water thus the defendants were not liable when an escape happened.

10.5.2 Consent

A person who consents to the accumulation cannot later complain when the thing escapes and damages the land. This is commonly seen in the case of buildings in multiple occupation where a tenant will be taken to have consented to the accumulation of a thing from which that land benefits.

CASE EXAMPLE

Peters v Prince of Wales Theatre (Birmingham) Ltd [1943] KB 73

The defendant employed a sprinkler system to protect the building from fire. The claimant also occupied the building and complained when stock was damaged by water from the sprinklers. It was held that the water supply benefited both claimant and defendant. There could be no liability.

10.5.3 Act of a stranger

A defendant will not be liable for the consequences of an escape which has been caused by the act of a person over whom the defendant has no control.

CASE EXAMPLE

Perry v Kendricks Transport Ltd [1956] 1 WLR 85

The defendants stored motor coaches on their land. The petrol tanks of the coaches were empty. Children took off the fuel cap and threw in a lighted match. The claimant was injured in the resulting explosion.

Holding that the defendants were not liable to the claimant, Lord Jenkins explained (at 91) that to establish liability it would be necessary to show:

JUDGMENT

'in the circumstances . . . the dangerous thing was left in such a condition that it was a reasonable and probable consequence of their action, which they ought to have foreseen, that children might meddle with the dangerous thing and cause it to escape'.

Had the children's actions been foreseeable, the claimant would have been able to claim in negligence. As it was, on the facts, the defendants were not liable.

It seems therefore that a defendant may be liable in negligence for the foreseeable act of a stranger.

10.5.4 Act of God

An Act of God is an unforeseeable natural phenomenon. This was explained by Lord Hobhouse in *Transco v Stockport* as describing events:

- i which involve no human agency;
- ii which it is not realistically possible to guard against;
- iii which is due directly and exclusively to natural causes; and
- iv which could not be prevented by any amount of foresight, pains and care.

Two contrasting cases are instructive, both dealing with damage caused by flooding after exceptional rainfall.

CASE EXAMPLE

Nichols v Marsland [1876] 2 ExD 1

Four bridges were washed away when artificial lakes overflowed following rain 'greater and more violent than any within the memory of witnesses'.

It was held that the defendant could not reasonably have anticipated such an act of nature and she was not liable.

CASE EXAMPLE

Greenock Corporation v Caledonian Railway [1917] AC 556

The defendants constructed an artificial paddling pool by diverting a stream. There was a rainfall of extraordinary violence which caused the pool to overflow. This resulted in damage to the claimants' property.

It was held that the defendants were liable. Rainfall, even if exceptionally heavy, was not an Act of God.

The issue seems to be not whether the event could be anticipated but whether human prudence should have foreseen the possibility of the event and guarded against it. Thus the possibility of heavy rainfall or exceptionally strong winds which occur, even if rarely, within England can be anticipated. A person who accumulates something which may cause damage if it escapes as a result of such occurrence is unlikely to escape liability. Even an escape caused by an earthquake might be said to be capable of being anticipated when it is remembered that 25 earthquakes measuring 4.5 or greater occurred in Britain during the twentieth century (British Geological Survey, accessed at www.quakes.bgs.ac.uk/hazard/eqlst.htm).

The reasoning of the courts seems to point to the possibility of liability in negligence for failure to prevent a reasonably foreseeable risk.

10.5.5 Default of the claimant

A person who causes the damage cannot complain, nor can the defendant be liable in such circumstances.

CASE EXAMPLE

Ponting v Noakes [1894] 2 QB 281

The claimant's horse leant across a boundary fence to reach and eat from a poisonous tree. The horse died.

It was held the damage had been caused by the horse's intrusion into the defendant's land. The defendant could not be liable (additionally there had been no escape).

10.6 Problems with the rule

At first sight *Rylands v Fletcher* may be thought to have potential to ensure that dangerous things are properly controlled. The definition of the tort seems quite clear – people who accumulate something that is potentially dangerous will be liable if damage is caused as a result of an escape even in the absence of negligence. The potential for dealing with the effects of pollution is clear. However, when the tort is looked at in depth, its effectiveness in dealing with anything other than a local, individual problem is questionable.

10.6.1 Strict liability?

Over the years, the courts have refined the requirements so that what appeared to be a tort of strict liability has gradually become one where some element of fault is required. We see this in the requirement that the potential for damage, should an escape occur, must be foreseen at the time the thing is accumulated (*Cambridge Water v Eastern Counties Leather*). It can perhaps be suggested that this, when taken into account with the restrictions on the defences of act of a stranger and Act of God, mean that the tort is now fault based.

Lord Hobhouse endeavoured to explain the present position in *Transco v Stockport* at 64:

JUDGMENT

'It is . . . the creation of a recognisable risk to other landowners which is an essential constituent of the tort and the liability of the defendant. But, once such a risk has been established, the liability for the foreseeable consequences of failure to control and confine it is strict.'

The matter continues to be confused – the likelihood is that examiners will continue to ask questions based on this issue!

10.6.2 Effective to protect the environment?

It is obvious that as the tort was originally envisaged, it could serve as a potent protection against pollution of the environment. By way of the various arguments concerning natural and non-natural use it can be argued that the potential has been substantially eroded if not completely eliminated. Elements such as benefit to society (*British Celanese v Hunt*) or to society generally (*Read v Lyons*) have been held to be sufficient to protect the defendant from liability. The question can be asked – does it really matter in the twenty-first century?

A statement by Goff LJ in *Cambridge Water v Eastern Counties Leather* at 305 may provide a clue. He took the view that while the preservation of the environment was an issue of:

JUDGMENT

'crucial importance to mankind . . . it does not follow . . . that a common law principle . . . should be developed or rendered more strict to provide for liability in respect of such pollution . . . given so much well-informed and carefully structured legislation is now being put in place for this purpose, there is less need for the courts to develop a common law principle to achieve the same end'.

Goff LJ's view is supported by the legislation coming from the European Union which is gradually ensuring that development must be sustainable and that any polluter should pay for damage to the environment. These principles are seen to be upheld by the regime governing planning decisions, which now requires an environmental impact assessment for major development proposals and by legislation governing industries which create an especial risk, for example the Nuclear Installations Act 1965 that governs liability caused by the escape of ionising radiations and the Merchant Shipping Act 1995 that governs liability for oil pollution caused by ships. Goff LJ is clearly of the view that the tort should be restricted to 'private' issues as he said 'it is more appropriate for strict liability in respect of operations of high risk to be imposed by Parliament'.

It has been decided in Australia that *Rylands v Fletcher* serves no useful purpose and should be subsumed into negligence (*Burnie Port Authority v General Jones Pty Ltd* [1994] 179 CLR 520). The tort is no longer part of Australian law.

The Australian approach was considered by the House of Lords in *Transco v Stockport*. Lord Hoffmann suggested that the tort has a residuary role to play despite the extension of statutory regulation and control over hazardous activities. Lord Hobhouse discussed this in more detail (at 56) when he said that the tort is still useful despite the ever-increasing amount of statutory regulation:

JUDGMENT

'The area of regulation is not exhaustive; it does not necessarily give the third party . . . an adequate or, even, any say; the Government decision may give priority to some . . . need which it considers must over-ride . . . individual interests; it will not normally deal with civil liability for damage to property; it does not provide . . . adequate knowledge and control to [enable a person] to evaluate and protect himself from the consequent risk.'

In *Transco v Stockport* the judges were unanimous in their opinion that the tort continues to exist and in its way continues to provide an element of protection of the environment.

It seems therefore that *Rylands v Fletcher* may continue to develop but only in connection with what can be described as 'local' or 'individual' problems, wider issues remaining the province of Parliament and the EU.

ACTIVITY

Self-assessment questions

1. Explain the key elements in *Rylands v Fletcher*.
2. What must 'reasonably be foreseen' in order to establish liability for the tort?
3. Explain the current position in respect of liability for personal injury in relation to the tort.
4. What distinctions can be drawn between the concepts of 'natural' and 'non-natural' use of land?
5. What useful purpose if any does the tort serve in the twenty-first century?
6. Describe the defence of 'Act of God' and give examples of when it may apply.

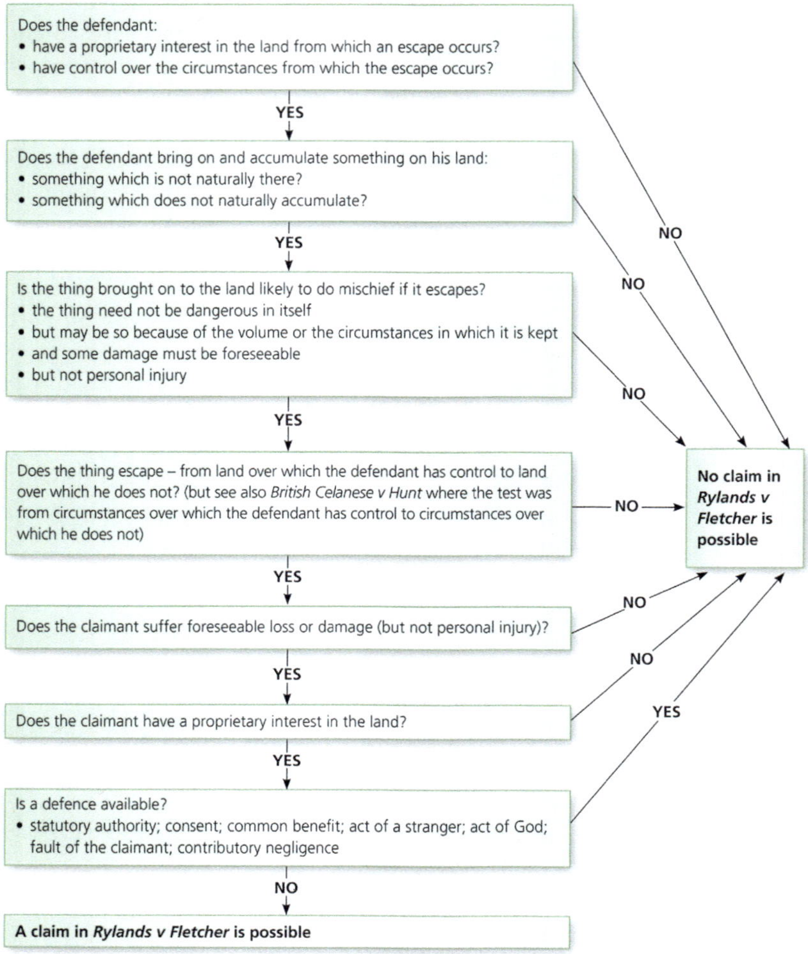

Figure 10.1 The essential elements of a claim in *Rylands v Fletcher*.

Table 10.1 The similarities and differences between the torts relating to land.

	Trespass to land	*Private nuisance*	*Public nuisance*	Rylands v Fletcher
Claimants	A person in possession of land	A person with a proprietary interest in land	A member of a class of Her Majesty's citizens	A person harmed by the escape of the dangerous thing
Defendants	Any person carrying out the trespass	A landowner, or a person creating or adopting nuisance	A person creating nuisance	A person in control of land from which thing escapes
Duration of interference	A single trespass is enough	Must be continuous	A single interference is enough	A single escape is enough

(Continued)

Table 10.1 (Continued)

	Trespass to land	*Private nuisance*	*Public nuisance*	Rylands v Fletcher
Directness	Must be direct	Must be indirect	Could be direct or indirect	Could be direct or indirect
Need to prove fault	Actionable per se – so no need to prove fault	Requires unreasonable use of land – which is similar to fault	Fault need not be proved	Cambridge Water says foreseeability is required – so suggest fault
Locality of interference	Not relevant	Relevant unless damage is caused	Could be relevant, e.g. to losing client connection	Could be relevant in deciding what is non-natural
Availability of damages	Any damage related to the trespass – and no need to show damage	Physical harm, economic loss	Physical harm, personal injury, economic loss	Physical loss
Defences	Customary right to enter, common law right, statutory right, consent, necessity, licence	Statutory authority, prescription, consent, act of stranger, public policy, over-sensitivity of claimant	General defences	Consent, common benefit, act of a stranger, or God, statutory authority, contributory negligence
Whether also a crime	Yes – possible under some statute	No – unless statutory	Yes – can be	No

KEY FACTS

Key facts on Rylands v Fletcher

Definition	Case
Bringing on to land and keeping there anything which it is foreseeably likely may cause damage if it escapes.	
Elements of the tort	**Case**
Bringing on to land – generally a thing which is naturally on land will not give rise to liability. Note there can be liability under nuisance for escape of something naturally on land.	*Giles v Walker* [1890]; *Ellison v MOD* [1997] *Leakey v National Trust* [1980]

(Continued)

(Continued)

Something likely to cause damage if it escapes	Case
Anything can be dangerous in certain circumstances – the thing need not be dangerous in itself – e.g. water. It must be reasonably foreseeable that should the thing escape, damage may be caused. Damage must be of type or kind that is reasonably foreseeable. No claim is possible for personal injury.	*Rylands v Fletcher* [1868] *Cambridge Water v Eastern Counties Leather* [1994]; *Transco v Stockport MC* [2003]; *Gore v Stannard (trading as Wyvern Tyres)* [2012] EWCA Civ 1248 *The Wagon Mound (No 1)* [1961] *Hunter v Canary Wharf* [1997]; *Transco v Stockport MC* [2003]
The thing must escape	**Case**
The thing must move from land under defendant's control to claimant's land. Contrast the thing must move from circumstances controlled by defendant to circumstances where defendant does not have control.	*Read v Lyons* [1947] *British Celanese v Hunt* [1969]
Defendant's use of land must be 'non-natural'	**Case**
Originally simply a test of whether the thing occurred naturally on the land or not. Could vary according to circumstances at the time – e.g. making munitions in time of war a natural use. Must be more than ordinary use. Proper for benefit of the community. Now apparently settled by – Use must be extraordinary and unusual, something quite out of the ordinary in that place and at that time.	*Rylands v Fletcher* [1868] *Read v Lyons* [1947] *Rickards v Lothian* [1913] *British Celanese v Hunt* [1969] *Transco v Stockport MC* [2003]
Claimant	**Case**
Must have proprietary interest in land affected.	*Hunter v Canary Wharf* [1997]
Defendant	**Case**
Unclear whether legal interest in land is necessary.	*Read v Lyons* [1947]; *British Celanese v Hunt* [1969]; *Rigby v Chief Constable of Northants* [1985]
Defences	**Case**
Statutory authority – if duty to accumulate imposed, no liability in the event of escape in the absence of negligence.	*Charing Cross Electricity v Hydraulic Power Co* [1914]; *Green v Chelsea Waterworks* [1894]

(Continued)

(Continued)

Consent – can be implied if claimant benefits from the accumulation.	*Peters v Prince of Wales Theatre* [1943]
Act of a stranger – no liability for action by person over whom defendant has no control.	*Perry v Kendricks Transport Ltd* [1956]
Act of God – no liability if escape caused by unforeseeable natural phenomenon which cannot realistically be guarded against.	*Transco v Stockport MC* [2003]
Default of claimant.	
Problems with the Rule	**Case**
Usefulness diminished by development from strict liability to requirement of foreseeability.	*Rylands v Fletcher* [1868]
Environment better protected generally by legislation specific to particular problems.	
Note Australian abolition of Rule but held in – Rule has residuary role in England.	*Transco v Stockport MC* [2003]

SAMPLE ESSAY QUESTION

Discuss the extent to which it is accurate to still refer to *Rylands v Fletcher* as a tort of strict liability.

Explain the original basis of the rule

- Defendant brings on to land and accumulates
- A thing likely to cause 'mischief' if it escapes
- And it does escape causing damage

Discuss how other requirements have been added

- Lord Cairns added non-natural use of land
- Things stored in large quantities are commonly non-natural while truly domestic uses are not
- Lord Macmillan narrowed the concept of escape – from land to land rather than circumstances to circumstances
- Goff LJ in *Cambridge Water* added foreseeability of harm

Consider the wide range of potential defences

- *Volenti non fit injuria*
- Common benefit – where the parties share the same premises
- Act of God – extreme weather
- Act of a stranger
- Statutory authority
- Damage caused through the fault of the claimant himself
- Contributory negligence under the Law Reform (Contributory Negligence) Act 1945 which reduces damages

Explain how the tort has developed

- The debate over the escape – may make it harder to claim
- The thing accumulated does not have to be what escapes – makes it easier to claim
- Things that naturally accumulate cannot lead to liability – may be unfair on a claimant
- The problem of identifying what amounts to a non-natural use of land – changes over time

Discuss the issue of whether the tort is still strict liability

- The effectiveness of the tort was limited straightaway by Lord Cairns by adding the requirement of non-natural use of land – which appears to vary according to the context in which the thing escapes
- Certain activities by their nature have been identified as always a non-natural use of land
- The meaning given to accumulation is not unlike fault liability
- The requirement of foreseeability makes it little different from negligence – rather than strict liability
- The tort has been described as a more specific type of nuisance – but again an action is harder to succeed in
- There is an unusually wide range of available defences for something described as strict liability

SUMMARY

- The basic rule according to Blackburn J was that a person should be liable for the damage caused by things brought on to and accumulated on the land which then escape – so concerned liability for dangerous things.
- There were originally three essential ingredients to the tort: a bringing onto and accumulating on the land (something not naturally there), of a thing likely to cause mischief if it escapes, and the thing does escape and causes damage.
- In the House of Lords in the case Lord Cairns added another requirement – that it must involve a 'non-natural' use of land.
- Later Goff LJ added the requirement of foreseeable damage – and the tort is now generally seen as a type of nuisance.
- Who will be a defendant and who can claim as a claimant will depend on whether the escape has to be from one person's land to another's or from the defendant's control to a situation outside his control.
- Although the tort is described as strict liability it clearly now requires proof of fault and there are also many defences including: act of God, act of a stranger, consent, common benefit and statutory authority.

11

Liability for animals

AIMS AND OBJECTIVES

After reading this chapter you should be able to:

- Critically explain the common law basis for liability
- Distinguish between dangerous species and non-dangerous species
- Explain the statutory basis for liability for either
- Apply the law to factual situations and reach conclusions as to liability

11.1 Introduction

By the middle of the twentieth century, the law relating to liability for damage or injury done by animals was confused. An owner could be liable under various torts on the requirements of those torts being established (see section 11.3). There were also other common law actions which imposed strict liability for harm done by animals. It was acknowledged that animals are by their nature unpredictable and that owners kept animals at their peril. Strict liability depended on whether the animals were 'ferae naturae' (loosely translated as wild animals) or 'mansuetae naturae' (loosely translated as tame animals). In the case of wild animals, the owner was presumed to know that they were dangerous and would be liable without fault, while in the case of tame animals, knowledge of the animal's dangerous tendency had to be proved before liability would be imposed. This is perhaps the origin of the saying 'Every dog is allowed one bite.'

It was hoped that there would be a thorough and wide-ranging reform of this area of law with liability being based either on the principles of negligence or strictly imposed for damage done by all animals. The opportunity was not taken, the Animals Act 1971 continuing a distinction between liability for dangerous and non-dangerous species alongside liability under various torts.

DOI: 10.4324/9781003202417-11

11.2 Statutory liability

11.2.1 Generally

The basic principle of the Animals Act 1971 is that a person who keeps a dangerous animal has strict liability for any damage which the animal may cause. A person who keeps an animal which is domesticated and is usually regarded as harmless will only be liable if the animal has given cause to fear that it has unusual characteristics which make it potentially dangerous.

11.2.2 Who is liable?

Liability is imposed on the 'keeper' of the animal. A person is a keeper of the animal if:

SECTION

's6(3)(a) he owns the animal or has it in his possession; or (b) he is the head of a household of which a member under the age of sixteen owns the animal or has it in his possession.'

If an animal strays, the original keeper remains liable unless and until another person fulfils the requirements of s6(3). A person who takes a stray into safekeeping to prevent it from causing damage or until it can be returned will not be regarded as the keeper (s6(4)).

11.2.3 Which animals are dangerous?

The definition is provided by s6(2).

SECTION

's6(2) A dangerous species is a species

a which is not commonly domesticated in the British Islands; and
b whose fully grown animals normally have such characteristics that they are likely, unless restrained, to cause severe damage or that any damage they may cause is likely to be severe.'

Potentially ferocious animals such as tigers clearly fall within the definition. Other animals, not known for ferocity, are also caught if any damage is likely to be severe. This would apply, for example, to elephants which rarely attack but whose sheer size means that any damage would be likely to be severe.

CASE EXAMPLE

Behrens v Bertram Mills [1957] 2 QB 1

The claimants ran a booth in a fun fair operated by the defendants who were the owners of a circus. The defendant's troop of elephants had to pass the booth on their way to the circus ring. One, elephant Bullu, was frightened by a small dog and in its fright trampled the booth injuring the claimants. Although Bullu was described as 'no more dangerous than a cow' the defendants were liable.

Although the case was decided before the Animals Act was passed, it is illustrative of the severity of damage which can be caused by a tame but very large animal.

CASE EXAMPLE

Tutin v Chipperfield Promotions Ltd [1980] 130 NLJ 807

The claimant agreed to take part in a camel race at the Horse of the Year Show. As the race started she was thrown off the camel by its awkward gait. It was held that the camel was a member of a dangerous species although the claimant did not succeed in this claim as on the facts the defence of voluntary assumption of risk applied. (She had also pleaded negligence on the part of the defendant and was successful on that basis.)

It is clear that whether or not an animal is a member of a dangerous species is a question of law and not one of fact. Neither the elephant in *Behrens v Bertram Mills* nor the camel in *Tutin v Chipperfield Promotions* was dangerous in the ordinary sense of the word but both species satisfied the legal test.

Any animal which is not covered by the definition is termed 'non-dangerous'.

11.2.4 Liability for dangerous animals

By s2(1):

SECTION

's2(1) Where any damage is caused by an animal which belongs to a dangerous species, any person who is a keeper of the animal is liable for the damage.'

This was explained by Lord Nicholls in *Mirvahedy (FC) v Henley and another* [2003] UKHL 16 when he said at 13:

JUDGMENT

'If you choose to keep a dangerous animal not commonly domesticated in this country, you are liable for damage done by the animal. It matters not that you take every precaution to prevent the animal escaping. You may not realise that the animal is dangerous. Liability is independent of fault. Liability is independent of knowledge of the animal's dangerous characteristics.'

By s5 the only defences available are that the damage was caused by the claimant's fault or occurred when the claimant had voluntarily assumed the risk (see section 11.2.5 for a full discussion of s5).

11.2.5 Liability for non-dangerous animals

The basis for liability is set out in s2(2).

SECTION

's2(2) Where damage is caused by an animal which does not belong to a dangerous species, a keeper of the animal is liable for the damage . . . if

a the damage is of a kind which the animal, unless restrained, was likely to cause or which, if caused by the animal, was likely to be severe; and

b the likelihood of the damage or of its being severe was due to characteristics of the animal which are not normally found in animals of the same species or are not normally so found except at particular times or in particular circumstances; and

c those characteristics were known to the keeper [or his servant having charge of the animal or to a member of his household who is the keeper but aged under sixteen].'

This sub-section is not a model of clear parliamentary draftsmanship. It has been described in various uncomplimentary ways by the judges who have had to try to interpret and apply it, s2(2)(b) in particular causing great difficulty. There have been a number of different approaches taken over the years but the section has recently come before the House of Lords for the first time in *Mirvahedy (FC) v Henley and Another*. To some extent the law has been clarified although no doubt problems will still arise in future cases. All three parts of s2(2) must be satisfied but, for convenience, each will be considered separately. The facts of *Mirvahedy* are given at this point for the sake of convenience. Relevant parts of the judgments are discussed later where appropriate.

CASE EXAMPLE

Mirvahedy (FC) v Henley and Another [2003] UKHL 16

Three horses were kept by the defendants in a field next to their house. Something frightened the horses and they bolted out of the field. They pushed over an electric fence and a surrounding wooden fence and then stampeded along a track on to a road. They ran for more than a mile onto a main dual-carriageway road where one of the horses collided with the car driven by the claimant. The claimant was seriously injured and the horse was killed. The claimant alleged that the defendants were liable under the Animals Act.

Section 2(2)(a): the nature of the damage

The damage must be 'of a kind which the animal unless restrained was likely to cause' or 'of a kind . . . which, if caused by the animal, was likely to be severe'. What does the word 'likely' mean? This has exercised judicial minds on several occasions.

CASE EXAMPLE

Smith v Ainger, The Times, 5 June 1990

The defendant's dog, an Alsatian cross, had a history of attacking other dogs. When it attacked the claimant's dog, the claimant was knocked over, breaking his leg. The Court of Appeal had to consider whether the injury was one which was 'likely' to occur unless the dog was restrained.

At first sight, the nature of the injury was unlikely – a bite would be more likely. The court held, however, that the words 'was likely' meant 'such as might well happen' rather than 'probable'. On this basis, on the facts, it was likely that the dog would attack another dog and that the owner of the other dog would intervene or, as in this case, get in the way. Were this to happen, there was a material risk that the owner would be bitten or buffeted and suffer injury. No distinction needed to be drawn between a bite and a buffet. The damage caused to the claimant was of a kind which the dog was likely to cause.

In many cases the severity of the damage can clearly be anticipated.

CASE EXAMPLE

Curtis v Betts [1990] 1 WLR 459

The claimant, aged 11, was attacked and bitten by Max, a bull mastiff weighing 70 kg. The child knew the dog and as he cycled past, he called to Max who was being put into a car. The dog leapt at the child and bit him on the face. It was held that s2(2)(a) was satisfied.

Slade LJ said:

JUDGMENT

'Max was a dog of the bull mastiff breed. If he did bite anyone, the damage was likely to be severe.'

As with dangerous animals, the damage need not be the result of anything other than the size and weight of the animal. Thus in *Jaundrill v Gillett, The Times*, 30 January 1996 the Court of Appeal accepted that horses were likely to cause damage by virtue of their weight.

While Lord Scott in *Mirvahedy* stated, *obiter*, that he had doubts as to earlier interpretations of s2(2)(a), the issue was not further considered and the Court of Appeal decisions continue to provide guidance.

Section 2(2)(b): is the behaviour normal or abnormal?

Once s2(2)(a) is satisfied, the cause of the animal's dangerousness must be established. This can be done in two ways:

i the danger was caused by characteristics 'which are not normally found in animals of the same species'; or

ii it was caused by characteristics which are not normally found in animals of the same species 'except at particular times or in particular circumstances'.

If the first approach is to be used, the characteristic which causes the danger must result from some abnormality. Lord Nicholls in *Mirvahedy* explained that this deals with 'a case where animals of the same species are normally docile but the particular animal is not'. The second approach covers animals which are not normally vicious but which may be dangerous at certain times. An example of this can be found in the case of a bitch with a litter who bites to defend her pups. While this is normal behaviour for a bitch in such circumstances, the second limb of s2(2)(b) means that there can be liability on the part of the keeper even though at other times the bitch is completely docile.

The judges have not been in agreement as to how s2(2)(b) should be interpreted.

CASE EXAMPLE

Cummings v Grainger [1977] QB 397

An Alsatian was loose in a scrap-yard to guard against intruders. The claimant went into the yard and was seriously injured by the dog. The Court of Appeal held that the dog had characteristics not normally found in an Alsatian dog except when it is being used as a guard dog. The second limb of s2(2)(b) was therefore satisfied.

In *Curtis v Betts* above, discussing whether the dog's behaviour fell within s2(2)(b), the Court of Appeal agreed with the trial judge:

JUDGMENT

'bull mastiffs have a tendency to react fiercely at particular times and in particular circumstances, namely when defending the boundaries of what they regard as their own territory'.

On the facts it was held that the accident occurred when the dog was defending its territory and therefore fell within the second limb of s2(2)(b).

These cases seem to make a clear statement that an owner cannot escape liability merely because the animal is potentially dangerous only at certain times and that all animals of that species share the same characteristic.

Other judges have argued that if all animals of the same species share the same characteristic at specific times then that cannot be termed an abnormal characteristic. This argument is based on the assumption that the requirement of abnormality in the first limb of the sub-section also applies to the second limb when the sub-section is read as a whole.

CASE EXAMPLE

Breedon v Lampard [1985] (unreported) 21 March, CA

The claimant was injured when a horse (Raffles) kicked out when the claimant approached either too quickly or too closely from behind. Raffles was wearing a red ribbon on his tail, a traditional warning to others that the horse is prone to kick. Accepting that it is normal for all horses to kick in some circumstances, the judges took the view that s2(2)(b) should be construed as imposing a single test, namely that the characteristic which led to the injury was abnormal.

Taking this view, the second limb merely serves to avoid attempts at escaping liability by arguing, for example, that all bitches bite sometimes.

The conflict has been partially resolved by the House of Lords in *Mirvahedy*. Each of the judges accepted that it is normal for horses to bolt when they are badly frightened. Three members of the court, Lords Nicholls, Hobhouse and Walker, held that the second limb of the sub-section applied. Although the horses were behaving normally for frightened horses, Lord Nicholls noted at 48:

JUDGMENT

'it was precisely because they were behaving in [an] unusual way caused by their panic that the road accident took place.'

This sufficed to bring their behaviour within the second limb of the sub-section. The minority judgments of Lords Slynn and Scott argue that the correct interpretation of the sub-section meant that liability could not be imposed when the behaviour was normal at the particular time. Only if it was abnormal at that time would the sub-section be satisfied.

Section 2(2)(b): what is a 'characteristic'?

While *Mirvahedy* seems to have settled the arguments about abnormality, another argument remains – what constitutes a 'characteristic' for the purposes of the sub-section? This question was considered by the Court of Appeal in *Gloster v Chief Constable of Greater Manchester* [2000] PIQR P114.

CASE EXAMPLE

Gloster v Chief Constable of Greater Manchester [2000] PIQR P114

A German shepherd dog (Jack) was a trained police dog rated as 'satisfactory' and 'not overaggressive'. His handler was about to release the dog to chase a car thief when he fell. Jack slipped his collar and set off after the innocent claimant who had not heard any warning not to run as the dog was about to be loosed. The claimant was bitten twice in the leg before Jack was called off. The issue was whether a dog which had been trained to be aggressive in certain circumstances had a 'characteristic' which would be caught by the sub-section. The defendant was not held liable as the requirement of s2 was not satisfied.

Lord Justice Pill argued that the relevant characteristic was the dog's ability to be trained, a normal characteristic for the breed and therefore not caught by the sub-section. The damage was due to the training and not to the dog's characteristic.

This approach was criticised in *Mirvahedy* by Lord Scott in his minority judgment when he referred to *Gloster* while discussing the meaning of s2(2)(b), at 128:

JUDGMENT

'The damage complained of was the bite. The likelihood of being chased and bitten was due to a characteristic of the police dog not normally found in German Shepherd dogs. There was, in my opinion, no more to be said about paragraph b [of the sub-section] than that.'

The other judges in *Mirvahedy* did not comment on this aspect of the *Gloster* judgment so that the issue of what amounts to a characteristic remains open.

It is clear that the characteristic need not be one which indicates a possibility that the animal will attack humans but it must be one which is not usually found in the particular species.

CASE EXAMPLE

Wallace v Newton [1982] 1 WLR 375

A horse which was known to be unpredictable lashed out and injured the claimant when being loaded into a trailer. It was held that this was a characteristic peculiar to the animal. The defendant was liable as he was aware of the characteristic which is not usually found in horses.

CASE EXAMPLE

Freeman v Higher Park Farm [2008] EWCA Civ 1185

The court had to consider whether s2(2)(b) included a horse that bucked when beginning to canter injuring an experienced rider. The court held that bucking was a normal characteristic of a horse and horses do not buck at any particular time. Liability was also denied because *volenti* under s5(2) applied.

Section 2(2)(c): does the keeper know?

The sub-section makes it clear that there will only be liability for damage caused by a non-dangerous animal if the dangerous tendency is known to the keeper. In the case of an animal's owner who is under 16, the child's knowledge will be imputed to the head of the household for this purpose. Apart from this exception, the requirement is of 'actual' rather than 'constructive' knowledge. Where a keeper 'should have' known, but did not know, of the likely consequences in particular circumstances, although there may be no liability under the Animals Act, there may be liability in negligence (see section 11.3.5).

11.2.6 Statutory defences

While liability under the Act is strict, it is not absolute. The Act sets out defences which can absolve the keeper from liability for injury or damage caused by either dangerous or non-dangerous animals.

Fault of claimant and voluntary assumption of risk

By s5(1):

SECTION

's5(1) a person is not liable . . . for any damage which is wholly the fault of the person suffering it.'

By s5(2) there is no liability to a person who 'has voluntarily accepted the risk' of damage.

The cases show that people can be very stupid at times. In *Marlor v Bell* [1900] 16 TLR 239 the claimant was injured when he stroked a zebra; in *Sylvester v Chapman Ltd* [1935] 79 SJ 777 the claimant went into a leopard's pen to remove a lighted cigarette.

More recently, in *Dhesi v Chief Constable of West Midlands Police, The Times*, 9 May 2000, both defences were held to apply.

CASE EXAMPLE

Dhesi v Chief Constable of West Midlands Police, The Times, 9 May 2000

The claimant and some other youths were involved in a confrontation with the police. The claimant was carrying a hockey stick which he was swinging from side to side in an angry and aggressive manner. He ran off and hid in some brambles.

Having been tracked by a police dog and its handler, he was warned three times that the dog would be loosed if he did not surrender. He did not do so and the dog was loosed. In his struggle to get away from the dog, the claimant was bitten several times.

It was held that he had voluntarily accepted the risk of being injured and that the resulting damage was entirely his own fault.

Liability to trespassers

By s5(3)(a) a person is not liable if a trespasser is injured by an animal which is not being kept for the purpose of protection. Where an animal is being kept on premises for the purpose of protection of persons or property, a keeper will not be liable to a trespasser 'if keeping [the animal] there for that purpose was not unreasonable' (s5(3)(b)).

CASE EXAMPLE

Cummings v Grainger [1977] QB 397

The defendant ran a breaker's yard and at night a German shepherd dog was allowed to run free for security purposes. The claimant knew about the dog when she entered the yard one night with a friend who also knew about the dog. The claimant, who had no right of entry and was a trespasser, was attacked and bitten by the dog.

The issue was whether the keeping of the dog for protection was reasonable. Lord Denning MR held:

JUDGMENT

'The only reasonable way of protecting the place was to have a guard dog. True it was a fierce dog. But why not? A gentle dog would be no good. The thieves would soon make friends with him. It seems to me that it was very reasonable – or at least not unreasonable – for the defendant to keep this dog there.'

The claimant was also held to have voluntarily accepted the risk when she entered the yard.

It must be remembered that the Guard Dogs Act 1975 has since come into effect setting stringent conditions for the use of guard dogs and making it a criminal offence to allow a guard dog to run freely unless it is under the control of a handler.

11.2.7 Liability for livestock

The term 'livestock' is defined by s11 as:

SECTION

's11 cattle, horses, asses, mules, hinnies, sheep, pigs, goats and poultry, and also deer not in the wild state.'

A keeper of livestock will be liable for damage caused by the animals to land or property belonging to someone else on to which the animals have strayed (s4). Additional rights of the person whose land or property has been damaged are set out in s7:

SECTION

's7 (i) a right to detain straying livestock which are not under someone's control but subject to notifying the police within 48 hours and giving the owner (if known) notice; (ii) after 14 days, the right to sell the livestock to recoup losses unless an appropriate amount has earlier been offered by the owner. This includes the right to recoup the cost of keeping the livestock safely and with proper care.'

The issue of fencing land has caused problems but the position is now reasonably clear. There is generally a duty to prevent livestock from straying on to the highway (s8) except in those areas such as some national parks where local people have a lawful right to graze animals on the highway. In such a case, adjoining land owners have no claim for any damage done by the animals straying on to their land from the highway (s5(5)).

11.2.8 Liability for injury to livestock caused by dogs

The keeper of a dog which causes damage to livestock is liable for that damage (s3). For the purpose of s3, the term 'livestock' includes 'pheasants, partridges and grouse' if these are in captivity. Further, by s9(1), a person who kills or injures a dog is not liable for that damage provided:

SECTION

's9(1) (a) that person acts to protect livestock and is entitled to do so; (b) notice is given to the police within 48 hours.'

A person is entitled to act provided the livestock is on their land or that of a person for whom they act, s9(2)(a), and at that time they reasonably believe:

SECTION

's9(3)(i) the dog is worrying or about to worry the livestock and there is no other reasonable means to end or prevent the worrying; or (ii) the dog has been worrying the livestock, is still in the area and not under anyone's control and there is no practicable way to find out to whom the dog belongs.'

11.3 Liability at common law

11.3.1 Trespass to land

The owner of animals which stray on to another's land may be liable in trespass to land. Examples are found in relation to fox-hunting.

CASE EXAMPLE

Paul v Summerhayes [1878] 4 QBD 9

The claimant had frequently informed the defendant, the local hunt, that it was not permitted to cross his land. The defendant persisted in doing so and was found to be liable for trespass.

CASE EXAMPLE

League against Cruel Sports Ltd v Scott [1986] QB 240

The defendant was liable for allowing fox hounds to run on to land owned by the claimant without the claimant's consent.

11.3.2 Trespass to goods

It may seem improbable, but in *Manton v Brocklebank* [1923] 2 KB 212 a person who had trained his dog to steal golf balls was held liable for trespass to goods.

11.3.3 Trespass to the person

An animal can be used against another person in the same way as any other weapon. It is likely that someone who deliberately sets an animal on a person will be liable for assault and/or battery.

11.3.4 Defamation

It has been suggested that a person who teaches a talking bird, for example a parrot, to say something which is defamatory of another will be liable for defamation.

11.3.5 Negligence

It is clear that there can be no liability under the Animals Act for damage caused by a non-dangerous species which has never previously shown evidence of potentially dangerous characteristics. This is of little comfort to the victim. It may be possible for the victim to obtain compensation by way of negligence. The usual rules as to duty, breach and causation must be satisfied (see Chapter 2).

CASE EXAMPLE

Fardon v Harcourt Rivington [1932] 146 LT 391

A dog had been left in a car during very hot weather. Trying to escape, the dog broke a window and a splinter of glass injured the claimant's eye. Lord Dunedin commented at 83:

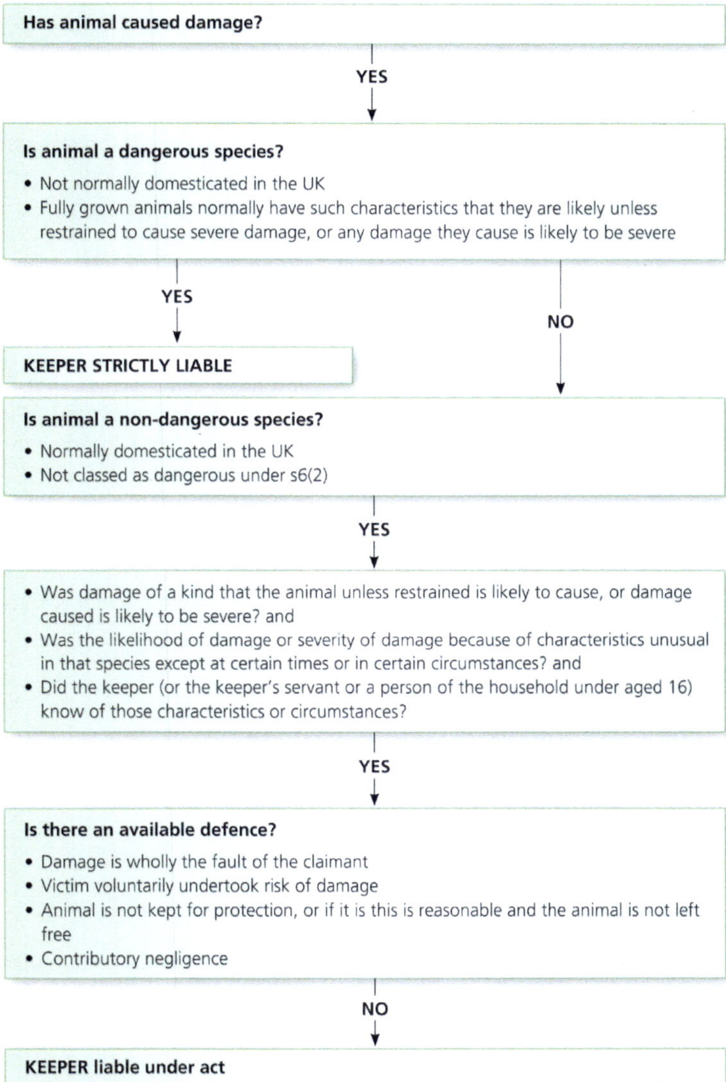

Figure 11.1 Liability under the Animals Act 1971.

JUDGMENT

'Quite apart from the liability imposed upon the owner of animals . . . by reason of knowledge of their propensities, there is . . . the ordinary duty to take care in the cases put upon negligence.'

On the facts the defendant was not liable as he could not guard against a 'fantastic possibility'.

An action in negligence is possible where the defendant's failure to control an animal leads to a foreseeable risk that it may cause harm.

CASE EXAMPLE

***Birch v Mills* [1995] 9 CL 354**

The claimant was walking dogs on leads along a public road when a herd of cows in an unfenced field chased the dogs and hurt the claimant. It was held that as the cattle were known to be frisky and to chase dogs, it was reasonably foreseeable that a person leading the dog was likely to get hurt.

CASE EXAMPLE

***Draper v Hodder* [1972] 2 QB 556**

A pack of Jack Russell dogs owned by the defendant got into his neighbour's garden and savaged a child playing there. It was impossible to identify which dog or dogs had actually injured the child. Knowledge by the defendant that any individual dog had dangerous propensities could not be proved.

The defendant was found liable for negligence. A pack of terriers is liable to attack any moving target and the defendant, an experienced dog breeder, knew this. The risk of injury if the animals were not sufficiently controlled was foreseeable.

However, there will be no liability where there is only a remote possibility of an injury and a claim has already failed under s2 of the Act, *Whippey v Jones* [2009] EWCA Civ 452.

11.3.6 Nuisance

Keeping animals on land can lead to a nuisance. Examples include offensive smells and/or noise. In *Leeman v Montague* [1936] 2 All ER 1677 the crowing of cockerels was held to amount to a nuisance. Today it is likely that such complaints would be dealt with as statutory nuisances but the possibility of using the common law still exists.

11.4 Other statutory provision

The Guard Dogs Act 1975 has already been mentioned (see section 11.2.6). Other statutes are intended to ensure that animals are not kept in such a way as to present a threat to people. The Dangerous Dogs Act 1991, for example, contains detailed provisions requiring proper control of certain breeds of dogs which are enforced by criminal sanction. The issue of control is addressed by the Dangerous Wild Animals Act 1976 and the Zoo Licensing Act 1981 requiring licences if such animals are to be kept and providing for compulsory insurance against liability for any damage such animals might cause.

SAMPLE ESSAY QUESTION

Discuss the argument that the Animals Act 1971 ensures that the keeper of an animal, whether of a dangerous or non-dangerous species, is fully liable for all the damage done by the animal.

Define keeper

- The owner of the animal or the head of a household in which a person under 16 is the owner of the animal

Explain the basis of liability for a dangerous species

- Defined in s6(2) – an animal not commonly domesticated in UK and with characteristics that, unless restricted, are likely to cause severe damage or any damage caused is likely to be severe
- Dangerous is a question of fact in each case
- The keeper is strictly liable

Explain where there is liability for non-dangerous species under the Act

- The damage is of a kind the animal is likely to cause unless restrained or if caused by animal is likely to be severe; and
- The likelihood or severity of damage is due to characteristics of the individual animal or species or of species at specific times; and
- The keeper knows of the characteristics

Discuss whether the provisions do ensure that the keeper is fully liable

- The definition of keeper is very broad
- For 'dangerous' animals liability is strict– so it does ensure liability
- It may even include animals that are not actually dangerous
- Rules on non-dangerous species – dependent on specific characteristics and knowledge of those characteristics so that, e.g. 'the dog always gets the first bite free' – so this may limit liability and be unfair in certain circumstances
- The court in *Mirhavedy* appears to have created a form of strict liability in the case of non-dangerous species
- There is no need for a link between characteristics and damage
- It is hard to distinguish between permanent and temporary characteristics

Discuss the possible impact of the defences on claims

- S5(1) – damage due entirely to fault of victim
- S5(2) – victim voluntarily accepted risk
- S5(3) – animal was either not kept for protection or if so then it was reasonable to do so
- S10 – contributory negligence
- May reduce the possibility of a successful claim even though the animal has caused damage

KEY FACTS

Key facts on liability for animals

Animals Act 1971	**Case/statute**
Who is liable?	
A person who owns the animal or has it in their possession. In the case of an owner under 16, the head of that household.	s6(3)
Dangerous animals	**Case/statute**
Not commonly domesticated in the British Islands which when fully grown have characteristics which mean that any damage they cause is likely to be severe.	s6(2)
Damage can be due to any characteristic including natural ferocity or size and weight.	*Behrens v Bertram Mills* [1957]; *Tutin v Chipperfield* [1980]
Non-dangerous animals	**Case/statute**
Any animal not included in definition of a dangerous animal.	
Liability for dangerous animals.	
Keeper has strict liability for any damage caused.	s2(1)
Liability for dogs	**Case/statute**
Keeper of dog liable for damage caused to livestock.	s3
Person responsible for livestock not liable if they kill or injure a dog which is worrying the livestock and there is no other reasonable means to stop the dog or if the dog has been worrying, is still in the area and not under anyone's control.	s9
Liability at common law	**Case/statute**
Owner may be liable for: • trespass to land • trespass to goods • trespass to person if animal 'set on' a person • defamation but unlikely • negligence • nuisance.	*Paul v Summerhayes* [1878] *Manton v Brocklebank* [1923] *Fardon v Harcourt Rivington* [1932]; *Birch v Mills* [1995]; *Draper v Hodder* [1972] *Leeman v Montague* [1936]

(Continued)

(Continued)

	Other statutory provision
	Guard Dogs Act 1975 Dangerous Dogs Act 1991 Dangerous Wild Animals Act 1976 Zoo Licensing Act 1981

SUMMARY

- Common law originally provided strict liability actions for damage caused by dangerous species of animals and for damage caused by straying livestock.
- These were replaced by the Animals Act 1971 although it is still possible to bring actions under other torts, e.g. negligence, trespass to the person.
- The Animals Act 1971 distinguishes between 'dangerous species' and 'non-dangerous' species.
- A dangerous species is one not domesticated in the UK and which is likely to cause severe damage unless restrained – and a keeper of such an animal is liable for all the damage it causes – so liability is strict.
- A keeper of a non-dangerous animal is liable if: damage is likely if the animal is unrestrained, or damage is likely to be severe; because of characteristics not normally associated with the species, or only at specific times or in specific circumstances; and these characteristics were known to the keeper.
- A keeper is somebody who is responsible for the animal or who is the head of the household where the actual keeper is a person under the age of 16.
- Possible defences are: consent, damage caused wholly by the claimant's own fault and contributory negligence.
- The Act also provides an action for damage caused by straying livestock and there is also an action for livestock killed by dogs, including the right to kill the dog in some circumstances to protect the livestock.
- There is a limited duty to prevent livestock from straying on the highway.
- Remoteness of damage is likely to be measured against the direct consequence test rather than the reasonably foreseeable test.

12

Torts relating to goods

AIMS AND OBJECTIVES

After reading this chapter you should be able to:

- Illustrate the common law basis for liability for defective products
- Explain the statutory basis for liability for defective products
- Identify and critically evaluate the bases of liability for interference with goods
- Apply the law to factual situations and reach conclusions as to liability

This chapter is divided into three sections: first, liability for defective products under common law; second, liability for defective products under statute; and third, liability for torts committed against goods.

12.1 Common law liability for defective products

12.1.1 Introduction

This area of law is partly dealt with by contract and consumer law and partly by torts, with a substantial contribution from statute. It is not appropriate to consider contract and consumer law in depth in a book on torts but it will be considered briefly. For detailed discussion, reference should be made to texts relevant to the specific area.

12.1.2 Liability in contract and consumer law

From the nineteenth century onwards, the courts have been concerned to prevent large businesses from taking advantage of their strength to 'bully' consumers. Consumers were first protected by the Sale of Goods Act 1893. Protection can in part be found in the Sale of Goods Act 1979 as amended

DOI: 10.4324/9781003202417-12

by the Sale and Supply of Goods Act 1994. The Act works by implying certain terms into all contracts for the sale of goods. An example is the requirement that the goods be 'fit for their purpose' (s14) which is not, however, implied into a private sale. Fitness for purpose includes a requirement that the goods should be free of defects and safe in normal use. People who are injured by goods which they have purchased have a remedy for breach of the term implied into the contract. Protection was extended by the Unfair Contract Terms Act 1977 which imposed strict limitations on the extent to which a business could exclude liability for defective products by means of an exclusion or limitation clause. This protection has subsequently been supplemented and superseded by the Consumer Rights Act 2015. The 2015 Act applies to business-to-consumer contracts and also to business-to-business contracts if the product is ultimately going to be supplied to a consumer. This means some provisions of the Sale of Goods Act continue to apply. Importantly, the Consumer Rights Act provides protection for when a consumer is left with a defective product, including digital products and the provision of defective services i.e. financial advice under s49. Many of these rights are implied into the contract and therefore cannot be excluded entitling the consumer to a remedy.

Where there is liability under the Sale of Goods Act, it is strict liability so far as the seller of the product is concerned. The buyer is entitled to be repaid the purchase price of the goods and to be compensated for further damage.

It sounds as if all situations are covered but there is one fundamental flaw – only a party to a contract can generally sue for breach of that contract. This means that a person injured by a product received as a gift cannot claim using the Sale of Goods Act. This is the doctrine of privity of contract. However, the Contracts (Rights of Third Parties) Act 1999 has remedied the situation whereby a third party can have rights under the contract between the buyer and seller of the products but only provided certain conditions are fulfilled. It is not likely that this will provide an effective remedy in many cases.

What then are the rights of a person injured by a defective product who is not the buyer of that product?

12.1.3 Liability in negligence

Liability for loss or damage caused by defective products is usually accepted as starting in 1932. However, in more limited form there are much older examples.

CASE EXAMPLE

Dixon v Bell [1816] 5 M & S 198

A master handed a gun to his young servant who had no experience of handling guns. The boy was injured when the gun went off. It was accepted that the goods were potentially dangerous and 'capable of doing mischief' so there was held to be liability for the injuries caused by putting dangerous and defective goods in circulation.

As was seen in Chapter 2, the case of *Donoghue v Stevenson* [1932] AC 562 gave rise to two rules:

i. the neighbour test which was intended to apply in all cases (the so-called wide rule); and
ii. the principle that a manufacturer owes a duty of care to the consumer (the so-called narrow rule).

The narrow rule was explained by Lord Macmillan when he said at 620:

JUDGMENT

> 'a person who engages in . . . manufacturing articles of food and drink intended for consumption by a member of the public in the form in which he issues them is under a duty to take care in the manufacture of those articles. That duty . . . he owes to those whom he intends to consume his products.'

It has been clear since 1932 that a manufacturer owes a duty of care to the ultimate consumer where products reach the consumer in much the same form as they left the factory.

As Lord Atkin identified in the case at 599:

JUDGMENT

> 'a manufacturer of products which he sells in such form as to show that he intends them to reach the ultimate consumer in the form in which they left him with no reasonable possibility of intermediate examination, and with the knowledge that the absence of reasonable care in the preparation or putting up of the products will result in an injury to the consumer's life or property, owes a duty to the consumer to take reasonable care.'

So essentially there are three key elements that must be proved for a successful claim for product liability in negligence:

- the goods must reach the consumer and be intended to reach the consumer in the same form in which they left the manufacturer;
- there is no possibility of an examination of or interference with the goods between leaving the manufacturer and reaching the end consumer;
- the manufacturer knows that failing to take sufficient care of the goods may put the consumer at risk of foreseeable harm.

12.1.4 The scope of liability

Product liability in negligence concerns damage caused by or losses arising from the defect in the goods. Claims for replacement goods are made in contract law usually under the Sale of Goods Act 1979. We are not concerned here with the cost of replacing the faulty goods but rather the harm that the defective product causes.

Originally product liability in negligence was restricted to foodstuffs but this has subsequently been extended to cover the full range of products. For instance it has included:

- a range of manufactured consumer durables – in *Grant v Australian Knitting Mills Ltd* [1936] AC 85, woollen underpants contained a chemical which caused the consumer to develop dermatitis, a painful skin disease; in *Herschtal v Stewart and Arden Ltd* [1940] 1 KB 155 it included a defective motor car;
- defects in a house, which can also include the fixtures and fittings (*Batty v Metropolitan Property Realisations Ltd* [1978] QB 554);
- defective repair to a lift which then caused injury (*Haseldine v Daw & Son Ltd* [1941] 2 KB 343);
- computer software (*St Albans City and District Council v International Computers Ltd* [1996] 4 All ER 481).

12.1.5 Bringing a claim in negligence for damage caused by defective products

Product liability in negligence relies on proving the same essential elements as for claims in negligence generally: the existence of a duty of care owed by the manufacturer to the 'ultimate consumer' of the product; breach of duty by the manufacturer; and foreseeable damage caused by the defendant's breach of duty.

Duty of care

The duty of care only applies in respect of goods reaching the consumer in the same form that they left the manufacturer where there is no chance of an intermediate examination.

Breach of duty

A breach of the duty by the manufacturer will generally involve a failure in the production process or alternatively a failure to rectify a known defect before the product reaches the consumer. So this may include:

- failing to check products that have been exposed to chemicals during the manufacturing process that then may cause harm (*Grant v Australian Knitting Mills Ltd* [1936]);
- failing to remedy a known fault, which may include failing to recall defective products in sufficient time to avoid harm to the consumer (*Walton v British Leyland Ltd* [1978], *The Times*, 13 July).

Foreseeable damage caused by the defendant's breach of duty

The consumer can only recover compensation by proving that the damage was actually caused by the defect in the goods. If there is another possible cause of the damage then the consumer is unlikely to gain compensation.

12.1.6 Potential claimants

The original description in *Donoghue v Stevenson* given to those able to sue a manufacturer for damage caused by defective goods was 'ultimate consumers' or 'end users'. On the basis that the case exploded the so-called privity fallacy of *Winterbottom v Wright* [1842] 10 M & W 109 it was inevitable that Lord Atkin would produce a description that was sufficiently broad to cover people who had not bought the goods themselves.

In any case, applying the neighbour principle, a claimant is anybody that the manufacturer 'should have in his contemplation' as being likely to be harmed if the goods are defective. So over time the definition has been broadened to include other situations involving foreseeable harm:

- suppliers that are injured because of the defect in the goods – in *Barnett v H and J Packer & Co* [1940] 3 All ER 575 sharp metal protruding from a sweet injured a shopkeeper who was storing the sweets and the manufacturer was liable for the injury;
- bystanders – in *Stennet v Hancock and Peters* [1939] 2 All ER 578 a pedestrian was injured by a component that had been negligently reassembled by a garage and which then fell off a lorry.

12.1.7 Potential defendants

The original defendant in common law product liability was limited to the manufacturer of the defective goods. However, over time the law has expanded to include a wider range of potential defendants, including a number in the chain of production and distribution where they have a potential impact on the safety of the goods:

- wholesalers (*Watson v Buckley, Osborne Garrett & Co Ltd* [1940] 1 All ER 174);
- retailers (*Kubach v Hollands* [1937] 3 All ER 907);
- other suppliers of goods (e.g. through mail order) (*Herschtal v Stewart and Arden Ltd* [1940] 1 KB 155) – but only when the duty owed by the supplier goes beyond distributing the goods and requires that the goods are inspected;
- people who repair goods (*Haseldine v CA Daw & Son Ltd* [1941] 2 KB 343);
- people who assemble goods (*Malfroot v Noxal Ltd* [1935] 51 TLR 551).

The consumer has a reasonable range of potential defendants to sue as a result. However, it is a more limited range than under the Consumer Protection Act 1987.

The problem for a consumer who seeks to rely on negligence arises from the need to prove fault, i.e. breach of the duty of care. It will be remembered that a person will not be liable for negligence if they have taken all reasonable steps to avoid injuring someone else. In some cases it is clear that there must have been fault and the courts have to be able to draw an inference of fault from the facts. This rather difficult concept is illustrated by two cases.

CASE EXAMPLE

Grant v Australian Knitting Mills Ltd [1936] AC 85

The claimant purchased some woollen underwear manufactured by the defendants. The garment was contaminated by sulphites which would not normally be present. This caused the claimant to suffer severely from dermatitis.

Finding the defendant liable, Lord Wright said at 101:

JUDGMENT

'According to the evidence, the method of manufacture was correct, the danger of excess sulphites being left was recognised and guarded against . . . If excess sulphites were left in the garment, that could only be because someone was at fault . . . . Negligence is found as a matter of inference from the existence of the defects taken in connection with all the known circumstances.'

CASE EXAMPLE

Evans v Triplex Safety Glass Co Ltd [1936] 1 All ER 283

The claimant bought a car fitted by the makers with a windscreen of 'Triplex Toughened Safety Glass'. While he was driving the car the windscreen shattered injuring the claimant and his passengers. Holding that the defendant was not liable Mr Justice Porter explained that an inference of fault on the part of the manufacturers could not be drawn for several reasons:

- i the windscreen had been in place for more than a year before the accident;
- ii the disintegration could have resulted from another cause during the course of use of the car.

It could have been badly fitted in the first place.

Unlike the cases of *Donoghue v Stevenson* and *Grant v Australian Knitting Mills* [1936] AC 85 where the cause of the problem was clear, in this case there were a number of potential causes thus fault could not be inferred.

These cases illustrate the difficulties faced by a claimant in bringing a successful action. There can be no certainty that the court will find that the defect has arisen by virtue of the defendant's fault as it seems that the claimant has to show that all other possible causes have been eliminated.

Additional problems faced by a claimant arise from the globalisation of trade. Products are imported from all over the world. While in some cases it is theoretically possible to bring an action in negligence against a foreign manufacturer, the matter is fraught with difficulty.

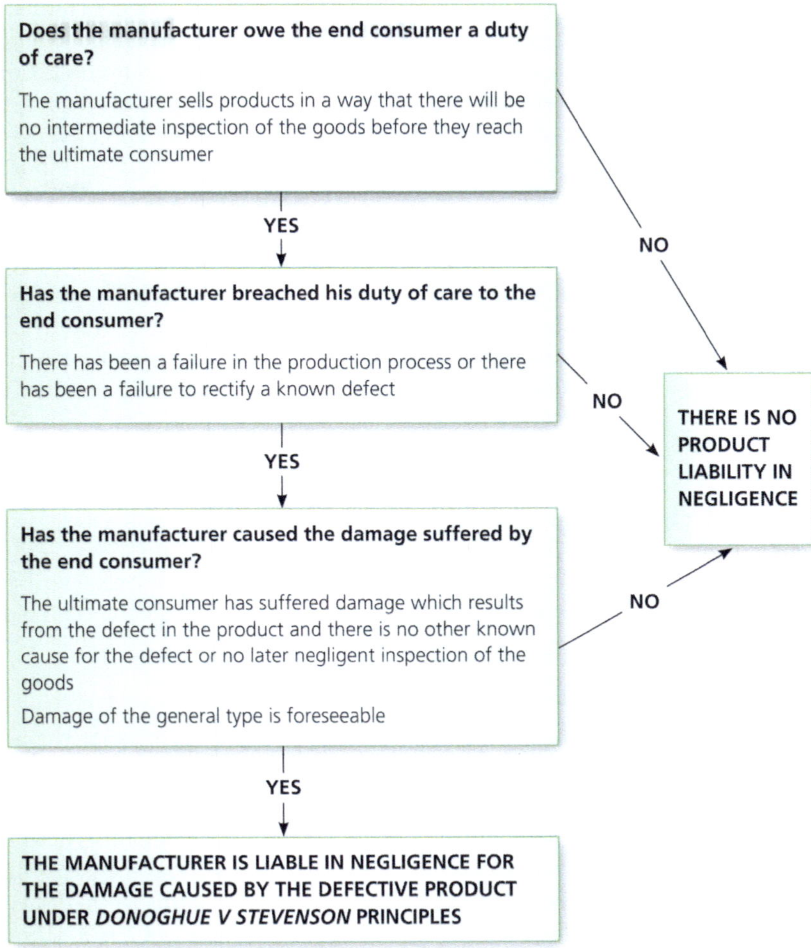

Figure 12.1 The requirements for a claim in product liability in negligence under *Donoghue v Stevenson*.

12.2 Strict liability under the Consumer Protection Act 1987

12.2.1 Background

The tort of negligence is not of much practical help in many cases. In the 1970s a number of babies were born in the United Kingdom who were seriously damaged by a drug taken by their mothers in the early stages of pregnancy for severe morning sickness. The drug, thalidomide, was suspected of causing birth defects and was, at the time it was prescribed in the United Kingdom, banned in many countries including the United States of America. Although eventually a compensation fund for the victims was created, it took many years during which time the victims had enormous difficulty in establishing the facts of the case. This and other concerns prompted the European Union (the UK was a member of the EU until January 2020) to consider creating a system which would allow consumers injured by defective products to obtain compensation more easily. Eventually Directive 85/374/EEC was created. The Preamble to the Directive states 'liability without fault on the part of the producer is the sole means of adequately solving the problem, peculiar to our age of increasing technicality, of a fair apportionment of the risks inherent in modern technological production'. The Directive was passed into UK law by the Consumer Protection Act 1987 Part I. The position following Brexit remains largely unchanged in this area as the Directive has been incorporated into national law via the Consumer Protection Act. However, the UK has updated its product safety regime by introducing the Product Regulation and Metrology Act 2025.

LEGISLATION

S1. (1) The Secretary of State may by regulations make provision, in relation to the marketing or use of products in the United Kingdom, for the purpose of –

(a) reducing or mitigating risks presented by products;

(b) ensuring that products operate efficiently or effectively;

(c) ensuring that products designed for weighing or measuring operate accurately.

The premise of the Act is to allow greater flexibility and scope to deal with product issues. For instance, it is intended that the Act will allow the government to hold online marketplaces to account for selling dangerous things, to consider the environmental impact of products and to consider the risks associated with selling certain products. Incidentally, this Act is similar to the EU's General Product Safety Regulation which came into force in December 2024. The Law Commission has launched a review of the UK's product liability framework with a view to consulting on proposed reforms in the second half of 2026.

Much has changed since the Consumer Protection Act 1987 came into force. For instance, many of us purchase our goods online, we also purchase more digital products, there are increased cyber security risks with some of products that we purchase and some of our purchases are made with AI embedded into the decision-making process. For example, a claim was pursued by a consumer against Amazon, a third-party online marketplace, in relation to a power tool that he had purchased which caused him significant personal injury resulting in the amputation of his index finger. The consumer argued that the power tool was defective under the 1987 Act. Amazon argued that the responsibility for the safety of the produce lay with the manufacturer and seller of the product who is based in China. Amazon argued that they are merely an online marketplace for a consumer to engage with a third-party seller. This case was settled out of court which therefore means that there was not the opportunity to explore how effective the 1987 Act could be in such a situation. However, it is hoped that the planned reforms should address such situations in the future.

At present, the Consumer Protection Act 1987 still governs this area and needs to be updated to reflect the current reality of consumer behaviour but until then the 1987 Act is the relevant law and is considered next.

12.2.2 Potential defendants under the 1987 Act

Section 2(1) of the Act states that there shall be liability 'where any damage is caused wholly or partly by a defect in a product'.

The class of those who may be liable is spelled out in s2(2) which provides that s2(1) applies to:

SECTION

's2(2)

a the producer of the product;

b any person who, by putting his name on the product or using a trade mark or other distinguishing mark in relation to the product, has held himself out to be the producer . . .;

c any person who has imported the product into [the United Kingdom] in order, in the course of any business of his, to supply it to another.

The producer of the product

A 'producer' is obviously the manufacturer of the product but the term is expanded to include those who win or abstract non-manufactured substances, for example coal and other mined substances. It also includes those who have subjected a non-manufactured product, for example food crops, to an industrial process which has created essential characteristics of the product, for example corn flakes from corn or frozen vegetables (s1(2)).

SECTION

's1(3) Where an essential component fails and damage is caused, both the manufacturer of the part and the manufacturer of the defective component will be liable.'

The 'own-brander' – section 2(2)(b)

An own-brander is someone who 'presents himself as the producer'. The effect of this description may mean that an own-brander who clearly states that the goods are produced 'for' that business rather than 'by' that business will escape liability. It will probably apply, for example, to the supermarket chain which markets its 'own brands' even though the goods are produced by a manufacturer.

The importer – section 2(2)(c)

Prior to Brexit, when goods were imported into the European Union from outside that area, the importer would be liable provided it has been imported with intent 'to supply it to another' (s2(2)(c)). For example, if goods have been imported from China into France and from there exported into the United Kingdom for sale to consumers, the original French importer would have liability. Following Brexit, this provision now means that if a person imports a product for supply in the UK in the course of any business and someone is hurt as a result of this product being defective, they may pursue a claim under this Act. However, if the product is imported for their private use which proves to be defective and causes harm to another, they cannot pursue an action under the Act as it was for private use.

CASE EXAMPLE

G v Fry Surgical International Ltd (unreported – cited in D Oughton and J Lowry, *Textbook on Consumer Law* (2nd edn, Blackstone Press, 2000), at p. 221).

The claimant was injured in an operation when a pair of surgical scissors broke. The scissors had been manufactured in Sweden, at that time not a member of the EU, and imported into the UK. The case was in fact settled without a judgment but the importer paid compensation.

Anonymous producers – section 2(3)

While the mere fact that a supplier has supplied the goods in question is not of itself enough to make the supplier liable (unlike the Sale of Goods Act which imposes liability on the supplier), a supplier has a duty to provide information which identifies the producer on request by a consumer (s2(3)). This is intended to enable a consumer to trace the goods back to the person who will have liability under the Act. The requirement is strengthened by the fact that should the supplier fail to provide the necessary information within a reasonable time; liability will rest on the supplier. As *Winfield and Jolowicz* suggests (W V H Rogers, *Winfield and Jolowicz on Tort* (16th edn, Sweet & Maxwell, 2002), p. 355) 'the importance of adequate record keeping can hardly be overemphasised', as the supplier could find that a substantial bill has to be met if those earlier in the chain of supply cannot be identified.

12.2.3 Products covered by the Act

Product is defined in s2(1) as 'any goods or electricity and (subject to subs (3)) includes a product which is comprised in another product, whether by virtue of being a component part, raw material or otherwise'.

Goods are defined in s45(1) as 'substances, growing crops, and things comprised in land by virtue of being attached to it and any ship, aircraft or vehicle'.

Buildings, nuclear power and agricultural produce which has not undergone an industrial process are all exempted from the scope of the Act.

12.2.4 The nature of the damage

By s5, damage means death or personal injury in all circumstances. While damage to property is also recoverable, this is limited. There is no liability for loss or damage to the product itself or to any product of which the defective product forms part (s5(2)).

Where damage to property has occurred, liability is restricted to those cases where the value of the claim exceeds £275 (s5(4)) and where the property which has been damaged is 'ordinarily intended for private use, occupation or consumption' and the claimant intended to use the property for such purposes (s5(3)).

The meaning of 'defect'

For the producer to be liable, the injury or damage must be caused 'wholly or partly by a defect in a product'. The meaning of 'defect' is accordingly of crucial importance.

The Act defines a product as being defective 'if the safety of the product is not such as persons generally are entitled to expect' (s3(1)). This is sometimes referred to as the public expectation test. In deciding whether or not a product is defective the court must take into account all the circumstances and in particular:

SECTION

'S3(1)

a the manner in which, and the purposes for which, it has been marketed, its get-up, the use of any mark in relation to the product and any instructions for, or warnings with respect to, doing or refraining from doing anything with or in relation to the product;

b what might reasonably be expected to be done with or in relation to the product; and

c the time when the product was supplied.'

Nothing is to be inferred from the fact that a product supplied at a later date is safer than the product in question.

While the Act (and the Directive from which it is derived) appears to impose a standard of safety, it is not in fact clearly explained what that standard is. The standard seems to be closely related to the tests in negligence, i.e. what standard would a reasonable producer maintain, but this disregards the requirement of the Directive that the producer should have strict liability for the defective product. The Directive provides some additional guidance by providing:

ARTICLE

A product is defective when it does not provide the safety which a person is entitled to expect, taking all circumstances into account including

a the presentation of the product;

b the use to which it could reasonably be expected that the product would be put;

c the time when the product was put into circulation.'

All of this needs to be considered against the background that the burden of proof is on the claimant and that the condition of the product is to be assessed not in terms of fitness for purpose but rather in terms of safety.

What will constitute a defect applying the test set out in s3, namely what persons are generally entitled to expect, has been extensively considered in the following cases.

CASE EXAMPLE

Abouzaid v Mothercare (UK) Ltd [2000] 12 WLUK 627

The claimant sustained a serious injury to his eye when attempting to fasten elastic straps to secure a sleeping-bag to a pushchair. As he was trying to fasten the buckle, the elastic slipped through his fingers and the buckle hit him in the eye. He claimed damages under the Consumer Protection Act.

The Court of Appeal considered the meaning of 'defective' and Lord Justice Pill concluded at 27:

JUDGMENT

'the product was defective within the meaning of the Act. . . . The product was defective because it was supplied with a design that permitted the risk [of an eye injury] to arise and without giving a warning that the user should not so position himself that the risk arose. Members of the public were entitled to expect better from the [defendants].'

The High Court had an opportunity to consider both of the meanings of s2 and s3. Most importantly Hinkinbottom J took time to provide guidance on the meaning of defect under s3 which has been much needed in this area.

CASE EXAMPLE

Wilkes v DePuy International [2016] EWHC 3096

The claimant underwent a hip replacement which involved a procedure to insert an artificial hip made up of metal components manufactured by the defendant. One component that made up the hip was a steel femoral shaft called a 'C-Stem'. Unfortunately, that stem fractured; and, when the artificial components were replaced, there was some evidence of metal debris having been shed around the joint. The claimant brought a claim under the CPA 1987 that the C-Stem component had a 'defect' in it, as defined in the Act, because its safety was not such as persons generally were entitled to expect.

Hinkinbottom J was of the view that previous authority in the area was not particularly clear in the area as he explained at 69 and 76–77:

JUDGMENT

'. . . the test for safety in this context requires an objective approach. Therefore, the relevant level of safety is not that which a particular patient considers the product should provide; nor even the level of safety which members of the public generally may consider it ought to provide. The level of safety is not assessed by reference to actual expectations of an actual or even a notional individual or group of individuals. Section 3(1) . . . defines "defect" in terms of "the safety of the product is not such as persons generally are *entitled* to expect . . ." [emphasis added]. That can only be a reference to an entitlement as a matter of law, not actual individual or even general expectation . . . In determining the level of safety which the public is entitled to expect in this sense, section 3 of the Act . . . requires "all circumstances" to be taken into account, "including" . . . "all relevant circumstances". . . . The circumstances which are relevant in a particular case is itself a matter of law. . . . The three specific matters set out in section 3(1)(a) are circumstances which must be considered . . . but they are clearly not intended to be an exhaustive list of relevant circumstances.'

In summary, applying the reformulated test, what then was the claimant entitled to expect in relation to the prosthetic hip as a matter of law? The circumstances that can be taken into account will vary from case to case depending on the facts concerned. In this case the following circumstances were considered:

- the product's risk-benefit assessment, costs – including the avoidability of the defect i.e. by adopting a different design;
- compliance with regulatory standards i.e. if met it would be difficult for the claimant to argue that a higher level of safety is required; and
- warning provided about the product's use.

Applying these circumstances to the facts, it was determined that there was not defect present in the prosthetic hip. Appropriate warnings were provided about the possibility of a fracture and the design was compliant with relevant standards and the benefits of this design outweighed any associated risks.

The clarity provided by this judgment has been welcomed as it has provided some much needed clarity in this area on the meaning of defect. This decision was closely followed by a decision from the Court of Appeal that also elaborated on the meaning and application of s3 of the CPA.

CASE EXAMPLE

Baker v KTM Sportmotorcycle UK Ltd & Anor [2017] EWCA Civ 378

The claimant bought a second-hand motorcycle that was manufactured by the defendant. The claimant was an experienced motorcyclist. A year after buying the motorcycle, the brakes failed and the claimant was thrown from the motorcycle and sustained injuries. The claimant argued that there was a defect in the motorcycle contrary to s3(1). At trial the court found in the favour of the claimant on the basis that the cause of the seizing of the brakes was galvanic corrosion which had happened as a result of a design defect combined with faulty construction or the use of inappropriate or faulty materials. The defendants appealed the decision on the basis that there was not sufficient evidence of the presence of a defect which caused the corrosion. They also argued that to prove his case Mr Baker had to show that there was a particular feature of the design or manufacture of the braking system which led to galvanic corrosion and that he had not done so. Lord Justice Hamblen held at 36 and 37:

JUDGMENT

'. . . it is not necessary to show how a defect was caused; it is sufficient to find that there is a defect. Here the defect found was a susceptibility for galvanic corrosion to develop in the brake system when it should not have done. There must have been a defect for the galvanic corrosion to develop as it did.'

This case serves as a further iteration of the way the CPA operates, namely that liability for damage or injury caused by a defect is strict. It is not necessary for the claimant to demonstrate *how* the defect was caused it is enough for the claimant to demonstrate the inference of a defect. This is to say, the claimant was riding a motorcycle, the brakes failed and he was injured. Other than arguing that the claimant had failed to maintain the motorcycle, there was no other explanation as to why the brakes failed other than the possibility of there being a defect in the design of motorcycle which allowed for galvanic corrosion.

CRITIQUING THE LAW

Consider the difficulties presented to a claimant in identifying the correct person or body to sue in cases of defective goods.

12.2.5 Defences

Compliance with legal requirements

A producer will not be liable for damage caused by goods which conform to mandatory statutory requirements under UK legislation (s4(1)(a)).

Goods not supplied in the course of business

The Act only applies where goods have been supplied in the course of business. Home-made goods on sale at charitable fairs are not covered by the Act although other law, such as the tort of negligence, may apply.

Defects arising after the date of supply

Common sense suggests that the producer should only be liable for defects in the goods at the time they are put into circulation. The Act reflects this in s4(1)(d). The defence is limited to defects arising after the date of supply so that there will be liability for defects existing at that time, even though the producer was unaware of them.

The 'state of the art' defence

By s4(1)(e) it is a defence to show:

SECTION

's4(1)(e) that the state of scientific and technical knowledge at the relevant time was not such that a producer of products of the same description as the product in question might be expected to have discovered the defect if it had existed in his products while they were under his control.'

This mirrors the 'state of the art' defence to allegations of negligence (Chapter 3).

It was thought by some that the defence went further than intended by the Directive but these fears were allayed by *European Commission v United Kingdom* (Case C-300/95 [1997] All ER (EC) 481). The European Court of Justice found that although the wording of the Act could be read to permit a subjective judgment, the issue of the state of scientific knowledge and its availability to the producer at the relevant time was capable of being decided objectively.

This does not mean that simply because there is some evidence available somewhere in the world that the producer will be expected to be aware of it. In many cases it will take time for research findings to circulate outside the country of origin and to be translated into an accessible language.

In essence, what the Act requires is that a producer is required to guard against foreseeable risks identified by the scientific and technical knowledge available at the relevant time.

CASE EXAMPLE

A v National Blood Authority [2001] EWHC 446 (QB)

The action was brought by 114 claimants who had been infected with hepatitis C when given blood transfusions or blood products produced by the defendants. The infection was caused by the use of infected blood after 1988. The virus was not identifiable until 1988 and a screening test was not generally available until 1991. Nonetheless the risk was known from 1988.

The defendant argued that there could be no liability as although the risk was known, the state of scientific knowledge at the time meant that there was no means of identifying whether or not blood was infected. The court rejected the argument holding that the 'state of the art' defence could not apply. The defendants knew of the risk and chose to supply the product in spite of it. The defendants must therefore take the consequences when injury resulted.

It is unnecessary to show that previous accidents had occurred. In *Abouzaid v Mothercare (UK) Ltd* [2000] EWCA Civ 348 Lord Justice Pill explained that a defect can be found to be 'present whether or not previous accidents had occurred'. He went on to say that 'Knowledge of previous accidents is not an ingredient necessary to a finding that a defect . . . is present.' It is in any event doubtful that 'a record of accidents comes within the category of "scientific and technical knowledge"'.

Contributory negligence

By s6(4) the Law Reform (Contributory Negligence) Act 1945 applies so blame can be apportioned between the producer and the person suffering damage.

12.2.6 Limitation of actions

The general rules discussed in Chapter 19 apply but are modified by the Consumer Protection Act 1987 which inserted a new section into the Limitation Act 1980. By s11A of the Limitation Act the limitation period for claims under the Consumer Protection Act for personal injury or damage to property runs for three years from the date of the damage or from the date on which it could reasonably have been discovered. In the case of latent damage, there is a long stop of ten years from the date the product was put into circulation. This means that if damage is not discovered until more than ten years have elapsed, no remedy can be obtained using the Consumer Protection Act. The usual discretion to extend the limitation period in the case of personal injury (Limitation Act 1980 s33) cannot be exercised to allow a claim after the end of the ten-year period.

12.2.7 A problem

We have seen that the European Directive was prompted in part by the thalidomide tragedy. It was hoped that the new law would enable people damaged by drugs to have a simple and effective remedy without the need to prove negligence. It has not worked out that way. There have been a number of multi-party actions brought when a drug has allegedly caused damage to a number of people. Cases have been brought against the manufacturers of benzodiazepine tranquillisers, the manufacturers of Seroxat and most recently the manufacturers of the MMR vaccine. All have foundered but not because the legal case has been lost. None of the cases has come to trial because legal aid, although initially granted, has been withdrawn. There appear to be two reasons why this has happened:

- the spiralling costs and the uncertain prospects of success in what would amount to test cases;
- the requirement that the action be launched within ten years of the goods coming onto the market which has meant that there may well be cause for suspicion as to the safety of the product but little actual evidence of any link between the product and the damage.

It seems that without reform of the funding for large multi-group actions and an easing of the limitation period, at least one of the groups intended to benefit from the law has in reality seen no benefit at all.

(For an interesting article on this issue, see Jon Robins, 'Why have they let us down?' *Independent Review*, 23 September 2003, p. 12.)

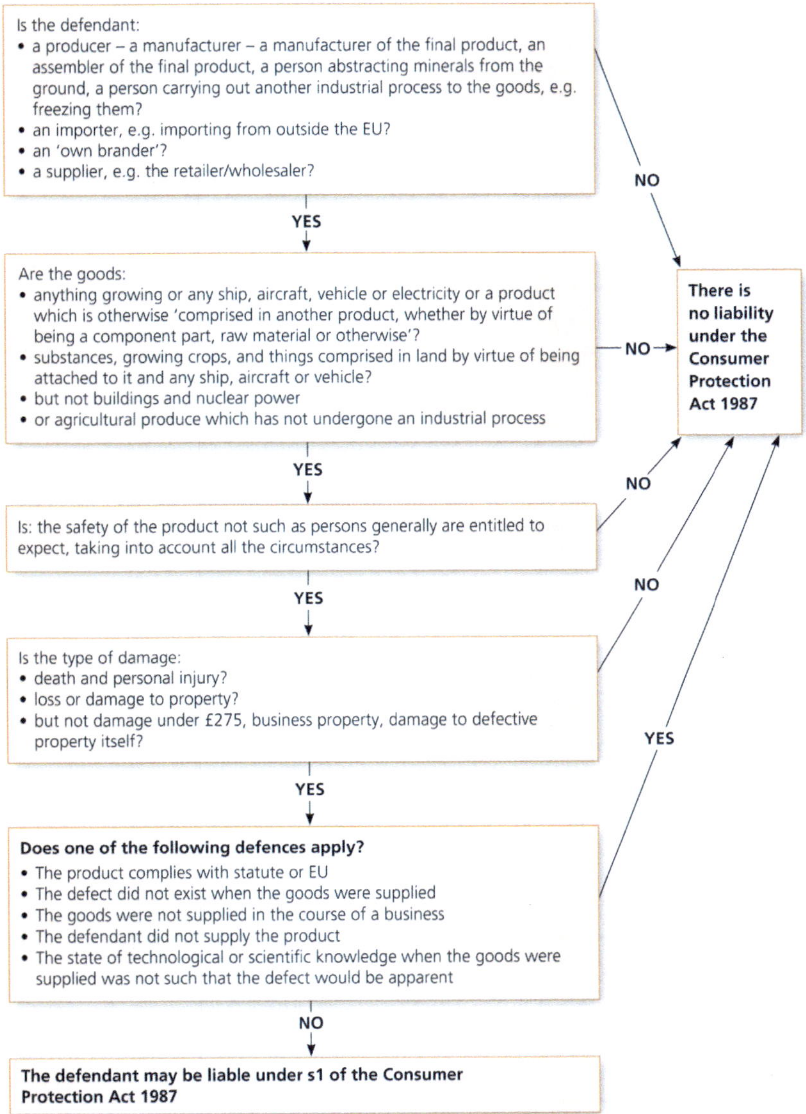

Figure 12.2 Product liability under s1 of the Consumer Protection Act 1987.

ACTIVITY

Self-assessment questions

1 What precisely is the 'narrow rule' derived from *Donoghue v Stevenson*?
2 Explain the difficulties faced by a claimant who seeks to rely on negligence for damages in respect of injuries caused by defective goods.
3 What is the purpose of Directive 85/374/EEC?
4 Explain precisely who may have liability for damage caused by defective products under the Consumer Protection Act 1987.

5 State the distinction drawn by the Act between compensation for personal injury and compensation for damage to property.
6 When will a product be regarded as 'defective' under the terms of the Act?
7 In the context of the 'state of the art' defence, what is the importance of *A v National Blood Authority*?

12.3 Interference with goods

12.3.1 Trespass to goods

Trespass to goods can be defined as any direct and intentional interference with goods in the possession of another without lawful authority.

Like other forms of trespass, the tort is actionable per se so that it is unnecessary to show that the goods have been damaged in any way or even that the owner has been permanently deprived of them.

Elements of the tort: direct and intentional

The act must be intentional in the sense that the person intended to do it. If this is the case, then the fact that the person mistakenly believed that he had the right to do so is irrelevant. In this sense the tort can be described as one of strict liability although damages are usually only nominal if no actual damage is done. Accidental interference will not amount to trespass but may amount to negligence. A person whose car or other property is damaged by the defendant's vehicle has to sue using negligence with its need to prove fault.

The act must also be direct; indirect damage may be actionable under some other tort, for example private nuisance or negligence.

Possession of goods

The essence of the tort is that there has been interference with a person's right to possess the goods. A person in actual possession, whether the owner or someone who has borrowed them, is able to bring an action against anyone who does not have a better legal title.

Interference

It has been seen that actual damage is not an essential element of the tort.

CASE EXAMPLE

Kirk v Gregory [1876] 1 ExD 55

Following the death of her brother-in-law the defendant moved jewellery belonging to the deceased to what she believed was a safer place. The jewellery was in fact stolen. It was held that the defendant was liable for trespass to goods by virtue of her act in moving the property.

There has been some debate as to whether or not a mere touching will suffice. Academic consensus appears to be that it will. The example given is that of a person who gently touches a museum exhibit without causing damage. To hold that mere touching is not enough would deprive the museum of any remedy.

Remedies

The remedies for trespass to goods are similar to those for the tort of conversion which is the subject matter of the next section of this chapter. For convenience, all remedies are dealt with later in section 12.3.4.

12.3.2 Conversion

Conversion (formerly known as 'trover') is now governed by the Torts (Interference with Goods) Act 1977 but the old common law rules are still very relevant.

Definition

The essence of the tort is: 'any dealing with another's property in a way which amounts to a denial of his right over it, or an assertion of a right inconsistent with his right, by wrongfully taking, detaining or disposing of it'. (S Deakin, A Johnston and B Markesinis, *Markesinis and Deakin's Tort Law* (5th edn, Oxford University Press, 2003), p. 438).

Quotation

Elements of the tort: the claimant's rights
The claimant must have title in the sense of:

- ownership;
- possession;
- an immediate right to possess;
- a lien or other equitable title.

Possession alone may be enough to found an action. An example occurs where goods are found. In such case, the finder will have an enforceable right to possession against everyone except someone with a better right.

CASE EXAMPLE

Armory v Delamirie [1721] 1 Stra 505

A chimney sweep's boy found a jewel. He took it to a jeweller for valuation and the jeweller refused to return it. The jeweller was liable for conversion.

CASE EXAMPLE

Parker v British Airways Board [1982] QB 1004

The claimant found a gold brooch on the floor of the executive lounge at Heathrow Airport. The Court of Appeal explained that the occupier of land upon which goods are found will have a better title than the finder if:

- the finder is a trespasser on the land;
- the property is in or attached to the land;

- the occupier of the land on which the property is found has prior to the finding 'manifested an intention to exercise control over the [land] and things which may be upon or in it'.

Although the defendants had a procedure for dealing with lost property and access to the lounge was restricted, this was not enough to establish intention to control the premises and things found on it. It was held that the claimant was entitled to the brooch.

Intention

The defendant must intend to do the act in question. As with trespass, it is not necessary for the defendant to intend to commit the tort. The fact that the defendant is unaware of the true facts will be no defence. An example occurs when an innocent person has acquired goods from a rogue who has no title to them. The true owner can sue the innocent party in conversion.

The act of conversion

An omission will not be enough; there must be an act of some sort which is inconsistent with the rights of the person in possession (from now on called the owner for the sake of brevity). The act must amount to a denial of title and may take many forms, for example:

- taking the goods;
- refusal to restore goods by a bailee on demand;
- wrongful delivery of goods to a third party;
- abuse of possession (for example, a bailee who delivers goods to the consignee after notice of stoppage in transit or changing a thing's character by making bread out of flour);
- destroying or disposing of the goods.

12.3.3 Defences to trespass and to conversion

Lawful authority

People who borrow books from a library have lawful authority for possession of that book provided they are a member. A person who takes possession of goods with the consent of the owner, for example as security for a debt, or pursuant to a court order, has lawful authority and is not liable for trespass. There will be liability for conversion if an act inconsistent with the extent of the authority is done.

Jus tertii

It is no defence for the defendant to show that another person has a better legal right to possession of the goods than the claimant. This caused problems where in fact this was the case and could leave the defendant facing two legal actions, one by the claimant and one by the person with a better title. To mitigate this difficulty the Torts (Interference with Goods) Act 1977 s8 enables a defendant to show that a named third party has a better right than the claimant. The rules of court enable directions to be given as to whether or not the third party should be joined as a party to the action.

12.3.4 Remedies

Retaking the goods

The owner can retake the goods from a person without a better title. This simple remedy may be helpful in some cases, but the owner needs to be wary of committing trespass to land in his efforts to retake the goods! The owner must act peaceably and use no more force than is reasonable in the particular circumstances.

It should be noted that a person onto whose land the goods have come is entitled to keep those goods until the owner pays for any damage done. Is this a possible remedy where cricket balls are hit on to land causing broken windows or other damage?

Damages: defendant no longer in possession

Where the defendant no longer has possession of the goods, damages will be for the value of the goods and any consequential loss which is not too remote.

CASE EXAMPLE

Bodley v Reynolds [1846] 8 QBD 779

A carpenter's tools were converted. He was awarded the value of the tools and an additional sum of £10 for his loss of earnings.

CASE EXAMPLE

Saleslease Ltd v Davis [1999] 1 WLR 1644

The test for remoteness of damage is whether or not the loss is reasonably foreseeable. The loss incurred by the claimant's inability to deliver the converted goods under a contract already concluded with a third party will be recoverable only if the defendant is aware of that contract.

Recently the courts have appeared to make a distinction in relation to consequential loss between those cases where the defendant acted dishonestly and those where he did not. In the former case, the defendant would be held liable for all the consequences which flowed directly and naturally from the wrongful conduct (*Kuwait Airways v Iraqi Airways (Nos 4 and 5)* [2002] 2 AC 883, HL).

Defendant in possession of the goods

By the Torts (Interference with Goods) Act 1977 s3 three orders are possible:

1. delivery of the goods and payment of any consequential damage;
2. delivery of the goods with the option for the defendant to pay damages made up of the value of the goods, in either case with the additional payment of damages for consequential loss;
3. damages.

While (1) will be ordered at the discretion of the court, the claimant can choose between (2) and (3). Generally the court will only order delivery of goods (specific restitution) where the goods are unique or of particular personal value to the claimant.

In some cases the value of the goods has been increased by the actions of the defendant. Where the defendant has acted honestly, believing that they have good title, the courts will generally allow the cost of improvements to be set against the value of the goods (Torts (Interference with Goods) Act 1977 s6).

ACTIVITY

Self-assessment questions

1 Define the tort of trespass to goods.
2 What precisely is meant by 'possession' in the context of the tort?
3 What is the essence of the tort of conversion?
4 Explain the principles which will guide the court in assessing damages for trespass to goods or conversion.

SAMPLE ESSAY QUESTION

Discuss the argument that the enactment of the Consumer Protection Act 1987 renders an action for product liability in negligence obsolete.

Identify the existence of a negligence action for defective products

- Derives from *Donoghue v Stevenson*
- A manufacturer of a product owes a duty of care to an end user or consumer of his products not to cause them harm

Discuss the essential elements for a successful claim

- The manufacturer owes the consumer a duty of care when the goods are received in the state that they left the manufacturer and there is no chance of an intermediate inspection of the goods
- The manufacturer has breached the duty of care by a failure in the manufacturing process or a failure to remedy a known defect in the goods
- The defect has caused foreseeable damage and there is no other possible cause of the damage

Identify the wider range of potential defendants under the Consumer Protection Act

- The consumer can sue producers – which includes manufacturers, people who assemble components, people who abstract minerals from the ground that go into making the product, people who carry out an industrial process etc.
- Suppliers
- Importers
- Own branders
- So can sue virtually anyone in the production and supply chain
- Which makes it more effective than negligence where the manufacturer was overseas

Discuss the range of defects and damage covered by the Act

- The consumer can sue for a defect in any goods which also includes a product comprised in another product
- Defect is defined as 'if the safety of the product is not such as persons generally are entitled to expect, taking into account all the circumstances'
- The Act covers death and personal injury and damage to property – but not small losses under £275, damage to business property, damage to the defective product
- So the Act is the same as negligence on the last but more restrictive on the first two

Discuss the range of available defences

- The product complies with EU or statutory requirements
- The defect did not exist when the product was supplied
- The product was not supplied in the course of a business
- The defendant did not supply the product
- The state of technological knowledge when the product was supplied
- So is possibly broader than that for negligence

KEY FACTS

Key facts on liability for defective goods

Liability for goods	**Case/statute**
Potential liability under Act as amended – generally remedy only available to buyer of goods.	Sale of Goods Act 1979
Liability in negligence dependent on ability to prove fault.	*Donoghue v Stevenson* [1932]; *Grant v Australian Knitting Mills* [1936]; *Evans v Triplex Safety Glass* [1938]
Consumer Protection Act 1987	**Case/statute**
Imposes liability where person injured by defective product.	s2(1)
Who may be liable	**Case**
Producer.	
Own-brander holding themselves out as producers of the goods.	
When goods imported into the EU with intent to supply them to another, the importer.	*G v Fry Surgical International Ltd* (unreported)
Supplier who fails to respond to request for information about producer or importer within reasonable time.	

(Continued)

(Continued)

Damage	Case
Includes death or personal injury.	
Damage to property where claim exceeds £275.	
Damage to the product excluded.	
Meaning of 'defect'	**Case/statute**
Product is defective if its safety is not what people generally are entitled to expect.	s3(1); *Wilkes v DePuy* (2016) EWHC 3096 (QB)
In deciding, all circumstances relevant but in particular: • marketing and instructions with product • what is reasonably likely to be done with the product • the time when it was supplied.	
Can be a design fault.	*Abouzaid v Mothercare (UK)* [2000]; *Baker v KTM Sportmotorcycle UK Ltd & Anor* [2017] EWCA Civ 378
Defences	**Case**
Compliance with legal requirements.	
Goods not supplied in the course of business.	
Defects arose after the date of supply.	
At the time the goods were put in circulation, scientific and technical knowledge was such that the producer could not be aware of the defect.	*A v National Blood Authority* [2001]
Limitation period	**Case**
Generally three years from the date of damage or date when it could reasonably have been discovered.	
Long stop of 10 years from date product was put into circulation.	

KEY FACTS

Key facts on interference with goods

Trespass to goods	Case
Direct and intentional interference with goods in possession of another.	
Actionable per se actual damage by defendant not necessary.	*Kirk v Gregory* [1876]
If act intended, it is no defence that defendant believed they had a right to the goods.	
Person in actual possession can sue all except someone with better legal right.	

(Continued)

(Continued)

Conversion	Case
Governed by Torts (Interference with Goods) Act 1977.	
Any dealing with another's property in such a way as to deny that person's rights in respect of the property.	
Person in actual possession can sue all except someone with better legal right.	*Armory v Delamirie* [1721]; *Parker v British Airways Board* [1982]
Dealing must be intended – no defence that defendant mistaken as to their rights.	
Defences to trespass and conversion	**Case**
Lawful authority.	
Jus tertii – right of a third party who has better title – court may direct third party to be joined to the action.	
Remedies	**Case**
Self-help by retaking the goods – acting peaceably and with no more force than necessary.	
Damages – value of goods if defendant no longer in possession together with consequential loss.	*Bodley v Reynolds* [1846]; *Saleslease v Davis* [1999]
Where defendant in possession court may order delivery of the goods and damages, claimant may ask for order for delivery with option for defendant to pay damages to make up value and to cover consequential loss or claimant may ask for damages alone.	
Where honest defendant has increased value of the goods cost of improvement generally allowed against value.	

SUMMARY

Liability for defective goods

- Consumers can recover compensation for damage caused by defective products through either negligence or the Consumer Protection Act 1987.
- In negligence the manufacturer of the goods owes a consumer a duty of care for defective goods that reach a consumer in the state that they left the manufacturer and there is no chance of any intermediate inspection.
- The Consumer Protection Act allows consumers to sue a wider range of defendants: producers, suppliers, importers, own-branders.
- The consumer can sue for a defect in any goods where 'the safety of the product is not such as persons generally are entitled to expect, taking into account all the circumstances'.
- Damages are possible for death and personal injury and damage to property but not small losses under £275, damage to business property or damage to the defective product.

- There are fixed defences: the goods comply with EU/statutory requirements; the defect did not exist when the product was supplied; the goods were not supplied in the course of a business; the defendant did not supply the product; the state of technological knowledge when the product was supplied was not such that the defendant could know of the defect.

Interference with goods

- Trespass to goods is the direct, immediate, intentional interference with personal property belonging to another.
- Conversion is now under the Torts (Interference with Goods) Act 1977 and involves ownership as well as possession – and it is the intentional, wrongful interference of a substantial nature with the claimant's possession or rights to possession, or dealing with the goods in a manner inconsistent with the rights of the owner.

Further reading

Eisler, J, 'One step forward and two steps back in product liability: The search for clarity in the identification of defects' (2017) *76(2) CLJ* 233–236.

Law Commission, *Product Liability*: https://lawcom.gov.uk/project/product-liability/.

Nolan, D, 'Strict product liability for design defects' (2018) *134 LQR* 176.

Smith, H, and Fotheringham, K, 'Exploring remedies for defective artificial intelligence aids in clinical decision making in post-Brexit England and Wales' (2022) *22(1) MLI* 33–51.

13

Trespass to the person

AIMS AND OBJECTIVES

After reading this chapter you should be able to:

- Explain the basic origins and character of trespass to the person
- Identify and distinguish the elements that are common to all forms of the tort
- Explain and apply the essential elements for proving assault
- Explain and apply the essential elements for proving battery
- Explain and apply the essential elements for proving false imprisonment
- Explain and apply the essential elements for proving an action for intentional indirect harm under *Wilkinson v Downton*
- Explain liability under the Protection from Harassment Act 1997
- Apply the law to factual situations and reach conclusions

13.1 The origins and character of trespass

13.1.1 Historical origins

Trespass was one of the two original forms of action (see section 1.1). The term has survived to the present day in the context of specific torts, one being trespass to the person. The essence of all modern forms of trespass can be found in the old idea that trespass was the appropriate remedy for any direct and forcible injury. As will be seen, trespass to the person relates to direct and forcible injury to the person. Before turning to the tort itself it is necessary to consider the legal meaning of:

- direct;
- forcible; and
- injury.

DOI: 10.4324/9781003202417-13

13.1.2 Direct

The traditional explanation of this word is that the injury must follow so closely on the act that it can be seen as part of the act. This is still true but perhaps implies that injuries caused by a car accident are also direct which is not legally the case. Such injuries are regarded as consequential. (For a more detailed discussion of this point see section 4.2.) As Lord Denning explained in *Letang v Cooper* [1964] 2 All ER 929, CA at 932:

JUDGMENT

'we divide the causes of action now according as the defendant did the injury intentionally or unintentionally. If one man intentionally applies force directly to another, the plaintiff has a cause of action in . . . trespass to the person . . . . If he does not inflict injury intentionally, but only unintentionally, the plaintiff has no cause of action today in trespass. His only cause of action is in negligence.'

This difficult proposition is easier to understand when the facts of the case are considered.

CASE EXAMPLE

Letang v Cooper **[1964] 2 All ER 929, CA**

While on holiday in Cornwall, Mrs Letang was sunbathing on a piece of grass where cars were parked. While she was lying there, Mr Cooper drove into the car park. He did not see her. The car went over Mrs Letang's legs injuring her. She claimed damages on the basis of both negligence and trespass to the person. It was agreed by both sides that the action in negligence was statute-barred, i.e. the action had not been commenced within the requisite three-year time limit. The question was therefore whether or not her claim could succeed in trespass to the person where the time limit of six years had not expired? Lord Denning explained at 932–934:

JUDGMENT

'If [the action] is intentional, it is the tort of assault and battery. If negligent and causing damage, it is the tort of negligence . . . [The plaintiff's] only cause of action here . . . (where the damage was unintentional), was negligence and not trespass to the person.'

The definitions of each of the three component parts of trespass to the person incorporate the word intentional as well as direct. The old meaning must, however, be understood if the rest of the law is to make any sense! These issues are discussed in more depth in Chapter 1.

13.1.3 Forcible

While the word itself conjures up a picture of force which causes or is capable of causing physical injury, in reality the law uses the term to describe any kind of threatened or actual physical interference with the person of another.

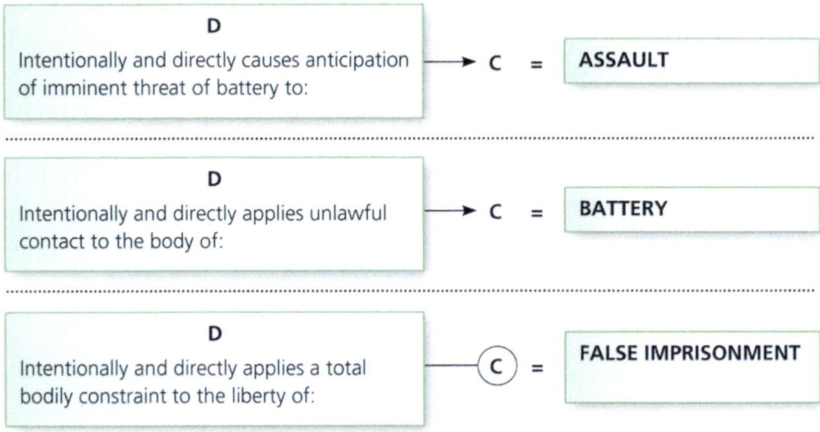

Figure 13.1 How liability is established in the different types of trespass to the person.

An unwanted kiss can be a trespass to the person (*R v Chief Constable of Devon & Cornwall, ex p CEGB* [1981] 3 All ER 826).

13.1.4 Injury

Given the explanation of forcible it comes as no surprise to learn that injury is interpreted widely and can include any infringement of personal dignity or bodily integrity. Actual physical harm is not an essential ingredient of trespass to the person although in many cases it may have occurred. The tort is actionable per se. In other words it is not necessary to prove actual damage. It is only necessary to prove that the actions of the defendant fulfil the requisite criteria.

13.1.5 The tort

Trespass to the person has three components which may occur together or separately. Each of itself gives rise to a cause of action. The components are:

- assault;
- battery;
- false imprisonment.

Assault and battery will each be defined and explained, the defences applicable to both these torts being considered together. False imprisonment will then be considered separately.

Trespass to the person can be committed in one of three ways (see Figure 13.1).

13.2 Assault

13.2.1 Definition

The tort can be defined in various ways. For example:

- 'The act of putting another person in reasonable fear or apprehension of an immediate battery by means of an act amounting to an attempt or threat to commit a battery amounts to an actionable assault' (R E V Heuston and R A Buckley, *Salmond and Heuston on the Law of Torts* (20th edn, Sweet & Maxwell, 1992), p. 127).

- 'Assault is an act of the defendant which causes the claimant reasonable apprehension of the infliction of a battery on him by the defendant' (W V H Rogers, *Winfield and Jolowicz on Tort* (16th edn, Sweet & Maxwell, 2002), p. 71).
- 'An assault is an act which causes another person to apprehend the infliction of immediate, unlawful, force on his person' (Goff LJ in *Collins v Wilcock* [1984] 3 All ER 374).

As will be seen, none of these definitions covers all the essential elements of the tort. A better definition is perhaps: an assault is some direct and intentional conduct by the defendant which causes the victim reasonably to fear that unlawful force is about to be used upon their person.

13.2.2 Ingredients of the tort

Direct and intentional

The words direct and intentional have the meaning discussed in section 13.1.

Conduct

Conduct in this context amounts to something which threatens the use of unlawful force. An obvious example is shaking a fist under someone's nose causing them to fear that they are about to be punched. In most cases it may be true that the assailant's actions clearly convey the necessary threat, but this is not always so.

In the modern world threats can be conveyed in many ways. Apart from physical action, the most obvious way is by means of a verbal threat. Traditionally, the use of threatening words alone could not amount to an assault (*R v Meade and Belt* [1823] 1 Lew CC 184). This may have been satisfactory in 1823 but in the twenty-first century there are other means of communication, for example by telephone and email. To the victim a verbal threat by these means may be just as credible as a gesture supported by threatening words. In criminal cases there has been recognition that words alone can indeed amount to an assault. In *R v Ireland* [1998] AC 147 the House of Lords held that silent telephone calls, sometimes accompanied by heavy breathing, could amount to a criminal assault. Lord Steyn, rejecting the proposition in *R v Meade and Belt*, said at 161:

JUDGMENT

'The proposition . . . that words can never suffice, is unrealistic and indefensible. There is no reason why something said should be incapable of causing an apprehension of immediate personal violence . . . Take now the case of the silent caller. He intends by his silence to cause fear and he is so understood. The victim is assailed by uncertainty about his intentions. Fear may dominate her emotions . . . She may fear the possibility of immediate personal violence. As a matter of law the caller may be guilty of an assault.'

Figure 13.2 Assault.

R v Ireland is of course a criminal case but it is very likely that if a civil action for assault based on words alone was to be brought, the decision would be that an assault had potentially been committed. Whether or not this would be the actual decision would depend on whether or not the other elements of the tort were satisfied.

Words can have the opposite effect by making it clear that the assailant does not intend to carry out the threat.

CASE EXAMPLE

Turberville v Savage [1669] 1 Mod Rep 3

The assailant put his hand on his sword and said 'If it were not assize-time, I would not take such language from you.' The victim alleged that he had been in fear that he was about to be attacked.

The statement was in fact a declaration by the assailant that he did not intend to attack the victim because the judges were in town. The intention as well as the act makes an assault.

Reasonable fear

The victim's fear that the threat is likely to be carried out must be reasonable. In part this depends on a subjective test which looks at the victim's perception of the situation. In *R v St George* [1840] 9 C & P 483 *Parke B* said:

JUDGMENT

'It is an assault to point a weapon at a person, though not loaded, but so near, that if loaded, it might do injury.'

The victim in such a case fears perfectly reasonably that he is about to be shot. If, however, the victim knew that the gun was unloaded, any fear would likely be held to be unreasonable.

It follows that the threat must be capable of being carried out at the time it is made. (In the case of telephone threats, the House of Lords in *R v Ireland* indicated that the fear should be that the assailant would be likely to turn up 'within a minute or two'.) What, however, would be the position if the defendant was to be prevented from carrying out the threat?

CASE EXAMPLE

Stephens v Myers [1830] 4 C & P 349

The claimant was acting as chair at a parish meeting and was seated at some distance from the defendant with other people seated between them. The meeting became angry and a majority decision was taken to expel the defendant. He said that he would rather pull the claimant out of the chair than be expelled and went towards him with a clenched fist. The defendant was stopped by other people before he was close enough actually to hit the claimant. The general opinion of others present was that the defendant would have hit the claimant had he not been stopped before he could do so.

The defendant was advancing in a threatening way so that had he not been stopped he would have hit his victim.

It is clear that Mr Stephens' perception that he was about to be hit was reasonable; at the time it was made, Mr Myers was in a position to carry it out. Where the assailant is not in such a position, the outcome may be different.

JUDGMENT

'if he was advancing with that intent, I think it amounts to an assault in law. If he was so advancing, that, within a second or two of time, he would have reached the plaintiff, it seems to me that it is an assault in law.'

Tindal CJ

CASE EXAMPLE

Thomas v National Union of Mineworkers (South Wales Area) [1985] 2 All ER 1

The claimant was a miner who continued to work during a particularly bitter strike by members of the NUM. The claimant and colleagues were bussed into work through a large crowd of striking miners who made threatening gestures and shouted threats at those on the bus.

For liability for assault to occur, there had to be the ability to carry out the threat at the time it was made. The crowd was kept away from the claimant and the others by a large number of police officers. They were also protected by being on a moving bus.

It seems therefore that ability to carry out the threat must exist at the time the threat is made. It has been seen, however, that this rule has been somewhat relaxed in the area of criminal law (*R v Ireland*). Whether this will enable the courts to devise an effective remedy for threats conveyed via email or the use of other technology remains to be seen. Abusive and threatening emails and text messages are being reported by the media as part of the growing problem of bullying in schools and the workplace. Perhaps it will not be long before this area of the law is reconsidered.

13.3 Battery

13.3.1 Definitions

Different definitions can be found in different sources. Thus:

- 'Battery is the intentional and direct application of force to another person' (W V H Rogers, *Winfield and Jolowicz on Tort* (16th edn, Sweet & Maxwell, 2002), p. 71).
- 'The application of force to the person of another without lawful justification' (R E V Heuston and R A Buckley, *Salmond and Heuston on the Law of Torts* (20th edn, Sweet & Maxwell, 1992), p. 125).
- 'Battery is the actual infliction of unlawful force on another person' (Goff LJ in *Collins v Wilcock*).

The problem is that none of these definitions covers all the requisite elements for liability. A better definition is where the defendant, intending the result and without lawful justification or the consent of the claimant, does an act which directly and physically affects the person of the claimant.

13.3.2 Ingredients of the tort

Intention

Life would be intolerable and the courts would be overloaded if every touch we received while going about our daily business was actionable. It is clear that the touching must be intentional if there is to be liability for battery, while non-intentional touching may amount to negligence. (See *Letang v Cooper* in section 13.1.2.) It must be remembered that it is the touching which must be intentional; it does not matter whether or not the defendant intended to cause injury although this may be relevant to the element of hostility discussed later in this section.

A problem can arise where the defendant intends to hit one person but misses and hits someone else. In such cases the doctrine of 'transferred malice' comes into play. The intention was to hit someone; the fact that the actual person hit was not the intended target is irrelevant.

CASE EXAMPLE

Livingstone v Ministry of Defence [1984] NI 356, NICA

A soldier in Northern Ireland fired a baton round targeting a rioter. He missed and hit the claimant instead. It was held that the soldier had intentionally applied force to the claimant.

Direct

The battery must be the direct result of the defendant's intentional act. This is easily seen when a punch or other form of physical touching occurs.

Case law dating back over the centuries shows just how widely the courts are prepared to stretch the meaning of direct.

CASE EXAMPLE

Gibbons v Pepper **[1695] 1 Ld Raym 38**

The defendant whipped a horse so that it bolted and ran down the claimant. The defendant was liable in battery for the claimant's injuries.

CASE EXAMPLE

Scott v Shepherd **[1773] 2 Wm Bl 892**

Shepherd threw a lighted squib into a market house. It landed on the stall of a ginger bread seller. To prevent damage to the stall, Willis picked it up and threw it across the market. Ryal, to save his own stall, picked it up and threw it away. It struck the claimant in the face and exploded, blinding him in one eye.

The defendant intended to scare someone although he did not intend to hurt the particular person who was actually injured. He was liable in battery, Willis and Ryal being held to be Shepherd's 'instruments'. W V H Rogers, *Winfield and Jolowicz on Tort* (16th edn, Sweet & Maxwell, 2002), p. 235 state that 'the law insists, and insists quite rightly, that fools and mischievous persons must answer for consequences which common sense would unhesitatingly attribute to their wrongdoing'.

CASE EXAMPLE

Pursell v Horn **[1838] 8 A & E 602**

The defendant threw water over the claimant. The force applied does not have to be personal contact and the defendant was liable in battery.

CASE EXAMPLE

Nash v Sheen **[1955] CLY 3726**

The claimant had gone to the defendant's hairdressing salon where she was to receive a 'permanent wave'. A tone rinse was applied to her hair, without her agreement, causing a skin reaction. The defendant was liable in battery.

Although, as the cases illustrate, the courts have been prepared to take a fairly wide view of what amounts to a direct touching, the one thing that does appear to be clear is that only a positive act will suffice. There is unlikely to be liability in battery for an omission.

CASE EXAMPLE

Innes v Wylie [1844] 1 Car & Kir 257

A policeman stood and blocked the claimant's entrance to a meeting of a Society from which the claimant had been banned. *Denman CJ* noted that:

JUDGMENT

'If the policeman was entirely passive like a door or a wall put to prevent the [claimant] from entering the room, and simply obstructing the entrance of the claimant, no assault has been committed on the claimant'.

Touching

Originally any touch however slight would amount to a battery. In *Cole v Turner* [1704] 6 Mod Rep 149 this appeared to have been qualified by Lord Holt when he said that 'the least touching in anger is a battery'. Does this mean that the touching, in addition to being intentional, must also be hostile?

Goff LJ, in *Collins v Wilcock* [1984] 3 All ER 374 (for facts see section 13.4.1), stated that 'the fundamental principle, plain and incontestable, is that every person's body is inviolate'. He went on to expound this by quoting from *Blackstone's Commentaries* in which Blackstone explained that the law cannot draw the line between different degrees of violence, and therefore totally prohibits the first and lowest stage of it; every man's person being sacred, and no other having a right to meddle with it, in any the slightest manner.

Goff LJ explained: 'a broader exception has been created . . . embracing all physical contact which is generally acceptable in the ordinary conduct of daily life'. While it may be a matter of personal opinion as to what constitutes generally acceptable conduct, it is clear from the judgment that actions such as tapping someone on the shoulder to gain their attention would not amount to a battery.

These relatively clear ideas were thrown into confusion in 1986 when the Court of Appeal seemed to prefer Lord Holt's explanation in *Cole v Turner*.

CASE EXAMPLE

Wilson v Pringle [1986] 2 All ER 440

A schoolboy admitted that he had pulled a bag which was over the shoulder of another boy. The other boy fell over and was injured. Summary judgment on the basis of battery was entered for the claimant, the defendant eventually appealing to the Court of Appeal. *Croom-Johnson LJ* at 447 explained that:

JUDGMENT

'it is not practicable to define a battery as "physical contact which is not generally acceptable in the ordinary conduct of daily life." In our view . . . there must be an intentional touching or contact in one form or another of the [claimant] by the defendant. That touching must be proved to be a hostile touching . . . Hostility cannot be equated with ill-will or malevolence. It cannot be governed by the obvious intention shown in acts like punching, stabbing or shooting. It cannot be solely governed by an expressed intention, although that may be strong evidence. But the element of hostility . . . must be a question of fact . . . It may be imported from the circumstances.'

In the event, the schoolboy's act of pulling the bag was merely a prank, the necessary element of hostility was lacking.

Wilson v Pringle created more questions than answers. The explanation given is not entirely helpful. It is still necessary to ask 'what does hostility mean?' The question was partially answered in *R v Brown* [1994] 2 All ER 75.

CASE EXAMPLE

R v Brown [1993] 2 All ER 75

The case concerned a group of sado-masochistic homosexuals who willingly cooperated in the commission of acts of violence against each other for sexual pleasure. The men were prosecuted for malicious wounding contrary to s20 Offences Against the Person Act 1861. The equivalent civil action would be based in battery. Following their conviction, the case reached the House of Lords where one of the issues considered was whether or not hostility on the part of the inflictor of an injury was an essential ingredient for battery.

Having seemingly approved the view in *Collins v Wilcock [1984]* 1 WLR 1172 that hostility could not be equated with ill-will or malevolence, Lord Jauncey at 90 went on to say that if the appellants' actions:

JUDGMENT

'were unlawful they were also hostile and a necessary ingredient of [malicious wounding] was present'.

It seems therefore that if the touching is unlawful, then it is hostile. As will be seen in the next part of this chapter, lawful authority in a variety of forms is a full defence to the tort. *R v Brown*, although a criminal case, appears to go some way to providing an explanation of when a touching will be regarded as hostile.

The question remains, however – is a hostile intent necessary in order to establish liability? Where does this leave medical treatment which has been given against the wishes of a patient? Doctors after all act with the intention of doing good for their patients. The issues raised by medical cases will be discussed in the next part of this chapter.

13.4 Defences to assault and battery

These are dealt with in one section as the same defences are available to each tort.

13.4.1 Lawful authority

If a person committing assault and/or battery has legal authority for the action, there can be no liability for that act. Statute gives two groups such authority.

Police officers

The powers of police officers are found in statute and, provided an officer acts within the scope of those powers, there can be no complaint for trespass to the person. If, however, the action goes beyond what is permitted, a police officer may be liable in the civil courts in the same way as any other person.

CASE EXAMPLE

Collins v Wilcock [1984] 3 All ER 374

A police officer needed to obtain a woman's name and address in order to caution her for soliciting for the purpose of prostitution. The officer detained the woman by holding her by the elbow. The woman scratched the police officer and was charged with assaulting a constable in the execution of her duty. The question was whether the police officer was acting lawfully when she held the woman's elbow to detain her. At 380 Goff LJ highlighted:

JUDGMENT

'The fact is that the [police officer] took hold of the [woman] by the left arm in order to restrain her. In so acting she was not proceeding to arrest the [woman]; and since her action went beyond the generally acceptable conduct of touching a person to engage his or her attention, it must follow . . . that her action constituted a battery on the [woman], and was therefore unlawful.'

Reasonable force may be used to make an arrest (Criminal Justice Act 1967 s3). What is reasonable depends on the facts. The general rule is that the force must be proportionate to the crime being prevented. The use of lethal force will seldom be necessary and might be thought to be a breach of Article 2 of the European Convention on Human Rights. In *McCann, Farrell and Savage v UK* [1995] 21 EHRR 97, ECtHR, arising from the deaths of three IRA suspects killed by members of the SAS in Gibraltar, it was accepted that lethal force can be used provided it is reasonably justifiable.

Health professionals treating people with mental illness

The Mental Health Act 1983 permits treatment for mental disorder to be given to patients who have been compulsorily detained using powers granted by the Act. By s63, treatment may be given without the consent of the patient, the Act including additional safeguards for extreme treatment such as psychosurgery and electro-convulsive therapy. Treatment otherwise than for the mental disorder is governed by the same rules which protect people who do not suffer from mental disorder.

13.4.2 Consent

If the claimant consents to the actions of the defendant, the claimant has no cause of action. Consent may be express or implied. It can be argued that there is implied consent to the jostling which occurs in a packed train during the rush-hour.

Sport

A person who takes part in a contact sport such as soccer, rugby or boxing consents to the touching that occurs when the sport is played according to the rules.

CASE EXAMPLE

Simms v Leigh Rugby Football Club [1969] 2 All ER 923

A broken leg resulted from a tackle during a rugby game.

By voluntarily taking part in a contact sport, players consent to touching which occurs provided it is within the rules of the game. In this case the tackle had been lawful therefore no battery had occurred.

If the touching is not permitted within the rules of the sport, then it is unlawful. The victim has not consented and the assailant may be liable for trespass to the person.

Medical treatment

For consent to be effective in relieving the defendant of liability, it must be real. The victim must understand what it is they are consenting to and the consent must be freely given. *J Cardoza Schloendorff v Society of New York Hospital* [1914] 211 NY 125, at 126I: 'Every human being of adult years and sound mind has a right to determine what shall be done with his own body, and a surgeon who performs an operation without his patient's consent, commits an assault.'

A person with capacity has an absolute right to give or withhold consent to treatment. In *Re T (Adult: Refusal of Treatment)* [1992] 4 All ER 649 Lord Donaldson MR said at 662:

JUDGMENT

'the patient's right of choice exists whether the reasons for making that choice are rational, irrational, unknown or even non-existent. That his choice is contrary to what is to be expected of the vast majority of adults is only relevant if there are other reasons for doubting his capacity to decide.'

This can give rise to some very difficult questions for health professionals as is shown in the case of Ms B.

CASE EXAMPLE

Ms B v An NHS Hospital Trust [2002] EWHC 429 (Fam)

Ms B was completely paralysed, able to move her head very slightly and to speak. She was being kept alive on a ventilator and had no hope of any recovery. She faced the rest of her life like this and informed those caring for her that she wanted the ventilator turned off. She was effectively saying that she withdrew her consent to the treatment. The doctors who had been caring for her for over a year found it impossible to accept her decision and argued that she lacked capacity to make her own decisions. Ms B sued for a declaration that she had the necessary capacity and that her continued treatment was a trespass to her person.

Having heard detailed evidence from the medical point of view and from psychiatrists who had examined Ms B as to her mental capacity, the judge, Dame Elizabeth Butler-Sloss P, said at 95:

JUDGMENT

'I am . . . entirely satisfied that Ms B is competent to make all relevant decisions about her medical treatment including the decision whether to seek to withdraw from artificial ventilation. Her mental competence is commensurate with the gravity of the decision she may wish to make.'

The defendants were therefore liable for trespass during the time Ms B had been treated against her will and a small sum by way of damages for battery was awarded. (Ms B was transferred to another hospital where her decision was respected and she died a few weeks later.)

On reading the facts of this case, there must be some sympathy for the doctors who knew that Ms B would die if they respected her refusal of treatment. This is an extreme example of the dilemma which is frequently faced by health professionals. Every case will depend on its own particular facts but some principles to assist in making decisions can be found in case law.

The fact that a person is suffering from mental disorder does not of itself mean that they lack capacity. The Mental Health Act 1983 only permits treatment without consent for the actual mental illness.

CASE EXAMPLE

Re C (Adult: Refusal of Treatment) [1994] 1 WLR 290

Mr C, suffering paranoid schizophrenia, was a patient in Broadmoor and unlikely to be well enough to be released from hospital. He developed gangrene in 1993 and the doctors believed that unless his foot was amputated, he would die. He applied for an injunction to prevent amputation then or at any time in the future. It was held that despite his illness, the court was satisfied that Mr C sufficiently understood the nature, purpose and effects of the proffered operation'.

JUDGMENT

The judge approved the test set out by the Law Commission (para. 2.20 Law Commission Consultation Paper No. 129 Mentally Incapacitated Adults and Decisions Making), namely:

- Does the patient understand and retain treatment information?
- Does the patient believe it?
- Can the patient weigh the information in the balance to make a choice?

The injunction was granted. Mr C in fact survived as the gangrene was successfully treated by other means.

Where a person genuinely lacks capacity to make their own decisions treatment will be lawful if it is in that person's best interests.

CASE EXAMPLE

Airedale NHS Trust v Bland [1993] 1 All ER 821

Tony Bland was in a persistent vegetative state and unlikely ever to improve. His brain stem continued to function but he had to be fed by artificial means. His parents and those caring for him wished to discontinue artificial feeding which had the inevitable consequence that he would die.

Goff LJ explained at 869:

JUDGMENT

'The question is whether it is in the best interests of the patient that his life should be prolonged by the continuance of this form of medical treatment or care.'

Lord Lowry took the view at 877:

JUDGMENT

'if it is not in the interests of an insentient patient to continue the life supporting care and treatment, the doctor would be acting unlawfully if he continued the care and treatment'.

Lord Browne Wilkinson argued at 883:

JUDGMENT

'the initial question is "whether it is in the best interests of Antony Bland to continue the invasive medical care." . . . This is a question for the doctor.'

The unanimous decision of the House of Lords was that the treatment, which was not in the best interests of Tony Bland, could lawfully be withdrawn.

Once capacity is established, then the patient must be given the information needed to make the decision, whether it is to have travel immunisation or to undergo major surgery. In the case of *Chatterton v Gerson* [1981] 1 All ER 257, Bristow J said at 265:

JUDGMENT

'In my judgment once the patient is informed in broad terms of the nature of the procedure which is intended, and gives her consent, that consent is real.'

It must be remembered that an action will only lie in assault or battery where there has been no consent, whether from the patient, the court or a person authorised by the patient to make decisions on their behalf. Failure to ensure that the patient is given sufficient information does not negate the consent which may have been given but may give rise to an action in negligence.

Consent can only be valid if it results from the exercise of free will. Coercion, whether by a relative or a health professional, will mean that the decision is invalid.

CASE EXAMPLE

Re T (Adult: refusal of medical treatment) **[1992] 4 All ER 649**

T had been seriously injured and required a caesarean section. She signed a form refusing a blood transfusion. Her condition deteriorated and a transfusion became necessary. At 662 Lord Donaldson MR said:

JUDGMENT

'the patient is . . . entitled to receive and indeed invite advice and assistance from others in reaching a decision . . . It is wholly acceptable that the patient should have been persuaded by others of the merits of such a decision . . . It matters not how strong the persuasion was, so long as it did not overbear the independence of the patient's decision.'

On the facts, the court held that T's decision was the result of over-persuasion by her mother. Her refusal of a transfusion was invalid.

13.4.3 Necessity

Trespass to the person may be justified where it is essential to prevent harm to others, for example pulling someone back from the path of a speeding car.

It may also be used in medical cases to justify treatment of a person without capacity. A health professional is entitled to do all that is necessary to deal with an emergency if a person is, for example, unconscious and there is nothing to indicate that the proposed treatment would be refused.

It is clear that this defence may overlap with the 'best interests' approach described in section 13.4.2 where the patient permanently lacks capacity.

CASE EXAMPLE

F v West Berkshire Health Authority [1989] 2 All ER 545

F, aged 36, had serious mental disability and the mental capacity of a child of four. She had formed a sexual relationship with another patient. The concern was that pregnancy would be disastrous for her and contraception was out of the question. Her doctors sought a declaration from the court that an operation for her sterilisation would be lawful. At 565–566 Goff LJ remarked:

JUDGMENT

'to fall within the principle [of necessity] not only (1) must there be a necessity to act when it is not practicable to communicate with the assisted person, but also (2) the action taken must be such as a reasonable person would in all the circumstances take, acting in the best interests of the assisted person . . .[I]n the case of a mentally disordered person . . . action properly taken . . . may extend to include such humdrum matters as routine medical or dental treatment, even simple care such as dressing and undressing and putting to bed.'

It was held that it was in F's best interests to be able to maintain the sexual relationship and thus, under the doctrine of necessity, the operation for sterilisation should take place to protect her from a possible pregnancy.

13.4.4 Parental authority

Despite the continuing debate over whether or not corporal punishment ought ever to be inflicted on a child, a parent will not be liable for assault or battery if the force used is by way of reasonable chastisement. The child must understand the purpose of the punishment, which must be proportionate to the wrong committed by the child.

The defence is only available to a parent. In *A v United Kingdom, The Times*, 1 October 1998 it was held by the Court of Human Rights that Article 3 of the Convention on Human Rights prohibited caning of a child by a step-parent on the basis that it amounted to 'inhuman and degrading treatment'.

As the debate about corporal punishment continues, it will be interesting to see whether the protection of Article 3 is extended to corporal punishment by parents. The Scottish Parliament has debated a Bill to outlaw smacking of young children by their parents but this foundered in part on the difficulty of defining what amounts to 'smacking' and on difficulties of enforcement.

13.4.5 Self-defence

The use of reasonable force to effect an arrest has been discussed above at section 13.4.1 and the rules are similar. Anyone is entitled to use reasonable force in self-defence or to protect others. The force used must be proportionate to the danger.

CASE EXAMPLE

Cockcroft v Smith [1705] 11 Mod 43

There was a scuffle in court between a lawyer and a clerk. The clerk thrust his fingers towards the lawyer's eyes so the lawyer promptly bit off one of the clerk's fingers. This was held not to be a proportionate response to the threat!

Whether or not the force used is proportionate is a question of fact. A recent criminal case has aroused a lot of discussion after a farmer, Tony Martin, was found guilty of manslaughter when he shot a burglar in the back from the top of the stairs. The jury was satisfied that this was a disproportionate response to the threat. In a similar case, *Revill v Newbery* [1996] 1 All ER 291, an allotment holder, fed up with frequent thefts from his allotment, was found to have used disproportionate force when he shot a thief through a hole which he had drilled in a shed.

The use of force in response to words is unlikely to be reasonable unless the words convey an immediate and real threat of the use of force.

CASE EXAMPLE

Lane v Holloway [1967] 3 All ER 129

A poor relationship existed between neighbours and when one came home drunk and rowdy, the woman next door told him to be quiet. He replied 'Shut up you monkey-faced tart.' This led to an argument between the neighbour and the woman's husband. The neighbour made a friendly and ineffectual shove at the husband who responded by beating him so badly that he needed 18 stitches for facial injuries. The beating was not a proportionate response to the drunken neighbour's gestures.

The defence can be raised in both criminal assaults and civil. However, there is a difference in approach between the criminal law and the civil law.

CASE EXAMPLE

Ashley v Chief Constable of Sussex Police [2008] UKHL 25

An armed police officer shot and killed a man during a raid on a house although the man was in fact not armed. He was initially charged with manslaughter but this was dropped. The man's father brought an action in assault and battery and the police claimed that the officer had acted in self-defence. It was held that the defence could not apply where it was based on facts that did not in fact exist and were unreasonably if honestly held because of things that had been said in briefings before the raid. This contrasts with the criminal law where the defence may have been available in the circumstances.

ACTIVITY

Self-assessment questions

1 Explain the importance of the judgment in *Letang v Cooper*.
2 Give a definition of
   a assault;
   b battery.
3 State precisely what is meant by the requirement of 'intention'.
4 Is hostile intent necessary to establish liability for battery?
5 Explain the criteria by which the courts will decide whether or not a person has capacity to give consent to medical treatment.

13.5 False imprisonment

13.5.1 Definition

False imprisonment occurs when a person is unlawfully restrained (whether by arrest, confinement or otherwise) or prevented from leaving any place.

The meaning of false imprisonment was considered by the Supreme Court in the case of *Jalloh*.

CASE EXAMPLE

R (on the application of Jalloh (formerly Jollah)) (Respondent) v Secretary of State for the Home Department (Appellant)

The claimant had been placed under an unlawful curfew after being released from a detention centre. The claimant was awarded damages for false imprisonment. The Secretary of State appealed on the basis that although the curfew was unlawful, this did not qualify as false imprisonment at common law and if it did, the common law concept of imprisonment should be modified and aligned with the more demanding concept of deprivation of liberty under article 5 of the ECHR. The Supreme Court dismissed the appeal stating that to restrict the classic understanding of imprisonment at common law to the very different and much more nuanced concept of deprivation of liberty under the ECHR would be a retrograde step. The Strasbourg court has needed to draw a distinction between the deprivation and the restriction of physical liberty. There is no need for the common law to draw such a distinction and every reason for the common law to continue to protect those whom is has protected for centuries against unlawful imprisonment, whether by the State or private persons. It is therefore possible for there to be false imprisonment without there being a deprivation of liberty under article 5.

13.5.2 Ingredients of the tort

Restraint

The restraint must be total. If there is a reasonable means of escape, the restraint cannot amount to false imprisonment.

CASE EXAMPLE

Bird v Jones [1845] 7 QB 742

Part of Hammersmith Bridge was closed off for seating to watch a regatta. Mr Bird insisted on walking on that part of the Bridge and climbed into the enclosure. He was prevented from getting out at the other end. There was nothing to stop him from going back the way he had come and crossing the Bridge on the other side which had not been closed off. Coleridge J at 744.

JUDGMENT

'A prison may have its boundary large or narrow, visible and tangible, or, though real, still in the conception only; it may be moveable or fixed: but a boundary it must have; and that boundary the party imprisoned must be prevented from passing.'

The claimant was not imprisoned as he was free to leave by the way he had entered.

It can be seen from this judgment that imprisonment need not be supported by physical barriers. A police officer who unlawfully tells someone that they are under arrest may be liable even if he does not touch the victim. The victim is not expected to risk being arrested should they try to escape. The detention in such circumstances is in 'conception only' but is nonetheless real. In fact a police cordon was held to be false imprisonment in *Austin v Commissioner of Police for the Metropolis* [2005] EWHC 480 (QB) (although in the case it was justified for the protection of others).

Surprisingly, false imprisonment can occur even if the victim is unaware of it at the time.

CASE EXAMPLE

Meering v Grahame-White Aviation Co Ltd [1919] 122 LT 44

The claimant was suspected of stealing paint. He was taken to a waiting room where he was told that he was needed to give evidence. He agreed to stay. Unknown to him, the works police had been told not to let him leave and waited outside the room to prevent him from doing so. The Metropolitan Police arrived and he was arrested. He claimed that he had been falsely imprisoned for the hour he had waited. Lord Atkin at 1507 commented:

JUDGMENT

'it appears to me that a person could be imprisoned without his knowing it. I think a person can be imprisoned while he is asleep, while he is in a state of drunkenness, while he is unconscious, and while he is a lunatic.'

The issue of knowledge was also considered in *Murray v Ministry of Defence* [1988] 2 All ER 521.

CASE EXAMPLE

Murray v Ministry of Defence [1988] 2 All ER 521

A woman's home was entered and searched in connection with terrorist matters. She knew the purpose of the visit but was not actually arrested until she left the house 30 minutes later. It was unclear whether or not she was aware that she was being detained throughout the period before the arrest.

Lord Griffiths at 528–529, while accepting that she was probably aware of her detention, said that it is not:

JUDGMENT

'an essential element of the tort of false imprisonment that the victim should be aware of the fact of denial of liberty . . . If a person is unaware that he has been falsely imprisoned and has suffered no harm, he can normally expect to recover no more than nominal damages.'

It is clear that the judges place great importance on the protection of the liberty of an individual. *Murray v MOD* was a case concerning terrorism in Northern Ireland. The Northern Irish Court of Appeal had been happy to conclude that there had been no false imprisonment, the House of Lords disagreed.

Intentional act

Until recently there was some doubt as to whether the detention had to be intentional or if negligence would suffice. In *Sayers v Harlow Urban District Council* [1958] 1 WLR 623 a woman who was accidentally locked into a cubicle in a ladies' toilet was held not to have been falsely imprisoned. However this view has changed, the House of Lords holding that false imprisonment is a tort of strict liability, thus intention is immaterial.

CASE EXAMPLE

R v Governor of Brockhill Prison, ex p Evans (No 2) [2000] 4 All ER 15

Ms Evans was sentenced to two years' imprisonment but had spent time in custody prior to sentence. This time entitled her to a reduction of the actual period spent in prison. Using Home Office guidelines, her release date was calculated as 18 November 1996. Judicial review established that the guidelines were wrong and her release date should have been 17 September 1996. The House of Lords held that she had been falsely imprisoned between those dates as false imprisonment is a tort of strict liability. Its consequences cannot be escaped even when, as in this case, the defendant had acted in line with law accepted as correct at that time.

In contrast in the following case it was not false imprisonment when a prisoner was restricted to his cell during an unofficial strike by prison officers.

CASE EXAMPLE

Iqbal v Prison Officers Association [2010] QB 732

A prisoner complained that he had been falsely imprisoned when he had been kept in his cell for six hours during a strike by prison officers and would normally have not been locked in his cell during those hours. The Court of Appeal dismissed his claim on the basis that the strike involved an omission not a positive act and therefore could be contrasted with the *Brockhill Prison* case.

Lord Neuberger MR stated at 23:

JUDGMENT

'a prisoner is no longer lawfully in the custody of a prison governor once his term of imprisonment expires: ergo he has a right, as against the prison governor, to be released, and it would therefore be unlawful for the governor not to release him. Once his term of imprisonment has expired a prisoner has an absolute right to leave prison, whereas . . . the claimant had no right to leave the Prison, and he had no even arguable right to leave his cell save if permitted by the Governor.'

13.5.3 Defences

Reasonable condition for release

A person is entitled to impose a reasonable condition for the release of the claimant. This may be a question of fact, as in *Robinson v Balmain New Ferry Co Ltd* [1910] AC 295 when the Privy Council held it was reasonable for a charge of 1d to be made when a passenger changed his mind about waiting for a ferry and wanted to leave. He would have had to pay a similar sum had he completed his journey.

The facts of *Robinson v Balmain* are perhaps unlikely to recur with any frequency. A more likely scenario in *Herd v Weardale Steel, Coal and Coke Co Ltd* [1915] AC 67 held that reasonable contractual provision could amount to a defence.

CASE EXAMPLE

Herd v Weardale Steel, Coal and Coke Co Ltd [1915] AC 67

A miner went underground at 9.30 a.m. for a shift ending at 4 p.m. After a dispute he demanded to be raised to the surface at about 11 a.m. He was in fact raised at about 1.30 p.m.

The House of Lords held his only right to be raised was at the end of his shift or in emergency. It mattered not that the cage could have been used before then as indeed happened. The House of Lords pointed out at 73: 'There were facilities [to raise him] but they were facilities which, in accordance with the conditions that he had accepted by going down, were not available to him until the end of his shift.'

Lawful arrest

A lawful arrest made in accordance with the Police and Criminal Evidence Act 1984 s24(4), as amended by the Serious Organised Crime and Police Act 2005 s110, cannot amount to false imprisonment. A police officer or private citizen who acts within the provisions will not be liable. A private citizen making a citizen's arrest should be wary as a private citizen only has protection if an arrestable offence has actually been or is being committed by the person arrested and the police have been speedily involved. Store detectives are particularly vulnerable.

CASE EXAMPLE

White v W P Brown [1983] CLY 972

A woman was locked up for 15 minutes by a store detective. This amounted to false imprisonment.

A police officer does not lose the protection if the arrest is mistaken, provided the arrest was reasonable in all the circumstances.

Detention for medical purposes

The Mental Health Act 1983 provides for the lawful detention of persons suffering from mental disorder. The provisions of the Act must be scrupulously followed as breach can mean that false imprisonment has occurred. This has caused difficulties where a person has been clearly ill and in need of treatment which can only be provided in hospital but whose illness does not meet the necessary criteria for compulsory detention. In *R v Bournewood Community and Mental Health NHS Trust, ex p L* [1999] AC 458 the House of Lords held that in such a case, the common law doctrine of necessity would apply to render the detention lawful. The case was then taken to the European Court of Human Rights as *HL v United Kingdom* (Application No. 45508/99) [2004]. The court found that the reasoning of the House of Lords could not stand and this provision of the Mental Health Act 1983 breached the applicant's rights under Article 5(1) of the European Convention on Human Rights.

The Mental Incapacity Act 2005 contains a provision that will ensure that all patients detained in a psychiatric hospital will have the right to challenge the legality of their detention by application to a Mental Health Review Tribunal.

Powers to detain persons suffering from physical disease also exist. The Public Health (Control of Disease) Act 1984, subject to strict safeguards, permits the removal to and detention in hospital of a person suffering from a notifiable disease.

Montgomery refers to a case where a person suffering from AIDS and 'bleeding copiously' was prevented, by court order under powers in the 1984 Act, from discharging himself from hospital. By the time the appeal was heard, the danger was past and the order was no longer needed, but the initial order was not criticised by the appeal court (J Montgomery, *Healthcare Law* (2nd edn, Oxford University Press, 2003), p. 35).

ACTIVITY

Self-assessment questions

1 Give a definition of 'false imprisonment'.

2 Consider whether the judgment in *R v Governor of Brockhill Prison*, ex p Evans means that false imprisonment should be regarded as a tort of strict liability.

13.6 Intentional indirect harm and protection from harassment

Trespass to the person deals with direct harm which is intentionally caused while negligence deals with direct harm which is caused unintentionally. This leaves a gap. What about the situation where harm is caused intentionally but indirectly? Nothing discussed so far in this chapter covers this situation. It would be wrong if a person were able to escape liability for harm which is caused intentionally but indirectly. The gap is partly filled by old law relating to wrongful interference and by the modern statute, the Protection from Harassment Act 1997.

13.6.1 Acts intended to cause harm

The law in this area is not very clear but it seems that a person who acts intentionally with the result that injury is indirectly caused, whether or not the injury is intentional, may be liable.

CASE EXAMPLE

Wilkinson v Downton [1897] 2 QB 57

The defendant, as a practical joke, told the claimant that he had been sent to tell her that her husband had been involved in an accident. Her husband as a result was lying in a public house with two broken legs. She was told that she was to take a cab to bring him home. As a result of this 'prank' the claimant suffered a violent shock causing serious physical consequences which threatened her reason. Her illness involved her husband, who was in reality at all times in the best of health, in substantial expense. Wright J held that a person who 'wilfully [does] an act calculated to cause physical harm to the [claimant] ie to infringe her right to personal safety and has thereby in fact caused physical harm' is liable if there is no justification for the act. 'This wilful injury is in law malicious, although no malicious purpose to cause the harm which was caused, nor any motive of spite, is imputed to the defendant.'

It must be noted that there was an acceptance by the judges that the defendant very probably had no intention of causing anything other than a laugh by his actions. The consequences were not intended by him nor could there be any liability for negligence. Despite its lack of clarity, the judgment was approved in the later case of *Janvier v Sweeney* [1919] 2 KB 316.

CASE EXAMPLE

Janvier v Sweeney [1919] 2 KB 316

During the First World War, a woman was told by a caller that he was a detective representing the military authorities and that she was the woman they wanted as she was suspected of corresponding with a German spy. She was extremely frightened and as a result suffered nervous shock, being ill for a prolonged period of time.

In the Court of Appeal it was held that the defendant was liable. Stating that this was a much stronger case than *Wilkinson v Downton*, Duke LJ acknowledged that in this case the defendant's intention was to terrify the victim for the purpose of obtaining an unlawful object.

The law was nonetheless left in a state of some confusion. Does the defendant's act have to be calculated to cause harm? Does actual physical or psychiatric harm need to result from the act? The issue has been further considered by the Court of Appeal in *Wong v Parkside Health NHS Trust and another* [2001] EWCA Civ 1721.

CASE EXAMPLE

Wong v Parkside Health NHS Trust and another [2001] EWCA Civ 1721

The claimant alleged harassment against her by three fellow employees and an inadequate response by the employer. One of the issues considered was the precise scope of the tort of intentionally causing harm.

Reviewing the authorities Lady Justice Hale considered whether actual injury needed to be established and whether there needed to be intention to cause injury. She stated at 12:

JUDGMENT

'for the tort to be committed . . . there has to be actual damage. The damage is physical harm or recognised psychiatric illness. The defendant must have intended to violate the claimant's interest in his freedom from harm. The conduct complained of has to be such that that degree of harm is sufficiently likely to result so that the defendant cannot be heard to say that he did not "mean" it to do so. He is taken to have meant it to do so by the combination of the likelihood of such harm being suffered as a result of his behaviour and his deliberately engaging in that behaviour.'

It seems therefore that for the tort to be established it must be proved:

1 that the defendant intended to infringe the claimant's 'right to personal safety' (*Wilkinson v Downton*) or 'interest in his freedom from harm' (*Wong v Parkside Health NHS Trust*); and
2 that actual injury, physical or psychiatric, occurred as a result.

This has subsequently been confirmed by the House of Lords.

CASE EXAMPLE

Wainright v Home Office [2004] AC 406; [2003] UKHL 53

The claimants, a mother and her son (who suffered from cerebral palsy and arrested development), went to prison to visit her other son who was on remand. The prison had a drug problem and the son on remand was suspected of supplying drugs so the governor had instructed that his visitors should be strip-searched and denied their visiting rights if they refused, though the claimants were unaware of this order in advance of the visit. They were taken to separate rooms. The mother's naked upper body was first examined and then her sexual organs and anus were visually examined, causing her great and visible distress. The son was at first reluctant to take off his underwear, suffered fits of sobbing and shaking, and when the officer examined his naked body that officer also lifted up his penis and pulled back his foreskin. The trial judge held that there was liability in battery and that the strip-search was a course of action intended to cause physical or psychiatric harm for which the defendant was also liable. The Court of Appeal disagreed with this latter point, doubted the existence of the tort of *Wilkinson v Downton* in the modern context and upheld the defendant's appeal. The claimants appealed to the House of Lords on the basis that, first, there was a tort of invasion of privacy (this was rejected by the House of Lords – see 14.6.2) and alternatively that damages could be awarded for emotional distress falling short of psychiatric harm where it was intentionally inflicted. The House of Lords accepted the continued existence of the tort in *Wilkinson v Downton* but held that there could be no liability for distress falling short of a recognised psychiatric injury and that, on the facts of the case, the intention essential for proving the tort could not be proved. The appeal was dismissed.

On the requirements for an action in *Wilkinson v Downton* Lord Hoffmann stated at 41 and 44–45:

JUDGMENT

'Commentators and counsel have been . . . unwilling to allow *Wilkinson v Downton* to disappear beneath the surface of the law of negligence . . . I do not resile from the proposition that the policy considerations which limit the heads of recoverable damage in negligence do not apply equally to torts of intention. If someone actually intends to cause harm by a wrongful act and does so, there is ordinarily no reason why he should not have to pay compensation. But I think that . . . you have to be very careful about what you mean by intend . . . imputed intention will not do. The defendant must actually have acted in a way which he knew to be unjustifiable and intended to cause harm or at least acted without caring whether he caused harm or not.'

Despite the attempts of the Court of Appeal in Wainright to abolish the tort, *Wilkinson v Downton* has been used even more recently as the sole basis of a successful claim.

CASE EXAMPLE

C v D [2006] EWHC 166 (QB); [2006] All ER (D) 329 (February)

A school headmaster was alleged to have sexually abused a pupil. The abuse took various forms, two of which could not be brought under trespass to the person. One was a video made by the defendant of the claimant in the school showers, the second involved the defendant pulling down the claimant's trousers and underwear in the school infirmary and staring at the claimant's genitals. While the trial judge did not feel that psychiatric injury was foreseeable as a likely consequence, he nevertheless did feel that the defendant was reckless as to whether he caused psychiatric harm to the claimant, conforming to the House of Lords in *Wainright*, and on this basis he held the defendant liable.

The most recent application and some might even say resurrection, of the rule in *Wilkinson v Downton* can be seen in the decision of *Rhodes v OPO* [2015] UKSC 32.

CASE EXAMPLE

Rhodes v OPO [2015] UKSC 32

The appellant is a well-known pianist, author and television film maker. He intended to publish a book about his life which included an account of how he suffered physical and sexual abuse including rape and his subsequent dependencies on drugs and alcohol and how he found redemption through music. The book is dedicated to his son from his first marriage. The son's mother had sight of the first draft of the book and insisted that there be significant changes made as she had serious concerns about the impact that this information could have on their son when he reads the book. She sought an injunction against its publication. There was a claim for intentionally causing harm under the rule in *Wilkinson v Downton* and the Court of Appeal allowed an interim injunction. Both of these matters were the subject of an appeal to the Supreme Court by the appellant. Lady Hale at 73–74 explained:

JUDGMENT

'. . . in relation to the tort in *Wilkinson v Downton*. It consists of three elements: (1) a conduct element; (2) a mental element; and, (3) a consequence element. . . . The conduct element requires words or conduct directed towards the claimant for which there was no justification or reasonable excuse, and the burden of proof is on the claimant. In this case, there is every justification for the publication. The Father has the right to tell the world about his story. The law places a very high value on freedom of speech. The right to disclosure is not absolute because a person may, for example, owe a duty to treat information as confidential, but there is no general law prohibiting the publication of facts which will distress another person. It is hard to envisage any case where words which are not deceptive, threatening or (possibly) abusive could be actionable under the tort recognised in *Wilkinson v Downton* . . .'

13.6.2 Protection from Harassment Act 1997

The problem faced by those who suffer harassment where there is no resulting injury is now dealt with by statute.

The Act provides that a person who pursues a course of conduct which he knows or ought to know amounts to harassment of another person may be guilty of the criminal offence of harassment. By s3 the Act gives the victim a remedy in civil law.

Conduct will amount to harassment if the course of conduct is such that 'a reasonable person in possession of the same information [as the defendant] would think the course of conduct would amount to harassment of the other' (s1(2)). The conduct can include causing the claimant to fear violence (s4(1)) or to cause the claimant alarm or distress (s7(2)). A 'course of conduct' means that the behaviour must occur more than once but it is clear that the defendant's intention is irrelevant as the judgment is that of the 'reasonable person'.

No actual physical or psychiatric harm need result from the harassment. Alarm or distress will suffice.

There is no remedy under the Act for a 'one-off' incident thus the defendant in *Wilkinson v Downton* would not be liable under the Act. The Act does however 'fill a gap' by providing a remedy for many situations where distress is caused, for example by means of 'stalking', telephone calls, emails or text messages.

13.6.3 A developing tort of harassment?

As the concept of harassment is gradually more closely defined, remedies are becoming available where the claimant has been subjected to conduct which does not amount to a threat but which nonetheless causes the claimant real harm. It may be that the Act will be enough to fill the gap but it is not yet clear that this will prove to be the case.

There has been much recent case law with quite different results. The best publicised of these cases is *Green*.

CASE EXAMPLE

Green v DB Group Services (UK) Ltd [2006] EWHC 1898

The claimant worked as an assistant company secretary for Deutsche Bank. She was subjected to constant abuse by a group of female staff, was constantly undermined by a male colleague and despite reporting this to her manager and seeking help, the company did nothing to support or help her. She suffered a period of sickness with depression as a result and on returning to work suffered a relapse and was unable to return to work. The judge awarded her £800,000 for personal injury and loss of future earnings for the mental illness resulting from the bullying. The award was based on both negligence and breach of the 1997 Act.

In *Howlett v Holding* [2006] EWHC 41 (QB) the Act was used to grant an injunction to put a stop to a campaign of victimisation waged against a former mayor by a disgruntled constituent. However, in *Merilie v Newcastle PCT* [2006] EWHC 1433 (QB) a dentist failed in a claim for harassment against her former employers because she suffered a lifelong personality disorder making her evidence unreliable since it was based only on her own perceptions.

Courts have accepted that the course of conduct must be sufficiently serious for a claim of harassment to succeed.

CASE EXAMPLE

Ferguson v British Gas Trading Ltd [2009] EWCA Civ 46

The claimant had been a customer of the defendant. After she changed to a different supplier British Gas continued to send her bills for gas that they had not supplied her with and later sent her several letters threatening to cut off her gas supply, to start legal proceedings against her and to inform a credit

Table 13.1 The differences between the different torts making up trespass to the person.

Tort	*Required state of mind*	*Whether direct or indirect*	*Whether contact required*	*Frequency*	*Whether damage needed*
Assault	Intention	Must be direct	No contact	Can be a single threat	No – only apprehension
Battery	Intention	Must be direct	Must have contact	Can be a single unlawful contact	No – can be harmless contact
False imprisonment	Question whether it always has to be intentional	Must be direct	Contact not necessary	Can be a single total restraint	No – need not even be aware
Wilkinson v Downton	Intention	Must be indirect	No contact	Can be a single infliction	Yes must suffer from physical or psychiatric harm
Harassment under the Protection from Harassment Act 1997	Intention	Can be either	Can be either	Must be more than one act of harassment (a course of conduct)	Only needs fear, alarm or distress – but could include psychiatric harm

rating agency. Despite the claimant contacting the company several times, the sending of the bills and threatening letters continued. They were in fact generated by a computer rather than by an individual. The claimant alleged harassment by the company. It argued that, since the claimant knew that the correspondence was unjustified and that it was generated by a computer she should not have taken it as seriously as if it came from an individual employee. The Court of Appeal held that, while the course of conduct must be serious for a claim under s3 of the Protection from Harassment Act, the fact of there being parallel criminal and civil liability was not generally significant in determining civil liability. The court considered that the conduct of the company was sufficiently serious to amount to harassment, and that there was no apparent policy reason why a corporation should be treated differently to an individual.

In *Jones v Ruth* [2011] EWCA Civ 804, a case involving neighbours, the Court of Appeal also identified that foreseeability of harm is not necessary when awarding damages under the Act. The conduct must be serious and deliberate and once that is proved damages can be awarded.

ACTIVITY

Self-assessment questions

1. Explain how the principle of *Wilkinson v Downton* differs from trespass to the person.
2. Consider how the principle of *Wilkinson v Downton* has been developed in later cases.
3. What are the basic requirements of the statutory tort created by s3 Protection from Harassment Act 1997?
4. Explain whether or not the principle of *Wilkinson v Downton* still has a role in protecting an individual from harm.

SAMPLE ESSAY QUESTION

Discuss the effectiveness of the tort of trespass to the person in protecting people's bodily integrity.

Outline the basis of an action in trespass to the person

- Three types – assault, battery and false imprisonment
- All are actionable per se so a remedy is available without proof of damage
- *Wilkinson v Downton* covers intentional indirect harm
- And also an action for harassment under the Protection from Harassment Act 1997

Explain the essential elements for assault

- Directly and intentionally causing the claimant to apprehend an imminent battery
- Involve threatening behaviour and the threat must be real and imminent
- And create a feeling of being threatened in the claimant
- Words can negate the fear of assault
- But words alone were traditionally insufficient
- Silent telephone calls have been accepted in criminal law

Explain the essential elements for battery

- Directly and intentionally applying unlawful force
- Judges have given direct a broad interpretation
- Hostility was identified as a requirement and has been said 'the least touching of another in anger is battery'
- But this could not apply in medical battery

Explain the essential elements of false imprisonment

- A total bodily restraint without safe means of escape
- But need not be physical
- And the claimant need not be aware of the restraint
- And the restraint may be justified by a contractual relationship or legitimate expectation

Discuss the range of available defences

- Defences to assault and battery include statutory authority, lawful arrest, Mental Health Act, consent, necessity parental authority, self-defence using reasonable force
- Defences include lawful arrest and detention under PACEA (as amended) (but note different rules for citizen's arrest), Mental Health Act and consent

Discuss the effectiveness of the tort

- Fact that the tort is actionable per se
- In assault damages are difficult to assess
- Difficulties associated with use of words
- Assault may be ineffective for threats of future harm
- In battery no need for actual harm to be proved
- And a broad view is applied to 'direct'
- Requirement of hostility is problematic
- Consent in sporting context and medical context
- Discuss how the defences may limit the effectiveness, particularly in relation to complaints about the police

KEY FACTS

Key facts on trespass to the person

Assault	Case/statute
Threat to use force against person of someone else.	
Actual harm need not be intended – intention to touch will suffice.	
Words alone traditionally not an assault.	*R v Meade and Belt* [1823]
But following verbal threat will suffice for criminal assault. Will this suffice for the tort?	*R v Ireland* [1997]

(Continued)

(Continued)

Words can negate threat.	*Turberville v Savage* [1669]
Victim must believe threat.	*R v St George* [1840]
It must be possible to carry out the threat – contrast with –	*Stephens v Myers* [1830] *Thomas v NUM* [1985]
Battery	**Case/statute**
Use of force against another person.	
Actual harm need not be caused – an unwanted kiss will suffice.	*R v Chief Constable of Devon & Cornwall* [1981]
Use of force must be direct but this is widely interpreted.	*Scott v Shepherd* [1773]; *Pursell v Horn* [1838] *Nash v Sheen* [1955]
There must be a touching – is hostility required?	
• no in	*Collins v Wilcock* [1984]
• but yes in	*Cole v Turner* [1704]
• and	*Wilson v Pringle* [1986]
(Note when HL held that if action is unlawful it is also hostile.)	*R v Brown* [1994]
Problem of medical cases – no hostile intent – does this case help?	*R v Brown* [1994]
Defences to assault and battery	**Case/statute**
Lawful authority – statutory powers given to police officers but any force used must be proportionate.	Police and Criminal Evidence Act 1984 *Collins v Wilcock* [1984]; *McCann, Farrell and Savage v UK* [1995]
Statutory powers given to those treating people with mental illness.	Mental Health Act 1983
Consent: sport – consent extends only to play within the rules of the game.	*Simms v Leigh RFC* [1969]
Medical treatment – every adult with capacity has right to consent to or refuse treatment.	*Re T (Adult: Refusal of Treatment)* [1992]; *Ms B v An NHS Hospital Trust* [2002]
Where person lacks capacity, treatment lawful if in the person's best interests.	*Airedale NHS Trust v Bland* [1993]
Necessity – act must be essential to prevent harm.	*F v West Berks HA* [1989]
Parental authority provided child understands why it is being punished and the punishment is proportionate; applies only to a parent.	*A v UK* [1998]
Self-defence – reasonable force proportionate to the threat may be used.	*Cockcroft v Smith* [1705]; *Revill v Newbery* [1996]; *Lane v Holloway* [1967]

(Continued)

(Continued)

False imprisonment	Case/statute
Total restraint preventing a person from leaving any place; not total if safe means of escape.	*Bird v Jones* [1845]
Restraint need not be physical; can occur even if claimant unaware.	*Meering v Grahame-White Aviation Co Ltd* [1919]; *Murray v Ministry of Defence* [1988]
Tort of strict liability.	*R v Governor of Brockhill Prison, ex p Evans (No 2)* [2000]
Defences to false imprisonment	**Case/statute**
Reasonable condition for release.	*Robinson v Balmain New Ferry* [1910]; *Herd v Weardale Steel* [1915]
Lawful arrest in accordance with Police and Criminal Evidence Act 1984 but note risk for private citizen if no crime actually committed by the arrested person.	*White v W P Brown* [1983]
Detention of people with mental illness under Mental Health Act 1983 or under common law doctrine of necessity.	*R v Bournewood Community and Mental Health Trust, ex p L* [1999]
Intentional harm	**Case/statute**
Provided act intended to cause harm, there can be liability even when elements of trespass to the person cannot be proved.	*Wilkinson v Downton* [1897]; *Janvier v Sweeney* [1919]
Actual injury, physical or psychiatric must occur.	*Wong v Parkside Health NHS Trust* [2001]
No liability for distress falling short of a recognised psychiatric injury.	*Wainright v Home Office* [2004]
Protection from Harassment Act 1997	**Case/statute**
Criminal offence to pursue a course of conduct which perpetrator knows or ought to know amounts to harassment of another.	s1
Statutory tort entitling victim to damages.	s3
Conduct can be anything which a reasonable person in the circumstances would think amounts to harassment.	s1(2)
Course of conduct means it happens more than once.	*Green v DB Group Services (UK) Ltd* [2006]
Defendant's intention is irrelevant.	
No actual harm need be caused.	

Conclusion

Trespass is an old tort which has to some extent been developed to deal with modern life. The gaps are partly filled by liability for intentional harm and by statute. It is likely that further developments will occur, partly resulting from the widespread use of information technology.

SUMMARY

- Trespass involves a direct interference with the claimant's person.
- It is actionable per se so there is no requirement to show that damage occurred.
- There are three types: assault, battery and false imprisonment.

Assault

- Intentionally and directly causing another to fear imminent unlawful contact.
- No contact is required but there must be threatening actions.
- Words alone are insufficient but can be a criminal assault – although words can negate an assault.
- The victim must believe the threat and it must be possible to carry it out.
- Consent, self-defence and necessity are all possible defences.

Battery

- Intentionally and directly applying unlawful force to a person.
- Courts have taken a broad view of what is direct.
- There is dispute over whether hostility is also a requirement.
- Battery is important in medical treatment – medical treatment in the absence of consent is generally a battery except where there is some justification for not obtaining consent – and it also has a context in sport where players act outside the rules.
- Consent, necessity and self-defence are all possible defences.

False imprisonment

- Involves total bodily restraint – with no safe means of escape.
- Can occur even where the claimant is unaware of the restraint.
- But it is not possible when the defendant has legitimate expectations that the claimant will remain for a set period of time.
- Consent, mistaken arrest (in the case of police officers) and lawful arrest are all possible defences.

Intentional indirect harm

- Possible where an action in trespass is impossible – but there must be personal injury whether physical or psychiatric.

Harassment

- Under the Protection from Harassment Act 1997 – but there must be a 'course of conduct' – so at least two events.

14

Defamation

AIMS AND OBJECTIVES

After reading this chapter you should be able to:

- Identify and distinguish between the elements required in proving a claim in defamation
- Identify relevant defences that may be available
- Explain the reasons for denying a general law of privacy
- Explain the basis of a claim for breach of confidentiality
- Critically analyse each tort
- Apply the law to factual situations and reach conclusions as to liability

14.1 Introduction

Defamation has undergone substantial changes under the Defamation Act 2013. This Act has changed the style of hearing, added a significant new element and also altered some of the defences as well as extending the law and the defences to new areas. The Act has put in place some much needed reforms.

Traditionally defamation actions were heard by juries with the judge's role being to decide whether the statement complained of was capable of having a defamatory meaning and the jury deciding whether the statement was defamatory. Now s11 of the 2013 Act repeals former legislation which gave a presumption of trial by jury in defamation cases, removes the presumption and identifies that a defamation trial will be without a jury unless a court orders otherwise. As will be seen, the question of what can amount to defamatory words is complex. Once this has been decided and it has then been decided that in the particular case the words of the claimant are defamatory, further considerations arise from the application

DOI: 10.4324/9781003202417-14

of Article 10 European Convention on Human Rights which protects the right to freedom of expression. In *Steel and Morris v UK* [2005] (Application no. 68416/01) ECHR two environmental campaigners who had lost a defamation action made against them by McDonalds and were ordered to pay extensive damages successfully proved that the trial had infringed their human rights under Articles 6 and 10 of the Convention. This was because the nature of English defamation law and the absence of any form of legal aid meant that the campaigners had to run their own defence against a large corporate body. The removal of jury trial is likely to be at least a small improvement in this respect since jury trials are inevitably expensive.

The balance between an individual's right to protect their reputation and the right to freedom of expression is a delicate one, involving the rights of individuals and the right of freedom of the press and other media to report on and draw attention to matters of public interest. This in turn involves consideration of what should constitute a matter of public interest in the sense of matters which are of public concern and in the sense of matters in which the public is interested. The latter may be simply because of the involvement of public figures in some type of allegedly scandalous situation.

14.2 The distinction between libel and slander

Defamation can take two forms

i. libel;
ii. slander.

Libel is usually written or takes some other permanent form.

CASE EXAMPLE

Monson v Tussauds Ltd [1894] 1 QB 671

The 'statement' consisted of a waxwork of the claimant. He had been charged with murder in Scotland and the verdict of 'not proven' had been given. Nonetheless the waxwork was placed near the entrance to the Chamber of Horrors. It was held that this amounted to a libel.

While libel is usually written, statute creates certain other forms. By the Defamation Act 1952, s1 broadcasts and television performances are to be treated as libel. Cable programmes are to be treated similarly (Cable and Broadcasting Act 1984) as are performances of a play (Theatres Act 1968). The issue of material in a film soundtrack was decided in *Youssoupoff v Metro-Goldwyn-Mayer Pictures Ltd* [1934] 50 TLR 581 when it was held that this could amount to libel.

Slander is a statement in some non-permanent form, usually in the form of spoken words although a gesture may suffice.

Other differences between libel and slander reflect the view that defamation in a permanent form is potentially more serious. Libel was traditionally actionable per se and general damages could be recovered without evidence that any actual loss had occurred.

By contrast, in the case of slander 'special damage' always had to be shown. A claimant who sought a remedy for slander had to show that some disadvantage or loss which was capable of being measured in money had resulted. This was not always easy to establish. In *Allsop v Allsop* [1865] 5 H & N 534 illness caused by the worry resulting from a slander was held to be too remote. Similarly in *Lynch v Knight* [1861] 9 HLC 597 the fact that a husband turned his wife out after hearing about a pre-marital relationship was also held to be too remote.

Slander was traditionally actionable per se in very specific circumstances:

- i where the imputation is that the claimant has committed a criminal offence punishable with imprisonment on the first conviction;
- ii where the imputation is of unchastity or adultery on the part of a woman or girl (Slander of Women Act 1891) (but this has now been repealed by s14(1) Defamation Act 2013);
- iii where it is imputed that the claimant is infected with a contagious or infectious disease likely to prevent others associating with the claimant (now under s14(2) Defamation Act 2013 special damage has to be shown);
- iv where the words impute unfitness, dishonesty or incompetence on the part of the claimant in relation to any office, profession, calling, trade or business.

Now under Section 1 Defamation Act 2013 in both libel and slander the claimant must show that he has suffered serious harm to his reputation. In the case of a body trading for a profit this must also show financial loss.

It is difficult to understand why the distinction between libel and slander remains even after reforms of the law by the Defamation Acts 1952 and 1996, but s14 Defamation Act 2013 makes a specific provision for slander. The position is further complicated by the Human Rights Act 1998 making Article 10, guaranteeing the right to freedom of expression, part of English law. As will be seen, the balance between the tort, whichever form it takes, and Article 10 is difficult to draw.

14.3 The elements of defamation

In all cases, the claimant must prove:

- a capacity to sue;
- b that the publication of the statement has caused or is likely to cause serious harm to the reputation of the claimant;
- c that the statement complained of is defamatory;
- d that the statement refers to the claimant;
- e that the statement has been published;
- f that the statement is false.

Table 14.1 The differences between libel and slander.

	Libel	*Slander*
How made	In permanent form.	In transient or temporary form.
Examples	• A written statement. • Film. • Statements broadcast on radio or television.	• A spoken statement. • Gestures. • Tape recordings of live performances.
Classification of law	• Tort. • Crime (in certain cases).	• Tort only.
When actionable	Is actionable if the publication of the statement causes serious harm to the claimant's reputation – in the case of a body trading for profit if serious financial loss is suffered.	Traditionally required that some damage must be proved which would now be serious harm to the claimant's reputation or financial loss in the case of a body trading for profit. Traditionally damage did not have to be proved in false allegations of: • a criminal offence involving imprisonment • a contagious or socially undesirable disease (but this now requires proof of special damage) • unchastity of women (this has now been repealed) • unfitness for any trade, profession or employment.

14.3.1 Who has capacity to sue?

Individuals

Any living person can bring a claim in defamation. A claim for defamation does not however, survive death as per Law Reform (Miscellaneous Provisions) Act 1934 s1(1).

Companies

Companies are also able to pursue a claim in defamation as they have a reputation to protect. This was confirmed in *South Hetton Coal Co v North Eastern News Assoc Ltd* [1894] 1 QB 133 where the claimant brought an action for libel against the defendant newspaper. Section 1(2) of the 2013 Act states that 'harm to the reputation of a body that trades for profit is not "serious harm" unless it has caused or is likely to cause the body serious financial loss.' This means that a company cannot sue for defamation unless the statement caused or is likely to cause serious financial harm.

Government bodies

Public authorities or governmental bodies are not able to sue for defamation. This position was affirmed by the House of Lords in the following case.

CASE EXAMPLE

Derbyshire County Council v Times v Newspaper Ltd [1993] AC 534 (HL)

The local authority brought an action for libel against the defendants in respect of two newspaper articles. These articles questioned the propriety of some investments that the claimant had made. It was held that actually it was in the highest interest of the public to subject a local authority to be subject to criticism and scrutiny. It follows then that it would be contrary to such interest to allow a local authority to have any common law right to bring an action for defamation.

The House of Lords emphasised that it is of great importance that a democratically elected governmental body should be open to uninhibited public criticism and the threat of a civil action of defamation must inevitably have an inhibiting effect on freedom of speech. For this reason, public bodies cannot bring an action in defamation. This approach is in line with Article 10 of the European Convention on Human Rights which protects the freedom of expression.

It is important to note that whilst local authorities and political parties may not be able to sue for defamation, individual politicians may be able to bring a claim for defamation in their personal capacity.

14.3.2 The statement must have caused serious harm to the reputation of the claimant

This is requirement that has been codified in section 1 of the Defamation Act 2013. Section 1(1) identifies that a statement is not defamatory unless it has caused or is likely to cause serious harm to the reputation of the claimant. The explanatory notes to the Act identifies the threshold at which a statement becomes actionable making clear that there must be really serious harm to the claimant's reputation.

Section 1(2) goes on to identify that in the case of a body that trades for a profit serious harm means that the body has suffered or is likely to suffer financial loss as a result of the publication of the statement. In this instance at least it is suggested that the tort of libel can no longer be said to be actionable per se since actual damage must be proved.

The common law had already been moving in this direction as in *Thornton v Telegraph Media Group Ltd* [2010] EWHC 1414 Tugendhat J said at 90:

JUDGMENT

'. . . whatever definition of "defamatory" is adopted, it must include a qualification or threshold of seriousness, so as to exclude trivial claims.'

Section 1 of the 2013 Act now puts this on a statutory footing so that any claim that does not make this threshold stage must be struck out early on.

CASE EXAMPLE

Lachaux v Independent Print Ltd [2019] UKSC 27

The claimant was engaged in bitter and acrimonious divorce proceedings. The claimant became aware of some articles in British newspapers that he contended were defamatory of him. The content of the articles suggested that the claimant carried out a campaign of intimidation and harassment against his wife, obtained a travel ban against her from leaving the UAE, and snatched their young son from her when he discovered where she was hiding from him. The preliminary matter that needed to be determined was whether, for the purposes of s1(1) of the 2013 Act, publication of the words complained of in all five articles satisfied the requirements of the statutory provision, namely that they caused 'serious harm'. Lord Sumption at paragraph 13 summarises the importance of s1:

JUDGMENT

'The Defamation Act 2013 unquestionably does amend the common law to some degree. Its preamble proclaims the fact ("an act to amend the law of defamation'). It is not disputed that there is a common law presumption of damage to reputation, but no presumption that it is 'serious'. So the least that section 1 achieved was to introduce a new threshold of serious harm which did not previously exist. The question on these appeals is what are the legal implications of that change, and what necessarily follows from it.'

Therefore, it was held that one cannot assume that harm has been suffered but rather it has to be demonstrated that the statement has caused serious harm on the balance of probabilities.

This is so to prevent trivial claims coming into the courts by raising the threshold of serious harm requiring the claimant to adduce further evidence of the harm. The harm complained of was serious enough to fall within the meaning envisaged in s1 of the 2013 Act. The section itself does indeed raise the threshold of seriousness from that as set out in the common law, namely in *Jameel* [2005] EWCA Civ 75 and *Thornton* and requires its application to be determined by reference to the actual facts and impact and not merely the meaning of the words.

Serious harm was the central issue in *Blake v Fox* [2025] EWCA Civ 1321. This case concerned posts on Twitter in October 2020 where Simon Blake, Colin Seymour, and Nicola Thorp (the claimants) each called Mr Fox (the defendant) racist or a racist. Mr Fox responded with three tweets of his own which called his accusers paedophiles. The claimants sued the defendant in libel.

Lord Justice Warby clearly explained the impact of and how to apply, s1(1) at paragraphs 32–33:

JUDGMENT

Blake v Fox [2025] EWCA Civ 1321

'Section 1(1) of the 2013 Act was intended to and did make the claimant's task harder . . . The court rejected the view . . . that section 1(1) merely required a tendency to cause "serious" as opposed to "substantial" reputational harm. The Supreme Court held that the sub-section did not amend the common law but supplemented it. The statute requires a claimant to go beyond proof of a defamatory tendency and to demonstrate as a fact on the balance of probabilities that the publication complained of caused (or was likely to cause) reputational harm that was serious. It further held that the common law presumption that a statement with a defamatory tendency caused actual harm to reputation has not survived the enactment of s 1 . . . it was possible to prove serious reputational harm by way of an inferential case. It upheld the decision of the High Court that the requirement was met on the facts of *Lachaux* on the basis of "(i) the scale of the publications; (ii) the fact that the statements complained of had come to the attention of at least one identifiable person in the United Kingdom who knew Mr Lachaux and (iii) they were likely to have come to the attention of others who either knew him or would come to know him in future; and (iv) the gravity of the statements themselves" or, putting it another way, "a combination of the meaning of the words, the situation of Mr Lachaux, the circumstances of publication and the inherent probabilities"' [21] (Lord Sumption, with whom the other Justices agreed).

Applying these four factors in the case of *Jameel,* there were only five people who read the story complained of it was held that the claim should be struck out as not disclosing a real and substantial tort. This is referred to as the *Jameel* principle: a claim which discloses no real and substantial tort is liable to be struck out for being an abuse of process of the court. If s1 were not to be interpreted in this way, then what would be the point of introducing that section? It was designed to introduce a new threshold of serious harm which did not previously exist. The extent of damage is now part of the test for a defamatory statement. Further guidance on how the courts will apply the *Jameel* principle can be found in the recent Supreme Court decision discussed below.

CASE EXAMPLE

Mueen-Uddin v Secretary of State for the Home Department [2024] UKSC 21

This libel action concerned a report entitled 'Challenging Hateful Extremism' which referenced the claimant as a war criminal relating to events that took place in 1971. The claimant denied any involvement in such events and brought a claim in libel. The Court of Appeal struck out the claim as an abuse of process for two reasons. The first was that since the claimant had been convicted of the said crimes in Bangladesh *in absentia*, to reconsider this would bring the administration of justice into disrepute by seeking to relitigate a criminal conviction in subsequent civil proceedings and it would be manifestly unfair to the Secretary of State to have to establish a defence of truth where the relevant events took place 50 years ago. Second, the claimant's reputation had already been badly damaged by his conviction by previous publicity that the resources required to litigate the matter would be so great that 'the game was not worth the candle' within *Jameel*. The Supreme Court however, allowed the appeal. They did so on the basis that the right of access to the courts was qualified by the court's power to prevent a misuse of its procedure and the extent of publication and its effect on the appellant's reputation were matters to be determined at trial. Unlike in *Jameel*, the claimant in this case is a UK citizen.

JUDGMENT

Lord Reed, paragraphs 34 and 81:

'The claimant had a clear and legitimate interest in vindicating his reputation against a most serious accusation made by the government of the state of which he was a citizen and where he resided. The publication was by no means minimal, and was from an authoritative and apparently trustworthy source.

. . .

The first important point about *Jameel* . . . is that the problem which gave rise to the need to strike out the claim was that for the court to allow the proceedings to continue in the absence of more than minimal damage would have been incompatible with the defendant's rights under article 10 of the Convention, and therefore contrary to the court's duty under section 6 of the Human Rights Act. The second point . . . is that . . . the explanation of *Jameel* given by Lord Sumption in *Lachaux*, did not import a test based upon weighing the value of the claim against the cost of the proceedings . . . The dicta focused upon the question whether the damage to the claimant's reputation was shown to be so trivial that the proceedings could not be regarded as serving the legitimate purpose of protecting the claimant's reputation, with the consequence that the interference with the defendant's freedom of expression could not be said to be necessary.'

It was held that the claimant had a legitimate interest in vindicating his reputation because if he were successful, it would be a major vindication for the claimant. In fact, this action culminated in an apology by the Home Secretary in the High Court together with an award of damages of £225,000.

A stark example of how the law of defamation applies equally to the realm of social media as much as it does to printed material can be found in the following case; students should take note and remind themselves of this point when using social media!

CASE EXAMPLE

Monroe v Hopkins [2017] EWHC 433

This is a well-publicised case that centred around the concept of serious harm. The defendant is a journalist for the MailOnline and the claimant is a food blogger. The defendant tweeted the following about the claimant although the defendant thought that she was tweeting about someone else:

'@MsJackMonroe scrawled on any memorials recently? Vandalised the memory of those who fought for your freedom. Grandma got any more medals?'

Considering what the reasonable reader would understand from this tweet, it is likely to mean that Ms Monroe condoned and approved of scrawling on war memorials, vandalising monuments commemorating those who fought for her freedom. Having determined that the tweet was defamatory of the claimant, the next step was to consider whether the tweets caused serious harm. Whilst the tweet was unsettling, injury to feelings alone is not enough. The claimant needs to establish that there has been serious harm to her reputation. This was established on these facts not least because the claimant received abuse over Twitter as a result of the tweet by the defendant.

This also serves as a useful reminder that it is irrelevant that the statement refers to someone other than to whom you intended. The law considers who is actually impacted by the statement regardless of whether the author of the statement intended to refer to them or not.

CRITIQUING THE LAW

Consider how a claimant may prove that they have suffered serious harm to their reputation. Do you think that this requirement helps or hinders claimants in bringing a claim in defamation?

14.3.3 The statement must be defamatory

In *Sim v Stretch* [1936] 52 TLR 669 Lord Atkin suggested that the test should be: would the words tend to lower the claimant in the estimation of right-thinking members of society generally?

The essence of the tort is that a person's reputation is seriously damaged by the statement so that others might think less of them. What this does not mean is that it is what the claimant thinks the statement means but rather what others in society might reasonably understand the statement to mean.

The difficulty is how this is to be decided. In *Parmiter v Coupland* [1840] 6 M & W 105 it was stated that the publication needed to 'be calculated to injure the reputation of another, by exposing them to hatred, contempt or ridicule'.

This narrow definition clearly does not cover all situations. The owner of a business can suffer loss if he is described as dishonest or unreliable. It is unlikely that such allegations would excite 'hatred, contempt or ridicule'.

This in turn raises the question of who are 'right-thinking members of society'. In some circles of society behaviour is admired which in other circles would be condemned.

CASE EXAMPLE

Byrne v Deane [1937] 2 All ER 204

A golf club kept illegal gambling machines, known as 'diddlers', in the club house. The police were told by someone that the machines were there and the club was ordered to remove them. The next day the following piece of doggerel was found on the wall:

'For many years upon this spot
You heard the sound of a merry bell
Those who were rash and those who were not
Lost and made a spot of cash
But he who gave the game away
May he byrnne in hell and rue the day.'

Diddleramus

The claimant alleged that the defendants meant and were understood by others to mean that he had 'grassed' to the police given the spelling of the word 'byrnne' and was consequently unfit to remain a member of the golf club.

Holding that it could not be defamatory to say that a person had reported a crime to the police Lord Justice Slesser said at 209:

JUDGMENT

'We have to consider . . . the view which would be taken by the ordinary good and worthy subject of the King . . . [who] would not consider such an allegation in itself to be defamatory.'

In other words, reporting on a crime is seen as commendable. It seems that the decision will reflect what the judges believe that an ordinary person would understand by the words used.

CASE EXAMPLE

Lewis v Daily Telegraph Ltd [1964] AC 234

The published statement said that the claimant's company was being investigated by the Fraud Squad. The claimant alleged that this would mean, to the ordinary reader, that the business was being carried on fraudulently. It was held that a reasonable person would not believe the business to be guilty merely on the basis of a police inquiry.

In the later case of *Hartt v Newspaper Publishing plc, Independent*, 27 October 1989 the ordinary reader was described as being one '. . . who is not unduly suspicious, but who can read between the lines. He might think loosely, but is not avid for scandal, and will not select one bad meaning where other non-defamatory meanings are available'.

Add humorous intent to the situation and it is difficult to know where to draw the line. Where the imputation is that the claimant has done something unlawful, the judgment of the ordinary citizen will probably be sufficient. *Byrne v Deane* [1937] 2 All ER 204 provides an example of this. In other cases, the position may not be so clear.

CASE EXAMPLE

Berkoff v Burchill [1996] 4 All ER 1008

The claimant, an actor, was described by the defendant as 'hideously ugly'. He alleged that this comment held him up to ridicule or meant that other people would shun or avoid him.

The majority in the Court of Appeal held that the words were capable of being defamatory, Lord Justice Neill saying at 1018:

JUDGMENT

'it would . . . be open to a jury to conclude that in the context the remarks about Mr Berkoff gave the impression that he was not merely physically unattractive in appearance but actually repulsive . . . to say this of someone in the public eye who makes his living . . . as an actor, is capable of lowering his standing in the estimation of the public and of making him the object of ridicule'.

Lord Justice Millett in his dissenting judgment said at 1018 and 1020:

JUDGMENT

'. . . mere chaff and banter are not defamatory, and even serious imputations are not actionable if no one would take them to be meant seriously . . . People must be allowed to poke fun at one another without fear of litigation'.

Lord Millett found that the words complained of were only a cheap joke at the claimant's expense.

The differing views of the judges in *Berkoff v Burchill* only serve to emphasise how difficult it is to decide how words may be seen by ordinary people. This can further be seen in the recent case of *Riley v Murray*.

CASE EXAMPLE

Riley v Murray [2022] EWCA Civ 1146 (CA)

The claimant was a television presenter who had conducted a high-profile campaign against antisemitism in the Labour Party while Jeremy Corbyn was its leader. The defendant was Corbyn's stakeholder manager. The claimant had posted a tweet which referenced an earlier tweet made by a journalist. The journalist's tweet referred to an incident in which an egg had been thrown at the former leader of the British National Party and stated 'if you don't want eggs thrown at you, don't be a Nazi'. The claimant's tweet, which captioned the journalist's tweet with the words 'good advice'. In response to the claimant's 'good advice' tweet, the defendant posted the tweet complained of. It read '[the claimant] tweets that Jeremy Corbyn deserves to be violently attacked because he is a Nazi. This woman is as dangerous as she is stupid. Nobody should engage with her. Ever.'

The court was tasked with determining the natural and ordinary meaning of the words, to what extent the words were a statement of fact or an expression of opinion, and to what extent they were defamatory of the claimant. At trial, Nicklin J applied the well-established and uncontroversial principles he had summarised in *Koutsogiannis v The Random House Group Ltd* [2019] EWHC 48 (QB), [2020] 4 WLR 25 [11]–[16]. An important aspect of these for present purposes is the "single meaning rule" explained in *Koutsogiannis* [11]:

'The Court's task is to determine the single natural and ordinary meaning of the words complained of, which is the meaning that the hypothetical reasonable reader would understand the words bear. It is well recognised that there is an artificiality in this process because individual readers may understand words in different ways: *Slim v Daily Telegraph Ltd [1968] 2 QB 157*, 173D–E, *per* Lord Diplock.'

The process of identifying the single natural and ordinary meaning of a statement is an objective one.

It was determined that the ordinary meaning of the defendant's tweet is:

1 Jeremy Corbyn had been attacked when he visited a mosque.
2 The Claimant had publicly stated in a tweet that he deserved to be violently attacked.
3 By so doing, the Claimant has shown herself to be a dangerous and stupid person who risked inciting unlawful violence. People should not engage with her.

Aside from determining the meaning of the usually written statement, the position can be further complicated if the statement is implied in a film so that the 'statement' makes society 'shun or avoid' the victim.

CASE EXAMPLE

Youssoupoff v Metro-Goldwyn-Mayer Pictures Ltd [1934] 50 TLR 581

A film imputed that the claimant, a Russian princess, had been raped by Rasputin, the so-called mad monk who was a figure of great and allegedly evil influence in pre-revolutionary Russia.

While the claimant was probably pitied, and certainly there was no suggestion that she was in any way to blame for the incident, the court held that the statement could tend to make people 'shun and avoid' her.

At the end of the day, the only certainty appears to be that the decision as to whether or not words are capable of being defamatory depends on what the judges in the particular case believe would be the reaction of those they believe to be ordinary citizens. A complicated sentence but one which reflects the complexity of the problem!

14.3.4 Innuendo

In many cases, the words used are clear and will be defamatory unless true, for example calling someone a thief. It is, however, possible for words to be inoffensive on the face of it and it is only with particular knowledge of other facts that the reader may reach a conclusion that is defamatory of the claimant. One example of this has already been given in *Byrne v Deane*. The following cases illustrate different outcomes which reflect, in the first case, individual knowledge of the claimant and, in the second, general knowledge available to all.

CASE EXAMPLE

Cassidy v Daily Mirror Group Newspapers Ltd [1929] 2 KB 331

A picture was published which showed Mr Cassidy with a young lady under a heading which stated that she and Mr Cassidy had just announced their engagement to be married. The claimant was Mr Cassidy's wife and this was generally known to be the case even though they led separate lives. She was able to prove that several people believed, as a result of the publication, that she was 'living in sin' with Mr Cassidy, a serious social problem for her in the 1920s. It was held that the words were capable of being defamatory and, once a jury considered the issue, it was decided that the defendant was liable.

CASE EXAMPLE

Tolley v Fry & Sons Ltd [1931] All ER Rep 131

The claimant was a well-known amateur golfer in the days when amateur status was regarded as very important. The defendant had published an advertisement for 'Fry's Chocolate Cream' which showed a sketch of the claimant in golfing gear with a packet of chocolate cream protruding from a pocket. The advertisement included a piece of verse:

> 'The caddie to Tolley said; "Oh, Sir!
> Good shot, Sir! That ball, see it go, Sir.
> My word, how it flies,
> Like a Cartet of Fry's.
> They're handy, they're good, and priced low, Sir."'

The words were not defamatory in themselves but implied that the claimant had been paid for letting his name be used in the advertisement. This was a serious matter which would have prevented him from taking part in golf competitions as an amateur. It was held that the meaning of the sketch and words combined was capable of being defamatory and indeed a jury found that he had been defamed.

Tolley indicates that in some cases, it is the perception of the ordinary reader, or the right-thinking member of society, which is important. This is illustrated by a modern case.

CASE EXAMPLE

Norman v Future Publishing [1999] EMLR 325

The claimant, a famous opera singer, complained that a passage in an article which said that she had told a joke using an Afro-American dialect, was defamatory because it appeared to show that she had used a derogatory stereotype or that she had mocked people of Afro-American heritage. Taking the comments in the context of the article as a whole, which appeared in a classical music magazine and which was generally complimentary to her talent, the court held that a reasonable reader could not have understood the words in the way alleged. The fact that the claimant denied ever using the words attributed to her was irrelevant, the relevant issue being whether or not the words used in the article were defamatory.

Norman also reiterates the point that an article must be read as a whole.

14.3.5 The statement must refer to the claimant

Claimants must prove that the words referred to them. The most straightforward way is obviously to show that they are named and sufficient other information such as their picture, is included so that the identity of the person referred to is clear. However, it is not always so straightforward. We have already seen, in *Cassidy v Daily Mirror Newspapers Ltd* that it will suffice that those who know the claimant believe that the claimant is the person referred to. Problems arise where the defendant either did not know of the claimant's existence or intended to refer to someone else. A person can be defamed 'by accident' if they happen to have the same or a similar name to a person referred to in the statement.

CASE EXAMPLE

E Hulton & Co v Jones [1910] AC 20

A Sunday newspaper published a fictitious article about 'Artemus Jones, a churchwarden from Peckham' who had spent a weekend in Dieppe with a lady who was not his wife. The real Artemus Jones was a barrister, unmarried and did not live in Peckham but he was able to bring witnesses who said that on reading the article they had believed it referred to him.

Giving judgment in the House of Lords, Lord Shaw quoted a passage from *Bourke v Warren* [1826] 2 C & P 307 with approval, at 26:

JUDGMENT

'It is not necessary that all the world should understand the libel; it is sufficient if those who knew the [claimant] can make out that he is the person meant.'

On this basis the claimant received damages of £1,750.

Newspapers and other parts of the media face particular risks. A news report may indeed be true of the person named. What about other people with the same name whose friends and associates believe that the report refers to them?

CASE EXAMPLE

Newstead v London Express Newspaper Ltd [1940] 1 KB 377

The newspaper carried a report of a case before the local court in which it stated that 'Harold Newstead, thirty-year old Camberwell man' had been convicted of bigamy. This was true but there was another Harold Newstead of about the same age who also came from Camberwell of whom it was not true.

The issue was whether or not the words were defamatory of the innocent man. The jury were asked: 'Would reasonable persons understand the words complained of to refer to the [claimant]?'

The jury having decided that the answer to the question was 'Yes' and that the claimant had been defamed, the matter went to the Court of Appeal. Dismissing the appeal, Sir Wilfred Greene MR said at 388:

JUDGMENT

'If there is a risk of coincidence, it ought I think, in reason to be borne, not by the innocent party to whom the words are held to refer, but by the party who puts them into circulation.'

The claimant can simply rely on the fact that others, reading an article in which the claimant is not named, may come across some fact or phrase which they connect to the claimant making it clear in their minds that the allegation is about that person.

CASE EXAMPLE

Morgan v Odhams Press Ltd [1971] 1 WLR 1239

The *Sun* newspaper contained an article in which it described how a Miss Murray, likely to be a major witness in a dog-doping trial, had gone into hiding after being kidnapped a week earlier by members of the dog-doping gang. A week earlier she had in fact been staying with the claimant. The claimant said that ordinary readers would assume that he was a member of the gang and witnesses who had seen the claimant with Miss Murray gave evidence that this was in fact what they believed. The question to be decided was: 'Would readers having knowledge of the circumstances reasonably have understood that the article referred to Mr Morgan?'

If the answer to this question was 'Yes' then Lord Reid observed at 1242:

JUDGMENT

'It does not matter whether the publisher intended to refer to the [claimant] or not. It does not even matter if he knew of the [claimant's] existence. And it does not matter that he did not know or could not have known the facts which caused the readers with special knowledge to connect the statement with the [claimant].'

As will be seen, the Defamation Act 1996, amending and replacing earlier legislation, now provides a defence of 'offer of amends', to alleviate the consequences of accidental defamation (see section 14.4.10).

14.3.6 The statement must be published

No action can be brought where the statement, no matter how untrue or offensive, is made only to the person about whom the allegation is being made. At least one other person must hear or read the statement and understand it. A deaf person who cannot lip-read would not 'hear' a slander, a foreigner who cannot read English would not understand an article in English. Newspapers and books are published so that any defamatory material they contain is published to the readers. A letter is published when it is dictated to a secretary and also when it is opened by someone other than the person defamed.

Publication can be defined as communication of the material to someone other than the person allegedly defamed. It is only when a publication is communicated to another that it can cause injury to reputation and when an assessment of serious harm can take place. The quality of the communication also has a bearing on whether this requirement is established. This point was highlighted in the following case.

CASE EXAMPLE

Webb v Jones [2021] EWHC 1618 (QB)

The claimant complained about some Facebook posts embedded within a thread made by the defendant. The posts in question were removed as a result of the claimant's complaint. The question for the court was whether the pleaded case is capable of showing that those posts pass the substantial publication test. Merely stating the number of people who are members of the group, without more, does not achieve that. The burden of proving substantial publication is on the claimant. The posts in question did not appear to identify the claimant, by her own or any other name by which she might be known. The court relied on the reasoning in the Supreme Court judgment in *Stocker v Stocker* [2020] AC 593 about the nature of social media browsing at 43:

'The imperative is to ascertain how a typical (i.e. an ordinary reasonable) reader would interpret the message. That search should reflect the circumstance that this is a casual medium; it is in the nature of conversation rather than carefully chosen expression; and that it is pre-eminently one in which the reader reads and passes on.'

The court goes on to conclude that the serious harm threshold is not met based on the quality of this type of publication at 69:

'Most of the reactions consisted only of an emoji click. It is not clear from the reactions or any other evidence that the person reacting knew that the claimant was the person referred to, or knew who she was. It is vanishingly unlikely, on the only evidence available or obtainable, that the claimant's reputation in the real world was damaged at all in the eyes of anyone by these posts; let alone to an extent which could conceivably be characterised as serious harm. This was confused and confusing ephemeral internet chatter, down thread, and swiftly lost in the surrounding hubbub. It is exactly the sort of case that section 1 of the Defamation Act 2013 was designed to stop.'

An exception to the rule concerns publication between spouses. A husband cannot make a publication to his wife, or a wife to her husband. As was said in *Wennhak v Morgan* [1888] 20 QBD 635 to hold otherwise 'might lead to disastrous results to social life'.

Publication usually occurs intentionally. There may also be liability for any publication which is not intended but which can reasonably be anticipated. A letter containing defamatory material will be published if it is opened in the usual course by anyone other than the addressee, for example by a post clerk. If it is not marked 'confidential' this can reasonably be anticipated.

CASE EXAMPLE

Theaker v Richardson [1962] 1 WLR 151

A defamatory letter written by the defendant was put into an envelope similar to those used for election addresses. The envelope was addressed to the claimant but was in fact opened by her husband, believing it to be election material. It was held by the jury that this was a natural and probable consequence.

On appeal Lord Justice Pearson explained that it was a question of fact at that time to be decided by the jury at 161:

JUDGMENT

'Was [the husband's] conduct something unusual, out of the ordinary and not reasonably to be anticipated, or was it something which could quite easily and naturally happen in the ordinary course of events?'

An interesting snapshot of domestic life in the early twentieth century is provided by the following case:

CASE EXAMPLE

Huth v Huth [1915] 3 KB 32

Mr Huth sent his wife a letter in an unsealed envelope alleging that they were not in fact married and that their children were illegitimate. At the time, a wife could not sue her husband in tort but the children could sue their father. They alleged that publication had occurred when the letter had been opened by the butler before he handed it to Mrs Huth.

As it is not part of a butler's duties to open letters addressed to his employers, Mr Huth could not reasonably have anticipated that the butler would in fact do so. Consequently there had been no publication and the children lost the case.

Single publication

It was the case under the common law that once defamatory material has been put into circulation by the original publisher, there could be liability for repeated publications by others unless the repetition was unauthorised and/or was not a natural and probable consequence which could reasonably be foreseen. This is to say that each separate publication gave rise to a separate cause of action even if it was the same publication. This is particularly problematic for a number of reasons:

- internet publications which create a sort of indefinite liability as time will start at the point of the fresh publication;
- print in hard copy which is then transferred into a digital format on the internet;
- publications in different jurisdictions at different times.

CASE EXAMPLE

Slipper v BBC [1991] 1 QB 283

The BBC made a film about the claimant's unsuccessful attempts to bring a robber back from Brazil. Preview tapes were sent to journalists and the film was subsequently broadcast on BBC. The claimant claimed that the film was defamatory and alleged that the BBC were responsible for the repetition of it in press material:

i that the BBC knew and would foresee that the preview tapes were likely to be reviewed in the national press; alternatively

ii that it was the natural and probable consequence that such reviews would be published.

The Court of Appeal held that whether or not the reviews reproduced the sting of the libel and whether or not repetition was invited or could have been anticipated were questions for the jury to decide.

CASE EXAMPLE

McManus v Beckham [2002] EWCA Civ 939

The defendant, Victoria Beckham, visited the claimant's memorabilia shop and claimed that the signed photographs of her husband were fake. This incident attracted significant media attention. The claimant brought an action for defamation but crucially relied on the subsequent publication of the incident to support his claim. The question here was whether the defendant knew that or appreciated the risk that what she had allegedly said was likely to be reported and likely repeated.

The issue of multiple publications has been addressed by section 8 of the 2013 Act. Section 8 introduced the single publication rule which states that any cause of action against the person for defamation in respect of the subsequent publication is to be treated as having accrued on the date of the first publication.

Publication and the internet

The courts have also been called on to consider the position of internet providers. Inevitably they have found that where the internet provider is unaware of the defamation then it cannot be held to be the publisher.

CASE EXAMPLE

Metropolitan International Schools Ltd v Designtechnica (T/A Corp (Digital Trends); Google UK Ltd; Google Inc [2009] EWHC 1765 (QB)

The claimant brought an action for defamation against the first defendant for comments made on a website bulletin board. The claimant also brought the action against Google, the internet search provider on the basis that the defamation had also been repeated in extracts of websites used in relation to searches. One issue for the court therefore was whether the internet provider could be considered to be a publisher of the defamation. The court held that it could not since it took an entirely passive role in facilitating the websites. It would need to have some awareness or some responsibility.

Internet service providers (ISPs) are considered to be merely passive as far as the requirement of publication goes. This was confirmed in the case of *Bunt v Tilley* [2006] EWCA 407 (QB). This is a sensible approach given the volume of activity that an ISP facilitates. However, the position is different, once an operator of a website is put on notice of hosting defamatory material.

CASE EXAMPLE

Tamiz v Google [2012] EWCA Civ 68

The defendant had allowed any internet users to create an independent blog. The claimant complained to the defendant that one of the blogs contained defamatory comments about him. However, the defendant did not promptly remove the blog post. It was considered that where the defendant fails to remove the post promptly after it has been notified, it may be that it will become the secondary publisher of the material. Ultimately in this case there was not a real and substantial tort.

The matter of internet publication has increasing importance in the area of defamation not least because publication through websites increases the frequency of repetition of potentially defamatory material.

CASE EXAMPLE

Lord McAlpine v Bercow [2013] EWHC 1342 (QB)

The claimant had been a high-profile Conservative politician and was incorrectly linked to allegations of child sex abuse in a TV programme (*Newsnight*). Newsnight made reference to a leading Conservative figure. The defendant published a post on social media (Twitter) which read:

'why is Lord McAlpine trending? *innocent face*'

The claimant was in fact innocent. The claimant argued that the ordinary meaning of the words and/or the meaning by innuendo was that he was guilty of sexually abusing children. The defendant had a large following most likely people interested in politics and who would be able to make an inference as to who the tweet was referring. The words 'innocent face' were to be read like a stage direction, directing the reader to imagine that the expression on the defendant's face was one of innocence as she asked the question, suggesting that that she does not know the answer to her own question.

What is interesting in this case is that the tweet in isolation probably would not have had as much impact. *Newsnight* referenced the accusation made not the alleged perpetrator. The tweet by the defendant, linked or repeated the accusation but implied that the claimant was the perpetrator. It was held that the effect of the repetition rule is that the defendant, as the writer of the tweet, is treated as if she had made, with the addition of the claimant's name, the allegation in the *Newsnight* and other media reports which had previously been made without his name. It is an allegation of guilt.

ACTIVITY

The 2013 Act introduced section 5 which addresses the position of operators of websites. This is discussed further below in the context of defences.

Self-assessment questions

1 What are the main differences between libel and slander?
2 Explain the difficulties faced by the judge in deciding whether or not the words are capable of being defamatory.
3 What precisely is meant by 'innuendo'?

14.4 Defences

It is for the defendant to prove that any of the relevant defences apply so the burden of proof is on the defendant to establish any that any relevant defences apply. The defendant needs to establish the defence on the balance of probabilities i.e. that it is more likely than not.

A statement that is true can never amount to defamation, however painful or embarrassing it may be. On this basis truth is a defence and is discussed next.

14.4.1 Truth

We have already seen that it cannot amount to defamation if what is published is the truth. It is for the defendant to prove the truth of the statement. What of the situation where most of what is published can be proved to be true but some parts of it cannot? The old common law defence of justification, namely that the substance of the statement is true even if there are some minor inaccuracies, has now been replaced in section 2 Defamation Act 2013 by a defence of truth. Section 5, Defamation Act 1952 which explained this last point is also replaced by s2(2) and (3) Defamation Act 2013.

SECTION

'2(1) It is a defence to an action for defamation for the defendant to show that the imputation conveyed by the statement complained of is substantially true

2(2) subsection (3) applies in an action for defamation if the statement complained of contains two or more distinct imputations

2(3) If one or more of the imputations is not shown to be substantially true, the defence under this section does not fail if, having regard to the imputations which are shown to be substantially true, the imputations which are not shown to be substantially true do not seriously harm the claimant's reputation.'

This means that this defence may be established if it can be shown

- the defendant must specify the defamatory meanings that they seek to justify;
- the imputation is one of fact;
- the imputation is one that is substantially true.

It is therefore possible for the defendant to justify the 'sting' of the statement by proving its truth even though some details may be inaccurate. The inaccurate details must not add to the 'sting' of the statement.

CASE EXAMPLE

Depp II v News Group Newspapers [2020] EWHC 2911 (QB)

The American actor Johnny Depp brought a claim in libel against the *Sun* newspaper, its associated website and the author of the article Dan Wootton. The claim concerned an article published on their website with the headline:

'GONE POTTY How Can J K Rowling be "genuinely happy" casting wife beater Johnny Depp in the new Fantastic Beasts film?'

The defendants sought to defend the claim by relying on the defence of truth. They sought to prove that the statement was substantially true by arguing that Depp beat his then wife, Amber Heard, causing her to suffer significant injury and on occasion leading to her fearing for her life. The defendants were able to establish that the statement was indeed substantially true as there were instances where Depp had hit his wife causing her to suffer significant injury and on occasion leading to her fearing for her life.

The words of the Act themselves must be applied so that past cases may no longer be binding but they are likely to be helpful for interpretation.

CASE EXAMPLE

Alexander v Eastern Railway Co [1865] 6 B & S 340

The claimant alleged that he had been libelled by a notice which stated that he had been convicted of travelling without paying his fare. It went on to say that he had been fined £9 1s 10d with an alternative of three weeks in prison if he failed to pay. The notice was accurate save that the alternative period of imprisonment was in fact only 14 days. It was held that the then defence of justification succeeded because the statement was substantially true.

It has been tempting for people to try to protect themselves by stating that 'it is rumoured that . . .' but this is unlikely to work. The fact that there is such a rumour may be true but the defendant will have to prove that the facts alleged in the rumour are true (*Shah v Standard Chartered Bank* [1999] QB 241).

It is by contrast possible for a defendant to succeed where the statement makes it clear that the defamatory imputation is in fact false. Whether or not this in reality removes the 'sting' of the charge is debatable as the following case shows.

CASE EXAMPLE

Charleston and Another v News Group Newspapers Ltd [1995] 2 AC 65

The claimants were actors who played husband and wife in *Neighbours*, a popular television show. The defendants published, in a mass circulation Sunday paper, photographs of the claimants, which showed the stars apparently engaged in sexual activity. The banner headline read 'Strewth! What's Harold up to with our Madge' while another headline read 'Porn Shocker for Neighbours Stars'. The photographs had in fact been taken from a computer game which had superimposed the faces of the stars on to pornographic photographs. This had been done without their knowledge or consent. The article beneath the headlines and the photographs made the circumstances clear and described the claimants as victims.

The issue was what inference a reader would have drawn. It was conceded that provided a reader had actually read beyond the first paragraph of the article, the falsity of the impression given by the photographs would have been clear. It was argued that a significant proportion of the readership would only in fact have read the headlines and looked at the pictures. Such people would have understood the publication in the defamatory sense.

The House of Lords held that the readership must be treated as a whole and the article read as a whole. This meant that the allegation of defamation could not be sustained, the truth was made clear. Commenting on the suggestions that a proportion of readers would not in fact read the whole article, Lord Bridge said at 73:

JUDGMENT

'if [such] readers, without taking the trouble to discover what the article was all about, carried away the impression that [the claimants] were . . . involved in making pornographic films, they could hardly be described as ordinary, reasonable, fair-minded readers'.

The judgments seem to show that the judges were aware that the publication was deeply offensive to the claimants but were 'not concerned to pronounce on any question of journalistic ethics' (per Lord Bridge). While this is undoubtedly true, the view can be of little comfort to the claimants.

It might also be thought that a claimant could ignore the true statements and bring an action based on only those parts of the statement which are untrue. Whether or not this can succeed depends on the nature of the charges. If they can be treated as distinct and separate (i.e. severable) this may work. If not, the defendant may be able to justify the actual charges complained of by showing that the charges, whether complained about or not, have a 'common sting' (*Polly Peck (Holdings) plc v Trelford* [1986] QB 1000).

It is for the defendant to show that the words complained of are substantially true. This is usually done in the course of the pleadings in which the defendant will set out the facts on which reliance is placed. The defendant cannot seek to justify a meaning of which the claimant has not complained.

CASE EXAMPLE

Bookbinder v Tebbit [1989] 1 WLR 640

The claimant, the leader of a Labour council, complained only of a specific charge that the leadership of the council had squandered public money by having a caption 'Support Nuclear Free zones' printed on school stationery. The defendant's attempt to justify this by reference to alleged general squandering of public money was struck out by the Court of Appeal. The claimant had based his complaint on a specific allegation and it was for the defendant to justify that allegation.

During the 1960s some cases were brought by criminals who alleged that a statement that they were guilty of the crime was in fact libellous. In one notorious case, *Hinds v Sparks* [1964] Crim LR 717, the civil jury found that an allegation of murder by the claimant was in fact untrue even though a criminal jury had convicted him on the same facts. It was clear that the civil route of defamation was allowing convicted criminals effectively to have a retrial in a court where the standard of proof was lower. The loophole was closed by the Civil Evidence Act 1968 (as amended by the Defamation Act 1996) which provides that evidence of conviction of a crime is conclusive evidence that the crime was in fact committed by the claimant in a defamation case.

14.4.2 Honest opinion

Section 3(1) Defamation Act 2013 has introduced a new defence of honest opinion which replaces the former defence of fair comment. It is similar to the old defence although it simplifies it and it does not include the former requirement that the opinion is a matter of public interest. This defence is one that applies to a comment or opinion which may not be considered to be fair as such but is an opinion that was honestly held. This is distinct from the defence of truth which concerns matters of fact.

Section 3(2), (3) and (4) introduce three conditions that must be met for the defence to succeed:

- The statement complained of must be a statement of opinion and not an assertion of fact.
- That the statement complained of indicated whether in general or specific terms the basis of the opinion.
- That an honest person could have held the opinion on the basis of:
  - a any fact which existed at the time that the statement complained of was published
  - b anything asserted to be a fact in a privileged statement published before the statement complained of.

Again the cases from the previous defence of fair comment may provide useful illustration of how the new defence will operate with the exception of the requirement of public interest.

Most people have opinions and express comments which may not always be reasonable. So-called experts and commentators, journalists, critics and others are no exception, but their comments are likely to be widely circulated.

An opinion can have as damaging an effect on reputation as an untrue statement of fact.

Opinion distinguished from fact

The first condition requires that the statement must be an opinion. It is sometimes difficult to distinguish between opinion and fact. For instance, calling a man a fornicator or a swindler looks like a statement of fact, but what is calling him immoral or dishonest? Are immorality and sin matters of fact or opinion?' The questions can only be answered by reference to the context in which the statements are made.

Opinions are based on facts which may be explicitly stated or which are referred to by implication. Where the facts are explicit, it is generally easy to distinguish between fact and opinion. Opinion based in implicit facts is more difficult. The House of Lords, in *Kemsley v Foot* [1952] AC 345, held that the old defence of fair comment could be pleaded where there was sufficient indication of the subject-matter on which the comment was based.

The issue has been further clarified by the following case.

CASE EXAMPLE

Telnikoff v Matusevitch [1992] 2 AC 343

A national newspaper published an article by the claimant in which he criticised the BBC, his employers, for employing too many employees from the ethnic minorities of the USSR rather than those who 'associate themselves ethically, spiritually or religiously with the Russian people'. The defendant wrote to the newspaper in response, attacking the claimant's article as racist and anti-Semitic. The defendant also said that the claimant was asking the BBC 'to switch from professional testing to a blood test' and to dismiss 'ethnically alien' employees. The defendant raised the defence of fair comment.

The issue was whether the letter should be judged alongside the article. Could the two be read together? The majority of the House of Lords held that the letter must be read alone. Lord Keith explained at 352:

JUDGMENT

'the readers of the letter must have included a substantial number of persons who had not read the article or who, if they had read it, did not have its terms fully in mind . . . The matter cannot turn on the likelihood or otherwise of readers of the letter having read the article.'

For this reason, the letter should be considered to decide whether or not the statements in the letter amounted to fact or opinion.

In any case the first condition under s3(2) means that the statement must be entirely recognisable as comment rather than an imputation of fact.

Moreover, the Court of Appeal in *British Chiropractic Association v Singh* [2010] EWCA Civ 350 considered in detail whether a statement published under the 'Comment and Debate' section in the *Guardian* newspaper formed an opinion or an assertion of fact. Moreover, this case illustrates the importance of our rights under Article 10, namely the freedom of expression which should not be suppressed easily.

CASE EXAMPLE

British Chiropractic Association v Singh [2010] EWCA Civ 350

Singh, a journalist, published an article under the 'Comment and Debate' section in the *Guardian* newspaper in which he wrote:

'The British Chiropractic Association claims that their members can help treat children with colic, sleeping and feeding problems, frequent ear infections, asthma and prolonged crying, even though there is not a jot of evidence. This organisation is the respectable face of the chiropractic profession and yet it happily promotes bogus treatments.'

There were two issues that required consideration. The first was whether the statement was defamatory and if it were, was this statement asserted as a fact or was it presented as the author's opinion. It was confirmed at first instance that the statement as read by the ordinary and reasonable reader, was in fact defamatory and that the statement was presented as a fact not an opinion and so could not avail himself of the defence of honest opinion as a result. The defendant appealed to the Court of Appeal not least because the BCA relied on the statement in question to demonstrate that it was defamatory in part because it was presented as a fact which also meant that if accepted, it would prevent Singh from relying on the defence of honest opinion. The statement, it was argued by Singh, should have been characterised as a value judgment as opposed to a fact per paragraphs 33–34:

JUDGMENT

'. . . the judge erred in his approach to the need for justification by treating the statement that there was not a jot of evidence to support the BCA's claims as an assertion of fact. It was in our judgment a statement of opinion, and one backed by reasons. We would respectfully adopt what Judge Easterbrook, now Chief Judge of the US Seventh Circuit Court of Appeals, said in a libel action over a scientific controversy, *Underwager v Salter* 22 Fed. 3d 730 (1994):

"[Plaintiffs] cannot, by simply filing suit and crying 'character assassination!', silence those who hold divergent views no matter how adverse those views may be to plaintiffs' interests. Scientific controversies must be settled by the methods of science rather than by the methods of litigation. . . . More papers, more discussion, better data, and more satisfactory models – not larger awards of damages – mark the path towards superior understanding of the world around us."

This is to say that the meaning of Singh's statement was that the BCA were promoting treatments without regard to evidence of their efficacy. Section 6 of the Defamation Act 2013, provides the defence of qualified privilege for statements made in scientific and academic context precisely because they encourage debate, are high value-laden and are expressed more often than not, as opinions. This is important to encourage debate and free speech.

The basis of the opinion must be stated in general or specific terms

The second condition in s3(3) is aimed at simplifying the law and providing a simple and straightforward test. In essence it is giving effect to the test approved by the Supreme Court in *Spiller and Another v Joseph and Others* [2010] UKSC 53 on the former defence of fair comment, that 'the comment must explicitly or implicitly indicate, at least in general terms, the facts on which it was based'.

Lord Walker commented at 131:

JUDGMENT

'The creation of a common base of information shared by those who watch television and use the internet has had an effect which can hardly be overstated. Millions now talk, and thousands comment in electronically transmitted words, about recent events of which they have learned from television or the internet. Many of the events and the comments on them are no doubt trivial and ephemeral, but from time to time (as the present appeal shows) libel law has to engage with them. The test for identifying the factual basis of honest comment must be flexible enough to allow for this type of case, in which a passing reference to the previous night's celebrity show would be regarded by most of the public, and may sometimes have to be regarded by the law, as a sufficient factual basis.'

An honest person might have held the opinion

This does not mean that everyone has to agree with the comment but that it must be a comment which an honest person could make on the basis of the facts.

The test now from s3(4) which identifies the third condition is that an honest person could have held the opinion where it was based on:

a any fact which existed at the time that the statement complained of was published;

b anything asserted to be a fact in a privileged statement published before the statement complained of.

The first is quite straightforward since if the facts were not a sufficient basis for an honest person to hold the opinion then an honest person could not hold them, and it is not an honest opinion. The second means that if the opinion was based on facts that would provide a complete defence in a privileged statement then an honest person could base his opinion on them.

In the case of *Riley v Murray* discussed above, the defence of honest opinion was rejected and the following provides an illustration of how the courts will apply this defence at paragraphs 39–41:

JUDGMENT

'Subsections (2), (3), (4) and (5) reflect the previous common law to this extent at least: the statement must be one of opinion rather than fact; it must indicate its basis in some way (I shall call this "the Basis Condition"); and there must be some fact on the basis of which an honest person could have held the opinion ("the Objective Honesty Condition"); but satisfaction of these conditions will not be enough if the claimant proves as a fact that the defendant did not hold the opinion she expressed (I will call this "the Dishonesty Disqualification").

The defendant had to satisfy the Judge that each of the three conditions in s 3(2)–(4) was met in relation to the imputation that "By so doing, the Claimant has shown herself to be a dangerous and stupid person who risked inciting unlawful violence. People should not engage with her." The Judge had decided at the preliminary trial that this was an expression of opinion, so the first condition was met. At the main trial, the Judge held that the Basis Condition was also met. But he held that the Objective Honesty Condition was not met because the Opinion was "expressly premised" on the truth of the Factual Statement and that, as he had already held, was untrue.

The Judge rejected the defendant's submission that on the true construction of s 3(4)(a) it was enough for her to prove that an honest person could have expressed the Opinion based on the terms of the GAT, and that "the reaction to the Good Advice Tweet more than demonstrates that an honest person could have expressed the Opinion". The Judge noted that the well settled position of the common law was that "if the alleged facts relied on as the basis for comment turn out to be untrue, a plea of fair comment avails the defendant nothing": *London Artists Ltd v Littler Grade Organisation Ltd* [1969] 2 QB 375, 395 (Edmund Davies LJ) approved in *Tse Wai Chun v Cheng* [2001] EMLR [31] (Lord Nicholls) . . . the Judge concluded that the literal reading of s 3(4)(a) relied on by the defendant would involve a "fundamental (and radical) departure from the settled position at common law" with surprising consequences which Parliament would not have intended.'

What this case tells us is that to successfully invoke this defence, this statutory provision is not be interpreted in the literal sense. The defendant has to prove that there is a true factual basis for their opinion and that is one that an honest person could hold. It is not enough for 'any fact' to be true but rather the fact that underlines the factual basis of the opinion must be true.

Others may believe that the comment is wrong or misguided but this is irrelevant. The issue was discussed by the House of Lords in *Reynolds v Times Newspapers Ltd* [2001] 2 AC 127. Suggesting that the word 'fair' is meaningless, Lord Nicholls said at 193:

JUDGMENT

'Comment must be relevant to the facts to which it is addressed. It cannot be used as a cloak for mere invective. But . . . [t]he true test is whether the opinion, however exaggerated, obstinate or prejudiced, was honestly held by the person expressing it.'

The need is for honesty. In discussing matters of public interest concerning public figures, Mr Justice Eady commented in *Branson v Bower* [2002] 2 WLR 452 that they must expect to have their motives 'subjected to scrutiny and discussed'. He went on to say at 461:

> 'Nor is it realistic today to demand that such debate should be hobbled by the constraints of conventional good manners – still less of deference. The law of fair comment must allow for healthy scepticism.'

The test is objective thus the defendant does not need to prove honesty, it is for the claimant to disprove it. While the defendant may be a crank, prejudiced or obstinate this alone does not make the comment dishonest but may well influence a jury in deciding whether or not the opinion is genuine.

On the basis of the matters discussed above, the defence is important to protect freedom of speech. It merely has to be decided whether or not the comment is honest, not whether the court agrees with it. In *Silkin v Beaverbrook Newspapers* [1958] 1 WLR 743, Mr Justice Diplock commenting on this as at that time the role of the jury at 747:

JUDGMENT

> 'it would be a sad day for freedom of speech in this country if a jury were to apply the test of whether it agrees with the comment instead of applying the true test: was this an opinion, however exaggerated, obstinate or prejudiced, which was honestly held by the writer.'

Section 3(5) shows that the defence will fail if the defendant does not in fact hold the honest opinion. This merely restates the previous law that the defence could be lost if the claimant could show malice on the part of the defendant. A good example of this under the former defence of fair comment is found in the following case.

CASE EXAMPLE

Thomas v Bradbury Agnew & Co Ltd [1906] 2 KB 627

A book was reviewed in *Punch* magazine published by the defendants. The review was extremely hostile but the defence of fair comment could perhaps have been used. However, the claimant was able to show, both from the words used in the review and from the demeanour of the reviewer in the witness box, that the reviewer was motivated by malice. The defence of fair comment failed.

For further discussion of the issue of malice see section 14.4.11.

14.4.3 Publication on matters of public interest

The Act in section 4 has introduced a defence related to matters of public interest. This is in relation to situations where it is felt that there should be debate about matters that are deemed to be in the interest of the public without fear of a libel action. This defence clearly aligns with our rights protected under Article 10. This defence replaces what was previously referred to as the *Reynolds* defence which is discussed further below in the context of qualified privilege.

SECTION

'4 (1) It is a defence to an action for defamation for the defendant to show that –

a the statement complained of was, or formed part of, a statement on a matter of public interest; and

b the defendant reasonably believed that publishing the statement complained of was in the public interest.'

This means that this defence may be established if it can be shown

- the statement must be or form part of, a matter of public interest;
- the defendant reasonably believed that publishing the statement complained of was in the public interest;
- the defence may be relied upon irrespective of whether the statement complained of is a statement of fact or a statement of opinion.

So the person publishing the statement must have believed both that it was a matter of public interest and that it was in the public interest to publish it. The term 'public interest' when used in a legal context is notoriously difficult to define or explain. Does it mean in essence something which it may benefit society generally to be aware of or does it simply mean something in which the public generally are interested? If it is the latter, then it would appear that for those in the public eye, whether politicians, religious leaders, celebrities etc. – the list could be endless – every aspect of their public and private life can be the subject of comment. In the absence of a law specifically protecting privacy (as to which see section 14.6.2), the courts have tried to draw some kind of line.

Lord Denning MR explained the concept of public policy in *London Artists Ltd v Littler* [1969] 2 QB 375 saying at 391:

JUDGMENT

'Whenever a matter is such as to affect people at large, so that they may be legitimately interested in, or concerned at, what is going on, or what may happen to them or others; then it is a matter of public interest on which everyone is entitled to make fair comment.'

This explanation appears to embrace both possible meanings. It is for the judge to decide whether or not the comment is on a matter of public interest. Recent years have seen a number of politicians subjected to comment about their private lives. It is not difficult to appreciate that the fact that a politician who lacks personal integrity in personal life may also lack integrity in public life and thus the private life can become a matter of public interest.

Clearly the new defence has both a subjective element, that the defendant believed the matter to be of public interest, and an objective one, that the court thinks that this is a reasonable belief. The defence replaces what has become known as the *Reynolds* defence (see section 14.4.5) and so the list of factors identified in the case which the court should take into account provide a useful guide for courts in applying the defence. This is explained by Warby J at paragraph 82:

JUDGMENT

Doyle v Smith [2018] EWHC 2935 (QB)

Several points from the *Reynolds* checklist of considerations relevant to the availability of the common law privilege are pertinent here: the Court will consider (among other things) (a) the reliability or credibility of the defendant's source(s); (b) what steps were taken by the defendant to verify the truth of the allegations before he made them; (c) whether the defendant sought any comment from the claimant; and (d) whether the defendant included the claimant's side of the story. Where the target of a publication has given an explanation, but the publisher fails to report it, it will be difficult if not impossible to claim the protection of the privilege.

For an illustration of the Supreme Court's approach to this defence the decision of *Flood v Times Newspapers Ltd* [2012] UKSC 11 serves as a useful example.

CASE EXAMPLE

Flood v Times Newspapers Ltd [2012] UKSC 11

Journalists were investigating a tip they had received that a member of the metropolitan police was corrupt and passing highly confidential information on to Russian oligarchs. The journalists thought that this could be the claimant which provoked an investigation by Scotland Yard into the conduct of the claimant with the possibility that he may be corrupt. Following this, the journalists then reported:

'Detective accused of taking bribes from Russian exiles. Police investigating the alleged sale to a security company of intelligence on the Kremlin's attempts to extradite opponents of President Putin, Michael Gillard reports'. The claimant brought proceedings on the basis that the article suggested that he had abused his position and taken bribes for improper purposes. The defendant newspaper defended its position by arguing that he was being investigated and that there were grounds for such an investigation. The investigation by Scotland Yard in fact did not find any evidence to substantiate the allegations.

The Supreme Court had to consider amongst other things, whether it was in the public interest to refer to the details of the allegations made to the police and what verification was required to discharge the requirements of responsible journalism. Lord Philips agreed with earlier formulations of public interest as expressed in *Reynolds* and particularly Lady Hale's formulation in *Jameel* at 125:

JUDGMENT

'In determining the public interest of material, the court considers both its subject matter and content and the appropriateness of publishing it as and when it was (or is to be) published. The speeches in *Jameel* [2007] 1 AC 359 discuss the extent to which it remains helpful to view the privilege in terms of the test (traditionally applied in cases of qualified privilege) of a reciprocal duty on the part of the press to publish and an interest on the part of the public to know. It is a truism that "what engages the interest of the public may not be material which engages the public interest": para 31 per Lord Bingham. . . . Lady Hale said at para 147 that "there must be a real public interest in communicating and receiving the information" and "in having [it] in the public domain", but that was "less than a test of what the public 'need to know', which would be far too limited".'

Moreover Lord Brown said at 113 that, the real question that needed to be asked was:

JUDGMENT

'. . . could whoever published the defamation, given whatever they knew (and did not know) and whatever they had done (and had not done) to guard so far as possible against the publication of untrue defamatory material, properly have considered the publication in question to be in the public interest?'

Overall this defence attempts to maintain a fair balance between the protection of one's reputation *vis-à-vis* the freedom of expression encouraging debate about matters deemed to be in the public interest but not necessarily what would be of interest to the public.

An example on how s4 has been approached by the Court of Appeal against the background of existing common law can be found in the following decision.

CASE EXAMPLE

Economou v de Freitas [2018] EWCA Civ 2591

In this tragic case, the defendant's daughter, Ms de Freitas, was engaged in a short relationship with the claimant following which she accused the claimant of raping her. The claimant argued that he was being falsely accused and brought a private prosecution against Ms de Freitas for perverting the course of justice. This claim was taken up by the CPS against Ms de Freitas but four days before the trial, she committed suicide. The defendant wanted an inquest into his daughter's death and sought to publicise information surrounding the circumstances around the death. The defendant made a series of media statements. It is against these that the claimant brought proceedings as he claimed that these statements suggested he falsely prosecuted Ms de Freitas for lying about being raped when he had in fact raped her. The claimant was not actually named in any such publications but he contended that there was sufficient innuendo in these for people who knew him and those who knew facts around the trial, to understand the publications to be referring to him. A central question in this case was whether the defendant could rely on the defence outlined in s4, namely that the publications were in the public interest. This was considered at paragraphs 75, 87–88, 95–96, 104–105 and 110:

JUDGMENT

'[This ground of appeal], raises difficult issues: in particular, the extent to which contributors to media publications or "citizen journalists" are subject to the same standard of "responsible conduct" that might be required of professional journalists, and the organs in which they publish, if they are to take advantage of the public interest defence.

There were three questions that had to be addressed in relation to each of the publications complained of. Was the statement complained of, or did it form part of, a statement on a matter of public interest? If so, did the defendant believe that publishing the statement complained of was in the public interest? If so, was that belief reasonable? We are principally concerned with the third question . . . the statements complained of were or formed part of a statement on a matter of public interest, and no issue is taken in this appeal with the judge's conclusion that the defendant believed that publishing the statement complained of, was in the public interest.

It follows the judge was right to approach the assessment of reasonableness, as he did, on the footing that a defendant's intended meaning may be relevant to his subjective belief . . . and to whether his belief was objectively reasonable. As the judge said, a reasonable belief that it is in the public interest to make statement "A" could be the basis for the public interest defence, even if the words unintentionally conveyed meaning "B". But this approach cannot be pressed too far, as the judge recognised: thus, in assessing whether a defendant's belief *is* reasonable, there are limits to the latitude to be allowed for unintended or ambiguous meanings. Against that background, I turn to the third question: was the defendant's belief that publishing the statement complained of was in the public interest, reasonable?

[I]t would not be appropriate to hold the defendant to the standard that might be required of a journalist because he was not one: his role was closer to that of a source or contributor . . . there is little scope under article 10(2) of the Convention for restrictions on freedom of expression in relation to questions of public interest.

The fact that information is present on the Internet, gives it permanence and reach, which may have profound implications for the life and future prospects of the person defamed. A successful public interest defence leaves a claimant whose reputation is damaged without vindication, damages or the ability to obtain injunctive relief . . . Section 4 requires the court to have regard to all the circumstances of the case when determining the all-important question arising under section 4(1) (b): it says the court must have regard to all the circumstances of the case in determining whether the defendant has shown that he or she reasonably believed that publishing the statement complained of was in the public interest.'

The Court of Appeal dismissed the appeal as it was felt that the defendant did indeed hold a reasonable belief that it was in the public interest to publish his statements.

CASE EXAMPLE

Banks v Callwalladr [2023] EWCA Civ 219

The claimant sued the defendant for libel in a TED talk and a tweet, both of which were published online to a substantial audience, each of which suggested that the claimant had secretly broken the law on electoral funding by taking money from a foreign power and lied about the matter. Following an official investigation, no evidence was found to suggest that there had been any such breach of the law. The defendant had apologised but she relied on the statutory defence of publication on matters of public interest under s4. At trial, it was found that the talk was defamatory but in the public interest. The Court of Appeal disagreed and Warby LJ commented at 47 that:

'The common law approach to the concept of "publication" accounts for the principle that a public interest defence, once established, does not necessarily endure for ever. A defendant has to show that at the time of each and every publication, he or she continued to believe that it was in the public interest to publish the statement and that this belief remained reasonable when those particular publications were made. The approach is a granular one. The public interest defence is not available in respect of publications made after the defendant ceases to hold the belief in question or such a belief ceases to be reasonable.'

What this case tells us is that the reasonable belief requirement is tested at the time at which the statement is published. If a publication continues to remain available online for instance, the defence available under s4 may no longer be applicable. Circumstances may change and therefore it may be difficult for the defendant to justify their belief that the statement published was in the public's interest.

14.4.4 Absolute privilege

It has long been believed that in certain circumstances people should be free to say whatever they wish without fear of being sued for defamation. The law recognises this and in limited circumstances will give the necessary protection by finding that the statement has absolute privilege; in other words the statement cannot be used as the basis of any legal action.

Parliamentary privilege

Statements made in either of the two Houses of Parliament have absolute privilege by virtue of the Bill of Rights 1688, Article 9. This will not protect a Member of Parliament who makes a defamatory statement outside the House but it covers statements made

i in the course of debate;
ii during committee proceedings;
iii by witnesses to committees.

By the Parliamentary Papers Act 1840, s1 publication of the reports, papers, votes or proceedings of either House also has absolute privilege.

While the privilege does not extend to statements made outside the House, a claimant cannot rely on reports of privileged statements to prove malice (*Church of Scientology of California v Johnson-Smith* [1972] 1 QB 522). This apparently unjust situation has been mitigated in part by the Defamation Act 1996 s13, which permits a member of either House to waive privilege to allow reference to be made to statements which could not otherwise be referred to. The Act only operates to permit a person to waive privilege in order to bring proceedings; it is of no help to a defendant (s13(4)). The privilege which is waived in fact belongs to Parliament which has its own powers of enforcement, but the Act permits an individual to waive that privilege so far as it concerns that individual. This can be done even after the person has ceased to be a Member of the House (*Hamilton v Al Fayed* [2000] 2 All ER 224).

Indeed a very topical example can be found when in 2018 when a newspaper reported that a well-known businessman was involved in allegations of sexual and racial harassment. The newspaper was careful not to name the businessman. The Court of Appeal had in fact issued an injunction to prevent the businessman being named. However, Peter Hain MP took a different view and claimed that it was in the public's interest to know who this individual is and that it is his duty under parliamentary privilege to name Sir Philip Green as the businessman in light of the fact the media have been prevented from naming him. This also serves as an extremely important example of how parliamentary privilege has been used in this instance to allow alleged victims of abuse to have their voices heard in Parliament where they have been unable to freely express their views through the media. There is nevertheless, a growing concern to maintain the rule of law and the separation of powers.

Judicial proceedings

Statements made in the course of proceedings before any court or tribunal whether by the judge, counsel, witnesses or the parties have absolute privilege (*Trapp v Mackie* [1979] 1 WLR 377). This can extend to statements made before the commencement of proceedings provided there is a link with possible proceedings (*Waple v Surrey County Council* [1998] 1 WLR 860) and to disclosure between opposing lawyers (*Taylor v Director of the Serious Fraud Office* [1999] 2 AC 177).

Absolute privilege also extends to 'fair and accurate report of proceedings in public before a court . . . if published contemporaneously with proceedings' (Defamation Act 1996, s14(1)). Originally under Defamation Act 1996, s14(1) now s7(3) Defamation Act 2013 substitutes a new list of courts from those covered by s14 which includes:

a any court in the United Kingdom;
b any court established under the law of a country or territory outside the United Kingdom;
c any international court or tribunal established by the Security Council of the United Nations or by an international agreement;

and in paragraphs (a) and (b) 'court' includes any tribunal or body exercising the judicial power of the State.

Communications between officers of state

State business might grind to a halt were there to be a risk of action for defamation. This means that communications between senior officers of State have absolute privilege.

CASE EXAMPLE

Chatterton v Secretary of State for India **[1895] 2 QB 189**

An official had written a letter to the Under-Secretary for State which contained an allegedly libellous statement about the claimant.

Dismissing the claimant's action on the basis that the letter had absolute privilege, Lord Esher MR explained at 191:

JUDGMENT

'[The law] does not exist for the benefit of the official . . . The reason for the law on this subject plainly appears [to be that] it is that it would be injurious to the public interest that such an inquiry should be allowed, because it would tend to take from an officer of state his freedom of action in a matter concerning the public [welfare].'

The extent of this rule is not clear. It covers communications between Ministers but it does not give blanket immunity for communications between civil servants. It seems that the rule is restricted to those few cases where it is essential that there should be total freedom of communication even though this results in a citizen losing any right to redress.

It should be remembered that the Crown can claim public interest immunity to prevent disclosure of certain classes of official documents (see a text on Constitutional and Administrative Law for details) although such a claim may well lead to political controversy.

The privilege also covers internal memoranda in a foreign embassy (*Fayed v Al-Tajir* [1988] QB 712) although it is likely that this is based on the idea that there should be no interference with the internal affairs of a foreign sovereign state rather than on the reasoning given in *Chatterton v SOS for India*.

14.4.5 Qualified privilege

The law recognises that there are other circumstances when a person needs to be free to tell the truth as they believe it to be, even though in reality they may be wrong. The protection which can apply in such circumstances is found in the doctrine of qualified privilege. Qualified privilege has the same effect as absolute privilege in that the statement cannot be used in a court of law.

The rules are to be found in both common law and in statute. While reading this section, remember that the defence can be defeated if it is shown that the maker of the statement acted maliciously (see section 14.4.11).

The defence generally

This means that this defence may be established if it can be shown

- that the defendant had a legitimate interest in informing readers of that statement;
- readers had a corresponding and legitimate interest in being informed of that statement – reciprocity is essential;
- the defendant was not motivated by malice.

Although in general an action will lie for publication of false and injurious statements, this will not be so where, as Parke B in *Toogood v Spyring* [1824–34] All ER Rep 735 explains at 738:

JUDGMENT

'[the statement] is made by a person in the discharge of some public or private duty whether legal or moral, or in matters where his interest is concerned . . . If fairly warranted by any reasonable occasion, and honestly made, such communications are protected for the common convenience and welfare of society.'

Whether or not such duty or interest exists will depend on the particular facts of the actual case in which the question arises.

The easiest example of how the defence works arises from giving an employment reference.

Few contracts of employment require an employer to give a reference to an employee so that there is no legal duty to do so; in reality many employers do so when requested. If a reference is to be any use to a potential future employer, it is essential that an honest picture is given of the employee's competence and character. The employer has a duty to communicate what is believed to be a true picture while the potential employer has an interest in protecting his business to employ a suitable person. Provided the reference is given honestly, the employee will have no redress if it is unfavourable. It should be noted that the employee may have a remedy in negligence if the person giving the reference has failed to take reasonable steps to check the accuracy of what was said (see *Spring v Guardian Assurance plc* [1995] 3 WLR 354).

Duty situations

It is for the judge to decide whether or not a duty situation exists. As the duty can be based on moral or social grounds, it is difficult to formulate specific principles. Lord Justice Lindley in *Stuart v Bell* [1891] 2 QB 341 suggested at 350:

JUDGMENT

'I take moral or social duty to mean a duty recognised by English people of ordinary intelligence and moral principle.'

In *Watt v Longsdon* [1930] 1 KB 130 Lord Justice Scrutton stated the problem at 144, as follows:

JUDGMENT

'Is the judge merely to give his own view of moral and social duty, though he thinks that a considerable portion of the community hold a different opinion? Or is he to endeavour to ascertain what view the great mass of right-minded men would take?'

It is clear that the judges try to be objective but inevitably their subjective view of what 'right-minded' people would think will influence the decision. Fortunately, some principles are apparent from case law.

In *Adam v Ward* [1917] AC 309 it was said that the person to whom the statement is communicated must have 'a corresponding interest to receive it. This reciprocity is essential.' A good example of how this works is found in the following case.

CASE EXAMPLE

Watt v Longsdon [1930] 1 KB 130

The claimant was the overseas director of a company of which the defendant was also a director. A letter was sent to the defendant from a foreign employee suggesting that the claimant was dishonest and immoral. The defendant wrote back making defamatory comments about the claimant and asking for confirmation of the allegations. Without waiting for a reply, he then showed the letter to the chairman of the company and to the claimant's wife. The statements were in fact untrue.

The Court of Appeal held:

- i the letter to the foreign employee was privileged – they had a common interest in the company;
- ii publication to the chairman was privileged – the defendant as an employee had a duty to pass the information on;
- iii publication to the claimant's wife was not privileged – there was no legal, social or moral duty to inform her about unsubstantiated allegations.

In his judgment Scrutton LJ held at 147 the 'the principle is that there must be an interest in the recipient and a duty to communicate in the speaker, or an interest to be protected in the speaker and a duty to protect it in the recipient'.

In deciding whether or not a duty situation exists the court will take into account all relevant circumstances, in particular:

- i Was there a relationship of confidentiality between the speaker and the recipient?
- ii Was the information given in response to a request or voluntarily?

From time to time defendants argue that certain types of statements should be treated generically as attracting qualified privilege. The courts have tended to reject this view.

In *Watts v Times Newspapers Ltd* [1996] 1 All ER 152 it was suggested that apologies by those making allegedly defamatory statements should form such a category. (The apology had in fact repeated details of the false accusations accompanied inadvertently by a picture of a third party totally unconnected with the matter.) Rejecting the idea that such apologies should generally attract qualified privilege, the Court of Appeal held that the usual principles must apply.

The courts have also considered whether there should be a generic category covering political information and debate.

CASE EXAMPLE

Reynolds v Times Newspapers Ltd [1999] 4 All ER 609

In 1994 a political crisis occurred in Ireland leading to the resignation of the claimant, the Prime Minister. The defendants published an article in the *Sunday Times* which the claimant said accused him of dishonestly and deliberately misleading the Irish Parliament about the reasons for the crisis and of lying to Parliament. The defendants claimed qualified privilege. At first instance the claimant succeeded. The defendants sought a new trial on the basis that the trial judge had erred when he refused to allow the defence of qualified privilege to be used. The Court of Appeal allowing the appeal suggested that qualified privilege can be argued by the press when:

- i the paper has a moral, social or legal duty to inform the public of the matter;
- ii the public has a corresponding interest in receiving the information; and
- iii the nature, status and source of the material and the circumstances of the publication are such as to warrant the protection of privilege.

The matter went to the House of Lords.

Holding that the question for the court is whether or not the duty-interest test is satisfied, the House of Lords found that the questions posed by the Court of Appeal were simply part of that test which takes account of all relevant circumstances. Emphasising the importance of freedom of expression and acknowledging the importance of the role played by the media to inform the public at large of political matters, Lord Nicholls said:

JUDGMENT

'The common law should not develop "political information" as a new "subject matter" category of qualified privilege, whereby the publication of all such information would attract qualified privilege, whatever the circumstances.'

He went on to list ten matters to be taken into account:

i the seriousness of the allegation;
ii the nature of the information and whether it is of public concern;
iii the source of the information;
iv steps taken to verify it;
v the status of the information;
vi the urgency of the matter;
vii whether comment is sought from the claimant;
viii whether the article contained at least the gist of the claimant's side of the story;
ix the tone of the article;
x the circumstances of the publication including the timing.

Lord Nicholls emphasised that the list is not exhaustive. The weight to be given to these and any other relevant factors will vary from case to case.

The House of Lords has subsequently considered the defence of public interest established in *Reynolds* in some detail. In *Jameel and others v Wall Street Journal* [2006] UKHL 44 it was held that the defence should be treated as a question of law and not as a matter of fact to be decided in each case.

The broad principles from *Reynolds* are now reflected in s4 Defamation Act 2013 and crucially, they should not be used as a rigid checklist. (see section 14.4.3).

Interest situations

The defence may apply where the communication is made by a person who has a lawful interest to protect, to a person who has a corresponding interest or duty to protect. The interest may be personal to either party or an interest common to both. The latter is most usually found in the context of business and commerce; for example, an employee who reports dishonesty or other malpractice to management can use the defence. Despite the availability of the defence, employees who 'blow the whistle' are likely to be apprehensive about the reaction of management or colleagues. This has been partly dealt with by the Public Interest Disclosure Act 1998 which protects such an employee from disciplinary action or victimisation provided the disclosure was made to an appropriate person and provided the employee had an honest and reasonable belief in the truth of the allegation.

Some the cases already discussed demonstrate that duty/interest situations are often closely related. Examples include *Watt v Longsdon* and *Reynolds v Times Newspapers Ltd*.

Statutory provision

The defence of qualified privilege has been extended by statute. By the Parliamentary Papers Act 1840 s3, extracts or abstracts of reports, papers, notes or proceedings published by order of Parliament have qualified privilege as, by the Broadcasting Act 1990 Sched. 20, para. 1 do publications of such extracts on television or radio.

The Defamation Act 1996 contains a Schedule that lists a wide range of documents which attract qualified privilege for any publication in any part of the media of any matter arising from such documents which are of public concern or of public benefit. Once this basic point of public interest is established, the extent of the protection is decided according to the part of the Schedule in which the document is listed.

Documents which appear in Schedule 1, Part 1 are privileged 'without explanation or contradiction'. These include fair and accurate reports of any parliament or court anywhere in the world and fair and accurate reports of proceedings at a public inquiry anywhere in the world.

Documents listed in Schedule 1, Part II are privileged 'subject to explanation or contradiction'. These include fair and accurate copies or extracts from documents produced by any parliament of a State which is a member of the European Union, by the European Parliament or by the European Court of Justice. It also includes fair and accurate reports of a general meeting of a United Kingdom public company and of the findings or decisions of various associations such as those formed for the promotion of sport, science, religion or learning. Under Defamation Act 2013 s7(4), the list extends to a fair and accurate copy of, extract from or summary of a notice or other matter issued for the information of the public by or on behalf of:

a a legislature or government anywhere in the world;
b an authority anywhere in the world performing governmental functions;
c an international organisation or international conference; and also to a fair and accurate copy of, extract from or summary of a document made available by a court anywhere in the world, or by a judge or officer of such a court, and also later in s7 to a number of other situations.

Part II privilege is lost if the defendant is shown to have refused or failed to publish in a suitable manner a reasonable letter or other document by way of the claimant's explanation or contradiction of the report. The defendant may also be required to give the claimant a 'right to reply'.

14.4.6 Operators of websites

The Defamation Act 2013 s5 created a new defence for operators of websites where an action for defamation is brought against them for something posted on their website. It also states the circumstances in which the defence will not be available:

SECTION

'5(2) It is a defence for the operator to show that it was not the operator who posted the statement on the website.

5(3) The defence is defeated if the claimant shows that –

a it was not possible for the claimant to identify the person who posted the statement, b the claimant gave the operator a notice of complaint in relation to the statement, and

c the operator failed to respond to the notice of complaint in accordance with any provision contained in regulations.'

Section 5(9) identifies that the defence may be lost if the operator of the website acts with malice, for example by encouraging the posting of the defamation or by colluding with the person posting it on the website.

This means that this defence may be established if it can be shown

- that the operator of the website is not the person who posted the statement on the website;
- the defence is excluded if it is not possible to identify who posted the statement;
- the defence is excluded if the operator of the website was given notice of the statement by the claimant;
- the defence is excluded if the operator failed to respond to such notice in accordance to the regulations (Defamation (Operators of Websites) Regulations 2013);
- the defence will be lost if the operator acted maliciously.

CRITIQUING THE LAW

Consider how you think that the law on defamation should respond to defamatory material being posted online that has been generated by AI. Is there a difference between a platform that generates potentially defamatory material and one that merely hosts such material?

14.4.7 Peer reviewed statements in scientific or other academic journals

Defamation Act 2013 s6 also introduced a new form of qualified privilege attached to statements in peer reviewed journals.

SECTION

'6(1) The publication of a statement in a scientific or academic journal (whether published in electronic form or otherwise) is privileged if the following conditions are met.

(2) The first condition is that the statement relates to a scientific or academic matter.

(3) The second condition is that before the statement was published in the journal an independent review of the statement's scientific or academic merit was carried out by –

a the editor of the journal, and

b one or more persons with expertise in the scientific or academic matter concerned.'

The new defence is designed to reflect the proper process of peer reviewing in academia. By s6(4) a defence is provided to those who review the work. Under s6(6) the defence is lost if malice can be shown.

This means that this defence may be established if it can be shown

- that the statement is published in a scientific or academic journal
- that the statement is about a scientific of academic matter
- that the statement has been independently reviewed by the editor or another relevant expert
- the defendant was not motivated by malice

14.4.8 Innocent publication

In theory some material is published many times over, for example in a book or newspaper – by the author to the editor, by the editor to the printer, by the printer to the wholesaler, by the wholesaler to the retailer and by the retailer to the reader! To deal with this situation, when in reality at least some of those involved may have no reason to know of the defamation, a defence is provided by the Defamation Act 1996 s1. This states that it is a defence for the defendant to show:

- they were not the author or that they were not the editor or publisher, in a commercial sense, of the material;
- all reasonable care was taken;
- they did not know nor had they reason to believe that the material contained a defamatory statement.

The Act restates an older defence, thus earlier cases can be helpful.

CASE EXAMPLE

Vizetelly v Mudie's Select Library Ltd [1900] 2 QB 170

The defendants subscribed to a publication in which publishers placed a notice asking for the return of copies of a book which contained defamatory material. The library ignored the notice and no member of staff had read the book.

The defendants had failed to make out the defence of innocent dissemination and were held to be liable for the publication. In order to succeed Romer LJ said at 180 that a defendant must show:

SECTION

'(1) that he was innocent of any knowledge of the libel in the work disseminated by him;

(2) that there was nothing in the work or the circumstances under which it came to him or was disseminated by him which ought to have led him to suppose that it contained a libel; and

(3) that, when the work was disseminated by him, it was not by any negligence on his part that he did not know that it contained the libel.'

The defence extends to those who provide access to information on the internet if the information is provided by a person over whom the service provider has no control. This is subject to certain limitations.

CASE EXAMPLE

Godfrey v Demon Internet Ltd [1999] EWHC 240 (QB)

The claimant was defamed when an anonymous person sent an obscene message to an internet user newsgroup which purported to come from him. He faxed the ISP, the defendant, telling them that the message was a forgery and asking for it to be removed. The defendant failed to do so. The claimant sought damages from the time he had given the necessary information to the defendant.

In his judgment Morland J commented at 206:

JUDGMENT

'after receipt of the [claimant's] fax the defendant knew of the defamatory posting but chose not to remove it from its . . . service . . . In my judgment the defamatory posting was published by the defendant and, as . . . it knew of the defamatory content of the posting, it cannot avail itself of the protection provided by . . . the Act and its defence under section 1 is in law hopeless.'

It appears that an internet service provider will be liable once the defamatory content is drawn to its attention if it then does nothing to remove the offensive material.

14.4.9 Consent

A person who consents to publication cannot later complain that it is defamatory. This would cover someone who has given the defamatory material to the publisher or who has had editorial control over an article about themself.

CASE EXAMPLE

Moore v News of the World [1972] 1 QB 441

The newspaper actually failed in its use of this defence when it reproduced a private account of Dorothy Squires' (a singer) private life with Roger Moore (an actor). She believed that she was being interviewed about her comeback and was not prepared for personal details which were later published. Otherwise the defence may have been available.

14.4.10 Offer of amends

This is not strictly a defence as it involves the defendant acknowledging that a defamation has occurred but it can have the effect of avoiding litigation and will therefore, in certain circumstances, have a similar effect.

Under the Defamation Act 1996 s2, a person who accepts that a complaint of defamation is well-founded may make a written offer of amends which includes offers to:

- make a suitable correction and a sufficient apology;
- publish the correction, etc. in any way which is reasonable and practical;
- pay compensation and costs.

In the case of *Monroe v Hopkins* discussed above in relation to the serious harm requirement, Monroe suggested that Hopkins make amends to avoid litigation by tweeting:

> 'Dear @KTHopkins, public apology +£5k to migrant rescue & I won't sue. It'll be cheaper for you and v. satisfying for me.'

Justice Warby made the following observation at paragraph 83:

JUDGMENT

> '[T]he case could easily have been resolved at an early stage. There was an open offer to settle for £5,000. It was a reasonable offer. There could have been an offer of amends under the Defamation Act 1996. Such an offer attracts a substantial discount: up to half if the offer is prompt and unqualified. Such an offer would have meant the compensation would have been modest. The costs would have been a fraction of those which I am sure these parties have incurred in the event. Those costs have largely been incurred in contesting the issue of whether a statement which on its face had a defamatory tendency had actually caused serious harm.'

Under s3, acceptance of the offer of amends brings the matter to an end save that the aggrieved party can apply to the court for an order that the terms of the accepted offer are fulfilled. If the necessary steps to fulfil the offer cannot be agreed, the defendant may make a statement in open court in terms approved by the court accompanied by an undertaking to the court for the manner of publication. In *Nail v News Group Newspapers* [2005] 1 All ER 1040 a newspaper had made false allegations about the sexual history of a well-known actor. It made an offer of amends and the parties agreed the wording of an apology but could not agree on compensation. This was then determined by the court under s3(5).

If the claimant does not accept the offer, by s4 it can be pleaded as a defence provided that it can be proved that at the time the statement was made the defendant knew or had reason to believe:

a the statement referred to the claimant or was likely to be understood as doing so; and
b it was false and derogatory.

If this defence is pleaded, the defendant cannot rely on any other defence.

The offer can also be used in mitigation of damages, whether or not it has been relied on as a defence.

14.4.11 The role of 'malice'

It is only rarely that a person's motive for their actions is relevant in tort. One such situation arises in the context of private nuisance (see section 9.4.2), another arises in relation to the defences of fair comment and qualified privilege in defamation.

In the context of fair comment, it is open to the claimant to prove that some improper motive lay behind the defendant's statement (see *Thomas v Bradbury Agnew & Co Ltd*, section 14.4.2, for an example of such a case).

Where the defence is qualified privilege it must be remembered that when the defence succeeds, what would otherwise be held to be defamatory is excused. To establish malice the claimant needs to prove that the defendant took advantage of the nature of the material to make statements which were not believed to be true or to vent spite or ill-will on the claimant or for some other improper motive. The protection of the defence is not lost because the defendant was negligent in checking the facts but in such a case the claimant may have an alternative action for negligence (*Spring v Guardian Assurance plc* [1993] 2 All ER 273).

The burden of proving malice rests on the claimant, who will seek to establish it from evidence of such matters as the relationship between the parties both before and after publication, from the words actually used which may be very excessive in the circumstances and from the defendant's demeanour when giving evidence.

Where more than one defendant is sued, malice on the part of one will not remove the availability of the defence to other, non-malicious defendants (*Telnikoff v Matusevitch* [1992] 2 AC 343).

ACTIVITY

Self-assessment questions

1 Explain the defence of 'truth'.
2 What is the important principle established by *Charleston v News Group Newspapers*?
3 To what extent does the defence of 'honest opinion' uphold the principle of freedom of speech?
4 Outline the circumstances in which a statement may be subject to 'absolute' privilege.
5 In the context of 'qualified' privilege explain how the courts approach the task of deciding whether a defendant has a 'duty' or 'interest' in making the statement complained of.
6 What are the limitations imposed in relation to the defence of 'innocent' publication?
7 Explain the effect of 'malice' in relation to defamation.

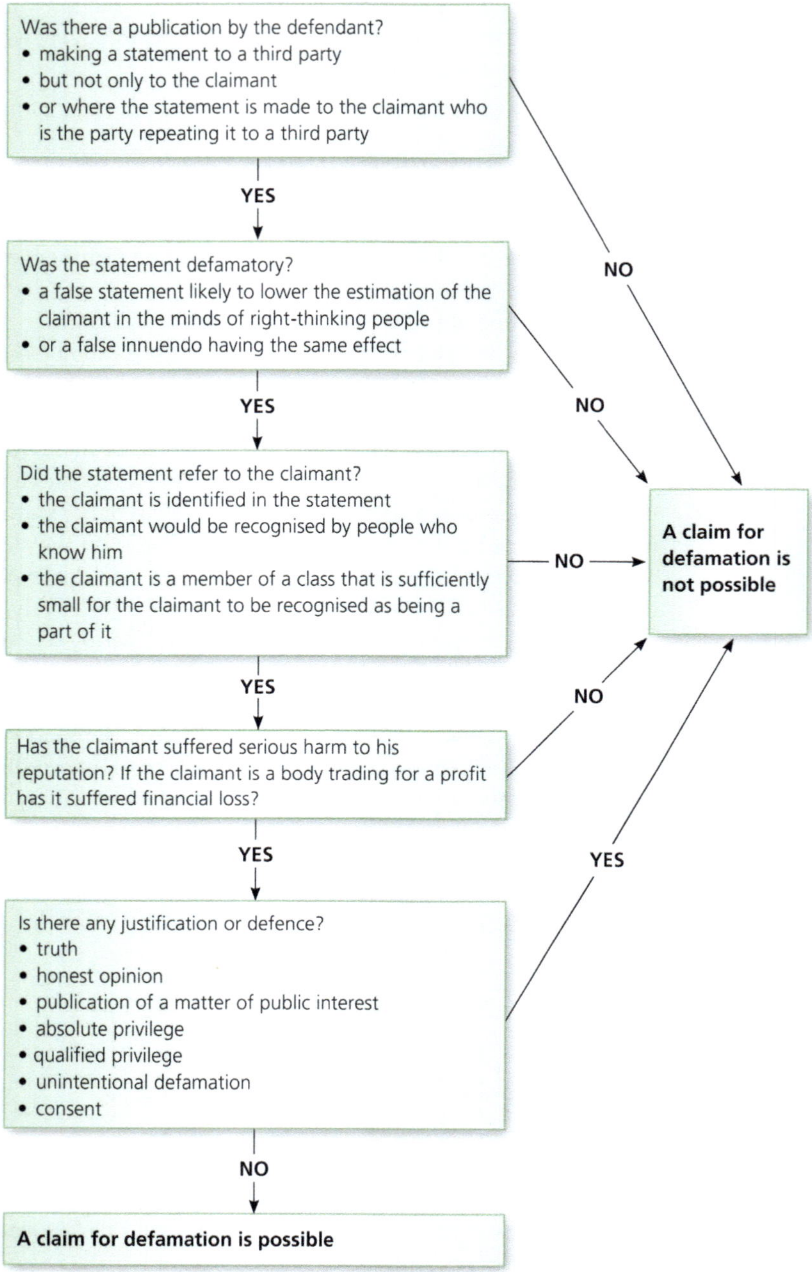

Figure 14.1 The essential elements for a claim in defamation.

14.5 Remedies

14.5.1 Injunction

An injunction may be sought by the claimant in two circumstances:

1 in rare cases to prevent publication of a defamatory statement;

2 to prevent the statement being repeated.

When a claimant becomes aware that a defamatory statement is about to be published, it would be natural to seek an interlocutory injunction to prevent that publication. The nature of an interlocutory injunction means that the substantive issue between the claimant and the defendant is not at that stage considered in detail – there is no trial of such issues. The result of this is that such injunctions are unlikely to be granted where a defendant can show that a defence, for example justification or fair comment, may be pleaded with some hope of success at the full trial.

CASE EXAMPLE

Holley v Smyth [1998] QB 726

A squabble occurred between two people involved in a financial transaction. The defendant alleged that the claimant had acted dishonourably and sent him a copy of the press release which he proposed to issue. The claimant sought an interlocutory injunction but his application was refused. The defendant made it clear that were he to be sued after publication, he would be able to establish that what was said was true. The Court of Appeal said that an interlocutory injunction should only be granted when it was clear that the statement was untrue. The claimant's application was refused.

These rules have to take account of European Convention on Human Rights Article 10, which guarantees freedom of expression and of the Human Rights Act 1998 s12, which prevents prior restraint 'unless the court is satisfied that the applicant is likely to establish that publication should not be allowed'. The reader may well feel that the statutory provisions merely restate the common law position. Unless it is clear that any defence is likely to fail, no interlocutory injunction will be granted.

When an injunction is applied for after trial of the substantive issues, the claimant is more likely to be successful if it can be shown that damages alone will not provide a sufficient remedy in the particular circumstances. In *Tolstoy Miloslavsky v UK* [1995] 20 EHRR 442, ECtHR the Court of Human Rights held that the grant of a permanent injunction to prevent repetition would not be a breach of Article 10.

14.5.2 Damages

While the purpose of damages is to compensate the claimant for loss, defamation is one of the few torts in respect of which exemplary damages may be awarded. The usual award is compensatory damages as explained by Sir Thomas Bingham MR in *John v Mirror Group Newspapers Ltd* [1996] 2 All ER 35 at 48:

JUDGMENT

'. . . compensate [the claimant] for the loss of his good name; and take account of the distress, hurt and humiliation which the defamatory publication has caused . . . the extent of publication is also very relevant; a libel published to millions has a greater potential to cause damage than a libel published to a handful of people.'

Exemplary damages will only be awarded where the claimant can prove that the defendant knew that a tort was being committed (or was reckless on this point) and even so went ahead on the basis that the profits to be made from the publication would far exceed any damages which might be payable. In such cases, the award will include a sum designed to ensure that the defendant is 'punished'. There may be little difficulty in proving the necessary knowledge by the defendant but the question of recklessness is not straightforward. It is most easily explained by an attitude of total disregard for the question of whether the statement is true or false. This becomes more believable when the defendant's awareness of profit to be made from publication is brought into consideration.

Previously, damages were determined by a jury. Section 11 Defamation Act 2013 confirms that trials are to be without a jury unless the court orders otherwise. The cases before the 2013 reference juries but are still relevant for the purposes of understanding how the level of damages has been determined.

The Courts and Legal Services Act 1990 gave the Court of Appeal power to review the level of damages awarded by a jury and to substitute its own assessment of an appropriate figure. The use of this power has led to some fairly spectacular reductions. In *John v Mirror Group Newspapers* [1996] 146 NLJ Rep 13 the figure was reduced from £75,000 to £25,000 while in *Rantzen v Mirror Group Newspapers (1986) Ltd* [1994] QB 670 the figure was brought down from £250,000 to £110,000. The Court of Appeal does not always disagree with a jury assessment.

CASE EXAMPLE

Kiam II v MGN Ltd [2002] EWCA Civ 43

The claimant had succeeded in a libel action in respect of a leading article published in the *Mirror* newspaper. The article was untrue in every material respect and the jury awarded damages of £105,000. The defendant appealed against the level of the award.

The jury award was upheld. Lord Justice Simon Brown restated a basic principle at 49:

JUDGMENT

'this court should not interfere with the jury's award unless it regards it as substantially exceeding the most that any jury could reasonably have thought appropriate'.

In earlier cases a comparison with the level of damages awarded in personal injury cases had been ruled out. However, by the time this appeal was heard the maximum amount for general damages in such cases had been increased to £200,000. Lord Justice Simon Brown and Lord Justice Waller recognised that a comparison with the level of damages in personal injury cases was a relevant consideration but found that the award was not excessive and dismissed the appeal. Lord Sedley, giving a minority judgment, went so far as to say at 78:

JUDGMENT

'I would allow this appeal on the narrow ground that even by comparison with other libel awards, but especially by comparison with personal injury awards, the figure awarded by the jury as compensatory damages is wholly excessive.'

It is also important to note that for some claimants, it is less about the damages that they may secure from a claim in defamation and more about being vindicated. Going to trial will inevitably draw attention to the statement and this may drive the need for vindication even further.

CASE EXAMPLE

Cairns v Modi, KC v MGN [2012] EWCA Civ 1382

This case concerned the level of compensation awarded in libel proceedings in these conjoined appeals. *Cairns v Modi* involved a sustained attack on the professional reputation of a world-famous cricketer who was awarded £90,000. By contrast, *KC v MGN Ltd* involved a blunder by a newspaper which led to a false accusation that a man of good character had been convicted in the 1970s of raping a 14-year-old girl. Fortunately, he was and remains anonymous, and after an early apology, the allegation was quickly withdrawn. He was awarded £75,000. The issue before the judge was the level of compensation to be awarded under s3 Defamation Act 1996 following the newspaper's acknowledgment of error and offer of amends under the statutory regime.

The reasoning for the level of damages is explained at paragraph 32 where £75,000 was awarded plus an additional £15,000 for the manner in which the trial was conducted. It was held that this award was proportionate to the seriousness of the allegation, the impact on the claimant and sufficient to vindicate his reputation:

JUDGMENT

'In any event it cannot be right in principle for a defendant to embark on a wholesale attack on the character of a claimant in a libel action heard by a judge without having to face the consequences of the actual and potential damage done to the victim both in the forensic process and as a result of further publicity . . . The judge will be well placed to assess whether the terms of the judgment do indeed provide sufficient vindication in the overall context of the case . . . the general public (or rather, interested "bystanders" who need to be convinced) will be concerned to discover what might be called the "headline" result. What most people want to know . . . is simply "how much did he get?"'

By contrast, in the second appeal in *KC v MGN*, the original award was discounted by 50 per cent from £150,000 to £75,000 to reflect that the claimant's anonymity had been maintained and, that an early apology was offered to vindicate the claimant very soon after the offending statement was published.

At paragraphs 49–50 it was explained that:

JUDGMENT

'If the circumstances of publication and the conduct of the defendant in this case had approximated to that of Mr Modi, with all the attendant publicity, directly and expressly repeating that KC was a sexual predator, and identifying him, or providing the means for his identification, an award of £150,000 would have been inadequate. However, given the limited number of those who might have read or heard of the false allegation made against him, and appreciate that it did indeed refer to him, the starting point was too high. We propose to reduce it to a level which, consistently with the limited publication and early apology, would nevertheless adequately reflect the abhorrent nature of the crime falsely alleged against KC and the damage done to and its impact on him . . . The offer of amends was made with reasonable promptitude in this case and the first apology published even earlier. KC therefore knew very soon after the date of publication that he was vindicated, and that this was bound to have "a major deflationary effect" on any award.'

(For more detailed discussion of the principles governing awards of damages, see Chapter 19.)

14.6 Privacy, confidentiality and human rights

14.6.1 Introduction

It should be clear to the reader that almost the last thing that the existence of the tort of defamation does is to protect privacy or confidentiality. It is true that the tort allows for a remedy in the event that something which is not true is published. This may have a deterrent effect but in order to obtain a remedy, the claimant will be faced with bringing court action which more often than not is likely to have the effect of making even more people aware of the false allegation. We have seen that it is very rarely that an interim injunction will be issued to restrain publication.

Defamation provides no remedy for people who face publication of a fact which they would rather keep private but which is true. Even where the publication relates to a conviction which is 'spent' by virtue of the Rehabilitation of Offenders Act 1974, a defendant who has disclosed the existence of the spent conviction can use it to support a defence of fair comment or justification (s8(3)), provided the publication was made without malice (s8(5)).

A person who has something which they choose to hide may have some help available but as we shall see it is very limited.

14.6.2 Privacy

English law does not recognise a general right to privacy. The House of Lords in *Wainright v Home Office* [2004] AC 406; [2003] UKHL 53 (discussed earlier) considered this in detail and rejected the notion that there was such a right in English law. The European Court of Human Rights in *Wainright v UK* ECHR (Application No 12350/04) has subsequently held that there was no breach of Article 3 but there were breaches of Article 8 and of Article 13. This is partly the result of the difficulty in framing an adequate definition. The difficulty is increased when it is remembered that too wide a definition could lead to:

- the opening of the floodgates to large volumes of litigation;
- an unreasonable restriction on the freedom of the media to report matters of public interest.

Too narrow a definition would fail to give adequate protection in all circumstances.

The issue was considered by the Calcutt Committee in 1990 which was investigating incidents of press intrusion. The Commission did not recommend the creation of a general tort of invasion of privacy considering that the right to privacy could be adequately protected by other means (Report of the Committee on Privacy and Related Matters (1990) Cm 1102).

The issue continues to be one which regularly troubles the courts. Currently in 2026, Prince Harry together with other high profile individuals including Liz Hurley, Elton John and Doreen Lawrence are pursuing a claim for the intrusion into their private lives by the press and the parameters of what really constitutes 'in the public's interest'.

In previous high-profile cases of *Campbell v MGN plc* [2004] 2 AC 457; [2004] 2 WLR 1232; [2004] UKHL 22 and *Douglas and Others v Hello! Ltd and Others* [2003] EWHC 786 (Ch) the judges were all concerned with the problem of giving effect to what they generally viewed as an underlying principle that privacy should be respected and protected. The conclusions were that this could be achieved by using existing English law rather than by developing a new general tort. In both cases the courts were prepared to accept that there were breaches of confidence.

Breach of privacy is in fact protected in various ways, most importantly by the development of the equitable remedy available for breach of confidence. Other protections include:

- Trespass to land, for example where the media has come on to land to take photographs or seek other 'evidence' although *Bernstein v Skyviews and General Ltd* [1977] QB 479 suggests that this protection can be limited.
- Breach of copyright as, for example, in *Williams v Settle* [1960] 1 WLR 1072 where a claimant obtained damages for unauthorised use of a photograph in which he owned the copyright. (See also Copyright, Designs and Patents Act 1988 s85, which gives the person who commissions a photograph or film for private and domestic purposes a right of privacy, in that publication of the work without consent is unlawful.)
- Breach of contract provides a simple remedy where the terms of the agreement are clear and impose a duty of confidentiality.
- Various statutes may also provide protection by regulating the way in which and the purposes for which information may be obtained (for example, the Interception of Communications Act 1985 regulates the use of telephone tapping and the Data Protection Act 1998 sets out a detailed scheme for obtaining, storing and use of personal data).

14.6.3 Confidentiality

Breach of confidence is a concept established in equity and has not yet been recognised as a tort. Many cases are based on breach of confidentiality in commercial and business cases which often involve industrial espionage or inappropriate disclosure of information to a rival concern. These are not dealt with in this book. The concept is also available to those whose personal privacy has been invaded or is threatened by disclosure of information which they regard as private. The general circumstances were explained in *Argyll v Argyll* [1967] Ch 302. Mr Justice Ungoed-Thomas explained at 304:

JUDGMENT

'(1) . . . a contract or obligation of confidence need not be expressed but can be implied . . .;
(2) . . . a breach of confidence . . . can arise independently of any right of property or contract . . .;
(3) . . . the court in the exercise of its equitable jurisdiction will restrain a breach of confidence independently of any right at law.'

While the action remains rooted in equity, it will continue to allow the principle of privacy to be protected in various novel circumstances arising in a fast-changing world.

The right to confidentiality can be overridden where this is necessary on the ground of public interest. We have already seen the difficulties faced by the courts in such cases, especially when a balance has to be found between the public interest in maintaining a free press and the private rights of individuals. An interesting example is found in the following.

CASE EXAMPLE

X v Y [1988] 2 All ER 648

A newspaper had found out that two doctors at a local hospital were being treated for AIDS. The paper argued that the names of the doctors should be disclosed in the public interest, that is so that patients could decide whether or not to be treated by the doctors.

Mr Justice Rose stated that he kept in the forefront of his mind 'the very important public interest in freedom of the press' but went on to say at 661:

JUDGMENT

'in my judgment those public interests are substantially outweighed when measured against the public interests in relation to loyalty and confidentiality both generally and with particular reference to AIDS patients' hospital records'.

The judge was also concerned that to leave AIDS patients vulnerable to disclosure of their medical records would act as a deterrent to others who would be reluctant to come forward to seek diagnosis. Public interest would be better served by diagnosis of as many as possible of those infected by the disease.

14.6.4 Human rights

It is popularly thought that Article 8 of the Convention on Human Rights grants a right to privacy. In fact it guarantees a right to 'respect for private and family life'. We have seen in Chapter 1 that Article 8 can be used in a very wide range of cases. In the context of privacy, the European Court of Human Rights has considered the extent to which protection of privacy is granted.

CASE EXAMPLE

Peck v UK [2003] ECtHR, 36 EHRR 41

The claimant, while suffering from depression, was walking in a town centre with a knife in his hand and attempted to cut his wrists. The fact that he was carrying a knife was picked up on CCTV and the police were sent. The claimant received necessary help. The film was subsequently used to promote the use of CCTV and still photographs were published in a local paper. In neither case was the claimant masked and indeed people recognised him. The UK courts, while sympathetic to the claimant, found that he had no remedy. The claimant applied to the European Court alleging breach of Article 8.

Noting that the claimant did not allege that the use of CCTV as such infringed his rights under Article 8, the Court held that 'the disclosure of [the] record of his movements to the public in a manner in which he could never have foreseen' gave rise to such infringement. At paragraph 720 it was held that:

JUDGMENT

'The disclosure . . . of the relevant footage constituted a serious interference with the . . . right to respect for his private life.'

14.6.5 Conclusion

The debate about privacy will continue but evidence to date suggests that the concept of privacy will continue to be regarded as a principle which underpins other aspects of the law. Equity is flexible so that confidentiality can be protected and the effect of Article 8 is gradually being understood in the context of English law. What is certain is that statute will play an important part. The Data Protection Act 1998 and the Freedom of Information Act 2000 have now been fully implemented. It may be that the statutory provisions and the codes of practice which are being developed at the present time will make a substantial contribution to the establishment of some clear rules.

ACTIVITY

Self-assessment questions

1. Why may a claimant be unable to obtain an interim injunction to restrain publication of defamatory material about the claimant?
2. When will the courts be likely to award exemplary damages for defamation?
3. Explain the equitable remedy for breach of confidentiality and the extent to which this can safeguard privacy of an individual.
4. In what circumstances is it likely that Article 8 of the European Convention of Human Rights will be used successfully to protect privacy?

SAMPLE ESSAY QUESTION

Discuss the extent to which the law on defamation achieves a balance between the right of a person to protect his reputation and the right of freedom of speech.

Outline the essential elements for a claim in defamation

- Publication
- Of a defamatory statement
- Which has caused or is likely to cause serious harm to the reputation of the claimant
- Referring to the claimant
- Which is untrue
- And has no defence

Distinguish between the two forms

- Libel – permanent form
- Slander – transitory form – proof of damage required except imputation of criminal conviction, unfitness for office
- Discuss any associated problems

Discuss the limitations of the tort

- Truth is always a defence so protects freedom of speech but could damage reputation
- Expensive to bring action so could limit ability to protect reputation
- Reputation is damaged as soon as the defamation occurs – unless prohibitory injunction is possible – but people rarely know about the defamation before publication

Discuss the effect of the defences

- Wide range favours freedom of speech possibly at expense of protecting reputation
- Absolute privilege and qualified privilege support freedom of speech at the expense of reputation
- Question whether defences of honest opinion and publication of a matter of public interest give too much licence to the press and media
- Printed apologies rarely have the same space or impact as the defamatory comment

Discuss other relevant issues

- The difficulty in bringing a class action or being a member of a defamed class
- The rules relating to innuendo make it harder for a claimant to prove the defamation – so more difficult to protect reputation
- Lack of intention is no defence – so this restricts freedom of speech
- The effect of the Human Rights Act

KEY FACTS

Key facts on defamation

Libel generally	Case/statute
Untrue statement in permanent form.	Defamation Act 1952
Not necessarily in writing – includes broadcasts and TV performance of a play.	Theatres Act 1968 *Youssoupoff v MGM* [1934]
Film.	
Actionable where serious harm has been caused or is likely to be caused to the claimant's reputation (in the case of a body trading for a profit this must be financial loss).	
Can be a crime but rare.	
Slander generally	**Case/statute**
Untrue statement in transient form.	
Usually verbal but can be gesture.	
Traditionally special damage required but with some exceptions.	
Elements of defamation	**Case/statute**
Statement must be defamatory.	
The statement must have caused or be likely to cause serious harm to the claimant's reputation (or some financial loss in the case of a body trading for a profit).	*Lachaux v Independent Print Ltd* [2019] *Monroe v Hopkins* [2017]
It must refer to claimant.	s1 Defamation Act 2013
It must be published.	
It must be false.	
Meaning of defamatory	**Case/statute**
Statement is untrue.	*Cassell v Broome* [1972]
It tends to lower a person in the eyes of others	*Parmiter v Coupland* [1840] *Youssoupoff v MGM* [1934]
or to expose them to ridicule or contempt.	*Byrne v Deane* [1937]
or to cause others to shun them.	*Hartt v Newspaper Publishing* [1989]
Note problem of deciding who is 'right-thinking member of society':	*Cassidy v Daily Mirror* [1929]; *Tolley v Fry & Sons* [1931]; *Norman v Future Publishing* [1999]
• the ordinary good and worthy person • the ordinary reader who is not unduly suspicious.	

(Continued)

(Continued)

Additional knowledge held by hearer or reader can make inoffensive statement defamatory.	
Reference to claimant	**Case/statute**
Usually explicit.	*Cassidy v Daily Mirror* [1929]
Can be implied from other information.	*Hulton v Jones* [1910]; *Newstead v London Express Newspaper* [1940]; *Morgan v Odhams Press* [1971]
Publication	**Case/statute**
Statement must be communicated to a person other than the claimant.	*Huth v Huth* [1915]; *Slipper v BBC* [1991]
Communication between spouses is not publication.	
Can be liability for unintentional publication where it can be reasonably anticipated that the material will be communicated.	
Defences: truth	**Case/statute**
The statement is true in substance.	S2 Defamation Act 2013
So must be substantially true.	*Alexander v Eastern Railway* [1865]
The untruthfulness of the statement is clearly stated.	*Charleston v News Group Newspapers* [1995]
Burden on defendant to prove truth.	*Bookbinder v Tebbit* [1989]
Note special provisions concerning criminal convictions.	*Hinds v Sparks* [1964] Civil Evidence Act 1968
Defences: honest opinion	**Case/statute**
The statement is one of opinion.	S3(2) Defamation Act 2013
Facts on which comment is based must be indicated expressly or by implication.	S3(3) Defamation Act 2013; *Telnikoff v Matusevitch* [1992]
An honest person could have held the opinion on the basis of: • facts which existed at the time the statement was published • things from a privileged statement published before the statement complained of.	S3(4) Defamation Act 2013 *Thomas v Bradbury Agnew* [1906]
The comment must be honestly made even if no one else agrees with it – claimant must disprove honesty.	*British Chiropractic Association v Singh*
Note that malice will defeat this defence. because it would not then be an honest opinion.	

(Continued)

(Continued)

Publication of a matter of public interest	Case/statute
The statement included a matter of public interest.	*London Artists v Littler* [1969]; *Flood v Times Newspapers Ltd* [2012]
The defendant believed that it was in the interest of the public to publish it.	*Reynolds v Times Newspapers* [2001]; *Economou v de Freitas* [2018]
The first is a subjective question and the second is objective for the judge to determine.	
Has replaced the *Reynolds* defence and codified it.	S4 Defamation Act 2013
Defences: absolute privilege	**Case/statute**
Statement cannot be used as the basis for any legal action.	Bill of Rights 1688
Applies to statements in either House of Parliament and to reports, etc. published by order of either House.	Parliamentary Papers Act 1840
Applies to statements made in proceedings before any court and to fair, accurate and contemporaneous reports of such proceedings.	*Chatterton v Sec of State for India* [1895]
Certain communications between officers of state.	
Defences: qualified privilege	**Case/statute**
No action can be based on statement with qualified privilege.	*Toogood v Spyring* [1834]
Statement must be made by someone who has a duty to make it to someone who has a duty to receive it.	*Stuart v Bell* [1891]
Duty may be legal, moral or social.	*Watt v Longsdon* [1930]
	Watts v Times Newspapers [1996]; *Reynolds v Times Newspapers* [2001]
Defences: innocent publication	**Case/statute**
Defendants will not be liable provided they are not the author, publisher or editor of the material, that they took all reasonable care and did not know of the defamatory material.	Defamation Act 1996, s1
Defence extends to internet service providers but note –	*Vizetelly v Mudie's Select Library* [1900]; *Godfrey v Demon Internet* [1999]
Defences: consent	**Case/statute**
Extends to those who are able to exercise editorial control.	

(Continued)

(Continued)

Defences: offer of amends	**Case/statute**
Defendant acknowledges defamation has occurred but makes written offer to apologise, to publish the correction and to pay compensation and costs.	
Acceptance ends matter.	
Refusal allows offer to be pleaded as defence.	
Defences: malice	**Case/statute**
Negates qualified privilege.	
Remedies	**Case/statute**
Injunction to prevent repeated publication but rarely available in advance of publication.	*Holley v Smyth* [1998]
Note effect of –	European Convention on Human Rights, Art. 10
and	
Damages – can be exemplary where defendant knew or was reckless that the material was defamatory – a matter for the jury but Court of Appeal has power to review and substitute a lower figure.	Human Rights Act 1998, s12

KEY FACTS

Key facts on privacy, confidentiality and human rights

Privacy	**Case/statute**
No general legal right to privacy.	
Judicial view it is not needed as other parts of the law can be used.	*Campbell v MGN* [2003]; *Douglas v Hello!* [2003]
Confidentiality	Case/statute
Equity may give remedy for breach of confidence.	*Argyll v Argyll* [1967]
Human rights	**Case/statute**
Protects right to respect for private and family life.	European Convention on Human Rights, Art. 8; *Peck v UK* [2003]

SUMMARY

- There are two types of defamation: libel (a permanent form) and slander (a transitory form).
- Defamation requires proof that a claimant has suffered or is likely to suffer serious harm to his reputation as a result of the statement (and for a body trading for profit this must be financial loss).
- Defamation is defined as a publication to a third party of a defamatory statement which refers to the claimant and causes serious harm to the claimant's reputation and with no lawful justification.
- A defamatory remark is one that lowers the estimation of the claimant in the minds of right-thinking people or would cause them to shun or avoid him.
- Implying decency or honesty cannot be defamatory.
- Defamation can be by an innuendo.
- The claimant must be able to show that the statement referred to him personally so class actions usually fail and only succeed where the claimant can show that he is identifiable as a member of the class.
- There are many defences available including: justification (the truth can never be defamatory however hurtful), honest opinion publication of matters of public interest, absolute privilege (generally proceedings in Parliament or in court), qualified privilege (in certain confidential communications between privileged parties), unintentional defamation and innocent dissemination.
- Remedies include both damages and injunctions.

Further reading

Bogle, S, and Lindsay, B, 'Serious harm: Six lessons since *Lachaux*' (2024) *16*(2) *JML* 417–439.

Erdos, D, 'Serious harm to reputation rights? Defamation in the Supreme Court' (2019) *78*(3) *CLJ* 510–513.

15

The economic torts

AIMS AND OBJECTIVES

After reading this chapter you should be able to:

- Identify and explain the essential elements for proving deceit
- Define the requirements for proving malicious falsehood
- Explain the essential elements for proving passing off
- Identify and explain the requirements for proving conspiracy and inducing a breach of contract
- Critically analyse each tort
- Apply the law to factual situations and reach conclusions as to liability

We are used to the law of torts dealing with interference that has caused loss or damage to property or physical injury. We have already seen from the law on pure economic loss that the courts are less willing to become involved where economic loss is concerned (see section 6.2). One of the traditional reasons given for this was that in character such loss was more appropriately compensated in the law of contract.

However, there are a number of torts that can be loosely grouped together and which are concerned with interference with a person's economic interests. They may represent an interference with a person's livelihood and include deceit and malicious falsehood and also can include passing off and a range of other specific ways of interfering with a person's trade.

15.1 Deceit

Deceit has a lot in common with and indeed is often associated with misrepresentation in contract law. It is a well-established tort that occurs when an entirely false representation is made that causes loss to a claimant who relies on the false statement. It was first recognised as early as the eighteenth century.

DOI: 10.4324/9781003202417-15

CASE EXAMPLE

Pasley v Freeman [1789] 3 Term Rep 51

The defendant falsely represented to the claimant that a third party to whom the claimant wished to sell goods on credit was in fact creditworthy. In fact this was entirely false and the claimant suffered loss as a result of the transaction. He was nevertheless able to recover for his loss through the tort of deceit.

The significance of the tort is that a successful claimant is able to recover not just for financial loss but for physical loss or injury also.

CASE EXAMPLE

Burrows v Rhodes [1899] 1 QB 816

The claimant was persuaded through a false representation to take part in the 'Jameson Raid'. He was able to recover under the tort for the physical injuries he sustained.

The tort is interrelated with the action for negligent misstatement and with misrepresentation in contract law. On this basis its significance may have reduced somewhat as a result of the *Hedley Byrne* principle and of the Misrepresentation Act 1967 since it is arguably harder to prove than either. However, the tort does enjoy a different measure of damages which may still make it a worthwhile cause of action.

The requirements of the tort of deceit are:

- that the defendant makes a false statement to the claimant or a class of people including the claimant;
- that the defendant knows that the statement is false or is reckless in making it;
- that the defendant intends that the claimant will rely for his conduct on the false statement;
- that the claimant does indeed suffer damage as a result of having relied on the statement.

15.1.1 The making of a false statement

Generally a misrepresentation must concern a material fact in order to be actionable and must not be only a mere opinion.

CASE EXAMPLE

Bisset v Wilkinson [1927] AC 177

Here in response to a request by the purchaser of land the vendor made a false statement concerning the number of sheep that the land being sold would support. There was no liability. The statement could not be relied upon since the vendor had no knowledge or expertise in the area and it was merely an unsupported opinion.

Of course a misrepresentation concerning a material fact may be actionable where the person making it has specialist knowledge.

CASE EXAMPLE

Esso v Marden [1976] QB 801

In this case the petrol company represented the likely sales of petrol to the person who was contracting to take a franchise of a petrol station. The statement could be relied upon because of the superior specialist expertise of the party making it.

While opinions are not classed as statements of fact it may be a false statement of fact to misrepresent an opinion or knowledge which is not actually held.

CASE EXAMPLE

Edgington v Fitzmaurice [1885] 29 Ch D 459

The directors of a company falsely stated that a loan would be used to improve the company. In fact their intention all along was to use the money to repay very serious debts that were owed by the company. The misrepresentation of a future intent in these circumstances was sufficient to amount to an actionable falsehood.

It will also amount to a false statement to fail to correct a true statement that has later become false.

CASE EXAMPLE

With v O'Flanagan [1936] Ch 575

A doctor was selling his practice which was said during the negotiations for the sale to be worth an annual income of £2,000. The practice actually lost patients, and thus income, prior to the completion and the doctor's failure to inform the purchaser of this fact amounted to an actionable misrepresentation.

It is also possible that a person who makes a false statement can be personally liable for deceit even though the misrepresentation is made on behalf of another party if all of the other elements of the tort are satisfied.

CASE EXAMPLE

Standard Chartered Bank v Pakistan National Shipping Line (Nos 2 and 4) [2002] 3 WLR 1547

A company, Oakprime Ltd, agreed to supply bitumen to a Vietnamese buyer with payment to be by letter of credit issued by Vietnamese bankers and confirmed by the claimant bank. The letter of credit required delivery before a specific date but loading of the bitumen was delayed until after that date. Mr Mehra, the managing director of Oakprime, then agreed with the shippers to insert a false shipping date in the documents. The claimant bank then authorised payment but was unable to recover from the Vietnamese bank because it had failed to notice that the documents were not in order. The claimant successfully sued both the shippers and Mehra. Mehra was held liable even though he had engaged in the deceit for the company. The court rejected a defence of contributory negligence since the defence was held not to be available in the case of a fraudulent misrepresentation.

15.1.2 Knowledge that the statement is false

The appropriate test of knowledge is the classic definition explained by Lord Herschell in *Derry v Peek* [1889] 14 App Cas 337. The test identifies the need to show a fraud which is hard to show.

CASE EXAMPLE

Derry v Peek [1889] 14 App Cas 337

A tram company was licensed to operate horse drawn trams by Act of Parliament. Under the Act the company would also be able to use mechanical power by first gaining a certificate from the Board of Trade. The company made an application and also issued a prospectus to raise further share capital. In this, honestly believing that permission would be granted, the company falsely represented that it was able to use mechanical power. In the event the application was denied and the company fell into liquidation. Peek, who had invested on the strength of the representation in the prospectus and lost money, sued. His action failed since there was insufficient proof of fraud. Lord Herschell in the House of Lords defined the action as requiring actual proof that the false representation was made 'knowingly or without belief in its truth or recklessly careless whether it be true or false'.

The test required that fraud must be proved which would mean that the misrepresentation had been made:

- knowingly; or
- without belief in its truth; or
- reckless as to its truth.

It would appear that where an employee acts in the course of his employment in committing a deceit then the employer is likely to be vicariously liable for the false statement. The same principle is likely to apply in the case of agents and their principals also.

15.1.3 Intention that the statement should be acted upon

For the deceit to be actionable the defendant must also have intended that the statement would be acted upon. However, only those people falling within the class that intended to act upon the statement are able to sue.

CASE EXAMPLE

Peek v Gurney [1873] LR 6 HL 377

Statements in a share prospectus were not intended to be acted upon other than by those to whom the prospectus was actually issued. As a result the court could not find that there was any liability for deceit.

In this way the representation need not be made personally to the person who relied on its truth.

CASE EXAMPLE

Langridge v Levy [1837] 2 M & W 519

The claimant bought a gun from the defendant who knew that the claimant intended his son to use it. The defendant falsely stated that the gun was sound and when the gun blew up in the son's face injuring him the defendant was held to be liable.

However, for the false statement to be actionable it is insufficient merely that it is foreseeable that the claimant might act on the statement.

CASE EXAMPLE

Caparo v Dickman [1990] 1 All ER 568

Here shareholders in a company bought more shares and then made a successful takeover bid for the company. When they wished to back out of the takeover they failed in their claim that they relied on the audited accounts prepared by the defendants that had shown a sizeable surplus rather than the deficit that was in fact the case. The House of Lords decided that the false statement could not found an action since the company accounts were a requirement of company law and are not prepared for those taking over the company. The fact that it was foreseeable that there was a possibility of the claimants relying on the audit was insufficient on its own for liability. It must have been in the defendant's mind at the time of the falsehood that the claimant was intended to rely on the falsehood.

Reliance on the statement

Actual reliance is also a necessary feature of the tort. The claimant must show that he did in fact act on the statement and suffer detriment as a result.

CASE EXAMPLE

Smith v Chadwick [1884] 9 App Cas 187

The claimant bought shares in a company whose prospectus falsely stated that a certain known influential person was a director of the company. In fact this false statement was of no significance at all since it was shown that the claimant had not in fact heard of that person and so could not have relied on the statement in entering the transaction. There was no liability.

The false statement need not be the only reason that the claimant acted as he did. It is sufficient in demonstrating reliance that it was one reason for acting.

Damage suffered by the claimant

For any action the claimant must inevitably have suffered loss or damage as a result of relying on the false statement for his course of conduct. The loss may be economic loss, or personal injury or property damage or indeed even distress and inconvenience.

CASE EXAMPLE

Archer v Brown [1984] 2 All ER 267

The claimant entered a partnership as a result of the defendant's deceit. In his successful action the court held that he should recover the cost of shares, interest on a loan needed to buy the shares, as well as loss of earnings and damages for injury to feelings all of which were losses caused by the deceit.

The claimant is able to recover for all losses that can be seen as a direct consequence of the deceit.

CASE EXAMPLE

Doyle v Olby (Ironmongers) Ltd [1969] 2 QB 158

In this case Lord Denning indicated that the measure of recoverable loss was based on direct consequences irrespective of whether or not the loss was foreseeable. The case involved a deceit made during the sale of a business that the business involved counter sales when it was in fact based on employment of a sales representative. The claimant was able to recover a sum equivalent to the difference in the value of the business acquired from that represented as being true during the sale and also expenditure in running the business, including the cost of employing a representative. The measure of damages was thus far superior to that which would have applied to the breach of contract.

ACTIVITY

Self-assessment questions

1 Is the action for deceit still relevant since Hedley Byrne and the Misrepresentation Act 1967?
2 What effect does specialist knowledge have in bringing an action for deceit?
3 What state of mind must a defendant have in order to be liable for deceit?
4 What degree of reliance does the claimant have to show in order to recover on the deceit?
5 For what loss can a claimant recover in a deceit action?

KEY FACTS

Deceit	**Case**
The tort has a lot in common with misrepresentation.	
The requirements of the tort of deceit are: • the defendant makes a false statement to the claimant or a class of people including the claimant • the defendant knows that the statement is false or is reckless in making it • the defendant intends that the claimant will rely for his conduct on the false statement • the claimant does rely on the false statement • the claimant suffers damage as a result	*Derry v Peek* [1889] *Derry v Peek* [1889] *Peek v Gurney* [1873] *Smith v Chadwick* [1884] *Archer v Brown* [1984]
Damages can be recovered for all loss that is a natural consequence of the breach.	*Doyle v Olby (Ironmongers)* [1969]

In simple diagram form the tort can be shown as in Figure 15.1.

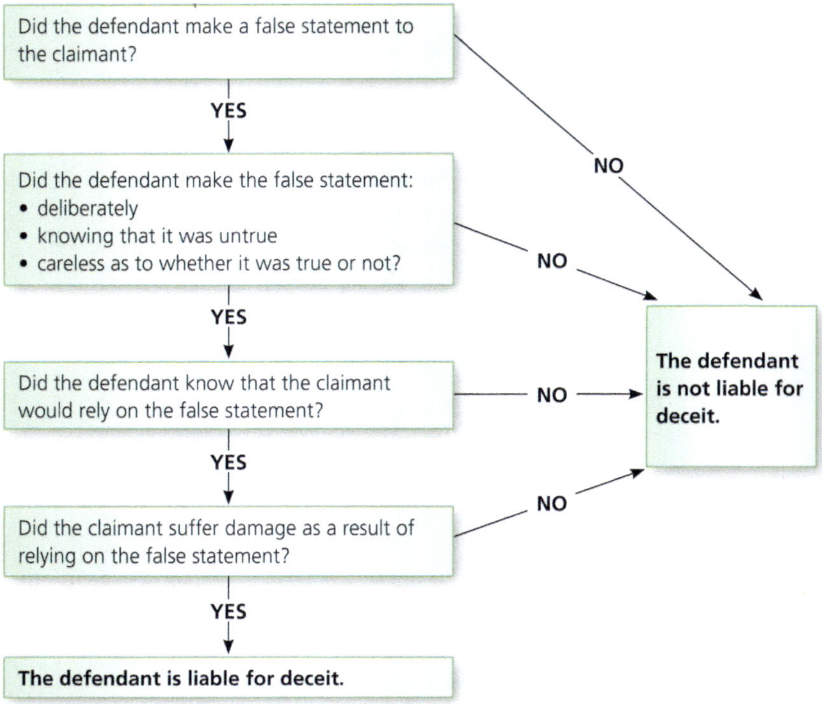

Figure 15.1 Liability for deceit.

15.2 Malicious falsehood

15.2.1 Introduction

The tort is in fact probably less an individual tort in its own right and more a generalisation of specific cases and is also sometimes referred to as injurious falsehood. Inevitably it is to do with loss caused to a claimant's livelihood or reputation as a result of a false statement made by another. The significant addition is the 'malice'.

CASE EXAMPLE

Ratcliffe v Evans [1892] 2 QB 524

A newspaper printed an article falsely stating that the claimant had gone out of business. It did so with the intention of causing harm to the claimant and his business. He sued successfully for his resultant business losses. The Court of Appeal distinguished from the very specific requirements of defamation and decided that the tort could result in liability in respect of any malicious statement that resulted in damage even where defamation could not be shown.

The tort has its origins in an action formerly referred to as slander of title. This was a very specific action based on the false questioning of a person's title to land with the result that it became less saleable or even unsaleable. In the nineteenth century the tort extended to include slander of goods, based on similar principles.

More recently the tort has developed in a more general sense as a protection of people's economic and commercial interests.

CASE EXAMPLE

***Kaye v Robertson* [1991] FSR 62**

This involved a famous television actor, Gordon Kaye. He was injured and journalists published photographs and a story about his injuries, falsely stating that the story was produced with the actor's permission. An action for malicious falsehood succeeded, the loss being that it prevented him from marketing the story himself and receiving payment for it.

In this way the tort can be used even where the loss is somewhat speculative in character.

CASE EXAMPLE

***Joyce v Sengupta* [1993] 1 All ER 897 CA**

Here the claimant had been falsely accused in a newspaper article of stealing private letters from her former employer, Princess Anne. Her action was successful because of the potential damage to her employment prospects.

Even though it is potentially very broad in its scope, the tort has a number of distinct elements:

- the defendant must have made a false statement about the claimant;
- the statement must have been calculated to cause damage to the claimant;
- the statement must have been made to a third party;
- the statement must have been made maliciously;
- the statement must have caused damage to the claimant.

15.2.2 A false statement about the claimant

The statement must be false. A mere advertising puff is not accepted as being believable by the courts and so is not actionable, for example 'Carlsberg, probably the best lager in the world' need not be problematic.

However, false statements that actually run down a competitor's goods may well be.

CASE EXAMPLE

De Beers Abrasive Products Ltd v International General Electric Co of New York [1975] 2 All ER 599

Here the defendants published what was alleged to be a 'scientific study' falsely denigrating the claimant's products in order to boost sales of their own products. They were liable under the tort.

Where the statement does not refer to the claimant at all then it will not be actionable even if it causes damage to the claimant.

CASE EXAMPLE

Cambridge University Press v University Tutorial Press [1928] 45 RPC 335

The claimants argued that they had suffered damage when the defendants had falsely stated that it was their own book that was recommended by an examination board, when in fact it was the claimants' book that was recommended. There could be no liability within the tort since there had been no reference to the claimants, even though they had allegedly suffered a loss of sales.

15.2.3 Calculated to cause damage to the plaintiff

The word calculated in the context of the tort merely means that loss or damage to the claimant was foreseeable.

In this way only specific references to the claimant rather than general ones are likely to be actionable. Two cases can be compared on this point.

CASE EXAMPLE

Lyne v Nicholls [1906] 23 TLR 86

False and derogatory remarks made by a newspaper about the circulation of one of its rivals were specific and were, therefore, actionable.

CASE EXAMPLE

White v Mellin [1895] AC 154 HL

Here labels attached to containers of baby food stated that it was better than any other baby food. The statement was very general in character and as such did not attach any liability.

15.2.4 Statement made to a third party

Although different in other ways, the tort has some similarity with defamation. One of the obvious common characteristics is the requirement of publication of the statement to a third party.

The reasoning behind this requirement is that the claimant is only likely to suffer loss or damage if the false statement has had an impact on third parties.

15.2.5 The presence of malice

To succeed, the claimant must also show that the statement was made with malice and has the burden of proof on this.

Malice, as elsewhere in tort, is a difficult concept to define. It need not necessarily involve dishonesty on the part of the defendant. It does, however, involve the absence of just cause or of belief in the statement.

CASE EXAMPLE

Joyce v Motor Surveys Ltd [1948] Ch 252

The defendant wished to evict the claimant from a tenancy in order that he could sell the property with vacant possession. The defendant then falsely informed the Post Office that the claimant had changed address and also falsely stated to the Tyre Manufacturers Association that the claimant had ceased trading as a retailer of tyres. Both statements were clearly false and there could have been no belief in their truth. The defendant was held to have acted with malice and was liable for malicious falsehood.

15.2.6 Damage actually suffered by the claimant

The claimant also has to show that he suffered actual loss. The loss need not be a particular loss as in loss of a specific customer. A more general loss as in a reduction in overall takings is sufficient. The damage can include damage to property as well as a pecuniary loss.

The test of remoteness of damage is based on reasonable foreseeability. In certain circumstances there is no requirement for the claimant to prove special damage:

- where the statement is in a written or permanent form and was calculated to cause a pecuniary loss;
- where the statement was calculated to cause a pecuniary loss to the claimant in respect of any office or profession, calling, trade or business he is in at the time of its publication – this is by s3(1) Defamation Act 1952.

It is at times of course advantageous to sue in defamation rather than claim for damages for malicious falsehood.

CASE EXAMPLE

Fielding v Variety Incorporated [1967] 2 QB 841

The defendants in their magazine published a false statement about the play *Charlie Girl* and called it a 'disastrous flop' when it was in fact a success. The claimant was able to recover £1,500 in defamation but only £100 in malicious falsehood because the former included a sum for injury to feelings where the latter was based purely on the actual loss.

ACTIVITY

Self-assessment questions

1. What was the original purpose of an action for malicious falsehood?
2. Is this purpose still the same or has it changed?
3. What exactly does malice mean for the purposes of the action?
4. What advantages are there in bringing such an action rather than claiming under defamation?

KEY FACTS

Malicious falsehood	Case/statute
A general class of torts covering loss to reputation through false statements – the elements are: • the defendant made a false statement about the claimant • the statement was calculated to cause damage to the claimant • the statement was made to a third party • the statement was made with malice • the statement caused damage to the claimant.	*Ratcliffe v Evans* [1892] *De Beers Abrasive Products Ltd v International General Electric Co of New York* [1975] *Joyce v Motor Surveys Ltd* [1948] *Fielding v Variety Incorporated* [1967]

15.3 Passing off

Passing off is often classed as a separate tort to either deceit or malicious falsehood, although some writers class it as an example of the latter. It does in any case have much in common with these two torts.

Where deceit refers to those situations where a person is specifically a victim of a misrepresentation causing him loss and where malicious falsehood is concerned with any loss of reputation, passing off is a more precise tort. It can occur when the defendant has literally 'passed his goods off' in a way

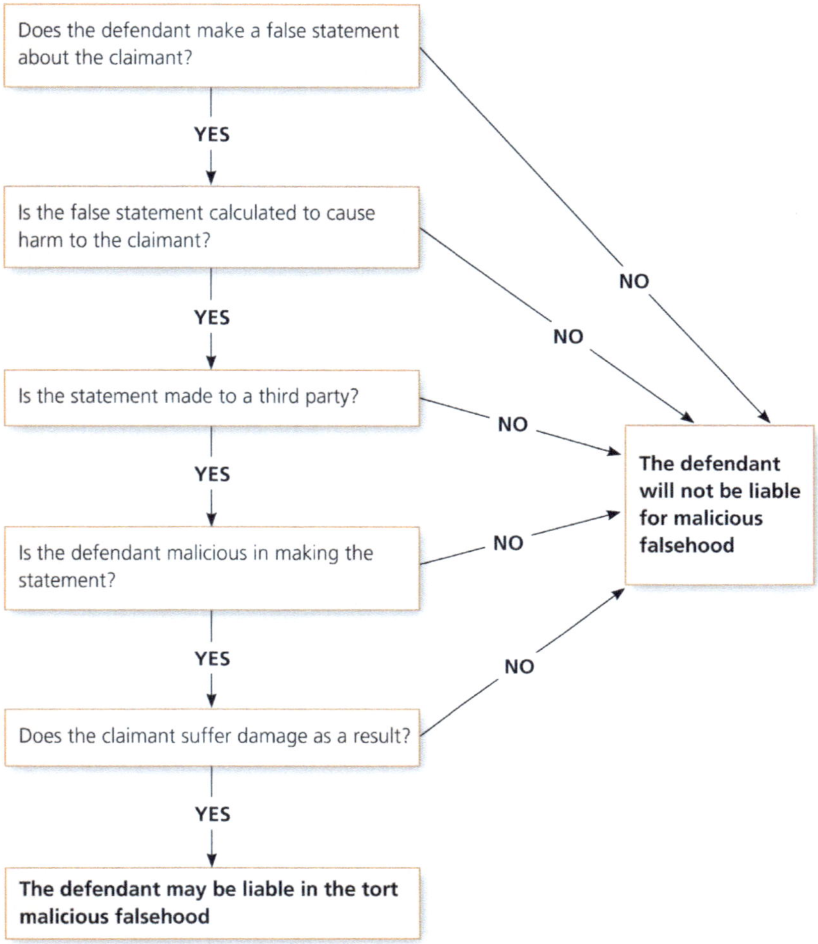

Figure 15.2 The essential elements for a claim in the tort of malicious falsehood.

that suggests that the goods are those of the claimant. In this way the defendant is taking commercial advantage of the claimant's goodwill or commercial reputation and in effect profiting from it.

Traditionally the tort would involve the defendant using the claimant's brand name or trademark in order to fool a customer into purchasing goods. As such in effect then it amounts to an unfair trading practice and is unacceptable and actionable because the claimant is likely to lose his legitimate trade as a result.

15.3.1 The characteristics of the tort

The tort has developed to include a variety of situations in which the defendant can be said to be trading unfairly at the expense of the claimant's legitimate business interests. The House of Lords has produced a comprehensive test in a judgment in 1979 of what it is necessary to prove in order to establish the tort.

CASE EXAMPLE

Erven Warnink BV v J Townend & Sons (Hull) Ltd [1979] AC 731

The claimants were the manufacturers of 'advocaat', an alcoholic drink made from egg yolks, spirit and wines. The defendants had for many years produced a drink called 'egg-flip', made from eggs and fortified wine which was significantly cheaper than advocaat. The defendants then introduced a drink known as 'Keeling's Old English Advocaat', which had the effect of capturing some of the advocaat market in the UK. The claimants sought an injunction to restrain the defendants from using the name 'advocaat', which they believed was specifically identified with their product. The House of Lords considered that nobody would be deceived into thinking that they were in fact buying Dutch advocaat. Nevertheless, the House also held that advocaat was still seen as a particular kind of drink and so the public had indeed been induced into buying the product as advocaat at the expense of the claimant's trade.

Lord Diplock in his judgment identified that the true test for passing off contained five essential elements:

- a basic misrepresentation;
- made by a trader in the course of pursuing his trade;
- directed towards prospective customers or ultimate consumers of his products;
- that was calculated to, or would foreseeably damage the business of, another trader;
- and that damage was in fact caused to the trader bringing the action.

15.3.2 The ways of committing the tort (the basic misrepresentation)

The tort is about misrepresenting the truth in order to take advantage of the claimant's trade and goodwill. In this way the misrepresentation can actually arise in a number of different ways.

By using the claimant's trade name.

CASE EXAMPLE

Maxim's Ltd v Dye [1977] 1 WLR 1155

Here the defendant was prevented from opening a restaurant called 'Maxim's' because there was also a very famous French restaurant called 'Maxim's'. The court held that in the circumstances the public would inevitably be led to believe that the restaurant was associated in some way with the French business.

By using the claimant's trademark or brand name.

CASE EXAMPLE

J Bollinger v Costa Brava Wine Co Ltd [1960] Ch 262

Here the defendants were trading a product under the name of Spanish Champagne. Champagne, while it is often used in a general sense to refer to sparkling wines, in fact refers to the sparkling wines of a very specific region of France where the wine is produced by a very specific process, 'methode champenoise'. The defendants were held not to be able to apply the word 'champagne' to their product which was merely taking advantage of the goodwill of the other product.

By claiming that the goods are those produced by the claimant when they in fact are not.

CASE EXAMPLE

Lord Byron v Johnston [1816] 2 Mer 29

Here the defendant sold books of poems and advertised them as being the works of Lord Byron, when someone else in fact wrote them. The court held that there was a clear misrepresentation designed to take advantage of a famous name.

By imitating the appearance of the claimant's product.

CASE EXAMPLE

Reckitt & Coleman Products v Borden Inc [1990] 1 All ER 873, HL

Here the claimants, among other things, were producers of lemon juice. They had marketed their product for more than 30 years in a yellow plastic container shaped like a lemon and thus the public very clearly identified with their product. When the defendants also sold lemon juice in a similar container the House of Lords held that this was passing off. The claimants were entitled to protect the very distinctive and original packaging of the product as well as the product itself. The court felt that it was clear that the public would be induced into believing that the lemon juice was produced by the same manufacturer and that the claimant's trade and goodwill was therefore threatened by the imitation.

By imitating the claimant's promotional or advertising material.

CASE EXAMPLE

***Cadbury Schweppes Pty Ltd v Pub Squash Co Pty Ltd* [1981] 1 All ER 213 PC**

Here the claimants had introduced a new canned lemon drink, 'Solo', using an extensive and very effective television and radio advertising campaign to do so. The following year the defendants introduced a similar product, 'Pub Squash', and also advertised on both television and radio using very similar material and even slogans. The court was prepared to accept that such behaviour could amount to passing off. However, the case itself failed because the court was unable to find that there was in fact a specific misrepresentation that would have induced the public into believing that the goods were the claimants'. There was no possibility that the public would be confused into thinking that the two products were in fact the same.

By using a product name too similar to that used by the claimant.

CASE EXAMPLE

***United Biscuits (UK) Ltd v Asda Stores Ltd* [1997] RPC 513**

Here the defendants produced and advertised a chocolate biscuit which they called 'Puffin'. The claimants had for a long time produced and sold a very popular chocolate biscuit snack called 'Penguin'. The court was prepared to accept that the two names were too close together and that the public could be deceived into believing that they were connected and that as a result the claimants' trade and goodwill was threatened. The product name was therefore held to amount to passing off.

The list is not exhaustive. Anything that imitates, or takes advantage of the claimant's product or even that suggests that the claimant's product is in any way inferior and that would have the effect of taking advantage of the claimant's trade or goodwill could amount to a passing off and be actionable as a result.

15.3.3 The other essential elements

It will not be a passing off unless the party accused is taking advantage of the claimant's goodwill for his own profit and is therefore passing off, unless the event occurs within a trade. Nevertheless, trade is quite liberally defined but not to the extent that it will cover every activity.

CASE EXAMPLE

Kean v McGivan [1982] FSR 119, CA

Here a political party was not able to protect itself against another person calling his own party the Social Democrat Party even though this could in effect lead to confusion. The court held that the concept of 'trade' did not extend this far.

The passing off must also be aimed at the customers or eventual consumers of the claimant's products for it to be actionable. Where the claimant and the defendant are involved in totally different businesses or activities then the court will not accept that damage could be caused to the claimant and there will be no actionable passing off.

CASE EXAMPLE

McCullough v May [1947] 2 All ER 845

A children's radio programme of the time was hosted by a person who was affectionately known as 'Uncle Mac'. The broadcaster failed in his attempt to show that a company producing a breakfast cereal which it called 'Uncle Mac's Puffed Wheat' could interfere with or take advantage of the goodwill that he had built up with the listening audience. The court held that there was no passing off because, even though the name was similar, it could not be shown to be aimed at the listeners in order to take advantage of the presenter's name.

The next requirement is at the very heart of passing off. The misrepresentation must be calculated to harm the trade or goodwill of the claimant. In this sense the tort is different from deceit where the intention to deceive is an essential element. With passing off the important thing is only that a misrepresentation has been made that will foreseeably deceive the customer of the claimant's product. If the consumer is unlikely to be confused by the misrepresentation then there can be no actionable passing off.

CASE EXAMPLE

Newsweek Inc v BBC [1979] RPC 441

An action was brought against the BBC on the basis that calling a news and current affairs programme *Newsweek* injured the trade and goodwill of the claimants, who for some time had published a magazine of the same name. The court would not accept that there was a passing off because it would not be foreseeable that the readers of a magazine could confuse the product with a programme. The two were too distinctly different.

Finally it is sufficient that damage is a probable result of the passing off. There is no requirement that the claimant should show actual damage. To hold otherwise would prevent the most usual remedy, an injunction, from having any great effect. In *H P Bulmer Ltd and Showerings Ltd v Bollinger SA* [1978] RPC 79, CA the use of the term 'Champagne' could obviously have a misleading and damaging effect when applied to an inferior product. The key point of the action is that the defendant has taken unfair advantage of a market that has been created by another party.

15.3.4 Defences and remedies

While a number of defences may be possible, the obvious and potentially the most effective defence is consent. If the claimant is a willing participant to the deception then he cannot complain afterwards that it is unfair.

There are two potential remedies:

- damages;
- injunction.

In the case of damages the claimant will obviously be seeking compensation for the loss of profits suffered as a result of any passing off and may also obtain damages for loss of reputation. It is also possible to use the equitable remedy of account on the profits made by the defendant out of the deception.

In the case of an injunction this will be used as a remedy to restrain the defendant from practising the deception. In this way the claimant is able to prevent the misrepresentation and protect his trade and goodwill.

ACTIVITY

Self-assessment questions

1. What is a defendant actually doing in order to be classed as 'passing off'?
2. What is the defendant hoping to achieve by the 'passing off'?
3. How does the effect of the deception differ between passing off and deceit?
4. In what ways is an injunction the best remedy for passing off?

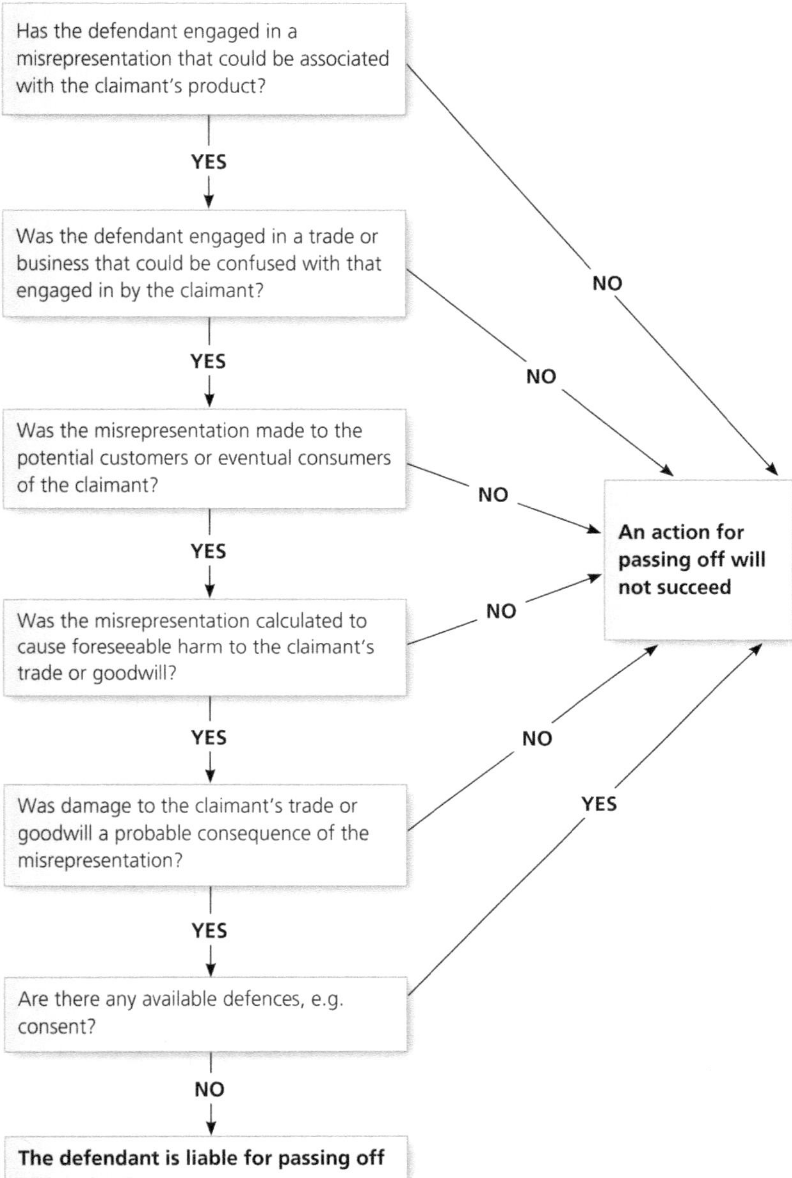

Figure 15.3 How an action for passing off is proved.

KEY FACTS

Passing off	Case/statute
Occurs where the defendant through misrepresentation unfairly takes advantage of the claimant's trade or goodwill causing damage – the elements of the tort are defined in the misrepresentation, e.g. • using the claimant's trade name or • imitating the appearance of the claimant's product or • using a product name too similar to that used by the claimant.	*Erven Warnink BV v J Townend & Sons (Hull) Ltd* [1979] *Maxim's Ltd v Dye* [1977] *Reckitt & Coleman Products v Borden Inc* [1990] *United Biscuits (UK) Ltd v Asda Stores Ltd* [1997]
The defendant must be acting in a trade or business.	*Kean v McGivan* [1982]
The misrepresentation is directed at the claimant's customers.	*McCullough v May* [1947]
The misrepresentation must be calculated to damage the claimant's trade or goodwill.	*Newsweek Inc v BBC* [1979]
It is sufficient that damage is a foreseeable consequence.	*H P Bulmer Ltd and Showerings Ltd v Bollinger SA* [1978]

15.4 Interference with trade

15.4.1 Introduction

This heading includes a strange and uncertain group of torts some of which were in former times used freely but have been overtaken by statutory rules, particularly those governing the actions of trade unions in trying to advance the conditions of their members. The common characteristic is that they concern interference with a person's trade or business by means other than a false representation that seems to characterise the three distinct torts in the three previous sections.

In the nineteenth century actions for numerous different torts were brought but there were two main ones:

- conspiracy;
- inducement to a breach of contract.

Both were used successfully over a long period of time. More recently Lord Diplock suggested that there is a general class of torts of interfering with the trade or business of another person by doing unlawful acts (see *Merkar Island Shipping Corporation v Laughton* [1983] 2 AC 570).

What would actually fall within this general tort is unclear. Quite clearly a party will be held liable in tort for unlawful acts that damage a person's economic interests. However, there are problems in defining precisely what economic interests can be protected and what amounts to unlawful means.

With the former there may be a difficulty in showing that conspiracy and inducing a breach of contract are covered. The requirements of both conspiracy and inducing a breach of contract are quite specific and the torts possibly still exist independently.

With the latter there may for instance be the problem of demonstrating that statutory crimes also give rise to civil liability. At one point at least intimidation might have come within the necessary unlawful means in certain circumstances where there is a third party involved.

CASE EXAMPLE

Rookes v Barnard [1964] AC 1129

At one time it was possible for trade unions to operate what was known as a 'closed shop'. By agreement with the employer all employees of a business were required to be members of a trade union. The union in question threatened a strike against an employer unless it dismissed an employee who had left the union. The employer did so and the employee then sued the employer. The House of Lords applied the law of intimidation and held that the union, by threatening an unlawful breach of contract by its members was liable. (The area of such trade union action is now covered by a variety of statutory rules.)

15.4.2 Conspiracy

A conspiracy in this context generally occurs when two or more people agree to injure another person in the course of his trade that will cause damage as a result.

There are three essential elements to the tort:

- the conspiracy itself – this is a combination of parties with a common purpose (conspiracy law has been used to control a variety of combinations for unlawful purposes besides just a conspiracy that is aimed at harming someone's trade);
- the purpose of the conspiracy – that the claimant's trade should be damaged;
- that there is no justification for this – the law is not seeking to prevent competition, even fierce competition, but to prevent unlawful means being used.

The conspiracy

The conspiracy is rarely hard to show as it is merely a joining together with a common purpose to harm the other party. It might include husbands and wives (*Midland Bank Trust Co Ltd v Green (No 3)* [1982] Ch 529), and directors of a company (*Belmont Finance Corporation Ltd v Williams Furniture Ltd* [1979] Ch 250) and a variety of other combinations.

The important point is that the conspiracy has an unlawful purpose that is aimed at harming another party's trade.

The purpose of the conspiracy

Where a 'simple' conspiracy is involved (where the act is not unlawful in itself) the courts will only accept that the tort has been committed where the clear and major purpose of the combination is to damage the claimant's trade.

CASE EXAMPLE

Crofter Hand Woven Harris Tweed Co Ltd v Veitch [1942] AC 435

The claimants produced tweed cloth in the Outer Hebrides for export using spun yarn from mainland Scotland. The defendants were trade union officials working for a rival firm that, as did most local firms, used yarn that was spun on the island. This firm was rejecting the men's demand for a wage rise, arguing that the competition provided by the claimants made it impossible. The union officials then pressured dockers at the port not to handle the yarn imported by the claimants, though the dockers were not in breach of contract when they agreed to do this. The claimants sought to prevent what they argued was an actionable conspiracy. The House of Lords considered that the major purpose of the combination was to promote the interests of the defendants, not to damage the claimants' interests, and the action failed.

In simple conspiracy therefore it will not matter that the conspirators are protecting their own interests if the major purpose of the conspiracy is damaging another party's trade. If that is the case then the conspiracy is actionable.

At one point it appeared that there was little difference when the conspiracy is to do an unlawful act by unlawful means. The courts would not accept that the conspiracy was actionable unless the conspiracy to do the unlawful act was not for the purposes of promoting or protecting the interests of the conspirators but was to damage the claimant's trade.

CASE EXAMPLE

Lonrho Ltd v Shell Petroleum Co Ltd (No 2) [1982] AC 173

At one point the government in Rhodesia (now Zimbabwe) had broken away from British rule and unlawfully declared independence. As a result the British Government imposed sanctions preventing UK companies from trading with the illegal regime. The defendants had traded with the regime in breach of the sanctions and made profits as a result that would not be available to those lawfully following the order, including the claimant. The House of Lords, however, held that even though the conspiracy was based on unlawful means, it could not be actionable unless the major purpose was to harm the claimant's trade rather than to advance its own.

The House of Lords has more recently identified that intention and motive are different. In this way where unlawful means are used, the defendant will not be able to excuse these means merely because the major purpose of the conspiracy was to advance the interests of the defendants.

CASE EXAMPLE

Lonrho plc v Fayed [1992] 1 AC 448

Here there was competition for the takeover of the House of Fraser, the chain owning the well-known department store Harrods. The defendant eventually won control and the claimant complained that this was only the result of false representations made to the Secretary of State for Trade and Industry by the defendant. The House of Lords accepted that an actionable conspiracy could be shown whenever there was sufficient proof of intent to harm the claimant's trade, and that, where the conspiracy was effected by unlawful means the fact that this intention to harm the defendant was not the major aim was irrelevant.

Justification

In a simple conspiracy it is sufficient to show that the major purpose of the conspiracy was to promote the interests of the conspirators. If this is shown then the action fails.

In the case of conspiracy by unlawful means it is much more difficult to show justification. In any case the use of the tort may be more limited in the light of the general tort of interference with trade.

15.4.3 Inducing a breach of contract

This tort originally developed so that there would be liability whenever one party knowingly induced a third party to breach his contract with the defendant causing the claimant a loss. Unlike conspiracy it would have been irrelevant whether or not the breach of contract was induced by unlawful means. The law seeks to protect freedom of contract. Once parties have entered a contract then interference with that contract can lead to liability in tort.

The origins of the tort in effect had more to do with the master and servant laws of the nineteenth century, as it had been recognised for some time that there could be liability for enticing a servant away from his master. However, there was no general liability for interference with a contract, but this was eventually developed to give an action to a party who had suffered loss because the other party had been persuaded to breach the contract.

CASE EXAMPLE

Lumley v Gye [1853] 2 E & B 216

A singer who was contracted to sing exclusively for the claimant was persuaded, in breach of that contract, to perform for the defendant. The court accepted that this gave rise to liability.

There are six essential elements to the tort:

- there is a breach of contractual obligations;
- the defendant induces the breach by either direct or indirect means;
- the defendant knows of the contract;
- the defendant intends that the contract should be broken;
- the claimant suffers loss as a result of the breach of contract;
- there is no justification.

Breach of contract

It was originally felt that the tort would only apply in the case of breaches going to the root of the contract and in effect destroying its purpose. However, it is now accepted that any breach of obligations is sufficient.

CASE EXAMPLE

Torquay Hotel Co Ltd v Cousins [1969] 1 All ER 522

During a dispute union action was used to prevent an oil supplier from fulfilling its contract with the claimant. The contract actually included an exclusion clause for damage caused by events beyond either party's control so there was in effect no actual breach of contract. An injunction was still granted to the claimant because there was still in effect interference with the contract. The exclusion clause only meant that the parties could be excused for breaches of their obligations. It did not mean that there were no obligations.

Inducement

The inducement will usually be either of two types:

- the defendant has persuaded a party to breach the contract or the defendant has prevented a party from completing his contract (direct means); or
- the defendant has prevented the party from carrying out his obligations often through industrial action (indirect means).

Lumley v Gye [1853] 2 E & B 216 is a classic example of the defendant persuading a party to breach his contract and the weight of the persuasion can be seen in the financial advantages on offer for breaching the contract. However, the persuasion can take a subtler form.

CASE EXAMPLE

Bent's Brewery Co Ltd v Hogan [1945] 2 All ER 570

Here a trade union official sent a questionnaire to pub managers for details of the trade and profits of the pubs they managed. This was held to have induced the managers into breaching their contracts by encouraging them to disclose confidential information.

Other forms of direct inducement include those making it impossible for a contracting party to perform his contract.

CASE EXAMPLE

GWK Ltd v Dunlop Rubber Co Ltd [1926] 42 TLR 593

Here car manufacturers had contracted with tyre manufacturers to use their tyres on cars exhibited at a motor show. The defendants actually removed those tyres and replaced them with their own. This unlawful action made it impossible for the car manufacturer to keep to their contract and was held to be an actionable inducement to a breach of contract.

Where the inducement is indirect then the inducement must also be achieved through unlawful means for the inducement to a breach of contract to be actionable. Historically many of the cases involve industrial action led by trade unions where members are in dispute with their employers.

CASE EXAMPLE

J T Stratford & Co v Lindley [1965] AC 269

Officials of the Waterman's Union were in dispute with the claimant. They instructed their members not to handle the claimant's barges as a result of which his business was damaged, as he was unable to complete contracts that he had formed with various customers. The House of Lords held that there was an inducement to a breach of contract, the breaches of contract by the union members with their employers, and this made it impossible for the employer to keep contracts with his customers, and that this had been achieved by unlawful means.

Knowledge of the existence of the contract by the defendant

This requirement is inevitably tied in also with the requirement that the defendant intends to cause the loss. It has generally developed that it is sufficient that the defendant has either actual or constructive knowledge of the existence of the contract. It is not for instance necessary that the defendant knew the terms of the contract. In this way it must have been obvious to the union in the *Stratford v Lindley* case that the barge company would have contractual arrangements with customers and that these would be breached and therefore cause loss to the claimants as a result of the industrial action by the members.

The intention that the contract should be breached

It is sufficient that the defendant intends that the contract should be breached. There is no requirement that the defendant should act with malice. Motive is in any case generally taken to be irrelevant in tort.

CASE EXAMPLE

Exchange Telegraph Co v Gregory & Co [1896] 1 QB 147, CA

Here the claimants were in exclusive possession of Stock Exchange prices which they sold under contract to subscribers who agreed not to reveal the information to others. The claimants also published the prices in a newspaper. The defendant, a stockbroker, then induced a subscriber to breach the arrangement and used the information for the benefit of his own clients. The court held that there was an actionable inducement to breach of contract.

Damage resulting from the breach of contract

The claimant must show that he has suffered loss resulting from the breach of contract, so standard principles of causation apply.

CASE EXAMPLE

Jones Bros (Hunstanton) Ltd v Stevens [1955] 1 QB 275

The defendant, after hiring an employee, then realised that the employee was in breach of contract with the claimants by working for the defendant. Nevertheless, he continued to employ him. However, there was held to be no actionable inducement to breach of contract because the claimant could not be shown to have suffered damage when it was shown that the employee would not have returned to his employment with the claimant even without the new employment.

Justification

The tort is actionable because there is no justification for the defendant's actions. In rare circumstances, where justification can be shown, this might provide a defence.

CASE EXAMPLE

Brimelow v Casson [1924] 1 Ch 302

Here a trade union representing theatrical workers persuaded a theatre manager to breach his contract with a theatrical company that was paying such poor wages that many of its chorus girls were forced into prostitution in order to make ends meet. The court held that the inducement to breach a contract was justified in the circumstances.

The common remedies in the tort are obviously damages or an injunction.

CRITIQUING THE LAW

Do economic torts still play a useful role in the law?

ACTIVITY

Self-assessment questions

1 What is the general characteristic common to all of the cases in this section?
2 What are the essential elements of a conspiracy?
3 What are the essential elements of an inducement to a breach of contract?
4 Why do so many of the cases involve trade unions?
5 What are the problems associated with Lord Diplock's suggestion of a general tort of interfering with trade through unlawful means in the *Merkar* case?

KEY FACTS

Nature of the tort
There are a number of torts that involve interfering with a person's trade or business by means other than a false representation. Two traditional ones are conspiracy and inducing a breach of contract.

The elements of conspiracy	**Case**
Two or more parties agreeing to damage another party's trade.	*Belmont Finance Corporation Ltd v Williams Furniture Ltd* [1979]
The purpose of the conspiracy is to damage the claimant's trade.	*Crofter Hand Woven Harris Tweed Co Ltd v Veitch* [1942]
If the conspiracy involves unlawful means then this is an absolute requirement.	*Lonrho Ltd v Shell Petroleum Co Ltd (No 2)* [1982]
There is no justification.	

The elements of inducement to breach a contract	**Case**
The defendant induces the breach by either:	*GWK Ltd v Dunlop Rubber Co Ltd* [1926]
• direct means, or	*J T Stratford & Co v Lindley* [1965]
• indirect means.	*J T Stratford & Co v Lindley* [1965]
Knowledge of the existence of the contract. Intention that the contract should be broken. The breach of contract causes the claimant loss.	*Exchange Telegraph Co v Gregory & Co* [1896] *Jones Bros (Hunstanton) Ltd v Stevens* [1955]
There is no justification.	*Brimelow v Casson* [1924]

A general tort	**Case**
Lord Diplock identified that there could be a general class of torts covering causing damage to a person's trade by unlawful means. The scope of this tort is uncertain – it probably cannot cover conspiracy and inducing a breach of contract, and it is uncertain what sorts of loss could be covered and what the definition of unlawful means would include.	*Merkar Island Shipping Corporation v Laughton* [1983]

ACTIVITY

Quick quiz

In the following examples consider which economic tort might be involved and the likelihood of a successful claim.

1 Dodi has begun to market a set of computer games covering football, cricket, rugby, athletics and other major sports. He is using the name 'Super Sports' as a brand name. There is already a national company manufacturing and retailing sportswear called 'Super Sports'.
2 Officers of the Allied and Amalgamated Union of Lecturing and Teaching Staff have called on members to strike because the Midshires University is paying its lecturing staff only 70 per cent of the usual rate for lecturing staff in universities.
3 Easyyears is a national company specialising in private warden patrolled residential housing for retired persons. In order to reduce overheads the company set up without gaining local authority licences for health and safety and minimum care standards as required by law. In its share prospectus Easyyears proclaimed to be local authority registered. The company has now had its homes shut because of breaches of safety and care standards after a local authority inspection. Adrian invested in what he thought was a very worthwhile project and has now lost his investment as a result of the local authority action.
4 Alan was a strong applicant for a position as Officer in Charge of a registered charity children's home. He failed to get the position after Belinda falsely stated that he had previous convictions for assaults on young children.

SUMMARY

Deceit

- Similar to misrepresentation but the defendant makes a false statement to the claimant or a class of people including the claimant, knowing that the statement is false or being reckless in making it, intending the claimant to rely on it, and the claimant does so and suffers damage as a result.
- Damages are for all loss that is a natural consequence of the breach.

Malicious falsehood

- Covers loss to reputation through false statements.
- The defendant makes a false statement about the claimant to a third party, calculated to cause damage to the claimant, the statement is made with malice and causes damage to the claimant.

Passing off

- Involves unfairly taking advantage of the claimant's trade or goodwill.
- The defendant acting in a trade or business misrepresents the truth by using the claimant's trade name or imitating the claimant's product, and directs the misrepresentation at the claimant's customers, and this is calculated to damage the claimant's trade or goodwill.

Interference with trade

- There are two main types of interference.
- Conspiracy – where two or more parties agree to damage another party's trade.
- Inducing a breach of contract – either by direct or indirect means intending that the contract should be broken.

Further reading

Cooke, Professor J, *Law of Tort* (14th edn, Pearson, 2019), Chapter 22.
Witting, C, *Street on Torts* (16th edn, OUP, 2021), Chapters 14 and 15.

16

Breach of a statutory duty

AIMS AND OBJECTIVES

After reading this chapter you should be able to:

- Identify the general character of statutory torts
- Explain the circumstances in which these will give rise to civil liability
- Critically analyse the area
- Apply the law to factual situations and reach conclusions as to liability

16.1 Statutes creating civil liability

Commonly statutory duties are regulatory in character and in the case of breach a body such as the Health and Safety Commission will bring an action leading to a criminal sanction, usually a fine. However, often a statute imposing a duty may also give rise to civil liability. The ensuing civil action is then known in tort as an action for breach of a statutory duty.

Such actions can appear very similar to basic negligence actions but can differ in a number of key ways:

- The standard of care appropriate to the duty is fixed by the statute and so is different from that in negligence where it is measured against the 'reasonable man'.
- The duty may be strict (in which case there will be no requirement for the claimant to prove that the defendant was negligent); or alternatively the burden of proof may be reversed (in which case it is for the defendant to prove that he did not breach the duty); and either of these, or both, may be advantageous to the claimant by comparison to normal negligence actions.

DOI: 10.4324/9781003202417-16

- Since the statutes in question are usually regulatory and often criminal in character the existence of civil liability is in any case often debatable.
- In America a breach of a statutory duty may even be used as conclusive proof of negligence in a civil action – but in England this is not the case, if the statute gives rise to civil liability at all then in effect it gives rise to a separate tort action.

The result of all the above is that it is common to plead such a breach with negligence in the alternative in the same claim.

Certain statutory provisions more obviously concern civil liability than others as when they merely modify the existing common law. An obvious example of this is the Occupiers' Liability Acts 1957 and 1984 and also the Consumer Protection Act 1987.

With others it is much harder to determine that civil liability is intended since the statute is predominantly regulatory and any civil liability that does exist may form only a very minor part of the statute as a whole. An example of this would be the Data Protection Act 1998.

Consequently the area is heavily dependent on statutory interpretation and therefore unpredictable since it is not always possible to assess which rule of interpretation a judge will rely on. Following the judgment in *Pepper v Hart* [1993] 1 All ER 42 there is also the question as to whether *Hansard* should be consulted.

The most common actions in which a claim for breach of statutory duties is made is industrial safety law. This itself runs alongside the basic common law principles of employers' liability (see Chapter 17). There is less evidence of success in other fields of law.

16.2 Proving liability

Actions are more complex than for normal negligence actions since the duty itself is invariably more complex. Claimants have a more complicated series of requirements that must be proved.

These propositions include:

- Does the statute create civil liability?
- Is there a duty of care owed to the claimant?
- Is there a duty of care imposed on the defendant?
- Has the defendant breached that duty by falling below the standard identified in the statute?
- Is the breach of duty the cause of the damage suffered by the claimant?
- Is the damage of a type which is contemplated in the statute?

16.2.1 Does the statute create civil liability?

First of all the claimant has to show that the Act in question actually confers an action for damages. This is not a problem where the Act gives specific guidance, an example of this being the Health and Safety at Work etc Act 1974. Here the general duties contained in ss1–9 of the Act clearly do not give rise to any civil action because this possibility is expressly excluded by s47.

However, s47 also states that certain regulations made under the statute do give rise to civil liability unless the regulation states otherwise.

However, problems can occur when the statute is silent on the issue. In this instance it is the role of the court in all cases to give effect to the intention of Parliament and again the claimant is subject to the application of the rules of statutory interpretation. This in itself can and has led to inconsistency in approach.

The modern test of whether a statute gives rise to civil liability is that of Lord Diplock in *Lonrho Ltd v Shell Petroleum Co (No 2)* [1982] AC 173:

- First, the court should presume that if the Act creates an obligation which is enforceable in a specific manner then it is not enforceable in any other manner. In this way if the Act was intended for the general benefit of the community rather than for the granting of individual rights then it will not usually be possible to use the Act to bring an action in tort.

There are two exceptions to this basic principle:

- where an obligation or prohibition is imposed under the Act to benefit a particular class of individuals;
- where the provision in the Act created a public right but the claimant suffered particular, direct and substantial damage different from that which was common to the rest of the public.

The test has been criticised because of two significant problems:

- It gives the court significant discretion in determining how to define a particular class.
- There does not appear to be a particular principle to determine the distinction between a statute creating a public right and one merely prohibiting what had formerly been lawful.

The courts in any case determine Parliament's intent by reference to various factors:

- The more precise the wording of the statute the more likely it is that the breach of the duty will give rise to a civil action for damages. Two cases can be compared to illustrate this point.

CASE EXAMPLE

Monk v Warby [1935] All ER 373

This case involved breach of a duty under what is now s143 of the Road Traffic Act 1988 not to allow an uninsured driver to drive a vehicle. The claimant, who had been injured through the negligence of the driver, was able to sue the owner of the car where there would have been no point in suing the uninsured driver. This was possible because the car had been used with the owner's knowledge.

CASE EXAMPLE

***Atkinson v Newcastle Waterworks* [1877] 2 ExD 441**

Here no civil action was available where statute imposed a £10 fine for failing to keep water at a certain pressure. The claimant's premises had caught fire and burned down but, despite the breach of statutory duty no part of the fine was payable to an individual so the statute did not create individual rights to a civil action.

- If the Act imposes a duty but there is a failure to mention a specific penalty then it is likely to give rise to a civil action.

CASE EXAMPLE

***Cutler v Wandsworth Stadium Ltd* [1949] AC 398**

Here a breach of a statutory duty to allow a bookmaker entry to a dog-racing track gave rise to a civil action. There was no mention of a fine or a penalty.

- Some groups commonly benefit from statutory duties and so in certain instances there are well-established principles of civil liability.

CASE EXAMPLE

***Groves v Lord Wimbourne* [1898] 2 QB 402**

Here the statutory duty was to fence machinery. The employee was injured as a result of a breach of that duty. A £100 fine was possible with part at least payable to the claimant, although there was no guarantee that he would receive it.

- A civil action is also more likely where the duty of the welfare of an identifiable group is concerned.

CASE EXAMPLE

***Thornton v Kirklees MBC* [1979] QB 626**

A statute creating an obligation to house homeless people was enforceable despite the fact that no specific remedy was identified.

- However, there must be a direct link between the group and the purpose of statute.

CASE EXAMPLE

McCall v Abelsz [1976] QB 585

Here residential occupiers did not count as a class for the purposes of harassment actions.

- For a civil action to be possible the purpose of the statutory provision must be for benefit of that class.

CASE EXAMPLE

R v Deputy Governor of Parkhurst Prison, ex parte Hague [1992] 1 AC 58

Here prisoners could not use alleged breaches of the Prison Rules to bring a civil action. The Prison Rules were for the regulation of prisons and did not provide any private law rights for the prisoners.

- But a civil action will not be possible in any case where the court feels that the duty is intended to be enforced by other means.

CASE EXAMPLE

Cullen v Chief Constable of the Royal Ulster Constabulary [2003] 1 WLR 1763

Cullen was arrested and his right to see a solicitor was denied under s15 Northern Ireland (Emergency Provisions) Act 1987. He was later given access to a solicitor and pleaded guilty to criminal charges. He then sought damages for the delay in giving him access to a solicitor. The trial judge and the Northern Ireland Court of Appeal held that the police had reasonable grounds to delay access and although they had breached the statutory requirement to give the claimant reasons for this delay at the time, this did not give rise to an action in tort. The House of Lords upheld the decision and held that there was no civil law duty because there would have been a possibility of judicial review. The House also commented that there was no issue under the Human Rights Act 1998 as there was no breach of Article 5 or Article 6 of the Convention on Human Rights.

One interesting recent development is the removal of the exclusion from civil liability in the Management of Health and Safety at Work Regulations 1999 under the Management of Health and Safety at Work and Fire Precautions (Workplace) (Amendment) Regulations 2003. Employees will now be able to bring a claim of breach of statutory duty where the regulations are not complied with. A particular requirement of the 1999 Regulations is risk assessment. In future a failure to assess risks or an inadequate risk assessment might give rise to liability. The changes in the regulations clearly give employees much broader scope to claim.

16.2.2 Is there a duty of care owed to the claimant?

Unless the claimant can show that by the statute it was intended that a duty should be owed to him as an individual or as a member of a specific class of individuals then an action in tort will fail.

CASE EXAMPLE

Hartley v Mayoh & Co [1954] 1 QB 383

A fireman was injured in a fire at a factory. His claim for damages failed. No duty was owed under the industrial safety provisions on which he tried to rely since the fire was not at his place of employment which the precise wording of the statute required.

Even though a statute does appear on its wording to confer civil rights on an individual leading to a possible tort action this may not extend as far as the family of that individual. So an action by a relative might fail.

CASE EXAMPLE

Hewett v Alf Brown's Transport [1992] ICR 530

Here the wife of a lorry driver contracted lead poisoning through washing her husband's overalls. Safety regulations did create a duty of care in favour of employees such as the lorry driver here. Nevertheless the duty could not be extended to cover the wife in the case. Slightly different reasoning applied in *Maguire v Hartland & Wolff plc* [2005] EWCA Civ 01 in respect of a wife who had contracted mesothelioma after washing her husband's overalls which had been exposed to asbestos dust. At the time she was exposed to the dust it would not have been reasonably foreseeable that she was at risk.

Nevertheless the scope of the duty may be used in certain circumstances to recover damages.

CASE EXAMPLE

Atkinson v Croydon Corporation [1938] (unreported)

Here a father was able to recover damages when his daughter contracted typhoid as the result of a failure to provide a clean water supply. No duty was actually owed to the girl. However, the father, who was paying for the service, was owed a duty and could recover damages on that basis.

The scope for establishing the existence of a duty is in any case potentially very wide.

CASE EXAMPLE

Garden Cottage Foods v Milk Marketing Board [1984] 2 All ER 770

The duty in this action arose as a result of EU law.

However, in a series of joined appeals the House of Lords has clearly restated the need to show that Parliament intended to create private law rights before any action is possible: *X (minors) v Bedfordshire County Council; M (a minor) v Newham London Borough Council; Keating v Bromley LBC* [1995] 3 All ER 353.

16.2.3 Is there a duty of care imposed on the defendant?

The statute must impose civil liability on the defendant or there can be no possible action. This can only be established by reference to the precise wording of the statute.

CASE EXAMPLE

R v Deputy Governor of Parkhurst Prison, ex parte Hague [1992] 1 AC 58

Here a claim by prisoners that civil law rights were infringed was rejected. The Prison Rules were passed for the purposes of regulating the administration of prisons not in any way to impose duties on prisons that would operate in favour of prisoners.

However, it is of course possible the civil duty might extend to a broad range of defendants.

CASE EXAMPLE

Shell Tankers v Jeremson [2001] EWCA Civ 101

In this case the Court of Appeal recognised that regulations covering the asbestos industry would also extend to users of asbestos in other industries.

Quite simply if there is no civil duty on the defendant that is identifiable from the words of the statute then there can be no civil action.

Has the defendant breached that duty by falling below the standard identified in the statute?

In the case of breaches of statutory duties there is no single standard of care, since the standard is identifiable from the individual statutory provision, so the court must assess the exact standard by construing the statute itself.

This is inevitably subject to inconsistency in approach and inevitably policy has a key role to play. As Lord Denning remarked in *Ex parte Island Records* [1978] 3 WLR 23 'you might as well toss a coin in order to decide the cases'.

Of course there are times when the words are so specific that the standard is self-evident.

CASE EXAMPLE

Chipchase v British Titan Products Co Ltd [1956] 1 QB 545

In this case the precise wording proved fatal to a claim. The defendant's injury was sustained when he fell six feet to the ground from a nine-inch wide platform. The regulations required that platforms over six feet six inches from the ground should be at least 34 inches wide. The specific wording of the provision was not breached and there was no possible action.

A precise and imperative wording in the provisions is likely to lead to liability being strict. Words such as 'must' or 'shall' are obvious examples of this general principle.

CASE EXAMPLE

John Summers & Sons v Frost [1955] AC 740

Section 14(1) of the Factories Act 1961 required fencing of machinery. The court refused to accept a plea that it was impracticable to fence machines. Liability was regarded as strict.

However, very often the standard may be only vaguely stated.

CASE EXAMPLE

Brown v NCB [1962] AC 574

Here the duty was to 'take such steps as may be necessary for keeping the road or working place secure'. There was held to be no liability when the court accepted that the manager had exercised reasonable skill and care.

Is the breach of duty the cause of the damage suffered by the claimant?

Causation is measured in similar ways to common law negligence. In this way the 'but for' test is significant in establishing a causal link.

CASE EXAMPLE

McWilliams v Sir William Arrol & Co Ltd [1962] 1 WLR 295

Here the claimant fell while not using a safety harness. Statute required that harnesses should be supplied. The defendant company was able to avoid liability because it was able to show that the claimant would not in any case have worn the harness.

So there must be a direct causal link between the defendant's breach of the statutory duty and the damage suffered by the claimant in order for a claim to succeed.

CASE EXAMPLE

Sussex Ambulance NHS Trust v King [2002] EWCA Civ 953

The claim was that injury was caused because of lack of specialist training required by regulations. The court accepted evidence showing that even without this specialist training the likelihood was that the claimant would still have suffered the injury. The court held that the employer was not liable.

However, the result might be different where the duty also extends to ensuring that the potential claimant complies with the safety provisions, for example by using or wearing safety equipment.

CASE EXAMPLE

Ginty v Belmont Building Supplies Ltd [1959] 1 All ER 414

While a failure to ensure that safety equipment is used may lead to liability, in this case the claim failed because the employer had done everything possible to ensure that the employee should use crawling boards provided for working on roofs. The claimant fell through the roof when not using the boards. The case is controversial however.

16.2.4 Is the damage of a type which is contemplated in the statute?

The final test for a claimant in respect of liability under a statutory duty in some senses mirrors the principle of remoteness of damage in normal negligence actions. The damage must be of a type that was contemplated by the statute or there can be no liability.

CASE EXAMPLE

Gorris v Scott [1874] LR 9 Ex 125

Here the claimant lost his sheep when they were swept overboard from the ship on which they were being carried. Even though there was a duty owed by statute, this was to prevent the loss of livestock through contagious diseases so there could be no liability.

The House of Lords in *Cullen v Chief Constable of the Royal Ulster Constabulary* also identified that the breach of duty in failing to warn of reasons for delaying access to a solicitor did not give rise to the type of damage that would normally be associated with a civil action. Tort damages are awarded for damage to property, personal injury and sometimes economic loss. The only possible action would have been for false imprisonment but the failure to warn would not amount to an unlawful detention.

On the issue of remoteness the case of *Young v Charles Church (Southern) Ltd, The Times*, 1 May 1997, CA is also relevant. Here a claim was possible because nervous shock which was suffered by the claimant was a type of damage contemplated in the Construction (General Provisions) Regulations 1961.

16.3 Defences

There are generally two defences available in claims for breach of a statutory duty.

16.3.1 *Volenti non fit injuria* (voluntary assumption of a risk)

Consent is not normally available as a defence and this is on policy grounds. However, it may be in two situations:

- where the claimant's wrongful act puts the defendant in breach – and *Ginty v Belmont Building Supplies* [1959] 1 All ER 414 is a good example of this;
- where the claimant tries to claim the defendant's vicarious liability as an issue.

CASE EXAMPLE

ICI Ltd v Shatwell [1965] AC 656

Two brothers who both worked in blasting ignored instructions and tested detonators without taking shelter as required by regulations. One brother who was injured as a result had ignored safety instructions and followed the guidance of the other brother. He then tried to fix the employer with vicarious liability for his brother's tort. The action failed because he had consented to the possible harm by accepting his brother's flawed advice and ignoring safety regulations himself.

16.3.2 Contributory negligence

The courts only very reluctantly accept this defence because regulations are often designed to protect workmen from their own carelessness. As Lord Denning remarked in *Caswell v Powell Duffryn Collieries* [1940] AC 152:

JUDGMENT

'the employee's sense of danger will have been dulled by familiarity, repetition, noise, confusion, fatigue, and preoccupation with work'.

The defence is still possible, however, where the claimant is genuinely at fault but liability is strict. Liability is not removed but the claimant's damages can be reduced to the extent to which he is at fault for his own loss or injury.

CASE EXAMPLE

Jayes v IMI (Kynoch) Ltd [1985] ICR 155

Reduction in damages of 100 per cent was awarded. The employer's obligation was not only to provide guards on machines but to ensure their continuous use when the machinery was turned on. The employee lost fingers when he failed to turn the machine off and tried to clear a blockage in the machine while it was still working.

ACTIVITY

Self-assessment questions

1 In what ways is the action similar to negligence?
2 In what ways is it different?
3 What advantages are there to a plaintiff in using the action?
4 What problems are there in proving the statute gave rise to an action in damages?
5 How imperfect is the test in *Lonrho*?
6 When will a claimant fail to show that a duty applies to him?
7 How is the standard of care measured?
8 How limiting are defences to the action?

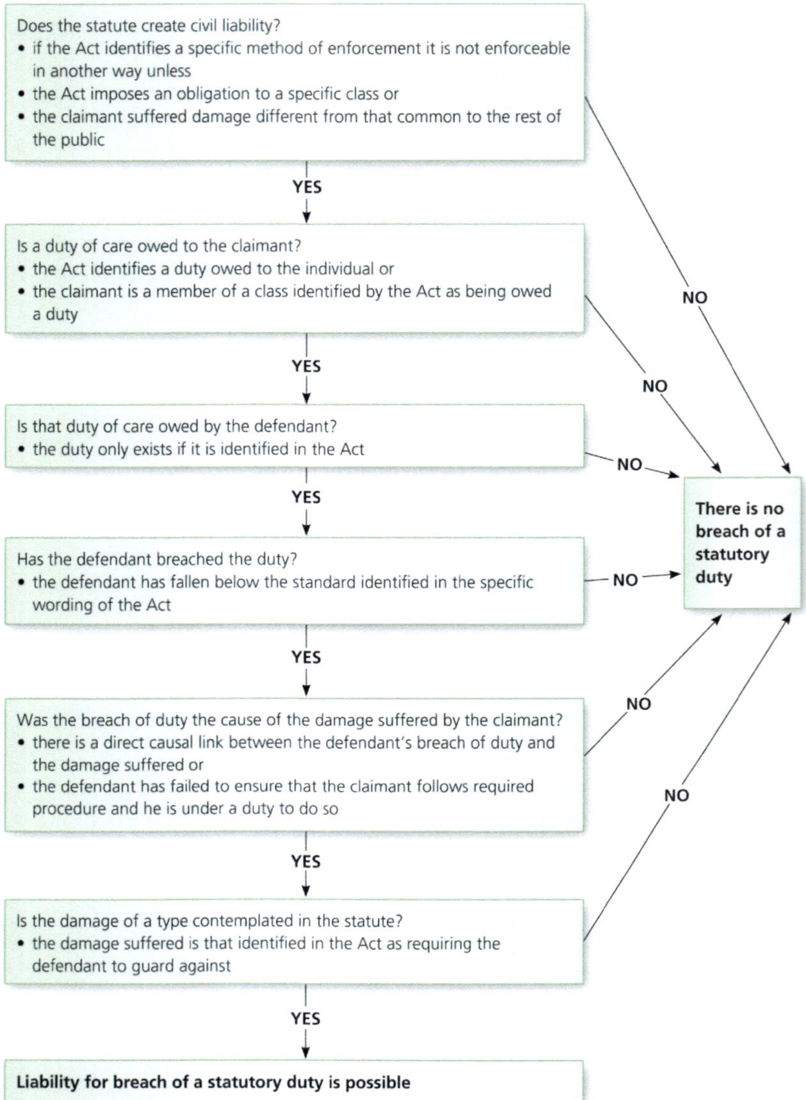

Figure 16.1 The essential elements of a claim for breach of a statutory duty.

KEY FACTS

The nature of breach of a statutory duty	Case
Concerns areas mainly like industrial safety law, but can include, e.g. consumer protection.	
Breaches of statutory duties usually lead to criminal sanctions so the main problem is proving that there is also civil liability.	

(Continued)

(Continued)

The nature of breach of a statutory duty	Case
A test has been developed by Lord Diplock in –	*Lonrho Ltd v Shell Petroleum Co* [1982]
Determining whether there is civil liability	**Case**
The courts will look at: the precise wording of the statute whether a precise penalty is indicated whether the welfare of a definable class is a purpose of the statute.	*Monk v Warby* [1935] *Cutler v Wandsworth Stadium* [1949] *Thornton v Kirklees MBC* [1979]
The essential questions to ask are: whether a duty is owed to the specific claimant whether a duty is imposed on the defendant whether the defendant has fallen below the appropriate standard of care whether the breach of duty has caused the damage suffered by the claimant whether the damage was of a type contemplated in the statute.	*Hewett v Alf Brown's Transport* [1992] *R v Deputy Governor of Parkhurst Prison, ex parte Hague* [1992] *Chipchase v British Titan Products Co Ltd* [1956] *McWilliams v Sir William Arrol & Co Ltd* [1962]
The courts will in any case not impose a duty where they feel that an alternative remedy was intended in the statute.	*Gorris v Scott* [1874]; *Cullen v Chief Constable of the Royal Ulster Constabulary* [2003]
Defences	**Case**
Volenti non fit injuria if the claimant has genuinely accepted the risk.	*Ginty v Belmont Building Supplies* [1959]
Contributory negligence – in which case damages will be reduced to the extent that the claimant contributed to his own harm.	*Jayes v IMI (Kynoch)* [1985]

SAMPLE ESSAY QUESTION

Discuss the difficulties associated with bringing a civil action for a breach of a statutory duty.

Explain when a breach of a statutory duty might occur

- Often occurs in health and safety, industrial safety law, consumer protection etc.
- Usually the statute is regulatory and makes criminal sanctions available to regulatory bodies

Discuss the basic problem

- Action for breach of statutory duty similar to negligence – but other considerations apply
- It is not always clear whether the statute does create civil liability since usually criminal in nature

Discuss how the courts decide if there is civil liability

- Examine precise wording of Act to see whether it intended to create civil liability
- Consider whether the claimant is owed a duty of care and that duty is imposed on the defendant
- Consider whether the defendant has breached his duty
- Decide whether the breach caused the damage and was a type of damage contemplated in the Act

Discuss the available defences

- *Volenti* which is only available only if the claimant's wrongful act caused the defendant breach

Discuss the difficulties associated with proving the existence of a civil action

- They usually impose criminal sanctions so the existence of civil liability is debatable
- It is often not stated whether it is civil liability in the Act
- Civil liability is more obvious where the Act modifies the common law
- But with other Acts it is harder to determine so the area is dependent on statutory interpretation
- As a result the area is unpredictable

Discuss the difficulties involved in succeeding in a claim

- The action is similar to negligence but it differs in significant ways
- The standard of care is usually fixed by the statute
- The duty can be strict, or the burden of proof may be reversed, either being advantageous to a claimant
- Treated as a separate tort
- So often it is pleaded together with negligence

ACTIVITY

Applying the law

Using the guide in Appendix 2 try the following problem question:

> Gary works for Careless Contractors. On 14 November 2003 the foreman, John, ordered him to replace a glass panel in the seventh-floor window of Storer Tower where the contractors had completed re-glazing on 10 November 2003. Scaffolding on three sides of the building had already been disassembled. Gary took up position on scaffolding outside the window and waited for the new pane to be winched down to him from the roof. As it came to rest on the scaffolding boards they collapsed, and Gary fell on to the boards below injuring himself.

The manager of the scaffolders suggested to John that the scaffolding was secure to work on but subjecting it to any great stresses should be avoided. Gary is hoping to claim under the Construction (Working Places) Regulations 1966 which state:

> 'it shall be the duty of every contractor, and every employer or workmen, who is undertaking any of the operations or works to which these regulations apply –

a To comply with such requirements as affect him, or any workman employed by him . . . provided that the requirements shall be deemed not to affect any workman if his presence in the place is not in the course of performing any work on behalf of his employer . . . and it shall be the duty of every contractor and every employer of workmen who erects or alters any scaffold to comply with such of the requirements as relate to the erection or alteration of scaffolds.'

Does Gary have an action for breach of statutory duty?

SUMMARY

- Mainly involves industrial safety law and some consumer protection.
- Usually involves criminal sanctions so the problem is proving civil liability exists.
- Courts consider the wording of the statute, whether a precise penalty is indicated, whether one purpose of the statute is the welfare of a definable class, whether the claimant is owed a duty of care and the defendant owes the duty, whether the defendant has breached the duty, whether the breach caused the damage, whether the damage was of a type contemplated in the statute, whether an alternative remedy was intended in the statute.
- *Volenti non fit injuria* and contributory negligence are possible defences.

Further reading

Cooke, Professor J, *Law of Tort* (14th edn, Pearson, 2019), Chapter 13.
Witting, C, *Street on Torts* (16th edn, OUP, 2021), Chapter 19.

17

Employers' liability

AIMS AND OBJECTIVES

After reading this chapter you should be able to:

- Identify the essential elements of the common law duty
- Explain the ways in which the common law duty has been expanded
- Critically analyse aspects of employers' liability
- Apply the law to factual situations and reach conclusions as to liability

17.1 Origins of liability

Employers' liability is a well-developed principle that is to be found in both the common law and statute. It developed initially in the nineteenth century through very limited statutory controls following the Industrial Revolution. The very first industrial safety law was Sir Robert Peel's Health and Morals of Apprentices Act 1802.

Most often those controls applied only to children and sometimes to women and were aimed more at regulating employment practices than at providing legal rights for employees. The first Acts to protect adult male workers were the Factory Act 1833 (which created a Factory Inspectorate) and the Factory Act 1844 (which introduced the idea of fencing off dangerous machinery).

So it took a long time for civil liability to develop in the area, not until the Workmen's Compensation Act 1897, and workers rarely had the means of suing or gaining compensation for the injuries that they sustained through negligent practices.

The nature of the development has also meant that the area is quite complex and involves consideration of both common law and statutory provision.

Employment was traditionally seen, as it still is, as a contractual relationship, based on freedom of contract, so no remedies were available in

DOI: 10.4324/9781003202417-17

tort. Employees were free to negotiate their own contractual terms, at least in theory, so if no reference to industrial safety was made in the contract then no civil action was available.

In the nineteenth century there were three further major barriers to workers' claims in respect of injuries sustained at work:

- The defence of *volenti* – the worker in accepting the work was said also to have consented to the risks and dangers inherent in the specific type of work.
- The defence of contributory negligence – this was a complete defence at that time so that if the employer could show that the employee was engaging in unsafe working practices then there could be no claim and this would be the case even though the worker had been directed to pursue those practices by the employer.
- The so-called fellow servant rule and the common law doctrine of common employment – where an employee was injured as the result of an unsafe practice of a fellow employee the employer could disclaim responsibility for that employee's actions and there could be no claim against the employer (and there would be little point in claiming against the 'fellow servant' who would inevitably be a 'man of straw').

The common law was generally hostile to workers and applied these three defences rigorously. Gradually, however, their severity was limited:

- In *Smith v Baker* [1891] AC 325 the court accepted that *volenti* would only be available if the claimant freely accepted and understood the specific risk.
- The Law Reform (Contributory Negligence) Act 1945 altered the character of the defence of contributory negligence making it a partial defence only affecting the amount of damages to be received rather than removing liability altogether as had formerly been the case.
- Finally in *Groves v Lord Wimbourne* [1898] 2 QB 402 the 'fellow servant' rule was held not to be available as a defence to a breach of a statutory duty; and in the Law Reform (Personal Injuries) Act 1948 the defence was finally abolished altogether.

There were also further major positive developments in the law:

- In *Wilsons & Clyde Coal v English* [1938] AC 57 the court identified that the employer owed a personal and non-delegable duty of care towards his employees.
- Employers became liable for defective plant and equipment in the Employers' Liability (Defective Equipment) Act 1969.
- The principle of the employer insuring workers against injury that was introduced in the Workmen's Compensation Act 1897 in respect of a limited range of named occupations was at a later stage extended to include all employees by the Employers' Liability (Compulsory Insurance) Act 1969.

Subsequent to all these developments there are in principle three means by which an employee might impose liability on an employer:

- for a breach of a statutory duty, for example under the Health and Safety at Work etc Act 1974 or other regulatory provisions where they include civil liability (see Chapter 16);
- for the tortious acts of another employee through the principle of vicarious liability (see Chapter 18);
- for a breach of the employer's personal non-delegable duty of care.

All three have been subject to significant development. Proving the complexity of the area in a claim for an injury at work the pleadings will very often involve all three.

17.2 The employer's non-delegable duty

17.2.1 Introduction

First, it is important to remember that the whole area of employer's liability is complicated by virtue of there being not only basic common law duties but that these are interspersed with a huge number of statutory duties and regulatory provisions. Either might prove beneficial to a claimant since commonly with statutory duties, liability is strict or the burden of proof is reversed. Often also a common law duty is contained in any case within a statutory provision. For these reasons a claim is often a mixture of both, pleaded as alternatives.

With statutory duties there is the added complication of demonstrating that the statute does indeed provide a civil remedy (as seen in Chapter 16).

The basic common law duty in essence derives from the judgment of Lord Wright in *Wilsons & Clyde Coal Co Ltd v English*. The basic duty is to take reasonable care for the safety of all employees while acting in the course of their employment.

Lord Wright identified the duty as personal and non-delegable and at the time saw the duty as having four key aspects:

- the duty to provide competent staff as working colleagues;
- the duty to provide a safe plant and equipment;
- the duty to provide a safe place of work;
- the duty to provide a safe system of work.

As the law has developed there has also now been established a general common law duty to protect the health and safety of the worker. This duty extends not only to physical health and well-being but also to ensure the psychiatric health of the worker.

One significant fact that must be remembered is that these categories are quite simply stated and do not necessarily fully reflect the complexities of the modern workplace. In this sense the separate duties can quite easily overlap. In any case the likelihood is that a claim that an employer has breached his duties towards an employee will likely contain elements of more than one duty. Besides this, as has already been indicated, there is likely to be overlap also with many of the statutory duties and, if there are civil remedies attached, the claim will possibly include a range of evidence of the employer's breaches, both common law and statutory.

17.2.2 The different aspects of the duty

The duty to provide competent staff

It is clear that the employer must ensure that all employees are competent to carry out the duties they are required to undertake in their employment.

CASE EXAMPLE

General Cleaning Contractors Ltd v Christmas [1953] AC 180

Here a window cleaner was injured while cleaning sash windows, having been improperly instructed on the safest method of undertaking the work. The employer was held liable.

An employer must also ensure the good behaviour of all employees while at work. In this way an employer should not tolerate unsafe practices, including the playing of practical jokes that might cause harm to other employees. All unsafe practices should be dealt with and an employee who indulges in such practices should be disciplined and in extreme cases even dismissed.

CASE EXAMPLE

Hudson v Ridge Manufacturing Co [1957] 2 QB 348

An employee was injured when a fellow employee well known for such behaviour carried out a practical joke on him. The employer was in breach of his duty and liable for failing to discipline the employee at fault and prevent him from repeating such activity and was held liable.

However, the employer may not be liable if he is unaware that the employee causing damage or injury is likely to behave in that way.

CASE EXAMPLE

O'Reilly v National Rail & Tramway Appliances [1966] 1 All ER 499

Here labourers breaking up a disused railway line found what they believed to be an unexploded shell of some sort from the Second World War, some nine inches long and one inch in diameter. The claimant was injured when he followed the suggestion of work colleagues that he hit the object with a sledgehammer. One had said 'Hit it: what are you scared of?' The employer had no idea that his employees would be so silly and thus escaped liability for the severe injuries sustained by the claimant.

In modern times actions using this basic common law duty are rare because of the principle of vicarious liability. However, it may still be useful when the employee's act causing injury or damage falls outside the scope of employment.

The duty to provide safe working conditions is now supplemented by successful actions under s3 Protection from Harassment Act 1997 – *Green v DB Group Services (UK) Ltd* [2006] EWHC 1989 (Ch) (see section 13.6.2) and *Majrowski v Guy's & St Thomas's NHS Trust* [2006] UKHL 34 (see section 18.3.1).

It also of course is an example of where vicarious liability applies within the employment. In recent times with the creation of the close connection test (see section 18.5.1) the courts appear to have widened the scope of what the employer may be vicariously liable for. One aspect of this has been in the case of violent attacks on one employee by another.

CASE EXAMPLE

Weddall v Barchester Healthcare Ltd; Wallbank v Wallbank Fox Designs [2012] EWCA Civ 25

This involves joined appeals both involving violent behaviour by employees towards other employees and whether this gives rise to vicarious liability. In the first a health assistant in a care home was telephoned at night while he was off duty asking if he would do an extra shift. The employee, who had a poor relationship with the manager who rang him, was drunk at the time, became angry and went back to work and attacked the manager who had called him. In the second an employee was reprimanded and given an instruction by a senior employee and the employee responded by pushing him into a table and injuring his back. The court held that in the case of the first there was no liability because the employee was not in the course of his employment. In the second it was held that there was a sufficiently close connection between the work and the employee's reaction for there to be vicarious liability, since it was an instantaneous response, albeit a violent one to a legitimate instruction.

The duty to provide safe plant and equipment

The basic duty is that the employer must take care both to provide safe equipment and of course to properly maintain it.

CASE EXAMPLE

Smith v Baker [1891–94] All ER Rep 69

A quarry worker was hurt when stones fell on him from hoppers that crossed over the quarry bottom on a conveyor system. The employer was liable because the machinery was not properly maintained.

Lord Halsbury LC at 74, identified the position that the employee was faced with:

JUDGMENT

'The question of law that seems to be in debate is whether . . . on occasion when the very form of his employment prevented him from looking out for himself, he consented to undergo this particular risk . . . I do not think the plaintiff did consent at all. His attention was on a drill, and while he was unable to take precautions himself, a stone was negligently slung over his head without due precautions against its being permitted to fall.'

The employer may need to train employees how to use equipment properly.

CASE EXAMPLE

Mountenay (Hazzard) & Others v Bernard Matthews [1993] (unreported)

Here the employee developed a clinical wrist problem as the result of continuously handling dead poultry on a production line. There had been no attempt to rotate work to prevent workers constantly using the same wrist actions or to educate workers to the natural risks of the work, so the employer was liable.

However, the employer can still avoid liability if he actually provides adequate equipment but the employee misuses the equipment or fails to make proper use of it.

CASE EXAMPLE

Parkinson v Lyle Shipping Co Ltd [1964] 2 Lloyd's Rep 79

Here an employee was badly burned while trying to light a boiler. There was no defect in the boiler. It was quite safe and the employee had been properly instructed in how to light it. So there was no liability.

The provisions of the Employers' Liability (Defective Equipment) Act 1969 have now possibly superseded the common law duty in many respects. The Act has a seemingly precise definition of equipment. Section 1(3) defines 'equipment' as 'any plant and machinery, vehicle, aircraft and clothing'. Nevertheless, even the Act itself has been subject to conflicting interpretation.

CASE EXAMPLE

Coltman v Bibby Tankers [1988] AC 276

In this case the Court of Appeal held that an injury sustained because of a defect in the hull of a ship was not actionable, not falling within the definition. The House of Lords later reversed this and accepted that the definition within the Act could include the circumstances of the case.

As with all statutory provisions the definitions within sections of Acts may be challenged and the court will be called on to interpret. This may lead to some surprising results.

CASE EXAMPLE

Knowles v Liverpool City Council [1993] ICR 21

In this case the court found no problem in bringing a kerbstone within the definition for the purposes of imposing liability under the Act. The employee had been injured because of the negligence of the council in failing to ensure that kerbstones were not raised and it was liable as a result of the broad interpretation accepted by the court.

The duty to provide a safe place of work

The general duty here is to take all steps that are reasonably practicable to ensure that premises are safe.

CASE EXAMPLE

Latimer v AEC [1953] AC 643

An employee was injured when slipping on a greasy patch on the factory floor following flood damage. The employer was not liable, having done everything practicable to ensure that the floor was safe for use.

Since many forms of work depend on employees being mobile, the duty may also extend to premises other than the employer's own premises.

CASE EXAMPLE

Wilson v Tyneside Window Cleaning Co [1958] 2 QB 110

Window cleaners were injured while working on a client's premises. The employer had done everything within his capability to ensure that the men were safe so could not be liable.

It is also true, however, that most industrial premises, if not other places of work, are potentially hazardous. Where the employee exercises a particular skill or enjoys specific expertise liability may be avoided where the worker has failed to take account of his own safety. All people with a skill are expected to have an awareness of the risks that are associated with exercising that particular skill.

CASE EXAMPLE

Roles v Nathan [1963] 1 WLR 1117

Chimney sweeps were killed by fumes when they were cleaning flues in an industrial chimney stack while boilers under the chimney were still alight. Their own expert knowledge should have alerted them to the dangers, and claims for their deaths failed.

Lord Denning explained the position at 1123:

JUDGMENT

'These chimney sweeps ought to have known that there might be dangerous fumes about and ought to have taken steps to guard against them. They ought to have known that they should not attempt to seal up the sweep hole whilst the fire was still alight. They ought to have had the fire withdrawn . . . they ought not to have stayed in the alcove too long when there might be dangerous fumes about. All this was known to these two sweeps; they were repeatedly warned about it, and it was for them to guard against it.'

One final point is that since employers very often will be in control of the premises within which they operate there may also be liability under the Occupiers' Liability Act 1957 (see Chapter 7).

The duty to provide a safe system of work

There are two key aspects to the duty:

- the creation of a safe system in the first place;
- a proper implementation of the system.

It is a question of fact in each case whether the work requires that a system is necessary and should be devised for safety purposes or whether safe practices should be obvious to the employee.

The employer is not able to rely on an unsafe practice merely because it is a common practice.

CASE EXAMPLE

Re Herald of Free Enterprise, Independent, 18 December 1987

It was irrelevant that it was not unusual for bow doors to be left open on roll-on roll-off ferries when entering or leaving port. Vessels could and did capsize as the result of such a practice.

The general duty is to provide an effective system of work which is sufficient to meet any foreseeable dangers.

CASE EXAMPLE

General Cleaning Contractors Ltd v Christmas [1953] AC 180

Holding on to the sill and without wedges while cleaning sash windows was clearly an unsafe system, although it was the one that had been explained to the employee by his immediate superior. In the event the sash cord failed and the window fell onto the window cleaner's hands, leading to the injuries and liability.

Inevitably in certain types of employment there are actual dangers presented by the nature of the work or by the people with whom the employee has to work. If the employer fails to operate systems to effectively avoid these dangers then the employer will be liable.

CASE EXAMPLE

Cook v Bradford Community NHS Trust [2002] EWCA Civ 1616

Here the employee worked in a psychiatric ward and was assaulted by a violent patient which in itself was a foreseeable risk. Because the systems in place failed to adequately address this risk the employer was liable.

The duty is also not just to devise the system but may also be to ensure that the system is carried out. A safe system is only safe if it is in fact followed. Thus, for instance, there is no point in an employer possessing safety equipment if employees are not provided with it.

CASE EXAMPLE

Bux v Slough Metals [1974] 1 All ER 262

An employee was provided with safety goggles but would not use them because he claimed that they misted up. The employer knew of this and when the employee was injured by a splash of molten metal the employer was liable for failing to ensure that the goggles were worn.

Again it is insufficient that an employer claims to have created a safe system if the employees are unaware of it. On this basis an employer might still be liable for a failure to warn of dangers inherent in the work.

CASE EXAMPLE

Pape v Cumbria CC [1992] 3 All ER 211

The employer was liable here for failing to warn that not wearing gloves might lead to dermatitis as a result of continuous contact with irritants.

The advances in modern technology and its effect on working practices may also have an impact on working conditions. In the case of use of VDUs for instance there are a range of provisions under regulations requiring safe working practices. The common law also demands that the systems for using such equipment should not damage the health and safety of the employee.

CASE EXAMPLE

Alexander and Others v Midland Bank plc [2000] ICR 464

Here employees worked under high pressure processing and continuously inputting information into computer databases. The employees successfully complained that the employer had consistently increased the work rate demanded and that as a result of unsafe practice they had suffered muscular injuries.

Where the employment involves contact with the public this in itself can very often present a potential hazard to the employee. The employer may well be expected to operate a system of work where the employee's safety was not unnecessarily threatened by public contact.

CASE EXAMPLE

Rahman v Arearose Ltd [2000] 3 WLR 1184

A restaurant worker was violently assaulted and seriously injured by customers. The employer was liable because it was identified that other members of staff had also been assaulted, the employer was aware of this and had not introduced any effective system to prevent it.

Much of the duty here has probably now been superseded, for example by the duty to undertake risk assessment under the 'six pack' and other regulatory requirements on an employer.

One possible recent development of the duty is to ensure that the system of work does not cause undue stress to the employee.

CASE EXAMPLE

Walker v Northumberland CC [1995] 1 All ER 737

A second nervous breakdown of a senior social worker resulted in liability for the employers. This was because after the first they were aware of his susceptibility to stress and did nothing to reduce his workload or the pressure associated with it.

Colman J explained the development at 749:

JUDGMENT

'It is clear law that an employer has a duty to provide his employee with a safe system of work and to take reasonable steps to protect him from risks which are reasonably foreseeable . . . there is no logical reason why risk of psychiatric damage should be excluded from the scope of an employer's duty.'

ACTIVITY

Quick quiz

Consider which aspect of the employers' duty may have been breached in the following circumstances.

1 Eric breaks his leg at the start of his shift at 6.00 a.m. in December on his way into the factory when he stumbles into a pothole near to the main door. The entrance to the factory has not been resurfaced for many years and it is very dark because the bulb in the light outside the entrance has gone and has not been replaced.
2 Tariq suffers a severe back injury when a fellow employee, Angus, pulls Tariq's chair away as Tariq is about to sit down. Other employees have complained about Angus's practical jokes in the past but he has never been disciplined for them.
3 Bronwen has been forced to give up work because of a permanent bronchial complaint that has been caused in her work drilling panels of a toxic material. She has never been provided with a mask, there is no mechanism on the machine to prevent dust and she has never had any warnings about the dangers of inhaling the dust or received any health and safety training.
4 Olga works in a café. She has been badly burned and injured when the new cappuccino machine spurted hot liquid all over her.

17.2.3 The character of the duty

As already identified the duty is entirely personal and non-delegable.

CASE EXAMPLE

Wilsons & Clyde Coal Co Ltd v English [1938] AC 57

Colliery owners had tried to delegate their responsibilities and liability under various industrial safety laws to their colliery manager by contractually making him entirely responsible for safety. However, when a miner was injured the colliery owners were held liable, the court refusing to accept that their personal liability could be delegated to a third party, who was in any case an employee.

17.2.4 Breach of duty

Once a duty of care has been established, the other elements of the claim also need to be established. The standard of care applied here is that of a reasonable employer and the duty extends only as far as what is reasonable. There is inevitably no requirement to guarantee the safety of employees as seen in *Latimer v AEC* [1957] AC 643.

The duty will extend to all reasonable and ancillary activities.

CASE EXAMPLE

Davidson v Handley Page Ltd [1945] 1 All ER 235

An employee slipped on a greasy duckboard on his way to his tea break and the employer was held liable. Breaks were a necessary part of the working day and even though the break might be out of the course of employment there must be a safe access to wherever the break is taken.

While the duty protects the employee it appears that the duty will not extend as far as protection of the employee's property.

CASE EXAMPLE

Deyong v Shenburn [1946] KB 227

The employee's clothing was stolen from a theatre in which he worked. There was held to be no liability on the employer.

Injuries that are sustained in the course of carrying out customary trade practices will not escape liability unless the practice itself is reasonable.

CASE EXAMPLE

Cavanagh v Ulster Weaving Co [1960] AC 145

Here the employee was expected to climb on a pitched roof while carrying a bag of cement and was injured when he fell. The employer argued that this was customary practice but it was clearly unsafe and he was held liable.

17.2.5 Causation and remoteness

The usual tests for causation and remoteness apply as set out in Chapter 4.

As in other areas of tort the 'thin skull' rule applies so the employer's duty extends to considering the possible extent of the injury to the particular employee.

CASE EXAMPLE

Paris v Stepney BC [1951] AC 367

Here the employee was already without sight in one eye. When failure to wear safety goggles resulted in the loss of his other eye the employer was liable to the extent of causing total blindness.

The employer of course is obliged only to guard against foreseeable risks and may take into account the practicability of any possible precautions.

CASE EXAMPLE

Charlton v Forrest Printing Ink Co Ltd [1978] IRLR 331

An employee was injured in an ambush while taking money to the bank on foot. The employer could have avoided the risk to the employee by arranging for a safer method of delivering the money and so was held liable.

The duty ultimately is to prevent accidents that are reasonably foreseeable. This is the basic *Wagon Mound* test. In this respect it is possible to compare two cases in determining how foreseeability is measured.

CASE EXAMPLE

Doughty v Turner Manufacturing Co Ltd [1964] 1 QB 518

In this case workmen were injured in an explosion when an asbestos lid negligently fitted on a chemical tank fell into the chemical. There was no liability because at the time it was not known that the specific chemical reaction causing the injuries would occur.

We have already seen in negligence that the precise damage or the precise circumstances in which it arises need not be foreseen as long as damage of the general kind caused can be foreseen.

CASE EXAMPLE

Bradford v Robinson Rentals [1967] 1 All ER 267

In this case, on the other hand, a driver was required to drive from Exeter to Bedford in a blizzard in a van with no heater and a broken window. The employer tried to claim that the resulting injury, frostbite, was unforeseeable. The court rejected the defence since some form of cold related illness was entirely foreseeable.

17.3 Developments in the common law duty

Judges have begun to expand the boundaries of the employer's duties towards the employee's health and safety. These developments apply in both a general sense and in relation to more specific injuries.

Extreme pressures of work and excessive workloads have led to the introduction of a general duty to protect the health and safety of the employee.

CASE EXAMPLE

Johnstone v Bloomsbury Health Authority [1991] 2 All ER 293

A junior doctor brought an action against the health authority that employed him, complaining that the fact that he was expected as a matter of course to work up to 48 hours of overtime per week and had to be on call had damaged his general mental health. The court held that there had been a breach of a non-excludable implied term in his contract to take reasonable steps to care for his health and safety. The employer could not exclude this implied term by use of the specific express terms in the contract and was liable as a result.

This has opened up a whole field of law on stress-related illnesses and psychiatric damage caused at work. The action was not entirely novel. It is accepted now that there is a general duty to protect both the psychiatric health and well-being of the employee.

CASE EXAMPLE

Petch v Commissioners of Customs and Excise [1993] ICR 789

Here the employee was claiming for a breakdown that he argued was due to the stressful nature of the work undertaken. Dillon LJ in the Court of Appeal held that the employer was not negligent because the event was unforeseeable and also because the employer had done everything possible to try to persuade the employee not to return to work. Nevertheless the court did accept that an employer could be liable if he knows that the employee is susceptible to stress and allows the employee to continue working in stressful circumstances.

The result of these recent cases is that an employee is entitled to treat a psychiatric injury caused by negligent work practice in the same way that a physical injury would be dealt with.

CASE EXAMPLE

Walker v Northumberland CC [1995] 1 All ER 737

Here the case was actually given leave for an appeal to the Court of Appeal but was settled beforehand for £175,000. The significant feature of the case was that the employee had already suffered a nervous breakdown as a result of work-related stress. On returning to work he had been promised that his workload would reduce but was actually faced with a huge backlog of work from his absence. The result was that he suffered a second breakdown causing him to leave work permanently after he was dismissed on sickness grounds. The employer was clearly liable because of placing a person who was already known to suffer from stress under even more stressful conditions and without having done anything about the understaffing and excess of work that had caused the first breakdown.

The *Walker* criteria can be straightforwardly applied. The employer is liable because he is aware of the employee's susceptibility to stress and has worsened that condition by unsafe practices or unnecessary pressures of work.

CASE EXAMPLE

Young v Post Office [2002] EWCA Civ 661

After changes in work practices involving a change to computer systems without adequate training the employee became stressed, was put on anti-depressants, suffered a nervous breakdown and was absent from work for months. The employer then agreed that the employee should return with a gradual reintroduction to work. In fact he had to attend a week's residential training course, and cover for a manager in his absence and suffered more stress, forcing him to leave permanently. The employer was liable because it did not follow its own agreed treatment of the employee.

The developments in this field have led to a variety of claims based on different aspects of stress at work that can be found reported in a variety of journals and newspapers.

Negligence claims in employment do not in any case have to result only from the workload. It is also possible for claims to be related to abuse or even physical danger in the workplace where the employer fails to protect the employee.

CASE EXAMPLE

Ingram v Worcestershire County Council, The Times, 11 January 2000

Here a council worker who supervised a gypsy camp site as warden was attacked by residents of the site after the council changed its policies on the treatment of the residents. He had dogs set on him and was also shot at and was unable to work from 1997 onwards. The council was liable and the employee received considerable damages of £203,000.

Quite obviously bullying and harassment in the workplace can also be a breach of the employer's duty and can lead to liability in a similar way to the cases above.

CASE EXAMPLE

Ratcliffe v Dyfed County Council, The Times, 17 July 1998

Here a claim for a stress-related injury was accepted when a head teacher was found to have bullied a junior member of staff. The general duty to protect the health, safety and welfare of the employee applied.

Another category of stress claims has concerned the effects of redeployment and changing job roles. These are obviously stressful circumstances for an employee. If the employer fails to take care of the employee's general health and welfare in such circumstances then there may well be liability.

CASE EXAMPLE

Lancaster v Birmingham City Council [1999] 99(6) QR 4

The claimant was employed in a clerical capacity by a city council. She was redeployed but given no training or guidance in her new position as a housing officer. She then suffered three separate absences through stress and the employer failed to do anything about the problem so that she eventually had to retire on health grounds. The defendant council admitted liability 'in the door of the court' and compensated the claimant.

It is possible, however, that the courts are now pulling back and that there is no general duty to guard against psychiatric injuries. Instead courts are now accepting that a duty that arises when an ordinary bystander would foresee that the stress suffered is likely to be of such a degree as to cause a recognised psychiatric disorder.

CASE EXAMPLE

Rorrison v West Lothian College and Lothian Regional Council (Scottish Court of Session) IDS Brief 655, February 2000

The claimant was a nurse responsible for welfare duties and first aid in a college. A new personnel officer disciplined her, allegedly for no particular reason, took her first aid role off her and changed the usual method of dealing with sick students without ever informing her. The claimant's GP then diagnosed anxiety depression and gave her sick notes for six weeks. When she returned to work the personnel officer gave her mainly clerical duties, allegedly harassed her and frequently changed her duties afterwards. At one point she was given 30 minutes to accept a change of contractual terms or be fired. She then suffered distress, panic attacks and depression and was given beta blockers by her doctor. The court stated that her action against her employers could only succeed if she was able to show an identifiable psychiatric illness rather than mere stress, and was not prepared to accept anxiety depression as being the same as clinical depression. It was also suggested that the illness resulting from the work conditions should be foreseeable to a reasonable bystander, rather than to a doctor, to succeed. The case is only persuasive but it demonstrates a harsh application of the principles in *Walker*.

In any case *Walker* criteria must be satisfied before a successful claim can be made. This means that it is for the claimant to show that it is the actions of the employer, knowing of the employee's existing illness, that has caused the later illness.

CASE EXAMPLE

Sparks v HSBC plc [2002] EWHC 2707 (QB)

The claimant had worked for the bank for many years when he began to suffer depression. The bank offered him retirement but instead he chose to work part time. Mistakes were found in his work but he was not disciplined and eventually he was also promoted. He suffered further depression and his work deteriorated and he was seen by the occupational therapist who recommended support although this was not given. He later retired on health grounds and claimed loss of earnings. The Court of Appeal would not accept his claim that the employer had caused or worsened the illness.

The area is a difficult one for judges to determine and the Court of Appeal has now produced guidelines for determining liability which appear to make it very difficult for claimants to bring successful claims for stress-related psychiatric injuries.

CASE EXAMPLE

Sutherland v Hatton and Others [2002] EWCA Civ 76

This leading case involved a number of joined appeals on stress-related illnesses at work. Two claims involved teachers. One concerned a local authority administrator and one a factory worker. All were claiming that they had been forced to stop working because of stress-related psychiatric illnesses caused by their employers.

The Court of Appeal issued some important guidelines.

- The basic principles of negligence must apply including the usual principles of employers' liability.
- The critical question for the court to answer is whether the type of harm suffered was foreseeable.
- Foreseeability depends on what the reasonable employer knew or ought reasonably to have known.
- An employer is entitled to assume that an employee is able to cope with the pressures normally associated with the job unless the employer has specific knowledge that an employee has a particular problem and may not cope.
- The same test should apply whatever the employment.
- The employer will be obliged to take steps to prevent possible harm when the possibility of harm would be obvious to a reasonable employer.

- The employer will be liable if he then fails to take steps that are reasonable in the circumstances to avoid the harm.
- The nature of the employment, the employer's available resources, the counselling and treatment services provided are all relevant in determining whether the employer has taken effective steps to avoid the harm and in any case the employer is only expected to take steps that will do some good.
- The employee must show that it is the breach of duty by the employer that has caused the harm, not merely that the harm is stress related.
- Where there is more than one cause of the harm the employer will only be liable for that portion of damages that relates to the harm actually caused by his breach of duty.
- Damages will in any case take account of any pre-existing disorder.

A Collender, 'Stress in the workplace' (2003) 153 NLJ 248 notes that '[W]hilst it is possible to identify some jobs that are intrinsically physically dangerous, it is rather more difficult to identify which jobs are intrinsically so stressful that physical or psychological harm is to be expected more often than in other jobs . . . With that guidance [*Sutherland v Hatton* [2002] EWCA Civ 76], courts are likely to be all the more willing to apportion and limit damages, to take account of the factors noted and if they do, the decision . . . will mark a significant development in the law.'

The House of Lords has subsequently had the opportunity to review the principles laid down in *Hatton*.

CASE EXAMPLE

Barber v Somerset County Council [2004] UKHL 13; [2004] 1 WLR 1089

This appeal involved one of the original claimants in the joined appeals in *Hatton*, having lost his appeal in the Court of Appeal. The claimant was a maths teacher who was given additional coordinating and managerial responsibilities in order to maintain his current income following a restructuring of the school in which he worked. As a result his working hours increased to between 61 and 70 hours a week and after some months of trying to cope he complained of being overloaded to his deputy head teacher. Nothing was done and a few months later, after consulting his GP for stress and enquiring into the possibility of early retirement, he suffered a bout of stress and depression and was absent from work for three weeks. Again nothing was done by the school to address his problems and he continued to see his doctor for stress. He finally broke down, shook a pupil and left the school permanently. Psychiatrists agreed that he was suffering moderate to severe depression. The claimant had won at first instance on the basis that the school ought to have appreciated that the risk to the claimant's health was significantly greater than to another teacher with a high workload and yet had done nothing. This was reversed by the Court of Appeal in the joined *Hatton* appeals. The House of Lords held that the Court of Appeal had failed to pay sufficient attention to the claimant's three-week sickness absence and the medical reasons for it and held that the local authority was in breach of its duty of care by being aware of the difficulties that the increased workload was having on the claimant and the medical consequences but failing to do anything to remedy it.

Following *Barber* the Court of Appeal applied the *Hatton* criteria to individual cases in joined appeals, *Hartman v South Essex Mental Health & Community Care NHS Trust; Best v Staffordshire University; Wheeldon v HSBC Bank Ltd; Green v Grimsby & Scunthorpe Newspapers Ltd; Moore v Welwyn Components Ltd; Melville v The Home Office* [2004] EWCA Civ 06.

The Court of Appeal has more recently re-emphasised the point that a successful claimant must show that it was reasonably foreseeable that he would suffer a psychiatric illness as a result of the employer's breach of duty, not just that he would suffer from stress. However, in *Daw v Intel Corporation (UK) Ltd* [2007] EWCA Civ 76 the Court of Appeal held that 'indications of impending harm to health were plain enough for the [employer] to realise that immediate action was required'. The claimant had sent many notes to her employer drawing their attention to stress caused by overwork and confused lines of communication. The court also held that the mere fact of offering counselling was not sufficient to avoid liability.

Safety has always appeared to be a major preoccupation of the common law in the context of employment. Statutory obligations to the employee also demonstrate a clear concern with safety, but the health and general welfare of the employee are also key elements of the duty. It is significant that the common law is beginning to adopt a similarly broad attitude towards the employee's well-being.

CASE EXAMPLE

Bonser v RJW Mining (UK) Ltd [2003] EWCA Civ 1296

The claimant was employed as a technical support and training manager. She often was forced to work beyond her contractual hours and the court accepted that her supervisor was overbearing and insensitive to her stress. This was despite the fact that her reference on taking up the post had said that she might not cope in a highly stressful environment. In 1996 she was reduced to a public display of tears when it looked as if the unreasonable demands by her supervisor were likely to lead to her having to cancel a holiday. Eventually in 1997 she suffered a stress-related psychiatric illness and was forced to give up work. The trial judge held that, while in 1997 when the illness became obvious it was too late at that time for the employer to take steps to help the claimant, steps could have been taken after the crying episode in the previous year. They had not been and the employer was therefore liable. The Court of Appeal applied the *Hatton* criteria and held that there was insufficient in either the reference or the tears of 1996 to put the employer on notice of the foreseeability of a psychiatric illness resulting and found that the employer could not be liable in the circumstances.

The law has not only developed in this relatively narrow field. One area where employees may feel vulnerable is when they require references from employers in seeking new employment. Traditionally where an employee suffered from a poor and inaccurately written reference there was little chance of a remedy. The only action available was in defamation and the defence of qualified privilege might prevent the employee from seeing the reference unless he could show malice on the part of the employer (see section 14.4.5). However, there has now also been developed a duty not to negligently prepare references for an employee. This removes many of the obstacles that an employee would have formerly faced.

CASE EXAMPLE

Spring v Guardian Assurance plc [1995] 3 WLR 354

Here the employee was dismissed and prevented from gaining a position with another company because of a negligently prepared reference provided by his employer. The House of Lords held that an employer has a duty when preparing a reference not to act negligently. The employer was held liable in the case. One other consideration was whether liability should be under *Hedley Byrne* or traditional negligence principles. The House was split on this point.

The rule on negligently prepared references has subsequently been developed in *Bartholomew v London Borough of Hackney* [1999] IRLR 246. The Court of Appeal identified that the duty was to ensure that only accurate information is provided and the impression created is not unfair. Even more recently in *Cox v Sun Alliance Life Ltd* [2001] IRLR 448 Lord Justice Mummery identified other key ingredients of the duty. The employer must believe in the truth of any information that he divulges and must also have reasonable grounds for that belief and make a reasonably thorough investigation of the facts before providing the reference (see also section 6.3.3).

17.4 Defences

There are a number of defences that can apply from the general defences. However, there are two defences that are obviously very appropriate in the case of employer's liability.

17.4.1 *Volenti non fit injuria* (voluntary assumption of a risk)

Many if not most fields of work carry with them their own specific risks and dangers. Inevitably it is possible for the employer to argue that in accepting work the worker has accepted the risks that go with the work. However, the defence may be of more limited use since *Smith v Baker*.

However, the defence can still be claimed where the employee fully understands the risks involved and the agreement is free from pressure. There is contrasting case law to illustrate this.

CASE EXAMPLE

ICI Ltd v Shatwell [1965] AC 656

The claimant and his brother worked in the defendants' quarry. They ignored the defendants' orders and also statutory regulations by testing detonators without taking appropriate precautions. The claimant was then injured in an explosion and claimed that the defendants were vicariously liable on the basis of the claimant's brother, who instructed him not to follow the instructions, having been negligent and in breach of statutory duty. The court rejected his claim. By ignoring his employers and listening to his brother's unauthorised comments he had assumed the risk of injury by exercising his own free choice and the defence of *volenti* could apply.

Similarly, where the employer by his negligence creates emergencies it is not then appropriate to try to apply the principles of *volenti* to the actions of those people responding to the emergency.

CASE EXAMPLE

Baker v T E Hopkins [1959] 3 All ER 225

An employer's workmen were subjected to danger by being exposed to petrol fumes in a confined space when the fumes overcame the men. A doctor attempting to rescue the men died as a result of his own exposure to the fumes. The employer tried to claim *volenti* on the part of the doctor. The court would not accept the application of the defence to the case. The doctor had not agreed to the specific risks involved. He was merely trying to do his best for the unconscious men. He had not consented to the risk of death.

The Court of Appeal explained the principle by referring to part of the judgment of Cardozo J in the American case *Wagner v International Railway Co* 332 NY 176 [1921] where he said:

JUDGMENT

'Danger invites rescue. The law does not ignore these reactions . . . in tracing conduct to its consequences. It recognises them as normal. It places their effects within the range of the natural and the probable. The wrong that imperils life . . . is a wrong also to the rescuer.'

As a matter of policy the defence is generally unavailable for breach of a statutory duty. However, it may still be available where the claimant can be said to be the sole cause of his own misfortune.

CASE EXAMPLE

Ginty v Belmont Building Supplies Ltd [1959] 1 All ER 414

Here the appropriate safety equipment, duckboards, had been provided. It was the complete failure by the claimant to use safety equipment that actually led to injury.

17.4.2 Contributory negligence

As a partial defence only the defence may be available in the case of any of the duties where the claimant is partly responsible for his injury.

However, employees are generally treated more leniently by the courts (see *Caswell v Powell Duffryn Collieries* [1940] AC 152). This is because it is accepted that the pressures of work mean that workers may take less than full care of themselves and should be protected from their own carelessness.

Even where the employee is careless in helping to create his own injury the employer may still be in breach of the duty to protect the employee from such carelessness (see *General Cleaning Contractors v Christmas* [1953] AC 180).

Nevertheless, where it is accepted that the employee has contributed to his own harm and that contributory negligence should apply then damages will be reduced according to the extent to which the employee did contribute to his own injury.

CASE EXAMPLE

Jones v Livox Quarries Ltd [1952] 2 QB 608

Here where the employee was injured in a collision caused by the defendant's negligence damages were reduced by 5 per cent. This was because the employee had contributed to his own injury by riding on the tow bar of a traxcavator despite the express prohibition of his employer.

Lord Denning identified the principles of the defence in the case at 615:

JUDGMENT

'Although contributory negligence does not depend on a duty of care it does depend on foreseeability. Just as actionable negligence requires the foreseeability of harm to others, so contributory negligence requires the foreseeability of harm to oneself.'

The defence can be used even in situations where death has resulted from the negligent event but the employee also contributed to his own harm.

CASE EXAMPLE

Davies v Swan Motor (Swansea) Co Ltd [1949] 2 KB 291

Here a dustman was killed in a collision caused by the defendant's negligence. Damages were reduced because he had contributed to his injuries by riding on the step of the dustcart.

It is also possible for there to be liability on the defendant but 100 per cent contributory negligence awarded and consequent reduction in damages.

CASE EXAMPLE

Jayes v IMI (Kynoch) Ltd [1985] ICR 155

Here the employer was liable because a statutory duty in respect of guarding machinery was strict in terms of liability for ensuring that guards were maintained at all times when machines were working. A 100 per cent contributory negligence was awarded when the employee lost fingers because the employee himself had taken the guard off the machine in order to clear a blockage while the machine was still running.

ACTIVITY

Self-assessment questions

1. Why did employers' liability develop so long after it was needed?
2. What were the major defects in the early law?
3. Was the common law always hostile to employees?
4. To what extent is an employer responsible for the actions of practical jokers within the workforce?
5. Which is more important the common law or statute in relation to safe plant and equipment?
6. To what extent can an employer follow an established trade practice which is dangerous?
7. What is the standard of care appropriate to maintaining safe premises?
8. What effect does causation have on the duty of an employer?
9. How easy is it for an employer to defend a case of breach of a common law duty?
10. How has the scope of an employer's duty of care expanded recently?
11. What difficulties confront an employee who is trying to bring a claim for a stress-related injury?

ACTIVITY

Applying the law

Using the guide to answering problem questions in Appendix 2 try the following problems.

1 Bodgit & Fastfit Co. is a light engineering firm. Some of its work involves cutting sheet metal on power guillotines. One day Stanley cuts a panel incorrectly, and, since the job is urgent, he agrees with his foreman, Oliver, to re-cut it without the safety guard in place. Because of the shape of the panel it slips and Stanley loses his hand as a result. Stanley had already lost his other hand when a fellow employee, Buster, a known practical joker, let off a banger behind Stanley. The shock caused Stanley to lurch forward and catch his hand in an unguarded press.

Advise Stanley of any possible course of action.

2 Spinnet & Weavit Co. is a textile manufacturer, that has recently installed central heating in its mill after complaints about the cold from its employees. In the weaving machine room, which is always warm, Fred becomes too warm, falls asleep and injures his hand in the loom. The hot pipes cause some floorboards to warp. Jack, who is wheeling a trolley of hot dye, is badly burnt when a wheel catches an uneven board and the dye spills over his legs. This spillage also creates dangerous chemical fumes when the dye mixes with varnish on the floor. Tom, another worker, feels nauseous from the fumes and tries to open a window. This is impossible since the windows have been sealed following the complaints about the cold. Tom is overcome by the fumes and hits his head very badly when he passes out.

Advise Spinnet & Weavit Co. of any liability it may have to Fred, Jack and Tom.

KEY FACTS

The scope of the duty	Case
The employer owes a non-delegable duty for the health and safety of the employee, so:	*Wilsons & Clyde Coal Co v English* [1938]
• must provide competent staff for duties undertaken • must provide safe working colleagues • must provide safe plant and equipment and properly maintain it (but now Employers' Liability (Defective Equipment) Act 1969 applies) • must take reasonable steps to provide safe premises (which may extend to other premises) • must provide a safe system of work: • must create and implement safe system • and ensure system is carried out • and system must meet dangers.	*General Cleaning Contractors v Christmas* [1953] *Hudson v Ridge Manufacturing* [1957] *Smith v Baker* [1891] *Latimer v AEC* [1953] *Wilson v Tyneside Cleaning Co* [1958] *Bux v Slough Metals* [1974] *General Cleaning Contractors v Christmas* [1953]

(Continued)

(Continued)

Cannot rely on unsafe system just because it is common practice.	*Re Herald of Free Enterprise* [1987]
Developments in the duty	**Case**
The duty now applies also to psychiatric health and well-being.	*Walker v Northumberland CC* [1995] *Sutherland v Hatton* [2002]
The Court of Appeal has issued guidelines – must know of existing vulnerability, it must be foreseeable that the employment practices will lead to a stress-related psychiatric injury and the employment practices must actually cause or worsen the psychiatric illness.	
There is also now a duty to provide references that are not negligently prepared.	*Spring v Guardian Assurance Co* [1995]
The character of the duty	**Case**
The duty is non-delegable.	*Wilsons & Clyde Coal Co v English* [1938]
The employer only need take reasonable precautions.	*Latimer v AEC* [1953]
The duty extends to reasonable and incidental activities.	*Davidson v Handley Page Ltd* [1945]
Duty does not extend to employees properly.	*Deyong v Shenburn* [1946]
Trade practices can only be relied upon if reasonable.	*Cavanagh v Ulster Weaving Co* [1960]
The employer should consider the possible extent of injury.	*Paris v Stepney BC* [1951]
And may consider practicality of any precautions.	*Charlton v Forrest Printing Ink Co* [1978]
And must prevent only reasonably foreseeable accidents.	*Doughty v Turner Manufacturing* [1964]
Defences	**Case**
Volenti (consent) – has limited use – the employee must fully appreciate and consent to the actual risk.	*Smith v Baker* [1891]
This is possible if the agreement is free from pressure	*ICI v Shatwell* [1965]
and where the claimant is the sole cause of injury but it is not available for breach of a statutory duty.	*Ginty v Belmont Building Supplies Ltd* [1959]
Contributory negligence – this is a possible defence to any duty.	
It is covered by the provisions of the Law Reform (Contributory Negligence) Act 1945.	
Damages may be reduced when the worker contributed to own injury	*Jones v Livox Quarries Ltd* [1952]
and even 100 per cent reduction is possible.	*Jayes v IMI (Kynoch) Ltd* [1985]

SUMMARY

- There is a non-delegable common law duty to provide competent fellow employees, safe plant and equipment, safe premises, a safe system of work, and more recently to prevent psychiatric harm.
- The duty cannot be delegated, and is to do what is reasonable, even extending to ancillary activities, but not to property, only reasonable trade practices are accepted, and the employer must consider the possible extent of injury to an employee, and can take into account the practicality of any precautions since the duty is only to prevent foreseeable accidents.
- *Volenti non fit injuria* and contributory negligence are possible defences.
- The common law has also been supplemented with many statutory provisions regulating the workplace and some of these have originated in EU law.

Further reading

Collier, A, 'Stress in the workplace' (2002) *153 NLJ* 248.

Elvin, J, 'Can an employer be under a duty to dismiss an employee for his own good in order to protect his health?' (2003) *62 Cambridge Law Journal* 20.

Elvin, J, 'How should the law respond to stress-related claims?' (2010) *21 King's Law Journal* 41.

'Stress at work' IDS Brief 655, February 2000.

Zindani, J, 'Back to the future from the court of appeal' (2000) *150 NLJ* 1100.

18

Vicarious liability

AIMS AND OBJECTIVES

After reading this chapter you should be able to:

- Explain the purposes and justifications for imposing vicarious liability
- Critically analyse and apply the relevant tests for establishing employment status and distinguish between an employee and an independent contractor
- Identify the circumstances in which an employer will be liable for the acts and omissions of an employee
- Evaluate the law in this area and consider whether it should be reformed

18.1 Origins, purposes and criticisms

Vicarious liability is not an individual tort in the way that we have looked at other torts such as negligence or nuisance. It is a means of imposing liability for a tort on to a party other than the party causing the tortfeasor.

It was in fact originally based on the 'fiction' that an employer has control over his employees and therefore should be liable for torts committed by the employee. This was possibly less of a fiction in the nineteenth century when the 'master and servant' laws still accurately reflected the true imbalance in the employment relationship.

In a less sophisticated society with less diverse types of work control was indeed possible. In domestic service for instance the master could dictate exactly the method of the work done by the servant. This was in fact dramatically demonstrated by case law of the time.

DOI: 10.4324/9781003202417-18

CASE EXAMPLE

Latter v Braddell [1881] 50 LJQB 448

A young female domestic servant was asked to submit herself to an internal examination when her mistress suspected that the girl was pregnant. The girl very reluctantly and in great distress complied with the order as in the employment circumstances of the time she would have little chance to refuse. In her later action for assault her claim failed. She was held to have consented to the examination.

Modern forms of employment make control less evident. For instance the actual work done by a surgeon can hardly be said to be under the control of a hospital administrator with no medical expertise.

Nevertheless, the origins of the liability are important because it is rare that vicarious liability will exist outside the employment relationship.

The rule has been criticised for being harsh and 'rough justice' since an apparently innocent party is being fixed with liability for something which he has not done. On this level imposing liability by this method is a direct contradiction of the principle requiring fault to be proved to establish liability.

There are a number of justifications for the practice, many of which have to do with ensuring that the victim of a wrong has the means of gaining compensation for the damage or injury suffered.

- Traditionally, as we have seen, an employer may have had a greater degree of control over the activities of employees. Indeed it may well be that an employee has carried out the tort on the employer's behalf, so it is only fair that the employer should bear the cost.
- The employer, in any case, is responsible for hiring and firing and disciplining staff. The employer may have been careless in selecting staff, and, if employees are either careless or prone to causing harm and the employer is aware of this, then he has the means of doing something about it. The internal disciplinary systems allow the employer to ensure that lapses are not repeated, ultimately to the extent of dismissing staff. The employer is also responsible for ensuring that all employees are effectively trained so that work is done safely.
- The major concern of an injured party is where compensation is likely to come from. In this respect the employer will usually be better able to stand the loss than the employee will. In any case the employer is obliged to take out public liability insurance and can also pass on loss in prices.
- This is itself a justification for vicarious liability since it is also a means of deterring tortious activities.
- In certain instances imposing vicarious liability makes the conduct of the case easier for the injured party in terms of identifying specific negligence. This is particularly so in the case of medical negligence.

Proving vicarious liability first depends on satisfying a number of other basic tests:

- Was the person alleged to have committed the tort an employee? There is only very limited liability for the torts of independent contractors.

- Did that party commit the alleged tort 'during the course of his employment'? An employer is generally not liable for torts that occur away from work or while the employee is 'on a frolic on his own'.
- Was the act or omission complained of a tort? Again an employer will not generally incur liability for other wrongs such as crimes carried out by the employee.

18.2 Framework for analysis of vicarious liability

The law on vicarious liability has been developing significantly over the past 25 years in part because of the changing landscape of working relationships and partly because of the nature of the type of claims being brought most notably, sexual abuse claims. For a defendant to be held vicariously liable for the tortious acts of one of its employees, there are two stages that must be overcome:

Stage 1: the *relationship* between defendant and tortfeasor needs to be determined

Stage 2: the *connection* between the commission of the tort and the relationship needs to be determined

So for a claim in vicarious liability to be made out, the following elements must be established and it is under this framework that the rest of the chapter shall proceed:

i The employee committed a tort;

ii Stage 1: A relationship of, or akin to, employment;

iii Stage 2: A close connection between the employer and the employee and the employee's tort.

18.3 The employee committed a tort

An employee must have committed a tort. This may take the form of a negligent act but it may take the form of intentional torts such as assault or battery. All of the elements of the relevant tort need to be made out. This area has in recent times, been fraught with cases involving sexual assault which fall to be considered.

18.4 Stage 1 relationship: tests of employment status

18.4.1 Introduction

It is not always possible to determine at first sight whether in fact a person is employed under a contract of service or not. It will often be in the interest of an 'employer' to deny that the relationship is one of employment. Definitions such as that contained in the Employment Rights Act 1996 that the employer is a person employed under a contract of employment are no real help in determining a person's employment status. It has been suggested in *WHPT Housing Association Ltd v Secretary of State for Social Services* [1981] ICR 737 that the distinction lies in the fact that the employee provides himself to serve while the self-employed person only offers his services. This is no great help in determining whether or not a person is employed.

There is in any case inconsistency in the methods of testing employee status according to who it is that is doing the testing. For instance, the only concern of the tax authorities in testing employee status is in determining a liability for payment of tax, not for any other purpose. So the fact that a person is paying tax is not necessarily definitive of their status as self-employed. Again industrial safety inspectors may have less concern with the status of an injured party and more with the regulations that have been breached.

Besides this a number of different types of working relationship are not so easy to define. In recent times we have seen the rapid growth of the so-called gig economy which relies on the premise that those who work for businesses are not classified as employees but rather as either independent contractors or workers who are afforded less rights than employees.

Over the years the courts have devised a number of methods of testing employee status. Some are less useful in a modern society than others but all contribute in the determination of an employee's status. They all have shortcomings and remain relevant to informing the current test for exploring the relationship between the tortfeasor and the employer.

18.4.2 The control test

The oldest of these is the 'control test'. This test derived from the days of the 'master and servant' laws as we have already seen. In *Yewens v Noakes* [1880] 6 QBD 530 the test was whether the master had the right to control what was done and the way in which it was done. According to McArdie J in *Performing Right Society v Mitchell and Booker* [1924] 1 KB 762 the test concerns 'the nature and degree of detailed control'.

Lord Thankerton in *Short v J W Henderson Ltd* [1946] 62 TLR 427 identified many key features that would show that the master had control over the servant. These included the power to select the servant, the right to control the method of working, the right to suspend and dismiss, and the payment of wages.

Such a test is virtually impossible to apply accurately in modern circumstances. Nevertheless, there are circumstances in which a test of control is still useful, in the case of borrowed workers.

CASE EXAMPLE

Mersey Docks & Harbour Board v Coggins and Griffiths (Liverpool) Ltd [1947] AC 1

Here the test was applied when a crane driver negligently damaged goods in the course of his work. In this case the Harbour Board hired a crane and the crane driver out to stevedores to act as their servant. Under the contract between the Board and the stevedores the crane driver was still to be paid by the Board and only they had the right to dismiss him, but for the duration of the contract he was to be regarded as the employee of the stevedores. The Harbour Board was still held to be liable for his negligence, however, since he would not accept control from the stevedores.

In the case above Lord Porter (at 17) gave a very clear explanation of the control test:

JUDGMENT

'the most satisfactory [test] by which to ascertain who is the employer at any particular time, is to ask who is entitled to tell the employee the way in which he is to do the work upon which he is engaged . . . it is not enough that the task to be performed should be under his control, he must control the method of performing it.'

This can be seen in *Hawley v Luminar Leisure plc* [2005] EWHC 5 (QB) where a nightclub owner was held to be in control of and therefore vicariously liable for bouncers actually employed by a security firm. This was because the owner gave the men detailed instructions on how to do the job.

18.4.3 The integration or organisation test

Lord Denning in *Stevenson Jordan and Harrison Ltd v McDonald and Evans* [1969] 1 TLR 101 established this test. The basis of the test is that someone will be an employee whose work is fully integrated into the business, whereas if a person's work is only accessory to the business then that person is not an employee. The question here is whether the core business can operate without the contributions of the employee.

According to this test the master of a ship, a chauffeur and a reporter on the staff of a newspaper are all employees, whereas the pilot bringing a ship into port, a taxi driver and a freelance writer are not. For instance the freelance writer will send in contributions every now and then and the business is not reliant on their contribution to operate whereas it is reliant on the news reporter to operate its core business.

The test can work well in some circumstances but there are still defects. Part-time examiners may be classed as employed for the purposes of deducting tax, but it is unlikely that the exam board would be happy to pay redundancy when their services were no longer needed.

18.4.4 The economic reality or multiple test

The courts in recent times have at last recognised that a single test of employment is not satisfactory and may produce confusing results. The answer under this test is to consider whatever factors may be indicative of employment or self-employment. In particular, three conditions should be met before an employment relationship is identified:

- The employee agrees to provide work or skill in return for a wage.
- The employee expressly or impliedly accepts that the work will be subject to the control of the employer.
- All other considerations in the contract are consistent with there being a contract of employment rather than any other relationship between the parties.

CASE EXAMPLE

***Ready Mixed Concrete (South East) Ltd v Minister of Pensions and National Insurance* [1968] 2 QB 497**

The case involved who was liable for National Insurance contributions, the company or one of its drivers. Drivers were used under a new contract under which they drove vehicles in the company colours and logo that they bought on hire purchase agreements from the company. Under the contract they were also obliged to maintain the vehicles according to set standards in the contract. They were only allowed to use the lorries on company business. Their contracted hours, however, were flexible and their pay was subject to an annual minimum rate according to the concrete hauled. They were also allowed to hire drivers in their place. Although it might be seen to have operated unfairly on the claimant the drivers were held to be independent. The case is important because McKenna J developed the above test in determining their lack of employment status.

The test has subsequently been modified so that all factors in the relationship should be considered and weighed according to their significance. Such factors might include:

- The ownership of tools, plant or equipment – clearly an employee is less likely to own the plant and equipment with which he works.
- The method of payment – again a self-employed person is likely to take a price for a whole job where an employee will usually receive regular payments for a defined pay period.
- Tax and National Insurance contributions – an employee usually has tax deducted out of wages under the PAYE scheme under Schedule E and Class 1 National Insurance contributions also deducted by the employer. A self-employed person will usually pay tax annually under Schedule D and will make National Insurance contributions by buying Class 2 stamps.
- Self-description – a person may describe himself as one or the other and this will usually, but not always, be an accurate description.
- Level of independence – probably one of the acid tests of status as self-employed is the extra degree of independence in being able to take work from whatever source and turn work down.
- Determine who has the benefit of any insurance cover that might be available (see *British Telecommunications plc v James Thompson & Sons (Engineers) Ltd* [1999] 1 WLR 9).

All of these are useful in identifying the status of the worker but none of them is an absolute test or is definitive on its own.

18.4.5 Akin to employment

Certain working relationships do not appear to have an obvious employment relationship but when given detailed consideration, appear to be closer to an employment relationship rather than anything else. Where this is the case, the relationship is referred to as being 'akin to employment'. This is an area in which there has been significant judicial developments where the judiciary has been minded to achieve justice through a flexible approach rather than have its hands tied by taking a mechanical view of this area.

In the following case, it was argued that a church cannot be held vicariously liable for its priests because they do not count as employees; this was firmly rejected by the Court of Appeal.

CASE EXAMPLE

JGE v The Trustees of the Portsmouth Roman Catholic Diocesan Trust [2013] QB 722

The claimant who as a child had lived in a children's home run by nuns claimed to have been sexually abused by the priest. The court found that the bishop was vicariously liable and the church appealed this on the basis that there was no formal contract, no wages paid by the bishop and very little in the way of control so that the tests for employment status (see section 18.2 above) would fail. The Court of Appeal dismissed the appeal on the reasoning that the relationship was sufficiently close to employment and the abuse was possible because of his role. Justice Macduff noted at paragraphs 31 and 80–81:

JUDGMENT

'Because there is no relationship of employer/employee between them, then, if one is judging the question on conventional lines, the bishop is not vicariously liable for the tortious acts of the priest. But now we get to the nub of this appeal. Can the bishop be vicariously liable if the relationship is akin to employment? Can the law be extended that far? . . . I distilled the essence of being an employee to be that he is paid a wage or salary to work under some, even if only slight, control of his employer in his employer's business for that business. Father Baldwin may not quite match every facet of being an employee but in my judgment he is very close to it indeed. The result of each of the tests leads me to the conclusion that Father Baldwin is more like an employee than an independent contractor. He is in a relationship with his bishop which is close enough and so akin to employer/ employee as to make it just and fair to impose vicarious liability. Justice and fairness is used here as a salutary check on the conclusion. It is not a stand-alone test for a conclusion. It is just because it strikes a proper balance between the unfairness to the employer of imposing strict liability and the unfairness to the victim of leaving her without a full remedy for the harm caused by the employer's managing his business in a way which gave rise to that harm even when the risk of harm is not reasonably foreseeable.'

This particular method of identifying an employment relationship was considered again by the Supreme Court shortly after the Court of Appeal's decision in *JGE*.

CASE EXAMPLE

***The Catholic Child Welfare Society and others v Various Claimants (FC) and The Institute of the Brothers of the Christian Schools and others* [2012] UKSC 56**

The Catholic Child Welfare Society ran a school until 1994 when it was closed down which had formerly been run by other Catholic bodies. The institute was founded in 1680 with a mission of providing education for Catholics and provided teachers for schools such as the one in question and it also supplied the school with a headmaster. The school was not only staffed by brothers of the institute but by other lay teachers. For a number of years the school was run as a reform school for boys who were criminal offenders and later it became a home for children in care. In 1993 and again in 2004 the headmaster was convicted of a series of sexual abuse against the boys in his care over a period of 20 years. A total of 170 claims were brought by men who attended the school as boys who claimed that they had been abused by brothers. They claimed both against the managers of the school who were therefore employees and against the institute which provided the brothers. Both the High Court and the Court of Appeal held that the institute was not vicariously liable for the activities of the brothers and the Catholic Child Welfare Society appealed again to the Supreme Court. The court allowed the appeals. It held that because of the way it conducted its affairs it was not important that it was more like an unincorporated association; that it did not matter that it was not an employer if the relationship was sufficiently similar to an employment relationship; that there was nothing to prevent both parties being vicariously liable; that the abuse could be said to be sufficiently closely connected to the 'employer's' business if in the circumstances it increased the risk that the victim would suffer the abuse.

Lord Phillips explained at 21:

JUDGMENT

'. . . the test [to establish vicarious liability] requires a synthesis of two stages:

i The first stage is to consider the relationship of D1 and D2 to see whether it is one that is capable of giving rise to vicarious liability.

ii Hughes LJ identified the second stage as requiring examination of the connection between D2 and the act or omission of D1. . . . What is critical at the second stage is the connection that links the relationship between D1 and D2 and the act or omission of D1, hence the synthesis of the two stages. . . .

The brother teachers were placed in the school to care for the educational and religious needs of these pupils. Abusing the boys in their care was diametrically opposed to those objectives but, paradoxically, that very fact was one of the factors that provided the necessary close connection between the abuse and the relationship between the brothers and the Institute that gives rise to vicarious liability on the part of the latter.'

This is to say, that this particular criterion of employment relationship can be established by looking at whether the relationship has certain characteristics similar to those found in employment, subject to there being a sufficient connection between that relationship and the commission of the tort in question.

Looking at some different contexts it is telling of how the courts will approach the requirement of establishing an employment relationship.

CASE EXAMPLE

Cox v Ministry of Justice [2014] EWCA Civ 132

This case centred around the relationship between the defendant and the tortfeasor. The claimant worked as the catering manager at HM Prison Swansea. There were about 20 prisoners who worked in the kitchen and came under her supervision. One day the claimant was working in the kitchen and instructed four prisoners to take some supplies upstairs to the kitchen stores. One of the prisoners, Mr Inder, negligently dropped a sack of rice onto her back causing her injury. The claimant brought an action against the Ministry of Justice as the *de facto* employer of the prisoner. The MoJ argued that there was no contractual relationship between the prisoner and the prison. The Court of Appeal, however, made clear that the prison service took the benefit of this work, and there was no reason why it should not take its burdens.

The employment relationship has been applied in another context where there is no obvious formal employment relationship but the situation is such that it is closer to an employee and employer relationship than that of an independent contractor. The Supreme Court set out some helpful guidelines as well in this area in the following decision.

CASE EXAMPLE

Armes v Nottinghamshire CC [2017] UKSC 60

In this case the claimant was in the care of the defendant local authority who placed her into foster care at the age of seven. Whilst in foster care, the claimant was both emotionally and sexually abused by those who supposedly cared for her. The claimant brought an action against the defendant local authority arguing *inter alia*, that the authority was vicariously liable for the actions of the foster parents. The key question in this case became whether the relationship between the local authority and the foster parents was akin to that between an employer and an employee. The Supreme Court relied on its decision in *The Catholic Child Welfare Society and others* and employed Lord Phillips' five-stage test to examining whether the relationship between the foster carers and the defendant had the incidents of an employment relationship:

i the employer is more likely to have the means to compensate the victim than the employee and can be expected to have insured against that liability;

ii the tort will have been committed as a result of activity being taken by the employee on behalf of the employer;

iii the employee's activity is likely to be part of the business activity of the employer;

iv the employer, by employing the employee to carry on the activity will have created the risk of the tort committed by the employee;

v the employee will, to a greater or lesser degree, have been under the control of the employer.

It was held by the Supreme Court that the abuse committed by the foster parents was committed in course of an activity carried on for the benefit of the local authority; the placement created a risk of abuse; the local authority exercised a significant degree of control over the foster parents such as powers of approval, inspection, supervision and removal; and the local authority had the means to pay damages. Therefore, the defendants were liable.

CASE EXAMPLE

Various Claimants v Barclays Bank plc ("Barclays Bank") [2020] UKSC 13

Barclays Bank engaged the services of medical practitioner, Dr Bates (now deceased), to conduct medical exams of prospective Barclays employees as part of their pre-employment process. Barclays arranged the appointments and provided the documents that needed to be completed. Dr Bates was paid by Barclays per assessment which he conducted at his practice in his house. It was alleged that Dr Bates sexually assaulted the claimants during these examinations. The claimants brought a claim against Barclays Bank for being vicariously liable for the sexual assaults allegedly committed by Dr Bates. As is well established, the employer of an independent contractor cannot be held liable for the negligence or torts committed by such a contractor in the course of the execution of the work. The claimants argued that Dr Bates was in a relationship akin to employment with Barclays Bank and therefore vicariously liable for his actions as per the decisions in *Catholic Child Welfare Society, Cox and Armes*. Lady Hale highlighted that in this case, it is not necessary to apply the five-stage test set out by Lord Phillips in *The Catholic Child Welfare Society* as this was not an ambiguous case in which it had to be determined whether it would be fair, just and reasonable to impose vicarious liability.

The appeal was allowed and vicarious liability could not be established as explained by Lady Hale at paragraph 28:

JUDGMENT

'Clearly, although Dr Bates was a part-time employee of the health service, he was not at any time an employee of the Bank. Nor, viewed objectively, was he anything close to an employee. He did, of course, do work for the Bank. The Bank made the arrangements for the examinations and sent him the forms to fill in. It therefore chose the questions to which it wanted answers. But the same would be true of many other people who did work for the Bank but were clearly independent contractors, ranging from the company hired to clean its windows to the auditors hired to audit its books. Dr Bates was not paid a retainer which might have obliged him to accept a certain number of referrals from the Bank. He was paid a fee for each report. He was free to refuse an offered examination should he wish to do so. He no doubt carried his own medical liability insurance, although this may not have covered him from liability for deliberate wrongdoing. He was in business on his own account as a medical practitioner with a portfolio of patients and clients. One of those clients was the Bank.'

The following case reminds us that we must rush to use the test for akin to employment where there are other factors indicating that the employee is in fact an independent contractor. The factors of control, how integral the work is payment and uniform still remain relevant.

CASE EXAMPLE

J D Wetherspoon Plc v Stephenus Bernadus Burger, Risk Solutions Bg Ltd. [2025] EWHC 1259 (KB)

The claimant had been at one of the defendant's pubs. He was restrained by two door supervisors with such force that he suffered a dislocated hip, requiring emergency surgery and a hospital stay. The door staff were employees of another company (Risk Solutions) contracted by the defendant to provide door security at the pub on certain nights, pursuant to a security services agreement. The defendant was held vicariously liable for the actions of the door staff. The court considered whether the door staff were effectively so integrated into the work of the pub that they were akin to being employed. Following the decision in *Barclays Bank*, it must be considered whether the relationship is genuinely one with an independent contractor carrying on their own business. If it is, there does not need to be any consideration of the five factors to determine whether this a relationship that is akin to employment. It was concluded that the nature of the contractual relationship should not be overlooked. This case did not necessarily warrant consideration of whether there was a relationship akin to employment since that question could be determined by considering which party exercised control over the staff.

The fact that security is integral to the operation of a pub or that the security staff have to co-operate with other staff does not transform the relationship with an external security provider into one akin to employment; it simply explains why the service is required and how is it necessarily to be provided. The agreement specified that Risk Solutions retained control over its employees, and there was no evidence that Wetherspoons had direct control over their actions. The control that was identified consisted in setting standards for the service which was to be supplied.

Gig economy workers

An increasingly popular mode of work can be found in the 'gig economy'. Work here is undertaken on the basis of short temporary engagements whereby the worker can determine the amount of work they would like to undertake. This model is largely dependent on the use of an app. This is also seen as a mode of work to supplement income dependent on the worker's availability. Modern-day examples include working as an Uber driver or as a delivery person for Deliveroo. The trouble with this model of work is that the status of the worker is not immediately clear. The relationship between the worker and employer is less formal than that of an employee and employer relationship and appears to be something more than that of an independent contractor. The government has commissioned report on this and the gig economy more generally which has considered the status of such workers. The report, 'Good work: the Taylor review of modern working practices', specifically considers the relationship between employers and those who work in the gig economy.

The report reminds us that under the present law there are three categories in which you can find yourself:

i employee; or

ii independent contractor i.e. self-employed; or

iii worker.

SECTION

Section 230 of the Employment Act 1996 states that:

'Employees, workers etc.

1 In this Act "employee" means an individual who has entered into or works under (or, where the employment has ceased, worked under) a contract of employment.
2 In this Act "contract of employment" means a contract of service or apprenticeship, whether express or implied, and (if it is express) whether oral or in writing.
3 In this Act "worker" (except in the phrases "shop worker" and "betting worker") means an individual who has entered into or works under (or, where the employment has ceased, worked under) –
   a a contract of employment, or
   b any other contract, whether express or implied and (if it is express) whether oral or in writing, whereby the individual undertakes to do or perform personally any work or services for another party to the contract whose status is not by virtue of the contract that of a client or customer of any profession or business undertaking carried on by the individual;

and any reference to a worker's contract shall be construed accordingly.'

The report recommends the following:

Government should retain the current three-tier approach to employment status as it remains relevant in the modern labour market, but rename as 'dependent contractors' the category of people who are eligible for worker rights but who are not employees.

It further recommends that 'control' and 'status' should be significant factors in determining who a 'dependent contractor' is.

CASE EXAMPLE

Uber BV (UBV) & Ors v Aslam & Ors [2021] UKSC 5

The claim in this case was brought by Uber drivers against Uber for failure to provide basic protections guaranteed under the Employment Rights Act 1996. Uber argued that in order to rely on the Act, the drivers first had to fall under the definition of employee or worker, and since the drivers were self-employed, they could not be considered as such and therefore could not benefit from the Act. The Employment Appeals Tribunal however agreed with the drivers that they held 'worker' status, Uber appealed to the Court of Appeal and to the Supreme Court. The Court of Appeal however agreed with the Uber drivers in that they were to be considered workers not least because of the level of control that Uber exerts over its drivers, the setting of fares and the operation of the app itself. Uber appealed to the Supreme court arguing that the drivers work for themselves as independent contractors. The Supreme Court explained that when considering such a claim, it is important not to interpret the terms of the contract as the starting point not least because the written documentation may not reflect the reality of the relationship and therefore the reality of the situation should be the focus. It is unlikely that the Uber drivers had even read the terms of the contracts that were drafted and presented to them by Uber, let alone fully understood their legal significance.

The Supreme Court emphasised five aspects which indicated that the drivers were working for Uber:

- i Uber sets the fare for the ride which cannot be changed by the driver so Uber dictates how much the drivers are paid.
- ii Drivers have to agree to the terms set by Uber without any negotiation.
- iii Once a driver is logged into the Uber app, the driver's choice about whether to accept requests for rides is constrained by Uber as if the driver's acceptance rate falls below a certain amount, they are subject to a penalty.
- iv Uber exercises significant control over the drivers via their rating system. If a driver does not achieve the requisite average rating, warning are issued with a risk of their relationship with Uber being terminated.
- v Uber restricts communications between a passenger and driver to the minimum necessary to perform the trip to prevent drivers from establishing any relationship with a passenger capable of extending beyond an individual ride.

All of these factors demonstrate that the drivers are subordinate and dependent on Uber indicating that the drivers are not just self-employed, and that they are workers.

This case reminds us of the importance of looking beyond the contract and actually looking at the working relationship between the company and its workers. This is also in line with what Lord Nicholls said in *Dubai Aluminium Co Ltd v Salaam* [2003] 2 AC 366 at 23 and 26:

CASE EXAMPLE

'Perhaps the best general answer is that the wrongful conduct must be so closely connected with acts the partner or employee was authorised to do that, for the purpose of the liability of the firm or the employer to third parties, the wrongful conduct *may fairly and properly be regarded* as done by the partner while acting in the ordinary course of the firm's business or the employee's employment.

This lack of precision is inevitable, given the infinite range of circumstances where the issue arises. The crucial feature or features, either producing or negativing vicarious liability, vary widely from one case or type of case to the next. Essentially the court makes an evaluative judgment in each case, having regard to all the circumstances and, importantly, having regard also to the assistance provided by previous court decisions. In this field the latter form of assistance is particularly valuable.'

Lending an employee

Another important development is that dual vicarious liability is now also a possibility.

CASE EXAMPLE

Viasystems (Tyneside) Ltd v Thermal Transfer (Northern) Ltd, S & P Darwell Ltd and CAT Metalwork Services [2005] EWCA Civ 1151

The claimant hired Thermal Transfer to install air conditioning in its factory. Thermal Transfer sub-contracted ducting work to Darwell which in turn hired fitters from CAT on a labour only basis. One of these fitters, through his negligence, caused a flood damaging the claimant's property. Thermal Transfer was liable to the claimant under its contract. The trial judge held that CAT was also liable as the fitter's employer. CAT appealed that Darwell should be considered the fitter's employer in the circumstances and the Court of Appeal agreed and held both liable.

ACTIVITY

Quick quiz

Consider whether the following would be classed as employees using the tests above.

1 Sarah, a machinist, who works from home stitching shirts from pieces of cloth pre-cut and delivered by Tej, who also deducts National Insurance payments from her pay but leaves her to settle her own tax. Tej owns the sewing machine that Sarah uses.
2 Eric, a plasterer, who travels round building sites and works for cash payments. Neither he nor builders that he works for pay tax or NI for him. He uses his own tools.

3 Coco, a circus clown, who also sells tickets before performances and helps to pack up the big top when the circus goes on to the next town. He also drives one of the lorries that transports the circus. The circus owner says that Coco is self-employed.

4 Alistair is a consultant orthopaedic specialist. He is paid a full time salary by an NHS Trust but spends three days per week seeing private patients.

18.5 Stage 2 connection: the test of liability

18.5.1 Connection between the tortfeasor and the employer when the tort is committed

Torts committed in the course of employment

We have already discussed whether it is fair to impose liability on an employer for torts committed by his employee. Since it is a potentially unjust situation, a mechanism is needed to ensure that the employer will only be liable for those torts committed by an employee where is can be demonstrated that there is a connection between the employer and tortfeasor when the tort takes place. In the past, an employer would be vicariously liable for the acts of its employee if it could be demonstrated that the tort was committed while the employee is 'in the course of the employment'. What is and is not in the course of employment has been a question of fact for the court to determine in each case. It is often difficult to see any consistency in the judgments. Judges have inevitably taken policy into account which may explain some of the apparent inconsistency.

It is very hard to find a general test for what is in the course of employment. However, courts have appeared to favour a test suggested by Salmond that the employer will be liable in two instances:

- for a wrongful act that has been authorised by the employer;
- for an act that, while authorised, was carried out in an unauthorised way.

It is the latter of the two has needed to be revised in order to respond to the different type of cases that have emerged in recent years most notably, cases involving intentional torts such as sexual abuse. This second scenario has had to be amended to consider how close the connection is between the tortious act and the actual work of the tortfeasor.

Authorised acts

An employer was said to be liable for acts that they have expressly authorised, and, since an employee is only obliged to obey all reasonable and lawful acts, they could refuse to carry out tortious acts that the employer instructed them to do.

The more difficult aspect of this rule is whether the employer can be said to have authorised a tortious act by implication and should therefore be liable. At least one case has suggested that this is possible.

CASE EXAMPLE

Poland v Parr [1927] 1 KB 236

The employee was a carter. He assaulted a boy in order to stop him from stealing from his employer's wagon. The boy fell under the wagon and was injured as a result. The employer was held to be vicariously liable for the assault since the employee was only protecting the employer's property, which by implication he had authority to do. He was acting reasonably and honestly in protection of the employer's property.

As Lord Atkin explained at 244:

JUDGMENT

'Any servant is, as a general rule, authorised to do acts which are for the protection of his master's property.'

Authorised acts carried out in an unauthorised manner

Most employment involves some form of discretion on the part of the employee. The employer may direct the specific work to be done and even to an extent the method by which it should be carried out. Almost inevitably employees will carry out work making decisions of their own as they go along. In some circumstances they may carry out acts that are completely unauthorised. The significant point to establish that the employer is still liable for their tortious acts is that they are actually still engaged in the work for which they are employed and that the tort arises out of this work. An employer can be liable then for unauthorised acts in a variety of ways.

- Where the employee is still engaged in his own work but does something even though this has been expressly prohibited by the employer.

CASE EXAMPLE

Limpus v London General Omnibus Company [1862] 1 H & C 526

At the time of the case buses were horse drawn. Bus drivers had been specifically instructed not to race because of the dangers to themselves and to the public. When they did and the claimant was injured the employer was held vicariously liable. The drivers were authorised to drive the buses but not in the manner they did.

- Where the employee carries out work that is authorised but is doing the work negligently.

CASE EXAMPLE

Century Insurance Co Ltd v Northern Ireland Transport Board [1942] AC 509

A driver of a petrol tanker was delivering to a petrol station. In lighting a cigarette he carelessly threw down a lighted match causing an explosion. The employer was still held liable since the driver was in the course of employment, and merely doing his work negligently.

- Where the employee gives unauthorised lifts contrary to instructions.

CASE EXAMPLE

Rose v Plenty [1976] 1 WLR 141

Here a milkman continued to use a child helper despite express instructions from the employer not to allow people to ride on the milk floats. When the boy was injured partly through the milkman's negligence his employer was held liable. The milkman was carrying out his work in an unauthorised manner.

Lord Scarman applied the principle to the case at 148:

JUDGMENT

'Why was the plaintiff being carried on the float when the accident occurred? [He] was there because it was necessary that he should be there in order that he could assist, albeit in a way prohibited by the employers, in the job entrusted to the servant by his employers.'

- Where the employee exceeds the proper boundaries of the job.

CASE EXAMPLE

Fennelly v Connex South Eastern Ltd [2001] IRLR 390

A ticket collector got into an argument with a customer whom he believed had not paid the appropriate fare and he then assaulted the customer. The Court of Appeal held that, since the act occurred within the course of employment, the employer was liable for the assault.

- Where the employee applies force in order to achieve the employer's objectives.

CASE EXAMPLE

***Bayley v Manchester, Sheffield and Lincolnshire Railway Co* [1873] LR 8 CP 148**

Part of a porter's work was to ensure that passengers got onto the correct train. Here the porter pulled the claimant from the train in order to do so and the employers were vicariously liable for the assault.

- Where the employee identifies himself as an employee even though the act is not to do with the employment.

CASE EXAMPLE

***Weir v Chief Constable of Merseyside Police* [2003] EWCA Civ 111**

A police officer was helping his girlfriend to move to a flat and he used a police vehicle without permission for the purpose. He then caught a young man interfering with the girlfriend's property which was outside the flat. He assaulted the young man, identifying himself as a police officer at the same time. The court held that in the circumstances the young man was entitled to believe that he was being assaulted by a police officer and the employer was liable.

It is now possible to impose vicarious liability where there is a breach of a statutory duty imposed on the individual employee rather than also on the employer. In this way a successful claim of vicarious liability can be made under s3, Protection from Harassment Act 1997.

CASE EXAMPLE

***Majrowski v Guy's and St Thomas' NHS Trust* [2006] UKHL 34; [2006] All ER (D) 146**

The claimant who was employed by the NHS trust claimed that he had been bullied and harassed by his departmental manager because of his homosexuality. He complained internally and following investigation his complaints were accepted and the Trust accepted that there had indeed been harassment. The claimant brought an action against the Trust under s3, Protection from Harassment Act 1997. At first instance the claim was struck out but the claimant won his appeal in the House of Lords.

The case of *Green v DB Group Services (UK) Ltd* [2006] EWHC 1898 (Ch) (see section 13.6.3) also represents a major development in respect of use of s3.

Torts committed outside the course of employment

An employer will not be liable where an employee's tortious act falls outside the actual scope of employment or where the employee was 'on a frolic on his own' (in other words they were acting on their own account which had nothing to do with the employment). There is a variety of circumstances in which the employer has be found not to be liable.

- Where the employee engages in expressly prohibited acts that have nothing to do with their own work.

CASE EXAMPLE

Beard v London General Omnibus Co [1900] 2 QB 530

Here a bus conductor drove the bus despite express orders to the contrary and injured the claimant. The employers were not vicariously liable. The conductor was not carrying out his own work but doing something outside the scope of his own employment.

- Where the employee is 'on a frolic of his own'. An employer will not be responsible for acts that occur outside the normal working day such as travelling into work. The same will apply where the employee does something outside the scope of the work. An employee who leaves work unofficially and goes off on an unauthorised escapade may be said to be 'on a frolic'.

CASE EXAMPLE

Hilton v Thomas Burton (Rhodes) Ltd [1961] 1 WLR 705

Workmen took an unauthorised break and left their place of work. On returning to work one employee, who was driving the work's van, crashed the van and killed somebody. The employer was held not to be liable since the workmen were 'on a frolic'.

- Activities that are nothing to do with the employer's business.

CASE EXAMPLE

Storey v Ashton [1869] LR 4 QB 476

A delivery driver was persuaded to divert from his journey to pick up coal for another man. Through his negligence the driver then caused an accident. The court would not accept that there could be vicarious liability. The employee was 'on a frolic on his own'.

- Giving unauthorised lifts.

CASE EXAMPLE

Twine v Beans Express [1946] 62 TLR 458

A hitchhiker was injured through the negligence of a driver who had been forbidden to give lifts. The employers were held not to be liable. This contrasts with what appears to be a fairly similar situation in *Rose v Plenty* [1976] 1 WLR 141. The significant difference is that here the employer was gaining no benefit from the prohibited lift.

- Acts that exceed the proper boundaries of the work and cannot be said to form part of the employment.

CASE EXAMPLE

Makanjuola v Metropolitan Police Commissioner, The Times, 8 August 1992

The claimant was persuaded into allowing a police officer to have sex with her in return for not reporting her to immigration authorities. The court accepted that there could be no possible liability on the employer. The actions of the employee were anything but part of his job and the officer was not doing anything that could be described as falling within his work responsibilities.

Some situations still defy easy analysis. As we have seen an employer will generally not be responsible for the employee while the employee is travelling to and from work. In some situations, however, this may not be the case. This for instance might include where the employee works from home and travelling is an essential part of the work.

CASE EXAMPLE

Smith v Stages [1989] 2 WLR 529

The employees in question were laggers and were sent from where they were working in the Midlands to deliver some urgent supplies to a power station in Wales. They were paid wages and also travelling expenses equivalent to rail fare, although there was no stipulation as to how they should travel. They went by car and as a result of one employee's negligent driving they were both seriously injured in a car crash. The employer was held to be liable here because the employees were paid both travelling expenses and travelling time and therefore the journey was accepted by the court as falling within their employment.

Goff LJ of Chieveley identified the operation of the principle at 938:

JUDGMENT

'[this involves] an employee, who has for a short time to work for his employers at a different place of work some distance away from his usual place of work . . . in all the circumstances of the case, S was required by the employers to make this journey . . . and it would be proper to describe him as having been employed to do so.'

ACTIVITY

Applying the law

Consider whether the employer would be liable in the following circumstances.

1 Roger is employed by 'Eazi-build', a DIY warehouse. While driving to work one morning his negligence causes a car crash in which Parminder is injured and her car is damaged beyond repair.

2 Simon is a travelling salesman for 'Eazi-build' who works from home. While driving to his first call he negligently collides with a car driven by Oona, injuring her and damaging her car.

3 Taru is a delivery driver for 'Eazi-build'. One day after completing his last morning delivery instead of returning to work as he should he goes to the Red Lion for a few beers. On driving back to work he negligently runs over a pedestrian, Nellie, killing her.

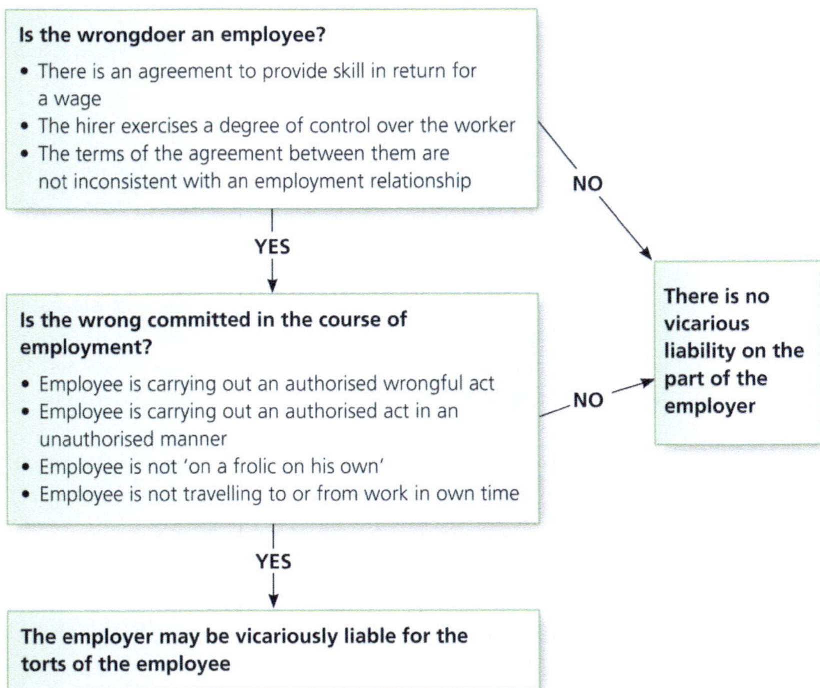

Figure 18.1 The straightforward process of testing vicarious liability.

18.5.2 The close connection test: liability for the intentional torts of an employee

Do the intentional acts of an employee give rise to liability of the employer or do they fall outside the course of employment for being intentional?

CASE EXAMPLE

Warren v Henleys [1948] 2 All ER 935

Here a petrol pump attendant assaulted a customer who he believed was intending not to pay. The court was not prepared to hold that the assault took place in the course of employment. It was not an essential part of his employment that he engaged in criminal activity.

The courts are more prepared to consider that the dishonesty of an employee falls within the course of employment and therefore to impose liability on the employer. This might apply in the case of fraud.

CASE EXAMPLE

Lloyd v Grace Smith & Co [1912] AC 716

The employee was an unsupervised conveyancing clerk. The solicitors who employed him were held liable for the fraud when the clerk fraudulently induced a client to convey her property to him. The court identified that the clerk was engaged in the job that he was hired for and the fraud occurred because he was given insufficient supervision by his employers.

However, the courts will generally not make an employer liable for an employee's fraudulent activities where they occurred partly in and partly outside the course of the employment.

One area that has caused difficulty for the courts in recent years is where public institutions are accused of being responsible for abuses carried out by their employees. The difficulty of identifying abuse as an 'unauthorised mode of carrying out an authorised act' had already led the Court of Appeal to rejecting claims of vicarious liability for sexual abuse.

CASE EXAMPLE

Trotman v North Yorkshire County Council [1999] IRLR 98

Here the claimant was a pupil at a special school. He alleged vicarious liability against the local authority after being sexually abused by his deputy headmaster while on a holiday with the school. The teacher was sharing the boy's bedroom for nocturnal supervision because of the boy's fits. Butler Sloss LJ found it difficult to reconcile the case with either the harassment cases based on an employer's implied duties to the employee, or with the cases based on fraud. The general feeling of the court was that the more extreme the act of the employee, the less likely that the employer would be held vicariously liable for it.

When the House of Lords was presented with a similar case in *Lister v Hesley Hall Ltd* [2001] 2 All ER 769, it developed a test based on inherent risk to cover such situations and enable liability to be imposed more easily. The case overruled the decision in *Trotman*.

CASE EXTRACT

In the case extract below a significant section of the judgment has been reproduced in the left-hand column. Individual points arising from the judgment are briefly explained in the right-hand column. Read the extract including the commentary in the right-hand column and complete the exercise that follows.

Extract adapted from the judgment in *Lister v Hesley Hall Ltd* [2001] 2 All ER 769	
Facts	
Between 1979 and 1982 the appellants were resident at Axeholme House. At that time the appellants were aged between 12 and 15 years. The school and boarding annex were owned and managed by Hesley Hall Ltd as a commercial enterprise. In the main children with emotional and behavioural difficulties were sent to the school by local authorities. Axeholme House is situated about two miles from the school. The warden was responsible for the day to day running of Axeholme House and for maintaining discipline. He lived there with his wife, who was disabled. The employers accept that, unbeknown to them, the warden systematically sexually abused the appellants in Axeholme House. The sexual abuse took the form of mutual masturbation, oral sex and sometimes buggery. The sexual abuse was preceded by 'grooming' . . . to establish control over the appellants. Neither of the appellants made any complaint at the time. In 1982 the warden and his wife left the employ of the respondents. In the early 1990s a police investigation led to criminal charges in the Crown Court. [The warden] was sentenced to seven years' imprisonment for multiple offences involving sexual abuse.	*Facts: two young boys were sexually abused by the warden of the home in which they were resident*
Judgment	
LORD STEYN:	
Vicarious liability is legal responsibility imposed on an employer, although he is himself free from blame, for a tort committed by his employee in the course of his employment. Fleming observed that this formula represented 'a compromise between two conflicting policies: on the one end, the social interest in furnishing an innocent tort victim with recourse against a financially responsible defendant; on the other, a hesitation to foist any undue burden on business enterprise'.	*Definition: employer responsible for wrongful acts of his employees* *Justification: allows victim to gain compensation*

For nearly a century English judges have adopted Salmond's statement of the applicable test as correct. Salmond said that a wrongful act is deemed to be done by a 'servant' in the course of his employment if 'it is either (a) a wrongful act authorised by the master, or (b) a wrongful and unauthorised mode of doing some act authorised by the master' . . . Situation (a) causes no problems. The difficulty arises in respect of cases under (b). Salmond did, however, offer an explanation which has sometimes been overlooked. He said . . . that 'a master . . . is liable even for acts which he has not authorised, provided they are *so connected* with acts which he has authorised, that they may rightly *be regarded* as modes – although improper modes – of doing them'. It is not necessary to embark on a detailed examination of the development of the modern principle of vicarious liability. But it is necessary to face up to the way in which the law of vicarious liability sometimes may embrace intentional wrongdoing by an employee. If one mechanically applies *Salmond's* test, the result might at first glance be thought to be that a bank is not liable to a customer where a bank employee defrauds a customer by giving him only half the foreign exchange which he paid for, the employee pocketing the difference. A preoccupation with conceptualistic reasoning may lead to the absurd conclusion that there can only be vicarious liability if the bank carries on business in defrauding its customers. Ideas divorced from reality have never held much attraction for judges steeped in the tradition that their task is to deliver principled but practical justice. How the courts set the law on a sensible course is a matter to which I now turn.	*Basic test: wrongful act must occur during the course of employment. Could be authorised act or authorised act done in unauthorised manner The second causes the problem* *Salmond test includes idea of 'close connection'* *Salmond test may mean employer not liable for intentional wrongdoing by employee*
It is easy to accept the idea that where an employee acts for the benefit of his employer, or intends to do so, that is strong evidence that he was acting in the course of his employment. But until the decision of the House of Lords in *Lloyd v Grace, Smith & Co* [1912] AC 76 it was thought that vicarious liability could only be established if such requirements were satisfied. This was an overly restrictive view and hardly in tune with the needs of society. In *Lloyd v Grace, Smith & Co* it was laid to rest by the House of Lords. A firm of solicitors were held liable for the dishonesty of their managing clerk who persuaded a client to transfer property to him and then disposed of it for his own advantage. The decisive factor was that the client had been invited by the firm to deal with their managing clerk. This decision was a breakthrough: it finally established that vicarious liability is not necessarily defeated if the employee acted for his own benefit. On the other hand, an intense focus on the connection between the nature of the employment and the tort of the employee became necessary.	*Traditionally vicarious liability only where employee acts for benefit of employer* *But vicarious liability possible where employee acts dishonestly on his own behalf* *Because employer has placed injured party in hands of employee so requires investigation of connection between employment and the tort*

It remains, however, to consider how vicarious liability for intentional wrongdoing fits in with Salmond's formulation. The answer is that it does not cope ideally with such cases. It must, however, be remembered that the great tort writer did not attempt to enunciate precise propositions of law on vicarious liability. At most he propounded a broad test which deems as within the course of employment 'a wrongful and unauthorised mode of doing some *act* authorised by the master'. And he emphasised the connection between the authorised *acts* and the 'improper modes' of doing them. In reality it is simply a practical test serving as a dividing line between cases where it is or is not just to impose vicarious liability. If this approach to the nature of employment is adopted, it is not necessary to ask the simplistic question whether in the cases under consideration the acts of sexual abuse were modes of doing authorised acts. It becomes possible to consider the question of vicarious liability on the basis that the employer undertook to care for the boys through the services of the warden and that there is a very close connection between the torts of the warden and his employment. After all, they were committed in the time and on the premises of the employers while the warden was also busy caring for the children.	*Salmond test not easy to apply to intentional wrongdoing (intention generally required in crimes)* *Purpose of test is to identify whether it is just to impose vicarious liability* *The sexual abuse is a mode of carrying out his employment because the nature of the employment gave him the opportunity*
In my view the approach of the Court of Appeal in *Trotman v North Yorkshire County Council* [1999] IRLR 98 was wrong. It resulted in the case being treated as one of the employment furnishing a mere opportunity to commit the sexual abuse. The reality was that the county council were responsible for the care of the vulnerable children and employed the deputy headmaster to carry out that duty on its behalf. And the sexual abuse took place while the employee was engaged in duties at the very time and place demanded by his employment. The connection between the employment and the torts was very close. I would overrule *Trotman v North Yorkshire County Council*. Employing the traditional methodology of English law, I am satisfied that in the case of the appeals under consideration the evidence showed that the employers entrusted the care of the children in Axeholme House to the warden. The question is whether the warden's torts were so closely connected with his employment that it would be fair and just to hold the employers vicariously liable. On the facts of the case the answer is yes. After all, the sexual abuse was inextricably interwoven with the carrying out by the warden of his duties in Axeholme House. Matters of degree arise. But the present cases clearly fall on the side of vicarious liability.	*Trotman overruled because employer had duty to care for the vulnerable children and the abuse occurred when the employee was at work* *Vicarious liability is justified in the case because the employee could only do the wrong because of the nature of his employment*

Key points from **Lister v Hesley Hall Ltd** [2001] 2 All ER 769

- Vicarious liability is when an employer (who is not the wrongdoer) is made liable for the wrongful acts of his employee.
- It is justified because it allows a claimant to be compensated.
- The traditional Salmond test was that there could be liability for acts that were in the course of employment.
- These were of two types: acts authorised by the employer, or wrongful and unauthorised modes of carrying out an authorised act – it is the second that causes problems.
- So the employer traditionally might not be liable for intentional wrongdoing.
- Salmond did recognise the possibility of close connection as a test.
- Traditionally vicarious liability was possible where the employee in effect acted for the benefit of the employer but not for his own benefit.
- But the Salmond test was not easy to apply because intent is required for most crimes and negligence is not enough.
- *Trotman* is overruled.

ACTIVITY

In the checklist above two significant points arising from the judgment are missing. Using both the judgment and the commentary in the right hand column consider:

1 why vicarious liability has been possible in the case of crimes involving dishonesty;

2 why vicarious liability is possible in the case of crimes involving sexual abuse.

Place these as key points in the Key Points checklist above.

The judgment in *Lister v Hesley Hall* is clearly a major development of the law on vicarious liability in respect of the victim of such torts. The close connection test is justified in the case because the House of Lords was satisfied that there was an inherent risk of abuse and the employer should have guarded against this.

R Coe, 'A new test for vicarious liability' (2001) 151 NLJ 1154 commented that: 'Whatever the reluctance of their Lordships to set forth the social and policy considerations behind the principle of vicarious liability, it is to be concluded from the decision that the question "who should be the loser" between the "two innocent parties", namely the employer and the victim, is answered by a finding that the risk should fall upon the enterprise . . . provided that there is a sufficient connection between the acts of the employee and the employment. The suggestion that the greater the fault of the servant, the less the liability of the master reflects the wrong approach.'

Nevertheless it has also been argued that the case leaves both legal difficulties unanswered and has far reaching practical implications. R Coe, *'Lister v Hesley Hall Ltd'* (2002) 65 MLR 270 argues that *Lister* fails to resolve the underlying rationale of vicarious liability and, if anything, adds further difficulties. The decision fails to distinguish between primary and vicarious liability in an area of law in which an institution may be sued on both bases. *Lister* has inevitably raised concerns as to the application of the "close connection" test, which has given rise to a risk of the floodgates opening up.

The principle from *Lister* was given further explanation in *Dubai Aluminium v Salaam* [2003] 2 AC 366. Lord Millet stated at 121 it would be no answer to a claim of vicarious liability that:

JUDGMENT

'the employee was guilty of intentional wrongdoing, or that his act was not merely cautious but criminal, or that he was acting exclusively for his own benefit, or that he was acting contrary to express instructions, or that his conduct was the very negation of his employer's duty'.

The reasoning in both cases has subsequently been approved and applied.

CASE EXAMPLE

Mattis v Pollock [2003] EWCA Civ 887; [2003] 1 WLR 2158; [2003] ICR 1335

A bouncer employed by a nightclub got involved in a fight with customers and the claimant intervened. The bouncer then left the club went home, returned with a knife and intent on revenge stabbed the claimant outside the club. In the Court of Appeal Lord Justice Judge identified that the simple question that the court had to decide was whether what the bouncer did was so closely connected to what his employer expected of him that the employer should be held vicariously liable. The court held that this was indeed the case. The whole point of the bouncer's employment was that he should physically manhandle customers and he was encouraged and was supposed to intimidate them and be able to win any fight.

The close connection test has subsequently been used with quite different results. In *Gravill v Carroll and Redruth Rugby Club* [2008] EWCA Civ 689 the club were held vicariously liable for a punch by one of its players causing a serious eye injury to the claimant. The court held that the punch was very closely connected with the type of employment, and that the club had various measures at its disposal, including disciplinary sanctions, to deter misconduct.

In *N v Chief Constable of Merseyside Police* [2006] EWHC 3041 (QB), however, there was no vicarious liability when an off-duty police officer, dressed in his uniform, agreed with a first-aider from a night club to take a young woman who was ill for medical attention but instead took her to his home, drugged her and raped her over a period of hours. The police officer's actions were held not to be closely connected with his employment. He had merely been using his uniform as a way of being able to commit assaults against women.

The area has also developed to cover instances of sexual abuse by Roman Catholic priests. Besides being instances of the close connection test the cases also raise the issue of what types of relationship give rise to vicarious liability since it is not always easy to apply the term 'employee' to the wrongdoers in question. The cases of *JGE* and *The Catholic Child Welfare Society* and others discussed above are also relevant here.

In *Maga v The Trustees of the Birmingham Archdiocese of the Roman Catholic Church* [2010] EWCA Civ 256 the Archdiocese was held liable for sexual abuse of the claimant by one of its priests. The claimant was 12 years old when the abuse began. It was held that the nature of the role of priest gave the opportunity to engage in abusive activities.

Lord Neuberger MR identified at 50:

JUDGMENT

'It is not merely that the abuse started and continued in the employer's premises where the employee resided because of his employment. It is also that the employee's . . . priestly duty, involved spending time alone with individuals such as the claimant. [The Vicar-General of the Archdiocese] said, "the normal course of a priest's work" would involve him "spend[ing] some time alone with people who were searching for truth" . . . the fact that [the priest] was spending time alone with the claimant for illegal sexual purposes is not the point: the opportunity to spend time alone with the claimant, especially in the presbytery, arose from Father Clonan's role as a priest employed as such by the Archdiocese.'

A significant decision in this area was handed down by the Supreme Court in 2016 which courted much attention – this was the decision of *Mohamud v WM Morrison Supermarkets Plc* [2016] UKSC 11. The Supreme Court took time to remind us that 'vicarious liability in tort requires, first, a relationship between the defendant and the wrongdoer, and secondly, a connection between that relationship and the wrongdoer's act or default, such as to make it just that the defendant should be held legally responsible to the claimant for the consequences of the wrongdoer's conduct.' In this case there was a clear employment relationship so there was no issue in relation to the first point but rather the central issue in this appeal centred around whether there was a sufficient connection between the wrongdoer's employment and his intentional actions (assault) against the claimant.

CASE EXAMPLE

Mohamud v WM Morrison Supermarkets Plc [2016] UKSC 11

In this case the claimant approached the employee of Morrisons Supermarket (Mr Khan) at its petrol station counter with a request to find out whether it would be possible to have some documents on his USB stick printed. The claimant was of Somali origin. Mr Khan used foul and racist language in response to the request and asked the claimant to leave. The claimant returned to his car but was followed by Mr Khan who got into the claimant's car on the passenger side and specifically told him in a threatening manner never to return here and subjected him to a serious and violent attack. Meanwhile, Mr Khan's supervisor came to the scene instructing Mr Khan to desist. It appeared to have been an unprovoked attack. Both the trial judge and Court of Appeal concluded that such actions fall outside the course of his employment and it is difficult to see a close connection between what he was employed to do and his tortious and rather violent conduct to justify Morrisons being held liable in line with the judgment in *Lister*. Such actions were deemed to be so far removed from what he was asked to do namely to serve customers that it was difficult to see how such grotesque violence could be connected to make the employer liable. Clarke LJ in the Court of Appeal decision held that just because Mr Khan's job entailed interaction with the public, this could not in itself be enough to generate a close connection and he went on to say '[i]f Morrisons were liable it would mean that in practically every case where an employee was required to engage with the public, his employer would be liable for any assault which followed on from such an engagement. That appears to me to be a step too far.' This was not however the approach that the Supreme Court took, who did in fact find Morrisons liable for its employee's actions. Lord Toulson essentially said that the court has to make an evaluative judgment in each case, having regard to all the circumstances and to the assistance provided by previous court decisions on the facts of other cases. He explains at 44–45:

JUDGMENT

'In the simplest terms, the court has to consider two matters. The first question is what functions or "field of activities" have been entrusted by the employer to the employee, or, in everyday language, what was the nature of his job. As has been emphasised in several cases, this question must be addressed broadly. . . . Secondly, the court must decide whether there was sufficient connection between the position in which he was employed and his wrongful conduct to make it right for the employer to be held liable under the principle of social justice . . . The cases in which the necessary connection has been . . . are cases in which the employee used or misused the position entrusted to him in a way which injured the third party.'

In this case, it was Mr Khan's job to attend to customers and to respond to their inquiries. His conduct in answering the claimant's request in a foul mouthed way and ordering him to leave was inexcusable but within the 'field of activities' assigned to him. What happened thereafter was an unbroken sequence of events. It was argued by the respondent and accepted by the judge that there ceased to be any significant connection between Mr Khan's employment and his behaviour towards the claimant when he came out from behind the counter and followed the claimant onto the forecourt. I disagree for two reasons. First, I do not consider that it is right to regard him as having metaphorically taken off his uniform the moment he stepped from behind the counter. He was following up on what he had said to the claimant. It was a seamless episode. Second, when Mr Khan followed the claimant back to his car and opened the front passenger door, he again told the claimant in threatening words that he was never to come back to the petrol station. This was not something personal between them; it was an order to keep away from his employer's premises, which he reinforced by violence. In giving such an order he was purporting to act about his employer's business. It was a gross abuse of his position, but it was in connection with the business in which he was employed to serve customers. His employers entrusted him with that position and it is just that as between them and the claimant, they should be held responsible for their employee's abuse of it. Mr Khan's motive is irrelevant. It looks obvious that he was motivated by personal racism rather than a desire to benefit his employer's business, but that is neither here nor there.

It is also a decision which stretches vicarious liability quite far especially when the Court of Appeal's position is considered in the same decision. There Clarke LJ stated that if Morrisons were to be found liable, then liability could be deemed to exist in almost every case in which an employee is required to engage with the public. The Supreme Court was not fazed by this and proceeded to find Morrisons liable. This is in part because it was the employment that provided the opportunity, setting, time and place for the tort to occur. Further comment on this point can be found in Giliker's 'Vicarious liability in the Supreme Court' who describes this ruling as having taken the course of employment test to its absolute limits. At this point, it can be seen that vicarious liability was on the move and enjoying a period of expansion in cases such as *Mohamud, Cox, Various Claimants v Catholic Child Welfare Society* to deal with very difficult factual circumstances requiring policy-based decisions. However, as can be seen below the law in this area has become well established and has been developed well enough for now, to deal with complex factual situations including cases involving intentional torts and sexual assaults.

The case of *Bellman v Northampton Recruitment* [2018] EWCA Civ 2214, involved a work Christmas party organised by the defendant. After the party, most of the guests went to a nearby hotel for further drinks where most of the guests were staying although not the claimant who was staying elsewhere nearby. The hotel and drinks were paid for by the defendant company. At these drinks, an argument arose between the company's managing director (Mr Major) who had a wide remit including decision over expenditure and the claimant over a work matter. The managing director assaulted the claimant by punching him which resulted in the claimant suffering from permanent brain injury. The question for the Court of Appeal was whether the defendant company could be held vicariously liable for the wrongful conduct its employee even though it occurred outside the workplace and outside office hours. The Court of Appeal applied Lord Toulson's analysis under *Mohamud* which asks whether there is a sufficient connection between the position in which the wrongdoer is employed and his wrongful conduct so as to make the employer liable under the principle of social justice and this requires the court to conduct an evaluative judgment. At paragraph 32 Asplin LJ held:

JUDGMENT

'. . . despite the time and place at which the assault occurred, Mr Major's position of seniority persisted and was a significant factor. He was in a dominant position and had a supervisory role which enabled him to assert his authority over the staff who were present and to re-assert that authority when he thought it necessary.'

In this case because the drinks party took place straight after the Christmas party, the managing director was asserting his authority and because it was all paid for by the managing director of the company, a close connection between his employment and the assault could be established. Again, this decision demonstrates another set of circumstances in which the employer may be liable.

The decision in *Bellman* was followed by the Supreme Court decision in *WM Morrison Supermarkets plc v Various Claimants* [2020] UKSC 12.

CASE EXAMPLE

WM Morrison Supermarkets plc v Various Claimants [2020] UKSC 12

In this case an employee, Andrew Skelton, who was a senior auditor, bore a grudge against his employer, the supermarket Morrisons, following disciplinary proceedings for minor misconduct. Skelton had access to the personal details of all of the employees at Morrisons. Skeleton copied this data and from his home, uploaded this to a publicly accessible file-sharing website. Once Morrisons became aware of this data being published, Skelton was arrested and Morrisons have spent £2.26 million dealing with the fallout from this including identity protection measures for its employees. The question for the Supreme Court to determine was whether Morrisons could be held vicariously liable for the wrongdoing of Skelton. It was argued by the claimants that Skelton's actions were within the field of activities assigned to him by Morrisons and presented a seamless and continuous sequence or unbroken chain of events. The Court of Appeal was persuaded by this argument, whereas the Supreme Court was not. The Supreme Court held that Skelton's disclosure of the data was not so closely connected with acts he was authorised to do. His wrongful disclosure cannot fairly and properly be regarded as done by him while acting in the ordinary course of his employment. Just because Skelton's employment gave him the opportunity to commit the wrongful act, that in of itself is not enough to impose vicarious liability of his employer. In *Mohamud* and *Bellman*, both tortfeasors were engaged in furthering their employer's business whereas in this case, Skelton was trying to harm his employer's business.

The position is summarised by Lord Reed at paragraph 47:

JUDGMENT

'All these examples illustrate the distinction drawn by Lord Nicholls at para 32 of *Dubai Aluminium* [2003] 2 AC 366 between "cases . . . where the employee was engaged, however misguidedly, in furthering his employer's business, and cases where the employee is engaged solely in pursuing his own interests: on a 'frolic of his own', in the language of the time-honoured catch phrase." In the present case, it is abundantly clear that Skelton was not engaged in furthering his employer's business when he committed the wrongdoing in question. On the contrary, he was pursuing a personal vendetta, seeking vengeance for the disciplinary proceedings some months earlier. In those circumstances, applying the test laid down by Lord

> Nicholls in *Dubai Aluminium* in the light of the circumstances of the case and the relevant precedents, Skelton's wrongful conduct was not so closely connected with acts which he was authorised to do that, for the purposes of Morrisons' liability to third parties, it can fairly and properly be regarded as done by him while acting in the ordinary course of his employment.'

The decision in *WM Morrison Supermarkets plc v Various Claimants* was welcomed by employers. It allays any fears that employers may have had following the decision in *Mohamud* that the close connection between the actions of the employee and the nature of employment could be easily established. The close connection test must be applied with careful reference to the facts of each case. However, how would this arguably less generous approach, apply in cases involving sexual abuse?

CASE EXAMPLE

Trustees of the Barry Congregation of Jehovah's Witnesses v BXB [2023] UKSC 15

In the case of *Trustees of the Barry Congregation of Jehovah's Witnesses v BXB* [2023] UKSC 15, the Supreme Court was asked to decide whether the Jehovah's Witness organisation could be held vicariously liable for a rape committed by one of its elders, Mark Sewell. Here the claimant and her husband made friends with Mark and his family with both families becoming very close, so much so that they went on holidays together. Later Mark became depressed and started abusing alcohol. The claimant had visited Mark at his house where a conversation took place but he pushed the claimant to the floor and raped her. Mark was convicted of raping the claimant and imprisoned. The claimant pursued an action against the defendant organisation alleging that they were vicariously liable for the rape. She was successful in her claim at trial and at the Court of Appeal but the Supreme Court reversed their decision on the basis that vicarious liability could not be established. At paragraph 58(v) Lord Burrows sets out the current position on vicarious liability in cases of sexual abuse:

JUDGMENT

'The same two stages, and the same two tests, apply to cases of sexual abuse as they do to other cases on vicarious liability. Although one can reasonably interpret some judicial comments as supporting special rules for sexual abuse, this was rejected by Lord Reed in *Cox*. The idea that the law still needs tailoring to deal with sexual abuse cases is misleading. The necessary tailoring is already reflected in, and embraced by, the modern tests.'

Lord Burrows goes on to explain that applying the correct tests liability cannot be established. At paragraphs 71, 73–74:

JUDGMENT

'The correct test that should have been applied . . . was whether the wrongful conduct, the rape, was so closely connected with acts that the tortfeasor, Mark Sewell, was authorised to do, that the rape can fairly and properly be regarded as committed by him while acting in the course of his quasi-employment as an elder.

. . . applying the correct close connection test . . . above, the claimant fails to satisfy that test. This is for the following reasons.

First, the rape was not committed while Mark Sewell was carrying out any activities as an elder on behalf of the Jehovah's Witnesses. He was at his own home and was not at the time engaged in performing any work connected with his role as an elder. So, eg, he was not conducting a bible class, he was not evangelising or giving pastoral care, he was not on premises of the Jehovah's Witnesses and the incident had nothing to do with any service or worship of the Jehovah Witnesses. The lack of direct connection to the role assigned to him as an elder makes these facts significantly different from the institutional sex abuse cases where, eg, as part of their jobs the warden was on the institutional premises looking after the children in *Lister* or the Brothers were living in the same institution as their victims in *Christian Brothers*.

Secondly, in contrast to the child sexual abuse cases, at the time of the rape, Mark Sewell was not exercising control over Mrs B because of his position as an elder. It was because of her close friendship with Mark Sewell and because she was seeking to provide emotional support to him, and not because Mark Sewell had control over her as an elder, that Mrs B went to the back room. The driving force behind their being together in the room at the time of the rape was their close personal friendship not Mark Sewell's role as an elder. Put another way, the primary reason that the rape took place was not because Mark Sewell was abusing his position as an elder but because he was abusing his position as a close friend of Mrs B when she was trying to help him.'

In the case of *MXX v A Secondary School* [2023] EWCA Civ 996 it had to be determined whether the a school was vicariously liable for the wrongful actions of someone who was on a one-week work placement. The tortfeasor was a former pupil at the school and undertook a placement at the school. During this placement he met the then 13-year-old claimant. Following the end of the placement, the claimant and the tortfeasor became friends on social media and shortly after, the tortfeasor had sexually abused the claimant. At trial it was held that the defendant school could not be held vicariously liable for the acts of the tortfeasor. Applying the two-stage test, Nicola Davis LJ held that there was a relationship between the defendant and the tortfeasor that was akin to employment. In relation to the second limb at paragraph 88 she explains:

JUDGMENT

'In my judgment, given the limited nature of PXM's role during the course of one week, the facts do not begin to satisfy the requirements of the close connection test. The grooming which led to the sexual offending was not inextricably woven with the carrying out by PXM of his work during his week at the defendant's school such that it would be fair and just to hold the defendant vicariously liable for the acts of PXM.'

The tortfeasor's work during the placement was not closely connected to the abuse of the claimant. He had no caring responsibilities towards the pupils or any authority over them.

Lord Burrows provides a clear summary of the current law on vicarious liability in the *BXB* at paragraph 58, which is worth replicating here to help explain the different stages of analysis.

JUDGMENT

Summary of the modern law on vicarious liability

i There are two stages to consider in determining vicarious liability. Stage 1 is concerned with the relationship between the defendant and the tortfeasor. Stage 2 is concerned with the link between the commission of the tort and that relationship. Both stages must be addressed and satisfied if vicarious liability is to be established.

ii The test at stage 1 is whether the relationship between the defendant and the tortfeasor was one of employment or akin to employment. In most cases, there will be no difficulty in applying this test because one is dealing with an employer-employee relationship. But in applying the 'akin to employment' aspect of this test, a court needs to consider carefully features of the relationship that are similar to, or different from, a contract of employment. Depending on the facts, relevant features to consider may include whether the work is being paid for in money or in kind, how integral to the organisation is the work carried out by the tortfeasor, the extent of the defendant's control over the tortfeasor in carrying out the work, whether the work is being carried out for the defendant's benefit or in furtherance of the aims of the organisation, what the situation is with regard to appointment and termination, and whether there is a hierarchy of seniority into which the relevant role fits. It is important to recognise, as made clear in *Barclays Bank*, that the 'akin to employment' expansion does not undermine the traditional position that there is no vicarious liability where the tortfeasor is a true independent contractor in relation to the defendant.

iii The test at stage 2 (the 'close connection' test) is whether the wrongful conduct was so closely connected with acts that the tortfeasor was authorised to do that it can fairly and properly be regarded as done by the tortfeasor while acting in the course of the tortfeasor's employment or quasi-employment. This is the test, subject to two minor adjustments, set out by Lord Nicholls in *Dubai Aluminium*, drawing on *Lister*, and firmly approved in *Morrison*. The first adjustment is that, to be comprehensive, it is necessary to expand the test to include 'quasi-employment' as one may be dealing with a situation where the relationship at stage 1 is 'akin to employment' rather than employment. The second adjustment is that it is preferable to delete the word 'ordinary' before 'course of employment' which is superfluous and potentially misleading (eg none of the sexual abuse cases can easily be said to fall within the 'ordinary' course of employment) and was presumably included by Lord Nicholls because 'in the ordinary course of business' were the words in section 10 of the Partnership Act 1890. The application of this 'close connection' test requires a court to consider carefully on the facts the link between the wrongful conduct and the tortfeasor's authorised activities. That there is a causal connection (ie that the 'but for' causation test is satisfied) is not sufficient in itself to satisfy the test. Cases such as *Lister* and *Christian Brothers* show that sexual abuse of a child by someone who is employed or authorised to look after the child will, at least generally, satisfy the test. But, as established by *Morrison*, the carrying out of the wrongful act in pursuance of a personal vendetta against the employer, designed to harm the employer, will mean that this test is not satisfied.

iv As made particularly clear by Lady Hale in *Barclays Bank*, drawing on what Lord Hobhouse had said in *Lister*, the tests invoke legal principles that in the vast majority of cases can be applied without considering the underlying policy justification for vicarious liability. The tests are a product of the policy behind vicarious liability and in applying the tests there is no need to turn back continually to examine the underlying policy. This is not to deny that in difficult cases, and in line with what Lord Reed said in *Cox*, having applied the tests to reach a provisional outcome on vicarious liability, it can be a useful final check on the justice of the outcome to stand back and consider whether that outcome is consistent with the underlying policy . . . Lord Phillips referred to five policies in *Christian Brothers* but, as Lord Reed recognised in *Cox*, a couple of those have little, if any, force. At root the core idea . . . appears to be that the employer or quasi-employer, who is taking the benefit of the activities carried on by a person integrated into its organisation, should bear the cost (or, one might say, should bear the risk) of the wrong committed by that person in the course of those activities.

v The same two stages, and the same two tests, apply to cases of sexual abuse as they do to other cases on vicarious liability. Although one can reasonably interpret some judicial comments as supporting special rules for sexual abuse, this was rejected by Lord Reed in *Cox*. The idea that the law still needs tailoring to deal with sexual abuse cases is misleading. The necessary tailoring is already reflected in, and embraced by, the modern tests.

CRITIQUING THE LAW

Consider the recent expansion of the law of vicarious liability which had the potential to overexpose employers which the courts now appear to have now halted. Do you think that claims based on vicarious liability that involve sexual abuse should be treated differently not least because they likely to be brought some years later from the actual occurrence of the abuse?

18.5.3 The employer's indemnity

Where the employer is vicariously liable then both he and the employee are in effect joint tortfeasors. The consequence of this is that the claimant could actually sue either. One further consequence is that the employer who is sued may then sue the employee for an indemnity.

CASE EXAMPLE

Lister v Romford Ice & Cold Storage Ltd [1957] AC 555

A lorry driver knocked over his father who at the time was his driver's mate. The father then claimed compensation from the employers. The employers' insurers on settling the claim then exercised their rights of subrogation under the insurance contract and sued the driver. The House of Lords accepted that this was possible.

The case has been strongly criticised, not least because it destroys the purpose of imposing vicarious liability. As a result insurers do not generally exercise their rights under the principle.

18.5.4 Liability for the torts of independent contractors

An employer will not usually be liable for the tortious acts of independent contractors whom he has hired. The reason is the lack of control that the employer is able to exercise.

Nevertheless there are some very limited circumstances in which an employer has been shown to be liable for the acts of independent contractors. These include:

- If the contractor has been hired for the purpose of carrying out the tort then the employer may be liable, as he would be for his employees.

CASE EXAMPLE

Ellis v Sheffield Gas Consumers Co [1853] 2 E & B 767

The defendants without having sought any actual authority to do so hired contractors to dig a hole in the road. The contractors failed to properly replace the hole and the claimant was injured as a result. The defendants were held vicariously liable because the contractor had only been carrying out the task set by the defendants who had in effect sanctioned the tort.

- Where the employers are under a non-delegable duty of care imposed by statute. This might for instance apply where there is an obligation not only to provide but also to ensure that industrial safety equipment is used.
- Where a similar non-delegable duty of care is owed in common law.

18.6 Vicarious liability of lenders of cars

Another area that creates problems apart from travelling to and from work is the practice of lending vehicles. The area includes a strange group of cases, not easily classified and in many ways quite confusing. In establishing whether the owner of the vehicle is vicariously liable for the acts of the driver, the defining difference appears to be whether or not the vehicle is being used for a purpose in which the owner has an interest.

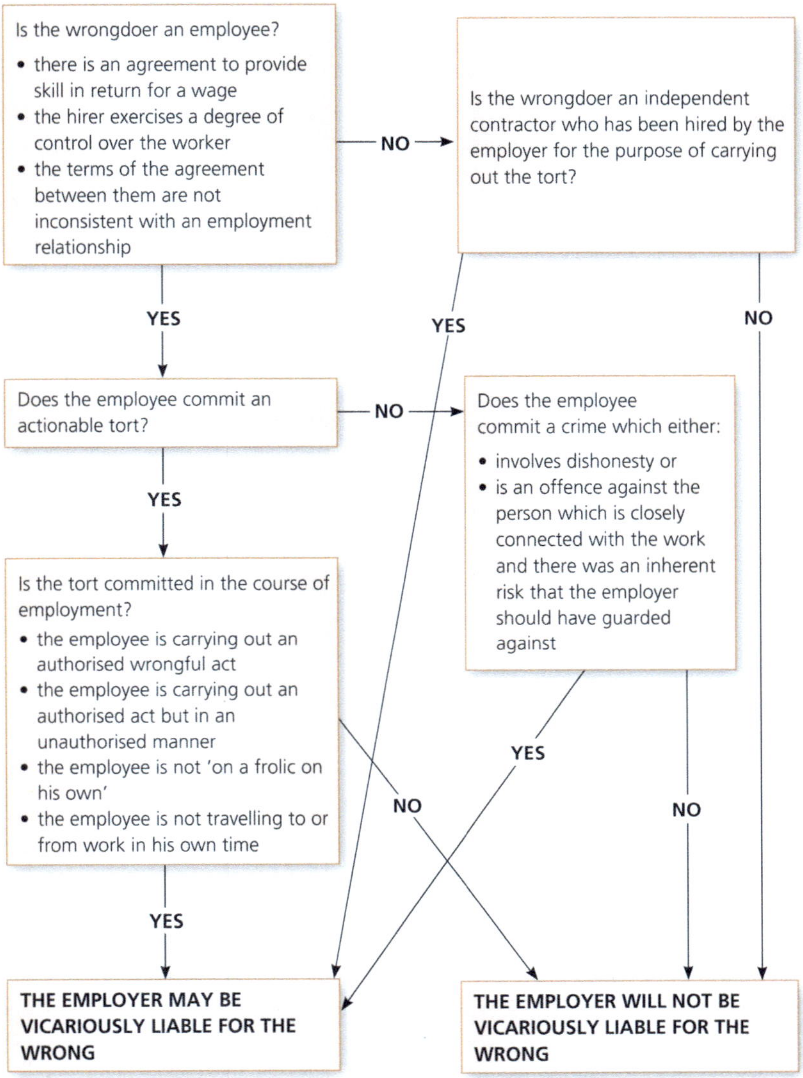

Figure 18.2 The process of establishing vicarious liability including more complex situations.

CASE EXAMPLE

Britt v Galmoye [1928] 44 TLR 294

Here there was no liability on an employer when the car was lent to the employee for the employee's own personal use.

The result will be different where the owner has requested that the other party should borrow the car to carry out the purposes of the owner.

CASE EXAMPLE

Ormrod v Crosville Motor Services Ltd [1953] 1 WLR 1120

In this case the owner of a car asked another party to take the car to Monte Carlo where the owner would later join him and other friends for a holiday. The friend drove the car negligently and collided with a bus, causing damage to both vehicles and injuries to the occupants of the car. The Court of Appeal held that the owner of the car was liable. Even though the driver was benefiting from the use of the car and using it for his own purposes he was also driving the car with the express authority and for reasons of the owner, who was thus vicariously liable for the accident.

As Lord Denning explained at 1123:

JUDGMENT

'The trip to Monte Carlo must be considered as a whole . . . it was undertaken with the owner's consent for the purposes of both of them, and the owner is liable for any negligence of the driver in the course of it.'

Though in some instances it appears that the logic of the decision is merely that the judges wished there to be liability, which does not necessarily produce a fully justifiable result.

CASE EXAMPLE

Morgans v Launchbury [1973] AC 127

A wife allowed her husband to use her car knowing that he was going out drinking on the express promise that he would not drive while drunk. The husband did have too much to drink and so he allowed another drunk and uninsured driver to drive him home. When there was an accident the Court of Appeal imposed vicarious liability on the wife in order that a claim could be made against her insurance. Lord Denning felt that the fact that the wife had given permission to use the car was sufficient to make her responsible. In the House of Lords Lord Wilberforce rejected this argument because it was impossible to pinpoint the exact basis on which a court could fix liability in such circumstances. He also felt that it was not for judges to interfere with the interrelationship between liability and insurance.

Lord Wilberforce identified the unfairness of the Court of Appeal's reasoning in making the owner of the car liable when put in the context of the general rules on vicarious liability (at 135):

JUDGMENT

'The owner ought to pay, it says, because he has authorised the act, or requested it, or because the actor is carrying out a task duly delegated, or because he is in control of the actor's conduct. He ought not to pay (on accepted rules) if he has no control over the actor, has not authorised or requested the act, or if the actor is acting wholly on his own purposes.'

ACTIVITY

Self-assessment questions

1 What justifications are there for making an employer liable for the torts of his employee?
2 In what ways can vicarious liability be said to be unfair?
3 What will a claimant need to show in order to establish liability on the part of the employer?
4 To what extent is it easy to demonstrate that a person is an employee?
5 Why is the 'control test' an ineffective test on its own?
6 How does the 'economic reality' test operate?
7 What factors are useful indicators of whether a person is employed or self-employed?
8 Is an employer liable for acts done in protection of his property?
9 Explain what is meant by an authorised act done in an unauthorised manner.
10 Why exactly was the dairy liable in *Rose v Plenty*?
11 What exactly is a 'frolic on his own'?
12 Why were *Limpus* and *Beard* decided differently?
13 In what circumstances is an employer liable for the crimes of his employee?
14 Why is *Lister v Hesley Hall* such an important case?
15 Why is the principle in *Lister v Romford* criticised and why is it not followed?
16 What consistency, if any, is there between *Morgans v Launchbury* and other cases on vicarious liability?

KEY FACTS

The nature of vicarious liability	Case
Vicarious liability is where one person is held liable for the torts of another. This is usually where an employer is liable for the tortious acts of an employee. For the employer to be liable two stages need to be considered: Stage 1: the *relationship* between defendant and tortfeasor needs to be determined Stage 2: the *connection* between the commission of the tort and the relationship needs to be determined	

(Continued)

(Continued)

The tests of employment status	
Various tests have been developed to determine whether or not someone is an employee rather than an independent contractor (self-employed) – these include the 'control' test, the 'integration' test and the 'organisation' test.	
The 'economic reality' test – all factors should be considered and their importance weighed. Relationships with the incident of an employment relationship that may be 'akin to employment' test can be considered.	*Ready Mixed Concrete v Minister of Pensions and National Insurance* [1968] *JGE v The Trustees of the Portsmouth Roman Catholic Diocesan Trust* [2013] *The Catholic Child Welfare Society and others v Various Claimants (FC) and The Institute of the Brothers of the Christian Schools and others* [2012] *Cox v Ministry of Justice* [2014] *Armes v Nottinghamshire CC* [2017] *Various Claimants v Barclays Bank plc ("Barclays Bank")* [2020] *J D Wetherspoon Plc v Stephenus Bernadus Burger, Risk Solutions Bg Ltd.* [2025]
A number of types of work defy easy description, e.g. casual workers, those who work in the gig economy.	*Uber BV (UBV) & Ors v Aslam & Ors* [2018] EWCA Civ 2748
The test of liability	**Case**
Course of employment can include: • authorised acts • acts done in an unauthorised manner • negligently carried out work • exceeding the proper bounds of the work.	*Poland v Parr* [1927] *Limpus v General London Omnibus Co* [1862] *Century Insurance v Northern Ireland Transport Board* [1942] *Bayley v Manchester, Sheffield & Lincolnshire Railway* [1873]

(Continued)

(Continued)

Torts outside the course of employment	Case
There is no liability for: • being on a 'frolic on his own' • things outside the scope of employment.	*Hilton v Thomas Burton* [1961] *Twine v Beans Express* [1946]
Liability for intentional torts of an employee	**Case**
An employer is not usually liable for an employee's crimes.	
This will apply to fraud.	*Lloyd v Grace Smith* [1912]
This will apply to crimes generally.	*Warren v Henleys* [1948]
A distinction is made where the criminal act of the employee is an inherent risk that the employer should guard against.	*Lister v Hesley Hall* [2001]
The close connection test: It will apply to intentional torts of an employee even if not directly motivated by a desire to further the employer's business but rather by their own motives.	*Mohamud v WM Morrison Supermarkets Plc* [2016] *WM Morrison Supermarkets plc v Various Claimants* [2020] *Trustees of the Barry Congregation of Jehovah's Witnesses v BXB* [2023]
Liability for torts of independent contractors	**Case**
There is usually no liability for torts of independent contractors.	*Ellis v Sheffield Gas Consumers* [1853]
It is rare but possible to recover the loss from the employee.	*Lister v Romford Ice* [1957]
In some cases it is possible for owners to be liable for torts committed in cars that they have lent to the tortfeasor.	*Morgans v Launchbury* [1973]

ACTIVITY

Applying the law

Using the guide in Appendix 2, try the following problem question.

Barry recently secured work as a delivery driver for 'Dodgy Transport' driving a 15 hundredweight Luton bodied Transit van, the only qualification being production of a valid driving licence. Barry has a clean licence but expressed concern at the time of his interview as he was only used to driving motor bikes. He signed a document called 'Document of Service' in which it was written that he must work such hours as the firm require, wear their uniform at all times while at work and that he accepts work from no other delivery business, except as authorised by 'Dodgy' officials. 'Dodgy' owns the van that Barry drives and they pay him a gross amount, leaving him to settle his own tax and National Insurance contributions. In his first week Barry was delivering to 'Rocky Co', a very good customer of 'Dodgy'. Alex, the manager of Rocky, asked Barry if he would take a parcel in need of urgent delivery to 'Steady Co', a customer of 'Rocky' that is five miles away and in the opposite direction to Dodgy's premises. Despite being unable to contact Dodgy on his mobile phone, Barry took the parcel. When he arrived at Steady's offices Barry had to reverse into their loading bay and negligently ran over the warehouseman, Stan.

Advise Dodgy whether it will be liable for the injuries caused by Barry's negligence.

SAMPLE ESSAY QUESTION

Discuss the argument that vicarious liability is unjust as it places liability on someone other than the person at fault.

Explain the basis of vicarious liability

- One party (usually an employer) is fixed with liability for the torts (and sometimes the crimes) of another party (usually an employee)

Explain the requirements for liability

- There is an established tort
- The tortfeasor is an employee
- The tort occurred in the course of employment

Describe the tests of employment status

- Control test
- Integration test
- Economic reality (multiple) test

Discuss the meaning of 'in the course of employment'

- Authorised acts
- Authorised acts carried out in an unauthorised manner
- Authorised acts carried out carelessly
- Where the employer benefits from the tort *Rose v Plenty*
- Paid travelling time
- But not frolics, activities not within the scope of employment and giving unauthorised lifts

Discuss whether the principle is unjust

- It contradicts the basic fault principle
- An employer can incur liability even though he has expressly prohibited the unsafe practice
- The rule may operate inconsistently or arbitrarily
- The tort often occurs before the employer realises that the employee has behaved badly and should be disciplined

Discuss whether the rule can be justified

- The employer benefits from work so should be responsible
- The employer should ensure that work is carried out safely
- The employer can more easily stand the loss
- It ensures that the claimant can be compensated
- The fact of compulsory insurance so only pays the premiums
- Increased premiums may act as a deterrent
- The employer can discipline employees for unsafe practices

Discuss the close connection test and its application – and whether it is any more or any less just

SUMMARY

- Vicarious liability is not a tort but refers to liability being with a person other than the tortfeasor usually an employer.
- And it is possible now for there to be joint vicarious liability.
- For the employer to be liable there must be a tort carried out by an employee during the course of employment.
- Tests of employee status include the 'control' test, the 'indicia' test and the 'organisation' (or integration) test, but the most commonly used now is the 'economic reality' test.
- Acts in the course of employment can include: authorised acts, acts done in an unauthorised manner, negligently carried out work, exceeding the proper bounds of the work.
- But there is no liability for being on a 'frolic on his own', or anything outside the scope of employment.

- An employer is not usually liable for an employee's crimes, but may be in the case of fraud and dishonesty – and now also where there is a close connection with the work and the criminal act of the employee carries with it an inherent risk that the employer should guard against.
- In rare situations a person can be vicariously liable for the torts of independent contractors.
- There is a theoretical possibility of the employee indemnifying an employer.

Further reading

Coe, R, 'A new test for vicarious liability' (2001) *151 NLJ* 1154.

Coe, R, 'Lister v Hesley Hall Ltd' (2002) *65 MLR* 270.

Giliker, P, 'Vicarious liability in the UK Supreme Court' (2016) *7 UK Supreme Court Yearbook* 152–166.

Good Work: The Taylor Review Modern Working Practices: https://assets.publishing.service.gov.uk/government/uploads/system/uploads/attachment_data/file/627671/good-work-taylor-review-modern-working-practices-rg.pdfJuly 2017.

Good Work: A Response to the Taylor Review of Modern Working Practices: https://assets.publishing.service.gov.uk/government/uploads/system/uploads/attachment_data/file/679767/180206_BEIS_Good_Work_Report__Accessible_A4_.pdfFebruary 2018.

Giliker, P, 'Analysing institutional liability for child sexual abuse in England and Wales and Australia: Vicarious liability, non-delegable duties and statutory intervention' (2018) *77(3) CLJ* 506–535.

Giliker, P, 'Can the Supreme Court halt the ongoing expansion of vicarious liability? Barclays and Morrison in the UK Supreme Court' (2021) *37(2) PN* 55–72.

'Vicarious liability' IDS Brief 655, February 2000.

19

Remedies and limitations

AIMS AND OBJECTIVES

After reading this chapter you should be able to:

- Explain the different remedies that are available
- Understand the significance of limitation periods
- Critically evaluate the remedies that can be awarded
- Apply the law to factual situations and reach conclusions

19.1 Damages

19.1.1 Nature and purpose of damages

In many cases where physical damage to property has occurred, the purpose of damages is clear – to compensate the claimant for the loss suffered, which usually means the cost of repairs and other quantifiable financial loss caused by the tort. It is less clear where personal injury is involved, as the court may also seek to compensate for future financial loss which can only be estimated as well as the pain and suffering which has been caused.

In the case of torts actionable *per se* no actual damage needs to be proved. So what then is the purpose of an award in such cases? Here the court seeks to mark its disapproval of the interference with the claimant's legal interest whether in relation to bodily integrity (trespass to the person), goods (trespass to goods), land (trespass to land) or reputation (libel and those situations where slander is actionable per se). The award is compensation for violation of such interest.

One particular feature of the system raises a very real difficulty. As a general rule, all awards of damages are final. The case cannot be reopened and the award reassessed at a later date. How can one predict the

DOI: 10.4324/9781003202417-19

future? This is of real concern in personal injury cases. As we shall see, this rule has been somewhat relaxed in such cases but a crystal ball is still needed.

special damages
not to be confused with special damage – generally refers to damages for financial losses and expenses incurred up to the date of trial which have to be pleaded separately from the claim itself

loss of amenity
damages are awarded where the claimant is unable to do things that he could before the wrong occurred

19.1.2 Types of damages – general and special

Damages are either general or **special damages**. Special damages must be specifically pleaded and consist of quantifiable financial losses including loss of wages, value of clothing or other property which has been lost or destroyed, cost of repairing damaged property and other out of pocket expenses. General damages are by their nature unable to be quantified precisely and cover such things as pain and suffering and **loss of amenity**. In certain circumstances general damages may be awarded in different forms to achieve slightly different purposes:

- contemptuous;
- nominal;
- aggravated;
- exemplary.

Contemptuous damages

The award of contemptuous damages, often the value of the smallest coin in the realm, marks the fact that

- the claimant has established that a right has been infringed;
- in the court's view the action should never have been brought.

The latter may be because of the actual circumstances of the case, for example where a 'one-off' trespass to land has occurred but was no more than a limited incursion causing no actual damage. The court may also use contemptuous damages to mark its belief that morally at least, although not legally, the claimant 'got what they deserved'. Such awards are not uncommon in libel actions.

One consequence of contemptuous damages is that the claimant may find that the award of costs is affected. Although an order is usually made in favour of the successful party, the judge has a discretion to order that both sides bear their own costs or even to order the claimant to pay the costs of both sides.

nominal damages
a small sum of damages awarded where there has technically been a wrong but no actual damage has been caused

Nominal damages

Where **nominal damages** are awarded the claimant's right has been infringed but little damage has occurred. The judge will be satisfied that the claimant has acted reasonably in bringing the case. Such awards are not unusual in cases where the tort is actionable per se such as trespass or where the remedy of choice is an injunction or a declaration. In the case of *Ms B v An NHS Trust* [2002] EWHC 429 (Fam) the declaration sought by the claimant was granted and a nominal sum awarded for damages for the trespass to her person. In that case the claimant also received full costs but it should be remembered that the judge may exercise discretion whether or not to award costs and may decline to do so.

Aggravated damages

Aggravated damages are awarded to compensate the claimant for injury to feelings and distress which have been increased by the defendant's bad motive or wilful behaviour.

The Court of Appeal gave an explanation of the circumstances in which aggravated damages should be awarded in the case of *Thompson v Metropolitan Police Commissioner* [1997] 2 All ER 762. Explaining that aggravated damages are awarded in addition to the basic figure which would usually be the sum for general damages, Lord Woolf MR said at 775:

JUDGMENT

> 'Such damages can be awarded where there are aggravating features about the case which would result in the [claimant] not receiving sufficient compensation for the injury suffered . . . Aggravating features can include humiliating circumstances . . . or any conduct of those responsible . . . which shows that they had behaved in a high-handed, insulting, malicious or oppressive manner.'

Aggravated damages have been awarded for claims relating to torts such as battery, trespass to land, deceit and racial or sexual discrimination but there is authority to say that this should not happen in cases involving claims of negligence (*Kralj v McGrath* [1986] 1 All ER 54 – a case involving medical negligence).

As the award is basically for hurt feelings, it would be inappropriate for a company to receive such an award – a company has no feelings to be hurt!

Exemplary damages

The purpose of exemplary damages is twofold:

i to punish the defendant; and

ii to deter others from similar behaviour.

At first sight, the difference between exemplary and aggravated damages is not clear. In both cases, the disapproval of the defendant's action is seen to merit an additional award based largely on the view taken of the defendant's behaviour. The distinction is drawn between behaviour which adds to the claimant's hurt feelings (aggravated damages) and behaviour which deserves punishment even if the additional hurt to the claimant is minimal.

The availability of exemplary damages

The modern approach dates from a case in 1964.

CASE EXAMPLE

Rookes v Barnard [1964] AC 1129

The case involved an industrial dispute at Heathrow Airport. The claimant was an employee who had left the union which operated an informal closed shop agreement with the employers, British Overseas Airways Corporation. The defendant was an unpaid union official and as a result of union action, the employers were told that unless the claimant was dismissed there would be a strike. The claimant was dismissed and brought a civil action against the defendant and others for conspiracy. The claimant succeeded in his action. The important point for discussion here was whether he could be awarded exemplary damages.

Lord Devlin explained the distinction between compensatory damages and exemplary damages. The former, including aggravated damages, are intended to compensate the claimant for loss suffered. The latter are awarded to mark disapproval of the defendant's conduct and to deter others from similar behaviour. Lord Devlin concluded at 1131 that there are two categories of cases where an award of exemplary damages could be appropriate:

JUDGMENT

i 'oppressive, arbitrary or unconstitutional action by the servants of the government';

ii 'those [cases] where the defendant's conduct has been calculated by him to make a profit for himself which may well exceed the compensation payable to the [claimant]'.

The judge noted that a third category of case existed where 'exemplary damages are expressly authorised by statute'.

The availability of exemplary damages has continued to be controversial. Lord Devlin in *Rookes v Barnard* took the view that there were 1226:

JUDGMENT

'certain categories of cases in which an award of exemplary damages can serve a useful purpose in vindicating the strength of the law . . . and thus admitting into the civil law a principle which ought logically to belong to the criminal'.

When it is remembered that the general purpose of damages in civil law is to provide compensation rather than to punish a defendant, the basis for this view is clear. However, what about those cases where the criminal law provides no remedy but the conduct of the defendant is in the eyes of many people deserving of punishment? It is in this area that the issue of exemplary damages becomes of particular importance and, at the same time, particularly controversial. The courts have struggled with the problem and have shown reluctance to allow any extension of the categories for which exemplary damages can be awarded.

In *Broome v Cassell & Co Ltd* [1972] AC 1027 it was held that the categories of torts for which exemplary damages could be awarded was limited to those cases where such an award had been possible prior to 1964 (the 'cause of action approach'). This view, although the subject of academic argument and criticism, has been reconsidered by the House of Lords in *Kuddus v Chief Constable of Leicestershire* [2002] UKHL 29.

CASE EXAMPLE

Kuddus v Chief Constable of Leicestershire [2002] UKHL 29

The claimant had come back to his flat to find that many items were missing. The police officer attending the scene said that the matter would be investigated but two months later forged the claimant's signature on a statement withdrawing the complaint of theft. The claimant brought an action for misfeasance in a public office against the defendant as the employer of the police officer. The issue for the courts was whether the actions of the police officer could be the basis of an award of exemplary damages.

In considering its judgment, the members of the House of Lords bore in mind the report of the Law Commission which in 1997 recommended that the availability of exemplary damages should extend to all torts regardless of whether such categories had been recognised prior to 1964 ('Report on aggravated, exemplary and restitutional damages', Law Com. No. 247, 1997). Discussing this issue, and supporting the view of the Law Commission, Lord Mackay said at 45:

JUDGMENT

'The issue is determined by whether the factual situation is covered by either of Lord Devlin's formulations.'

Rejecting the 'cause of action' approach taken in *Broome v Cassell*, Lord Nicholls said that it represented at 55:

JUDGMENT

'an arbitrary and irrational restriction on the availability of exemplary damages'.

Lord Nicholls went on to say at 63:

JUDGMENT

'an arbitrary and irrational restriction on the availability of exemplary damages. . . . On occasion conscious wrongdoing by a defendant is so outrageous, his disregard of the [claimant's] rights so contumelious, that something more is needed to show that the law will not tolerate such behaviour. Without an award of exemplary damages, justice will not have been done.'

The present position

Accepting as one must, that the position is now that explained by the House of Lords in *Kuddus v Chief Constable of Leicestershire*, it is informative to consider examples of those cases where the courts have considered the issue of exemplary damages in those circumstances suggested by Lord Devlin in *Rookes v Barnard*.

In the case of oppressive, arbitrary or unconscionable action by servants of the government it is clear that there can be a punitive remedy for blatant abuse of power by civil servants or other agents of the government. An example of this is found in the following case.

CASE EXAMPLE

Huckle v Money [1763] 2 Wils 205

The defendant was detained pursuant to a search warrant for no more than six hours, during which time he was given 'beefsteaks and beer'. Notwithstanding this good treatment, the court held that the fact that the warrant was issued to obtain evidence at 207:

JUDGMENT

'is worse than the Spanish inquisition . . . it is a more daring public attack upon the liberty of the subject'.

The purpose of the category seems to be to ensure that executive powers are not exercised in an abusive way. Police officers are not strictly servants of the government but their actions are covered by these rules. Actions by publicly owned corporate bodies are only covered if the body is exercising an executive function. In *AB v South West Water Services Ltd* [1993] 1 All ER 609 it was held that a publicly owned monopoly supplier of water did not exercise executive functions and was not covered.

Lord Devlin's second category is intended to catch behaviour by the defendant which shows:

i cynical self-interest in calculating that profit will exceed any compensation to which the claimant may be entitled; and

ii knowledge that the action is against the law or a blatant disregard of whether the action is or is not lawful.

Mere carelessness by the defendant will not suffice. No precise definition of what will suffice can be given but it seems that the courts are looking for some evidence of deliberate, calculated action. It is clear that there is no need to show that the defendant made any precise calculation.

In *John v MGN Ltd* [1997] QB 586, a case in which the singer Elton John was the subject of a libel, it was suggested:

i a general calculation that publication would aid sales of the newspaper; and

ii any negotiated settlement or even any award of damages would be less than the profit from the increased sales was enough.

19.1.3 Damages for personal injury

pecuniary loss
damages that can be calculated in financial terms, e.g. loss of earnings

non-pecuniary loss
compensation for pain, suffering and loss of amenities where judges have developed rates of compensation

Assessing unliquidated damages for personal injury is fraught with difficulty. How can such injury be compensated for by money? The award is divided into three parts:

1 pre-trial **pecuniary loss;**
2 loss of future earnings; and
3 **non-pecuniary loss.**

We will look at the first two categories together and then turn to the third. Before turning to these, it should be remembered what the purpose is of damages by way of compensation.

JUDGMENT

Lord Blackburn, in *Livingstone v Raywards Coal Co* (1880) 5 App Cas 25, at 39 stated:

> [W]here any injury is to be compensated by damages, in settling the sum of money to be given in reparation of damages you should as nearly as possible get at that sum of money which will put the party who has been injured, or who has suffered, in the same position as he would have been in if he had not sustained the wrong for which he is now getting his compensation or reparation.

Pecuniary loss

It is possible for losses falling into this category to be assessed in money terms. The claimant will be able to provide evidence of actual expenditure relating to the injury and future earnings can be quantified.

Expenses

Many items of expenditure can simply be proved by the production of receipts or similar evidence. This can include the cost of private medical treatment actually incurred as there is no requirement to use the National Health Service (Law Reform (Personal Injuries) Act 1948, s2(4)). Where it is used, the NHS has the right to recover costs relating to treatment resulting from a road traffic accident from the third party's insurers (Road Traffic (NHS Charges) Act 1999) but this does not apply to the cost of future treatment.

The claimant may claim the cost of future private medical care but once the award has been made, the court has no supervisory powers and it is for the claimant to decide whether or not to use NHS facilities after all. At the time of the award, the court may take into account the cost of care which the claimant will be unable to receive privately and, indeed, if the court is satisfied that private treatment will not in fact be used for whatever reason, no award can be made to cover private costs.

Apart from the choice to use private medical care, there is a requirement that the expenditure is reasonably incurred. By way of example, a claimant is free to choose between permanent care in an institution or at home. The difference in cost is not decisive but the basis of the choice must be reasonable. It will be more difficult for the claimant to show that the choice of home-care is reasonable where the alternative cost of institutional care is much less.

Where a relative or other person provides necessary care rather than a person employed for that purpose, the carer has no direct claim. Since *Donnelly v Joyce* [1974] QB 454 the cost of such services, whether actually paid for or not, has been recoverable by the claimant. This would certainly cover net loss of earnings by a family member who has given up work to care for the claimant but will not otherwise amount to the commercial rate for the services.

Loss of future earnings

It is unfortunately the position, that in cases of personal injury caused by negligence, the claimant may have their earning capacity reduced because of injury sustained. The injury may also reduce the life expectancy of the claimant resulting in lost years or in other words, additional years of life which the claimant would have enjoyed if they had not been injured.

The court has to calculate the sum which will, when invested, produce a sum representing the claimant's lost earnings. This is done in two stages:

1 assessment of net annual loss; and

2 multiplying this figure by the number of years such loss is likely to continue.

The net annual loss is usually gross wages less tax, social security contributions, pension contributions and any other deductions which would have been made from gross income. At first sight this looks simple but how many people can be certain of what the future holds? Opportunity may knock, enabling the claimant to increase earnings, or unemployment may strike, causing a drastic reduction. A claimant may argue that the injury has resulted in the loss of a chance of fame and/or fortune. In such cases, the court will make as realistic assessment as possible of the chances of the claimant actually achieving the goal. This happened in the following case example.

CASE EXAMPLE

Doyle v Wallace [1998] PIQR Q146

The claimant was unable to work following a car accident. She had been planning to qualify as a drama teacher but, if she was not successful, to work as a clerk. As it was too early to say on the basis of her studies to that date whether or not she would have qualified, the court assessed her chances of qualifying at 50 per cent and her net future income at halfway between what she would have earned as a clerk and the higher pay she could have expected as a teacher.

Once the net annual loss has been calculated it would seem a simple calculation to multiply this figure by the relevant number of years throughout which it might have been earned. The courts will, however, take account of what have been described as 'the normal vicissitudes of life', for example, that the claimant might not have worked until retirement age.

Even after these figures have been assessed, it is not simple to calculate the lump sum payable. The court needs to decide what capital sum must be invested to produce an annual income of the right amount. This takes into account the fact that interest will accrue on the investment and the fact that the claimant will be expected to use part of the capital to supplement the income. A major problem is caused by inflation, which can fluctuate widely over a long period of time with the result that the return on the invested income can be seriously affected. The courts use actuarial tables (the Ogden Tables) prepared by insurance experts as well as guidance issued by the Lord Chancellor as to the likely rate of return on investments. By the Damages (Personal Injury) Order 2017 (SI 2017 No. 206) the rate of return is presently set at −0.75 per cent. Previously this had been set at 2.5 so this is quite a change. The courts do not have to follow the guidance, the Damages Act 1996 s1 granting discretion to depart from it where appropriate. This change has been made in order to reflect the amount that claimants could expect to earn by investing their compensation.

Lost years

In cases where a claimant has lost years or in other words been deprived of the additional years of life which they would have enjoyed but for their injury, adults can usually claim for their loss of earnings for these years. Historically, child claimants could not successfully claim for lost years. In *CCC v Sheffield Teaching Hospitals NHS Foundation Trust*, [2026] UKSC 5 which was a leapfrog appeal from the High Court directly to the Supreme Court, the Supreme Court delivered a landmark ruling has determined that lost years particularly by a child claimant, can be recovered contrary to previous authority.

LEAPFROG

A leapfrog appeal is where an appeal can be made from a lower court directly to a higher court bypassing or leaping over the court in the middle. For example, an appeal can be made from the High Court or a Divisional Court directly to the Supreme Court bypassing the Court of Appeal. A leapfrog appeal is usually used when there are exceptional circumstances which require a direct appeal to the higher court and that it is in the interests of justice.

A leapfrog appeal was necessary in this case because if the case had been appealed to the Court of Appeal, the Court of Appeal would have been bound by its previous decision hence why the Supreme Court was asked to review the correctness of the decision in *Croke v Wiseman* [1982] 1 WLR 71.

CASE EXAMPLE

CCC v Sheffield Teaching Hospitals NHS Foundation Trust, [2026] UKSC 5

The child claimant in this case suffered a severe brain injury at birth and was not expected to live beyond the age of 29. The defendants accepted responsibility for their negligence but disputed the damages that should be awarded. The defendants agreed that *loss of earnings* to age 29 should be awarded but disputed that earning for *lost years* should be awarded. The argument for the claimant was that but for the negligence, she would have worked and retired aged 68 considering the family's background and environment, when she would have been entitled to a pension. It was argued that earnings for these lost years, should be recoverable. Previously, the House of Lords in *Pickett v British Rail Engineering Ltd* [1980] AC 136 held that *adults* can recover for loss of earnings where their life expectancy has been reduced due to negligence, not least because they are likely to have dependants. By contrast, the decision in *Croke* meant that *children* could not recover for such future loss of earnings if their life expectancy had been reduced due to negligence. One reason advanced for this distinction is that a child is unlikely to have dependents. The reason given for this distinction is that to determine how much a child would go on to earn was too speculative. What education would the parents have been able to give the child? What if one or other of them died, would the education have been interrupted? If not, how far would the child have succeeded? By a majority of 4–1, the Supreme Court decided that children must be treated the same as adults when assessing lost years.

Lord Reed in *CCC* commented at paragraphs 48–49 that:

JUDGMENT

'The decision of the majority in *Croke v Wiseman* that no award for the lost years should be made where the claimant was a young child was based, as explained above, on the absence of dependants. That reasoning is inconsistent both with legal principle and with the relevant authorities. There is no reason of legal principle why a claimant's ability to obtain an award in respect of his own pecuniary losses should depend on the existence of dependants. The claim for lost years is in respect of the claimant's own loss, not in respect of anyone else's, and his or her right to damages is not in any way dependent on how they might be used.'

Lord Reed went on the say at paragraph 58 that evidential difficulties caused by the defendant, in inflicting a severe injury on a young child, should not be allowed to deprive the child of just compensation. This approach offers a sense of fairness and justice since the defendant who caused the harm should not be able to benefit from the difficulties that the claimant may encounter in proving their loss. Remember, this is distinct to establishing causation earlier in the claim which requires the claimant to prove their case on the balance of probabilities usually using the but for test. By contrast, Lady Rose in her dissenting judgment at paragraph 164–165 maintained that:

JUDGMENT

'". . . there is a principled distinction between the position of [an adult]. . . and young children . . ." The difference is that for an adult claimant, the court has before it some evidence of the individual characteristics and abilities of the person whose loss is being compensated. Based on that evidence, the court can make findings about what that person would have achieved in their working life if their life had not been irrevocably changed by the defendant's negligence. The court can then assess the value of what the person has lost. Where the claimant is a child and there is no evidence about how that individual would have grown and developed, the court is required instead to calculate damages on the basis of assumptions about the child's future abilities, opportunities and earning power, based on factors such as their gender and their family background, including their social class.

Not only does that push the court into uncomfortable territory . . . but it contradicts a fundamental principle of tort law which is that the loss to be compensated is the loss suffered by this individual claimant.'

CRITIQUING THE LAW

Do you think that Lady Rose is correct? Do you think that a child claimant who has not yet suffered loss but has been deprived of earning potential and capacity should be awarded damages?

Deductions

It is a basic principle that a person should not be compensated from more than one source for the same injury. There are exceptions for certain social security benefits and for some other sources of compensation.

Social security benefits. For many years the sum awarded to the claimant was reduced by the amount of social security benefits payable. In 1989 this was changed to enable relevant benefits to be recouped from the defendants or their insurers but the result was that on occasions the claimant would be left without any compensation and it continued to allow the insurers to avoid payment of compensation in full. The position is now governed by the Social Security (Recovery of Benefits) Act 1997 which provides that damages may only be reduced if certain benefits equivalent to particular heads of damage have been paid. Schedule 2 specifies the relevant benefits which will be set against loss of earnings, the cost of care and the loss of mobility. By way of an example, attendance allowance is taken into account against the heading 'loss of care' and income support is set against 'loss of income.'

The result of this complex legislation is that the claimant will receive full compensation although some of it may come from social security benefits which are then paid back to the State by the defendants or their insurers.

Other sources of compensation. Sums paid by way of sickness benefit by an employer are taken into account but not a disability pension paid by an employer, insurance payouts from personal accident cover taken out by the claimant or payments made on a charitable basis. This obviously means that the claimant does in fact 'profit' in the sense that income is increased.

The approach has been criticised by the Law Commission ('Damages for personal injury: collateral benefits', Consultation Paper 147, 1997) but continues to be used by the courts. The reasoning seems to be that to do otherwise would:

i discourage employers from making proper arrangements for their employees;

ii discourage people from obtaining sensible insurance cover;

iii be an unreasonable rebuff to those seeking to act benevolently in response to another's misfortune;

iv allow tortfeasors to escape full liability.

CASE EXAMPLE

Parry v Cleaver [1970] AC 1

Considering the issue of collateral benefits, the House of Lords held that by ignoring insurance payments under an employer's scheme the court acknowledged the fact that the claimant had in fact 'paid for' the benefit either directly through contributions or indirectly through past service to the employers. In relation to policies taken out by the claimant, the public interest was served by encouraging people to protect themselves in this way, and to deduct such sums might discourage them from doing so.

Discussing charitable payments Lord Reid said at 14:

JUDGMENT

'It would be revolting to the ordinary man's sense of justice, and therefore contrary to public policy, that the sufferer should have his damages reduced so that he would gain nothing from the benevolence of his friends or relations or the public at large, and that the only gainer would be the wrongdoer.'

Non-pecuniary loss

The difficulty of assessing such awards is immense. In an Australian case, *Todorovic v Waller* [1987] 37 ALR 481, Gibbs CJ and Mr Justice Wilson in a joint judgment commented that: 'Although the aim of the court . . . is to make good to the [claimant], as far as money can do, the loss which he has suffered, it is obvious that it is impossible to assess damages for pain and suffering and loss of amenities . . . by any process of arithmetical calculation.'

Despite the difficulties some principles have evolved to enable the courts to assess such damages. This is dealt under two heads, namely damages for:

i pain and suffering; and
ii loss of amenity.

The meaning of pain and suffering is clear and will include worry about the future as well as mental suffering caused by knowledge that life expectancy may have been reduced. It can also include awareness of impending death unless the circumstances of the accident are such that the claimant would have been unaware (*Hicks v Chief Constable of South Yorkshire* [1992] 2 All ER 65 – one of the Hillsborough cases where no award was made for the victims of suffocation for the pain preceding death). A victim who remains unconscious may receive a reduced sum taking account of the fact that there is no awareness.

The term 'loss of amenity' refers to the changes in lifestyle which the claimant will suffer as a result of the injury. A keen amateur sportsperson may recover under this head for inability to continue the sport. It is an objective judgment so that an award under this head will be made to someone who is permanently unconscious. While it may seem odd that a person is compensated even when unable to comprehend their loss, the award for loss of amenity continues.

The principles governing awards under these heads were explained by the House of Lords in 1980.

CASE EXAMPLE

Lim Poh Choo v Camden and Islington Area Health Authority [1980] AC 174

The claimant was the victim of medical negligence which caused her to suffer extensive and permanent brain damage. As a result for most of the time she was barely aware and at all times she needed total care.

Lord Devlin explained that damages for pain and suffering (at 188):

JUDGMENT

'depend upon the [claimant's] personal awareness of pain, her capacity for suffering. [Damages for loss of amenity] are awarded for the fact of deprivation, a substantial loss, whether the [claimant] is aware of it or not'.

He went on to acknowledge at 189:

JUDGMENT

'comparability matters. Justice requires that such awards . . . be consistent with the general level accepted by the judges.'

The consequence of the requirement that awards should be comparable is that the courts have created a 'tariff' of the amounts appropriate to different categories of claim involving loss of amenity. This normally takes the form of lower and upper brackets within which the particular award will fall. Over the years, the awards decreased in value and the Law Commission concluded that they were far too low ('Damages for Personal Injury: Non-pecuniary Loss', Law Com. No. 257, 1999). This finding was accepted by the Court of Appeal in *Heil v Rankin* [2001] QB 272. Although the Court refused to raise the tariffs by the amount suggested by the Law Commission, it recommended that certain categories of awards should be increased where the injuries were more serious. The scale amount will now be increased by about one-third for very serious cases, for example quadriplegia and severe brain damage, tapering down to no increase in awards of £10,000 and below.

Once for all settlement

We have seen the difficulties inherent in calculating an appropriate amount of compensation. The claimant, the defendant and the court are forced to rely on assessments of what the future holds. The need for a crystal ball to predict the future may be particularly acute in the context of certain types of injury where later deterioration may occur, but whether or not it does in fact do so is unpredictable.

Only one award can be made

Public policy dictates that only one action can be brought based on the same wrong. A later action cannot be brought if the consequences turn out to be worse than was taken into account at the time of the trial.

In the case of compensation for personal injuries, the problem has been partly addressed by the Senior Courts Act 1981 s32A. This applies where there is a known chance that the claimant's health may seriously deteriorate at some time in the future but where there is no certainty when or if it will happen. In such cases an award of provisional damages can be made based on the assumption that such deterioration will not occur, but allowing the claimant to obtain further compensation should it do so.

Another way to address the problem is found by splitting the hearing into two parts, the first concerned with liability, the second with assessment of damages. This allows the medical situation to become clearer and a more accurate assessment of the claimant's loss to be made.

Structured settlements

An obvious solution to the problem would be to introduce a mechanism for reassessment of the claimant's position at fixed intervals. This has been rejected by the Law Commission (Law Com. No. 56 HC 373, 1973) although it was supported by the Pearson Commission.

In the meantime one potentially helpful development has occurred with the creation of structured settlements. These are governed by the Damages Act 1996, s5 which provides:

SECTION

's5(1) . . . a "structured settlement" means an agreement settling a claim . . . for personal injury on terms whereby

a the damages are to consist wholly or partly of periodical payments; and
b the person to whom the payments are to be made is to receive them as the annuitant under [annuities] purchased for him by the person against whom the claim is brought . . . or his insurer.'

The section goes on to provide that the amounts may be for life or specified periods and may be for a fixed sum subject to increases or reassessment to ensure that its value in real terms is maintained.

The court has no power to order structured settlements, nor is there any mechanism to take account of later deterioration in the claimant's health. Not surprisingly, the Law Commission did not recommend that the court should have power to impose such settlements ('Structured settlements and interim and provisional damages', Law Com. No. 224, 1994).

19.1.4 Damages for damage to property

The basic rule is that the claimant must be restored to the position prior to the damage to, or destruction of, the property.

In the case of damage to property, the claimant is entitled to a sum which represents the amount by which the value of the property has been diminished. This will usually be the cost of repair unless this outweighs the market value of the property. In the latter case only the diminution in value will normally be payable. Where property has been destroyed, the market value of property at the time of destruction will be awarded.

In both cases an additional sum for loss of use until repair or replacement will be awarded where this is reasonable. In the case of a business this can include a sum for loss of profit.

19.1.5 Damage to land and buildings

Although the basic principle is the same as for other damage to property, the issue of reasonableness is more important when the cost of restoration exceeds the value of the land. It may make commercial sense to rebuild on the same site rather than move elsewhere in which case the cost of rebuilding might well be reasonable and thus the basis of the award (for a more detailed discussion of this issue see section 8.7.1).

19.1.6 Some general principles

We have already seen the first important principle that the claimant should only be compensated for actual loss. This was reaffirmed by Lord Justice Otton in *Indata Equipment Supplies Ltd (t/a Autofleet) v ACL Ltd* [1998] FSR 248 when he said (at 249) that the correct measure of tortious damages is:

JUDGMENT

> 'such sum as would . . . put the [claimant] into the position it would have been in had it not been for the tort'.

The second principle is that the claimant has a duty to mitigate their loss by taking any steps which it is reasonable for them to take. A claimant seeking compensation for personal injury is expected to undergo medical treatment which may improve the situation. Where such treatment has unreasonably been refused, damages will be assessed as if the treatment had been given and effected the anticipated improvement.

A claimant who is unable to pursue former employment because of the injury is expected to take reasonable steps to obtain alternative employment. The fact that the new work may be lower paid will be reflected in the calculation of lost earnings.

Where property has been damaged, we have already seen that consequential losses will only be recoverable if they have been reasonably incurred. A business which is deprived of the use of essential equipment may recover the cost of hiring similar equipment if by that means the loss of profit is minimised.

19.1.7 The problem of death

As a general rule, the fact that the claimant or the defendant has died will not affect liability as the cause of action will survive for the benefit of or against the estate (Law Reform (Miscellaneous Provisions) Act 1934, s1). A deceased claimant's estate cannot benefit from an award of exemplary damages, nor can loss of income include any period after the date of death. Funeral expenses can be claimed where the defendant's tort is responsible for the death.

By virtue of the Fatal Accidents Act 1976 (as amended) certain relatives of a deceased person may bring a separate action against a person who has caused the death. The action, which is brought by the personal representatives of the deceased, lies for the benefit of:

i a surviving spouse, former spouse or common law spouse;

ii a parent or person treated by the deceased as a parent;

iii children;

iv a brother, sister, uncle or aunt of the deceased.

Damages are assessed on the basis of the extent to which the claimant was dependent on the deceased. The purpose of the award is to compensate for the loss of financial support, although an additional sum can be awarded for loss of services and emotional support.

A surviving spouse or a parent of a deceased child is entitled to damages for bereavement. The amount of such damages is set by statute and currently stands at £15,120 pursuant to s1(1) Fatal Accidents Act 1976.

19.2 Injunction

19.2.1 Generally

An injunction is an order of the court which must be obeyed. Breach of injunction amounts to contempt of court and as such is punishable by imprisonment in more serious cases. The remedy is theoretically available in respect of all torts but is perhaps most commonly used to prevent recurrence in cases of private nuisance, trespass to land and defamation.

It must be remembered that the remedy is equitable which means that it is discretionary. The court must be satisfied that the grant of an injunction is appropriate in the particular circumstances. Unlike damages, which are granted as of right where a legal right has been infringed, there is no right to an injunction. It will be refused, for example, where the claimant has acquiesced in the sense that the defendant has been led to believe that the claimant does not object to the infringement of the claimant's right. Where the claimant has acted to mislead the court or the defendant in some way, the order may well be refused. It must be remembered that the maxims of equity will always apply. (For further discussion of equitable maxims, you may care to consult a text on Equity and Trusts.)

19.2.2 Damages in lieu?

While there is discretion to award damages in lieu of an injunction, the courts are concerned to ensure that the right to break the law should not be available for purchase by those who are in a position to pay. This could amount to endorsing the conception that there is one law for the rich and one for the poor. As Lord Justice Lindley commented in *Shelfer v City of London Electric Lighting* [1895] 1 Ch 287 at 315:

JUDGMENT

> 'the court has always protested against the notion that it ought to allow a wrong to continue simply because the wrongdoer is able and willing to pay for the injury he may inflict'.

(For a more detailed discussion of this principle in the context of nuisance see section 9.6.2.)

We have already seen that in cases of nuisance the courts may 'tailor' an injunction to reach a sensible compromise between the interests of the claimant and the defendant (*Kennaway v Thompson* [1980] 3 WLR 361).

The courts also try to balance the public interest against private rights. In *Miller v Jackson* [1977] QB 966 Lord Denning MR took the view that where public and private interests conflict, the public interest should prevail (at 981):

JUDGMENT

> 'The public interest lies in protecting the environment by preserving our playing fields in the face of mounting development, and by enabling our youth to enjoy all the benefits of outdoor games such as cricket and football.'

Lord Denning's view was criticised and the principles set out in *Shelfer* were reaffirmed. An injunction should only be refused and damages awarded in lieu where:

1 if the injury to the plaintiff's legal rights is small;

2 and is one which is capable of being estimated in money;

3 and is one which can be adequately compensated by a small money payment;

4 and the case is one in which it would be oppressive to the defendant to grant an injunction – then damages in substitution for an injunction may be given.

As discussed earlier in Chapter 9, the guidance had come to be treated as the law as opposed to simply guidance to assist judges in exercising their discretion. So it was the position prior to *Coventry v Lawrence*, that the four criteria are normally to be applied, so that if all four tests are satisfied, there is little jurisdiction to award an injunction but if they are not satisfied then an injunction may be awarded. This is contrary to the point that an injunction is a discretionary remedy. It was held in *Coventry v Lawrence* that it requires an exceptional case before damages should be awarded in lieu of an injunction and the conduct of the parties should be considered when the court exercises its discretion. This matter was again reviewed in *Fearn*.

Where the wrong is trivial or very temporary, damages may be awarded in lieu of an injunction. Sometimes public interest will prevent an injunction from being awarded as was explained by Lord Leggatt in *Fearn v Tate Gallery* [2023] UKSC 4 at 120–122:

JUDGMENT

> 'The correct approach – for which the leading authority is now this court's decision in *Lawrence* – where significant considerations of public interest are raised is for the court to take this factor into account, not in determining liability, but, where liability is established, in deciding whether to grant an injunction or to award damages . . . But it is fundamental to the integrity of any system of property rights that, in any such case, the individuals whose rights are infringed or overridden receive compensation for the violation of their rights. In other words, the public interest may sometimes justify awarding damages rather than granting an injunction to restrain the defendant's harmful activity, but it cannot justify denying the victim any remedy at all.'

19.2.3 Types of injunctions available

Mandatory injunctions

A mandatory injunction requires the defendant to take some active step to put matters right. It is rarely granted. The principles which will guide the court were set out in the following case example.

CASE EXAMPLE

***Redland Bricks Ltd v Morris* [1970] AC 652**

Excavations by the defendants on their land had meant that part of the claimant's land had subsided and the rest was likely to slip. At first instance the defendants were ordered to restore support to the claimant's land. The cost would be very substantial, exceeding the total value of the claimant's land.

On appeal to the House of Lords Lord Upjohn set out some general principles:

i there must be a very strong probability that substantial damage will be caused;

ii damages would be inadequate as a remedy;

iii the defendants' behaviour is relevant – have they tried to 'steal a march' on the claimant or the court or have they behaved reasonably albeit wrongly?

iv it must be possible to frame a mandatory injunction in such a way that the defendants are very clear as to precisely what needs to be done.

For further discussion of these issues, particularly the reasonableness of the defendants' action, see section 8.7.

Prohibitory injunctions

This is an order of the court to prevent a recurrence of the tort. It is most commonly found in actions for nuisance, trespass to land and defamation where there is a risk that the tortious behaviour may be repeated.

Quia timet *injunctions*

In rare cases it may be clear that a tort is about to be committed. In such cases, it is possible for the claimant to anticipate matters and to ask the court to prevent the defendant from proceeding. The injunction is rarely granted as the claimant must show:

i there is a high probability of substantial damage; and

ii the probability is imminent.

It is tempting to believe that this would be an effective remedy to prevent publication of allegedly defamatory material in those rare cases where the claimant has prior warning. This has become less likely since the Human Rights Act 1998 came into effect. The provisions of s12 are very relevant and are discussed in the next paragraph.

interim (interlocutory)
An injunction given before the actual dispute is heard – to avoid harm that may be caused to the claimant before the action comes to court

Interim (interlocutory) injunctions

Where it can be shown that an order is urgently necessary to prevent substantial damage, the court can sometimes be persuaded to grant an interim injunction. This has the effect of stopping the allegedly tortious behaviour for a short time pending a full hearing of an application for a prohibitory injunction. If an interim injunction is granted, the claimant will normally be required to give an undertaking to the court to pay damages and costs if the later action fails. In cases involving alleged defamation, the Human Rights Act 1998 s12 is very relevant. The Act provides that where the court is considering a matter which raises the right to freedom of expression:

SECTION

's12(3) no [interim] relief is to be granted so as to restrain publication before trial unless the court is satisfied that the applicant is likely to establish that publication should not be allowed'.

The Act goes on in s12(4)(a) to require the court to consider the extent to which the material is likely to be available to the public and whether it is in the public interest that the material should be published.

The court will not grant such an injunction where the defendant alleges an intention to rely on the defence of justification or fair comment.

19.3 Other remedies

We have already discussed self-help remedies which are applicable to specific torts:

i self-defence in the context of trespass to the person;

ii necessity in the context of trespass to the person, negligence and trespass to land;

iii abatement in the context of nuisance;

iv and reference should be made to the appropriate sections for further detail.

19.4 Limitation periods

19.4.1 Generally

It is a fundamental principle that people should not be at risk of having an action brought against them for an indefinite period of time. In addition to the unfairness caused to that person, a very practical difficulty can arise in finding the evidence. Documents may have been lost or destroyed, witnesses may have disappeared and memories fade with time. For this reason a claimant is required to seek a remedy within a specified period. In Chapter 1 we saw the effect that this requirement can have in *Letang v Cooper* [1965] 1 QB 232 where the claimant sought to use the old forms of action in order to avoid a limitation period. As we shall see, in some cases it may be possible for the claimant to obtain the court's leave to bring an action after the limitation period has expired. The court will in such cases be very concerned to ensure that justice is done to both parties.

The present law is found in the Limitation Act 1980 as amended by the Latent Damage Act 1986 and the Defamation Act 1996.

19.4.2 The basic periods

These are as follows:

- claims which do not involve personal injury – six years;
- claims involving personal injury, even if only part of the claim – three years.

In each case the time is calculated from the date on which the cause of action accrued. In most cases this is clear – the event happens, damage is immediately known to have happened and it is immediately possible for an action to be brought. The cause of action accrues on the date the event happened.

This is easy to see in relation to those torts which are actionable per se and in many others, but what of the cases where the damage lies hidden for some time? Special rules dealing with these cases are considered in the next sections.

19.4.3 Latent damage to property

In those cases where damage has to be proved, the damage can lie hidden for some time and not become apparent within the limitation period.

The problems became apparent in cases about defective buildings heard during the 1970s and 1980s. In *Sparham-Souter v Town & Country Developments (Essex) Ltd* [1976] QB 858 it had been held, by the Court of Appeal, that the limitation period would run from the date on which the claimant knew or ought reasonably to know that damage had occurred. This was known as the 'reasonable discovery' test. Some years later, in *Pirelli General Cable Works Ltd v Oscar Faber & Partners* [1983] 2 AC 1, the House of Lords overruled the reasonable discovery test.

CASE EXAMPLE

***Pirelli General Cable Works Ltd v Oscar Faber & Partners* [1983] 2 AC 1**

The defendants were consulting engineers who had designed tall chimneys. As a result of negligent design, cracks appeared in the chimneys. The damage was not discovered for some considerable time by which date the limitation period for a claim in negligence had expired. The claimants argued that time did not begin to run until the damage could have been discovered using reasonable diligence.

Time would start to run when physical damage occurred regardless of whether or not it was at that time discoverable. The claim was accordingly out of time and barred.

As a result of the confusion and apparent injustice, the Latent Damage Act 1986 was passed which inserted new provisions into the Limitation Act 1980.

By s14A(4)(b) a new period was available of three years from the date on which the claimant knew or reasonably could have known about the defect and that it was due to the defendant's negligence. This meant that a claim could be brought many years after the expiry of the usual limitation period of six years.

It was still considered that it would be unjust for defendants to be at risk for an indefinite time. To deal with this, s14B provides that there is a 'long stop' of 15 years running from the date of the last act of negligence which could be the basis of the claim. By way of example, in *Pirelli* the defendants would have remained at risk for a total period of 15 years from the date of the negligence which caused the defect.

Property may well have changed hands during the limitation period. This could mean that the right to bring an action was lost as the person who originally had a cause of action would no longer be able to bring a claim. This has been dealt with by the Latent Damage Act 1986 s3(1), which provides that the right of action vests in a successor in title to the property. The limitation period is still calculated from the date on which the original owner would have been able to claim.

19.4.4 Personal injuries

As we have seen, the basic limitation period for any claim which is concerned wholly or partly with personal injury is three years from the date the cause of action accrues. This has always caused problems, particularly in the case of certain industrial diseases, where the injury may not become apparent for many years.

When an injury has occurred the Limitation Act 1980, s11(4) provides that the limitation period runs for the period of three years from the date of the injury or, where this is not immediately apparent, for a period of three years from the date on which the claimant has knowledge of the injury. A claimant is deemed to have the necessary knowledge in circumstances set out in s14(1) namely:

- the claimant is aware that the injury is significant; and
- the injury is due in whole or in part to the defendant's negligence, nuisance or breach of duty; and
- the claimant knows the identity of the defendant; and
- if the alleged wrongdoer was someone other than the defendant, for example an employee in cases where the defendant has vicarious liability, the claimant knows the identity of that person and the necessary additional facts to support the claim, for example the fact that the person was employed at the relevant time by the defendant.

Injury is regarded as 'significant' if a claimant would reasonably have regarded it as sufficiently serious to bring an action against a defendant who did not dispute liability. This complicated meaning was interpreted by the Court of Appeal in *Spargo v North Essex District Health Authority* [1997] PIQR P235:

1. The claimant needs broad knowledge of the act or omission which caused the injury.
2. There must be a real possibility that the act or omission in question is the cause of the injury.

3 The claimant will be regarded as having the necessary knowledge when matters have reached the stage where it would be reasonable for the claimant to investigate whether or not there is a cause of action, for example by seeking legal advice.

4 A claimant who:

- believes that the cause is known but who is mistaken; or
- one whose knowledge is so vague that they cannot reasonably be expected to investigate a possible claim; or
- one whose knowledge is such that they would need to check with an expert for more information

will not have the necessary knowledge to start the limitation period running.

A claimant must seek the advice and information which it is reasonable to seek but will not be deemed to have knowledge of matters only available as the result of failure by an expert to identify the problem.

CASE EXAMPLE

Marston v British Railways Board [1976] ICR 124

The claimant suffered injury when a piece of metal flew off a hammer. An expert who conducted a hardness test on the hammer failed to notice the defect which caused the accident. It was held that the claimant was not deemed to be aware of the cause of action and a later claim was allowed.

Where death has resulted and a claim is to be made under the Fatal Accidents Act 1976, the limitation period is three years from the date of death or the date on which the deceased had the necessary knowledge whichever is the later (Limitation Act 1980, s12(2)).

19.4.5 Other statutory provisions

Various statutes impose specific limitation periods

By the Defamation Act 1996, which inserted s4A into the Limitation Act 1980, an action for defamation or malicious falsehood must be brought within a period of 12 months from the date of the publication. A cause of action in defamation does not survive the death of the person defamed.

As we have seen, an action under the Consumer Protection Act 1987 is subject to a 'long stop' of ten years from the date the product is put into circulation (Limitation Act 1980, s11A(3)).

The Merchant Shipping Act 1995 ensures that actions brought for damage to a vessel, cargo or persons on board the vessel caused by another vessel must be brought within two years.

19.4.6 The court's power to extend the limitation period

By the Limitation Act 1980, s33 the court has power to override the statutory time limits where it is equitable to do so. This power cannot be exercised in cases:

- brought under the Consumer Protection Act 1987;
- involving trespass to the person where the limit is six years.

The court must have regard to all relevant circumstances and in particular, but not exclusively, to:

- the length of and reasons for the delay;
- the effect, if any, on the evidence in the case, for example have documents been lost or destroyed or have witnesses become untraceable or unavailable;
- the behaviour of the defendant after the cause of action arose, for example what replies were given to requests for information;
- if the claimant has been disabled for any cause arising after the cause of action, how long that disability lasted;
- did the claimant act promptly and reasonably once the possibility of an action was known;
- steps taken by the claimant to obtain appropriate information from, for example, doctors, lawyers or other experts.

The discretion can only apply where no proceedings have been issued within the relevant period. A claimant who issues a claim and then does not proceed with it, will usually be unable to take advantage of s33. This is of particular importance now that the courts are taking a proactive role to ensure that claims are dealt with expeditiously. In such cases the claimant may have an action in negligence against professional advisers who have failed to take steps required. This is likely to mean that s33 cannot be used, but there is no general rule that this will follow. The judge's discretion is unfettered and the decision will reflect a balancing act between the prejudice caused to both parties by the delay.

The issue of discretionary extension of the limitation period has recently been considered by the House of Lords in a series of joined appeals, *A v Hoare and conjoined appeals* [2008] UKHL 6, which involved claims for sexual abuse brought out of time. While discretionary extension of the three-year period for personal injury claims applies to 'negligence, nuisance or breach of duty' the House of Lords in *Stubbings v Webb* [1993] AC 498 had held that there was no such discretion in the case of deliberate assault. In *Hoare* the House of Lords overruled *Stubbings v Webb* arguing that there was no rational explanation why Parliament would make the law harder for a person bringing a personal injury claim caused by a deliberate assault than one caused by negligence.

19.4.7 Legal disability

A claimant who suffers legal disability is not thereby disadvantaged. The limitation period will run for the relevant period from the time the disability ceases or the claimant dies. This means that a minor can bring an action for personal injury within three years of attaining majority (18 years of age) unless an action has previously been brought on their behalf. Someone who is of unsound mind when time begins to run is similarly protected. Where a person becomes of unsound mind after the date of accrual, the disability has no effect.

19.4.8 Fraud and concealment

The law is concerned to ensure that a person cannot benefit from fraud or other dishonest behaviour. The limitation periods are therefore subject to extension in some cases.

Where the claimant's action is based on fraudulent action, for example the tort of deceit, time only begins to run once the claimant has discovered, or ought by reasonable diligence to have discovered, the fraud.

In cases where the claimant's right of action has been deliberately concealed by the defendant, time will only start to run once the claimant has discovered, or ought to have discovered, the concealment.

19.4.9 The future?

The reader will have realised that the law in this area is extremely complex and confused. The Law Commission ('Law Commission, limitation of actions', Report No. 270, July 2001) has recommended:

1 the limitation period in all cases should be three years running from the date the cause of action is discoverable;
2 there should be an absolute 'long stop' of ten years;
3 in personal injury cases, the court should continue to have a discretion to extend the limitation period and no long stop would apply.

The reforms would continue to make special provision for actions under the Consumer Protection Act 1987 allowing for an absolute long stop of a different period.

In the case of those suffering legal disability, the Law Commission proposes:

1 In the case of infancy (minority) although the initial period would not run, the long stop would apply provided it did not come to an end before the minor reached 18.
2 In the case of adults, the initial period would not run but the overall long stop would apply.
3 Where a claimant is under a disability and has suffered personal injury but is in the care of a responsible adult ten years after the date of accrual or the date when they became disabled whichever is the later, the periods will run from the date the responsible adult knew or ought to have known the relevant facts. This would be subject to the court's discretion to grant leave to bring proceedings even after the end of the limitation period.

The reader is likely to agree that reform is needed. Whether the proposals would in reality simplify the situation is a matter to be seen if and when reform is implemented. To date, there is little sign that the Law Commission's proposals will be adopted.

KEY FACTS

Key facts on damages

Damages for personal injury	**Case/statute**
Pecuniary loss – covers actual expenditure including cost of medical treatment or private care if actually incurred or to be incurred in the future if reasonable.	
Loss of future earnings involves assessment of actual net annual loss multiplied by number of years of productive life – figure needs to represent that which will produce the necessary income over the period taking into account the gradual use of capital and the rate of inflation.	
Certain sums can be deducted from net loss of earnings including social security benefits and sickness benefits but not employers' disability pension, claimant's own health insurance or charitable payments.	*Parry v Cleaver* [1970]
A good example of the court's approach.	
Non-pecuniary loss	**Case/statute**
Includes a sum for pain and suffering which claimant must actually experience.	*Hicks v Chief Constable of S Yorks* [1992]
Additional sum is awarded for loss of amenity, i.e. necessary changes in lifestyle – awarded even when claimant unaware of the changes.	
For court's approach in particular see judgment of Lord Devlin.	*Lim Poh Choo v Camden & Islington AHA* [1980]
Problems with damages for personal injury	**Case/statute**
Only one award can be made – claimant cannot go back to court if situation changes.	
Problem partly alleviated by voluntary use of structured settlements which can be subject to reassessment.	Damages Act 1996, s5
Damages for damage to property	**Case/statute**
Sum represents diminution of value of the property.	
Usually cost of repair plus sum for loss of use until repair or replacement.	
Loss in value of property usual award where cost of repair outweighs value.	
Market value where property destroyed.	
General principles	**Case/statute**
Claimant is only compensated for actual loss – there should be no element of profit.	

(Continued)

(Continued)

Claimant under a duty to take reasonable steps to mitigate the loss.	
Death	**Case/statute**
Generally action will survive death of claimant or defendant, personal representatives acting on behalf of the estate.	Law Reform (Miscellaneous Provisions) Act 1934, s1
Deceased claimant cannot receive exemplary damages or loss of income after the date of death.	
Relatives who were financially dependent on deceased claimant have action in their own right.	
Surviving spouse or child entitled to damages for bereavement, presently £12,980.	

KEY FACTS

Key facts on injunction

Generally	Case/statute
Equitable order breach of which amounts to contempt of court and is punishable.	
Cannot be granted as of right – court must be satisfied that it is appropriate in the particular circumstances.	
Damages can be awarded in lieu but court must be wary not to allow a wrongdoer to buy the right to continue the wrong.	*Shelfer v City of London Electric Lighting* [1895]
Modern tendency for court to tailor the injunction to try to achieve balance between parties	*Coventry v Lawrence* [2014] UKSC 13
Mandatory injunction	**Case/statute**
An order to do something.	
For principles see –	*Redland Bricks v Morris* [1970]
Risk of substantial damage, damages would be inadequate, defendant's behaviour is relevant, defendant must know exactly what needs to be done.	
Prohibitory injunction	**Case/statute**
Prohibits wrongful act.	
Quia timet – granted in anticipation to prevent future wrongdoing – very rarely available.	
Interim (interlocutory) injunction	**Case/statute**
Will stop allegedly unlawful action pending full hearing for prohibitory injunction.	

(Continued)

(Continued)

Claimant usually required to give undertakings as to costs and payment of damages if action unsuccessful.	
Rarely available in defamation cases.	Human Rights Act 1998, s12(3)
Generally	**Case/statute**
Law found in –	Limitation Act 1980 as amended
Action must be started within prescribed period.	
Failure to do so means action barred.	
Basic period six years for claims not involving personal injury, three years for claims any part of which relates to personal injury.	
Latent damage to property	**Case/statute**
Time runs from when claimant knows or ought reasonably to have known the damage has occurred due to defendant's negligence.	s14A(4)(b)
Long stop of 15 years running from the date of the last act of negligence which could be the basis for the claim.	s14B
Personal injuries	**Case/statute**
Normally three years from the date of injury.	
In cases where injury is not immediately apparent, e.g. industrial disease, three years from date claimant has knowledge of the injury and the potential for a claim against the defendant.	s14(1) *Spargo v North Essex DHA* [1997]
Other limitation periods	Case/statute
Defamation – 12 months from date of publication.	Defamation Act 1996
Consumer protection – long stop of ten years from date product put into circulation.	Consumer Protection Act 1987
Damage to shipping cargo or person on board – two years. Trespass to the person – six years.	Merchant Shipping Act 1995
Power to allow action out of time	**Case/statute**
Found in –	Consumer Protection Act 1987
Cannot be used in relation to action under or in cases of trespass to the person.	
Court must be satisfied that it is reasonable in all the circumstances to grant leave taking into account relevant history and the conduct of both parties as well as the likely availability of evidence.	Limitation Act 1980, s33

(Continued)

(Continued)

Legal disability	Case/statute
A child has three years from attaining 18 if no previous action brought on the child's behalf.	
Someone of unsound mind has three years from recovery unless previous action brought on their behalf.	
Fraud and concealment	**Case/statute**
Time will only begin to run from the date when the claimant discovers or ought to have discovered the fraud or the concealment.	

SUMMARY

Remedies include:

- Damages – which can be general, special, contemptuous, nominal, exemplary, non-pecuniary.
- Injunctions – which can be mandatory, prohibitory, interim (interlocutory).

There are statutory limitation periods beyond which no action can be brought:

- Six years generally from the tort.
- Three years from the tort or the date of knowledge in personal injury claims.
- There are other fixed periods for other specific torts.
- There is also the means for a court to allow an action that is out of time in very strict circumstances.

Appendices

Appendix 1

Activity: essay writing

What follows is a sample essay title and guide on how to prepare to answer it.

It has been suggested that 'it is generally recognised that the rules governing recovery for damages for nervous shock (psychiatric harm) lack coherence, logic, justice and even plain common sense' (F A Trindale, 'Reformulation of the nervous shock rules' (2003) 119 *LQR* 204). In the light of the above *statement*, compare and evaluate the different rules applied by the courts to primary and secondary victims in cases of psychiatric harm.

Answering the question

There are usually two key elements to essays in law:

- First, you are required to identify and explain the areas of law as identified in the question.
- Second, you are required to answer the question set, which usually is in the form of some sort of critical element, that is you may very probably see the words 'discuss', 'analyse', 'critically consider', 'explain', etc.

Students for the most part seem quite capable of doing the first, but slightly less skilled at the second. The important points in any case are to ensure that you only deal with relevant legal material in your answer and that you do answer the question set, rather than one you have made up yourself, or the one that was on last year's paper.

For instance, in the case of the first point, in this essay you might say the following: psychiatric harm is an area of negligence. Negligence requires proof of the existence of a duty of care and breach of that duty and damage caused by the defendant that is not too remote a consequence of the breach. But you do not need to treat the examiner to everything that you know about the standard of care, or the 'but for test', etc., because none of that is directly relevant. In the case of the second point, the essay asks you to 'compare and evaluate' the rules applicable to different types of claimants in psychiatric harm. This clearly indicates that you must compare the different rules for dealing with primary and secondary victims, and since you are asked to evaluate, you will need to pass some sort of comment on whether the law treats both fairly, adequately, etc.

Relevant law

The appropriate law appears to be:

- Psychiatric harm is one of those novel duty situations in negligence and thus all the other rules of negligence apply.
- Psychiatric harm involves recognised psychiatric illness such as PTSD but not mere grief or other distress – compare *Reilly* and *Tredget*.
- Psychiatric harm involves recognised psychiatric illnesses such as PTSD but not mere grief or other distress.
- The rules on who can recover in what situation are now contained in *Alcock*.
- The law distinguishes between primary victims – those present at the scene of an incident and directly affected or injured by the defendant's negligent act or omission – and secondary victims – those indirectly affected by the trauma caused by the defendant's negligent act or omission.
- Primary victims can recover if they suffer physical as well as psychiatric injury, or if physical harm is foreseeable and they suffer nervous shock as a result – *Dulieu v White* or *Page v Smith*.
- Secondary victims must have a close tie of love and affection with a primary victim and close proximity in time and space to the traumatic event or its immediate aftermath – *McLoughlin v O'Brian and Paul v Wolverhampton* – or be a professional rescuer – *Chadwick v British Railways Board* and *Hale v London Underground*. Note also that such people must be of reasonable fortitude – *Bourhill v Young* – and that the psychiatric injury must result from the trauma being witnessed by their own unaided senses, either seeing or hearing.

Evaluation

The commentary in the essay requires you to compare the treatment of primary and secondary victims and to evaluate their treatment. Relevant comments might include:

- that the range of injuries that will allow liability is limited, although floodgates argument and state of medical knowledge may justify this and it has had some expansion – *Vernon v Bosley*;
- the primary victims generally have no problem recovering;
- consideration that since *White v Chief Constable of South Yorkshire*, professional rescuers must be identifiable as genuine primary victims in order to claim;
- consideration that, according to *Greatorex v Greatorex*, a rescuer could also claim if he could be classed as a genuine secondary victim, that is conform to all the requirements in *Alcock*;

- that close tie of love and affection is quite limited in scope – *Alcock;*
- and perhaps unfairly does not include close friendships or working relationships – *Robertson and Rough v Forth Road Bridge* and *Duncan v British Coal;*
- the immediate aftermath is quite narrowly defined – *Alcock* – and the widest point pre-dates the test – *McLoughlin v O'Brian but now see Paul v Wolverhampton;*
- that bystanders are treated unfairly in comparison to professional rescuers although they may suffer the same psychiatric injuries – *McFarlane v EE Caledonia;*
- that professional rescuers were originally treated more fairly in determining liability than were the relatives of primary victims – *Alcock* – but that the courts recognising the possible injustice have changed their stance on professional rescuers in relation to the 'Hillsborough' litigation – compare the Court of Appel in *Hicks v Chief Constable of South Yorkshire;*
- that public policy plays an important role in deciding on liability in nervous shock, particularly the 'floodgates' argument;
- that numerous cases seem to be out of line with the 'strict' rules – for example *Attia v British Gas* and nervous shock following witnessing damage to property, *Owens v Liverpool Corporation* and primary victim being a corpse, *Dooley v Cammell Laird* and primary victim being a work colleague of the claimant, *Tredget v Bexley Heath Authority* where the nervous shock seemed to be based on profound grief at the death of a child, *Hevican v Ruane* [1991] 3 All ER 65 where the nervous shock followed the claimant being informed of the death of his son and witnessing the body, was long after the immediate aftermath.

Of course it will usually be required of you in producing a discussion that you make references also to the arguments of academic commentators either in leading texts or journal articles.

You should also take care to follow whatever system for citation and use of tables and bibliography you have been given.

Appendix 2
Activity: applying the law

What follows is a reasonably straightforward problem question and a guide on how to answer it.

There are always four essential ingredients to answering problem questions:

- First, you must be able to identify which are the key facts in the problem, the ones on which any resolution of the problem will depend.
- Second, you will need to identify which is the appropriate law which applies to the particular situation in the problem.
- Third, you must apply the law to the facts.
- Finally, you will need to reach conclusions of some sort. If the question asks you to advise, then that is what you need to do. On the other hand, if the problem says 'Discuss the legal consequences of . . .' then you know that you should offer advice and guidance which illustrates and advises on any problems the parties may encounter whether they are in their favour or not.

Problem

Homer, his wife Marge and children Bart and Lisa go to the Springfield Holiday Camp for two weeks in August. In their holiday contract is the following clause: 'Neither the Springfield Holiday Camp nor their servants or agents will be liable for death or injury to visitors, howsoever caused.' A large notice to the same effect is placed at the entrance to the camp. The camp is owned and managed by Springfield Leisure Co.

Late one night while returning to the holiday chalet, which is high up on a slope, Homer falls down the steep steps that lead to the chalet from the road below. There is no guardrail to the steps, and the steps are also unlit. Homer suffers severe head injuries in the fall. Marge is electrocuted and badly burnt when she plugs in the kettle in the chalet's kitchenette. The socket has actually been left live due to the negligence of Shoddy Electric Co. who recently rewired the chalet.

Bart cuts himself badly and wrecks his jacket with a sharp knife when he sneaks into the kitchen in the camp restaurant to make himself a sandwich. The door is not locked but a notice on the door of the kitchen reads: 'Danger. Staff only'. Lisa suffers a very bad stomach upset when she eats berries on a bush growing by the chalet front door. The berries are poisonous.

Advise Homer, Marge, Bart and Lisa of any remedies that they might have for their injuries and against whom.

The facts

It is important to have a clear idea of what the principal facts are, particularly here where there are several different people and different problems involved. The main facts seem to be:

1. Springfield Leisure Co. own and manage the Springfield Holiday Camp.
2. Homer, Marge and their children Bart and Lisa contract for a holiday at the camp for two weeks in August.
3. The contract contains an exclusion of liability for death or injury, howsoever caused.
4. A notice to the same effect is posted at the entrance to the camp.
5. Homer is injured when he falls at night down steep unlit steps to his chalet with no handrail.
6. Marge is electrocuted and badly burnt when plugging in the kettle.
7. The socket is live due to the negligence of Shoddy Electric Co. who rewired it.
8. Bart cuts himself on a knife in the restaurant kitchen.
9. A notice on the kitchen door reads: 'Danger. Staff only'.
10. Lisa is poisoned when she eats berries growing on a bush by the front door.
11. Bart and Lisa are both children.

The appropriate law

It is very important when answering problem questions that you use only the law that is relevant to the precise facts, if for no other reason than that you are not getting any marks for using law that is irrelevant and so you are wasting valuable writing time. By looking at the various facts, we can say that the following law may be relevant in our problem here:

1. The area involved in the Occupiers' Liability Acts.
2. a The 1957 Act covers liability towards 'visitors' – those lawfully on the premises.
   b The 1984 Act concerns trespassers – and covers liability only to personal injury, not property damage.
3. There are three key issues:
   a what counts as premises;
   b who is an 'occupier' and so who can be sued;
   c who can claim under the Acts and under which one.
4. There is no real definition of premises in either Act – the common law applies and is widely defined (i.e. wide enough to include a ladder in *Wheeler v Corps*).
5. Occupier is again not defined in either Act – again the common law applies, an occupier is 'anybody who is in control of the premises' – *Wheat v Lacon*.

6 Under the 1957 Act a 'visitor' is anybody with a lawful right to be on the premises.

7 Under s.2.2(1) a 'common duty of care' is owed to all visitors.

8 Under s.2(2) the duty is to take all reasonable care to keep the visitor safe for the purposes for which he has legitimately entered the premises.

9 The standard of care is as for negligence, so the same sort of principles apply.

10 Under s.2(3) an occupier must be prepared for children to be less careful than adults would be.

   a The occupier must not do anything to 'allure' the child into danger – *Taylor v Glasgow Corporation.*

   b An occupier may be able to rely on the duty of parents to supervise very young children – *Phipps v Rochester Corporation.*

11 An occupier will not be liable for the harm caused by the work of independent contractors provided:

   a itis reasonable for the occupier to entrust the work to someone else – *Haseldine v Daw;*

   b a competent contractor is hired – *Ferguson v Welsh;*

   c the occupier carries our checks on the work if appropriate – *AMF v Magnet Bowling.*

12 An occupier may avoid liability under s.2(1) in a number of ways:

   a Warning notices, provided they are effective – Rae v Mars (and nothing short of a barrier may possibly be sufficient for children).

   b Exclusion clauses in contracts – but these would be subject to s.65 of the Consumer Rights Act 2015, and a clause excluding liability for death or injury caused by negligence is invalid under s.65(1).

   c The defences of contributory negligence and consent (not relevant here).

13 The 1984 Act applies by s.1(1)(a) to persons other than visitors.

14 Under the 1984 Act an occupier is liable under s.1(1) in respect of dangers 'due to the state of the premises or things done or omitted to be done on them'.

15 Under s.1(3) the occupier will be liable if:

   a he is aware of the danger;

   b he knows that the trespasser may come into the vicinity of the danger; and

   c the risk is one against which the occupier might be expected to provide some protection.

Applying the law to the facts

1 We know that Springfield Leisure Co. owns and manages the holiday camp so we can feel that it 'controls' the premises and is occupier and therefore defendant under the Act.

2 We know also that Homer and his family have paid for their holiday and so will be 'visitors' and therefore may claim under the 1957 Act. The common duty of care applies to them all and they are entitled to expect the same standard of care.

3 'Premises' presents no problems here – the holiday camp clearly is.

4 It is easier past this point to take each individual in turn.

Homer:

- The question is whether not providing a handrail on the steep steps and not having them lit is a breach of Springfield's duty – it would certainly seem to fall below an appropriate standard of care and the facts in any case seem to resemble those in *Wheat v Lacon*.
- The exclusion clause cannot apply because of s.65(1) CRA.
- Similarly, the warning notice outside the camp would fail to relieve liability unless it covered specific risks – *Rae v Mars*.

Marge:

- Leaving sockets 'live' clearly falls below an appropriate standard of care.
- The question here is whether it is Springfield or Shoddy who is responsible.
- It will obviously depend on whether Shoddy is a reliable contractor or not.
- Clearly it is appropriate for Springfield to delegate that type of work, and they do not have the expertise to check it, they are relying on the contractors – *Haseldine v Daw*.
- The exclusion clause and warning notice would fail for the same reasons.

Lisa:

- Lisa is a child so under s.2(3) is entitled to expect greater care than an adult.
- The bush appears to be possible 'allurement', certainly if we compare it with the facts in *Taylor v Glasgow Corporation*.
- It would be hard to expect the parents to take full responsibility here where the bush is outside the front door and so it is unlikely that *Phipps v Rochester Corporation* could apply in the circumstances.
- Again, the exclusion clause cannot apply and the notice is even less appropriate here because Lisa is a child.

Bart:

- Bart has entered a part of the premises from which he is barred – this may make him a trespasser.
- Bart is a child and a kitchen may well be an allurement to a hungry child – Springfield may expect some risk of trespassers to such parts of the premises if they do not keep them locked up – *BR Board v Herrington*.
- Furthermore, kitchen implements, sharp knives, etc. are clearly dangerous if unattended.

- The notice on the door is unlikely to be sufficient warning since it is imprecise in respect of the risk and in any case, Bart is a child.
- The 1984 Act applies only in respect of injuries so Bart may be unable to claim in respect of his damaged jacket.

Conclusions

We have shown how the law applies to each of our four central characters and would be able to advise them to sue with confidence.

- Homer and Lisa could both sue Springfield for their injuries under the 1957 Act.
- Marge can sue for her injuries, but unless Shoddy are disreputable contractors whom Springfield should not have hired, then her action will be against Shoddy rather than Springfield.
- Bart is a trespasser and will sue Springfield under the 1984 Act, but for his injuries only, not for his other damage.

You should also remember to use references and citations and tables and bibliography in the accepted way.

Glossary of legal terminology

actionable per se an action for a tort where the claimant does not have to prove that damage occurred, only that the tort occurred

'but for' test the main test for establishing factual causation in an action for negligence – but for the defendant's breach of duty the damage would not have occurred

claimant the person who brings an action in tort

damages refers to the compensation awarded by the court in a successful claim

defendant the person against whom a claim in tort is made

economic loss refers to a loss that is purely financial, e.g. loss of profit – in contrast to personal injury or damage to property

exemplary damages a form of damages which is not related to compensation for damage suffered but which the court makes to show its disapproval of the defendant's action

ex turpi causa non oritur actio a defence that may be raised against a claimant whose claim arises from their own criminal actions

interim (interlocutory) an injunction given before the actual dispute is heard – to avoid harm that may be caused to the claimant before the action comes to court

joint tortfeasors where the wrongful act is carried out by more than one person, they are joint tortfeasors and any or all of them can be sued

loss of amenity damages are awarded where the claimant is unable to do things that he could before the wrong occurred

malice motive is generally unimportant in most torts but in some circumstances acting maliciously is an element of the tort, e.g. malicious falsehood and nuisance

mesne profits used in trespass to land – allowing the claimant to claim for damage done by the trespasser and for any costs incurred in recovering possession of the land

misfeasance this is where the defendant has acted wrongly

neighbour principle a test used in negligence to establish whether a duty of care is owed

nervous shock a recognised psychiatric injury such as clinical depression and post-traumatic stress disorder caused by a single shocking event

nominal damages a small sum of damages awarded where there has technically been a wrong but no actual damage has been caused

non-feasance this is where the defendant has a duty to act and is liable for a failure to act

non-pecuniary damages compensation for pain, suffering and loss of amenities where judges have developed rates of compensation

novus actus interveniens means 'a new act intervenes' – refers to situations where the defendant is excused liability because another intervening act has broken the chain of causation

occupier in liability for damage caused by the state of premises the occupier is the person in actual control of the premises when the damage occurs – so there can be dual occupation

pecuniary damages damages that can be calculated in financial terms, e.g. loss of earnings

prescription a defence in private nuisance where the thing complained of had been active for 20 years or more and the claimant had known about it and not complained before

proximity refers to the fact that the defendant should contemplate that his actions may have an effect on potential claimants – rather than physical closeness

remoteness of damage also known as causation in law – refers to damage which is foreseeable and therefore which the courts are prepared to compensate – they would not compensate for damage that was too remote a consequence of the defendant's breach

res ipsa loquitur literally means 'the thing speaks for itself' – where the claimant is unable to show details of the negligence but the damage was obviously caused negligently, the defendant will be required to show that he was not negligent

several liability where there are joint tortfeasors each one can be separately liable for the whole damage – so if one lacks funds to pay compensation the claimant can bring the action against the one that can pay

special damage occurs in slander where the claimant usually has to prove that he has suffered damage as a result – also occurs in public nuisance where the claimant has to show that he has suffered damage over that suffered by the public generally

special damages not to be confused with special damage – generally refers to damages for financial losses and expenses incurred up to the date of trial which have to be pleaded separately from the claim itself

strict liability refers to torts where the claimant does not have to show fault on the part of the defendant – the most obvious ones are under the Animals Act 1971 and the Consumer Protection Act 1987

thin skull rule also known as the 'eggshell skull rule' – means that the defendant has to take extra care of a claimant who is susceptible to a certain type of harm

tort a French word meaning 'wrong' – so is a general word used to describe civil wrongs

tortfeasor will be the defendant in a tort action – the person who commits the wrong

trespass torts based on trespass tend to involve interference, e.g. with rights over land, or property or indeed with their 'bodily integrity'

trespass ab initio in the case of people who have a legal right to enter land such as a meter reader if they commit wrong while on the land they are said to be trespassers from when they entered

trespasser a person who enters premises without permission or who exceeds the permission they are given

vicarious liability not a tort in itself but a means of imposing liability on somebody who is responsible for the tortfeasor usually an employer

visitor usually refers to somebody who enters premises lawfully

volenti non fit injuria literally means 'no injury can be done to a willing person' – so is a defence where the claimant understands the risk of harm and willingly accepts it.

Index

Note: Page numbers in *italics* indicate figures, and page numbers in **bold** indicate tables in the text

For Product Safety Concerns and Information please contact our
EU representative GPSR@taylorandfrancis.com Taylor & Francis
Verlag GmbH, Kaufingerstraße 24, 80331 München, Germany